Employment Law
in Context

We work with leading authors to develop the strongest educational materials in business and management, bringing cutting-edge thinking and best learning practice to a global market.

Under a range of well-known imprints, including Financial Times Prentice Hall, we craft high quality print and electronic publications which help readers to understand and apply their content, whether studying or at work.

To find out more about the complete range of our publishing, please visit us on the World Wide Web at: www.pearsoneduc.com

Employment Law
in Context

An Introduction for HR Professionals

BRIAN WILLEY

Second edition

FT Prentice Hall
FINANCIAL TIMES

An imprint of **Pearson Education**
Harlow, England • London • New York • Boston • San Francisco • Toronto • Sydney • Singapore • Hong Kong
Tokyo • Seoul • Taipei • New Delhi • Cape Town • Madrid • Mexico City • Amsterdam • Munich • Paris • Milan

Pearson Education Limited
Edinburgh Gate
Harlow
Essex CM20 2JE
England

and Associated Companies throughout the world

Visit us on the World Wide Web at:
www.pearsoned.co.uk

First published 2000 by Pitman Publishing, a division of Pearson Professional Ltd
Second edition published 2003 by Pearson Education Limited

ISBN: 0 273 67859-0

British Library Cataloguing-in-Publication Data
A catalogue record for this book is available from the British Library

10 9 8 7 6 5 4 3
08 07 06 05 04

Typeset in 9.5/12pt Stone Serif by 35
Printed in Malaysia, KHL
The publisher's policy is to use paper manufactured from sustainable forests.

Contents

Preface   xiv
Publisher's acknowledgements   xvii
List of abbreviations   xviii
Table of cases   xx
Table of statutes   xxvi
Table of statutory instruments   xxviii
Table of statutory codes of practice   xxx
Table of European Community Law   xxxi
List of useful websites   xxxiii

1 An introduction to employment law   1
Learning objectives   1
1.1 Structure of the chapter   1
1.2 Introduction   2
Substantive aspects · Procedural aspects
Exercise 1.1 *Future changes – where will the UK be in 2006?*
Political perspectives
1.3 The nature of legal regulation   8
Standards in law
Exercise 1.2 *How much freedom of expression?*
Processes for complaint · Effective remedies
1.4 The nature of voluntary regulation   31
Employer discretion · Grievance procedures · Disciplinary procedures ·
Consultation and collective bargaining · Third parties
1.5 Some underpinning principles   34
Substantive issues · The processes of employment relations
1.6 Conclusion   40
Further reading · References

Part One The changing employment relationship   43

Introduction to Part One   45
Economically driven change · Changes in employment status ·
'New model' employment regulation · Conclusion

2	**Regulating the employment relationship**	**47**
	Learning objectives	47
2.1	Structure of the chapter	47
2.2	Introduction	47

Defining the employment relationship · Frontier of control ·
The parties' expectations · Three sets of 'rules' · The role of the
contract of employment

| 2.3 | The context | 50 |

Concepts of work and employment · The psychological contract ·
Individualism and collectivism · Diversity of employment status
Exercise 2.1 *A flexible workforce?*

| 2.4 | The legal framework | 62 |

Introduction · Status: employee, worker or independent contractor? ·
The characteristics of the contract of employment · The terms of a
contract of employment · Written information about contracts of
employment · Terminating a contract of employment · Employment
protection for 'atypical' workers

| 2.5 | Conclusion | 88 |

Exercise 2.2 *Who has employment rights?*
References

3	**Managing change in the employment relationship**	**91**
	Learning objectives	91
3.1	Structure of the chapter	91
3.2	Introduction	92
3.3	Context	92

Private and public-sector change: an overall view · The
organisation's culture · Strategic considerations · Operational
factors · Economic considerations · Employment relations matters ·
Tensions with legal requirements · The incidence and experience
of changes

| 3.4 | The legal framework | 102 |

Variation of contracts of employment · Flexibility in existing
contractual terms
Exercise 3.1 *Some problems of managing variation*
Transfers of undertakings
Exercise 3.2 *Some problems of managing transfers of undertakings*
Redundancy and redeployment
Exercise 3.3 *Some problems in managing redundancies*

| 3.5 | Employment policies and practices | 126 |

Variation · Transfers · Managing redundancies
Case study 3.1
Exercise 3.4
Further reading · References

| Part Two | **Discrimination and equal opportunities** | **133** |

Introduction to Part Two — **135**
The concepts · The law · Voluntary action by employers · Conclusion ·
Further reading · References

4 **Sex discrimination in the workplace** — **149**
Learning objectives — 149
4.1 Structure of the chapter — 149
4.2 Introduction — 150
    Historic situation of women · Changing perspectives
4.3 The context — 152
    Participation in the labour market · Women's pay · Social trends and
    influences · Political approaches
4.4 The legal framework — 160
    Structure of discrimination law · Grounds of unlawful discrimination ·
    Access to statutory rights · Direct discrimination · Indirect
    discrimination · Claims relating to equal pay · Victimisation · Positive
    action and positive discrimination · Special provisions · Liability ·
    Enforcement procedures · Remedies
4.5 Employment policies and practices — 180
    Human resource strategy · Recruitment and selection · Terms and
    conditions of employment · Working time · Training and development ·
    Promotion and career progression · Dress and appearance ·
    Retirement and pensions · Dismissal
4.6 Conclusion — 187
    Exercise 4.1 *Some discrimination problems*
    Further reading · References

5 **Race discrimination in the workplace** — **191**
Learning objectives — 191
5.1 Structure of the chapter — 191
5.2 Introduction — 192
    Population profile of Britain · The concepts
5.3 The context — 198
    The social background · Political approaches · Labour-market
    participation · Social issues
5.4 The legal framework — 205
    Grounds for unfair discrimination · The areas of employment
    protection · Direct discrimination · Indirect discrimination ·
    Victimisation · Special provisions: 'genuine occupational qualification' ·
    Positive action and positive discrimination · Liability · Enforcement ·
    Remedies · Employing workers from overseas

5.5 Employment policies and practices   220
Human resource strategy · Recruitment and selection · Pay and
benefits · Working time · Training and development, promotion and
transfers · Dress codes · Dismissal
Case study 5.1
Exercise 5.1
Further reading · References

6 **Disability discrimination in the workplace**   **229**
Learning objectives   229
6.1 Structure of the chapter   229
6.2 Introduction   230
6.3 The context   230
Defining disability · The social context · Disability and the labour
market · The employment context · Technological context · The
political and historical background · The developing political and
legislative context · Social welfare support
6.4 The legal framework   242
The coverage of the legislation · The meaning of disability · The
meaning of discrimination · The duty to make reasonable adjustments ·
Liability · Burden of proof · Enforcement procedures · Remedies ·
The Disability Rights Commission · Managing long-term
sick absence
6.5 Employment policies and practices   253
Management approach · Implications for contracts and agreements ·
Practical steps: the 1996 *Code of Practice*
Exercise 6.1 *Some discrimination problems*
Further reading · References

Part Three **Regulating performance and conduct**   **259**

Introduction to Part Three   **261**

7 **Harassment and bullying at work**   **263**
Learning objectives   263
7.1 Structure of the chapter   263
7.2 Introduction   264
Growing concern about harassment · Definitions
7.3 The context   265
Power relations · Cultural factors · The characteristics of the workplace ·
The parties involved · Possible consequences

7.4   The legal framework   269
      The contract of employment · European equal treatment legislation ·
      Direct discrimination and detriments · Dismissal · Liability for the
      harassment · Harassment by third parties · Action against the
      perpetrator · Possible remedies in law for the victim
7.5   Employment policies and practices   277
      Defining harassment and bullying · Who might be possible victims? ·
      Approach to allegations of harassment and bullying · Managerial
      roles and responsibilities · Informal procedures and counselling ·
      Role of grievance procedure · Training · Communications · Role of
      disciplinary action · Consultation with trade unions · Monitoring
7.6   Conclusions   281
      Case study 7.1
      Exercise 7.1
      Further reading · References

  8   Information, privacy and surveillance   **284**

      Learning objectives   284
8.1   Structure of the chapter   284
8.2   Introduction   285
8.3   The context   285
      Technological developments · Social values and human rights ·
      Economic and security considerations
8.4   The legal framework   288
      The Data Protection Act 1998 · Privacy and surveillance ·
      Whistleblowing and public interest disclosure legislation
8.5   Employment policies and practices   296
      The Data Protection Act: the *Employment Practices Data
      Protection* Code · Privacy and surveillance · Whistleblowing
8.6   Conclusion   312
      Further reading · References

  9   Discipline and dismissal   **313**

      Learning objectives   313
9.1   Structure of the chapter   313
9.2   Introduction   314
9.3   The context   315
      The nature of the employment relationship · The common law of
      contract · Social standards · Political action · Assessing the law's
      effectiveness
9.4   The legal framework   321
      Introduction · The nature and purpose of discipline at work · Circumstances
      in which contracts of employment end · Fair and unfair dismissal ·

Fair reasons for dismissal · Unfair reasons for dismissal ·
Reasonableness in the circumstances · Procedural fairness
Exercise 9.1 *Misconduct cases: Scenarios*
Procedures for redress · The remedies

9.5   Employment policies and practices   342
The context: expectations and norms · Handling discipline and dismissal
Exercise 9.2 *Discipline at work: Scenarios*
Further reading · References

Part Four   Terms and conditions of employment   **353**

Introduction to Part Four   **355**

10   Pay regulation   **358**
Learning objectives   358
10.1   Structure of the chapter   358
10.2   Introduction   358
10.3   The context   359
Economic issues · Political policy: the 'free play' of the market? ·
Social welfare factors · Social policy
10.4   The legal framework   366
Definitions · Regulating the pay transaction · Statutory national
minimum wage
10.5   Employment policies and practices   378
Contracts of employment and collective agreements ·
Special agreements · Information and records
Exercise 10.1 *Pay regulation: Scenarios*
References

11   Regulation of working time   **382**
Learning objectives   382
11.1   Structure of the chapter   382
11.2   Introduction   383
11.3   The context   385
The historic use of voluntary measures · A growing long-hours
culture · Social issues · Economic considerations
11.4   The legal framework   389
Piecemeal legal regulation · The Working Time Regulations 1998 ·
Working people with entitlements · The employer · Defining 'working
time' · Some key working-time provisions · Paid annual leave ·
Implementing the Regulations · Records · Enforcement · Are the
Working Time Regulations working?

11.5 Employment policies and practices   401
      A strategic approach to implementation
11.6 A checklist for action   403
      Exercise 11.1 *Some scenarios*
      Further reading · References

12 Health and safety at work   **407**

      Learning objectives   407
12.1 Structure of the chapter   407
12.2 Introduction   408
      The concepts
12.3 The context   410
      The economics of health and safety · Technology and ergonomic
      factors · Work-related stress · The incidence of major accidents ·
      The European dimension
12.4 The legal framework   417
      Introduction: a diversity of legal action · The common law ·
      Statute law · Some key regulations
      Exercise 12.1 *Assessing the risks?*
      Rights of employees · Consultation and representation
12.5 Employment policies and practices   439
      Creating a safety culture · A safety policy · Safety consultation and
      communication · Occupational health service · Employee assistance
      programmes and counselling
      Case study 12.1 *The VDU operators: a safety grievance*
      Exercise 12.2 *The VDU operators: a safety grievance*
12.6 Conclusion   449
      Further reading · References

13 Work-life balance, parental and dependency rights   **451**

      Learning objectives   451
13.1 Structure of the chapter   451
13.2 Introduction   451
13.3 The context   452
      Labour market and social trends · Work-life balance · Political initiatives
13.4 The legal framework   461
      Pregnancy · Maternity leave entitlements · The status of the contract
      of employment · Returning to work · Requesting flexible working ·
      Parental, paternity, adoption and dependency leave · Detrimental
      treatment and unfair dismissal · Statutory pay
13.5 Employment policies and practices   473
      Workplace culture · Facilitating work-life balance · Leave entitlements ·
      Flexible working time · Place of work · Facilities · Communication and
      consultation about 'work-life balance'

Case study 13.1 *Dependency scheme in the Royal Borough of
Kingston upon Thames*
Exercise 13.1 *Developing a dependency policy*
References

| Part Five | Collective rights at work | 483 |

Introduction to Part Five   **485**
Preliminaries · The role of trade unions · The traditional model of
British industrial relations · The 'British disease' · A 'new model' of
employee relations? · International influences · Conclusion · References

14   Employee participation   **499**
Brian Willey and Huw Morris

Learning objectives   499
14.1   Structure of the chapter   499
14.2   Introduction   500
       The concept of consultation · The concept of collective bargaining ·
       The concept of industrial democracy
14.3   The context   507
       The development of employee participation in the UK ·
       Employee participation policy and practice in the UK
14.4   The legal framework   516
       Low-level participation · Financial participation ·
       Higher-level participation
       Exercise 14.1: *Implications of the Information and Consultation Directive*
       Statutory rights for representatives · Statutory recognition
       for collective bargaining
14.5   Employment policies and practices   534
       Traditional managerialist · Progressive managerialist ·
       'Industrial democrat' or partnership · Social inclusionist ·
       Summary of employer approaches
14.6   Conclusion   544
       Further reading · References

15   Industrial action   **547**
Learning objectives   547
15.1   Structure of the chapter   547
15.2   Introduction   547
       What is industrial action? Sociological definitions ·
       What is industrial action? Definitions from legislators ·
       The phenomenon of industrial action

15.3 The context 551
1945–79 · 1979 to date · A 'dual track policy' · The position of
individual employees
15.4 The legal framework 556
Individual employees · Trade unions
15.5 Conclusion 572
Case study 15.1
Exercise 15.1
Further reading · References

16 Conclusion **576**
16.1 Ethical standards 576
16.2 Minimum standards 576
16.3 Juridification 577
16.4 Business interests 577
16.5 Labour-market flexibility 579
16.6 The accommodation of non-work life 580
16.7 Individualisation and collectivism 580
16.8 Representation rights 581
16.9 Qualified access to statutory rights 582
16.10 Enforcement processes 583
16.11 The value of the remedies 584
16.12 The future 585
References

Appendix Feedback on case studies and exercises 586
Glossary 601
Index 609

Preface

Particularly in the past twenty-five years, employment law has had a growing significance for managers – whether general managers or human resource practitioners. Potentially, it influences and may constrain action they want to take. One principal aim of this textbook is to help those with day-to-day responsibilities for employee relations and human resource management to manage within the law.

Its purpose is to promote understanding of three aspects:

- the application of the law to employment relations (in policy making and problem solving);
- the social purposes behind the legislation (what Parliament and the European Union are trying to achieve); and
- the contextual issues that affect the implementation of the law (e.g. social trends and economic considerations).

Applying the law (through problem solving and policy making) involves a good understanding of the other two areas. A manager advising on the handling of a dismissal, for example, is more likely to produce an effective and lawful outcome if s/he does not focus exclusively on the problem in hand (terminating the employment for employee misconduct). Remembering the purposes behind the legislation (to provide fair reasons, fair treatment and natural justice and consideration of all the circumstances) is important. Similarly, a recognition of the business context and organisational needs is important.

Likewise, the development of corporate policies is more likely to be effective and well informed if they are not seen, narrowly, as a series of conditions of employment to be applied mechanistically. For example, when parental and dependency leave policies are formulated, an understanding of the social trends against which they are developed is important (e.g. greater economic activity by women, longer working hours, difficulties of reconciling work and non-work life). Furthermore, the social purposes behind this legislation (to promote family-friendly policies and provide a better balance between work and non-work life) should be acknowledged to ensure that the corporate policies achieve the statutory objectives. A manager who understands these purposes is better able to defend and argue for policy developments with colleagues.

So, this textbook aims to be integrative. It is hoped that those concerns that exist (particularly among HR managers and general managers) about the impact of employment law can be addressed and that they can gain both a familiarity with and an enthusiasm for the subject and, also, the confidence to analyse and handle a greater range of problems.

Market for the book

This textbook is designed, principally, for those engaged in academic study. It is written for non-lawyers who wish to gain a basic understanding of the key areas of employment law. Principally, it is for students on postgraduate and post-experience courses. This would obviously cover those on programmes leading to graduate membership of the Chartered Institute of Personnel and Development, those on Diploma of Management Studies courses and those studying employment law modules on, for example, Masters in Business Administration courses. It would also be useful to students on BA Business Studies courses who are undertaking an employment law option.

Furthermore, an additional, related and important market is tutors on these courses – particularly non-lawyers who themselves are developing an understanding of the subject area.

Approach to learning

In attempting to bridge knowledge of legal provisions, on the one hand, and consideration of employee relations and human resource issues, on the other, the textbook provides a number of opportunities for the reader to undertake exercises and case studies.

The structure of each chapter

- Learning objectives: The reader is given a list of objectives that should be attained once the chapter and associated exercises have been completed.
- Introduction: This sets out the broad issues to be considered.
- The context: This identifies and discusses, as appropriate, the social, economic, political and technological issues that form the background against which a particular body of law is developing. Included in this section will be an outline of the social purposes of the legislation.
- The legal framework: The essential framework is outlined and discussed. As appropriate, material is drawn from European law, statute law, case law and codes of practice.
- Employment policies and practices: This will consider the application of the law to the workplace. It will consider the experiences of organisations and the difficulties that have been encountered. It will provide assistance for policy

formulation and ways in which problems with employee relations might be dealt with.

■ Case studies and scenarios: Most chapters have exercises, which invite the reader to apply the concepts and legal provisions to the circumstances that are set out. The exercises are suitable for both individual and syndicate work in the classroom. Feedback is provided in Appendix 1, which outlines the key issues that should have been considered.

Other features of the book

■ Further reading: Apart from the references quoted in the discussion, supplementary reading is indicated at the end of each chapter.

■ Glossary: This provides definitions of terms that are used on several occasions in the book.

■ Index: This is designed to enable the reader to search quickly for relevant information when tackling problems in class, preparing for examinations or working on assignments.

■ Instructor's Manual: This is provided as an accompaniment to the textbook. It comprises a range of further exercises and material that might to used by tutors.

Acknowledgements

The initial idea for this book arose from a previous collaborative text, *The Corporate Environment, a guide for human resource managers* (Pearson Education), written in 1995 with my colleague, Huw Morris. The discussions we held about that textbook stimulated ideas about this present one as a complementary piece of work. Also, my involvement over a number of years in teaching the Employment Law option on the Personnel Management Diploma at Kingston University and discussions with students further reinforced my view that such a textbook could be useful. Furthermore, my teaching on the MA/LLM in Employment Relations and Law helped me recognise more fully the complexity of issues that non-lawyer HR practitioners often have to manage. My thanks to them for helping to germinate and sustain the idea, and my admiration to many of those who wrestle with the application of the law on a day-to-day basis.

The responsibility for the text is obviously mine. But it could not have been written without the contributions, comments and advice of various people in relation to both the first edition and this new edition. From Kingston University, I would like to thank Professor Robert Upex, Vera Sacks (in the School of Law), Jasmine Pidduck, Sanjiv Sachdev and, a former colleague, David Stannard (in the School of Human Resource Management). All kindly considered drafts of chapters and made very helpful comments on structure and content.

Contributions to the text was written by three other people. Huw Morris contributed ideas and material for Chapter 14 (Employee Participation); David Stannard wrote the Case Study in Chapter 3; and Jasmine Pidduck contributed the scenarios in Chapter 6. I am most grateful to them for their contributions.

In addition, I would like to thank Jasmine further for allowing me to draw heavily on unpublished written work she had undertaken on disability discrimination. Avril Doyle kindly arranged permission to include material for a case study from her Masters' dissertation and Catriona Banting from Croner Publications Ltd gave permission to use the scenarios on working time regulation in Chapter 11. Bruce McDonald, Chief Executive at the Royal Borough of Kingston upon Thames, kindly gave his time to discuss the Authority's dependency policy.

A number of people facilitated the completion of this book and also deserve thanks. Professor Christine Edwards, my Head of School, gave her support and enthusiasm for the project. Within the operational constraints of timetabling and my responsibilities as a course director, she provided me with as much space as was possible to undertake the task. Sadie McClelland and, previously, Penelope Woolf, from Pearson Education, had sufficient faith to commission the project initially and to help in its achievement. My thanks to them. For the second edition thanks are owed to all the editorial and production team at Pearson Education.

Finally, such textbooks are rarely written without the support of families. In this case, I would like to thank my wife, Ann. It is a pain to have a family member apparently welded to a PC over a summer vacation! Also, I want to thank my children, Ian, David and Helen for their continued interest.

I hope that readers will find the textbook useful and, above all, that it will give them the confidence to deal with the issues that employment law will present.

Brian Willey
Kingston University
February 2003

Publisher's acknowledgements

We are grateful to the following for permission to reproduce copyright material:

Figure 2.1 from *Strategic Prospects for HRM*, reproduced with permission of the Chartered Institute of Personnel and Development, London; Figure 2.2 from *Whose flexibility? the costs and benefits of non-standard working arrangements and contractual relations*, by Kate Purcell, Terence Hogarth and Claire Sim, published in 1999 by the Joseph Rowntree Foundation, reproduced by permission of the Joseph Rowntree Foundation; Figure 5.2 reproduced with permission from Glover, S. *et al.* (2001) 'Migration: an economic and social analysis' RDS Occasional Paper No. 67, London: Home Office; The controller of Her Majesty's Stationery Office for all Crown copyright material; extracts from *Equal Opportunities Review* and IRS *Employment Trends* reproduced by permission of Reed Elsevier (UK) Ltd trading as Lexis Nexis UK. Permission has been granted to reproduce data from the Department of Trade and Industry *Employment Relations Research* Series; the findings do not represent the views of the Department.

List of abbreviations

ACAS	Advisory, Conciliation and Arbitration Service
BPR	Business process re-engineering
CA	Court of Appeal
CAC	Central Arbitration Committee
CBI	Confederation of British Industry
CEEP	Centre européen d'études de population
CIPD	Chartered Institute of Personnel and Development
CRE	Commission for Racial Equality
DDA 1995	Disability Discrimination Act 1995
DPA 1998	Data Protection Act 1998
DfES	Department for Education and Skills
DRC	Disability Rights Commission
DTI	Department of Trade and Industry
EA 2002	Employment Act 2002
EAT	Employment Appeals Tribunal
EC	European Community
ECHR	European Convention on Human Rights
ECJ	European Court of Justice
EEC	European Economic Community
EOC	Equal Opportunities Commission
EqPA 1970	Equal Pay Act 1970
ERDRA 1998	Employment Rights (Dispute Resolution) Act 1998
ERA 1996	Employment Rights Act 1996
ERA 1999	Employment Relations Act 1999
ET	Employment Tribunal
ETUC	European Trade Union Confederation
EU	European Union
EWC	European Works Council
GOQ	Genuine occupational qualification
HC	High Court
HL	House of Lords
HASAWA 1974	Health and Safety at Work etc. Act 1974
HRM	Human resource management
HSC	Health and Safety Commission

HSE	Health and Safety Executive
HSI	Health and Safety Inspectorate
ILO	International Labour Organisation
IRA 1971	Industrial Relations Act 1971
IT	Industrial Tribunal
LPC	Low Pay Commission
NDC	National Disability Council
NICA	Northern Ireland Court of Appeal
NIRC	National Industrial Relations Court
NMWA 1998	National Minimum Wage Act 1998
PPP	Public-private partnership
QMV	Qualified majority vote
RRA 1976	Race Relations Act 1976
RR(A)A 2000	Race Relations (Amendment) Act 2000
RIPA 2000	Regulation of Investigatory Powers Act 2000
SAP	Statutory adoption pay
SDA 1975	Sex Discrimination Act 1975
SMP	Statutory Maternity Pay
SOSR	Some other substantial reason
SPP	Statutory Paternity Pay
TICER 1999	Transnational Information and Consultation of Employees Regulations 1999
TQM	Total quality management
TUC	Trades Union Congress
TULRCA 1992	Trade Union and Labour Relations (Consolidation) Act 1992
TUPE 1981	Transfer of Undertakings (Protection of Employment) Regulations 1981
UNICE	Union des industries de la communanté européenne
WERS	Workplace Employee Relations Survey
WIRS	Workplace Industrial Relations Survey
WTR 1998	Working Time Regulations 1998

Table of cases

Adekeye v Post Office (No. 2) [1997] IRLR 105, CA 208
Airfix Footwear v Cope [1978] ICR 210, EAT 85
Alexander v Home Office [1988] IRLR 190, CA 178, 179
Anglia Regional Co-operative Society v O'Donnell, EAT 655/1991 105
Arbeiterwohlfahrt Der Stadt Berlin v Botel [1992] IRLR 423, ECJ 161
Armitage and Others v Johnson [1997] IRLR 162 218
Auguste Noel Ltd v Curtis [1990] IRLR 326, EAT 330
Avon County Council v Howlett [1983] IRLR 171, CA 369
Aziz v Trinity Street Taxis Ltd [1988] ICR 534, CA 170
Balamoody v United Kingdom Central Council for Nursing, Midwifery and
    Health Visiting [2002] IRLR 288, CA 210
Barber v Guardian Royal Exchange [1990] IRLR 240, CA 14, 161, 186
Barber v RJB Mining (UK) Ltd [1999] IRLR 308, HC 393
Barclays Bank plc v Kapur [1995] IRLR 87, CA 168
Barry Allsuch and Co v Harris [2001] HC 76
Bartholomew v London Borough of Hackney [1999] IRLR 246, CA 74
Bass Leisure v Thomas [1994] IRLR 104, EAT 120
BBC v Souster [2000] IRLR 150, Court of Session 206
BECTU v Secretary of State for Trade and Industry C–173/99, ECJ 14, 394
Beneviste v University of Southampton [1989] IRLR 122, CA 170
Bernadone v Pall Mall Services group and another [1999] IRLR 617 114
Bex v Securicor Transport Ltd [1972] IRLR 68 107
Bilka-Kaufhaus GmbH v Weber von Hartz [1986] IRLR 317, ECJ 161, 169
Bladon v ALM Medical Services Ltd, ET Case 2405845/99 297
Bolton Roadways Ltd v Edwards and Others [1987] IRLR 392, EAT 560
Bork (P) International A/S v Foreningen af Arbejdsledere i Danmark [1989]
    IRLR 41, ECJ 116
Bowden and others v Tuffnells Parcels Express Ltd, C–133/00, ECJ 391
BPCC Purnell Ltd v Webb, EAT 129/1990 106
B.P. Chemicals v Gillick [1995] IRLR 511, EAT 89
Bracebridge Engineering Ltd v Darby [1990] IRLR 3, EAT 271
Briggs v NE Education and Library Board [1990] IRLR 181, NICA 467
British Home Stores Ltd v Burchell [1978] IRLR 379 273, 330
British Nursing Association v Inland Revenue (National Minimum Wage
    Compliance Team) [2002] IRLR 480, CA 373
British Telecommunications plc v Ticehurst [1992] IRLR 219, CA 562
British Telecommunications plc v Roberts and Longstaffe [1996] IRLR 601 467

Brown v Rentokil [1998] IRLR 31, ECJ   182, 462
Burdett-Coutts and Others v Hertfordshire County Council [1984] IRLR 91   104
Burton and Rhule v de Vere Hotels [1996] IRLR 596, EAT   275
Byrne v BOC Ltd [1992] IRLR 505, EAT   332
Byrne Brothers (Formwork) Ltd v Baird and others, EAT case 542/01   391
Caisse Nationale d'Assurance Vieillesse de Travailleurs Salariés v Thibault [1998]
   IRLR 399   465
Caledonia Investment and Property v Caffrey [1998] IRLR 110, EAT   471
Callaghan v Glasgow City Council [2001] IRLR 724, EAT   248
Carmichael and Leese v National Power plc [2000] IRLR43, HL   66, 85
Cast v Croydon College [1998] IRLR 318, CA   176
Cheeseman and others v R Brewer Contracts Ltd [2001] IRLR 144   109, 111
Chessington World of Adventures v Reed [1997] IRLR 556   273
Chief Constable of West Yorkshire v Khan [2001] IRLR 830, HL 170   213
Church v West Lancashire NHS Trust [1998] IRLR 4, EAT   120
Clark v TGD Ltd t/a Novacold [1999] IRLR 318, CA   246
Clark v Oxfordshire Health Authority [1998] IRLR 125, CA   85
Clarke v Eley (IMI) Kynoch Ltd [1982] IRLR 482, EAT   121
Coleman v Skyrail Oceanic Ltd [1981] IRLR 398, CA   178
College of Ripon and York St John v Hobbs [2002] IRLR 185, EAT   244
Commission for Racial Equality v Dutton [1989] IRLR 8, CA   206
Coote v Granada Hospitality Ltd, C–185/97, ECJ   171, 207
Cosgrove v Caesar and Howie [2001] IRLR 653, EAT   246
Courtaulds Northern Textiles Ltd v Andrew [1979] IRLR 84, EAT   75
Cox v Sun Alliance Life Ltd [2001] IRLR 448, CA   75
Cresswell and Others v Board of Inland Revenue [1984] IRLR 190, HC   105, 557
Crofton v Yeboah [2002] CA   216
Cross and another v Highlands and Islands Enterprise and another [2000]
   Court of Session   74
Dawkins v Department of Environment [1993] IRLR 284, CA   206
Defrenne v Sabena [1978] C–149/77, ECJ   163
Dekker v Stichting Vormingscentrum [1991] IRLR 27, ECJ   136, 175, 462
De Souza v Automobile Association [1986] IRLR 103, CA   271
Dietrich v Westdeutscher Rundfunk [2000] C–11/99, ECJ   430
Dimbleby and Sons Ltd v National Union of Journalists [1984] IRLR 161   565
DJM International v Nicholas [1986] IRLR 76   114
East Lindsey District Council v Daubney [1977] ICR 566, EAT   331
ECM (Vehicle Delivery Service) Ltd v Cox and others [1999] IRLR 559, CA   110
Egg Stores v Leibovici [1976] IRLR 376, EAT   325
European Commission v United Kingdom, C–383/92 [1994] IRLR 392, ECJ   13,
   100, 123
Fairchild v Glenhaven Funeral Services Ltd [2002] HL   420
Flack v Kodak Ltd [1986] IRLR 255, CA   67
Ford v Warwickshire County Council [1983] IRLR 126, HL   67
Foster v British Gas [1991] ICR 84, HL   12
Foster v Hampshire Fire and Rescue Service [1997] EAT 1303/97   244
Francovich and Bonifaci v Republic of Italy [1992] IRLR 84, ECJ   13
Gillespie v Northern Health and Social Services Board [1996] IRLR 214   465
Goodwin v the United Kingdom [2002] Applicaton 28957/95, ECHR   18, 19

Grant v SW Trains Ltd [1998] IRLR 188, ECJ   24

Grimaldi v Fonds des Maladies Professionnelles [1990] IRLR 400, ECJ   270

Halford v United Kingdom [1997] IRLR 471, ECHR   294

Hall (HM Inspector of Taxes) v Lorimer [1994] IRLR 171   65

Hammersmith and Queen Charlotte's Special Health Authority v Cato [1987]
    IRLR 483, EAT   161

Hampson v Department of Education and Science [1989] IRLR 69, CA   169

Handles-og Kontorfunkionaerernes Forbund i Danmark v Dansk
    Arbejdgiverforening [1991] IRLR 31, ECJ   462

Harrods Ltd v Remick [1997] IRLR 9, EAT   89, 208

High Table Ltd v Horst and Others [1997] IRLR 513, CA   120

Home Office v Holmes [1984] IRLR 299, EAT   183

Hussein v Saints Complete House Furnishers [1979] IRLR 337   212

Iceland Frozen Foods Ltd v Jones [1982] IRLR 439, EAT   35

ICTS (UK) Ltd v Tchoula [2000] IRLR 643, EAT   179

Initial Contract Services Ltd v Harrison and others, EAT case 64/01   109

Insitu Cleaning Company v Heads [1995] IRLR 4, EAT   271

James v Eastleigh Borough Council [1990] IRLR 288, HL   37, 165, 210

Jenkins v Kingsgate (Clothing Productions) Ltd (No. 2) [1981] IRLR 388, EAT   170

J.H. Walker Ltd v Hussein [1996] IRLR 11   206, 224

Johnstone v Bloomsbury Health Authority [1991] IRLR 118, CA   421

Jones v Associated Tunnelling Co Ltd [1981] IRLR 477   105

Jones v the Post Office [2001] IRLR 384, CA   250

Jones v Tower Boot Co Ltd [1997] IRLR 68, CA   175, 274, 421

Kalenke v Freie Hansestadt Bremen [1995] IRLR 660, ECJ   171

Kenmir Ltd v Frizzell [1968] 1 All ER 414, HC   111

Kerr v Nathan's Wastesavers Ltd [1995] EAT 91/95   434

Kigass Aero Components Ltd v Brown [2002] IRLR 312, EAT   395

King v Great Britain-China Centre [1991] IRLR 513, CA   217

Kowalska v Freie und Hansestadt Hamburg [1992] C–33/89, ECJ   161

Landsorganisationen i Danmark v Ny Molle Kro [1989] IRLR 37   110

Lange v Georg Schunemann GmnH C–350/99, ECJ   77

Lane v Shire Roofing Co (Oxford) [1995] IRLR 493   64

Leonard v Southern Derbyshire Chamber of Commerce [2001] IRLR 19, EAT
    244

Lewen v Denda [2000] IRLR 67, ECJ   465

Lewis v Motorworld Garages Ltd [1985] IRLR 465   273

Lewis Woolf Griptight Ltd v Corfield [1997] IRLR 432, CA   472

Linfood Cash and Carry Ltd v Thomson and Another [1989] IRLR 235, EAT
    330

Litster v Forth Dry Dock [1989] IRLR 161, HL   113, 116

Lommers v Minister van Landbouw Natuurbeheer en Vissejj [2002] IRLR 430,
    ECJ   172

London Borough of Harrow v Cunningham [1996] IRLR 256, EAT   330

London Underground Ltd v Edwards (No. 2) [1998] IRLR 364, CA   167, 168,
    169, 183

Mandla v Dowell Lee [1983] IRLR 209, HL   205, 213

Marleasing SA v La Comercial Internacional de Alimentación C–106/89, ECJ   13

Marschall v Land Nordrhein-Westfalen [1998] IRLR 39, ECJ   171

Marshall *v* Harland and Wolff Ltd [1972] IRLR 90, NIRC   325

Marshall *v* Southampton and SW Hampshire Area Health Authority [1986] IRLR 140, ECJ   14, 186

Marshall *v* Southampton and SW Hampshire Area Health Authority (No. 2) [1993] IRLR 445, ECJ   14, 178, 179

McMeechan *v* Secretary of State for Employment [1997] IRLR 353, CA   87

McPherson *v* Rathgael Centre for Children and Young People and Northern Ireland Office (Training Schools Branch) [1991] IRLR 206, CA   170

Meer *v* London Borough of Tower Hamlets [1988] IRLR 399, CA   167

Merckx *v* Ford Motor Company Belgium SA [1996] IRLR 467, ECJ   111

Methven & Musiolik *v* Cow Industrial Polymers Ltd [1980] IRLR 289, CA   170

Metropolitan Borough of Solihull *v* National Union of Teachers [1985] IRLR 211   558

Middlesbrough Borough Council *v* Transport and General Workers' Union and another (EAT 26/00)   123

Midland Plastics Ltd *v* Till and Others [1983] IRLR 9, EAT   560

Miles *v* Enterprise Glass Ltd, IT case 538/89   269

Ministry of Defence *v* Cannock and Others [1994] IRLR 509   178

Mirror Group Newspapers Ltd *v* Gunning [1986] IRLR 27, CA   164

Morgan *v* Staffordshire University [2002] IRLR 190, EAT   243

Morrow *v* Safeway Stores plc, EAT case 275/00   75

Morse *v* Wiltshire County Council [1998] Case 1279/97, EAT   248

Mowatt-Brown *v* University of Surrey [2002] IRLR 235, EAT   245

Nagarajan *v* Agnew [1994] IRLR 61, EAT   210

Nethermere (St. Neots) Ltd *v* Jardiner & Taverna [1983] IRLR 240   85

Niemietz *v* Germany [1992] 16 EHRR 97, ECHR   294

Norton Tool Co Ltd *v* Tewson [1973] 1 All ER 183   341

Ojutiku *v* MSC [1982] ICR 661, CA   169

O'Kelly and Others *v* Trust House Forte plc [1983] IRLR 369, CA   66, 85

Oy Liikenne Ab *v* Pekka Liskojarvi and Juntunen [2001] IRLR 171, ECJ   109

P *v* National Union of Schoolmasters/Union of Women Teachers [2001] IRLR 532, CA   571

P *v* S and Cornwall County Council [1996] IRLR 347   14, 137, 163

Panesar *v* Nestlé Co [1980] ICR 144, CA   169, 213

Patefield *v* Belfast City Council [2000] IRLR 664, NICA   472

Perera *v* Civil Service Commission and Department of Customs and Excise (No. 2) [1983] IRLR 166, CA   167, 212

Pickstone *v* Freemans plc [1988] IRLR 357, HL   13

Polkey *v* A.E. Dayton Services Ltd [1987] IRLR 503, HL   4, 123

Porcelli *v* Strathclyde Regional Council [1986] IRLR 134, Court of Session   264, 271

Preston *v* Wolverhampton Healthcare Trust (No. 2) [2001] 1 CR 217   81

Price *v* Civil Service Commission [1978] IRLR 3, EAT   167, 168

Quinnen *v* Hovels [1984] IRLR 227, EAT   164

Qureshi *v* Victoria University of Manchester and another [1997] Case 01359/93   218

R *v* Associated Octel Ltd [1994] IRLR 540, CA   427, 428

R *v* Birmingham City Council ex parte Equal Opportunities Commission [1989] IRLR 173, HL   165

R v Board of Trustees of the Science Museum [1993] IRLR 853, CA   424

R v British Coal Corporation and Secretary of State for Trade and Industry ex parte Price [1994] IRLR 72, CA   122

R v Central Arbitration Committee and another ex parte Kwik-Fit [2002] IRLR 395, CA   534

R v Immigration Appeal Tribunal ex parte Antonissen [1991] ECR 1–745   219

R v Secretary of State for Employment ex parte Equal Opportunities Commission [1994] IRLR 176, HL   14, 38, 168, 184

R v Secretary of State for Employment ex parte Seymour-Smith and Perez [1997] IRLR 315   13, 167, 168

Rainey v Greater Glasgow Health Board [1987] IRLR 26, HL   170

Rask and Christensen v ISS Kantineservice A/S [1993] IRLR 133, ECJ   109–11

Raval v Department of Health and Social Security and Civil Service Commission [1985] IRLR 370   211

Rawlings v Barraclough t/a Independent Delivery Services Ltd [1995] 15595/95, IT   434

Rigby v Ferodo [1988] ICR 29, HL   104

Rinner-Kuhn v FWW Special-Gebaudereinigung GmbH and Co [1989] IRLR 493, ECJ   161

Risk Management Services (Chiltern) Ltd v Shrimpton [1977] EAT 803/77   107

Robertson and Jackson v British Gas Corporation [1983] IRLR 202, CA   72

Rossiter v Pendragon [2002] CA   116

Royle v Trafford Borough Council [1984] IRLR 184, HC   562

Sartor v P&O European Ferries (Felixstowe Ltd) [1992] IRLR 271, CA   332

Schmidt v Austicks Bookshops Ltd [1977] IRLR 360, EAT   186

Schmidt v Spar und Leihkasse der Früheren Ämter Bordesholm, Keil und Cronshagen [1994] IRLR 302, ECJ   110

Secretary of State for Employment v ASLEF (No. 2) [1972] 2 All ER 949, CA   557

Secretary of State for Employment v Spence and Others and Spencer and Sons (Market Harborough) Ltd (in liquidation) [1986] ICR 651, CA   113

Showboat Entertainment Centre Ltd v Owens [1984] IRLR 7, EAT   205

SIMAP v Conselleria de Sanidad y Consumo de la Generalidad Valenciana [2000] IRLR 598, ECJ   14, 86, 392

Sim v Rotherham Metropolitan Borough Council [1986] IRLR 391, HC   558

Simmons v Hoover Ltd [1976] 3 WLR 901, EAT   557

Singh v Rowntree Mackintosh [1979] ICR 554, EAT   169

Smith v Carpets International UK plc [1997] case 18005007/97   250

Smith v Safeway plc IRLR 457, CA   186

Snowball v Gardner Merchant Ltd [1987] IRLR 397, EAT   271

Sophie Redmond Stichting v Bartol [1992] IRLR 366, ECJ   109–11

Spafax Ltd v Harrison [1980] IRLR 442, CA   107

Squibb UK Staff Association v Certification Officer [1979] IRLR 75, EAT   491

Stadt Lengerich v Helmig [1995] IRLR 216, ECJ   80

Spijkers v Gebroeders Benedik Abattoir CV and Another [1986] 2CMLR 296, ECJ 109–11

Steel v UPW [1978] ICR 181, CA   169

Stewart v Cleveland Guest Engineering Ltd [1994] IRLR 440, EAT

Suzen v Zehnacker Gebaudereinigung GmbH Krankenhausservice [1997] IRLR 255, ECJ

Tariq *v* Young [1989] COIT 24773/88   206
Taylor *v* Connex South Eastern Ltd, EAT case 1243/99   115, 116
Thompson *v* SCS Consulting Ltd and others [2001] IRLR 801, EAT   117
Tidman *v* Aveling Marshall Ltd [1977] IRLR 218   342
Tottenham Green Under Fives' Centre *v* Marshall [1989] IRLR 147   214
United Association for the Protection of Trade Ltd *v* Kilburn EAT 787/84   107
United Bank *v* Akhtar [1989] IRLR 507, EAT   106
United Kingdom *v* European Council C–84/94 [1996] ECJ   13
Voteforce Associates *v* Quinn, EAT case 1186/00   395
W.A. Goold (Pearmak) Ltd *v* McConnell and Another [1995] IRLR 516   4, 32
Walker *v* Northumberland County Council [1995] IRLR 35, HC   74, 420
Weathersfield Ltd t/a Van and Truck Rentals *v* Sargent [1998] IRLR 14, EAT   209
Webster *v* Ministry of Defence [1991] 2628/91   179
Westbrook and Others *v* Building and Property Limited and Others
    COIT/2300437/98   114
Western Excavating Ltd *v* Sharp [1978] IRLR 27   116
West Yorkshire Police *v* Vento [2001] EAT case 522/01   178, 179
Whelan and Another t/a Cheers Off Licence *v* Richardson [1998] IRLR 114,
    EAT   342
Wheeler *v* Patel and J. Golding Group of Companies [1987] IRLR 211   116
Whent *v* T. Cartledge [1997] IRLR 153, EAT   118
Whiffen *v* Milham Ford Girls School and another [2001] IRLR 468, CA   121
White *v* Reflecting Roadstones Ltd [1991] ICR 733, EAT   107
Wileman *v* Minilec Engineering Ltd [1988] IRLR 144, EAT   271
Williams *v* Compair Maxam Ltd [1982] IRLR 83, EAT   120
Williams *v* Watsons Luxury Coaches Ltd [1990] IRLR 164, EAT   325
Williams *v* Western Mail and Echo [1980] IRLR 222, EAT   560
Wilson and Others *v* St Helens Borough Council; Baxendale and Meade *v* British
    Fuels Ltd [1998] IRLR 706, HL   115, 116
Wiluszynski *v* London Borough of Tower Hamlets [1989] ICR 493, CA   561
Winnet *v* Seamarks Brothers Ltd [1978] IRLR 387, EAT   560
Wren *v* Eastbourne Borough Council [1993] ICR 955, EAT   111
Wright *v* Scottbridge Construction Ltd [2001] IRLR 589, EAT   373
Wynnwith Engineering Co Ltd *v* Bennet [2001] EAT case 480/00   109
Young, James and Webster *v* UK [1982] 4 EHRR 38   496
Zafar *v* Glasgow City Council [1998] IRLR 36, HL   211, 217

Table of statutes

Asylum and Immigration Act 1996   220
Children and Young Persons Act 1933   390
Children and Young Persons Act 1963   390
Chronically Sick and Disabled Persons Act 1970   238
Companies Act 1985   516
Data Protection Act 1998   284, 288–92, 306
Disability Discrimination Act 1995   10, 26, 89, 140, 180, 207, 229–42, 246–57, 270, 274, 326, 328, 332, 390
Disability Rights Commission Act 1999   252
Employment Act 1989   225
Employment Act 2002   4, 32, 46, 123, 176, 315, 347, 467, 582
Employment Agencies Act 1973   87, 302
Employment Relations Act 1999   9, 33, 78, 333, 341, 348, 356, 526
Employment Rights Act 1996   9, 30–1, 62–70, 74, 77, 85, 89, 96, 105, 116, 119–25, 137, 186, 253, 295–6, 319, 321, 324–30, 335–45, 349, 367–74, 379, 380, 383, 389, 395, 432, 434, 435, 462–6, 469, 471, 472, 530, 531, 560, 561
Employment Rights (Dispute Resolution) Act 1998   21
Equal Pay Act 1970   25, 49, 73, 137, 155, 161–3, 170, 207, 363, 367
European Communities Act 1972   9, 24
Health and Safety at Work etc. Act 1974   9, 26, 36, 75, 76, 407–9, 412, 417, 419, 422–8, 438, 440–1, 443, 445–6, 510, 525
Human Rights Act 1998   9, 15–19, 24, 34, 285, 292–3, 576
Immigration Act 1971   219
Industrial Relations Act 1971   491, 509
Misuse of Drugs Act 1971   445
National Minimum Wage Act 1998   26, 46, 78, 89, 328–9, 356–7, 366–7, 370–8
Pensions Scheme Act 1993   526
Protection from Harassment Act 1997   264, 275
Public Interest Disclosure Act 1998   295
Race Relations Act 1976   10, 25, 137–40, 165, 172, 180, 198, 200, 205–20, 225–6, 270–1, 274
Race Relations (Amendment) Act 2000   137, 145, 164, 200, 209, 221, 304, 328
Rehabilitation of Offenders Act 1974   307
Regulation of Investigatory Powers Act 2000   292, 308
Sex Discrimination Act 1975   9, 10, 25, 89, 137–40, 160–77, 180–1, 184, 186, 207, 209, 271, 274, 328, 390
Sex Discrimination Act 1986   161

Trade Union and Labour Relations (Consolidation) Act 1992   10, 24, 49, 89, 118, 120, 122, 318, 320, 325, 328–9, 336, 338–9, 367, 397, 489, 491, 510, 523–4, 527–32, 548, 554, 559, 562, 564–8, 570, 572, 582
Unfair Contract Terms Act 1977   421

Table of statutory instruments

Collective Redundancies and Transfer of Undertakings (Protection of Employment) (Amendment) Regulations 1995 (SI 1995/2587) 123

Collective Redundancies and Transfer of Undertakings (Protection of Employment) (Amendment) Regulations 1999 (SI 1999/1925) 123

Companies (Director's Report) (Employment of Disabled Persons) Regulations 1980 (SI 1980/1160) 239

Conduct of Employment Agencies and Employment Business Regulations 1976 (SI 1976/715) 87

Control of Substances Hazardous to Health Regulations 1999 (SI 1999/437) 423, 433

Disability Discrimination (Meaning of Disability) Regulations 1996 (SI 1996/1455) 242–5

Disability Discrimination (Employment) Regulations 1996 (SI 1996/1456) 242, 247

Employment Equality (Sexual Orientation) Regulations 2003 (draft) 138, 161

Employment Equality (Religion or Belief) Regulations 2003 (draft) 138

Fixed-term Employees (Prevention of Less Favourable Treatment) Regulations 2002 (SI 2002/2034) 82–4, 89, 513, 530

Flexible Working (Eligibility, Complaints and Remedies) Regulations 2002 (SI 2002/3236) 468

Flexible Working (Procedural Requirements) Regulations 2002 (SI 2002/3207) 468

Health and Safety (Consultation with Employees) Regulations 1996 (SI 1996/1513) 436–7, 439, 443, 526

Health and Safety (Display Screen Equipment) Regulations 1992 (SI 1992/2792) 407, 428, 430–2

Health and Safety (Young Persons) Regulations 1997 (SI 1997/135) 429

Management of Health and Safety at Work Regulations 1999 (SI 1999/3242) 9, 407, 424, 428–9, 432, 441

Manual Handling Operations Regulations 1992 (SI 1992/2793) 433

Maternity and Parental Leave etc. Regulations 1999 (SI 1999/3312) 466, 468, 530

Maternity and Parental Leave (Amendment) Regulations 2002 (SI 2002/2789) 463

National Minimum Wage Regulations 1999 (SI 1999/584) 373

Noise at Work Regulations 1989 (SI 1989/1790) 433

Offshore Safety (Safety Representatives and Safety Committees) Regulations 1989 (SI 1989/971)   436, 526

Occupational Pension Schemes (Disclosure of Information) Regulations 1996 (SI 1996/1655)   526

Part-Time Workers (Prevention of Less Favourable Treatment) Regulations 2000 (SI 2000/1551)   9, 46, 79–81, 89

Paternity and Adoption Leave Regulations 2002 (SI 2002/2788)   470

Personal Protective Equipment at Work Regulations 1992 (SI 1992/3139)   433

Provision and Use of Work Equipment Regulations 1992 (SI 1992/2932)   433

Race Relations Act 1976 (Statutory Duties) Order 2001 (SI 2001/3458)   304

Race Relations Act 1976 (Amendment) Regulations 2002 (draft)   138

Race Relations (Questions and Replies) Order 1977 (SI 1977/842)   217

Reporting of Injuries, Diseases and Dangerous Occurrences Regulations 1995 (SI 1995/3163)   423, 433

Safety Representatives and Safety Committees Regulations 1977 (SI 1977/500)   427, 436–9, 443

Sex Discrimination (Gender Reassignment) Regulations 1999 (SI 1999/1102)   137

Sex Discrimination (Indirect Discrimination and Burden of Proof) Regulations 2001 (SI 2001/2660)   166

Telecommunications (Lawful Business Practice) (Interception of Communications) Regulations 2000 (SI 2000/2699)   292

Transfer of Undertakings (Protection of Employment) Regulations 1981 (SI 1981/1794)   9, 45, 67, 100, 108, 111–18, 126–7, 261, 327–8, 524–5, 528, 530

Transnational Information and Consultation of Employees Regulations 1999 (SI 1999/3323)   513, 521–2

Working Time Regulations 1998 (SI 1998/1833)   5, 9, 12, 27, 46, 72, 78, 82, 86, 89, 328–9, 338, 356, 382–3, 390–8, 402, 404, 529

Workplace (Health, Safety and Welfare) Regulations 1992 (SI 1992/3004)   433

Table of statutory codes of practice

ACAS Code of Practice on Disciplinary and Grievance Procedures (2000)   4, 10, 30, 32, 35, 38, 278, 280, 311, 314, 320, 322–7, 332–3, 337, 345–7, 419, 582

ACAS Code of Practice 2: Disclosure of information to trade unions for collective bargaining purposes (1997)   510, 529

ACAS Code of Practice 3: Time off for trade union duties and activities (1997) 530

Commission for Racial Equality: Code of Practice for the elimination of racial discrimination and the promotion of equality of opportunity in employment (1983)   10, 171, 215, 220–4, 280

Commission for Racial Equality: Code of Practice on the duty to promote race equality (2001)   140, 200, 215, 220

Equal Opportunities Commission: Code of Practice for the elimination of discrimination on the grounds of sex and marriage and the promotion of equality of opportunity in employment (1985)   10, 171, 181–2, 184, 280

Equal Opportunities Commission: Code of Practice on equal pay (1997)   162, 183

Code of Practice: Picketing (1992)   568–70

Code of Practice: Industrial action ballots and notice to employers (2000) 566–7

Code of Practice for the elimination of discrimination in the field of employment against disabled persons or persons who have had a disability (1996)   10, 243, 246, 248–9, 253–7

Table of European Community Law

Treaties and charters

Treaty establishing the European Community (1957) (The Treaty of Rome)
10–11, 37, 138, 141, 172, 186, 415
Treaty of European Union (1992) (The Treaty of Maastricht) 10–11, 511–12
Treaty of Amsterdam (1997) 10, 11, 138, 172
Treaty of Nice (2000) 10
Community Charter of the Fundamental Social Rights of Workers (1989) 497
Single European Act 1987 11, 37, 357, 415

Directives

Burden of Proof in Sex Discrimination Cases 1997 (Council Directive 97/80/EC)
11, 166, 176
Collective Redundancies 1975 (Council Directive 75/129/EEC) 11, 497
Collective Redundancies 1992 (Council Directive 92/56/EEC) 11, 123, 497
Contract of Employment Information 1991 (Council Directive 91/553/EEC)
11, 77
Data Protection 1995 (European Parliament and Council Directive 95/46/EC)
11, 288
Display Screen Equipment 1989 (Council Directive 89/391/EEC) 11
Employment 2000 (Council Directive 2000/78/EC) 11, 38, 137, 161, 200, 240,
251
Equal Pay 1975 (Council Directive 75/117/EEC) 11, 138
Equal Treatment 1976 (Council Directive 76/207/EEC) 11, 24, 136, 138, 160,
175, 178, 462
European Works Council/Information and Consultation Procedures in
Community-scale Undertakings 1994 (Council Directive 94/45/EC) 5, 11,
497, 512–13
Fixed-term Workers 1999 (Council Directive 99/EC) 11, 12, 78, 82
Informing and Consulting Employees 2002 (European Parliament and Council
Directive 2002/14/EC) 11, 33, 497–8, 513, 518
Insolvency of an Employer 1980 (Council Directive 80/987/EEC) 11
Parental Leave 1996 (Council Directive 96/34/EC) 11, 12, 357

Part-time Workers 1997 (Council Directive 97/81/EC)   11, 12, 38, 78, 79
Posted Workers 1996 (European Parliament and Council Directive 96/71/EC)
   11
Pregnant Workers 1992 (Council Directive 92/85/EEC)   11, 137–8, 175, 357,
   462
Race Discrimination 2000 (Council Directive 2000/43/EC)   11, 137, 200, 211,
   217
Safety and Health 1989 (Council Directive 89/391/EEC)   11, 357, 408, 416–17,
   428, 436, 497
Transfers of Undertakings (acquired rights) 1977 (Council Directive 77/187/EEC)
   11, 100, 108, 112, 115, 497, 524
Transfers of Undertakings (acquired rights) 1998 (Council Directive 98/50/EC)
   11, 100, 108, 111, 113–14
Working Time 1993 (Council Directive 93/104/EC)   4, 11–12, 356–7, 383, 387,
   391–4, 497
Working Time for Seafarers 1999 (Council Directive 99/63/EC)   391
Young People at Work 1994 (Council Directive 94/33/EC)   11, 394, 429

Recommendations

Dignity of Women and Men at Work (Council Recommendation 91/131/EEC)
   261, 270

Council of Europe: conventions

The European Convention for the Protection of Human Rights and
   Fundamental Freedoms (1950)   15–19, 24, 34, 54, 138–9, 185, 198, 285–7,
   293, 299, 495–6

List of useful websites

Advisory Conciliation and Arbitration Service
www.acas.org.uk

Cabinet Office
www.cabinet-office.gov.uk

Central Arbitration Committee
www.cac.gov.uk

Confederation of British Industry
www.cbi.co.uk

Chartered Institute of Personnel and Development
www.cipd.co.uk

Commission for Racial Equality
www.cre.gov.uk

Department for Education and Skills
www.dfes.gov.uk

Department of Trade and Industry (employment relations sites)
www.dti.gov.uk/er

Disability Rights Commission
www.drc-gb.org/drc/default.asp

Employment Tribunal Service
www.ets.gov.uk

Equal Opportunities Commission
www.eoc.org.uk

European Commission
www.europea.eu.int/comm

European Court of Human Rights
www.echr.coe.int

European Court of Justice
www.curia.eu.int

European Parliament
www.europarl.eu.int

European Union
www.europa.eu.int

Health and Safety Executive
www.hse.gov.uk

Home Office (Human Rights Act issues)
www.homeoffice.gov.uk/hract

Information Commissioner
www.dataprotection.gov.uk

Inland Revenue
www.inlandrevenue.gov.uk

Institute of Employment Studies
www.employment-studies.co.uk

Joseph Rowntree Foundation
www.jrf.org.uk

Low Pay Commission
www.lowpay.gov.uk

National Association of Citizens Advice Bureaux
www.nacab.org.uk

Office of National Statistics
www.statistics.gov.uk

Public Concern at Work
www.pcaw.demon.co.uk

Stationery Office
www.thestationeryoffice.com

Trades Union Congress
www.tuc.org.uk

United Kingdom Parliament
www.parliament.uk

Work Foundation
www.indsoc.co.uk

CHAPTER 1

An introduction to employment law

Learning objectives

This chapter considers the ways in which the employment relationship is regulated by both voluntary and legal measures. Having read it you should understand:

■ The nature and purpose of both voluntary and legal regulation in general.

■ The underpinning principles that derive from law.

■ The relationship that can exist between voluntary and legal regulation.

■ The various roles of the courts and tribunals.

It will provide the basis for understanding the central role of employment contracts in legal regulation of the individual employment relationship (which is explored in Chapter 2), and the role and contribution of collective bargaining as a key instrument for voluntary regulation (in Chapter 14).

1.1 Structure of the chapter

The chapter comprises the following sections:

■ *Introduction*: The role of legal and voluntary regulation, political influences.

■ *The nature of legal regulation*: Common law, statute law, European law, the European Convention on Human Rights, processes for complaint, the roles of tribunals and courts and effective remedies.

■ *The nature of voluntary regulation*: Terms and conditions of employment, and procedures in employment relations.

■ *Some underpinning principles*: Ethics, human rights, fairness, reasonableness, equal treatment, harmonisation, natural justice, consent and freedom.

1.2 Introduction

Broadly speaking, the employment relationship is regulated by both voluntary and legal measures. Voluntary measures comprise agreements and other decisions which derive from collective bargaining, arbitration, conciliation, grievance and disciplinary handling. They also include voluntarily accepted standards of good practice. Legal measures cover European Union (EU) treaties and directives, British statute law, the common law of contract and of tort, statutory codes of practice and some international standards. In practice, these are not isolated sets of measures. They invariably interlink and influence each other.

These voluntary and legal mechanisms achieve two broad purposes. First, at various points, they influence the function of management – i.e. the ways in which managers exercise power, control workforces and manage conflicts of interest. This influence can be illustrated in the following way. It is widely accepted that the employment relationship is characterised by an imbalance of power in favour of the employer. Both voluntary and legal regulation can restrain the unfettered exercise of this employer power. So, for example, collective bargaining can minimise the exploitation of individuals at work by agreements on pay and conditions and, also, by helping to process grievances. Furthermore, the law can establish both minimum conditions of employment and also set limits on the action an employer might take against employees. (This is discussed more fully in Chapter 2.)

The second purpose is to assert certain principles. On the one hand, there are those principles that influence the nature and quality of decisions that are made (for example, fairness, equal treatment, reasonableness, etc.). In addition, there are those principles which mould the regulatory process itself – for example, the fundamental importance of consent to the contract of employment, and of procedural fairness in disciplinary cases (*see* sections 1.4 and 1.5).

The interlocking of voluntary and legal measures of regulation is explored more fully in Fig. 1.1. The balance in favour of (or against) voluntarism or legalism shifts over time. It is particularly susceptible to changes in political opinion. In Britain, there has been a long-term trend away from a voluntary system of employment regulation, where the law was said to 'abstain'. This has been a result of both government policy and also, increasingly, of EU Social Action Programmes.

Figure 1.1 plots the impact of voluntary and legal regulation on both the substantive aspects of employment relations (i.e. terms and conditions of employment) and the procedures which are used for determining and influencing these terms and conditions and for dealing with any disagreements which might arise. Any system of employee relations, at any point in time, can be located in one or other of the quadrants in Fig. 1.1. In order to do this, two questions have to be answered:

1 To what extent does the law prescribe in detail, or only in principle, issues affecting terms and conditions of employment?

2 To what extent does the law prescribe in detail, or only in principle, the procedures to be adopted in the management of employee relations?

Let us explore both these questions further.

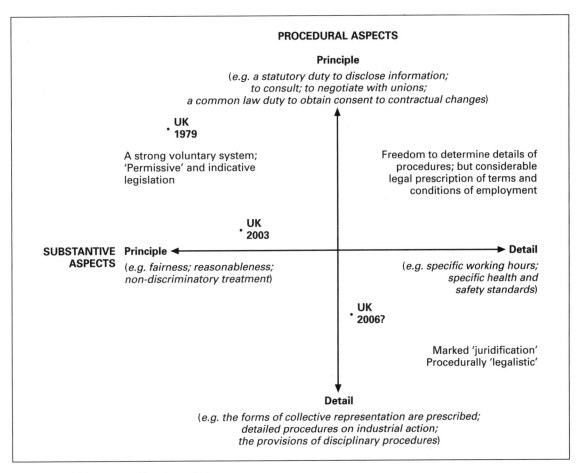

Figure 1.1   Voluntary and legal regulation

1.2.1   **Substantive aspects**

It has been traditionally accepted within British employment relations that, as far as terms and conditions of employment are concerned, the law may set a general framework, but the details would be determined either by employers alone or after negotiation with trade unions. Indeed, in 1954, one academic lawyer was able to make the following comment: 'There is, perhaps, no major country in the world in which the law has played a less significant role in the shaping of (industrial) relations than in Great Britain and in which the law and legal profession have less to do with labour relations' (Kahn-Freund, 1954).

However, this characterisation soon began to change. Increasingly, over the following five decades, statute law was enacted to establish certain principles to guide ways in which employers behave and also the terms and conditions of employment offered to staff. For example, fairness is now a basic criterion used to judge the reason for sacking an employee. Reasonableness is widespread as a reference point in health and safety law for assessing the standards to be implemented. The prohibition of unfair discrimination is fundamental to the law on sex, race and disability discrimination.

There has, however, also been a growing tendency towards more detailed pre-scription of certain terms and conditions of employment. This has arisen, in part, from case law and, also, from European law. We will look at each of these in turn.

Where the courts have interpreted the general framework of law on, for example, sex discrimination or unfair dismissal, they have set detailed requirements that then have an impact on all employers. So, for example, the requirement not to discriminate indirectly against women or on racial grounds has been elaborated to rule that certain employment practices might be discriminatory and unfair and would need to be justified (e.g. seniority-based promotion).

The impact of European law on the details of terms and conditions of employment is felt, particularly, in four areas: discrimination, the rights relating to pregnancy and parenting, health and safety and working-time regulation. In the case of the first two, there is a growing body of detailed requirements arising from Directives and from decisions of the European Court of Justice. The Working Time Directive has a considerable range of detailed provisions.

So, as far as the substantive aspects of employment relations, there is evidence to show Britain moving from a strongly 'voluntarist' position (i.e. at the left of the horizontal axis in Fig. 1.1) along towards a middle position. Academic commentators have said that this indicates growing evidence in Britain (as in other European countries) of juridification. This is defined as the tendency to which the behaviour of employers and unions is determined by reference to the legal standards. Indeed, it is suggested that a 'minimum standards' contract of employment has now been created through the continued intervention of statute law (*see* Chapter 2).

1.2.2 Procedural aspects

The procedural aspects can be subdivided into those that concern the individual employee, and those which concern collective relationships.

Individual employees work under a contract of employment agreed with the employer. Consent is at the heart of contract formation. It is also central to contract variation. The courts have asserted, in numerous cases, that when an employer wishes to change terms and conditions of employment, then, procedurally, the employee must be consulted and his/her agreement must be sought (*see* Chapter 2). In disciplinary matters involving individuals, procedural fairness is essential. This is specified in the ACAS *Code of Practice on Disciplinary and Grievance Procedures* and has been affirmed in case law (*Polkey* v *A.E. Dayton Services Ltd* [1987] IRLR 503, HL). The Employment Appeals Tribunal has also ruled on the right of an individual, through an implied term in the contract of employment, to raise grievances through an appropriate procedure (*W.A. Goold (Pearmak) Ltd* v *McConnell and Another* [1995] IRLR 516). A worker also has a statutory right to be accompanied in a grievance and a disciplinary hearing (ERA 1999, s 10). Finally, the Employment Act 2002 introduces, as an implied term of the contract of employment, a statutory minimum grievance procedure and dismissal and disciplinary procedure.

As far as collective relations are concerned, Britain has, historically, had a strong tradition of voluntarism for determining the procedures to be adopted in employment relations. So, employers could freely decide whether or not to negotiate with trade unions and on which terms and conditions of employment; the type of consultation arrangements to be introduced; and the structure of grievance and disciplinary procedures. There is still considerable freedom in this area for employers. However, it is not total. Changes, arising from British and European law, have introduced certain detailed procedural standards and requirements.

First of all, European law now sets a statutory duty upon employers to consult with employee representatives on collective redundancies, health and safety and transfers of undertakings. (To a large extent, the consultation mechanism is not prescribed in detail.) Secondly, the EU, in developing social partnership, has enacted a detailed information disclosure and consultation system for specified multinational companies, under the European Works Council Directive 1994. Thirdly, a framework of law on rights of statutory trade union recognition for collective bargaining provides some limitation on employers' freedom of action. Fourthly, the Working Time Regulations 1998 provide for an innovative collective arrangement – the right, in non-union organisations, to negotiate 'workforce agreements'. Fifthly, a European directive on informing and consulting employees is to be implemented in Britain between 2002 and 2008. Finally, the framework of British law governing industrial action has enacted many detailed procedural requirements – particularly for trade unions (*see* Chapters 14 and 15).

There has been some shift towards more detailed legal prescription of procedures. However, there remains a degree of discretion for management in the conduct of collective employment relations. So, in looking at the vertical axis in Fig. 1.1, there is a slight, but perceptible, movement down towards the centre.

Overall, then, British employment relations have changed in the balance between voluntary and legal regulation and the comparative significance of these two aspects. Suggested positions, for 2003 and 2006, have been indicated in Fig. 1.1. Further change is likely to continue.

Exercise 1.1	**Future changes – where will the UK be in 2006?**
	Investigate the changes that are likely to occur in employment law through action of the UK government and the European Union. Consider the extent to which these affect substantive and procedural issues. Estimate where the UK could be positioned in Fig. 1.1 in the year 2006.

1.2.3 Political perspectives

Shifts in approach to employment regulation reflect various political views held by British governments and the European Union. They are views about, for example, the nature of employment law, the extent of voluntarism and the degree of protection accorded to working people. It is possible to identify three different models to consider the underpinning politics of employment law (Morris, Willey and Sachdev, 2002: 229):

■ the free collective bargaining model;
■ the free labour market model;
■ the employee protection or social justice model.

Each of these models, in different ways and with different emphases, considers a range of economic, social, political and human rights issues: the management of the economy, the economic consequences of collective bargaining, the concept of social justice, the entitlement to job security, anti-discrimination policies, the human rights of freedom of association and freedom of expression.

The models are designed to review and analyse broad trends in the development and structure of employment law. 'None of these models exists in its pure form. Contemporary employment relations in Britain are, in fact, governed by the interpenetration of the three models' (Morris, Willey and Sachdev, 2002: 232).

The free collective bargaining model reflects the traditional pattern of British industrial relations which developed, particularly, from the First World War onwards. Collective bargaining was seen as the central process of employee relations. Usually, this resulted in voluntary agreements between an employer and particular trade unions. The role of consultation was comparatively marginal. This model reflected, in part, the international standards on freedom of association set in the 1940s and 1950s by the International Labour Organisation (ILO) and which British governments signed.

Philosophically, it emphasised voluntarism, which was characterised by the general, though not complete, 'abstention of the law' (Kahn-Freund, 1954). The limited law enacted had two principal functions. First, it created a permissive framework in which trade unions could exist lawfully, engage in collective bargaining and call for and organise industrial action. Public policy promoted collective bargaining as an acceptable method of conducting the employment relationship. For short periods in the 1970s, the law was used to provide statutory recognition rights for trade unions. This strongly reinforced the promotion of collective bargaining. The second function of law was to provide limited support for workers in vulnerable situations, e.g. through minimum pay set by Wages Councils for some workers (until 1993), and also through a partial framework of health and safety legislation.

A consensus on voluntarism was broadly subscribed to by employers, unions and governments of both major political parties. The generally accepted view was that employers and trade unions should be free voluntarily to negotiate and agree both terms and conditions and also the procedures for handling their industrial relations.

Voluntarism was subject to numerous strains in the post-war years. Government increasingly tried to balance the sectional interests and claims of trade unions and their members, on the one hand, and the public interest, on the other. So when, for example, the level of pay settlements achieved through free collective bargaining was perceived to be inflationary and economically damaging, governments, both Conservative and Labour, enacted statutory incomes policies and also introduced legislative attempts to limit trade union power. After 1979, under Thatcherism, this free collective bargaining model became subject to a major political onslaught.

The free labour market model was gradually implemented from 1979 to support the wider economic policies of the Thatcher government. It decisively broke the prevailing consensus on industrial relations policy – which, admittedly, had been subject to considerable strains since the late 1960s. The principles underlying this second model were reflected in several broad policy approaches:

- deregulation of the labour market: involving the removal of certain protective measures for employees which were seen as 'burdens on business'. Many employee protection policies of the European Union, seen as obstructing this overriding economic objective, were challenged (notably, the Working Time Directive 1993);

- the promotion of economic objectives encouraging cost effectiveness, competitiveness and flexibility in the use of labour;
- the primary importance of individualism in the employment relationship and the marginalising of collective interests and collective representation;
- the curbing of trade union power by abolishing, rather than reforming, recognition rights and by constraining unions' ability to organise industrial action.

The policies pursued were principally driven by the economic interests of employers. Arguably, the countervailing interests of working people received little consideration – except, perhaps, in the area of sex, race and disability discrimination policies and health and safety at work. To a considerable extent, however, these improved protections (in sex discrimination and health and safety) were a result of EU policies and rulings by the European Court of Justice (ECJ).

The employee protection or social justice model reflects the broad approach adopted by the EU. It infuses the growing range of the individual employment rights in force in Britain. The principles underlying European law and the EU's approach to social policy are founded upon the following precepts:

- protection for employees throughout the employment relationship by the creation of a regulatory framework;
- a recognition that employees have both individual and collective interests and that these have to be accommodated in a framework of employment law;
- harmonisation of conditions of employment across member states – complementing economic convergence;
- consideration given to economic issues (cost effectiveness, competitiveness and labour flexibility) in the formulation of employee protection measures;
- the promotion of consensus between the social partners – i.e. employers and their organisations and employees and their trade unions;
- an acceptance of the principle of subsidiarity – that is to say that some issues are more appropriately regulated at the level of the member state rather than at the level of the EU.

Consequently, European law (principally, through the Treaties and Directives) has led to the enactment of, for example, equal treatment on the grounds of sex, race, sexuality, age, religion and disability, equal pay, the protection of pregnant workers, the establishment of health and safety standards, restrictions on working time, job security and the protection of part-time and fixed-term workers.

As far as the procedures of employee relations are concerned, the EU has been less interventionist in relation to trade union recognition for collective bargaining, and dispute resolution. Detailed arrangements are, generally, the responsibility of individual member states. However, the concept of social partnership has been developed through EU legislation on duties to consult (*see* Chapter 14).

Since the election of a Labour government in 1997, contemporary British employment relations continues to be characterised by the interpenetration of all three models. Collective bargaining still has a significant function (particularly in the public sector). The statutory rights for trade unions to claim recognition for collective bargaining go some way towards maintaining this as a characteristic in British employment relations. The government, however, also supports aspects of the free market model. At the 1997 Trades Union Congress the Prime Minister, Tony Blair, committed the government to 'the flexibility of the present labour market'. He spoke of a 'crusade for competitiveness' and the intention 'to build the most educated, skilled, adaptable and creative country in the western world'. A central question remains: how can flexibility in all its forms be promoted and achieved and, at the same time, accommodate the concerns of working people for income and job security and for career development? With the rescission of the 'opt-out' from the Social Chapter and a commitment to enact further European employee-protection measures, it is clear that a difficult balance has to be struck between some apparently divergent policy directions.

1.3 The nature of legal regulation

Legal regulation of employment consists of three areas: frameworks of law that set standards, processes for dealing with complaints about infringements of legal rights, and the provision of remedies. We will look at these three areas in turn.

1.3.1 Standards in law

Standards for the employment relationship are set in the common law, statute law, regulations and European law. Additionally, statutory codes of practice are approved by Parliament.

Common law

This is formulated by judges through case law. They set and develop various principles (e.g. the concept of reasonableness). They can create various legal tests (e.g. to define an employee). Common law is used in interpreting statute law. It has two aspects: the law of contract and the law of tort.

Law of contract: A contract is an agreement between two or more parties. These parties create their own rights and duties. So, they voluntarily decide the content of the contract. Courts may be involved in discovering the intention of the parties (i.e. what they meant by a particular provision), and whether the contract was breached. Within the employment relationship (*see* Chapter 2) this branch of law has considerable significance through the contract of employment.

Law of tort: A tort is a civil wrong other than a breach of contract. Obligations here are imposed by law. This branch of law concerns the interests of a person which may be injured by another. So, a person may be injured by another's negligence (e.g. as a result of poor health and safety management), or an employer's economic interests may be damaged by unlawful industrial action organised by a trade union. A central concern for courts, in this branch of the law, is the issue of liability (i.e. who is liable for causing the injury). In some instances, the issue of vicarious liability arises – where one person assumes liability for another's action or inaction (e.g. where an employer is liable for all breaches of health and safety standards – even where they may be committed by a manager or another employee). Vicarious liability is also of particular importance in the enforcement of anti-discrimination law (Chapters 4–6).

Statute law

This is primary legislation. It refers to Acts of Parliament which may set new legal requirements and can also overturn case-law decisions of the judges. It is the most common way through which new general rights and duties are established. There are many examples in the field of employment relations (e.g. the Sex Discrimination Act 1975; the Employment Rights Act 1996). The issues for the courts, in respect of statute law, are:

- Does the complainant have a remedy?
- Has a provision of the legislation been infringed?
- Has the specific legislative provision been interpreted in previous judgments (particularly by the Court of Appeal, the House of Lords or, if European law is involved, the European Court of Justice)?
- Does the legislation have to be interpreted to conform with European law?
- What are the implications of the Human Rights Act 1998?

Regulations

It is important to note that Acts of Parliament can enable new legal standards to be created in the form of regulations (statutory instruments). These are laid before Parliament and approved through a simpler process than that necessary for enacting a statute. This is known as secondary or subordinate legislation. In employment law, there are a number of important regulations, many of which have been made under the European Communites Act 1972 or the Health and Safety at Work Act 1974 or the Employment Relations Act 1999. Examples include:

- Transfer of Undertakings (Protection of Employment) Regulations 1981.
- Management of Health and Safety at Work Regulations 1999.
- Working Time Regulations 1998.
- Part-Time Workers (Prevention of Less Favourable Treatment) Regulations 2000.

In the judicial process, when Acts and regulations are interpreted, legal standards are clarified and are applicable for future reference. In essence, legal precedents are established.

Statutory codes of practice

In hearing complaints, tribunals and courts may be required to take account of statutory codes of practice. These have been approved by Parliament. The main ones for individual employment rights currently in force are:

- ACAS Code: Disciplinary and Grievance Procedures (2000).
- Commission for Racial Equality: Code of Practice for the elimination of racial discrimination and the promotion of equality of opportunity in employment (1983).
- Equal Opportunities Commission: Code of Practice for the elimination of discrimination on the grounds of sex and marriage and the promotion of equality of opportunity in employment (1985).
- Code of Practice for the elimination of discrimination in the field of employment against disabled persons or persons who have had a disability (1996).
- Equal Opportunities Commission Code of Practice on equal pay (1996).

The status of statutory codes is as follows:

- failure of a person to observe any provision of a code 'shall not of itself render him liable to any proceedings';
- however, in any proceedings before an employment tribunal, any appropriate code of practice 'shall be admissible in evidence, and if any provision of such a code appears to the tribunal to be relevant to any question arising in the proceedings it shall be taken into account in determining that question'.

So, for example, if an employer fails to permit a dismissed employee the opportunity to be represented by a fellow worker at the disciplinary hearing, this will not be an offence for which the employer might be sued. However, a tribunal, in considering the fairness of such a dismissal will take into account this failure by the employer when determining whether or not the dismissal is fair (TULRCA 1992, s 207; RRA 1976, s 47; SDA 1975, s 56A; DDA 1995, s 51).

European law

In employment regulation, four elements of European law are relevant: the Treaties of the European Union; Directives; rulings of the European Court of Justice; and, to a much lesser extent, non-binding instruments.

Treaty articles: The original Treaty of Rome 1957 created the then European Economic Community. This was subsequently amended – notably by the Single European Act 1987, the Treaty on European Union 1992 (the Maastricht Treaty), the Treaty of Amsterdam 1997 and the Treaty of Nice 2000. A treaty article can be enforced as a direct right in the courts of member states where it is 'sufficiently clear, precise and unconditional as to require no further interpretation'. Such a treaty article can have direct effect both 'vertically' and 'horizontally'. This means, in the first instance, that the article confers rights for the citizen against the state. In the second instance, it confers rights for one private citizen to exercise against another. 'The most important use of direct effect in the field of social policy has been in relation to the principle of equal pay for equal work between men and women' (Deakin and Morris, 1998: 114).

Among the key Treaty articles that have implications for employment relations are the following. The first group deal with standards of treatment advocated by the European Union. The second group deal with the procedures used to adopt new European law.

Standards of treatment

■ prohibition of discrimination on the grounds of nationality;

■ promotion of improved working conditions and approved standard of living for workers (Art 136);

■ the principle of 'equal pay for equal work' (Art 141).

Procedures

■ the requirement of unanimity in the adoption of harmonisation measures (Art 94);

■ the provision of 'qualified majority voting' for the adoption of health and safety at work measures (Art 138);

■ action that can be taken against member states who persistently fail to implement Directives, which can result in a reference to the European Court of Justice.

(The Treaty of Amsterdam 1997, implemented from 1 May 1999, consolidated the original Treaty of Rome 1957, the Single European Act 1987 and the Maastricht Treaty 1992.)

Directives: these are the principal means for establishing employment rights within the European Union (*see* Table 1.1). They are proposed by the Commission. After many ministerial meetings, ultimately, they may be agreed and adopted by the Council of the European Union (which comprises the heads of government of all member states). Traditionally, agreement had to be unanimous. However, in 1987 amendments were made to permit the adoption by 'qualified majority vote' (QMV) of certain Directives (those defined as health and safety

Table 1.1   Some key European Directives on employment policy

1975	Equal Pay	1994	Protection of Young People at Work
1975	Collective Redundancies	1995	Data Protection
1976	Equal Treatment	1996	Parental Leave
1977	Acquired Rights	1996	Posted Workers
1980	Insolvency	1997	Part-time Workers
1989	Health and Safety	1997	Burden of Proof in Sex Discrimination Cases
1990	Display Screen Equipment	1998	Business Transfers Directive
1991	Contract of Employment Information	1999	Fixed-Term Work
1992	Collective Redundancies	2000	Race Discrimination (July 2003)
1992	Pregnant Workers	2000	Employment (phased in by 2 Dec. 2006)
1993	Working Time	2002	Information and Consultation (phased in by 2008)
1994	European Works Councils		

Notes:

1 Dates in brackets are those by which the new Directives must be implemented by Britain; the other Directives have already been transposed into law.

2 The details of many of these Directives will be considered, as appropriate, in other chapters of the book.

measures). The Treaties of Amsterdam and Nice envisage extensions to QMV to certain employment protection measures (notably equal opportunities and equal treatment).

It is also possible, under procedures adopted in the Maastricht Treaty, for the 'social partners' to negotiate a 'framework agreement' on a particular policy proposed by the Commission. These 'social partners' are UNICE, the European private-sector employers' confederation; CEEP, the public-sector equivalent; and ETUC, the European confederation of trade unions. Framework agreements may then be adopted by the Council of the European Union as the basis of a new Directive. In recent years, three significant examples have been the 1996 Directive on Parental Leave, the 1997 Directive on Part-time Workers and the 1999 Directive on Fixed-Term Work. There have also been unsuccessful attempts to introduce Directives (for example, that relating to agency work).

The main advantage of such framework agreements is the ability to take into account, at the drafting stage, the practical implications (reflecting the experiences of employers and unions) of such policies proposed by the Commission. It may be that rather than provide detailed provisions, general principles are agreed which can guide employment practice at individual workplaces. This is particularly the case with the 1997 Part-time Workers Framework Agreement and Directive (*see also* Chapter 2).

Generally, Directives are enforceable against member states. Each country is obliged to transpose a Directive into national law within a specified number of years. In Britain this is achieved by passing an Act of Parliament or laying regulations before Parliament for approval. So, for example, the Working Time Directive 1993 was enacted through the Working Time Regulations 1998.

The enforcement of Directives has particular significance for those employed in the public sector (and in certain private-sector companies which carry out public functions under law). They may use a Directive in a national court without it having been transposed into national law. This arises because they work for the state (the civil service) or 'an emanation of the state' (e.g. a local authority, a hospital trust or an agency created from the reorganisation of the civil service). The Directive is said to have 'direct effect'. However, the Directive must be 'sufficiently precise and unconditional' to be enforced without the need for domestic legislation. In practical terms, this means that a person employed in any public-sector body can complain that a specific right has been infringed even is there is no British legislation. Unlike a Treaty article, a Directive can only have 'vertical direct effect' – i.e. against the state or an emanation of the state.

The concept of 'emanation of the state' has been interpreted by the courts to embrace certain privatised corporations (notably British Gas and water companies). Three tests have been developed to help establish whether an organisation can be so defined:

1 Is there a public service provision?
2 Is there control by the state?
3 Does the organisation have special powers?

It was ruled in a House of Lords judgment that 'a state body is a body, whatever its legal form, which has been made responsible, pursuant to a measure adopted by the state, for providing a public service under the control of the state, and which has, for that purpose, special powers beyond those which result from the normal rules applicable in relations between individuals' (*Foster* v *British Gas plc* [1991] ICR 84).

Rulings of the European Court of Justice: With Treaty articles and Directives, these have been the other most significant influence on the development of employment regulation within Britain. These are binding on all member states, irrespective of the country of origin of a particular case. The ECJ is responsible for determining the application and interpretation of European law (*see* Table 1.2). Its main functions are:

- *To decide whether a member state has failed to fulfil a treaty obligation.* For example, it decided that because of the failure of the Italian government to implement the 1980 Insolvency Directive by the due date in 1983, citizens could sue their government for the loss they had sustained, provided there was a clear link between a government's failure and the damage suffered by an individual (*Francovich and Bonifaci* v *the Republic of Italy* [1992] IRLR 84). The consequence of this case is that 'Frankovich claims' can now be made in the British courts, subject to certain conditions.

- *To deal with infraction proceedings.* For example, the failure of the United Kingdom to provide for full consultation rights in respect of redundancies and business transfers was referred by the Commission to the Court for a ruling (*EC Commission* v *United Kingdom* C–383/92 (1994)). Ultimately, it resulted in the adoption of new consultation regulations in 1995. These were further amended in 1999.

- *To review the legality of decisions of the Council of the European Union and the Commission.* For example, the court determined that the Working Time Directive 1993 was properly made under the treaty procedures (*United Kingdom* v *the European Council* (1996) ECJ C–84/94).

- *To review the failure to act of the Council of the European Union and the Commission where the treaty obliges them to act.*

- *To give preliminary rulings on points of European law at the request of a national court.* For example, the House of Lords referred the issue of the two-year qualifying period for unfair dismissal claims to the ECJ (*R* v *Secretary of State for Employment ex parte Seymour-Smith and Perez* [1997] IRLR 315).

- *To hear complaints on the application and interpretation of European law.*

- *To determine the wider application of European law.* For example, in 1990, the ECJ ruled that national courts are obliged to interpret that country's domestic legislation in the light of European Directives regardless of whether the domestic legislation pre-dates or post-dates the Directives. This wide view of interpretation also concerns law enacted in the member states prior to that country's entry into the EU (*Marleasing SA* v *La Comercial Internacional de Alimentación* C–106/89).

In interpreting the law, the ECJ adopts a 'purposive' (as opposed to 'literal') approach to interpretation. So, it will consider the intention and the 'spirit' of the legislation, rather than the strict 'letter'. This is compatible with the character of

Table 1.2 The impact of European law: some key cases

Non-discriminatory retirement ages as between men and women	The House of Lords judgment in the *Marshall* case resulted in amendments to British law in the Sex Discrimination Act 1986 (*Marshall* v *Southampton and SW Hampshire Area Health Authority* [1986] IRLR 140).
Discrimination on the grounds of pregnancy defined a 'direct discrimination'	This arose from the ECJ ruling in the *Dekker* case and elaborated equal treatment law (*Dekker* v *Stichting Vormingscentrum* [1991] IRLR 27). The concept was also incorporated in the Pregnant Workers Directive 1992.
Protection of workers against dismissal during a business transfer	In *Litster* v *Forth Dry Dock* [1989] IRLR 161 the House of Lords clarified the situation under European law about whether contracts could be terminated and the circumstances where an employee had continuity of service.
Obligation of employers to consult employee representatives or union representatives in collective redundancies and transfers of undertakings	This complaint about the UK's non-compliance with European law to the ECJ (*EC Commission* v *United Kingdom* C–383/92 [1994] IRLR 392) resulted in new regulations being approved by Parliament under the previous Conservative government. The government amended these in 1999.
Pensions defined as 'pay'	This resulted in superannuation payments being defined, by the Court of Appeal, as subject to the European equal pay provisions (Art 119 of the Treaty of Rome) in *Barber* v *Guardian Royal Exchange* [1990] IRLR 240.
Part-time workers' access to statutory rights	It was ruled by the House of Lords (*R* v *Secretary of State for Employment ex parte Equal Opportunities Commission* [1994] IRLR 176) interpreting equal treatment law that it was indirect discrimination against women to have hours qualifications for access to redundancy pay and unfair dismissal compensation. New regulations were introduced. These provided one qualification for all employees (full-time or part-time) – two years' continuous service with an employer.
The removal of the ceiling on compensation in sex discrimination cases	A ceiling on compensation payments was ruled as limiting the effective implementation of the principle of equal treatment (*Marshall* v *Southampton and SW Hampshire Area Health Authority* (*No. 2*) [1993] IRLR 455). As a consequence, ceilings on compensation in all discrimination actions – both sex and race – were removed in new regulations (SI 1993/2798; SI 1994/1748).
Discrimination on the grounds of transsexual status ruled contrary to equal treatment law	This was determined by the ECJ in *P* v *S and Cornwall County Council* [1996] IRLR 347. The Sex Discrimination (Gender Reassignment) Regulations came into force on 1 May 1999 (SI 1999/1102).
Defining 'working time' when 'on call'	This interpretation of the Working Time Directive 1993 was determined in *SIMAP* v *Conselleria de Sanidad y Consumo de al Generalidad Valenciana* [2000] IRLR 598.
Entitlement to paid annual leave	The 13-week qualifying period for this was ruled to be unlawful in *BECTU* v *Secretary of State for Trade and Industry* ECJ, C–173/99. The entitlement was ruled to accrue from the first day of employment.

much European law which is in the form of broad statements of overriding aims and principles. The House of Lords has accepted that such an approach might be accepted in the British courts for complying with European law (Templeman LJ in *Pickstone* v *Freemans plc* [1988] IRLR 357).

Non-binding instruments: Principally these are Recommendations and Resolutions.

European Convention on Human Rights

From 2 October 2000, the European Convention on Human Rights was incorporated into law in the United Kingdom through the Human Rights Act 1998. This Convention was drafted under the auspices of the Council of Europe – an intergovernmental body, founded in 1949, primarily to promote democracy, human rights and the rule of law throughout Europe. It is separate from the European Union, although member states of the EU are also members of the Council of Europe and the EU accepts the Convention.

The Convention was ratified by the UK in 1951. Until 2000, people who alleged that their human rights had been infringed needed to embark on a lengthy process to the European Court of Human Rights in Strasbourg. Following the implementation of the Human Rights Act 1998, the Convention is gradually woven into the fabric of law in the UK and complainants have easier access to possible redress in the domestic courts. (Figure 1.2 sets out the key Convention rights.) The Human Rights Act 1998 has three fundamental effects:

■ *Common law*: This must be developed compatibly with Convention rights. This means that previous judgments can be questioned. In respect of

---

The detailed provisions of these rights are in Schedule 1 to the Human Rights Act 1998

Absolute rights
These have no restrictions or limitations:
Article 7: Protection from retrospective criminal penalties
Article 3: Protection from torture, inhuman and degrading treatment and punishment
Article 4: Prohibition of slavery and enforced labour

Limited rights
These can be limited in specific circumstances defined in the Convention:
Article 5: The right to liberty and security
A person may be detained if the detention is lawful. It covers, for example arrest by the police and imprisonment following conviction by a court.

Qualified rights
Many rights with a bearing on employment relations are in this category:
Article 8: Right to respect for private and family life
Article 9: Freedom of thought, conscience and religion
Article 10: Freedom of expression
Article 11: Freedom of assembly and association

It is permissible to interfere with these qualified rights in the following circumstances:

■ If the interference is provided for in law
■ If the interference is necessary in a democratic society. It must fulfil a pressing social need; pursue a legitimate aim; be proportionate to the aims being pursued; and be related to a permissible aim set out in the relevant Article (e.g. the prevention of crime or the protection of public order). (*See* Exercise 1.2.)

Other rights
Article 6: Right to a fair trial
Article 14: Prohibition of discrimination

Figure 1.2 Key Convention rights

employment this is likely, in time, through case law, to affect the common law of contract.

■ *Legislation*: All legislation (Acts of Parliament, Regulations and Orders) must be interpretated and implemented in compliance with the Convention 'so far as it is possible to do so' (HRA 1998, s 3(1)). Where there are two possible interpretations of a statutory provision (i.e. one compatible with the Convention and one not), that which is compatible must be adopted. Previous interpretations, under case law from courts in the United Kingdom, may no longer be relied upon. Where it is not possible to interpret particular legislation compatibly, a court (in England and Wales, the High Court and above; and in Scotland the Court of Session and the High Court of Justiciary) may:

– Quash or disapply secondary legislation (i.e. Regulations and Orders).

– Issue a 'declaration of incompatibility' (HRA 1998, s 4) for primary legislation (i.e. an Act of Parliament). This will not rescind the legislation. It will remain in force. However, the declaration will draw the issue to the government's attention and enable the appropriate minister to invoke the 'fast track' procedure to amend the legislation in Parliament by a remedial order.

– Require UK courts and tribunals to take account of case law from the European Court of Human Rights in Strasbourg but not necessarily be bound by it.

(In the employment context, neither employment tribunals nor the Employment Appeals Tribunal have power to quash or disapply secondary legislation nor to issue declarations of incompatibility. If this was done in an employment law case, it would be, at the appeal stages, in the Court of Appeal or the House of Lords. Nevertheless, employment tribunals and the EAT must interpret the law compatibly with the Convention.)

■ *Activities of public authorities*: It is unlawful for a public authority to act incompatibly with Convention rights. An aggrieved person or 'victim' (HRA 1998, s 7) can bring a case against a public authority before a court of tribunal in the United Kingdom. The Act covers all activities of a public authority: for example, policy-making; rules and regulations; personnel issues; administrative procedures; decision-making.

There are three broad categories of public authorities:

– *'Obvious' or 'pure' public authorities*: This describes, for example, a government department or statutory agency; a Minister of the Crown; local authorities; NHS trusts; education authorities; fire and civil defence authorities; the armed forces; the police and the immigration service; and the prison service. Everything done by these (whether in their public functions or in their private functions – e.g. offering an employment contract) is covered by the Human Rights Act.

– *Courts and tribunals*.

– *'Hybrid' or quasi-public bodies*: These are bodies which carry out some functions of a public nature. So, they are not a public authority for all their activities, but only when carrying out public functions. Examples include the privatised utilities (the gas, electricity and water companies).

Exercise 1.2	How much freedom of expression?

Article 10: Freedom of expression
This is a qualified right. It means that it can be interfered with. The first paragraph states:

Everyone has the right to freedom of expression. This right shall include the freedom to hold opinions and to receive and impart information and ideas without interference by public authority and regardless of frontiers. (Art 10.1)

- Write down those circumstances in which you think it might be appropriate to inter-fere with a person's freedom of expression. These can relate to the workplace or social relations in general.
- Say why you have selected these particular circumstances.
- How would you restrict freedom of expression?
- What problems do you think might arise from curtailing freedom of expression?
- Now read the second paragraph of Article 10 and check whether or not the restric-tions you were proposing fit.

The exercise of these freedoms, since it carries with it duties and responsibilities, may be subject to such formalities, conditions, restrictions or penalties as are prescribed by law and are necessary in a democratic society, in the interests of national security, territorial integrity or public safety, for the prevention of disorder or crime, for the protection of health or morals, for the protection of the reputation or rights of others, for preventing the disclosure of information received in confidence, or for maintaining the authority and impartiality of the judiciary. (Art 10.2)

Were the restrictions that you were proposing provided for in law; fulfilling a pressing social need; pursuing a legitimate aim; and proportionate to the aims being pursued?

Feedback on this exercise is provided in the Appendix to this book.

In addition to the rights and freedoms outlined above, two other important Convention articles are that ensuring a fair trial (Article 6) and the prohibition against discrimination (Article 14). The latter is not a free-standing right. It can only be invoked in conjunction with an allegation that another Convention right has been infringed. It states that 'the enjoyment of the rights and freedoms set forth in this Convention shall be secured without discrimination on any ground such as sex, race, colour, language, religion, political or other opinion, national or social origin, association with a national minority, property, birth or other status'. This list of potential discriminatory grounds is not comprehensive. The phrases 'such as' and 'or other status' show that it is illustrative.

Remedial action: The Human Rights Act 1998 creates two effects:

- *A direct effect*: This where a person (i.e. a victim) can enforce Convention rights directly in court through starting legal proceedings. Such action can only be taken against a **public authority**. A victim may be a company or other organ-isation as well as a private individual. The complaint has, normally, to be made within one year of the act complained of (HRA 1998, s 7(5)). If a court finds that a public authority has breached a person's Convention rights, it can award whatever remedy is available to it within its existing powers and is just and equitable (HRA 1998, s 8(1)). This may include the award of damages;

quashing an unlawful decision; ordering the public authority not to take the proposed action.

■ *An indirect effect*: There is no means of enforcing Convention rights directly against **private individuals** (including private companies or quasi-public bodies when they are carrying out their private functions). In these cases where a private individual or organisation is involved, there is an indirect effect. This means that the law (statute and common law and any secondary legislation) in the cases involving such private 'individuals' must be applied and interpreted compatibly with the Convention.

Complaints under the Human Rights Act may be initiated in a number of courts or tribunals, depending on which is appropriate. If the claim is based on a contract or in tort (e.g. a claim for personal injury), action should start in the High Court or the County Court (or the Sheriff Court or Court of Session in Scotland). Where the case relates to the decision of a public body, the appropriate action will usually be judicial review in the High Court.

An illustration of the implications of the Convention can be seen in the case of Christine Goodwin (Fig. 1.3). Although the complaint originated prior to the implementation of the Human Rights Act 1998, it shows the implications for UK law of Convention rights and the need for public authorities to behave compatibly.

(The implications of Convention rights and freedoms for employment relations will be considered further in appropriate chapters of this textbook).

The complainant
Christine Goodwin, a post-operative male to female transsexual, is a UK citizen, born in 1937. Her treatment and surgery were provided for and paid for by the National Health Service between 1985 and 1990.

The complaint
She alleged violations of the European Convention of Human Rights. (The hearing was held in the Court of Human Rights in Strasbourg because the complaint was lodged in 1995 – prior to the ECHR's incorporation into UK law.) The complaint related to British law affecting the treatment of transsexuals in employment, social security, pensions and marriage.

Details of the complaint
Having been dismissed from one employer in the early 1990s (she believes for her transsexual status), she started a new job and was required to provide her National Insurance number. She was concerned that from this number the new employer could have traced details of her history. The Department for Social Security refused her request for a new number. She was also told that she would be ineligible for a state pension at 60 years (1997) – the age of entitlement for a woman. So, she reached an agreement to pay national insurance contributions directly and not through her employer. A transsexual continues to be recorded for social security, national insurance and employment purposes as being of the sex recorded at birth. She was not able to obtain a new birth certificate. Finally, although she had a continuing relationship with a man, she could not marry because the law treated her as a man.

Relevant articles of the Convention
Article 8, the right of privacy; Article 12, the right to marry; Article 13, the provision of an effective remedy; and Article 14, non-discrimination.

Figure 1.3 The case of Christine Goodwin

Source: Summarised from judgment of European Court of Human Rights – Application No. 28957/95. The number in brackets refer to paragraphs in the judgment.

The Court's approach
It recognised that this case was at the heart of social changes. Implicitly, it acknowledged that the ECHR is a 'living instrument' – i.e. it should be interpreted in the light of changing circumstances, values and social attitudes. It noted that it was not bound to follow its own previous decisions.

The Court's key decisions
- *Right to privacy*: Balancing the interests of individuals and the state, it stated, unanimously, that 'society may reasonably be expected to tolerate a certain inconvenience to enable individuals to live in dignity and worth in accordance with the sexual identity chosen by them at great personal cost' (91). 'Exceptions are already made to the historic basis of the birth register system . . . in the case of legitimisation or adoptions . . . To make a further exception in the case of transsexuals . . . would not, in the Court's view, pose the threat of overturning the entire system' (87). So, 'the fair balance that is inherent in the Convention now tilts decisively in favour of the applicant. There has, accordingly, been a failure to respect her right to private life in breach of Article 8 of the Convention' (93).

- *Right to marry*: 'The applicant . . . lives as a woman, is in a relationship with a man and would only wish to marry a man. She has no possibility of doing so. In the Court's view, she may therefore claim that the very essence of her right to marry has been infringed' (101). Finding a breach of Article 12, the Court, unanimously 'finds no justification for barring the transsexual from enjoying the right to marry under any circumstances'.

Implications
- *A legally binding decision?* The rulings of the European Court of Human Rights are not formally binding on the UK Government in the way that those of the European Court of Justice are. (Non-compliance with the decisions of the latter would breach our Treaty obligations.) However, a British court deciding a human rights issue is required, in deciding on compatibility with the ECHR, to take account of Strasbourg case law.

- *Moral commitment?* In conformity with the ratification of the ECHR and its incorporation into domestic law, the UK will take action. To date, employment law has changed to bring transsexuals under the protection of the Sex Discrimination Act 1975 (*see* Chapter 4). In terms of more general legislation (e.g. the ability to have a new birth certificate and the implications of this for employment), action is under consideration.

- *Legal consistency*: A further consideration for the British government may be the need to establish some consistency in law. The Court commented that 'where a state has authorised the treatment and surgery alleviating the condition of a transsexual, financed or assisted in financing the operations and indeed permits the artificial insemination of a woman living with a female-to-male transsexual . . . it appears illogical to refuse to recognise the legal implications of the result to which the treatment leads' (78).

- *Redress for 'victims' now*: Christine Goodwin made her claim in June 1995. A ruling by the European Court of Human Rights was made in July 2002. The Human Rights Act 1998 improves the process available to UK citizens. Since October 2000, an applicant can now lodge complaints about incompatibility with the ECHR in the UK courts. Appeal to the Strasbourg Court is still available to those who argue that the UK courts have failed to identify a breach of the ECHR.

Figure 1.3 (*cont'd*)

1.3.2 Processes for complaint

Normally, complaints about individual employment rights are made to an employment tribunal. It is possible for either an applicant (the employee or worker) or a respondent employer to appeal, on a point of law, to the Employment Appeals Tribunal and then, usually with permission, to the Court of Appeal and to the House of Lords. If the complaint has involved the application of European law

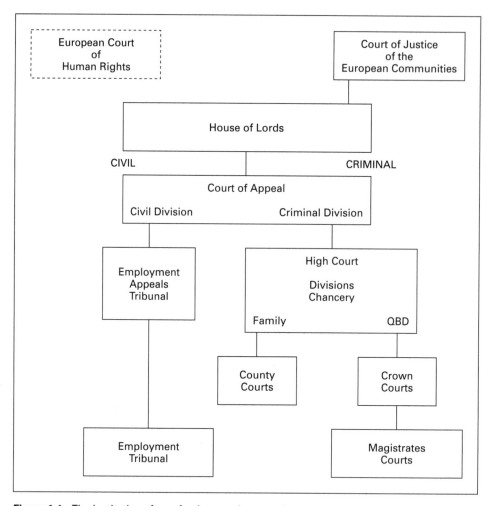

Figure 1.4 The institutions for enforcing employment law

(e.g. on sex discrimination, working time, transfers of undertakings or equal pay), an ultimate appeal would be to the European Court of Justice (in Luxembourg). The Court of Appeal or the House of Lords can refuse leave (or permission) to appeal further (*see* Fig. 1.4).

In addition, various statutory agencies have responsibility for assisting in specified ways in the enforcement of employment law. The most notable are the Advisory Conciliation and Arbitration Service, the Equal Opportunities Commission, the Commission for Racial Equality, the Health and Safety Commission and the Health and Safety Executive, the Low Pay Commission, the Disability Rights Commission and the Central Arbitration Committee. The key institutions of employment law are reviewed below.

Employment tribunals

Originally set up in 1964, as industrial tribunals, to deal with training levy complaints, their jurisdiction was extended to unfair dismissal in 1972 and now covers a very wide range of employment rights (e.g. discrimination on the grounds of sex, race and disability, equal pay, maternity rights, rights of trade union membership and unlawful pay deductions). Under recent legislation they will also hear certain working-time complaints and infringements to the statutory minimum wage. They deal with individual employment rights complaints. In 1998, they were renamed 'employment tribunals'.

The use of tribunals to deal with employment rights complaints was supposed to be beneficial in offering informality and speed. This has not proved to be (see later discussion on Effective remedies). A tribunal comprises three people. The chairperson is legally qualified and the two lay members are drawn from either side of industry.

Analysis of the cases lodged at these tribunals in 2001–2 (*ACAS Annual Report 2001–02*) shows the following:

- The major allegation against employers was unfair dismissal (52 000 cases from a total of 165 093), followed by 37 591 protection of wages applications.
- Discrimination cases tend to be few: sex (7525), race (3825), disability (5057) and equal pay (2614).
- Of the original applications, 57 660 were resolved through ACAS conciliation, and 44 842 were withdrawn. Roughly, one-quarter of completed cases went on to a tribunal hearing.
- Success for applicants in cases that go to a hearing is reported as follows: 48 per cent of all cases, 36 per cent of unfair dismissal cases, 59 per cent of wage deduction cases, 27 per cent of sex and race discrimination cases, 24 per cent of disability discrimination cases and 77 per cent of redundancy cases (Employment Tribunal Service, 1999–2000 – *see* DTI (2001)).
- Median compensation is £2244 for unfair dismissal (DTI); £5125 for sex discrimination, £5000 for race discrimination and £7218 for disability discrimination (*Equal Opportunities Review* no 108, August 2002).

Because employment tribunals are the most likely legal forum before which an employer might appear, we will look at some details of the complaints process for unfair dismissals (the most common complaint) (*see* Fig. 1.5). It is important to remember that for other types of application there may be some variant on this process. The Employment Rights (Dispute Resolution) Act 1998 provides for various circumstances in which it is possible to proceed without a full hearing (s 2) and it adds to the list of cases in which a chairman might hear certain matters alone (e.g. statutory redundancy pay) (s 3).

Since 1993, it has been possible for the dismissed employee and the employer to make a compromise agreement. This is a binding agreement. The ex-employee must have received independent advice from a lawyer who has insurance cover. They must be legally advised about the provisions of the agreement and its implications, and particularly about the foregoing of their right to go to an employment tribunal. ERDRA 1998, s 9 widens the range of competent advisers to include certified trade union officials and advice workers). (For further information see the Employment Tribunal Service website: www.ets.gov.uk.)

1 Dismissal by the employer
Dismissal must have taken place for an application to be heard.

2 Application to the employment tribunal on the appropriate form
An applicant must have the appropriate qualifying length of service (one year). If the dismissal infringes discrimination law, then no qualifying period is necessary (but employees in organisations employing fewer than 15 people cannot make disability discrimination claims). The complaint must be made within three months of the dismissal.

3 Response invited from the employer on the appropriate form
This must be returned within 14 days. If an employer does not contest an application, a tribunal can proceed without a full hearing.

4 ACAS involvement

Conciliation
ACAS has a statutory duty to promote a settlement. The outcomes will be:

■ settlement
■ withdrawal
■ progress to a tribunal hearing.

Arbitration
An optional scheme of arbitration, for ordinary (non-discrimination) unfair dismissal cases, was launched in 2001. Both applicant and respondent must agree in writing to go to arbitration. The arbitrator's decision is final. There can be no appeal to an employment tribunal (details from ACAS website).

5 Possible preliminary hearing to resolve jurisdictional issues
The tribunal determines whether a party is entitled to bring or contest a matter. Each party has the opportunity to submit representations in writing and to advance oral arguments before the tribunal.

6 Possible pre-hearing review to assess weight of evidence
A tribunal considers the application and response and also written representations, documents and oral argument – but not the details of the evidence. If it decides the claim or defence has no reasonable prospect of success, it may order the relevant party to pay up to £500 deposit to be permitted to continue with the proceedings. This must be paid within 21 days. Possible outcomes at this stage are *withdrawal* or *progress to full hearing*. (An applicant disregarding the tribunal's advice can proceed to a full hearing but may be liable for up to £10 000 costs if unsuccessful at that hearing.)

7 Full hearing before employment tribunal
Normally, the applicant goes first. The applicant may make a statement, be questioned by the employer's representative and the tribunal, and may call witnesses. The evidence before the tribunal can comprise: written reasons for the dismissal; the employer's written response form; further particulars of the employer's reasons for the dismissal; and various relevant documents.
    A tribunal may order an employer to provide more information; and may order a witness summons. Since 1994, it has been able to require a written answer to any question to help clarify matters and progress the proceedings.
    The outcomes of a tribunal hearing are:

■ rejection of application
■ claim upheld
    – compensation
    – re-engagement
    – reinstatement.

Figure 1.5 Processing a tribunal application: unfair dismissal

Overall, half of tribunal hearings are won by applicants. This pattern has remained stable over the years.
   (The importance of remedies is considered later in this chapter. Furthermore, there is more detail on remedies in Chapters 4–6 on discrimination law and in Chapter 9 on dismissal.)

8 Possible appeal (on a point of law only) to Employment Appeals Tribunal
In 1995/6, the EAT registered 1358 appeals, of which 669 related to unfair dismissal, 127 to sex discrimination and 112 to race discrimination. Of the total appeals, 176 were allowed or remitted back to the employment tribunal.

Figure 1.5 (cont'd)

The Employment Appeals Tribunal (EAT)

This was established in 1976 as a superior court of record to hear appeals on points of law from (then) industrial tribunals. It comprises judges, nominated by the Lord Chancellor (drawn from the High Court and Court of Appeal) and lay members who have experience of employee relations. In various areas of employment law, it has provided guidance for tribunals on particular issues of law. (For further information see the Employment Tribunal Service website: www.ets.gov.uk.)

The Court of Appeal

Created in the late nineteenth century, it comprises two divisions: the Civil Division (presided over by the Master of the Rolls) and the Criminal Division (presided over by the Lord Chief Justice). Under employment law, appeals against rulings of the Employment Appeals Tribunal are heard in the Civil Division. In most cases, appeals can be made against its decisions to the House of Lords – with leave (permission) of the Court of Appeal or the House of Lords.

The House of Lords

A panel of five Law Lords sit to hear appeals from 'inferior' courts. For most British cases, this is the final court of appeal. However, if the law derives from the European Union, there is a further appeal stage to the European Court of Justice.

The European Court of Justice

Based in Luxembourg, this is the principal judicial body in the European Union. It is officially known as the Court of Justice of the European Communities (ECJ). It has jurisdiction in Britain under the European Communities Act 1972 to deal with a range of competition, company law and employment law matters. It is competent to deal with such European employment law as that involving the Equal Treatment Directive and the Treaty article on equal pay. Its significance in moulding and interpreting European law was discussed above. A member state is obliged to comply with the rulings of the ECJ, irrespective of the country of origin of the original claim.
   The ECJ comprises 15 judges and nine Advocates-General who assist the court. The judges are nominated by member states for a six-year term. They make the

final rulings on the application of European law. The role of Advocates-General has no equivalent in the English and Scottish legal systems. They provide a reasoned submission (an Opinion) in open court. These are preliminary views about the points of law involved in a specific case. They will refer to other relevant rulings and recommend a judgment. Some months later, the court will pronounce its ruling. It is usual for it to accept an Advocate-General's view. However, there have been occasional cases where the Opinion has been overturned (*Grant v SW Trains Ltd* [1998] IRLR 188. (For further information contact the European Union website: www.europa.eu.int.)

The European Court of Human Rights

Based in Strasbourg, this court operates under the Council of Europe, which is separate from the European Union. Its responsibility is to adjudicate on alleged violations of the 1950 European Convention for the Protection of Human Rights and Fundamental Freedoms. Britain is a signatory of this Convention. To date, its decisions have *not* automatically become part of British law. However, the government incorporated the Convention into British law under the Human Rights Act 1998. 'Bringing these rights home will mean that the British people will be able to argue for their rights in the British courts . . . It will also mean that the rights will be brought much more fully into the jurisprudence of the courts throughout the United Kingdom and their interpretation will thus be far more subtly and powerfully woven into our law' (Home Office, 1997: 6) (see earlier section).

The Advisory Conciliation and Arbitration Service

Established initially in 1974, ACAS became a statutory body in 1975. It is an independent service, charged with the general duty 'to promote the improvement of industrial relations (in particular, by exercising its functions in relation to the settlement of trade disputes)' (TULRCA 1992, ss 209–14). It is governed by a Council, comprising a full-time chairperson; three members appointed after consultation with the Confederation of British Industry (CBI) and other specified employers' organisations; three after consultation with the Trades Union Congress and other specified employees' organisations; and three appointed by the Secretary of State for Trade and Industry. It publishes an annual report (TULRCA, ss 247–53).

Among its functions are the following:

- to offer conciliation in disputes over individual statutory employment rights between individual employees and their employers or ex-employers (e.g. unfair dismissal, equal pay, discrimination, etc.);
- to provide collective conciliation for industrial disputes;
- to provide facilities for arbitration, mediation and committees of investigation;
- to issue codes of practice providing guidance (e.g. on disciplinary and grievance procedures).

(For further information see the ACAS website: www.acas.org.uk.)

The Equal Opportunities Commission

Established in 1976 under the Sex Discrimination Act 1975 (ss 53–6), its duties involve:

■ working towards the elimination of discrimination;
■ promoting equality of opportunity between men and women generally;
■ keeping under review the Sex Discrimination Acts and the Equal Pay Act and making proposals for amending them;
■ undertaking or assisting relevant research and education activities.

It is headed by a chairperson and a deputy and has 13 part-time commissioners. It operates through committees and working parties. It advises people on their rights in law and, in certain circumstances, can assist them take a case to a tribunal or court. This is usually where there is a legal point to be tested. It can conduct formal investigations, issue non-discrimination notices enforceable in the courts, issue codes of practice and institute proceedings both in relation to advertising and in cases where there have been instructions or pressure to discriminate. It publishes an annual report. (For further information see the EOC website: www.eoc.gov.uk.)

The Commission for Racial Equality

Established in 1977 under the Race Relations Act 1976 (ss 43–6), the CRE has the following duties:

■ working towards the elimination of discrimination;
■ promoting equality of opportunity and good relations between persons of different racial groups generally;
■ keeping under review the Race Relations Act and making proposals for amending it;
■ undertaking or assisting relevant research and educational activities.

The CRE has similar powers and duties to the EOC – including assistance in taking cases to tribunal or court. It provides advice to employers, unions and other organisations. It co-ordinates the work of about 100 racial equality councils, established in areas with a significant presence of non-white ethnic groups. It is required to produce an annual report. (For further information see the CRE website: www.cre.gov.uk.)

The Disability Rights Commission

The DRC was established in 2000, replacing the National Disability Council. The Commission comprises 15 members, 10 of whom have a disability. They have been recruited for the particular expertise that they can bring to the Commission's work. It has the following duties:

- working towards the elimination of discrimination against disabled persons;
- to promote the equalisation of opportunities for disabled persons in all fields of activity;
- to encourage good practice in the treatment of disabled persons;
- to review the working of the Disability Discrimination Act 1995.

As with EOC and the CRE, it has the power to conduct formal investigations; issue non-discrimination notices; and can assist individual claims of unlawful discrimination.

(For further information see the DRC website: www.drc-gb.org.)

The government indicated in December 2001 that it was considering the creation of a unified Equality Commission. This could embrace the work of the the EOC, CRE and DRC. Additionally, it could have responsibility for new European laws on discrimination on the grounds of sexuality and age (for implementation in 2003 and 2006 respectively).

The Health and Safety Commission

Established in 1974 under the Health and Safety at Work Act 1974 (ss 10–14), it is responsible for taking appropriate steps to secure the health, safety and welfare of people at work and to protect the public generally against dangers to health and safety arising from work activities.

It is headed by a chairperson and has up to nine commissioners. In formulating its policies, the Commission organises widespread consultation on all aspects of health and safety. It publishes an annual report. The Commission is responsible for the Health and Safety Executive. Its inspectors advise on health and safety legislation and have powers of enforcement. (For further information see the HSE website: www.hse.gov.uk.)

The Low Pay Commission

The LPC was initially set up as a non-statutory body in July 1997 to report on the introduction of a national minimum wage. Under the National Minimum Wage Act 1998 the LPC is now established in a statutory framework. It comprises a chairman and eight other members. These generally consist of nominees from employer bodies, trade unions and academics with low pay expertise.

The role of the LPC is to carry out tasks as specified by the Secretary of State. These will include reviews of the impact of the national minimum wage since its introduction in April 1999. Specific tasks will include consideration of proposed regulations. Before making recommendations it is required to consult employers' and workers' organisations. It is also obliged to have regard to 'the effect of this Act on the economy of the United Kingdom as a whole and on competitiveness' (NMWA 1998, s 7). (For further information see the LPC website: www.lowpay.gov.uk.)

The Central Arbitration Committee

The CAC has been in existence since the mid-1970s. It is an independent tribunal with statutory powers to adjudicate in various disputes relating to statutory employment rights. In recent years it has played a low-profile role in employment relations. Its principal responsibility has been dealing with complaints relating to the disclosure of information for collective bargaining. It also provides voluntary arbitration in industrial disputes.

In 2000, it assumed significant additional responsibilities for two important areas of collective representation: statutory rights for trade unions to be recognised for collective bargaining purposes; and information disclosure and consultation rights in respect of European-based multinational companies (*see* Chapter 14).

The current chairman is a High Court judge. There are 10 deputy chairmen and 32 members of the Committee (16 representing employers and 16 representing workers). They reflect a wide range of experience in human resource management, trade union representation, academic life and the legal profession. (For further information see the CAC website: www.cac.gov.uk.)

1.3.3 Effective remedies

It is, of course, pointless enacting employment rights without ensuring adequate redress. Two aspects are discussed here: access to legal redress, and effectiveness of complaints procedures.

Access to legal redress

There are, currently, limitations on access to statutory employment rights. A person may have to satisfy two requirements: that of being an employee (*see* Chapter 2); that of having one year's continuous service with the employer. The hours qualification which further restricted rights for part-timers who worked less than 16 hours per week was rescinded in 1994. This was as a result of a successful claim, under European equal treatment law, that it was indirectly discriminatory on grounds of sex, because part-timers are overwhelmingly female. The present service qualification of one year is of particular significance for complaints alleging unfair dismissal and unfair redundancy selection.

Exceptions to this service qualification exist under all discrimination law. Here, rights apply from the first day of employment. Indeed, they also cover the recruitment and selection process prior to the start of employment. Discrimination law also extends to all workers – whatever employment relationship or contract they have. So, self-employed contract workers are covered. Claims about unlawful deductions from wages and entitlements under the Working Time Regulations are, likewise, not subject to a service qualification.

Complaints under common law, in respect of the contract of employment, are not restricted by length of service or hours worked. Technically, an employee who sustains a breach of contract can take one of three courses of action:

1 Accept the breach of contract by the employer and carrying on working.
2 Object to the breach and sue the employer for damages in the County Court.
3 If the breach is fundamental (e.g. non-payment of wages, or dismissal without due notice) resign and complain to an employment tribunal, alleging constructive dismissal and also sue for breach of contract. (However, the constructive dismissal claim may be subject to the qualifying period of service.)

Effectiveness of complaints procedures

Effective remedies also depend upon effective complaints procedures. We will consider this by looking at the tribunal process, as the primary route for processing employment rights complaints. Many commentators have pointed to the complexity of both the tribunal procedure and, in certain respects, the employment rights issues themselves.

Originally, tribunals were commended in comparison with the ordinary courts because they were said to offer 'cheapness, accessibility, freedom from technicality, expert knowledge of a particular subject' (Franks Committee, 1957). Over the past 25 years, all these characteristics have been increasingly questioned in various academic studies (Dickens *et al.*, 1985; Leonard, 1987; Lewis and Clark, 1993). The characteristics of the employment tribunal process are as follows:

■ *Access*: May be formally limited by employment status and service qualifications.

■ *Procedure*: May be slow – taking up to a year to deal with many cases.

■ *Resources*: Those available to applicants and respondent employers differ widely. Many applicants are unrepresented. Of applicants, 78 per cent were not members of a union or staff association (DTI 2002). Forty-nine per cent of applicants consulted an external law firm (DTI 2002). Some applicants use the services of the Citizens' Advice Bureaux. Having said this, 10 per cent of applicants did not discuss their case with either a solicitor or a professional adviser (i.e. in the CAB, union or welfare rights centre). Employers, on the other hand, are more likely to have either expertise in a personnel department or access to external legal advice. Of employers, 63 per cent consulted an external law firm (DTI 2002).

■ *Technicality*: Increasingly, this has become the hallmark of the tribunal process. The presence of lawyers has encouraged tribunals to appear more like courts. Indeed, by the mid-1980s they were described as 'quasi-courts' (Dickens *et al.*, 1985). Also, the provisions of employment law, with growing bodies of case law and precedent, have made some issues particularly difficult for the lay person. Two principal examples of this are the issues of equal pay and transfers of undertakings cases.

■ *Stamina*: Applicants need stamina and resources to enter and remain in the tribunal complaints process. Nearly two-thirds of applicants said they had experienced stress as a result of their application and a third reported damaged employment prospects. Applicants bringing unfair dismissal or discrimination cases were most likely to report stress (DTI 2002). Half of all applicants reported spending longer than 20 hours of their own time on the case. The mean time spent was 42 hours compared with a mean time of 31 hours reported by directors and senior managers. Discrimination cases absorb most management time (DTI 2002).

■ *Remedies*: If applicants are successful, these are insignificant. Under discrimination law, the remedies are unlimited compensation; an award for injury to feelings; a declaration; reinstatement or re-engagement if dismissal is involved. Under unfair dismissal law, limited compensation and reinstatement or re-engagement are available. However, in practice, the primary remedy is compensation. Despite some well-publicised cases, even that available in discrimination cases is small – at around £5000. The median figure for successful ordinary dismissal cases is under £2700. Reinstatement as a remedy is, in practice, virtually non-existent. It is ordered in 0.3 per cent of cases but in practice re-employment does not arise – partly because some ex-employees do not wish to return, but primarily because of employers' reluctance. In these circumstances, additional compensation is the remedy.

■ *Employment consequences*: This relatively limited redress must also be seen in the context of the reality of employment after the tribunal application. Nearly two-thirds of applicants said that they worked for a different employer and almost a quarter were out of work. Of those who changed jobs or became self-employed 45 per cent saw their new job as a 'stop gap'. Half of these applicants reported earning lower pay and just over a third reported higher pay.

Some consideration has been given to improvements and the possible use of non-legal and voluntary processes. Governments have, for the past ten years or so, become increasingly concerned about the effectiveness of dispute resolution concerning employment rights. This concern has been strongly related to cost but, linked with that, also to the need to encourage employers to take greater responsibility for effective in-company resolution of grievances and disciplinary matters. The aim is to make employment tribunals the last and not the first resort in dispute resolution.

Research evidence reveals some of the problems. For example, in 62 per cent of all applications, there was no attempt by employer and employee to meet to resolve the dispute before the claim is made (DTI, 2002: 24). A significant aspect of the problem with dispute resolution is the size of the employer. Small organisations are particularly deficient. Of those employing 10–19 employees, 18 per cent had no grievance procedure. Employees of small employers accounted for 'a disproportionately high share' of tribunal applications. One-third of applications come from those working in micro-organisations (between 1 and 9 employees) – although such organisations account for 18 per cent of total employment (DTI 2001). Detailed statistics show, for example, that organisations employing up to 49 employees accounted for 54 per cent of employers who were involved in an unfair dismissal, 68 per cent of breach of contract claims and 71 per cent of cases of unlawful deduction of wages.

Governments have evolved a four-pronged strategy for attempting to reduce tribunal applications:

■ *Financial penalties*: These were introduced in the mid-1990s by the Conservative government to deter 'misconceived' claims. The rates were increased in July 2001. They involve:

 – A maximum deposit after a pre-hearing review (where the tribunal advises against proceeding to a full hearing): £500 (previously £150).

 – The maximum award of costs (without any assessment) when, after a pre-hearing review, a party proceeds to a full hearing and loses: £10 000 (previously £500).

■ *Alternative dispute resolution*: ACAS's duty to conciliate in tribunal applications was supplemented in May 2001 by an Arbitration Scheme for Unfair Dismissal applications. With agreement of both the applicant and the respondent employer, this provides an alternative to an employment tribunal hearing for determining an unfair dismissal claim by a final and binding decision.

■ *Effective in-company procedures*: In 1999, tribunals were empowered to reduce compensation in successful unfair dismissal cases where the applicant had not used the company's appeal procedure; and increase compensation where the employer prevented the use of the procedure (ERA 1996, s 127A). This is repealed under the Employment Act 2002 and a wider provision is enacted. To promote effective in-company dispute resolution, a revised statutory Code of Practice on Discipline and Grievance Procedures (encompassing guidance on the statutory right to be accompanied) was published by ACAS in 2000. The promotion of workplace dispute resolution is also a significant element in the Employment Act 2002 through two measures:

  – *Implied terms of the contract*: The introduction into all contracts of employment of two procedural requirements: a statutory dismissal and disciplinary procedure (DDP) and a grievance procedure (GP). It will be unfair for an employer to dismiss an employee without complying with the DDP.

  – *The written statement of terms and conditions*: These statutory provisions (ERA 1996, s 1) are amended, including the removal of the exemption for employers with fewer than 20 employees in providing detail on disciplinary rules and procedures. Tribunals will be able to increase a compensation award by between 5 and 25 per cent where the written statement is incomplete, inaccurate or non-existent.

■ *Access to information and expertise*: This is an issue for all employers but it is of particular concern for small employers. The incidence of in-house expertise is strongly dependent on the size of the organisation. The Workplace Employee Relations Survey 1998 found evidence of personnel specialists in 17 per cent of organisations with fewer than 100 employees. It rose steeply to 53 per cent for those employing 100–999 employees; and peaked at 95 per cent for those employing over 10 000 employees (Cully *et al.*, 1999: 52). For smaller employers, expertise from consultants and lawyers tends to be bought in as required.

At present, the government's approach is developing. ACAS provides an advisory service and information covering the range of employment rights issues. The Department of Trade and Industry provides guidance in a range of publications as do the various statutory agencies. In addition, the Better Regulation Task Force (Cabinet Office, 2002) has recommended that the government run pilot scheme providing HR resources to groups of small employers to help ensure compliance with employment law. In some ways the role of ACAS may be pivotal. Overwhelmingly, small (as well as large) employers see its conciliation officers as trustworthy and even-handed in dealing with tribunal applications. The Better Regulation Task Force recommends a wider role for ACAS: '[it] should be brought into the dispute process before a tribunal application is made. In businesses with less than 50 employees, where there is no management chain, either party should be able to call upon mediation services. It would encourage disputes to be resolved in the workplace rather than having to go to tribunal.'

The nature of voluntary regulation

Despite the growth of legal regulation over the past 25 years or more, voluntary regulation of the employment relationship is still significant. There are several key aspects of voluntary regulation: the extent to which employers have discretion in determining pay and conditions of employment and the procedures they use; the use of grievance procedures; the use of disciplinary procedures; the roles of consultation and collective bargaining; and the contribution of third parties to the regulation of employment relations.

1.4.1 Employer discretion

Earlier in this chapter, it was shown how the law is increasingly influential in defining the standards with which the employer must comply. However, there is still scope for employer discretion or freely negotiated terms. This can be considered by looking at four functions of employment law: to set minimum standards, to establish certain principles for employment practice, to specify a general approach to determining certain matters and to set absolute requirements.

An example of *minimum standards* is the statutory minimum periods of notice required to terminate contracts of employment (ERA 1996, s 86). These do not preclude an employer from stipulating more favourable notice periods. The national minimum wage sets a threshold hourly rate of pay which an employer can exceed but must not fall below. An example of establishing *principles* arises in redundancy selection. The law does not specify the details of the criteria by which people are chosen. It is for the employer to determine and to justify if challenged. The law asserts the principles that these criteria must be non-discriminatory and objectively justifiable. An example of specifying *a general approach* can be seen in the legal concept of reasonableness. In dismissal cases, tribunals inquire to see whether the respondent employer has behaved, in arriving at the decision to dismiss, like a reasonable employer. Under health and safety law, the general duties upon employers must be complied with as far as is reasonably practicable.

Law can also set *absolute requirements*. These remove employer discretion. One example of this is the obligation to provide specific maternity leave to a pregnant employee. However, having said that, an employer might offer more generous leave entitlements. Overall, there are still few provisions in this area.

In exercising discretion, in the areas indicated above, employers may rely on an appropriate statutory code of practice (e.g. those on discipline at work, sex, race and disability discrimination law). These can help in action to be taken. An employer might also use a relevant voluntary code of practice or guidance note. For example, the Chartered Institute of Personnel and Development has published various guides on the following topics: recruitment, harassment at work, age and employment, psychological testing and substance misuse. These provide advice on acceptable standards of personnel management within the relevant law.

Just as the employer can have discretion in establishing terms and conditions of employment, so, too, there can be discretion in respect of employment procedures. Theoretically, this discretion can exist in respect of the choice of procedures to be used and in the ways in which specific procedures operate. In practice, as we will see, employers are expected to have and to operate both grievance and disciplinary procedures, and their freedom of choice about whether to engage in consultation or collective bargaining is becoming increasingly limited. We will look at each of these procedures in turn.

1.4.2 Grievance procedures

These voluntary procedures are influenced in two ways: through good practice guidance and through various legal requirements (*see* ACAS Code of Practice on Grievance Procedures, 2000). Law and good practice requires that several factors are taken into account. The procedure should be operated fairly. Among other things, this means that the grievance should be subject to serious investigation, dealt with by an appropriate manager and that the statutory right to be accompanied should be available for the worker (ERA 1999, ss 10–15).

The importance of good practice can be seen by a brief review of the legal context in which grievances are handled. First, each employee has, as an implied term of the contract of employment, access to a statutory minimum grievance procedure (EA 2002). Secondly, employers are obliged in the 'statement of initial employment particulars' (ERA 1995, ss 1–3) to notify an employee of the person a grievance can be raised with and the person to whom appeal can be made. Thirdly, the EAT has affirmed that there is an implied term in an employee's contract that a company 'would reasonably and promptly afford a reasonable opportunity' to enable the employee to have a grievance dealt with. Failure to provide adequate procedural redress is regarded as a fundamental breach of the contract of employment (*W.A. Goold (Pearmak) Ltd* v *McConnell and Another* [1995] IRLR 516).

Fourthly, in relation to complaints arising under discrimination law, an employer may have a defence if they can show that they 'took such steps as were reasonably practicable' to deal with the employee's complaint (of direct or indirect race or sex discrimination, harassment or victimisation). So, evidence of the effective use of a grievance procedure will be valuable. Given the possibility of unlimited compensation here, it is prudent for the employer to comply.

Finally, under contract law, where an employer wishes to vary contractual terms, case law suggests that the employer should provide information to the employee about the changes and provide a reasonable opportunity for the employee to make representations. The grievance procedure can be the forum.

1.4.3 Disciplinary procedures

The ACAS Code of Practice on Disciplinary Procedures (2000) and case law emphasising procedural fairness have created circumstances in which it is imperative for employers to have a formal procedure for discipline and dismissal. (This is discussed in more detail in Chapter 9.) Procedurally, employers are not completely free to do what they want. Under dismissal law, an employer is expected to conform to the principle of natural justice. This involves an employee knowing the allegation against them (e.g. an act of gross misconduct) and then being able to be represented, bring appropriate witnesses, have a full hearing and be given a proper right of appeal.

Under the Employment Act 2002 (Sch 2), the need to ensure universal coverage of discipline and dismissal procedures has resulted in a statutory minimum dismissal and discipline procedure being implied into individual contracts of employment. The requirements to comply with this procedure will significantly curtail employer discretion (*see* section 1.3).

1.4.4   Consultation and collective bargaining

As far as collective employment relations are concerned, employers have had long-standing freedom to determine whether or not they wish to engage in collective bargaining or in consultation. However, this choice is gradually being reduced. Since 1995, arising from a judgment in the ECJ, employers have a statutory duty to consult about collective redundancies (involving 20 or more people), about health and safety matters and about transfers of undertakings. The Information and Consultation Directive 2002 (to be phased in by 2008) extends the statutory duty to consult to all undertakings with 50 or more employees. In addition, the Employment Relations Act 1999 introduces a statutory right to collective bargaining (*see* Chapter 14). These developments on consultation and collective bargaining are likely, in time, to change the ways in which the employment relationship is regulated and managed. Furthermore, the Working Time Regulations 1998 provide for the negotiation of 'workforce agreements', with non-union employee representatives, as a means of implementing the provisions on working time, rest breaks and holidays (*see* Chapter 11).

Although collective agreements are voluntary and binding in honour, they do have some legal consequences. Specific terms are incorporated into individual contracts of employment and are, consequently, enforceable in respect of that individual employee. (The importance of this is explored in Chapter 2.)

1.4.5   Third parties

Voluntary regulation of employment relations, as considered so far, has concerned relationships *within* an employing organisation. However, it is much wider in scope. It embraces three other processes *external* to the employing organisation: conciliation, mediation and arbitration.

While ACAS has a statutory duty to offer conciliation to all parties who are involved in an employment tribunal complaint, it is up to the parties whether or not to use this service and agree a settlement. It is the conciliation officer's function to try and promote a settlement. This is achieved in about a third of cases. As a consequence, the matter does not proceed to a full hearing. As far as collective disputes are concerned, employers and unions can voluntarily seek ACAS help or not. On average (over a three-year period) there are 1447 such requests each year (ACAS *Annual Report 2001–02*).

ACAS can also assist in establishing arbitration. There are (on average over a three-year period) 65 references annually in relation to collective disputes (ACAS *Annual Report 2001–02*). But its use is rare for individual complaints. However, since May 2001, an arbitration scheme has been in operation to provide an alternative form of dispute resolution to an employment tribunal hearing. Its use has been limited. By February 2003, it had received 35 cases.

In addition, ACAS provides a service of mediation. This is effectively a 'half-way house' between conciliation and arbitration. The third party is more proactive in proposing likely courses of dispute resolution. 'Advisory mediation' is a development of this and is an in-depth problem-solving process which is based around a consultancy approach (Kessler and Purcell, 1995).

1.5 Some underpinning principles

In the previous sections, we have referred to various principles which infuse employment law. Here, we consider them more fully and indicate their relationship to human resource management and employee relations. These underpinning principles can be divided into those that concern the substantive issues of employment relations (i.e. the outcomes – terms and conditions of employment and other decisions), and those that affect the processes by which decisions on terms and conditions are made.

1.5.1 Substantive issues

In recent years, two overarching and interconnected policy perspectives have become increasingly influential: 'ethical standards' and 'human rights'. They are used to assess the treatment of employees and behaviour in society at large. Concern about business ethics not only covers the treatment of British employees but also extends to corporate behaviour in international supply chains, which may be founded, in part, upon child labour and exploitative conditions. 'Third World' charities have expressed strong concern about this; and, indeed, Oxfam has published a code of practice to encourage employers to address the issue and take steps to establish a more ethical supply chain.

The issue of human rights is likely to become more strongly entrenched in employment practice now that the European Convention on Human Rights 1950 is incorporated into British law under the Human Rights Act 1998 (*see* section 1.3.1). Essentially, four Convention Articles are likely to be relevant: freedom of expression (Art 10); rights of trade union membership (Art 11); as a factor in 'whistle-blowing', confidentiality and workforce surveillance, the right to privacy (Art 8); and the prohibition against discrimination (Art 14).

It is against this background, then, that a number of key principles will be discussed: fairness, reasonableness, equal treatment and harmonisation.

Fairness

In defining fairness, people are invariably subjective (considering the concept in relation to their own personal values). Also they tend to define it relatively or comparatively (e.g. this is fair and that is not). When asked why they say something is fair or unfair, the tendency is quickly to move away from the abstract and explore details and practical elements of what constitutes fairness.

For example, at the heart of the current debate on a statutory minimum wage is the notion of a fair wage. The idea of such a wage is long-standing. The Catholic Church has, historically, referred to a just wage; and the Council of Europe defines and quantifies a decency threshold – an acceptable level of pay. It is the latter that provides a clue to the practical ways in which the concept of fairness is defined. There are social expectations that pay should be sufficient, as a minimum, to enable a person to buy food, and provide adequate shelter and appropriate welfare care for himself/herself and any dependants.

Fair treatment, then, is determined against reference points. These, of course, are likely to change over time – particularly as social expectations shift. So, what is perceived to be fair in one period of history may be unacceptable at another time. A balance, then, has to be struck between was is perceived, on the one hand, to be fair and what is seen, on the other, to be exploitative.

The use of reference points is clearly seen in that other employment area where fairness is central: dismissal. Whilst the law distinguishes between fair and unfair dismissal, it does not define the concept. In the 1960s, various reports on the treatment of employees pointed to their vulnerability to arbitrary treatment by an employer; the consequent loss of employment, income, status and, possibly, loss of reputation; and to the widely held consensus of opinion that the situation was unsatisfactory. The eradication or minimisation of arbitrary treatment was, therefore, the goal. This could be achieved only through the adoption of a number of practical steps. Today, these are represented by the tests used at an employment tribunal: determining whether the reason for the dismissal was a prescribed fair reason; whether the employer behaved reasonably in all the circumstances in dismissing the person for that reason; and, finally, whether there were fair workplace procedures for handling the dismissal in conformity with the statutory code of practice.

This suggests that fairness, in the context of dismissal, is determined, to a large extent, by compliance with a pre-determined structure. In part this is true – in respect of the reason for the dismissal and compliance with the ACAS Code of Practice. However, the second test on whether the employer behaved reasonably can be highly contentious in determining whether treatment was fair or not. This issue is explored below in our discussion of the concept of reasonableness.

Reasonableness

Reasonableness is, likewise, an undefined term. It is a long-established concept in law generally. For example, in criminal law there are the concepts of reasonable force and reasonable chastisement of children. Additionally, the reasonable man test can be used in civil proceedings to make value judgements about a person's conduct. The fundamental difficulty with such a test, and with the concept of reasonableness, is that it is frequently measured against shifting criteria. As social attitudes change, even within 20 or 30 years, the socially accepted notion of reasonable behaviour changes. Also, at any one time, there will probably be differences in attitude between men and women, between older and younger people, and between people from different social and ethnic backgrounds on the standards that they have in mind when assessing reasonableness.

More specifically, within the employment arena, the concept occurs, primarily, in dismissal cases and in health and safety matters. Tribunals, in dealing with unfair dismissal applications, will consider, as outlined above, whether the employer behaved reasonably and determine the fairness or not of the dismissal. A structure for such a determination was set out in an EAT judgment (*Iceland Frozen Foods Ltd* v *Jones* [1982] IRLR 439):

- The starting point should be the legislation, which states that 'the determination of the question whether the dismissal is fair or unfair (having regard to the reason shown by the employer) (a) depends on whether in the circumstances (including the size and administrative resources of the employer's undertaking) the employer acted reasonably or unreasonably in treating it as a sufficient reason for dismissing the employee, and (b) shall be determined in accordance with equity and the substantial merits of the case' (now in ERA 1996, s 98(4)).

- The tribunal members must consider the reasonableness of the employer's conduct, not simply whether they consider the dismissal fair.

- In judging the reasonableness of the employer's conduct an industrial (now employment) tribunal must not substitute its decision as to what was the right course to adopt for that of the employer.

- In many (though not all) cases there is a range of reasonable responses to the employee's conduct within which one employer might reasonably take one view, another quite reasonably take another.

- The function of a tribunal is to determine whether in the particular circumstances of each case the decision to dismiss the employee fell within the range of reasonable responses which a reasonable employer might have adopted. If the dismissal falls within the range the dismissal is fair; if the dismissal falls outside the range it is unfair.

The implication of such a test is that in judging the employer's behaviour, account will be taken of the extent to which they considered all the circumstances of a case. So, for example, the following issues will arise: whether there were extenuating circumstances, whether proper consideration was given to these and to the employee's previous record and whether an appropriate investigation was undertaken. Having found out as much as possible about the circumstances, was the employer's response (a decision to sack) one that a reasonable employer might make? This, according to employment lawyers, provides an objective test for gauging reasonableness – i.e. the likely responses of other employers. It is based upon the tribunal's perceptions of employers at particular points in time. In part, the role of tribunal lay members is to inform on the practices and policies of reasonable employers.

Reasonableness is also at the heart of health and safety legislation. The general duties placed upon employers must be complied with as far as is reasonably practicable (HASAWA 1974, ss 2–4). This, again, involves a balancing of various factors. On the one hand, for example, there will be a safety hazard or a risk to be assessed. On the other hand is the cost, time and trouble that could be taken to eliminate that risk or hazard. There are also the practical steps that might be available (e.g. because of the existence of particular protective equipment). On the facts and in the particular circumstances, reasonableness is determined. What is the scale and probability of the risk? How much money is likely to be involved in tackling it? What alternative ways of dealing with a hazard are available? In this area, it is a matter for the courts or tribunals to determine on the facts.

The two key principles that remain, in relation to terms and conditions of employment, are equal treatment and harmonisation. Underlying both is a perception (and invariably the reality) that differential and inequitable treatment exists.

Equal treatment

Equal treatment as a concept has developed in British employment relations as a result of a number of parallel influences: social movements originating in the United States of America, and policy initiatives within the European Union. In the 1960s, in the USA, the women's movement critically questioned the role and status of women in society and the opportunities available. Simultaneously, the civil rights movement was challenging endemic racism and asserting social, voting and employment rights. The significance of these movements was felt in Britain and energised groups who sought changes here. It is no accident that anti-discrimination and equal opportunities law on sex and race was enacted in the 1970s. These statutory initiatives were pragmatic responses to particular contemporary social pressures (*see* Chapters 4 and 5).

Within the European Community (as the Union was then called), commitment to equal treatment has had an uneven history. The founding Treaty of Rome (1957) refers only to equal pay between men and women – and that as a result of a political compromise. No specific social provisions were included. The Community was conceived, initially, in primarily market economy terms as a free-trade area or 'common market'. Pragmatically, a Social Action Programme in the 1970s promoted equal treatment on grounds of sex and equal pay. By 1989, under the Community Charter of the Fundamental Social Rights of Workers, a clear shift had taken place in the importance of social policy. The preamble stated that 'the same importance must be attached to the social aspects as to the economic aspects and . . . therefore, they must be developed in a balanced manner'. Equal treatment on grounds of sex has developed significantly in this context and has been defined to cover the rights of not just men and women, but also pregnant workers, and transsexuals. British law on equal treatment has, therefore, since our membership of the European Community in 1973, been moulded not just by evolving social attitudes but also by European legislation and rulings in the ECJ.

There are two aspects to equal treatment law. First, 'like must be treated alike'. In this a basis of comparison is established. The objective legal test has been defined, in a House of Lords sex discrimination case judgment, in this way: 'would the complainant have received the same treatment but for his/her sex?' (*James* v *Eastleigh Borough Council* [1990] IRLR 288). The second aspect concerns policies and practices, which appear neutral in effect, but should be scrutinised to see if they create some institutionalised disadvantage for a person on the grounds of sex or race. These two sources of inequality are known, respectively, as direct and indirect discrimination. They form the basis for the principle of equal treatment in British employment law (*see* Chapters 4–6).

The principle of equal treatment is, of course, defined as widely or as narrowly as the legislators choose. As already said, it was enacted, initially in the 1970s, in relation to sex and race discrimination. Social trends and political lobbying have led to further measures, whereby equal treatment now encompasses other forms of discrimination: disability, pregnancy, and religion and political opinion in Northern Ireland. Between 2003 and 2006, the European Union Employment

Directive 2000 will also implement provisions against discrimination on grounds of sexual orientation, religion, age and disability.

Harmonisation

Harmonisation, as an issue in British employment relations, developed from the early 1970s, in a pragmatic way and on a voluntary basis, in negotiations between employers and trade unions. It concerned the establishment of single-status terms and conditions of employment and the removal of the differential status and treatment of manual and non-manual (i.e. blue-collar and white-collar) workers. In particular, it resulted in common holidays and working hours, and common access to sick pay and pensions. Previously, status distinctions had been the norm – with manual workers granted shorter holidays, working longer hours and, invariably, having no access to sick pay or pension schemes.

In terms of statutory employment rights, there has been no explicit differentiation between blue- and white-collar workers. The principal limitations on access have related the number of hours worked each week (which was ruled unlawful in 1994: *R* v *Secretary of State for Employment ex parte Equal Opportunities Commission* [1994] IRLR 176) and the length of continuous employment. This issue is now intertwined with both equal treatment law (because proportionately more part-timers are female than full-timers) and EU initiatives to establish pro-rota conditions for part-timers through the Part-time Workers Directive 1997.

1.5.2 The processes of employment relations

There are three key underpinning principles that can occur within these processes: the concept of natural justice, the issue of consent and the question of freedom.

Natural justice

Natural justice is a long-standing legal concept. There are two key rules: that no person may be a judge in their own case, and that a person must be given a fair opportunity to know the allegation against them, to state their case and to answer the other party. In the employment arena, these rules have a particular impact on the procedures for handling dismissal cases. Procedural fairness is as important a consideration to tribunals as the other tests (viz. whether the dismissal is for a fair reason, and whether the employer behaved reasonably in all the circumstances).

The reference document for disciplinary procedural matters is the ACAS *Code of Practice on Disciplinary Procedures* (2000). The House of Lords has confirmed that the Code should be regularly consulted in cases of disciplinary dismissal. Paragraph 9 indicates the practical steps to be taken through which the requirements of natural justice might be satisfied.

Consent

Consent or agreement features at various stages in the employment relationship: contract formulation, contract variation and in negotiated terms and conditions of employment with trade unions or other workforce representatives.

Consent is central to the law on contracts of employment. As detailed in Chapter 2, the contract of employment is an agreement and may not be changed without the agreement of the parties (the employer and the employee). Consent may be express (usually clearly and formally given) or implied (i.e. from the behaviour of the employee who works under particular terms and conditions without protest). If an employer changes a term of the contract of employment without agreement then they breach the contract. Where this has happened, courts have stated that the contract must be complied with until it is either changed by agreement or terminated.

The issue of consent also occurs in relation to negotiations with trade unions and in the resulting collective agreements, which, by definition, give the consent of the appropriate workforce to certain terms and conditions of employment. These agreements are, typically, in British industrial relations, voluntary agreements. Very rarely do they have legal status. Breach of a collective agreement, by an employer, is more likely to result in a dispute than in legal action.

Freedom

The final principle that infuses employment procedures is freedom. Largely, this is considered in relation to employer action. However, it does, also, to a much lesser extent, concern the activity of employees.

Traditionally, within British employment relations, employers have asserted their commitment to managerial freedom. This has often been encapsulated in the term, the right to manage. As such, this 'right' has no legal standing. It is, arguably, a moral right deriving from economic ownership. It is an assertion that management should have unfettered freedom and discretion to take whatever decisions are appropriate for the economic success of the business. Frequently, it is strongly associated with operational issues – particularly the deployment and organisation of resources, including employees. It embraces, for example, a 'right to hire and fire', rights to determine promotion, staffing levels, disciplinary matters, production control, technological change and quality issues.

There are, however, circumstances in which managements have been, and continue to be, willing to limit their freedom to act. In determining pay and conditions, some employers have felt that their interests could be met by agreeing to recognise trade unions. Although such a concession would reduce management's freedom of action, it would be compensated for by the creation of a more orderly system of industrial relations based on workforce consent. However, the concession has been seen as being in favour of free collective bargaining – a voluntary system to regulate pay and conditions, a system that could take directly into account the specific interests of that employer and their workforce. The decision to recognise a trade union for bargaining, then, continues to be seen, by most employers, as one to be taken freely by themselves – without any statutory compulsion.

Both of these elements of managerial ideology have been substantially challenged and changed in the past 20 years or more. The right to manage has been significantly constrained by the various frameworks of legal regulation (particularly those on discrimination and dismissal). Where collective bargaining continues to exist, its complete 'freedom' is open to question. Provisions of collective agreements are not isolated from the specifications of employment law.

In general terms, no collective agreement can infringe discrimination law. More specifically, certain legal provisions (e.g. on redundancies, maternity and working time) can and will mould the terms of collective agreements. The freedom of an employer to decide whether or not to engage in collective bargaining has, since 2000, and depending on the circumstances, been restricted.

The extent to which employers have freedom and discretion is, then, variable. It is dependent upon the combined extent to which employment law intervenes and the employer has conceded collective bargaining rights. Storey (1980: 45) described the right to manage as 'the residue of discretionary powers of decision left to management when the regulative impacts of law and collective agreements have been subtracted'.

For employees, the issue of freedom is more uncertain. Primarily, it arises when the contract of employment is formulated. Common law states that the contact is freely arrived at. However, most commentators regard this as a legal fiction. An employee's freedom to influence the terms of the contract are heavily constrained – unless the employee has particular skills and experience that are in short supply and great demand. The only freedom an employee is likely to have is to accept or reject the offered contract.

1.6 Conclusion

The interlocking of legal and voluntary measures remains an important feature of employment regulation. The balance has decisively swung towards significant juridification over the past 25 years or more. Managers are less likely to determine policies, employment practices and terms and conditions of employment without reference to legal standards. Nevertheless, there are still areas for management to exercise discretion and to determine some of their own standards above the statutory minima. It is unlikely that there will be a return to the high level of voluntarism that existed in Britain until the 1960s. Indeed, evidence of future developments suggests that voluntarism within a legal framework will continue to be the norm.

Further reading

Recent Annual Reports of:

- Advisory Conciliation and Arbitration Service
- Commission for Racial Equality
- Equal Opportunities Commission
- Health and Safety Commission
- Disability Rights Commission
- Low Pay Commission
- Central Arbitration Committee

Advisory Conciliation and Arbitration Service (2001) *Discipline and Grievances at Work; an advisory handbook*. London: Advisory Conciliation and Arbitration Service

References

Advisory Conciliation and Arbitration Service (2002) *Annual Report 2001–02*. London: ACAS.

Cabinet Office (2002) *Employment Regulation: Striking a Balance* (Better Regulation Taskforce). London: Cabinet Office.

Cully, M. *et al.* (1999) *Britain at Work*. London: Routledge.

Deakin, S. and Morris, G. (1998) *Labour Law*. London: Butterworths.

Department of Trade and Industry (2001) *Dispute Resolution in Britain: a background paper*. London: DTI.

Department of Trade and Industry (2002) *Findings from the 1998 Survey of Employment Tribunal applications*. London: DTI.

Dickens, L. *et al.* (1985) *Dismissed*. Oxford: Blackwell.

Franks, Lord (1957) *Committee on Administrative Tribunals and Enquiries: Report*, Cmnd. 218. London: HMSO.

The Home Office (1997) *Rights Brought Home: the Human Rights Bill*, Cm. 3782. London: Stationery Office.

Kahn-Freund, O. (1954) 'Legal Framework' in Flanders, A. and Clegg, H. (eds) *The System of Industrial Relations in Great Britain*. Oxford: Blackwell.

Kessler, I. and Purcell, J. (1995) *Joint Problem Solving*, Occasional Paper 55. London: ACAS.

Leonard, A. (1987) *Judging Equality*. London: The Cobden Trust.

Lewis, R. and Clark, J. (1993) *Employment Rights, Industrial Tribunals and Arbitration: the Case for Alternative Dispute Resolution*. London: Institute of Employment Rights.

Morris, H., Willey, B. and Sachdev, S. (2002) *Managing in a Business Context: an HR approach*. London: Prentice Hall.

Storey, J. (1980) *The Challenge to Management Control*. London: Business Books.

PART ONE

The changing employment relationship

Introduction to Part One

The chapters in Part One are concerned with three broad themes: economically driven change affecting employment relations, changes in employment status and a new legal model for regulating the employment relationship.

ECONOMICALLY DRIVEN CHANGE

Employers have increasingly initiated operational and employment changes as a result of competitive pressures – from within the United Kingdom, from within Europe generally and internationally. Many of the changes have frequently been designed to reduce unit labour costs. So they have had an impact on various aspects of the employment relationship.

First, technology has substituted for human labour (particularly, equipment using rapidly developing micro-electronic technology). Strategically, 'business process re-engineering' (BPR) has aimed at more systematic reappraisals of organisational structures. BPR has encompassed the redefining of organisations' core activities and has resulted in delayering and downsizing. Also, reconsideration has been given to the effectiveness of operational systems and to the importance of quality indicators including 'total quality management'. The legal consequences of many of these developments have been felt, particularly, in variation of contract of employment issues and in the application of redundancy law.

Secondly, many employers have reassessed the deployment and use of their remaining labour forces. One 'buzz word' that has infused this management activity is 'flexibility', which has affected, principally, job demarcations, the scheduling of working time and the location of work.

Thirdly, the use of tendering (and, particularly 'compulsory competitive tendering' in parts of the public sector under the previous Conservative government) has resulted in structural changes whereby employees have been transferred to new employers. As an alternative strategy in public service provision, the Labour government is promoting public-private partnership (PPP) initiatives. At the heart of these central government policies is the issue of protecting employees' existing terms and conditions of employment (under the Transfer of Undertakings (Protection of Employment) Regulations 1981); and the emergence of a two-tier workforce delivering public services.

CHANGES IN EMPLOYMENT STATUS

One aspect of 'flexibility' has been the growing use of 'non-standard' employment (i.e. those who are not permanent full-time employees). This has resulted in the creation of important minorities within the workforce – for example, those working part-time or on formal job share schemes; or on fixed-term or casual contracts; or as homeworkers/teleworkers; or as agency staff. The traditional model of continuous employment with one employer for long periods of time may be eroding. It is, however, still the norm for most working people. Nevertheless, for some, discontinuous employment is emerging as a clear feature of employment relations. The growth of this 'flexible workforce' has created two areas of concern in respect of employment protection: how to overcome restricted access to statutory employment rights; and how to deal with the inferior terms and conditions often provided under contracts of employment.

As we will see, this diversity of employment status is increasingly, but fitfully, being recognised within the legal regulation of the employment relationship. Part-time workers have acquired greater access to employment rights and, under the Part-time Workers Regulations 2000, are able to claim pro-rata contractual rights with full-timers. Continuity of employment provisions have, on occasion, been construed to protect casual workers and those on fixed-term contracts. Some statutory rights are being extended to atypical workers – for example, under the Working Time Regulations 1998 and the National Minimum Wage Act 1998.

'NEW MODEL' EMPLOYMENT REGULATION

The traditional vehicle for regulating the employment relationship is the contract of employment. However, this has shown itself to be imperfect in a number of ways. It does not, in itself, provide adequate protection for employees. Parliament has, over the past 40 years, developed a basic contract of employment that can be enforced under statute. Key elements of this 'new model' are already in existence. These include: the right to contractual information, the right not to have the contract unfairly terminated, the right that no term of the contract should be discriminatory under sex discrimination law, minimum periods of notice, the right not to have pay deducted unlawfully and a minimum right for maternity leave for women. Additions to this framework are rights to paid holidays, rest breaks, a maximum working week and statutory minimum pay. The Employment Act 2002 has incorporated, as implied contractual terms, minimum statutory procedures for grievance handling and for dismissal and disciplinary action. Increasingly, these statutory rights are being extended to 'workers' rather than to 'employees'. This widens the protective coverage.

CONCLUSION

It is against this background that Chapter 2 will discuss the diversity of employment relationships and the ways in which they are being regulated – by contract and statute law. Chapter 3 will focus on the consequences of business change – how the terms of individual contracts can be changed, the protections afforded to employees when there are business transfers and employee rights in redundancy situations.

CHAPTER 2 Regulating the employment relationship

Learning objectives

This chapter develops various themes introduced in Chapter 1. Having read it, you should understand:

- The nature and significance of changes affecting the employment relationship.
- The diversity of employment status in the 'flexible labour market'.
- Ways in which contracts of employment and statute law regulate the formation and operation of the employment relationship, and establish certain terms.

2.1 Structure of the chapter

This chapter comprises the following sections:

- *Introduction*: The character of the employment relationship and its legal regulation.
- *The context*: The concepts of work and employment, the psychological contract, the balance of individualism and collectivism and the diversity of employment status.
- *The legal framework*: Contracts for the regulation of work, the characteristics of the contract of employment, express and implied terms, the statement of initial employment particulars, terminating a contract of employment and protection for 'atypical' workers.

2.2 Introduction

In this chapter, we consider two broad, related issues: the character of the employment relationship and how it is changing, and the ways in which this relationship is regulated both in law and by voluntary measures.

2.2.1   Defining the employment relationship

The employment relationship is an exchange relationship: the exchange of work for payment. It is often known as the 'work-wage bargain'. The parties are an individual worker and an employing organisation. Because it is voluntarily entered into, it is different from other relationships under which work may be performed: e.g. slavery, serfdom, conscription.

It is also characterised as a power relationship. The two parties are often spoken of as if they are of equal status. However, the economic reality of employment shows that, in practice, there is, usually, no equality. In discussing the employment contract, Wedderburn (1986) described the situation this way: 'The individual employer is from the outset an aggregate of resources, already a collective power in social terms . . . In reality, save in exceptional circumstances, the individual worker brings no equality of bargaining power to the labour market and to this transaction central to his life whereby the employer buys his labour.'

Key to the operation of this relationship is the way in which power is exercised by an employer. The following questions are explored at various points in this chapter. Does an employer have unfettered power to impose conditions of employment? To what extent are employers expected or required to obtain consent from an employee about terms and conditions of employment? In which ways do law and/or agreements with unions (or other workforce representatives) constrain an employer's exercise of power?

2.2.2   Frontier of control

One aspect of power relations in sociological studies of the employment relationship is the concept, 'the frontier of control'. This refers to 'the range of issues over which workers have some degree of collective influence, primarily, but not exclusively, through trade unions' (Batstone, 1988: 218). It could, of course, also encompass work groups and teams. The frontier of control reflects the relative balance of power between managers and employees, which may shift as an organisation's economic and technological circumstances change; and/or if there are legislative restraints imposed on unions. Its location will probably be different for different issues. For example, management might grant considerable influence to a union in pay determination to achieve consent to reward systems and to defuse a potentially significant source of conflict. However, it may wish to retain 'the right to manage' over issues involving the deployment of resources including manning levels.

2.2.3   The parties' expectations

To the employment relationship, both parties bring various expectations and assumptions about how it will function (see 'The psychological contract' below). Also, they approach it having some interests in common and some in conflict. For example, it is probable that both parties will agree on the economic objective of business survival. This, after all, is the source of job security and income for both parties. However, they are likely to disagree about cost-cutting measures affecting job levels, the scheduling of working time or the flexibility of tasks that working people are expected to carry out. So, consensus and conflict coexist in this relationship. One essential task is the regulation and management of conflict, and the need to capitalise on consensus.

2.2.4   Three sets of 'rules'

The employment relationship is not a 'free for all'. It is regulated. Three formal instruments may be used: the contract of employment, statutory requirements and agreements with unions (or with other workforce representatives). All these instruments produce sets of 'rules'. The first two, clearly, have force of law. The third set, in origin, is a result of a voluntary decision by an employer to negotiate directly with a union or to accept the provisions of a collective agreement negotiated elsewhere. Whilst collective agreements are, invariably, voluntary agreements and are presumed to be so (TULRCA 1992, s 179), they can and do have legal force, in respect of terms and conditions of employment, through 'incorporation' into an individual's contract of employment. So, in practice, all three formal instruments for regulating the contract have legal significance.

We will be consider the contribution of statute law in all of the subsequent chapters. The regulatory role of collective bargaining is explored in a later section of this chapter. Initially, then, we will focus on the role of the contract of employment.

2.2.5   The role of the contract of employment

This is the central instrument for regulating the individual employment relationship. It is the starting point for so many issues: grievances, disciplinary action and complaints to tribunals. However, although it is so fundamentally important, it is still a flawed instrument.

First, it regulates an asymmetrical employment relationship – i.e. characterised by a power imbalance under which an employee can be vulnerable to employer action. Secondly, many aspects of the contract can reinforce employer power. It provides a means of direction and control of the employee and, consequently, has been described as 'a command under the guise of an agreement' (Kahn-Freund, 1983: 18). Indeed, various commentators have pointed to the considerable opportunities existing for employers not only in formulating of the contract; but in determining how it is carried out; and, also, in seeking to change it. Thirdly, when it is formulated and agreed, a legal fiction is adopted that it is 'freely arrived at'. Technically, this is so. No employee is forced to enter into a contract of employment, but rather, must 'take it or leave it'. In reality, few job applicants or employees have influence over the terms of the contract affecting them and, in the force of economic circumstances, most people accept. Fourthly, there are still echoes of the old 'master and servant' relationship in the way the employment contract is perceived. This submissive relationship, which governed employment law, was, during the nineteenth century, gradually replaced by the, theoretically, more egalitarian contractual relationship. However, occasionally, judges in their rulings reflect the old-fashioned perspective based on status.

Finally, the contract of employment has limitations as far as the adoption of universal minimum standards is concerned. Statute law can be necessary to ensure universal fair treatment. For example, the Equal Pay Act 1970 (s 1) deems that 'an equality clause' shall be included in contracts of employment if one is not provided for 'directly or by reference to a collective agreement or otherwise'. Effectively, this means that no term of a contract of employment can be discriminatory on grounds of sex. It will be void if it does so. Deakin and Morris (1998: 543) comment on how statute law on sex and race discrimination was necessary: 'The common law, with its emphasis on freedom of contract, sees nothing inherently wrong with discrimination . . . as long as no pre-existing contract or property right is infringed'. Through such statute law, Parliament is eroding 'contractual autonomy'.

2.3 The context

In recent years, several developments have had an impact on the employment relationship and, consequently, on contractual issues. These are of fundamental significance because they force a reappraisal of various traditional models and practices. The pace of change also continues to be rapid. Change poses, more sharply, the critical question: how far can the contract of employment accommodate business needs?

We will look at four major contextual issues: the concepts of work and employment; standards and expectations about employment in the psychological contract; the balance of individualism and collectivism; and the growing diversity of employment status. Whilst these areas reflect changing social attitudes, all are heavily influenced by economic considerations.

2.3.1 Concepts of work and employment

In the post-war period, employment has been the predominant model through which work has been carried out. Essentially, it involves a long-term arrangement between an individual and an organisation, with work provided on a continuing basis – 'day in, day out', 'week in, week out', even 'year in, year out'. Traditionally, in employment, a 'job for life' was presumed. Entitlements (e.g. to increased pay, holidays and other benefits and even access to promotion) were often service related – based on seniority and continuous service. For individuals, a job, in these terms, was, and remains, a very valuable asset.

This model is essentially based on male employment patterns. This gender-based perspective is important in considering the issues raised in this chapter. Linda Dickens (1992: 5) has commented that:

> A key to women's disadvantage in the labour market . . . is that structures of employment, although apparently neutral, are in fact moulded around the life patterns and domestic obligations of men. Our systems of labour law and social security have similarly taken the male as the neutral standard of the worker, to the disadvantage of women who, in not conforming to the male life and work pattern, fall outside various protections. The adoption of the male as the normal standard is revealed immediately we consider the label 'atypical' employee . . . The 'typical' employee is male; the 'atypical' employee female.

This model has been subject to considerable buffeting in the past two decades as a result of two related factors: employers' need for both greater flexibility in resource utilisation and also greater efficiency and cost effectiveness. These changes, initiated by employers, particularly from the early 1980s onwards, have been explored by academic writers in such theoretical models as 'the flexibile firm' (Atkinson, 1984); and 'the shamrock organisation' (Handy, 1991). (These are discussed below under the diversity of employment status.)

Handy (1991) contends that we should reconsider our attitude to work as a wider activity and 'stop talking and thinking about employees and employment'. His reason is that 'if work were defined as activity, some of which is paid for, then everyone is a worker, for nearly all their natural life'. He proposes a portfolio of five categories of work – the balance of which will constantly alter as people grow older:

1 *Wage or salaried work*: Where individuals are paid for the time given. This represents the traditional employment model, whether a person's contract is full-time, part-time or temporary.

2 *Fee work*: Where money is paid for results delivered. Its incidence increases as jobs move outside organisations.

3 *Home-work* (or *'domestic work'* to prevent confusion with the concept of 'homeworking'): This includes all tasks taking place in the home – cooking, cleaning, caring for children and other relatives, maintaining and improving the home. This area of work is particularly susceptible to the use of other providers. Depending on a person's economic circumstances and many other factors (including the levels of social welfare benefits or wider government policy) a person may, for example, use professional childcare, commission a self-employed plumber or employ a cleaner or gardener.

4 *Gift work*: This is done for free outside the home for relatives, friends, neighbours, charities, local groups and as a public service. This unpaid work is particularly significant for a growing range of charitable organisations providing personal services to those who are ill or disabled.

5 *Study work*: This involves education or training designed to improve skills and increase knowledge – e.g. learning a language or studying for a qualification. In an employment culture increasingly emphasising training and development, continuous improvement and life-long learning, then, this work is of great value to individuals and organisations.

This 'portfolio' concept of work clearly challenges the social convention that paid employment is the only appropriate definition both of people's contribution to society and of their status. So, the home-work (or domestic work), particularly of women caring for children, which is traditionally undervalued, would be recognised. The concept of 'unemployment' would be redefined. The notion of 'retirement', traditionally seen as disengagement from paid employment, would be reappraised.

2.3.2 The psychological contract

The second contextual issue is the psychological contract. This concept was initially outlined by Schein (1988) and has since been elaborated. Its state is regularly monitored by the Chartered Institute of Personnel and Development in an annual survey. Essentially, it is about the expectations and assumptions that the parties bring to an employment relationship. These are likely to be moulded by previous employment experiences; by the process of socialisation in the family and the education system; by a person's values; and by economic imperatives involving the need, for example, for income and an appropriate living standard.

One author, summarising the nature of this contract states that:

> within that implict contract are embedded three kinds of individual expectations and needs:
>
> 1   The need for equity and justice – that employees will be treated fairly and honestly and that information and explanation about changes will always be provided.
> 2   The desire for security and relative certainty – that employees can expect, in return for their loyalty, that they need not be fearful, uncertain or helpless (as they contemplate who might be the next to go).
> 3   The need for fulfilment, satisfaction and progression – that employees can trust the value that the organisation places on their current contributions and prior successes and relationships (Mant, 1995: 48).

Herriot (1995: 196) outlines how the psychological contract can shift over time and may, indeed, be shifting rapidly (*see* Fig. 2.1).

The achievement of 'deals' under the psychological contract is highly problematic. For the employee, it depends on several factors. First, there is the extent to which the employer is serious about what is on offer; and, through employment practices and the employment contract, aims to deliver on these 'offers'. It can be argued that 'many of today's employees have abandoned the idea that they have a deal with their organisation'. They experience 'feelings of

The individual offers		The organisation offers
	1970s	
Loyalty		security
Compliance		promotion
Good citizenship		care
	1990s	
Accountability		a job
Flexibility		higher salary
Long hours		
	2010s	
Learning		employability
Learning to learn		flexible contract
Clear added value		individualised rewards

Figure 2.1 Three psychological contracts

Source: Tyson, S. (1995) *Strategic Prospects for HRM*. London: Chartered Institute of Personnel and Development. Reproduced with permission.

powerlessness – powerlessness to exit or to loosen the ever-tightening systems of control' (Herriot, 1995: 197).

Secondly, there is the question of feasibly reconciling the expectations of employee and employer. Mismatches can be sources of conflict, demotivation and disaffection. Thirdly, in terms of successful delivery of the psychological contract, much will probably depend on organisational size and the grades of the staff concerned. So, larger organisations, with developed human resource management (HRM) policies may be more successful.

It is possible to comment on the actual state of the psychological contract from somewhat contrasting survey data published by the Economic and Social Research Council and the Chartered Institute of Personnel and Development.

The ESRC Future of Work Programme is based on in-depth interviews with 2466 employees across occupational groups. The report states that 'it is hard to find much evidence of any widespread "psychological" contract or mutually acceptable trade off between the needs of companies and the demands of employees' (Taylor, 2002: 7). Looking at the central concepts in the psychological contract, of trust, loyalty and commitment, 'the survey provides little evidence, however, that many of these progressive ideas usually associated with enlightened human resource management techniques are being translated into practical measures that are ensuring the growth of more high commitment workplaces' (Taylor, 2002: 11). One important gloss highlighted in this report is the importance of the different experiences of employees. 'It is hard not to reach the conclusion that class and occupational differences remain of fundamental importance to any understanding of our world of work' (Taylor, 2002: 8). For example, 'many people still regard their job as part of a career with distinct promotion prospects. Indeed, as our economy becomes increasingly dominated by the highly qualified in skilled work this perception is likely to grow and not decline' (Taylor, 2002: 14). However, only a tiny minority of manual workers take a similar view of career potential. Similar markedly different attitudes to employee commitment between managers and manual workers were found in the Workplace Employee Relations Survey 1998 (Cully *et al.*, 1999: 186).

The authors of the CIPD's most recent survey of the state of the psychological contract argue that at the core of this contract are three key elements: fairness of treatment, trust and delivery of the 'deal'. To achieve 'a positive psychological contract', they state, 'it is important to invest in human resource practices and to foster a climate of direct participation' (Guest and Conway, 2001: 54).

Its results (drawn from a telephone survey of 619 people working for organisations employing ten or more people) revealed, perhaps surprisingly, that 'the psychological contract is in fairly good shape'. They report that 'most workers remain satisfied, committed and motivated'. But, they added, 'if the decline in the use of the kind of key (human resource management) practices that make a difference continues, we can expect to see further rises in dissatisfaction and disaffection with negative consequenecs for consequent performance at work' (Guest and Conway, 2001: 54).

Certainly, when asked about the delivery of the promise of fair treatment by their managers and supervisors, 38 per cent said it was 'always kept' and 35 per cent said it was kept 'to a large extent'. The promise to deliver on fair pay 'for the work that you do' was said to have 'always' been kept by 40 per cent and kept 'to a large extent' by 26 per cent.

On other aspects of the delivery of the deal, the respondents were asked, 'To what extent has your organisation always kept its promises or commitments to you?' about a range of employment issues. The aggregate responses, 'always' or 'to a large extent' were given as follows: to provide you with a career (74 per cent), job security (80 per cent), to provide you with interesting work (61 per cent).

As far as trust is concerned, when respondents were asked, 'In general how much do you trust your organisation to keep its promises or commitments to you and other employees?', 33 per cent said 'a lot' and 50 per cent said 'somewhat'. There was a remarkable result to the related question, 'To what extent do you trust management to look after your best interests?': 27 per cent said 'a lot' and 48 per cent said 'somewhat'. It would have been interesting to explore these 'best interests' more thoroughly, given the evident conflicts of interest within employment relationships. In respect of loyalty, 47 per cent said they felt 'a lot of loyalty to the organisation' and 41 per cent 'some loyalty'. Seventy-eight per cent were 'very' or 'quite proud' to tell people who they worked for.

Many of the expectations referred to in the formulation of the psychological contract relate to principles which occur in employment law: fairness, equality of treatment and opportunity, job security. These, in turn, reflect standards, accepted internationally, in the conventions of the International Labour Organisation and the European Convention on Human Rights; and in European law (*see* Chapter 1). The contract of employment and statute law are likely, then, to be instrumentally important in giving effect to certain aspects of the psychological contract. However, there may also be circumstances in which law might be at variance with the expectations of the parties. For example, an employer's expectation of flexibility in the deployment and use of staff might be constrained by legal obligations.

2.3.3 Individualism and collectivism

The third contextual issue is the shifting balance between individualism and collectivism in management of the employment relationship. 'Individualism' has been promoted both politically and by employers – particularly in respect of pay and entitlement to benefits. It has also been evident in pay determination, where there has been a political drive towards 'decollectivisation' (constraining the power of trade unions). In essence, 'individualism' implies that the sole focus for workers is their own terms and conditions of employment. 'Collectivism' is an acknowledgement that working people have some interests in common. Normally, this view derives from the fact that work is invariably a social and co-operative activity. So collective interests may be expressed informally through workgroups or more formally through trade union representation.

Until the early 1980s, trade union recognition was extensive, with a density of unionisation of over 50 per cent (i.e. over 13 million working people). Collective bargaining was, consequently, a significant voluntary means for regulating employment relations. It covered some 70 per cent of the workforce. By 2000, the overall density of trade unionism was around 33 per cent and the coverage of collective bargaining was estimated at around 50 per cent.

However, although law was a factor in 'decollectivisation', there were broader economic changes, in the 1980s and 1990s, unfavourable to organised labour – notably, the substantial slackening of labour markets and higher and persistent levels of unemployment together with more competitive product markets. There were also changes in organisational structures in the public sector – a trade union heartland. Politically, since the election of a Labour government in 1997, there has been some shift in approach. There is an acknowledgement of both individual and collective interests (*see also* Chapter 14).

2.3.4   Diversity of employment status

The fourth issue is the diversity of employment status. This has been developing in the labour market over the past two decades. However, the use of part-time, temporary, casual work and homeworking are not new. They have a long history in the labour market, where they have been regarded as marginal or 'atypical' forms of working. Present-day interest in these forms of employment status derives from employers' drives for flexibility. Atkinson (1984) outlined an influential model, 'the flexible firm', encompassing various forms of flexibility.

The 'flexible firm'

This model describes a 'dual labour market'. It does not represent any particular firm. It can be used, essentially, as an analytical tool to understand the interconnections between different types of employment flexibility. Atkinson has denied that it is a prescriptive model. It is descriptive. It is 'the organisation structure which many UK firms are trying to introduce'; although it is arguable that few firms have systematically attempted to introduce it.

In the flexible firm model five flexibilities are identified: numerical, functional, reward, working time and geographic mobility. The emphasis given by any one organisation to any of these flexibilities is dependent on its product market, its customer demands and the technology used.

Numerical flexibility: This concerns the use and deployment of workers. It focuses on business needs to adjust workforce size to meet peaks and troughs in the provision of a service or the production of goods. The most notable examples involve the use of part-time, temporary or casual workers, as well as homeworkers. In some respects, these forms of 'peripheral', or 'atypical', employment can also meet individual workers' preferences – for example, helping accommodate work and domestic responsibilities.

Functional flexibility: This relates to the removal of job demarcations and the introduction of multiskilling or dual skilling. Some employers define wide 'job profiles' in order to broaden the range of tasks employees may be called upon to perform, so reducing overall labour costs.

Reward flexibility: Its adoption is designed to encourage individual performance and cost efficiency. It concerns the adjustment of remuneration to reinforce other flexibilities. Examples include merit pay, profit-related pay, performance-related pay, profit sharing and employee share ownership.

Working-time flexibility: This concerns the scheduling of working time to meet the peaks and troughs of production or service delivery. It can involve the introduction of annual hours scheduling, shiftworking, term-time contracts, zero-hours contracts and on-call contracts. It is also supplemented by employee demands for flexible working time, particularly to manage childcare.

Geographic flexibility: This relates to the location of work and the need for employees to be mobile. This may involve daily travelling in the course of work; the use of homeworking/teleworking; relocation within the United Kingdom, or even expatriate status.

The structure of 'the flexible firm' model encompasses four groups of working people:

The core group: This comprises full-time permanent career employees. Examples include managers, skilled and professional workers. They are offered a relatively high degree of employment security in exchange for being flexible about the work they perform (functional flexibility). A principal characteristic of the group is that they have skills which cannot be bought in and are likely to be specific to the organisation. Career development is generally good and training and development is facilitated for this group. Rewards are likely to comprise a performance-related element. The size of this group is likely to be under constant scrutiny because 'some managers are anxious to push as many jobs as possible into the peripheral or external categories' (Atkinson, 1984).

First peripheral group: This comprises full-time employees. They have fewer career opportunities and lower job security than staff in the core group. They can be found in, for example, administrative, supervisory and assembly jobs. Their numbers can be varied according to shift in customer demand. Job content is geared to a narrow range of tasks. According to Atkinson, functional flexibility is not sought from this group. Significant numbers of women predominate in these jobs.

Second peripheral group: This comprises temporary workers and those with short-term contracts. Such contracts might be used for a wide range of tasks, ranging from routine work to the completion of a major project requiring professional expertise. In most instances, the expectations of both parties are that, on completion of the task, commitment to the organisation ceases. Again, a significant proportion of women workers are located in this category.

Externals: This category may comprise self-employed workers, subcontractors, agency staff, consultants, homeworkers/teleworkers and 'public subsidy' workers (i.e. those on government-funded job creation schemes). Such outsourcing (i.e. buying in products and services rather than incorporating them into the organisation's own range of activities) is often used if the work is either very specialised (i.e. requires particular professional skills) or very mundane (e.g. cleaning, catering and security). It can result from an organisation's policy of 'getting back to the core business'. External workers have 'the entire responsibility for providing business support and training for themselves'.

Handy (1991) outlined the 'shamrock organisation'. This mirrors much of Atkinson's model. He adds one interesting dimension: *the displacement of work to customers*, e.g. filling cars with petrol, using automatic teller machines, scanning groceries in supermarkets and assembling your own furniture.

The models and evidence of labour market trends

Both Atkinson's and Handy's models have been criticised in varying ways. However, they usefully highlight the segmentation of contemporary labour markets and certain elements within them: the degree of job security, access to development opportunities and career progression; the use of technological change, and employers' policies to promote cost effectiveness; greater use of flexibility in all its forms; and the use of 'distancing strategies', whereby work is carried out by contractors or customers.

What the models do not reflect is the practice of specific industries or sectors. For example, the use of permanent part-time or temporary staff will vary between sectors depending on the nature of the goods or services provided, customer demands, the technology used and the organisation's operational systems. The feasibility of functional flexibility or the need to have flexible working-time scheduling is again dependent on these factors.

Furthermore, these models, if taken at their face value, in isolation from statistical analyses of the labour market, arguably, overstate the trend away from full-time permanent towards 'atypical' forms. A monograph reporting on some data from the ESRC Future of Work Programme states:

> the most startling overall conclusion to draw from the material is that many of the commonly held assumptions about today's world of work need to be seriously questioned . . . The evidence simply does not sustain the view that we are witnessing the emergence of a 'new' kind of employment relations, seen in the 'end of career' and 'the death of the permanent job for life'. The shift away from permanent and full-time jobs to temporary, short-term or part-time work is exaggerated (Taylor, 2002).

The detailed trends are considered below.

A snapshot of the labour market

The categories of employment status currently in frequent use are: permanent employment (full-time and part-time); temporary employment (full-time and part-time); casual work; agency work; zero-hours contract workers; homeworking/ teleworking; and self-employment. These categories are considered below to provide a background to the legal issues in the next section of the chapter.

Table 2.1 is an overall snapshot of the structure of the labour market. It is important to note that this snapshot obscures two important medium and long-term trends within the labour market which will influence employers' decisions on the resourcing of work: an ageing population and decreasing childbirth.

The actual and likely responses to these developments are:

- Encouraging greater participation of women in the labour market.
- Encouraging older workers to remain economically active for a longer period of time and possibly the introduction of flexible retirement.
- Encouraging more immigrant workers to participate in the labour market.

These issues will be considered at various stages later in the textbook.

Table 2.1 The labour market structure 2001 (million workers, Summer 2001 in United Kingdom)

	Total workers	Employees	Self-employed	Unpaid family workers	Government-supported training and employment programmes
All	28.3	24.8	3.2	0.10	0.13
Male	15.6	13.1	2.4	0.03	0.09
Female	12.7	11.8	0.8	0.07	0.04

Source: Labour Force Survey.

Full-time and part-time working (million workers)

	Total workers		Employees		Self-employed	
	FT	PT	FT	PT	FT	PT
All	21.2	6.8	18.7	6.1	2.5	0.7
Male	14.1	1.4	12.0	1.1	2.1	0.3
Female	7.1	5.5	6.7	5.1	0.4	0.4

Source: Labour Market Trends, Summer 2001.

Typical and 'atypical' forms of employment

Full-time workers: This represents what has been long regarded as the typical or 'standard' form of employment. It is invariably permanent employment (though some are working on fixed-term contracts). Full-time workers represent around three-quarters of the labour force.

Part-time workers: There are 6.8 million of these workers in the United Kingdom. Around 80 per cent are female, but the number of men working part-time has been increasing. By sector, two-thirds of part-time jobs are located in two specific categories: 'public administration, education and health' and 'distribution, hotels and restaurants'. Average working hours are some 15 per week. Some part-time employment is structured on a 'job share' basis. Also, the incidence of 'double-jobbing' is continuing to grow with 1.2 million workers having a second job (for, on average, nine hours per week). Typically, many of the terms and conditions of employment under which part-time workers have worked have been inferior in comparison with full-time workers, although, in some situations, the pro-rata principle has been established.

Temporary workers: Temporary jobs can take a variety of forms. They have in common the fact that the jobs are held by someone who has been recruited to do them for a finite period of time (although this may be up to several years). They include seasonal work, casual work, non-permanent jobs obtained through a temporary employment agency ('agency temps') and jobs carried out under a 'fixed-term contract'.

Temporary workers comprise 7.5 per cent of all employees (1.7 million people) (Labour Force Survey, Spring 1998). This contrasts with a proportion of 5.5 per cent of employees in 1992. Despite this modest growth, the UK has the third lowest proportion of temporary workers in the European Union. According to ESRC research, there were some specific shifts in the nature of this temporary work (Taylor, 2002: 12). In 2000, 5.5 per cent were on a temporary contract of less than twelve months (7.2 per cent in a comparable survey in 1992); and 2.8 per cent on fixed-term contract (between one and three years) (5 per cent in 1992).

Fifty-five per cent of temporary workers are female. By sector, 10 per cent of employees in the public sector are temporary (particularly in public administration, education and health care), compared with 6 per cent in the private sector. By occupation, the greatest concentrations of temporary employees are in the professional occupations.

The reasons most commonly cited by employers for recruiting temporary workers are: 'providing cover for the absence of permanent staff (e.g. on maternity leave); to cope with seasonal fluctuations in workload; to staff short-term projects; and to acquire people with specialist skills which are only needed on a short-term basis or which are only available on a non-permanent basis' (Sly and Stillwell, 1997: 349). Employees took temporary employment for the following reasons: 42 per cent could not find a permanent job, and 28 per cent did not want a permanent job (*ibid.*).

Agency workers: In terms of total numbers, they are a small group. However, in certain sectors and occupations, their incidence is significant (e.g. clerical and secretarial work, personal and protective services, and plant and machine operatives). There is a growth in 'banks' of professional agency staff (e.g. nurses, further education lecturers and supply schoolteachers). There are two categories of 'agencies': employment business and employment agencies (Employment Agencies Act 1973). The first supply their staff to work on a temporary basis for clients under the control of the hirer. They are usually paid by the agency. Those in the second category introduce working people to be employed by or to establish a business relationship with the client themselves.

Zero-hours contracts: This is not a new employment status. However, it has grown in importance as a result of variable customer demand, changing technology and managerial strategies to be more cost effective. The government reports that 'some 200 000 people in the UK work under zero hours contracts' (DTI, 1998: 18). It has been defined as an arrangement 'where the worker was not guaranteed any work at all but in some way was required to be available as and when the employer needed that person' (Cave, 1997). In such arrangements, the employee may have a right to refuse work. It was found in Cave's study that 22 per cent of employers used zero-hours contracts. It was also reported that women are more likely to be employed on such contracts; and that, in 91 per cent of organisations, zero-hours contract workers did not have the same benefits as other employees.

Self-employed workers: There are 3.2 million self-reported self-employed persons in the United Kingdom – three-quarters of whom are male. This category has grown fitfully since the early 1980s – depending on economic circumstances. Clearly, this term can, and does, encompass people who may be in certain of the preceding categories – particularly, homeworking and teleworking. Whether or not such a person is a 'genuine' self-employed person (an independent contractor) or an employee is a matter that the courts can be asked to determine (*see* later in this chapter).

Homeworking/teleworking: Homeworking is a long-established feature of certain parts of the manufacturing industry. It involves routine tasks carried out at home, principally by women, invariably for low pay. In 1994, it was reported that average hourly pay was £1.28, compared with £4.42 for female manual workers generally. 'In addition, they received no non-wage benefits and also incurred expenses as a result of their work, such as heating, lighting, telephone, purchase of machines and materials and electricity' (Stanworth, 1996: 15). National surveys on the extent of homeworking suggest between 300 000 and one million workers (Stanworth, 1996: 13). Women are estimated to represent 80 per cent of homeworkers and are more likely to have dependent children than women in the workforce generally. Overwhelmingly, female homeworkers undertake clerical and secretarial work; and craft and related work.

Teleworking is a 'high-tech' variant of this traditional model. Huws (1997) suggests that teleworking is, in fact, a component part of many kinds of work – some of which is carried out on the employer's premises or even in the context of full-time permanent employment. 'Pure' teleworking, however, like homeworking, can result in different, possibly inferior, terms and conditions of employment. Stanworth (1996: 4) states that 'the overlap with homework appears most clearly at the bottom end of the status hierarchy. Teleworkers performing clerical functions such as word processing or data entry working in their own homes are often women in a similar employment relationship to their employers as are homeworkers'.

The Labour Force Survey (Spring 2001) reported that 2.2 million people in the UK (i.e. 7.4 per cent of the total labour force) worked at home at least one day a week and used both a telephone and a computer to do their work. Around 74 per cent of all teleworkers worked in the private sector (e.g. in real estate, renting and business activities). Most are professionals, managers and senior officials. About two-thirds of teleworkers are men (Labour Market Trends, June, 2002: 311).

General conclusions

The context of employment relations, outlined here, shows, on the one hand, a diversity of employment status and contractual relationship and, on the other hand, a range of flexible working-time practices and work location arrangements. These two aspects can be presented, usefully, in a single diagram which categorises them in terms of differing degrees of structure. *Structured flexibility* is characterised by clearly defined boundaries of both working time and contractual status. So, a compressed working week is a highly structured way of organising working time; and a fixed-term contract puts a limit on the duration of that employment relationship. *Unstructured flexibility* refers to more loosely defined arrangements of working time and more tenuous employment relationships (Purcell *et al.*, 1999) (*see* Fig. 2.2).

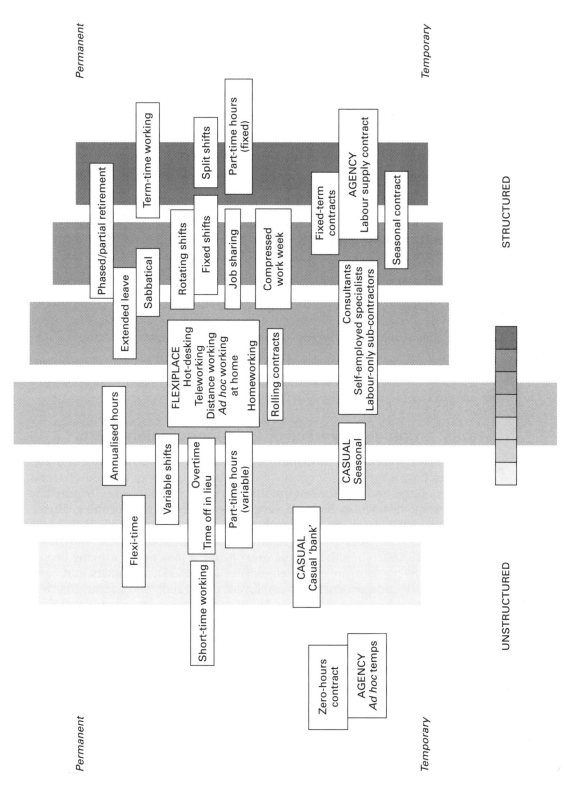

Figure 2.2 Typology of flexible working from *Whose flexibility? the costs and benefits of non-standard working arrangements and contractual relations* by Kate Purcell, Terence Hogarth and Claire Sim, published in 1999 by the Joseph Rowntree Foundation. Reproduced by permission of the Joseph Rowntree Foundation.

A flexible workforce?

1 Find the composition of your organisation's workforce according to employment status.

2 What are the significant differences in terms and conditions of employment between people of different employment status? Do you think that there are instances where your organisation might be liable for complaints at an employment tribunal?

3 What is the gender and racial composition of the workforce? When you have read Chapters 4 and 5 on sex and race discrimination, return to this exercise and consider whether or not your organisation has patterns of direct and/or indirect discrimination.

2.4 The legal framework

2.4.1 Introduction

In this section, we will consider four broad legal issues:

- employment status: employees, workers and independent contractors;
- different forms of contract used to regulate a working relationship;
- the characteristics of the contract of employment;
- employment protection for 'atypical' workers.

2.4.2 Status: employee, worker or independent contractor?

It has become increasingly important to appreciate the distinctions between these three broad categories of employment status. This arises because of access to statutory rights and also for determining contractual entitlements. Statute law helps draw the distinction, but to a very limited extent. Much of the guidance is set out in case law. Indeed, it is admitted by government that 'the definitions of "employee" and "worker" in legislation are not sufficiently clear and "user-friendly"' (DTI, 2002: 7). Although the overwhelming majority of working people (estimated at 80 per cent) are either 'employees' or 'dependent workers' and 7 per cent were clearly independently self-employed, 12 per cent 'had a status that was still unclear' (Burchell *et al.*, 1999: 64). So, the social policy reasons for clarifying this area are strong.

As indicated earlier, there are differences between work and employment. 'Work' is a wide term that includes any tasks carried out by a person for an organisation. It encompasses 'employment'. 'Employment' is generally thought of as a continuing relationship – whether full-time or part-time. This relationship, for the purposes of employment law, is regulated by a contract of employment. So, the term 'employee' refers to 'an individual who has entered into or works under (or, where the employment has ceased, worked under) a contract of employment' (ERA 1996, s 230(1)). This is a 'contract of service or apprenticeship' (s 230(1)–(2)). Establishing a person's 'employment' status is important for access to employment rights – particularly unfair dismissal rights (ERA 1996, s 94(1)). This statutory definition of 'employee' has been developed in case law and is explored below.

The wider term 'work' is not defined in law. However, the wider concept of 'worker' is.

> In this Act 'worker' (except in the phrases 'shop worker' and 'betting worker') means an individual who has entered into or works under (or, where the employment has ceased, worked under) –
> (a) a contract of employment, or
> (b) any other contract whether express or implied and (if it is express) whether oral or in writing, whereby the individual undertakes to do or perform personally any work or services for another party to the contract whose status is not by virtue of the contract that of a client or customer of any profession or business undertaking carried on by the individual (ERA 1996, s 230(3)).

The issues relating to these two categories and to the independent contractor (or self-employed person) are summarised in Fig. 2.3 and then explored below.

Employee	Worker	Independent contractor
Common law tests: is the person an employee?	**Common law tests**: how many of these does the person comply with?	Non-compliance with the *common law tests*.
Mutuality of obligation: does this exist in relation to current and future performance of work?	*Mutuality of obligation*: to what extent does this exist?	No *mutuality of obligation* to a particular employer
Duration of work: continuous or intermittent service?	*Duration of work*: continuous or intermittent service?	*Duration of work?*
Contract of employment: this exists if the person satisfies the common law tests and both levels of mutuality of obligation.	*Contract of employment*: a person thought to be a 'worker' may be an 'employee' if that person satisfies the common law tests and both levels of mutuality of obligation. However, if they are only partially satisfied, then, the person may be defined as a worker on some 'other contract' to work 'personally'.	No *contract of employment* exists. The person works under a contract for services – a commercial contract.
People in these categories are sometimes described as having '*an employment relationship*'.		
In determining a person's employment status against these tests and criteria, courts and tribunals look at *the facts and circumstances* of the individual case. They do not just accept the label that is given by the employer to a particular individual's employment relationship. This may be inaccurate. Determining employment status involves a mixture of law and fact.		

Figure 2.3   Establishing employment status

Common law tests

These tests attempt to distinguish whether the person is an employee or self-employed – i.e. in business on his/her own account. The various factors considered are:

- *The control test*: This concerns the degree of control exercised by the employer. This long-standing test was at one time considered conclusive of 'employee' status. However, it is now regarded by the courts as one of the factors to be taken into account. The nature of control has, in practice, changed, for example, as the result of human resource policies such as 'empowerment' and the need to recruit skilled and professional staff who exercise discretion and can work with some degree of autonomy. Courts and tribunals recognise that control may nowadays be more a question of the employer retaining 'ultimate authority' over the employee in relation to the performance of work. The Court of Appeal has indictaed that the test considers 'who lays down what is to be done, the way in which it is to be done, the means by which it is to be done and the time when it is done' (*Lane v Shire Roofing Co (Oxford)* [1995] IRLR 493). In respect of self-employed people, it has been argued that, according to this test, they have greater autonomy and discretion in respect of the way work is carried out. Alternatively, it is plausibly suggested that 'the right of control fails to distinguish employment from self-employment because its presence is entirely consistent with either type of contract' (Brodie, 1998: 140).

- *The integration test*: This test involves considering of the ways in which a person contributes to an organisation and is part of its structure: is the person 'integrated' into the organisation or 'accessory' to it? To what extent does the person contribute to service delivery or the production of goods? So, it focuses on the organisation of work and less on the issue of control or subordination. If integration is established, then, a person is likely to be an 'employee'.

- *The economic reality test*: This is closely associated with the integration test and covers the issue of who bears financial risks and, as appropriate, who provides the resources for work to be done (i.e. staff, tools and equipment). It should help provide a clearer answer to the question of whether the individual is in business on their own account – i.e. self-employed. It 'implies a test of economic dependence, in the sense that employee status is the result of "the extent to which the individual is dependent or independent of a particular paymaster for the financial exploitation of his talent" ' (Burchell *et al.*, 1999: 6). Genuine self-employed persons (or independent contractors) are likely to provide their own tools and be responsible for their own training; and not be integrated into the structure and operation of the employer's organisation. They may hire their own staff and/or make subcontracting arrangements to carry out work. However, in practice, it is not always possible to identify the genuine self-employed. Some self-employed may have a relationship of economic dependence on an employer. The category of 'dependent self-employed' 'potentially includes freelance workers, sole traders, home-workers and casual workers of various kinds' (Burchell *et al.*, 1999: 12).

- The extent to which a person under an *obligation* to work: The nature and the extent of this obligation is considered in the next section.

In addition to these tests, other issues are considered by courts and tribunals – principally:

■ Whether the work is on *a continuing basis*: Clearly, for some people, work is discontinuous. The significance and duration of breaks in employment is one of the factors to be considered (see section below).

■ Whether the employer deducts income *tax and social security* contributions.

According to these tests, the finding of whether a person is an employee working under a contract of employment depends on the balancing of these factors. No factor is seen as sufficient in itself, but some are seen as essential (e.g. control and payment of wages). All facts and circumstances of a particular case must be considered. The Court of Appeal has stated that any decision on employee status does not involve a mechanical checking off of factors. An overall view must be taken of the circumstances. This would involve weighing the significance of particular factors and considering, if appropriate, the intentions of the parties and their behaviour (*Hall* (*HM Inspector of Taxes*) v *Lorimer* [1994] IRLR 171).

Given the growth of atypical work (for example, homeworking and temporary contracts), a grey area has developed. As suggested in Fig. 2.3, a person may not comply with all the common law tests. For example, there may be breaks in the continuity of service. The person may make their own arrangements for tax and national insurance. In the circumstances of a particular case it might be difficult to define a person as an employee. But that person might be encompassed by the definition of worker in that they work under a contract where they agree to perform personally any work of services (ERA 1996, s 230(3)).

Mutuality of obligation

One important common law test is the obligation to work. The use of this test in the courts has grown since the late 1970s. In determining whether or not a person is an employee and whether or not a contract of employment exists, courts and tribunals will look at the mutuality of obligation – i.e. the obligations that the person working owes to the employer and vice versa.

Two levels of obligation have to be considered (Deakin and Morris, 1998: 164–8). The first is the obligation to provide work and to perform work. The second level involves mutual promises of future performance of the employment relationship. This provides stability and continuity. If this second level is missing, there is probably no contract of employment. The individual cannot be an 'employee'. He or she, however, may be defined as a 'worker' and there may be some 'other contract' to carry out work 'personally' (ERA 1996, s 230(3)). Clearly, casual workers, who work intermittently, may be in this situation. They are unlikely to have a promise of future work. However, such a promise could be made if the employer offers a 'global' or 'umbrella' contract (see below).

It has been commented that 'the "mutuality" test differs from the "economic reality" test in focusing on the terms of the individual hiring rather than on evidence of economic dependence. The mutuality test looks for formal evidence of subordination in the contract terms themselves' (Burchell *et al.*, 1999: 7). The difficulty often is that the contract may be silent on the issue of mutuality of obligation. The person working may have a long-established relationship with the employer;

and the person may have made assumptions that they are an employee because of their length of service, their economic dependence on the employer for pay and their integration into the employer's organisation – albeit intermittently. However, a court may look at the contract and fail to find an express term stating that there is mutuality of obligation. It will, then, draw inferences from the facts and imply terms into the contract. This may be sufficient to disadvantage the individual worker concerned. No global contract may be found and so each period of discontinuous employment stands alone.

The fine distinctions made in this area have been seen in two particular cases (*Carmichael* v *National Power* [2000] IRLR 43 and *O'Kelly* v *Trusthouse Forte plc* [1983] IRLR 369. The former is considered later (see also Fig. 2.5 p 86). The second case involved a group of wine waiters who were 'regular casuals'. This apparently contradictory phrase meant that they were kept on a list to be called for work when required – a practice commonly used in respect of 'bank' staff in teaching and nursing. Their claim for employee status fell because this 'was a purely commercial transaction for the supply and purchase of services for specific events, because there was no obligation for the applicants to offer their further services'. These cases are illustrations of the ' "grey zone" between employment and self-employment' (Burchell *et al.*, 1999: 7).

Genuine self-employed people (or independent contractors) are, in respect of mutuality of obligation, free to choose the work they do. Where they agree to do work, they need not provide it personally. They may delegate it to another person to undertake it. So, no mutuality exists which points to an employment contract.

Continuity of work

This is particularly significant in three related respects:

- Considering a person's status as an employee.
- Access to statutory rights – many of which are service related. It has been said that 'the rules on continuity of employment may interact with the "mutuality" test to deny protection to employees with irregular working arrangements' (Burchell *et al.*, 1999: 10).
- Qualifying for employment benefits under an employment contract (e.g. holidays, sick pay, access to a 'cafeteria' of benefits).

The statutory provisions on continuous employment are defined in the Employment Rights Act 1996 (ss 210–19). Generally, continuity is in relation to one employer. (The exceptions are considered below.) Also, continuous employment can encompass a number of contracts of employment with that one employer.

To calculate continuous employment, the legal starting point is set out as follows: 'Any week during the whole or part of which an employee's relations with his employer are governed by a contract of employment counts in computing the employee's period of employment' (ERA 1996, s 212). The importance of establishing the existence of a contract of employment is signalled in this provision. It is also clear that the number of hours a person works in each week is not relevant. There is a statutory presumption in favour of continuous employment, unless the contrary is shown by the employer.

Certain weeks count (under particular rules): where the employee is 'incapable of work in consequence of sickness or injury' (ERA 1996, s 212(3)(a)); or is 'absent from work wholly or partly because of pregnancy or childbirth' (s 212(3)(d)). In addition, and of more significance for atypical workers, are those weeks which may count where the employee is 'absent from work on account of a temporary cessation of work' (s 212(3)(b)), or 'absent from work in circumstances such that, by arrangement or custom, he is regarded as continuing in the employment of his employer for any purpose' (s 212(3)(c)).

It has been ruled in various cases that temporary cessation of work need not break continuity of employment. No time period is prescribed for the cessation. The cessation is a question of fact: did it or did it not take place? The cessation can be for any reason. The work referred to is the paid work of the individual employee – not the general work of the employer's business.

In the handling of such cases, two approaches have been used by the courts: the broad-brush approach, and the mathematical approach. In the former, the focus is on the whole employment history of the individual employee. This would, obviously, be done in retrospect and could take account of the expectations and intentions of the parties. The second approach considers proportions of time spent at work and times absent because of the temporary cessation. For example, in *Ford* v *Warwickshire County Council* [1983] IRLR 126, HL (a case involving a succession of fixed-term contracts for a further education lecturer), Diplock LJ, ruled that the interval when there was no work should be 'characterised as short relative to the combined duration of the two fixed-term contracts. Whether it can be so characterised is a question of fact and degree.' In fact, the interval was one month (August) between contracts of 11 months on either side covering an academic year. This situation had existed for nine academic years. For a person on a temporary contract, the recognition of nine years' continuous service was valuable.

In the *Ford* case, the mathematical approach was advantageous to the employee, but in other circumstances, it might lead to pedantic arguments of what 'short duration' meant. The broad-brush approach has more to commend it. The Court of Appeal subsequently adopted this latter approach in *Flack* v *Kodak Ltd* [1986] IRLR 255, CA, where an employee had a pattern of highly irregular work patterns. At present, both tests are available to courts.

The other issue of absence from work relates to that which is by arrangement or custom. This can cover secondment, special leave of absence, working-time scheduling such as job share or limited hours per week. 'It appears that the agreement or custom must exist when the absence begins, not as an *ex post facto* afterthought (Smith and Thomas, 2000: 154).

It was mentioned earlier that continuous service is normally with one employer. However, there are circumstances in which acquired service might be preserved if the employee changes employer:

- where there is the transfer of a trade, undertaking, business or part of a business (as specified in the Transfer of Undertakings (Protection of Employment) Regulations 1981 (as amended);
- where one corporate body replaces another as employer under Act of Parliament;
- where the employer dies and the employee is then re-employed by the personal representatives or trustees of the deceased;

- where there is a change in the partners, personal representatives or trustees who employ the individual;
- where the individual is taken into the employment of an 'associated employer'.

This final circumstance can create difficulties. Control is the central issue. For the purposes of the Employment Rights Act 1996, 'any two employers shall be treated as associated if – (a) one is a company of which the other (directly or indirectly) has control, or (b) both are companies of which a third person (directly or indirectly) has control' (s 231). A finding of 'control' can be difficult. There are technical ways of establishing it through majority shareholding. Some cases have explored the channels of influence exerted on corporate policy. The presence of these can be particularly important for employment relations issues. Although there is no authoritative guidance on this issue, there is clearly statutory authority for courts and tribunals to inquire into organisational decision-making structures.

Contracts to perform work

From the preceding discussion, three contracts have been identified (apart from the commercial contracts entered into by independent contractors). These are: the contract of employment under which an employee works; some 'other contract' under which a worker works; and a global contract.

The predominant form of contract in UK employment relations is the contract of employment. This will be the focus of the next section. 'Other contracts', as indicated earlier, are likely to have many of the elements of a contract of employment. However, a 'worker' working under such a contract may not be eligible for certain employment rights (see later section). A global or umbrella contract embraces work carried out for a particular employer in various discontinuous periods of employment. It recognises continuity of work and mutuality of obligation – including the promise of future performance.

2.4.3 The characteristics of the contract of employment

The contract of employment is usually defined in this way:

> It is a promise or an agreement. It is freely arrived at by the parties that make it. No one compels them to agree. The two parties are an employer and the individual employee. It is legally enforceable in the courts and is intended to be so. It is usually of indefinite duration. It involves 'consideration' – i.e. something, usually pay, which the employer gives to buy the promise of the employee to be ready, willing and able to undertake the agreed work. It may be in writing, verbally agreed or part verbal and part in writing. It need not be signed.

Some of the elements of this definition are considered in more detail below.

Parties to the contract

There are two: the individual employee and the employer. There is, however, no acknowledgement in law about the relative power of these two parties. The primary concern of the courts has been about definitions. Occasionally, this has been about who the employer is; but more commonly it has been to determine whether or not a person is an employee. The common law is silent about this and, as outlined above, common law tests have been formulated. Also, statute law defines an employee but not in any detail (ERA 1996, s 230(1)–(2)).

Is the contract of employment freely arrived at?

The idea that a contract of employment is freely arrived at has been described as a legal fiction. An individual will probably be offered employment on particular terms. The individual's choice will be to accept or refuse employment. To this extent, the answer to the question must be yes. However, the ability of any individual employee to influence the specific terms of a proposed contract are limited or non-existent, unless that person has skills, knowledge or experience which are scarce and in demand by employers.

Enforcing a contract of employment

A contract of employment is legally enforceable in the courts. Either party can complain that the other has breached a term of the contract. Usually, it is the employee who complains against the employer. Some breaches can be relatively minor. In such a case, the employee might raise a grievance against the employer. Others are described as fundamental, in the sense that they go to the heart of the contract and effectively destroy it. Such breaches are repudiatory. For example, if an employer fails to treat an allegation of workplace harassment seriously and does not take proper steps to investigate it and have the harassment stopped, this is seen by courts and tribunals as a breach of the mutual trust and confidence that should exist between an employer and an employee (see Implied terms below). Technically, an employee could sue for breach of contract. Often, though, the employee is likely to resign. Arguing repudiatory breach of contract, the person can then appeal to an employment tribunal alleging unfair constructive dismissal. If such harassment is based on sex or race there is no qualifying period for applications.

Where an employer believes an employee has breached the contract of employment – whether a minor or a fundamental breach – this is usually dealt with through disciplinary action and, possibly, dismissal.

A verbal contract

Entirely verbal contracts do exist – particularly for casual workers. Under these, the nature of the work and the pay rate is verbally offered and the person verbally agrees to it. Most employees, admittedly, will have something in writing as well as the verbal undertakings (*see* the Statement of initial employment particulars – Fig. 2.4). Nevertheless, it can be difficult to prove the terms of a verbal contract. A court or tribunal would hear evidence from the parties about how they behaved in the employment relationship. It would, then, infer from this, as far as it could, what the parties understood by the contractual terms and what they had agreed to.

The *Statement of Initial Employment Particulars* must provide the following information in one document:

1 Names of the employer and the employee.

2 Date when employment began.
 This is not necessarily the first day the employee turned up for work. It may be earlier.

3 Date when continuous employment began.
 This may include previous employment with that employer; or employment with a company involved in a business transfer; or employment with another company within a group.

4 Scale or rate of remuneration, or the method of calculating remuneration.
 Employees should be able to check the accuracy of their pay in detail and have the right to an itemised pay statement.

5 Intervals at which remuneration is paid.

6 Terms and conditions relating to hours of work (including normal hours of work).

7 Terms and conditions relating to holiday entitlement including public holidays and holiday pay.
 This should provide enough detail for the employee's entitlement, including entitlement to accrued holiday pay on termination of employment, to be precisely calculated.

8 Job title or brief job description.
 It is better not to include in the statement of particulars a job description as this will be evidence that the statement is intended to be contractual. Generally, the job description is treated as lawful instructions and can be more easily changed.

9 The place of work or, if the employee is required or permitted to work at various places, an indication of that fact and the employer's address.
 The following information may be provided in instalments, so long as this is done by the end of the second month. It is possible, in some cases (marked with an asterisk, *), to cross-refer to other documents, provided the employee has reasonable access and opportunity to read them.

10 Terms relating to sickness, injury and sick pay. (*)

11 Pensions and pension scheme. (*)

12 Period of notice that each party must give to terminate the contract. (*)

13 Where employment is temporary, how long it is likely to last, or the termination date of a fixed-term contract.

14 Collective agreements that directly affect terms and conditions. Where employer is not a party to the collective agreement, the person by whom they are made must be named.

15 Where employees are sent to work outside the UK for more than one month:
 – the period of work outside the UK;
 – the currency in which they will be paid;
 – special benefits available while they work abroad;
 – any terms relating to their return.

16 Disciplinary rules and procedures. (*)

17 Grievance procedure. (*)

Contractual information can and does, of course, exist in various other documents. The most likely sources of such information are an offer letter, a staff handbook, pension scheme documents, relevant memos and agreements with trade unions and other workplace representatives. These may help clarify terms and conditions of employment if there is any dispute. Such sources of information can be particularly helpful in those circumstances where an employer does not issue a statutory Statement of Employment Particulars.

Figure 2.4 Statement of Initial Employment Particulars (ERA 1996 s 1)

Signing a contract

Signature is not necessary. If an employee accepts an offer of employment; comes to work as requested; and carries out the tasks required; and the employer pays the wages due, then, this is sufficient evidence of the contract's existence and of its essential terms.

2.4.4 The terms of a contract of employment

The terms of a contract of employment fall into two categories: express terms and implied terms. *Express terms* are those provisions which normally are in writing and agreed. If they are not in writing, they will have been agreed verbally. Obvious examples are terms relating to rates of pay and the length of the working week.

Implied terms are those which have not been agreed to by the parties but which have been implied into contracts either by the courts or by statute law. Terms might be implied by judges for one of several reasons.

- for reasons of 'business efficacy' (i.e. where a term is necessary to make the contract work);
- where, on the facts, such a term is so obvious (even though it is not provided as an express term);
- on the basis of custom and practice (see below);
- to give effect to a statutory requirement;
- to meet changing circumstances.

The terms of contracts of employment derive from six sources – some of these from law, and some from voluntary regulation:

- management decisions on terms and conditions of employment;
- collective agreements between the employer and recognised unions;
- workplace rules;
- custom and practice;
- statute law;
- implied terms under common law.

Management's decision-making freedom on terms and conditions is considerable. It is, as we have already discussed (Chapter 1), subject to the provisions of statute law (e.g. on discriminatory treatment), to concepts of fairness and reasonableness and to the principles of variation of contract set out in case law. Taking account of relevant statute law, then, management may offer a job applicant a particular level of pay, decide the arrangement of working time and say how work is to be carried out. If the applicant agrees to the management's terms on offer then a contract will exist. This freedom of management to offer terms of employment can be modified in those organisations where trade unions are recognised for the purposes of negotiation (collective bargaining). Here, certain terms and conditions are jointly agreed with the union(s).

So, *collective agreements* also provide contractual terms. These are voluntary agreements. They are not legally enforceable because, normally, employers and trade unions decide this, but they do have legal significance in another way. The terms and conditions in collective agreements are incorporated, as appropriate, into the individual contracts of employment.

To illustrate this process of incorporation, we will consider the appointment of a new employee. This person will be offered a contract of employment. Some of the terms of this (for example, pay, the length of the working week, shift pay, sick pay arrangements) will, if the employer negotiates with a union for that grade of staff, derive from a collective agreement. It does not matter whether or not the individual employee is or is not a member of the union, the contract will include the relevant negotiated terms. The appropriate rate of pay and other provisions of the collective agreement are incorporated into the employment contract – i.e. they become contractual terms for that individual. As such they are legally enforceable in the courts (whether or not that individual is a union member). (The workforce agreements outlined in the Working Time Regulations 1998 for non-union organisations are also encompassed by the legal process of incorporation.)

The incorporation of collective agreements has two main implications when contracts of employment are changed: in conferring consent to the changes; and in the preservation of already established conditions. As we discuss in Chapter 3, an employer must obtain consent to change a term in the contract. It is possible for a union to provide this consent on behalf of employees if, for example, a person's contract states that they will work 'on terms negotiated from time to time with the XYZ Union'. If the contractual terms change through negotiation, then, for better or worse, the employee is deemed to have given consent.

The second implication relates to the continuing contractual life of established terms and conditions after a collective agreement has ended. One example of this derives from circumstances in British Gas in the 1980s. The company unilaterally terminated an incentive bonus scheme. It was a voluntary collective agreement with the union. The company was entitled to give notice to terminate this agreement. However, the provisions of the agreement had been incorporated into individual contracts of employment. These were, in law, unaffected by the end of the collective agreement. Kerr LJ said:

> the terms [of a collective agreement] are in this case incorporated into the individual contracts of employment and it is only if and when those terms are varied collectively by agreement that the individual contract of employment will also be varied. If the collective scheme is not varied by agreement but by some unilateral abrogation or withdrawal or variation to which the other side does not agree, then it seems to me that the individual contract of employment remains unaffected (*Robertson and Jackson* v *British Gas Corporation* [1983] IRLR 202, CA).

The law on *workplace rules* is so varied that it is impossible to provide anything but general guidelines. The rules are likely to be in an employee's contract if the employee signs them, or if they are posted in notices in the workplace. But, even if they are signed, the rules may not become contractual but merely be lawful and reasonable instructions on how a job is to be carried out.

The differences between a contractual rule and a lawful instruction can be described as follows:

- a rule can only be altered with the employee's consent. Instructions can be changed without consultation or agreement;
- by working to rule an employee is merely carrying out the contract. By disobeying instructions (which are lawful and reasonable) an employee is breaking the contract.

Custom and practice describes a customary way of working. This can be binding if it meets these conditions:

- it must be widely known and almost universally observed;
- it must be reasonable;
- it must be so certain that the individual employee can know exactly the effect that the custom has on him/her.

Statute law affects contracts of employment in a number of distinct ways:

- it can set minimum conditions which must be met by employers (e.g. notice periods for employees, maternity leave). An employer may provide conditions better than the minimum standard – but not lower;
- it can prescribe general obligations on employers which are designed to influence the way they behave in the employment relationship. This encompasses both non-discriminatory treatment in respect of sex, race and disability, as well as general duties under health and safety law to provide a safe and healthy working environment as far as is reasonably practicable;
- it might through a statutory imposition directly intervene in the contract of employment. For example, the Equal Pay Act 1970 (s 1) deems that an equality clause shall exist in contracts of employment.

The implied terms from common law are the final source of contractual terms. Common law, as indicated earlier, is judge-made law, under which the law of contract has generally developed. Over time, two sets of general obligations have been implied into contracts by the judges: those governing the behaviour of employers and those for employees. In some instances, these general duties have been modified by certain provisions in statute law.

The *general duties on employers* include the following.

To pay wages and salaries

Failure to pay wages that are due is regarded as a repudiatory breach of the contract of employment.

Not to make unauthorised deductions

An employer may only make deductions if there is authority to do so. This can be provided by Act of Parliament (e.g. the statutory right to make PAYE and National

Insurance deductions). Alternatively, the employee can agree in writing (e.g. the deduction of union subscriptions). Finally, there might be a provision in statute law and also a term in the contract of employment that permits deductions (e.g. covering stock shortages and cash deficiencies in the retail trade). The Employment Rights Act 1996 Part II provides protection against unlawful deduction of wages (*see* Chapter 10).

To take reasonable care of the employee

This implied term covers those issues categorised as health, safety and welfare issue (*see also* Chapter 12). It also has formed the basis of complaints relating to the provision of references.

In respect of health and safety, there can be difficulties in interpretation and applicability to various cases. It is the basis of complaints concerning work intensification, excessive workload, the onset of stress and recognised psychiatric illnesses and the incidence of physical injury to an employee. It is clear from case law that the key issues are: employer liability for the breach of the duty of care; the possible negligence of the employee in not complying with instructions; and the 'foreseeability' (on the facts) of the psychological or physical injury on the facts (*see* reference to the *Walker* case in Chapter 12).

This is still an evolving area of law. In a recent case (*Cross and another v Highlands and Islands Enterprise and another* [2000] Court of Session), in the Scottish Court of Session, Lord MacFadyen said: 'It seems to me that the common law duty of an employer to take reasonable care for his employee's safety and health, and to provide and maintain for him a safe system of working, ought to *extend* to include a duty to take reasonable care not to subject the employee to working conditions that are reasonably foreseeably likely to cause him psychiatric injury or illness' (author's italics).

There is no general duty on an employer to provide a reference. But where references are provided, they should comply with guidance under case law. This is developing and complex – to the extent that it involves three parties: the ex-employee, the employer who is the referee, the prospective new employer who receives the reference. It has been ruled and affirmed by the Court of Appeal (*Bartholomew v London Borough of Hackney* [1999] IRLR 246) that an employer is under a duty of care to provide a reference which is true, accurate and fair. It must not give an unfair or misleading impression when considered in totality. The burden of proof is on the referee to show that the contents were true. The referee might defend themselves by showing that they 'honestly believed' that the contents were true.

As a general rule, a reference does not have to provide a full and comprehensive report on all facts relating to the person in question. However, difficulties may arise in one particular set of circumstances. This is when an employee might resign under a threat of disciplinary action or before that action is complete. Again, case law has asserted that the principle of telling the truth is important. If the employer omits any mention of the disciplinary proceedings, it could be a breach of duty owed to the recipient of the reference and make the referee liable for legal action for neglient mis-statement. On the other hand, a referee should not make comments about an employee on matters which have not been properly investigated. In terms of natural justice, a proper investigation involves giving the employee a chance to state their case. In *Cox* v *Sun Alliance Life Ltd* [2001] IRLR 448, the Court of Appeal found that the referee was negligent in relying on unexplored allegations of dishonest conduct attributed to the ex-employee and the communication of these views to Mr Cox's new employer.

To co-operate with the employee

Originally, this meant not impeding employees in the performance of their contracts. Arising from unfair dismissal cases, it has been frequently stated that employers must not destroy the mutual trust and confidence upon which co-operation is built. The implied term of mutual trust and confidence has been stated in this way: an employer will not, without reasonable and proper cause, act in a manner calculated or likely to destroy or seriously damage the relationship of confidence and trust between employer and employee. It provides a test to judge the behaviour of the employer (*Courtaulds Northern Textiles Ltd* v *Andrew* [1979] IRLR 84, EAT).

So, employers have been held to be in breach of contract in the following situations: where an applicant for transfer had not been dealt with fairly; where there was a failure to investigate a genuine safety grievance; and where there was a false accusation of theft on the basis of flimsy evidence; where the right to suspend an employee was exercised unreasonably; where a mobility clause was not operated reasonably. The Employment Appeals Tribunal has held that breach of mutual trust and confidence will 'inevitably' be a repudiatory breach of the contract of employment and can result in employee resignation and a consequential claim for constructive dismissal (*Morrow* v *Safeway Stores plc* EAT 275/00).

The *general duties on employees* include the following.

To co-operate with their employer

Under case law, this has been construed to mean helping promote the employer's business interests by working according to the terms of the contract. In working to contract, employees must not wilfully disrupt the employer's business. Some Acts of Parliament have elaborated co-operation. For example, the Health and Safety at Work Act 1974 (s 7) refers to the duty of employees to co-operate with their employer in the implementation of safety requirements.

To obey any lawful and reasonable instructions

As indicated earlier, there is a distinction between contractual rules and instructions. The former cannot be changed without consent. The latter are in management's discretion. But any management instructions must be both lawful and reasonable. So, for example, an instruction which involved unlawful discrimination would be unacceptable. Whether or not an instruction is reasonable is dependent upon the circumstances and, perhaps ultimately, the view of a tribunal. Failure, by an employee, to comply with lawful and reasonable instructions can result in dismissal. Consequently, it is by this route that the issue can be scrutinised by tribunals and courts.

To be trustworthy

This duty is complementary to the employer's duty of mutual trust and confidence. The duty of fidelity, as it is also known, has four aspects:

- *A general duty not to be dishonest.* Acts of deception, theft, embezzlement, etc. are regarded as breaches of trust and as such are likely to lead to immediate dismissal. They are also regarded as serious offences before the criminal courts.

- *The obligation not to compete with the employer.* An employee may, in their spare time, work for a competitor where the first employer does not regard this as inconsistent or likely to cause substantial harm.

    The obligation not to compete can result in the inclusion as an express term, into some contracts of employment, of restrictive covenants. These restrict the activities of ex-employees. There are three likely types of restrictive covenant: *non-competition* (i.e. limiting the ex-employee from taking employment in competition with the former employer; *non-solicitation* (i.e. prohibiting contact with clients and customers of the former employer; and *non-dealing* (i.e. not engaging in business activities with such clients and customers). Such clauses are in restraint of trade. They will be void unless the employer can show that the restrictive covenant is necessary to protect a legitimate business interest and is not an excessive restriction.

    The reasonableness of restrictive covenants can be considered by the courts. For example, in *Barry Allsuch and Co v Harris* [2001], the High Court ruled that the prohibition by an estate agency on a former employee from working in a specified area for two years was unreasonable and unenforceable. No other estate agency in the area imposed a non-competition covenant for longer than six months. There was no evidence to suggest that the employer's business was so different from other estate agencies to justify a longer period.

- *The obligation not to disclose confidential information obtained in employment.* This can, of course, bind not only current employees but also ex-employees. In this way, it links with restrictive covenants. It needs also to be seen in the context of 'whistleblower' legislation (*see* Chapter 8).

- *The obligation not to benefit from work undertaken for the employer*, as covered by statutory legislation on patents, intellectual property rights and copyright. However, subject to this limitation, an employer cannot prevent a former employee from using the general knowledge and skill that has been acquired in the course of employment.

The duty of fidelity generally ends when the contract ends. However, exceptions involve the duty not to disclose trade secrets and confidential information. Breaches of trust by an employee are invariably regarded seriously and are likely to lead to dismissal and, in certain circumstances, criminal proceedings (*see* Chapter 9).

To take reasonable care

This is supplemented by a statutory duty under the Health and Safety at Work Act 1974 (s 7) whereby employees should take care of themselves and fellow workers and co-operate with the employer and other agencies in complying with health and safety requirements.

The significance of these sources of the contract of employment will vary in each organisation and for each grade of employee. Some sources are universally important: management decisions, rules, statute law and implied terms. In some areas of employment, custom and practice might also be significant. The importance of collective bargaining is restricted to those spheres where trade unions are recognised and negotiate terms and conditions of employment with the employer.

2.4.5 Written information about contracts of employment

In some organisations, for some (often senior and professional) grades of staff, employers may produce a legally drafted contract of employment. However, this is rare for most employees. Since 1963, statute law has required employers to provide information on certain contractual terms. Given that contracts of employment need not be in writing, this measure goes some way to reassure employees. It can help in the internal handling of grievances and disciplinary action; and also in hearings before employment tribunals.

This Statement of Initial Employment Particulars (required under the ERA 1996, s 1) (*see* Fig. 2.4 p 70) is not an employee's contract of employment. It is information about what the employer says are the terms of the contract. Lord Wedderburn (1986: 138) states that this statement 'constitutes very strong prima facie evidence of what were the terms of the contract between the parties . . . It is not "conclusive" but places "a heavy burden" on the party who alleges the real terms are different'. All employees, irrespective of hours worked, must receive such a statement within eight weeks of starting employment. There is an appeal to an employment tribunal for non-provision.

The requirements relating to the Statement must comply with the European Directive (91/533/EEC) on the employer's obligation to inform employees of the conditions applicable to the contract or employment relationship. In a case involving the absence of information on the employee's obligation to work overtime, the European Court of Justice ruled that the employee should be informed of any 'essential element' of the contract (*Lange* v *Georg Schunemann GmnH*, C–350/99).

2.4.6 Terminating a contract of employment

This issue will be explored further in Chapter 9. Here, it is sufficient to outline, briefly, those circumstances in which a contract might end.

Notice to terminate: Notice can be given, by either the employer or the employee, in accordance with the contract; or, if the contract is silent, then, by using the statutory minimum periods of notice (ERA 1996, s 86). These are that a person continuously employed for one month or more (but less than two years) is entitled to one week's notice. A person employed for two years or more (but less than 12 years) is entitled to one additional week's notice for each continuous year of employment.

Summary dismissal: This refers to the instant termination of the contract. It can arise after appropriate investigation and a disciplinary hearing relating to an employee's gross misconduct (e.g. theft, drunkenness).

Wrongful dismissal: This is a common law claim for breach of contract (e.g. the implied term of mutual trust and confidence). A claim can be made irrespective of length of service. The restrictions on unfair dismissal claims do not apply.

Constructive dismissal: This arises in circumstances where an employee resigns because of what is perceived to be a repudiatory breach of the contract by the employer (e.g. not paying wages that are due, providing hazardous working conditions, or failing to tackle workplace harassment of an individual worker). Because of an employer's behaviour or inaction, the employee feels forced to resign. This is regarded as the equivalent of dismissal.

The end of a fixed-term contract: This refers to a contract which has a date of termination. It contrasts with those short contracts that are for the purpose of carrying out a specific task and finish whenever that task finishes.

Frustration: This is a complex area and much will depend on the specific circumstances of the case. It involves termination of the contract as a result of some unforeseen event which makes it difficult for the contract to be carried out. Frustration would cover death, long-term ill-health or imprisonment.

2.4.7 Employment protection for 'atypical' workers

In this section, we will look at how employment protection is developing for various categories of 'atypical' workers. Increasingly, often echoing European law, protections and rights have been accorded to workers or those who have an employment relationship. This breaks the restriction to 'employees' who have a contract of employment. As indicated earlier, this restriction has often created legal problems in determining a person's status as an 'employee'. In some areas, the present government has decisively moved in the direction of wider rights (under the National Minimum Wage Act 1998 and the Working Time Regulations 1998). In the 'Fairness at Work' White Paper the government stated its intention 'to consult on the idea of legislation enabling it similarly to extend the coverage of some or all existing employment rights by regulation' (para 3.18). This wider access to statutory rights is provided for in the Employment Relations Act 1999 (s 23). In July 2002, the government consulted on the implementation of section 23 (DTI 2002).

In respect of statutory rights, the overall situation is summarised in Fig. 2.6 p 89. The following subsections look at the experience of particular categories of 'atypical' workers under case law and also the growing body of statutory employment protection.

A significant driver of employment protection in this area has been the European Union. The social partners concluded framework agreements (which formed the basis of Directives) on part-time work (1997) and fixed-term work (1999). Negotiations on an agreement on temporary agency work failed in 2001. In March 2002, the European Commission published proposals for a Directive. All European Directives take a broadly similar approach – establishing the principle of non-discrimination or equal treatment with specific comparators.

Part-time workers

There are three broad developments, in law, which have begun to improve protection and rights for part-time workers. First of all, the European Court of Justice ruled in 1994, in respect of statutory employment rights, that it was indirect sex discrimination for Britain to have differential qualifying rights for access (for full-time workers and for part-time workers) to unfair dismissal compensation and redundancy pay. As a consequence, the requirement for part-timers working under 16 hours per week needing five years service (as against two) was repealed in 1995. No hours qualifications now exist in access to any British employment rights.

Secondly, under the law on indirect sex discrimination, women returning from maternity leave have applied to vary the scheduling and number of working hours. The requirement to work full-time has been ruled to be a condition or requirement that has to be justified (*see* Chapter 4).

Thirdly, the European Union adopted a Directive (1997) implementing the social partners' Framework Agreement on Part-Time Work. This deals with the issue of contractual rights for part-timers. It concerns any part-timers who have a contract of employment or are in an employment relationship. Part-timers are workers whose normal hours of work, averaged over a period of up to a year, are less than the normal hours of comparable full-timers.

The Directive comprises certain general principles which must be transposed into national law:

- part-timers may not be treated less favourably than full-timers;
- member states should in consultation with the social partners work to remove obstacles to part-time work;
- employers should, as far as possible, make opportunities for part-time work at all levels; and should give consideration to requests from workers for changes from part-time to full-time work and vice versa;
- refusal to transfer from full-time to part-time work or vice versa is not in itself a valid reason for dismissal.

The Directive has been partially transposed into UK law through the Part-time Workers (Less Favourable Treatment) Regulations 2000 (which was amended in 2002). The key provisions are:

- *Who is a part-time worker?* This is defined by exemption – as a person who is not a full-time worker in a particular workplace. A full-time worker works for a particular employer and is 'paid wholly or in part by reference to the time he works and, having regard to the custom and practice of the employer in relation to workers employed by the worker's employer under the same type of contract, is identifiable as a full-time worker' (reg 2(1)). A part-time worker is a similar person but is *not* identifiable as a full-time worker.

- *Who is the comparator?* The Regulations specify that the part-time worker and their comparator are to be employed at the same time, by the same employer, at the same establishment, under the same type of contract, and be engaged in the same or broadly similar work (taking into account, as appropriate, whether they have a similar level of qualification, skills and experience) (reg 2(4)). An amendment was introduced in 2002 to clarify the phrase 'the same type of contract'. This enables comparison to be made with either a full-time worker on a *permanent* contract or a full-time worker on a *fixed-term* contract.

  If there is no comparator at the same establishment, a person who works at a different establishment of that employer can be chosen. It is not possible, as under sex discrimination law, to have a hypothetical comparator.

- *The principle of equal treatment*: A part-time worker has the right not be treated by the employer less favourably than the employer treats a comparable full-time worker. This is in respect of the terms of the contract (*see* below). It also prohibits a part-time worker being subject to any 'detriment by any act, or deliberate failure to act, of the employer' (reg 5(1)). Detriments would include, for example, denial of opportunities for promotion. This right applies only if the less favourable treatment 'is on the ground that the worker is a part-time worker' and that the discriminatory treatment is 'not justified on objective grounds' (reg 5(2)). To test whether there has been less favourable treatment, the pro-rata principle shall apply unless it is 'inappropriate' (reg 5(3)).

- *Objective justification*: Discriminatory treatment is only justified on objective grounds if it can be shown that the less favourable treatment is necessary to achieve a legitimate objective (e.g. a genuine business objective) and is an appropriate way of achieving that objective. This is broadly the same test used for justifying indirect sex discrimination.

- *Rate of pay*: A part-time worker must not receive a lower basic rate of pay than a comparable full-time worker. The protection also covers special rates of pay (e.g. bonuses, shift allowances and unsocial hours and weekend payments).

- *Overtime*: Under current case law (*Stadt Lengerich* v *Helmig* [1995] IRLR 216, ECJ) part-time workers do not have an automatic right to overtime payments once they work beyond their normal hours. However, once a part-time worker exceeds the normal hours of a comparable full-time worker, the part-timer has a legal right to the applicable overtime payments.

- *Contractual sick and maternity pay*: A part-time worker must not be treated less favourably than a comparable full-time worker in terms of calculating the rate of sick pay or maternity pay; the length of service required to qualify for payment; the length of time for which the payment is received. The benefits must be provided pro rata to a part-time worker unless differential treatment is justified on objective grounds.

- *Other contractual benefits*: A part-time worker must not be treated less favourably than a comparable full-time worker in terms of fringe benefits such as health insurance, company cars, subsidised mortgages and staff discounts.

- *Conditions of access*: There must be no discrimination over access to an occupational pension scheme, a profit-sharing scheme or a share option scheme between full-time and part-time workers unless different treatment is justified on objective grounds.

- *Leave entitlements*: Part-time workers are entitled, as appropriate, to statutory leave entitlements (annual leave, maternity leave, parental leave and time off for dependants). Where an employer provides enhanced arrangements under contractual terms, then, part-time workers should have the same entitlements as full-time workers – on a pro rata basis where appropriate.

- *Access to training*: Part-time workers should not be excluded from training. Training provision should be at convenient times for the majority of staff including part-time workers.

- *Redundancy*: The selection criteria and different treatment of full-time workers and part-time workers should not be discriminatory. If they are, they must be justified on objective grounds.

- *Conversion to part-time worker status*: A full-time worker who reduced their hours of work is entitled not to be treated less favourably than they were treated as regards terms and conditions of employment or being subject to any detriment (reg 3). This is not a right to become part-time. It is a matter for the employer to consider requests. If an employer allows women to reduce their hours of work (for childcare reasons), then, requests from a man must be treated in the same way under indirect sex discrimination law (*see* Chapter 4).

- *A written statement of reasons*: A worker who believes they have been discriminated against may ask the employer in writing for 'a written statement giving particulars of the reasons for the treatment' (reg 6). If there is a case for objective justification, this should be stated. This written statement is admissible under proceedings at an employment tribunal. A tribunal may draw 'any inference that it considers just and equitable, including an inference that the employer has infringed the right in question' if the employer has 'deliberately and without written excuse' not provided such a statement; or considers that 'the statement provided is evasive or equivocal' (reg 6(3)).

- *Protection against unfair dismissal and victimisation*: Dismissal or selection for redundancy is automatically unfair if the reason or principal reasons concern the exercise of rights under the Regulations. An employee may complain to an employment tribunal irrespective of their age or length of service. Similar protection is provided for against victimisation.

- *Application to employment tribunal*: A worker may complain to an employment tribunal of less favourable treatment or victimisation (reg 8). The application should be made within three months of either the date of the action complained of or the last in a series of discriminatory actions. Where a worker presents a complaint, it is for the employer to identify the ground for the less favourable treatment or detriment (reg 8(6)).

- *Liability*: An employer is vicariously liable for the behaviour of, for example, managers, supervisors and other workers, 'in the course of his employment' whether or not the behaviour was with the employer's knowledge and approval (reg 11(1)). An employer's defence before an employment tribunal is that they 'took such steps as were reasonably practicable' to prevent the discrimination (reg 11(3)). (This provision reflects those provided under other discrimination law. *See* Chapters 4–6.)

- *Remedies*: If an employment tribunal finds a complaint to be well founded, it is required, as it considers 'just and equitable' (reg 8):
  - To make a declaration of the rights of the complainant and the employer in relation to the complaint.
  - To order the employer to pay compensation to the complainant. An amendment was introduced in 2002 to remove a two-year limitation on remedies in relation to an occupational pension. This was ruled by the House of Lords to be incompatible with European law in *Preston* v *Wolverhampton Healthcare Trust (No 2)* [2001] ICR 217.
  - To recommend that, within a specified period, the employer takes action to deal with the discrimination against the complainant which appears to the tribunal to be reasonable in the circumstances of the case. Failure to comply with the recommendation may result in increased compensation.

Workers with fixed-term contracts

There are several legal issues involving these workers. The first and basic issue is continuity of service. This is of considerable significance for those workers on successive temporary contracts. To determine continuity, these contracts can be 'stitched together'. This is important in deciding access to benefits and calculating qualifying periods for complaints about employment rights (*see* earlier in this chapter).

The second area concerns statutory employment protection already provided for temporary workers within employment law. Examples include the following:

■ They are covered by discrimination law while in employment.

■ They are entitled to contractual information within the first eight weeks of employment.

■ They accrue paid annual leave from the first day of employment under the Working Time Regulations 1998.

■ Unlawful deductions from wages are prohibited.

■ A pregnant worker has an unqualified right to ordinary maternity leave.

■ They have specific health and safety protection.

Thirdly, there are the implications of the Fixed-term Employees (Prevention of Less Favourable Treatment) Regulations 2002. These came into effect on 1 October 2002. These Regulations transpose into UK law the Fixed-term Workers Directive 1999. The key provisions of the Regulations are:

■ *The principle of equal treatment*: A fixed-term employee should not be treated less favourably than a comparable permanent employee on the grounds that the employee is a fixed-term employee (reg 3). The fixed-term employee's terms and conditions should not be less favourable than those of the 'permanent' employee. The Regulations also prohibit the employee being subject to any 'detriment by any act, or deliberate failure to act, of the employer' (reg 3(1)(b)).

■ *Objective justification*: However, an employer will be able to treat fixed-term employees less favourably than comparable permanent employees where the treatment is objectively justified. Such justification depends on the circumstances of each case. The Regulations provide that discrimination in relation to a particular contractual term will be justified where the fixed-term employee's overall package of terms and conditions is not less favourable than the comparable permanent employee's (reg 4).

■ *Who is covered?* The Regulations apply to employees, defined in the usual way as someone who works under a contract of employment. The 1999 Directive provides protection for fixed-term workers. The limitation of the Regulations to employees means that the definition of an 'employee', under the common law tests, is likely to arise in some cases (*see* earlier discussion in this chapter).

■ *Which contracts are covered?* A fixed-term contract means a contract of employment which is one of the following (reg 1(2)):

  – a contract which is made for a specific term which is fixed in advance (e.g. three months, a year or three years); or

- a contract which ends automatically on the completion of a particular task or upon the occurrence or non-occurrence of any specific event. Examples of such circumstances are employees covering maternity leave breaks; those covering peaks in production demand or demands for a service; or tasks that are part of carrying out a particular project (e.g. setting up a database).

■ *Who is the comparator?* The comparator is a 'permanent' employee (reg 2). This is a person on a contract of employment which is of indefinite duration. It is sometimes referred to as an 'open-ended' contract that can be terminated by due notice by either the employer or the employee. The comparator should be employed by the same employer at the same establishment doing the same or broadly similar work. Where relevant, the comparator should have similar skills and qualifications to the fixed-term employee. Where there is no comparator in the same establishment, then, a comparison can be made with a similar permanent employee working for the same employer in a different establishment.

■ *Successive fixed-term contracts*: The use of successive fixed-term contracts is limited to four years, unless further fixed-term contracts can be justified on objective grounds. It will, however, be possible for employers and employees to increase or decrease this period through a collective agreement with a trade union or, in non-union organisations, through workforce agreement with employee representatives (reg 8 and Schedule 1). For the purpose of this Regulation, service accumulated from 10 July 2002 will count towards the four-year limit. There is no limit on the duration of the first fixed-term contract. However, if a first contract of four years or more is renewed, it will be treated from then as permanent unless the use of a fixed-term contract is objectively justified.

  Furthermore, if a fixed-term contract is renewed after the four-year period, it will be treated as a contract for an indefinite period unless the use of a fixed-term contract is objectively justified. A fixed-term employee has a right to ask the employer for a written statement confirming that their contract is permanent or setting out objective reasons for the use of a fixed-term contract beyond the four-year period. The employer must provide this statement within 21 days (reg 8).

■ *A written statement of reasons*: A fixed-term employee has a right to ask their employer for a written statement setting out the reasons for the discriminatory treatment that they believe has occurred. The employer must provide this statement within 21 days (reg 5). This written statement is admissible under proceedings at an employment tribunal. A tribunal may draw 'any inference that it considers just and equitable, including an inference that the employer has infringed the right in question' (reg 5(3)) if the employer has 'deliberately and without written excuse' not provided such a statement or considers that 'the written statement is evasive or equivocal'.

■ *Redundancy waiver*: Any such waiver that is included in a fixed-term contract which was agreed, extended or renewed after 1 October 2002 will be invalid.

■ *Protection against unfair dismissal and victimisation*: Dismissal or selection for redundancy is automatically unfair if the reason or principal reason concerns the exercise of rights under the Regulations. An employee may complain to an employment tribunal irrespective of their age or length of service. Similar protection is provided for against victimisation (reg 6).

- *Termination of a fixed-term contract*: From 1 October 2002, the end of a 'task contract' that expires when a specific task has been completed or a specific event does or does not happen will be a dismissal in law; as will be the non-renewal of a fixed-term contract concluded for a specific period of time. Employees on 'task contracts' of one year or more have the right to a written statement of reasons for the dismissal and the right not to be unfairly dismissed. If the contract lasts for two years or more and it is not renewed because of redundancy, the employee has the right to statutory redundancy pay.

- *Application to employment tribunal*: A worker may complain to an employment tribunal of less favourable treatment or victimisation (reg 7). The application should be made within three months of either the date of the action complained of or the last in a series of discriminatory actions. Where a worker presents a complaint, it is for the employer to identify the ground for the less favourable treatment or detriment (reg 7(6)).

- *Liability*: An employer is vicariously liable for the behaviour of, for example, managers, supervisors and other workers, 'in the course of his employment' whether or not it was done with the employer's knowledge and approval (reg 12(1)). An employer's defence before an employment tribunal is that they 'took such steps as were reasonably practicable' to prevent the discrimination (reg 12(3)). (This provision reflects those provided under other discrimination law. *See* Chapters 4–6.)

- *Remedies*: If an employment tribunal finds a complaint to be well founded, it is required, as it considers just and equitable (reg 7):
  - To make a declaration of the rights of the complainant and the employer in relation to the complaint.
  - To order the employer to pay compensation to the complainant which the tribunal considers just and equitable.
  - To recommend that, within a specified period, the employer takes action, which appears to the tribunal to be reasonable in the circumstances of the case, to deal with the discrimination against the complainant. Failure to comply with the recommendation may result in increased compensation.

Casual workers

In the flexible labour market, the role of casual workers is of growing importance in particular sectors (e.g. as nurses, supply teachers or in hotels and catering). 'Bank' staff and those 'on call' can have particular problems of employment protection in law. This can be compounded by an employer's reliance on 'regular casuals'. There is clearly an employment relationship. The question at issue is what kind of employment relationship? Is it one that confers access to statutory rights (particularly dismissal protection)?

The legal issues that have arisen in cases over the past 15 years have been (*see* earlier discussion also):

- whether the person is an 'employee' working under a contract of employment or an independent contractor;
- whether there is clearly 'mutuality of obligation' (i.e. an obligation on the employer to provide work and upon the employee to accept work offered). If this does not exist then there can be no contract of employment;
- whether there is an 'umbrella contract' or 'global contract' covering all assignments. Such a contract is dependent on 'mutuality of obligation' being established.

There have been cases where 'regular casuals' have been ruled not to have a contract of employment. For example, *O'Kelly and Others* v *Trust House Forte plc* [1983] ICR 728 concerned waiters whose names were on a list to be called first for banqueting functions. They worked only for THF and did so virtually every week for varying hours (from three to 57). They were paid weekly, deductions were made for tax and National Insurance and they also received holiday pay. They worked under the control of the head waiter and were provided with uniforms. However, they did not have to agree to work if they did not wish to. Likewise the company was not required to provide work. Refusal could, however, result in removal from the list. The Court of Appeal stated that there was no mutuality of obligation.

Following the established approach, the Court of Appeal ruled against a 'bank' nurse on the ground that there was no evidence of mutuality of obligation (*Clark* v *Oxfordshire Health Authority* [1998] IRLR 125). It was clearly stated that 'no "contract of employment" within the definition contained [in the Employment Rights Act 1996] (whether it can be given the extra-statutory name "global" or "umbrella" or any other name) can exist in the absence of some mutual obligations subsisting over the entire duration of the relevant period' (Sir Christopher Slade).

The vulnerability of casual workers was further seen in the House of Lords decision in the case of two tour guides who worked at a power station in Northumberland (*Carmichael and Leese* v *National Power plc* [2000] IRLR 43) (*see* Fig. 2.5).

Homeworking and teleworking

The critical issue for this group of flexible workers has been the establishment of an employment contract as an access to employment rights. Stanworth (1996: 15) reports in one survey that 'only about one-third of the homeworkers were regarded as employees by their employers and many would prefer this status'. She adds that 'most only knew their agent and not their employer's name. They were kept in a constant state of insecurity and confusion over their employment position.'

One notable case was *Airfix Footwear* v *Cope* [1978] ICR 210. In this case, Mrs Cope worked at home making shoe heels. The company provided her with tools and issued instructions and, over a seven-year period, she generally worked a five-day week. She was paid on a piecework basis without deductions for tax and National Insurance. She was held by the Employment Appeals Tribunal to be an employee (*see* the 'tests' earlier in this chapter). Another case covering this issue and coming to the same conclusion is *Nethermore (St. Neots) Ltd* v *Jardiner & Taverna* [1983] IRLR 240. Each case is determined on its facts using the common law tests (*see* earlier section).

Ms Leese had been employed as a tour guide since March 1989. She was obliged to supervise parties of visitors, explain various activities and answer questions. She also gave talks to schools. She was given training for the post. In her offer letter, she was described as working on a *casual as required basis*. The company did not have to provide work and Ms Leese could refuse work.

She worked as a guide for up to 25 hours per week. She was paid, after deduction of tax and national insurance contributions at an employed person's rate. But she was only paid when she worked. There was no sick pay nor pension provision. No notice to terminate the contract was indicated. She was provided with a uniform. She was accountable to the company for the quality of her work. The grievance and disciplinary procedures for regular staff did not apply. There was no written contract of employment nor any contractual information other than that in the offer letter.

The complaint of the two women to the employment tribunal was that the company had failed to provide a written statement of initial employment particulars (now under the ERA, s 1). The company contended that they were not employees. This issue was taken for determination through the Employment Appeals Tribunal and the Court of Appeal.

It was heard, in the proceedings, that Ms Leese had been unavailable for work on eight occasions. There had been no suggestion by the company of disciplinary action. The Court of Appeal ruled that there was mutuality of obligation, and hence a contract of employment, because the workers were under an obligation to take 'a reasonable amount of work' as a tour guide and the company was obliged to provde 'a reasonable share of work'. It found the existence of a 'global' contract.

However, the House of Lords said that the objective inference from the situation as described was that, when work was available, the applicants were free to undertake it or not as they chose. It saw the flexibility suiting both parties. The arrangement was based on mutual convenience and good will and had worked well in practice over the years. But it took the view that, in the circumstances of the case, there was no 'irreducible minimum of mutual obligation necessary to create a contract of service' – i.e. a contract of employment.

Figure 2.5   The *Carmichael and Leese* case

The present government's policy of broadening the scope of employment rights to those 'workers' who have 'an employment relationship' should assist this category to working people (*see* Chapter 10 on pay regulation and Chapter 11 on working time regulation).

Zero-hour contract workers

The legal problems for this category and potential abuse by employers – particularly, under the contract of employment – are recognised by the government in both the 'Fairness at Work' White Paper (paras 3.14–3.16) and the Working Time Regulations 1998. To date, there has been no resolution of the issues. The central issues for working people in this category are: What is regarded as 'working time'? What duties must they perform during this working time? What payment in respect of working time are they entitled to? A European Court of Justice case (*SIMAP* v *Conselleria de Sanidad y Consumo de la Generalidad Valenciana* [2000] IRLR 598) has provided some guidance on the definition of working time. Dealing with doctors who were 'on call', it was ruled that only time linked to the actual provision of primary care services was working time. (Outside of that time, even though they were at the disposal of their employer, they could, it was ruled, manage their time with fewer constraints and pursue their interests.)

Courts and tribunals must, inevitably, establish, on the facts of individual cases, whether a worker is 'on call'; if so, is the worker free to use their time until 'called' by the employer or must they remain on the employer's premises waiting to work? Furthermore, the courts and tribunals need to establish whether or not time waiting for work should be paid.

Agency workers

The position of agency workers can be ambiguous in respect of employment protection. Effectively, there are two models that may be adopted. First, there is that where the worker is clearly an employee of the agency and works on a temporary basis for a number of different client organisations. Under the Conduct of Employment Agencies and Employment Business Regulations 1976, the employment agency (defined in the Employment Agencies Act 1973, s 13) must provide a written statement of employment particulars and an indication of whether the person is employed on a contract of employment or a contract for services (as an independent contractor). While the employment contract may be with the agency, the client has a number of responsibilities to the worker under employment law – particularly discrimination and health and safety law.

The status of the worker under employment protection law is left to decisions of the courts considering the facts of each individual case. In *McMeechan* v *Secretary of State for Employment* [1997] IRLR 353, the Court of Appeal considered the status of an agency worker. Following the insolvency of the agency, he claimed entitlement to a payment from the National Insurance Fund as an employee. The court weighed the various facts in the case which point to or away from an employment relationship. Among the evidence was a document signed by McMeechan which stated that he would provide his services as a 'self-employed worker and not under a contract of service'. However, there was also evidence that the agency had power of dismissal for misconduct, the right to end assignments. It had the right to make deductions from an hourly rate of pay (for poor performance or bad timekeeping) and his pay was subject to deduction of tax and National Insurance contributions. Furthermore, the agency provided a grievance procedure, and McMeechan owed a duty of fidelity and confidentiality. The court found that there was an employment relationship with the agency but only for the purposes of the specific engagement.

The second model is simpler in that the agency places staff with an organisation, but has no obligations as an employer. The client organisation assumes that role.

In March 2002, following the breakdown of negotiations between the EU social partners in May 2001, the European Commission proposed a draft Directive for consideration by the Council of Ministers and the European Parliament. It is likely that this Directive, once formally agreed, will come into force in the UK in 2006. This proposal establishes the principle of non-discrimination in working conditions, including pay, between temporary agency workers and comparable workers in the client organisation as soon as the temporary agency worker has completed a period of service – six weeks is suggested. A 'comparable worker' is defined as a worker in the client undertaking who holds an identical or similar post to the agency worker, taking into account seniority, qualifications and skills.

It is proposed that exceptions to the principle of non-discrimination can arise in particular situations: where certain objective reasons can be applied and justified; where a collective agreement exists; where the agency worker has an open-ended contract with the agency; and where no comparable worker nor any collective agreements exist.

The overall state of employment protection outlined in the preceding discussion is summarised in Fig. 2.6.

2.5   Conclusion

The regulation of the employment relationship is being subjected to two parallel developments in law. First, statute law is progressively determining a framework of minimum rights which mould the terms of the contract of employment. Within the next few years, a 'new model contract' deriving from these statutory minima will be available in law to most 'employees' and many 'workers'. The general political thrust of British and European employment law is acknowledging that members of the 'flexible labour market' are entitled to minimum rights and that the general restriction of access to statutory rights to full-time permanent employees has ceased to be defensible. Consequently, legislation gradually recognises the circumstances of part-time workers, those on temporary contracts, agency workers and homeworkers.

Secondly, case law is taking some tentative steps in the direction of establishing protections for 'atypical' workers. Examples of this are found in the rulings on continuity of service, and on the contractual position of casual workers.

The practical effects of all these developments suggest that employers need to take much greater care in drafting contracts and in deciding on how they are to be operated.

Exercise 2.2   **Who has employment rights?**

Consider the following scenarios and say whether or not you think the person can claim that a statutory right has been infringed. What are the legal issues involved?

1   Mick has worked for three months as a hotel porter. He believes that he has been underpaid in his last monthly pay.

2   Marion has worked for a computer company on a succession of three-month fixed-term contracts with occasional gaps of several days between them. After 18 months her employer dismisses her.

3   Indira is a homeworker sewing garments. She works about 15 hours per week. She is paid £2.50 per hour.

4   Sharon has been employed for six weeks as a civilian administrator in a police station and objects to the sexual remarks of a custody sergeant. She resigns.

5   Jehan had worked, after training and briefings, for a call-centre on a 'regular casual' basis for just over a year. Work was offered to him when it was available and it was expected that he would not refuse it unreasonably. On two occasions in one month he rejected the offer of work. The company wrote to him and said that it was withdrawing his name from its lists.

Feedback on this exercise is provided in the Appendix to this book.

Access is no longer restricted by the number of hours a person works each week.

For those with 'employee' status
- Protection against unfair dismissal
  - A right qualified by age and length of service (ERA 1996, ss 94, 108, 109).
  - Restricted right when dismissal relates to industrial action (TULRCA 1992, ss 237–9).
- Basic maternity leave
  - An unqualified right (ERA, ss 71–8).
- Right to return to work
  - Qualified by length of service (ERA, ss 79–85).
- Shop and betting shop workers
  - Irrespective of age or length of service (ERA, ss 36–43, 45).
- Right to parental leave
  - Qualified by length of service.
- Protection for fixed-term employees against discrimination (Regulations 2002).

For 'workers'
- Protection against sex discrimination
  - Available 'in relation to employment' (SDA 1975, s 6). 'Employment' is defined as meaning 'employment under a contract of service or of apprenticeship or a contract personally to execute and work or labour and related expressions shall be construed accordingly' (s 82(1)).
  - An express provision is included in relation to 'contract workers' (s 9) (*BP Chemicals* v *Gillick* [1995] IRLR 511, EAT).
- Protection against race discrimination
  - Available, as sex discrimination law, in relation to 'employment' (RRA 1976, ss 4, 78(1)) and in relation to 'contract workers' (s 7) (*Harrods Ltd* v *Remik* [1997] IRLR 9, EAT).
- Protection against disability discrimination
  - Applies to 'employment' in terms reflecting sex discrimination law (DDA 1995, s 4).
  - Excludes an employer who employs fewer than 15 employees (s 7) until October 2004. There could be considerations here of the 'associated employer' issue.
- Right to equal pay
  - This covers 'the ordinary basic minimum wage or salary and any other consideration whether in cash or in kind which the worker receives directly or indirectly in respect of his employment from his employer' (Art 141, Treaty of Rome).
- Protection from deduction from wages
  - Available irrespective of length of service.
- Working time regulation
  - This provides for maximum working weekly hours (subject to an individual opt-out) (reg 4), and various rest entitlements (regs 9–11) – irrespective of length of service and hours worked.
- Right to paid annual leave
  - A minimum annual leave entitlement accruing from the start of employment (WTR 12).
- Right to statutory minimum wage
  - This provides for a national minimum wage for adults and for trainees (National Minimum Wage Act 1998, s 1).
- 'Whistleblowing' rights
  - This amends ERA 1996 and protects from detrimental treatment and dismissal those workers who make a protected disclosure.
- Protection for part-time workers against discrimination (Regulations 2000)

Figure 2.6 Access to certain key statutory employment rights*

* More details on these provisions are in the relevant chapters.

References

Atkinson, J. (1984) 'Manpower Strategies for Flexible Organisations', *Personnel Management*, August, 28–31.

Batstone, E. (1988) 'The Frontier of Control' in Gallie, D. (ed.) *Employment in Britain*. Oxford: Blackwell.

Brodie, D. (1998) *The Contract for Work*, Scottish Law and Practice Quarterly 2.

Burchell, B. *et al*. (1999) *The Employment Status of Individuals in Non-Standard Employment*, Employment Relations Research Series 6. London: Department of Trade and Industry.

Cave, K. (1997) *Zero Hours Contracts*. University of Huddersfield.

Cully, M. *et al*. (1999) *Britain at Work*. London: Routledge.

Deakin, S. and Morris, G. (1998) *Labour Law*. London: Butterworths.

The Department of Trade and Industry (1998) 'Fairness at Work', Cm. 3968. London: Stationery Office.

The Department of Trade and Industry (2002) *Discussion document on employment status in relation to statutory employment rights*. London: DTI.

Dickens, L. (1992) *Whose Flexibility? – Discrimination and Equality Issues in Atypical Work*. London: Institute of Employment Rights.

Guest, D. and Conway, N. (1997) *Employee Motivation and the Psychological Contract* (Issues in People Management No 21). London: Institute of Personnel and Development.

Guest, D. and Conway, N. (2001) *Organisational Change and the Psychological Contract*. London: Chartered Institute of Personnel and Development.

Handy, C. (1991) *The Age of Unreason*. London: Arrow Business Books.

Herriot, P. (1995) 'The Management of Careers', in Tyson, S. (ed.) *Strategic Prospects for HRM*. London: Chartered Institute of Personnel and Development.

Hotopp, U. (2002) 'Teleworking in the UK', Labour Market Trends, June.

Huws, U. (1997) *Teleworking: Guidance for Good Practice*. London: Institute of Employment Studies.

Kahn-Freund, O. (1983) *Kahn-Freund's Labour and the Law* (ed. P. Davies and M. Freedland). London: Stevens.

Mant, A. (1995) 'Changing Work Roles', in Tyson, S. (ed.) *Strategic Prospects for HRM*. London: Chartered Institute of Personnel and Development.

Marginson, P. *et al*. (1995) 'Strategy, Structure and Control in the Changing Corporation: a Survey-based Investigation', *Human Resource Management Journal*, 5(2).

Purcell, K. *et al*. (1999) *Whose Flexibility? The costs and benefits of non-standard working arrangements and contractual relations*. York: Joseph Rowntree Trust.

Schein, G. (1988) *Organisational Psychology*. London: Prentice Hall.

Sly, F. and Stillwell, D. (1997) 'Temporary Workers in Great Britain', *Labour Market Trends*, September, 347–54.

Smith, I. and Thomas, G. (1996) *Industrial Law*. London: Butterworths.

Stanworth, C. (1996) *Working at Home: a Study of Homeworking and Teleworking*. London: Institute of Employment Rights.

Storey, J. (1980) *The Challenge to Management Control*. London: Business Books.

Taylor, R. (2002) *Britain's World of Work – myths and realities*. London: Economic and Social Research Council.

Tyson, S. (1995) *Strategic Prospects for HRM*. London: Chartered Institute of Personnel and Development.

Wedderburn, Lord (1986) *The Worker and the Law*. Harmondsworth: Penguin Books.

CHAPTER 3

Managing change in the employment relationship

Learning objectives

This chapter considers the legal consequences for the employment relationship of changing managerial policies. Having read it you should understand:

- The ways in which terms in contracts of employment might need to be varied to accommodate changing business conditions.
- The ways in which an employer might build 'flexibility' into contractual terms.
- The employment protection for employees in business transfers.
- The circumstances under which an employer might lawfully make staff redundant.

3.1 Structure of the chapter

This chapter comprises the following sections:

- *Introduction*.
- *The context*: Private and public sector change – an overall view, the organisation's culture, strategic considerations, operational factors, economic considerations, employment relations matters, tensions with legal requirements, the incidence and experience of changes.
- *The legal framework*: Variation of contracts of employment, flexibility in existing contractual terms, transfers of undertakings, redundancy and redeployment.
- *Employment policies and practices*: The practicalities of contract variation, managing transfers of undertakings, and managing redundancies.
- *Case study 3.1*: Brideshead College.

3.2   Introduction

Changes to organisations and changes in their employment practices arise for various economic, technological and, occasionally, political reasons. The ways employers respond to these change-drivers can be affected by four broad frameworks of employment law:

- case law relating to variation of contracts of employment;
- case law relating to 'flexible terms' within contracts of employment;
- law, deriving from the European Union, on the transfers of undertakings; and
- law relating to redundancy and redeployment of employees.

Having considered the nature of the changing business context, we will look at each of these areas of law in turn.

3.3   The context

It is a commonplace to say that management is increasingly the management of change. Business is always in a state of flux. The principal drivers of change are pressures to compete more effectively in product markets; to respond to technological changes in product manufacture, service delivery, information storage and communication; and to achieve appropriate standards of quality. Additionally, changes may be a consequence of political decisions. Examples of the latter include the introduction of public-private partnerships by the Labour government and competitive tendering into public sector organisations by the previous Conservative government; the shifting of government funding and subsidies; the reorganisation and privatisation of public organisations; or changes in the state of the global economy. Furthermore, change may also be driven by the developing legal standards. For example, we will consider later in this textbook the significance for the management of employment relations of such measures as health and safety regulation, discrimination law, and the regulations on working time.

3.3.1   Private and public-sector change: an overall view

The scale of overall **private-sector** change is seen in data published from the second Company Level Industrial Relations Survey 1992 (Marginson *et al.*, 1995: 21). This involved 176 companies with more than 1000 employees. They were asked to identify the extent and sources of organisation change in the previous five years. The broad results were are shown in Table 3.1.

Data from the Workplace Employee and Industrial Relations Surveys 1990–8 showed that 29 per cent of private sector workplaces (on the survey panel for that period) had undergone change of ownership. The incidence was greater in private manufacturing (at 39 per cent) than in private services (at 25 per cent).

Table 3.1   Change in private-sector enterprises

Extent of changes in UK enterprises	Per cent
Merger and acquisition	70
Investment in new locations	65
Expansion at existing sites	66
Divestment	48
Closure of existing sites	62
Rundown of existing sites	40
Formation of joint ventures	36
Establishment of long-term contracts with suppliers or customers	37
Sources of change in internal structure	
Internal growth of business	53
New major acquisition	40
New major diversification	16
Shift from production to market logic	25
Increased accountability to business unit	53
Simplification/'delayering'	37
Decentralisation	26

Source: Adapted from Marginson *et al.* (1995: 21).

Forty-six per cent of all changes of ownership were the result of a takeover or merger; 34 per cent from sale by the parent organisation; and 14 per cent from management buy-out (Millward *et al.*, 2000: 23).

Within the **public sector**, over the past 20 years, there has been radical restructuring of many organisations. In local government, from 1988, 'compulsory competitive tendering' resulted in some contracting out of services. The National Health Service was reconstituted into trusts. The civil service was fragmented into various agencies. The previous Conservative government also sold public corporations' assets – the 'privatisation' of, for example, British Telecom, British Gas, the water supply and electricity industries and British Rail. The Labour government has, in a limited way, continued the process of privatisation with, for example, that of National Air Traffic Services in 2001.

Evidence from Workplace Employee and Industrial Relations Surveys (1990–8) showed that 18 per cent of those public sector organisations located in the surveys' panels over this period of time reported some change in ownership. 'Ownership changes were reported by around half of all public sector health establishments, one quarter of local government workplaces and one fifth of primary and seconday schools. Here we see the effects of the creation of self-managing trusts in the National Health Service, the reorganisation of local government and moves to grant-maintained status within state education' (Millward *et al.*, 2000: 23).

As a result of all these changes, the role of employer was often redefined and various legal issues arose concerning transfers of undertakings, redundancies and contractual variation.

At the time of writing, the Labour government is promoting public-private partnerships. These are defined as 'a risk-sharing relationship based on a shared aspiration between the public sector and one or more partners from the private and/or voluntary sectors to deliver a publicly agreed outcome and/or public service' (IPPR, 2001: 260).

In one review and critique of developments over the past twenty years or so, it has been commented that 'in both the private and public sectors, there has been a trend towards outsourcing; more recently, this trend has been more pronounced in the latter. Organisations were urged to concentrate upon their "core" activities. Some have argued that a "contract" state has emerged whereby an increasing proportion of public services are organised around market relations and commercial contracts between purchasers and providers. This approach raised a series of difficulties for the public sector, including issues of private sector "opportunism", problems of the monitoring of contracts, the commodification of the public realm and a lack of accountability' (Sachdev, 2001: 5).

The election of a Labour government in 1997 signalled the end of local authority compulsory competitive tendering. A system of 'best value' replaces it. The principles of 'best value' have been set out, recently, by the Department of the Environment, Transport and the Regions and include the following provisions:

- The duty of best value is one that local authorities will owe to local people, both as taxpayers and the customers of local authority services. Performance plans should support the process of local accountability to the electorate.

- Achieving best value is not just about economy and efficiency, but also about effectiveness and the quality of local services – the setting of targets and performance against these should therefore underpin the new regime.

- There is no presumption that services must be privatised and once the regime is in place there will be no general requirements for councils to put their services out to tender, but there is no reason why services should be delivered directly if other more efficient means are available. What matters is what works.

Whatever the source of the change (in private or public-sector organisations), there are several aspects that should be taken into account. These, to a greater or lesser extent, have implications in law. In brief, they are: the organisation's culture, strategic considerations, structural and operational factors, economic considerations, employment relations matters, tension with legal requirements, the incidence and experience of changes. We will look at each of these in turn.

3.3.2 The organisation's culture

An organisation's culture may be difficult to define. It has been described as 'the characteristic spirit and belief of an organisation, demonstrated, for example, in the norms and values that are generally held about how people should behave and treat each other, the nature of working relationships that should be developed and attitudes to change. These norms are deep, taken-for-granted assumptions which are not always expressed, and are often known without being understood' (Torrington and Hall, 1998: 100). Clearly, there is a strong connection with the elements of the 'psychological contract' outlined in the previous chapter.

Cultural norms develop over a long period of time. They can and do, for example, mould recruitment and selection policies, day-to-day working practices, and attitudes to reward systems. They can pose significant barriers to change – particularly in rooting out discriminatory treatment and patterns of harassment (*see* Chapters 4–7). Large organisations (particularly in the private sector) have reputations for promoting 'cultural change'. This is seen by chief executives and senior management as a means of eradicating what are perceived to be inefficient practices and failures to achieve corporate business objectives. Given the entrenched nature of cultures, such change programmes encounter considerable difficulties. Indeed, there is likely to be a cultural clash between what is believed by senior managers to be the new formal culture and the traditional cultural norms that staff seek to preserve. It may be that a 'counter-culture' emerges.

The extent to which an organisation's culture can facilitate change is particularly dependent upon the effectiveness of the techniques of communication, persuasion and consultation within that organisation.

3.3.3   Strategic considerations

'Strategy' is a term frequently used in management texts in an approving way. It is an *integrative* process that involves *planning*. Strategy decisions have a medium-to long-term perspective and are likely to have major resource implications. They bring together data and assessments from a wide range of organisational activities (production or service delivery, marketing, finance, employment relations, etc.). As a result of the fluidity of the business context, strategies are implemented in a context of uncertainty and risk. Finally, the outcome of strategic decision-making will tend to involve significant change in the size, equipment, staffing arrangements or other aspects of the organisation's physical and human resources.

So, to have any prospect of success a change in management strategy has to take account of various relevant factors: organisational culture, the political structures (both formal and informal) within the organisation, the nature and degree of resistance to change, ways of achieving both the anticipated economic and operational outcomes, and those provisions in the prevailing legal framework that will affect the management of change.

3.3.4   Operational factors

In dealing with the management of change, the repercussions of particular changes need to be anticipated and considered. This is particularly so when operational changes are initiated. One example will illustrate the wide range of consequences. If an organisation is considering the installation of new, more technologically advanced equipment, there are various implications:

- *economic factors*: the cost of purchase, the effect on unit costs and unit labour costs, the impact on product market competitiveness;
- *operational*: the nature of working practices to be adopted, the redefinition of jobs, staffing levels, the scheduling of working time;
- *health and safety*: compliance with general duties in law and with other appropriate specific regulations;
- *employee relations*: requirements to consult about changes, the impact of new technology on staffing levels and whether redundancy or redeployment is proposed, impact on payment systems, consequences for working practices and for the scheduling of working time, consequences for the contracts of employment of individual employees.

A coherent implementation plan would enable likely difficulties to be anticipated and appropriate action to be taken. It would also give due attention to legal issues (these are discussed in some detail in the next two sections on *economic considerations* and *employee relations matters*).

3.3.5 Economic considerations

Economic issues are important in certain aspects of the law governing the management of change. There can be economic justifications for particular courses of action:

- *Implied terms in the contract of employment* can have economic significance. One such term defines the employee's duty to co-operate with his/her employer. This is invariably interpreted as a duty to help achieve the employer's economic objectives. Another duty is the need to obey lawful and reasonable instructions. This has been construed to cover changes in operational and working practices designed to make an organisation more cost effective.

- When an employer terminates a contract of employment that he is seeking to vary, then the reason for the termination is usually '*business need*' (which falls within the category of 'some other substantial reason' ERA 1996 s 98(1)).

- When the transfer of an undertaking is envisaged, then, certain staff of the transferor may be *dismissed for an 'economic' reason*. The law allows dismissal for two other reasons ('technical' and 'organisational') which, in practice, are very likely to interrelate with economic factors.

- *Redundancy and redeployment decisions* invariably are founded on economic considerations. These could form part of the legal defence of such decisions.

While courts and tribunals have often supported an employer's economic rationale for change, there has been one area where they have not endorsed employer's action. Economic factors cannot be used as a justification for breaches of the employee's contract of employment (for example, by means of a pay cut). The integrity of the contract of employment must be preserved. Change can only be made by agreement (*see* later discussion).

3.3.6 Employment relations matters

There are several employment relations issues in change management: procedures for managing change; substantive issues; resistance to change; counselling and employee morale.

- *Procedures*: There are statutory duties upon an employer to provide information about proposed changes (e.g. in respect of redundancies, business transfers and changing health and safety measures) and to consult with appropriate employee representatives (Chapters 12 and 14). Under common law, it is expected that employers will consult with individual employees when proposing variations to an existing contract of employment. This is with a view to obtaining consent.

- *Substantive issues*: These involve changes the employer is seeking to achieve (e.g. changes in payment systems, working practices, working-time scheduling, staffing levels, promotion schemes, etc.). These, as we have seen in the earlier discussion, are associated with strategic business objectives, operational necessity and questions of unit labour cost. (These are considered further in the later section on the incidence and experience of the changes.)

- *Resistance to change*: Resistance can derive from the predisposition of an individual, fear of the unknown, the prevailing degree of trust between employees and their employer, anxiety about preserving status and maintaining job security, poor communications. This resistance can be managed.

  Psychologists have acknowledged that individuals go through a 'coping cycle' (Carnall, 1990). This has five stages: denial of the change, anger and defensive responses for self-protection, the discarding of commitment to the traditional ways of work, adaptation to the new ways and, finally, internalisation of the new ways. As individuals progress through these stages, initially, both their performance and their self-esteem drop. But gradually, as 'discarding' takes place, both recover. It is suggested that individuals vary in the speed with which they pass through the cycle – with some never completely passing through it.

  For management, two approaches are important here. First, it is advisable to facilitate the 'coping' for individuals. This can be achieved by explanation of the changes and providing opportunities for individuals to make representations. Secondly, collective action can produce some practical outcomes. For example, consultation and negotiation about change in a 'high trust' organisation should help maintain a climate of good employment relations. Negotiation with unions or other employee representatives can help deliver consent, tackle workforce anxieties and help smooth the change. It can be an exercise in conflict minimisation. So, significant sources of resistance to change can be managed.

- *Counselling employees*: This can be necessary for dealing with the consequences of change and, in particular, redundancies. In redundancies, the remaining workforce may experience 'the survivor syndrome' – feelings of guilt about not being selected for redundancy. So, in the medium term, low staff morale may need to be tackled.

3.3.7   Tensions with legal requirements

The legal framework, discussed later in this chapter is, then, set in the context of often rapid and substantial organisational and operational change. Given the speed of response often demanded by employers, it is not surprising that attempts may be made to short-circuit or deliberately ignore legal obligations. However, in some instances, with the growing complexity of legal requirements, employers may not fully understand the juridification of employment relations that has been taking place over the past 20 years or more.

So, at the heart of the management of change, in respect of the law, is a tension between, on the one hand, the economic imperatives of business and, on the other, employees' interests (e.g. in respect of job and income security, and fair treatment). This tension can be difficult to resolve at workplace level. It frequently surfaces in court and tribunal cases. Sometimes rulings have sought to balance these interests.

3.3.8 **The incidence and experience of changes**

Variation of individual contracts of employment

Changes are extremely common. Beneficial changes (e.g. pay increases, increased holidays and shorter working hours) continue to be evident in many workplaces. But, in the past ten years or so, adverse changes have also occurred. These have included relocation and redeployment, pay cuts, increased working time.

Such variations have been achieved by one of a number of ways – some lawful and some not:

- a negotiated collective agreement with a union or unions;
- individual agreement with an employee;
- the incorporation of a change to statute law into contracts of employment;
- unilateral imposition of changed terms which goes unchallenged by an employee.

During the 1980s, courts were called upon to deal with a number of claims about variation of contract. Usually, these concerned the allegation that an employer had breached the contract of employment by making the change without agreement. The principal issues concerned pay cuts, the unilateral removal of a specific contractual term, changing working practices or the introduction of new technology.

Other cases were documented by the National Association of Citizens' Advice Bureaux. These may not have resulted in court or tribunal action. 'Changes in pay and/or hours are the most common unilateral changes experienced by CAB clients'. It was accepted that 'in some circumstances, the employer may be entitled to make such changes – that is, where this discretion is part of the contract of employment itself' (NACAB, 1993: 12). The NACAB identified the problem for employees – particularly in the context of a general economic recession. 'Numbers of employees are faced with an impossible choice – accepting a severe deterioration in their working conditions or losing their job. With unemployment standing at over three million, the implications of this dilemma are obvious' (NACAB, 1993: 49).

Flexibility of contractual terms

The term 'flexibility' is used very widely to describe a number of employee relations features (*see* Chapter 2). Flexibility in respect of contractual terms covers such matters as mobility and working from home (*geographic flexibility*); the scheduling of working hours or *temporal flexibility* (annualised hours contracts, overtime working, shift working, part-time working, job share, weekend working and flexitime); payment by results and performance-related pay (*reward flexibility*); and *functional flexibility* (requirements to undertake a variety of tasks).

The incidence of such examples include the following:

- *Annualised hours contracts*: 4 per cent of male and female employees work on these contracts (Labour Force Survey, Spring 2000).
- *Shift-working*: worked by about four million people (16 per cent of the working population).

- *Night-working*: worked by one and a half million people (6 per cent of the working population).

- *Part-time working*: some six million people work on part-time contracts (over 25 per cent of the working population).

- *Job-sharing*: In the first findings of the Workplace Employee Relations Survey (Cully *et al.*, 1998: 20) it was reported that 16 per cent of all employees 'had access' to a job-sharing scheme. The incidence was much higher in the public sector – at 34 per cent for women and 23 per cent for men. However, the incidence of this is relatively uncommon at under one per cent of all employees (Labour Force Survey, Spring 2000).

- *Weekend working*: 52 per cent of men and 36 per cent of women work at least one day at the weekend.

- *Flexitime*: worked by 10 per cent of full-time staff (CSO, 1997: 80). The WERS 1998 first findings reported that 32 per cent of all employees 'had access' to such an arrangement.

- *Individual performance-related pay*: WIRS 1990 reported that 46 per cent of workplaces had payments by results for manual workers and 37 per cent had it for non-manual workers. In 1998, the respective figures were 37 per cent and 44 per cent (Millward *et al.*, 2000: 213).

- *Functional flexibility*: WIRS 1990 reported that 36 per cent of managers stated that, in the preceding three years, they had introduced changes in working practices that have reduced job demarcation or increased the flexibility of working (*ibid.*: 334).

- *Working at or from home*: the first findings of WERS 1998 reported that 9 per cent of all employees 'had access' to such an arrangement.

Transfers and contracting-out

Employee transfers can be viewed from three perspectives: the extent to which organisations have been contracting-out activities and services; the actual and perceived employee relations impact of transfers; and the extent to which the law on business transfers has provided employment protection.

The 1998 Workplace Employee Relations Survey reports on **the extent of contracting-out**. Around 90 per cent of workplaces contract out one or more services. This proportion was similar in both the public and private sectors. From a list of 11 possible services, 'on average, workplaces had subcontracted four of these eleven services. Foremost among these were building maintenance (61 per cent), cleaning (59 per cent), transporting of documents or goods (39 per cent), training (38 per cent) and security (35 per cent)' (Cully *et al.*, 1999: 36). Workplaces in the private sector were much more likely to contract out security and recruitment, whereas those in the public sector were more likely to contract out catering.

The researchers asked managers in workplaces which had contracted-out services whether contractors were doing work which five years previously would have been undertaken by direct employees of the workplace. One-third said that this was the case – and some of the contractors' staff were former employees. The survey concludes that 11 per cent of workplaces have transferred some employees to a different employer over the past five years. This proportion was far higher in the public sector (22 per cent) than the private sector (6 per cent).

When asked the reasons for the contracting-out of services, 'by far the most common reason', mentioned by 48 per cent, was the need to make cost savings. Twenty-seven per cent mentioned the ability to focus on core business activities, and 21 per cent the ability to offer an improved service. In the public sector, 38 per cent said that they did so because of government-led initiatives or regulations. 'Although this might imply that contracting out was foisted upon the public sector, there was no difference between the proportions of workplaces in the private and public sector saying they were motivated by potential cost savings . . . Overall, 42 per cent of workplaces said they made cost savings through contracting out, but 31 per cent were now paying more for the same services with the remainder paying the same' (Cully *et al.*, 1999: 36).

In respect of **employee relations**, the wave of change affecting the public sector over the past 20 years has resulted in many negative outcomes as far as terms and conditions are concerned. For example, many of the economic gains of CCT (for government and private contractors) 'appear to be at the expense of staff pay and conditions, rather than genuine productivity gains. Case studies, including those commissioned by the government, found that exposure to tendering led to the, often dramatic, erosion of terms and conditions of employment. This was particularly true of manual staff'. Job losses arising from CCT were 'considerable' and equal opportunities were a 'major casualty' (Sachdev, 2001: 5). There is, also, a strong trade union criticism about the development of a 'two-tier' workforce in local authority services. There are significant differences in pay between staff transferred out and those employees recruited after the contract has been awarded.

The government has shown some commitment to preventing PPPs resulting in adverse conditions of employment. Ways of achieving this include the extended application of the Transfer of Undertaking (Protection of Employment) Regulations 1981 and the 1998 Directive; giving legislative force to guidance on staff transfers in the public sector; and strengthening the Best Value guidance, its inspection and enforcement requirements (*see* section 3.4 below).

Until the early 1990s, **transfers of undertakings law** in Britain was accepted as governing only 'commercial ventures'. However, this view was increasingly challenged as being at variance with the Acquired Rights Directive 1977 which did not distinguish between private-sector organisations, on the one hand, and public-sector and charitable or voluntary organisations on the other hand. It was 'an unjustified restriction' (Cavalier, 1997: 6). Britain's non-compliance with European law was taken by the European Commission to the European Court of Justice. In 1993, the Transfer of Undertakings (Protection of Employment) Regulations 1981 were amended in conformity with European law. This was ahead of the ruling by the ECJ against Britain (*European Commission* v *UK* [1994] IRLR 392).

One consequence of the partial implementation of the Directive in the early years was that competitive tendering cases in local government and the NHS were not challenged. Many of these had resulted in changed and adverse conditions of service for staff who were transferred.

For a couple of years or so, until March 1997, the law on transfers became fairly clear-cut and, generally, predictable. It was accepted that it applied to most contracting-out situations. Since 1997, there has been a period of substantial uncertainty. This arose from the ECJ's decision in a German case involving second-generation contracting (*Suzen* v *Zehnacker Gebaudereinigung GmbH Krankenhausservice* [1997] IRLR 255). (The consequences of this are discussed in more detail in section 3.4 on the legal framework.) This uncertainty is gradually being resolved and the 1998 amending Directive is transposed into British law.

Redundancy

The **incidence of redundancies**, reported in *Labour Market Trends*, shows the annual number generally fluctuating between 200 000 and 400 000, depending on prevailing economic conditions. In the Workplace Employee Relations Survey 1998, one-third of all workplaces reported making some reduction in the size of their workforce in the year preceding the survey. Larger workplaces were twice as likely to have done so – 51 per cent in comparison with 28 per cent. There was no difference beween the public and private sector. Eighty-six per cent of workplaces reported that they had no guaranteed job security (Cully *et al.*, 1999: 79).

The Survey reported the use of several **methods to reduce the workforce:**

	% workplaces
Natural wastage	57
Early retirement or voluntary redundancy	37
Redeployment within the workplace	32
Compulsory redundancies	27

In respect of methods, there were differences between the public and private sectors. Public-sector workplaces were twice as likely to use early retirements and voluntary redundancies (63 per cent compared with 26 per cent of private-sector workplaces). By contrast, compulsory redundancies were more likely in the private sector (32 per cent in comparison with 15 per cent of public-sector workplaces) (Cully *et al.*, 1999: 80).

The **reasons** most commonly given by managers in 1990 for workforce reductions were not reported in the 1998 Survey. However, the 1990 Survey reported results similar to those given in 1984 (Millward *et al.*, 1992: 322):

	% workplaces
Lack of demand	37
Reorganised working methods	37
Improved competitiveness, efficiency or cost-reduction	29
Automation	10

Where redundancies were used, the **criteria for selecting staff** were reported as follows by managers (Millward *et al.*, 1992: 325):

	% workplaces
'Last in first out' (LIFO)	47
Employee's level of skills or qualifications	29
Performance record	23
Disciplinary record or attendance	19

LIFO has been the traditional and crude method for selection. It has been argued for as fair and objective. However, increasingly, employers have questioned its value to them in terms of business needs and particularly skill mix. One survey of 80, generally large, public- and private-sector organisations, shows diminishing reliance upon this criterion. Only 11 per cent of respondents used it (*IRS Employment Trends* 658, June 1998). Because it is based on continuity of service, it is also questionable in terms of the law on indirect sex discrimination.

The IRS survey reports the following 'most commonly cited factors' involved in reducing their workforce from 70 respondents:

	Respondents
Requests for voluntary redundancy	56
The skill level of the employee concerned	55
An assessment of past or potential performance	52
Ability to perform or be trained for alternative jobs	49
The job of the employee concerned	48
Attendance record	46
Length of service	44

Most organisations took account of two or more factors in their selection. Disciplinary records were used in six.

3.4 The legal framework

We will consider four aspects of employment law:

1 *Variation of contracts of employment*: This concerns those circumstances where an employer wishes to change an existing term or terms of a contract of employment.

2 *Flexibility available in existing contractual terms*: This covers situations where existing terms of a contract of employment are sufficiently flexible to help an employer achieve operational objectives (e.g. relating to the mobility of staff; or the range of tasks an employee carries out).

3 *Transfers of undertakings*: This relates to the protection of an employee's existing terms and conditions of employment when the business they work for is transferred.

4 *Redundancy and redeployment*: This concerns the policies of employers to reduce and reorganise their workforces. These changes may result in dismissal or new terms and conditions of employment.

3.4.1 Variation of contracts of employment

Employers are continually experiencing changes: in their product markets, in available technology, in the preferences of their customers and clients and in the attitudes and expectations of their workforces. Frequently, these changes promote a drive for cost effectiveness and for greater flexibility in the deployment and use of labour. Clearly, this state of business flux is likely to have an impact upon individual contracts of employment. Employers are likely to seek, for example, changes in location of work, in the reward systems, in the nature of tasks to be undertaken and in the hours to be worked and in the scheduling of these. Inevitably, the question arises: *how can a contract of employment be changed lawfully?*

A contract of employment is made at a specific point in time – reflecting an employer's policies, requirements and expectations at that time. It is also an agreement (*see* Chapter 2). Given this, it can only be changed by agreement. So, the issue of consent is central to contract variation. In some circumstances, employees are willing to give their consent. A pay rise or longer paid holidays are examples of acceptable, beneficial changes. However, contentious problems arise when employees perceive that the change is (or is likely to be) detrimental to them: a cut in pay, longer hours of work or the removal of some contractual benefits.

Because the contract of employment is the principal instrument for regulating the employment relationship, it is important that clear guidance exists, in law, on how changes are to be made. Over the years, courts have provided this by asserting certain principles. We will look at the issues involved. Broadly, there are two alternative courses of action available to employers who wish to make contractual changes:

- They may attempt to make the changes by discussion and agreement with the employees concerned, either individually or through trade unions or other employee representatives.
- They may terminate the existing contract, with due notice (i.e. whatever a particular individual is entitled to) and offer a new contract embodying the changed terms and conditions of employment.

Change by agreement

The first step that an employer needs to undertake is to clarify whether the change affects any *terms of an employee's contract* of employment or whether it could be covered by *lawful and reasonable instructions* (*see* Chapter 2).

In respect to **contractual terms**, there must be agreement to change – consensual variation. This consent can be either express (clear, unequivocal and perhaps written) or implied (inferred from an employee's behaviour). It can be provided by the employee individually or through trade union representatives.

The role of trade union representatives in such contractual change can be particularly important. This arises because of the incorporation of collective agreements into individual contracts of employment (*see* Chapter 2). The employer and the employees concerned (together with their recognised union) can intend to incorporate any agreed changes into existing contracts of employment. Usually such incorporation is express incorporation. So, an employment contract itself expressly provides that the collective agreement (as amended by agreement from time to time) is incorporated into that contract of employment. The employee will, then, be bound by any concession made by the union, regardless of whether s/he consents to the variation or is a union member.

But, of course, consent (by unions or individuals) is not always given – particularly to adverse contractual changes. For example, there have been cases where employers, without agreement, implemented pay cuts. Although they may have had sound economic reasons for reducing unit labour costs, courts have ruled the changes to be unlawful because they were a breach of the existing contract of employment. The employers had not sought nor obtained the agreement of the employees concerned. Damages, in the form of back-pay, were awarded to these employees. The action of the employers, in these cases, was described as *unilateral variation* – change of a contract by one party without agreement. It did not matter to the courts, in such cases, whether or not the employer could justify the pay cuts on economic grounds. The issue was: what does the existing contract of employment state that an employee should be paid? (*Burdett-Coutts and Others* v *Hertfordshire County Council* [1984] IRLR 91.)

If an employer unilaterally changes the term of a contract of employment, the employee has three possible courses of action:

1 reject the variation and **work under protest**;
2 **resign** and claim constructive dismissal; or
3 **accept** the new terms.

We will look at each of these in more detail.

Work under protest

The employee rejects the variation, holds the employer to the previously agreed terms of the contract and continues working. The courts or tribunals would expect the employee to have indicated clearly rejection of the imposed change. In *Rigby* v *Ferodo* [1988] ICR 29, a case involving an imposed pay cut, the House of Lords outlined the *essential elements of 'working under protest'*:

- The employer's action amounted to a repudiatory breach of contract but not to termination of the contract.
- The employees had not accepted the employer's proposed changes in terms and conditions of employment.
- The employees were entitled to sue for the difference between the amount of wages they should have received and that which they had in fact received.
- As long as there is a continuing contract, not terminated by either side, the employer will remain liable for any shortfall in contractual wages.
- If the employer wants to limit liability, he must bring the contract to an end, although in doing so, he will run the risk of unfair dismissal claims.

Resignation of the employee

The employee accepts the repudiation of their contract of employment. A claim for constructive dismissal might then be made; as might a claim for redundancy. (The issue of constructive dismissal is discussed in Chapter 9.)

Agree to the imposed change and continue working

There are two aspects to such agreement – whether it is implied or express. Where an employee continues to work without protest, after an imposed variation, they may be taken to have impliedly consented to the variation. Whether there has been implied consent would be judged on the facts of each case. Courts have been reluctant, on occasion, to find implied consent, particularly where the effect of a change had no immediate effect. For example, one case involved the implementation of a mobility clause some five years after it had been introduced. The employee did not understand why she had been sent the original change in terms and conditions and had left it unsigned. The EAT, confirming the industrial tribunal's decision, ruled that the fact that she had continued to work after 1987 did not necessarily mean that she had agreed to the mobility clause which was not applied to her until 1992 (*Anglia Regional Co-operative Society* v *O'Donnell*, EAT 655/1991). This approach reflects that stated some years earlier in the EAT: 'If the variation related to a matter which has immediate practical application (e.g. the rate of pay) and the employee continues to work without objection after effect has been given to the variation (e.g. his pay packet has been reduced) then obviously he may well be taken to have impliedly agreed' (*Jones* v *Associated Tunnelling Co Ltd* [1981] IRLR 477). So, to avoid doubt, an employer should obtain express agreement to contractual changes.

Change by termination

It is not always possible to agree change by consultation and/or negotiation. So, an employer may adopt the second course of action – terminating the existing contract with due notice (i.e. the notice that each individual employee is entitled to) and offering a new contract which incorporates the new terms. The employee may accept the new contract. Alternatively, the employee (providing there is a sufficient length of service) may challenge the termination at an employment tribunal. Tribunals have usually accepted business need as 'some other substantial reason' for dismissal – provided that the employer presents evidence of why the changes were required (ERA 1996, s 98(1)(b)). Reasonableness in handling the whole process is also expected – with the employer showing that the employee's interests had been considered and that reasonable procedures had been followed before the employer insisted on the adoption of the changes (*see also* Chapter 9).

3.4.2   Flexibility in existing contractual terms

The contract of employment can be drafted to provide some operational flexibility for employers. Such flexibility can derive from two sources: the implied terms of the contract and specific express terms. Two implied terms are of importance – that requiring an employee to obey lawful and reasonable instructions and the duty of an employee to co-operate with the employer.

   If the proposed change relates to **lawful and reasonable instructions**, then the employer has much greater freedom and discretion to implement. In the 1980s, as technical change was developing rapidly, the question of computerisation of work was considered by the courts. One notable case dealt with the computerisation of certain clerical and administrative tasks in the Inland Revenue (*Cresswell and Others* v *Board of Inland Revenue* [1984] IRLR 190). Walton J, in the High Court, stated that employees could not conceivably have a right to preserve their working obligations completely unchanged during their employment. They could reasonably be expected, after proper training, to adapt to new techniques. All that would happen with computerisation was that jobs would remain 'recognisably the same but done in a different way'.

This implied term does not, however, give an employer free rein to make changes. Instructions usually refer to operation and work practice matters. They must be reasonable. Courts and tribunals would judge this on the facts. They must, also, be lawful. One element of lawfulness would be whether or not a term of the contract of employment (particularly an express term) was likely to be breached.

On **the duty to co-operate**, it has been commented that 'although every contract of employment must contain a certain irreducible element of co-operation, including an obligation not to obstruct the introduction of new technology or forms or work organisation, this cannot be invoked to over-ride terms and conditions on such matters as pay, hours and employee benefits which are clearly understood to be mutually binding' (Deakin and Morris, 1998: 269).

If an employer wishes to be certain about the degree of flexibility available, the inclusion of appropriate express terms into the contract of employment would be helpful. Such express terms could cover, for example, place of work and mobility, or transfer between posts.

Place of work and mobility

At the heart of mobility clauses in contracts of employment is the implied term of *mutual trust and confidence*. Effectively, courts and tribunals consider the nature of the provisions of a mobility requirement; its application to the circumstances of an employee's employment; and the consequences for the employee. The employer's behaviour in implementing a mobility clause might constitute a repudiation of the contract of employment. Two cases illustrate the issues. One relates to geographic mobility – transfer to a different part of the country; the other concerns in-company mobility.

In the first case (*United Bank* v *Akhtar* [1989] IRLR 507, EAT), the employee resigned (claiming constructive dismissal) when he had been asked to relocate at very short notice and without financial assistance, which was in the employer's discretion. His contract of employment contained a clause which stated that he might be required to relocate within the United Kingdom on a temporary or permanent basis. The EAT, dismissing the employer's appeal, took the view that the lack of reasonable notice and of financial assistance made it impossible, in practical terms, for the employee to comply with the contractual obligation to move. The employee found the employer's behaviour intolerable. It was such as to damage mutual trust and confidence.

In the second case (*BPCC Purnell Ltd* v *Webb*, EAT, 129/1990), the employee was transferred from one pre-press department of a printing company to another. Because of the different nature of shift working in the new department, he was likely to lose £80 per week in earnings. His employment contract contained a clause requiring 'total flexibility between all pre-press departments'. The EAT, finding unfair constructive dismissal, stated that this term must not be used in such a way to destroy mutual trust and confidence. The £80 reduction in weekly wages, out of a total of £305, was unacceptable and was a clear breach of the term.

Transfers between posts

It may be that, within an employment contract, provision is made for internal company transfers. The Court of Appeal has held that when an employer acts within the contract, the fact that loss is thereby caused to the employee does not render that action a breach of contract (*Spafax Ltd* v *Harrison* [1980] IRLR 442). However, a malicious or grossly unfair transfer could amount to a breach of mutual trust and confidence.

Various cases, relating to express terms, illustrate the potential flexibility. For example, in one case (*Bex* v *Securicor Transport Ltd* [1972] IRLR 68), the nature of the employee's work was changed. Although he regarded this as a demotion, it was found that the company was expressly entitled to carry out these duties. There was no repudiation of the contract. In other cases, the transfer might be subject to a proviso. So, in *White* v *Reflecting Roadstones Ltd* [1991] ICR 733, EAT, redeployment to a less well-paid job was permissible provided operational efficiency made it necessary. In *Risk Management Services (Chiltern) Ltd* v *Shrimpton* 1977, EAT 803/77, short notice of changes in shifts and duties had to be 'in an emergency'.

This section has been concerned with specific express terms which permit variation. Sometimes, employers suggest a wider, more general express term to vary contracts. This is not advisable. This would allow the employer to vary all terms of the contract. It is doubtful whether an agreement including such a term could be regarded as a contract at all. There is, in effect, no agreement on the terms of the contract. In one case where there was a general express term, the EAT ruled that the employer's power was limited to changes of a minor and non-fundamental nature (*Untied Association for the Protection of Trade Ltd* v *Kilburn* 17.9.85, EAT, 787/84).

Exercise 3.1

Some problems of managing variation

Read these scenarios and decide on the following:

- *What legal issues do you think might be involved?*
- *What do you recommend that the employer do both in law and in practice?*

1 Samantha is employed as an assistant in the Gateshead branch of Listeria Foodmarkets. On Friday, her manager tells her that from the following Monday she is to work at the Newcastle branch.

2 Locksmith Engineering has been in severe financial difficulties over the past 12 months. As part of its response for dealing with the problems, the owner has decided not to award a pay increase from 1 April this coming year.

3 At the local health centre, patient records are to be computerised. Beryl, who has been the practice receptionist for 15 years, tells the practice manager that she will not use the computer: 'It's not my job. I was employed to deal with manual files'.

4 Staff in the Finance Department of Wavertree Borough Council have always had a 15-minute tea break at 10.30 am and at 3.00 pm. However, in practice the length of the break has drifted to half an hour. Required to deal with a heavy overload of council tax matters, the Director has issued a notice that forthwith the break will be 15 minutes and that anyone abusing the arrangement will be disciplined.

5 Jamila worked as a retail assistant in a large department store chain in Swansea. As a result of a change in policy, she was required to ask all customers who did not have a company charge card whether they would like information on the scheme. Increasingly, she came to dislike this aspect of her work. She did not see it as a task that she was employed to do. She also resented the attitudes of customers who made disparaging comments about the high rate of interest on the company's charge card. She resigned.

Feedback on this exercise is provided in the Appendix to this book.

3.4.3 **Transfers of undertakings**

The law relating to transfers of undertakings makes a critical contribution to employee protection when, for business reasons, an employee is transferred from one employer to another. It originates in the Acquired Rights Directive 1977, which has been transposed into British law through the Transfer of Undertakings (Protection of Employment) Regulations 1981. These regulations were amended in 1993. A new Directive (amending the original), adopted in 1998, is being transposed into British law.

In this section, we will consider:

- the coverage of the Directives and Regulations;
- the definition of a relevant transfer;
- information disclosure and consultation;
- the nature of employee protection.

Coverage

The TUPE 1981 Regulations define *'undertaking'* (reg 2.1) as *'any trade or business'*. It encompasses *'part'* of such undertakings. Since amendments in 1993, it now clearly includes non-commercial and public sector 'undertakings'. The individuals eligible for protection are 'employees'. This term was used in the originating Directive and is in the TUPE Regulations. Essentially, concern is with the effect of the transfer on the employee's contract of employment and any relevant collective agreements.

The employers involved in business transfers are *'the transferor'* (the organisation that currently is employing the employees) and *'the transferee'* (the organisation to which the staff will be transferred).

What is 'a relevant transfer'?

The 1998 Directive (Article 1(1)) explicitly defines relevant transfers (author's italics):

a) This directive shall apply to *any transfer* of an undertaking, business or part of an undertaking or business *to another employer as a result of a legal transfer or merger*.

b) Subject to subparagraph (a) and the following provisions of this Article, there is a transfer within the meaning of this Directive where there is *a transfer of an economic entity which retains its identity*, meaning an organised grouping of resources which has the objective of pursuing an economic activity, *whether or not that activity is central or ancillary*.

c) This Directive shall apply to *public and private undertakings* engaged in economic activities *whether or not they are operating for gain*. An administrative reorganisation of *public administrative functions*, or the transfer of administrative functions between public administrative authorities, is not a transfer within the meaning of this Directive.

What is *not* a relevant transfer under the Regulations?

- takeovers by share transfer;
- the transfer of assets only – for example, the sale of equipment alone is not covered;

- transfers of contracts to provide goods and services where no transfer of a business or part of a business is involved;
- transfers of undertakings located outside the United Kingdom.

There are two subsidiary questions involved in answering the principal question 'What is a relevant transfer?' These are: 'Is the *identity* of an economic entity preserved?' and 'Is the entity *a going concern*?'

Identity

The question of *identity* is decisive in determining whether or not a relevant transfer exists. To assess the preservation of identity 'a shopping list' of factors has developed from ECJ rulings (*Spijkers* v *Gebroeders Benedik Abattoir CV and Another* [1986] 2 CMLR 296; *Dr Sophie Redmond Stichting* v *Bartol* [1992] IRLR 366; *Rask and Christensen* v *ISS Kantineservice A/S* [1993] IRLR 133). In the *Cheeseman* 2001 case, the EAT outlined the key principles distilled from recent cases, in the form of a two-stage test. The elements of the test concern various factual circumstances of the undertaking concerned:

Stage one: before the alleged transfer, was there an identifiable economic entity?

- There should be a **stable economic entity**. In *Initial Contract Services Ltd* v *Harrison and others*, EAT 64/01, the EAT tested the stability of an entity. It found that the cleaning operation in question was characterised by extreme fluctuations in the number of employees over a period of 17 years and changes in the tasks carried out. It concluded that this was merely a group of employees carrying out part of the overall business under the control of the central organisation.
- The entity should be **sufficiently structured and autonomous**. In *Suzen* v *Zehnacker Gebaudereinigung GmbH Krankenhausservice* [1997] IRLR 255, the ECJ defined an economic entity as 'an organised grouping of persons and assets facilitating the exercise of an economic activity which pursues a specific objective'. In *Wynnwith Engineering Co Ltd* v *Bennett* [2001] EAT 480/00, the EAT accepted that there was no unity in the tasks carried out by a particular group of workers. So, there was no economic entity and, therefore, no transfer of an undertaking.
- The entity **need not necessarily have tangible or intangible assets**. This would depend on the sector. For example, in cleaning and surveillance, the assets are often reduced to their most basic and the activity is essentially based on manpower.
- The entity **may be characterised by the personnel performing it**. An organised group of wage-earners specifically and permanently assigned to a common task could (in the absence of other factors of production) be an economic entity.
- However, **an activity** is not of itself an economic entity. Consideration would have to be given to such factors as the workforce, management of staff, the organisation of work, resourcing and the method of operations. In *Oy Liikenne Ab* v *Pekka Liskojarvi* [2001] IRLR 171, the ECJ said that 'the mere fact that the service provided by the old and the new contractors is similar does not justify

the conclusion that there has been a transfer of an economic entity between two undertakings. Such an entity cannot be reduced to the activity entrusted to it. Its identity also emerges from other factors, such as its workforce, its management staff, the way in which its work is organised, its operating methods or, indeed, where appropriate, the operational resources available to it.'

■ An entity may cease to exist on the **expiry of a contract**.

Stage two: If there was such an entity, has it been transferred to the transferee?

The factors outlined here draw on and add to those in the *Spijkers*, 1986 case. In the *Redmond*, 1992 case, it was noted that the factors should form part of 'an overall assessment' and, therefore, no factor should be considered in isolation. The tests will be applied to each situation and the assessment will be made on the basis of the particular facts and circumstances. The decisive criterion to be considered as to whether or not a relevant transfer exists is whether the identity of the economic entity is preserved after the transfer – either by continuing in operation or by resuming operation.

■ The **type of undertaking** or business that was transferred. This can be *part of an undertaking* or business (*Redmond*, 1992; *Rask*, 1993). It can be an *ancilliary activity* for the transferor, which may not necessarily be related to the organisation's business aims. The Regulations apply irrespective of the size of the undertaking transferred. A relevant transfer can involve the *transfer of leases and franchises* (*Landsorganisationen i Danmark* v *Ny Molle Kro* [1989] IRLR 37). In *Suzen* 1997, the first distinction was drawn between labour-intensive services and other services. It was ruled that there would only be a transfer if either of the following transferred: significant tangible/intangible assets or a major part of the workforce – in terms of numbers and of skills – which provided the service prior to change of contractor.

■ Whether or not **tangible assets** (e.g. buildings and moveable property) are transferred. This was considered in various cases (*Redmond*, 1992; *Schmidt* v *Spar und Leihkasse der Früheren Ämter Bordesholm, Keil und Cronshagen* [1994] IRLR 302; *Suzen*, 1997). For example, in the *Redmond* case, 'part' of the Dr Sophie Redmond Foundation's activities were transferred, as a result of the redirection of local authority funding, to the Sigma Foundation. This transfer involved knowledge, resources, some employees and some clients and patients. The fact that certain assets or functions had not been transferred did not in itself seem to the ECJ to be sufficient to preclude the application of the Directive. It was possible for a relevant transfer to exist if there was a transfer of services (*Rask*, 1992; *Schmidt*, 1994). In the *Schmidt* case, a cleaning service by one person was ruled as a relevant transfer. The total absence of transferred assets was dismissed by the ECJ as not being a crucial issue. The decisive criterion was stated as being the preservation of identity.

■ The value of **intangible assets** (e.g. goodwill) at the time of the transfer.

■ Whether or not the **majority of employees** are taken over by the new employer. If no employees are transferred, the reason why can be relevant in determining whether or not there is a relevant transfer. (Following *Suzen*, 1997 and *ECM*, 1999, this is now *one* of the factors to be taken into account).

- Whether or not there is **a change of ownership**. This is not necessary. A **change in control** can be sufficient (*Spijkers*, 1986). It has been commented that 'applying this test, the ECJ has demonstrated great willingness to find relevant transfers in order to safeguard the positions of employees' (Linden, 1992). This approach was reaffirmed in the *Rask* case, 1992. Here, the ECJ ruled that the Directive applied whenever there was a change in the person or legal entity responsible for the running of the undertaking and who, as a result of the change, entered into *the obligations of an employer* in relation to the employees of the undertaking. It was not relevant whether the ownership of the undertaking was transferred. This was again reaffirmed by the EAT in *Cheeseman*, 2001.

- The **degree of similarity** between the activities carried on before and after the transfer. Similarity between the service provided by the old and new undertakings providing a contracted-out service or by the old and new contract-holders does not necessarily mean that there has been a transfer of an economic entity. Where it is a labour-intensive sector, it is recognised that an entity can maintain its identity post-transfer even if the transferee pursues more than the activity performed pre-transfer. The Regulations apply where, for example, two companies cease to exist and combine to form a third.

- Whether or not the **customers** are transferred. 'Customer' can be the specific organisation for which a service is provided – for example, a local authority or a hospital trust.

- The period, if any, for which those **activities are suspended**. No importance is attached to a gap between the end of work of one subcontractor and the start of a successor. A three-month closure of a tavern which was subsequently reopened by a new licensee (*Ny Molle Kro*, 1989) was ruled to be covered by the Directive.

- A transfer may exist without any **formal contract**. Evidence of this is seen in the *Redmond* case (1992) (involving the switching of funding) and in *Merckx v Ford Motors Co Belgium SA* [1996] IRLR 467 (involving a change in car dealerships). The absence of any contractual link between transferor and transferee may be evidence that there is no transfer but is certainly not conclusive as there is no need for any such direct contractual relationship. However, the 1998 Directive does state that 'this directive shall apply to any transfer of an undertaking, business or part of an undertaking or business to another employer as a result of *a legal transfer or merger*' (Art 1(1)).

A 'going concern'

The issue of an undertaking being a *going concern* is a general principle applied to transfers. It is a long-established concept in British law. Essentially, it means putting the transferee in possession of a concern, the activities of which could be carried on without interruption (*Kenmir Ltd* v *Frizzell* [1968] 1 All ER 414, HC). It involves looking at what is taken over by the new owner (e.g. premises, machinery, goodwill, work in progress, debts, accounts receivable, orders, etc.).

In various cases, the concept of 'going concern' has been modified. For example, the significance of 'goodwill' has been downplayed or ignored (*Wren* v *Eastbourne Borough Council* [1993] ICR 955, EAT). It has been commented that 'typically with service contracts there is no goodwill in the operation contracted out or the goodwill is retained by the customer and none arises from the running of the operation thereafter . . . If goodwill is to continue to be an important factor, then this will also militate against findings of business transfer in such cases' (Linden, 1992).

Information disclosure and consultation

In the context of European social partnership objectives, the Acquired Rights Directive 1977 outlined requirements to help employees and their representatives both understand and influence the impact of a business transfer on employees.

The Regulations identify the following key provisions (reg 10):

- **Information** to be given to employee representatives in both the transferor's and the transferee's undertakings of:
  - the reasons for the transfer;
  - the legal, economic and social implications of the transfer for the employees;
  - measures envisaged in relation to the employees.

  The transferor and the transferee must give such information to their employee representatives 'long enough' before the transfer is effective to enable consultation to take place. The information must be in writing.

- **Consultation** with employee representatives must take place if the transferor or transferee 'envisages measures in relation to his employees'; and the consultation must be 'with a view to seeking their agreement to measures to be taken'. So, parallel consultation processes may take place within the transferor's organisation and within the transferee's organisation where employees are to be affected by the transfer of the undertaking (reg 10(1)).

  Consultation must be genuine. This is outlined as follows: 'In the course of those consultations the employer shall – (a) consider any representations made by the (appropriate) representatives; and (b) reply to those representations and, if he rejects any of those representations, state his reasons' (reg 10(6)).

  The employer is obliged to allow the representatives access to the affected employees. Also, they should be given 'such accommodation and facilities as may be appropriate' (reg 10(6A)).

Complaint about an employer's failure to inform and consult can be made to an employment tribunal. It is not necessary to wait until the transfer has taken place. The effective implementation of this set of provisions into British employment law has been fitful and incomplete. (The issue of employee consultation is explored in more detail in Chapter 14.)

The nature of employee protection

There are various issues that arise in respect of individual employee protection under the law relating to business transfers. These are:

- a person's status as an 'employee';
- their employment 'immediately before' the relevant date of the transfer;
- preserving continuity of the employment contract and the transfer of rights and liabilities;

■ the issue of occupational pensions;

■ an employee's right to refuse a transfer;

■ variations of conditions of employment;

■ constructive dismissal;

■ protection against dismissal;

■ the status of collective agreements with trade unions in a transfer;

■ the status of agreements on trade union recognition.

Employee status

In Chapter 2, when discussing the parties to an employment contract, we considered the case law tests for determining whether or not a person was an 'employee'. Because TUPE employment rights accrue to employees alone, it may be necessary to use the tests for individuals whose employment status is unclear (reg 2). The 1998 Directive envisages broadening the coverage. It places obligations on both the transferor and transferee employers for rights in respect of a contract of employment or an employment relationship. In addition, it states that member states cannot exclude from the Directive's scope employees who are part-time workers, on fixed-term contracts or in temporary employment (Art 2(2)).

The relevant date

In deciding access to these employment rights, a person must be employed by the transferor employer 'immediately before' the transfer of the undertaking takes place (reg 5(3)). Essentially, such an employee, employed at the relevant date of the transfer, is entitled to have their contractual rights preserved and is protected from dismissal (except in specific circumstances which are discussed later). The relevant date of the transfer has been ruled as the date the sale of the business was completed and not the date that contracts for sale were exchanged, which will be earlier.

Two leading cases have set out guidance in this area (and also in respect of access to redundancy pay where a dismissal takes place). In the first case (*Secretary of State for Employment* v *Spence and Others and Spencer & Sons* (*Market Harborough*) *Ltd* (*in liquidation*) [1986] ICR 651), the Court of Appeal upheld a claim for statutory redundancy pay. The employee contracts were terminated at 11 am on 28 November 1983. The business was sold at 2 pm. The workforce was re-employed by the new owners on the following day, 29 November. It was ruled that the employees had not been transferred with the business. Their contracts of employment were not subsisting at the actual time of the transfer. This case is used as guidance where a dismissal is for 'economic, technical or organisational' reasons (reg 8(2)) (*see* pp 116–17).

In another case (*Litster and Others* v *Forth Dry Dock and Engineering Co Ltd and Forth Estuary Engineering Ltd* [1989] IRLR 161), the House of Lords ruled that, unless there is an economic, technical or organisational reason for dismissal, an employee who was dismissed before the transfer must be deemed to be still employed immediately before the transfer. In this case the employees were dismissed at 3.30 pm on the day of the transfer. Some were employed at 4.30 pm by the new company at lower pay.

Continuity of an individual's employment contract

The terms of the contract of employment with the transferor (the old employer) are continued with the transferee (the new employer). So, there is no break in an employee's continuity of service. This is important in respect of contractual rights and benefits and, also, access to statutory rights.

'On completion of a relevant transfer . . . all the transferor's rights, powers, duties and liabilities under or in connection with any such contract [of employment] shall be transferred . . . to the transferee' (reg 5(2)(a)). Most contractual rights are clear-cut. The Regulations cover those relating to pay, benefits, hours, holidays, etc. However, pensions are excluded (*see* below).

There has been difficulty about profit-related pay. This clearly relates to the transferor's circumstances and there could be difficulties about transferring such a scheme to the transferee. A tribunal found, in one case, that profit-related pay was a central part of the contracts of a group of transferred employees and that the money due from the transferor employer was due and should be paid by the new (transferee) employer. However, it was stated that this would not apply in future years, nor would the transferee be required to introduce an equivalent scheme (*Westbrook and Others* v *Building and Property Limited and Others*, COIT, 2300437/98).

This regulation, of course, covers a transferee's potential liability for a range of employment issues. A transferee may be liable for any personal injury claim or employment tribunal applications that are still in process. Cases that have been reported include liability for a transferred sex discrimination claim (*DJM International* v *Nicholas* [1986] IRLR 76); and liability for an accident at work (*Bernadone* v *Pall Mall Services Group and another* [1999] IRLR 617). Protection against such actions can be arranged through an indemnity scheme. Under the 1998 Directive, member states can require transferors to notify transferees of all the rights and obligations that will pass to them when the relevant transfer takes place (provided that they are known to the transferor).

Occupational pensions

Excluded from contractual protection is the preservation of an employee's rights under an occupational pension scheme (reg 7). This has been described as 'a gaping hole in the legislation – at European and national level' (Cavalier, 1997: 35). The Court of Appeal has ruled that while pension rights do not transfer, there is a duty to protect accrued pension rights that exist at the time of the transfer. The 1998 Directive gives discretion for member states to provide protection for future pension rights.

In the public sector, the government has given guidance that a private-sector transferee (i.e. a private-sector company to which existing public-service employees are transferred) offer a scheme that is 'broadly comparable' to that previously enjoyed by these employees. Whether or not this criterion is met in any particular case can be assessed in accordance with criteria from the government's Actuary's Department. Under current law, in respect of pensions, 'private sector employees, unlike public sector employees, may still in practice find themselves in a significantly worse position after a transfer than they were before it' (DTI 2001b: para 14). The government says that this 'uncertain legal position is unsatisfactory'. It aims at 'legal certainty' when the 1998 Directive is implemented (DTI 2001a: para 15).

Employee's right to refuse transfer

It is possible for an employee to decline transfer and terminate their own contract of employment (reg 5(4A), (4B)). The effect is that the transfer shall terminate the contract of employment but the employee 'shall not be treated for any purpose as having been dismissed by the transferor'. As a consequence, the employee is not entitled to any statutory or contractual right which would normally arise on a dismissal.

Variation of contracts

There are three principal legal issues here: the question of whether or not the changes relate to the transfer; protection against the worsening of conditions of employment; and the general case law relating to contract variation.

Changes relating to the transfer: The 1977 Directive and the Regulations do not set a period of time after which an employer might seek to vary contracts of employment. This leaves open to argument the issue of what is 'the transfer period'. The Court of Appeal has provided some guidance on the relationship of the changes to the transfer. In *Wilson* (1997) and *Meade* (1997), it drew an important distinction. In the first case, it was the survival of the transferee and not solely the transfer that resulted in the agreed contractual changes and this was therefore acceptable. In the second case, the transfer was the sole reason for the variation and, therefore, the change was ineffective. The House of Lords (*Wilson v St Helens Borough Council* [1998] IRLR 706) upheld the Court of Appeal decision on these cases.

In the House of Lords ruling on *Wilson* and *Meade* (1998), it was commented by Lord Slynn that 'it seems that there must, or at least may, come a time when the link with the transfer is broken or can be treated as no longer effective . . . If the transferee cannot safely agree terms to bring his new employees into line with existing employees' standard terms and conditions, that will discourage employers from taking over new businesses or lead to the transferee dismissing transferred employees'. The government has signalled its proposal to change the law. It 'proposes to improve the operation of the Regulations by making clear that they do not preclude transfer-related changes to terms and conditions that are made for an ETO reason – that is, an "economic, technical or organisational reason entailing changes in the workforce"' (2001b: para 25).

To date, there has been no resolution of how long the transfer period is. For example, in a dismissal case (*Taylor v Connex South Eastern Ltd*, EAT 1243/99), the EAT held that the dismissal of an employee who refused to accept his employer's standard terms and conditions two years after the transfer had taken place was automatically unfair. This was on the basis that the protection, conferred by regulation 8, still applied as the changes were made in connection with the transfer.

Protection against the unilateral worsening of conditions of employment: This protection is provided for in reg 5(5). This describes the right of an employee 'to terminate his contract of employment without notice if a substantial change is made in his working conditions to his detriment'. This relates to the body of law referred to earlier in this chapter where unilateral variation can constitute a repudiatory breach of a contract of employment, which can result in the employee resigning and claiming constructive dismissal. The employee may take action short of resignation for the unlawful variation of terms and conditions. This can include remaining in employment and, as appropriate, claiming unlawful deduction of wages (ERA, Part II), or a claim for breach of contract in the County Court.

Constructive dismissal

Regulation 5(5) refers to the 'right of an employee . . . to terminate his contract of employment without notice if a substantial change is made in his working conditions'. This could form the basis of a constructive dismissal claim to an employment tribunal. Such a claim involves a repudiatory breach of contract by the employer; resignation by the employee (because they accept the repudiation); and, subject to one year's qualifying service, a claim for constructive dismissal (ERA 1996, s 95(1)(c); and *Western Excavating Ltd* v *Sharp* [1978] IRLR 27). The Court of Appeal (in *Rossiter* v *Pendragon* [2002] CA) reaffirmed these requirements. In transfer cases, an employee must show that a substantial and detrimental change in working conditions constitutes a repudiatory breach of contract.

Dismissal

Protection against dismissal in a transfer situation is available to any employees of the transferor or the transferee. However, the right to make a claim before an employment tribunal is restricted to those with one year's continuous service. 'Where either before or after a relevant transfer, any employee or the transferor or transferee is dismissed, that employee shall be treated . . . as unfairly dismissed if the transfer or a reason connected with it is the reason or principal reason for his dismissal' (reg 8(1)).

Automatically unfair dismissal: If an employee is dismissed in breach of the 1977 Directive (Art 4(1)), he must be considered still to be employed by the undertaking at the date of the transfer (*Bork (P) International A/S* v *Foreningen af Arbejdsledere i Danmark* [1989] IRLR 41, ECJ). To give effect to this under the Transfer of Undertakings Regulations, the House of Lords implied into the Regulations that where a person has been dismissed for an automatically fair reason relating to the transfer, then, that person continues to have protection as if they were an employee (*Litster and others* v *Forth Dry Dock and Engineering Company Ltd and another* [1989] IRLR 161). Protection against automatically unfair dismissal connected with a transfer can extend over a considerable period of time (see the *Taylor* v *Connex South Eastern Ltd* (1999) case mentioned earlier).

ETO reasons for dismissal: The only exemption from this unfair dismissal protection is 'where any economic, technical or organisational reason entailing changes in the workforce of the transferor or transferee before or after a relevant transfer is the reason or principal reason for dismissing an employee' (reg 8(2)). (*See* Fig. 3.1.) From case law, it is clear that attempts to cut pay and other labour costs to obtain a better price for the business are not admissible reasons. In *Wheeler* v *Patel and J. Golding Group of Companies* [1987] IRLR 211, it was ruled that economic reasons were to be given a narrow interpretation. They should not relate to attempts to achieve a better price or achieve a sale. In the *Wilson* (1998) case, a school was unable to remain open without a radical reorganisation which would reduce its running costs.

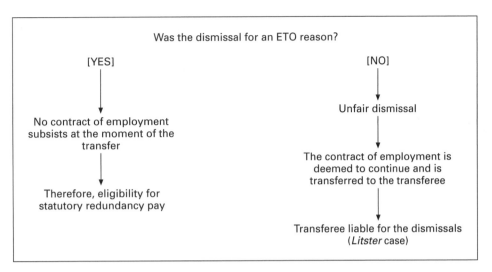

Figure 3.1 Dismissals 'immediately before' a transfer

The critical phrase 'entailing changes in the workforce' is linked closely with the ETO reason for dismissal. It is likely that this would cover a change in the numbers employed arising from changed business needs. It may well be that the employee is entitled to redundancy compensation for an ETO dismissal.

The EAT, in *Thompson* v *SCS Consulting Ltd and others* [2001] IRLR 801, outlined the steps to be taken:

- In deciding whether an ETO reason was or was not the reason or principal reason for the dismissal, the tribunal is making a factual decision.
- In making that factual decision, the tribunal must consider whether the reason was connected with the future conduct of the business as a going concern.
- The tribunal is entitled to take into account as relevant factual material whether there was any collusion between the transferor and transferee and whether the transferor, or those acting on its behalf, had any funds to carry on the business or any business, at the time of the decision to dismiss.
- An appellate tribunal should only interfere with such a factual decision if the (employment) tribunal erred in law by applying the wrong test, by considering an irrelevant factor, by failing to consider a relevant factor or by reaching a perverse decision.

In the *Thompson* (2001) case, involving the insolvency of a business that was to be sold by the receivers, the EAT ruled a dismissal to be fair for an ETO reason. The fact that the transferee imposed a precondition upon the sale agreement that led to the dismissal of Mr Thompson and 24 other employees did not undermine the view that the dismissal was for an ETO reason. The employment tribunal's fact-finding showed that the business could only be viable for the future and continue as a going concern if the workforce was reduced in size. Indeed, all of the employees would inevitably have been dismissed if this arrangement had not been reached with the transferee.

Collective agreements

Collective agreements can make an important contribution to the formulation of terms and conditions of employment. Provisions in collective agreements can be incorporated into contracts of employment and so be legally enforceable in respect of that individual employee (*see* Chapter 2). Regulation 6 recognises the importance of these agreements as an instrument of employment regulation. The transferee takes over those collective agreements negotiated with the transferor and in force immediately before the transfer.

In a recent case involving local authority staff transferred to a private contractor (*Whent* v *T. Cartledge* [1997] IRLR 153), the EAT ruled on the right to a pay increase (in line with local authority national conditions) as a contractual entitlement. It was a term of the employees' contracts of employment that their conditions of employment were set through the National Joint Council for local authority manual workers. On transfer, the private contractors were bound by the existing terms and also any future nationally agreed terms. 'This protection of the right to future pay increases only applies where the collective agreement providing for those rises is incorporated into the individual employee's contract and where the collective agreement (or other machinery) establishes an entitlement to receive a pay increase, not merely a discretion for the employer to follow or implement an award' (Cavalier, 1997: 30).

The issue of change in respect of collective agreements might arise in a number of ways. The first issue is at what stage an employer might terminate a collective agreement. Collective agreements usually include a termination clause – providing for notice of between three and twelve months to be given. Whether this is outside the 'transfer period' would be a matter for a tribunal to determine on the facts. The second issue concerns the continuity of the contractual terms deriving from the 'old' collective agreement. The means of changing these was discussed above.

Trade union recognition

Regulation 9 deals with the related issue of trade union recognition agreements.

> Where before . . . a transfer an independent trade union is recognised to any extent by the transferor in respect of employees of any description who in consequence of the transfer become employees of the transferee, then, after the transfer, (a) the union shall be deemed to have been recognised by the transferee to the same extent in respect of employees of that description so employed; and (b) any agreement for recognition may be varied or rescinded accordingly.

If an undertaking (where an independent trade union is recognised) is transferred and it retains a distinct identity, then, the union can expect the transferee to continue to recognise it in respect of the transferred employees and to the same extent that it was recognised by the previous employer (i.e. the same issues being negotiated about). However, if the undertaking does not retain its identity, then, the matter of recognition is a matter for the transferee and the union, subject to the law on statutory recognition for collective bargaining (TULRCA 1992, s 70A) (*see* Chapter 14).

| Exercise 3.2 | **Some problems of managing transfers of undertakings** |

Read these scenarios and decide on the following:

- *What legal issues do you think might be involved?*
- *What do you recommend that the employer do both in law and in practice?*

1 A hospital trust is transferring its security staff to the security division of a large American-owned multinational. The transferee is not keen on employing a number of long-serving security guards. It suggests that they be made redundant by the trust before the transfer.

2 A non-union catering company, has successfully bid for the contract to provide catering facilities at Somerset University. The existing terms and conditions of the staff to be transferred have been negotiated with UNISON. The collective agreements have been incorporated into the individual employees' contracts of employment. The managing director tells the personnel director that he wants to preserve a union-free company.

3 A facilities management company has acquired a contract cleaning company. The managing director tells the personnel manager that he wants there to be a common pay structure for existing and recently acquired cleaning staff. In addition, the work rotas and holiday arrangements must be harmonised.

4 Some weeks after the transfer the facilities management company receives a copy of an employment tribunal application (concerning an allegation of race discrimination). The discrimination is said to have occurred several months before the transfer of the staff from the contract cleaning company.

5 A company which manages parks and gardens is to acquire staff who work in a large privately owned garden attached to a country house. Some of the staff are permanent employees, some are on seasonal contracts and some are called 'self-employed' (although they work for most of the year at the park). The personnel director of the transferee questions whether these 'self-employed' staff should be transferred.

Feedback on this exercise is provided in the Appendix to this book.

3.4.4   Redundancy and redeployment

There are several key aspects of the law on redundancy that we will consider: the definition, criteria for selection, the use of alternative employment strategies, consultation about redundancies, fair dismissal provisions, the right to time off work and the availability of redundancy pay.

Definition

A person is dismissed for reason of redundancy if the dismissal is 'wholly or mainly attributable', first of all, to 'the fact that his employer has ceased or intends to cease (i) to carry on the business for the purposes of which the employee was employed by him, or (ii) to carry on that business in the place where the employee was employed' (ERA 1996, s 139(1)(a)).

Secondly, and alternatively, the reason for the dismissal is 'wholly or mainly attributable' to 'the fact that the requirements of that business (i) for employees to carry out work of a particular kind or (ii) for employees to carry out work of a particular kind in the place where the employee was employed by the employer, have ceased or diminished or are expected to cease or diminish' (s 139(1)(b)).

Two significant issues have arisen from the interpretation of these provisions. First, the words 'cease' or 'diminish' mean 'either permanently or temporarily and for whatever reason' (s 139(6)). A second issue involves 'place of work' and the use of mobility clauses. For most employees, 'place of work' is clear-cut. It is usually one permanent location. Where this is not so, difficulties can arise in determining the application of redundancy law. Two approaches have been adopted by courts and tribunals over the past 30 years: the factual test and the contractual test. These have invariably come into conflict.

The factual test requires investigation into where the employee actually works (irrespective of the provisions of the mobility clause). The contractual test gives weight to the details of the mobility clause and its stipulations that the employee might work at any location designated by the employer. Such a provision can obstruct an employee's redundancy claim because an employer can argue that if work ceases at one location, then the employee is contractually obliged to work elsewhere. Increasingly, courts and tribunals have recognised that employment reality is not as straightforward as that may suggest. In 1994, the EAT questioned the contractual test (*Bass Leisure* v *Thomas* [1994] IRLR 104), asserting that the statute (s 139) defined *one* place of work. In a subsequent case, the Court of Appeal ruled that if an employee genuinely moves around in his/her employment (in a case involving silver-service waitresses) then the mobility clause can assist in defining the extent of 'the place of work' (*High Table Ltd* v *Horst and Others* [1997] IRLR 513). Essentially, a blend of the tests is resulting. There must be an investigation of the facts (what actually happens) and part of this inquiry will take into account the contractual terms.

Thirdly, 'bumping' dismissals have been ruled as not falling within the statutory definition of redundancy. (These involve circumstances where an employee is dismissed in order to make way for another employee whose job is redundant.) The EAT stated that the proper meaning of 'work of a particular kind' (s 139(1)(b)) is 'work of a particular kind which the relevant employee was required to do' (*Church* v *West Lancashire NHS Trust* [1998] IRLR 4).

Selection criteria

In selecting employees for redundancy, an employer must have fair and objective criteria against which an individual's selection can be defended. The selection criteria must be disclosed to employee representatives (TULRCA 1992, s 188(4)(d)). The EAT has ruled that reasonable employers should use criteria 'which as far as possible do not depend solely upon the opinion of the person making the selection, but can be objectively checked against such things as attendance record, efficiency at the job, experience or length of service' (*Williams* v *Compair Maxam Ltd* [1982] IRLR 83). There is no statutory obligation to follow customary arrangements such as LIFO.

Clearly, there are three dangers that an employer should be aware of: the likelihood of detrimental treatment against a specific employee; direct discriminaton; and the possibility of indirect discrimination. Selection for redundancy can be challenged if it is seen to victimise or discriminate against an individual on various grounds (e.g. infringing sex, race, disability, pregnancy, trade union membership, and specific health and safety rights) (*see* later relevant chapters). In addition, it should not be used against an employee who is asserting certain statutory employment rights (ERA 1996, s 104).

The issue of direct discrimination is relatively clear-cut. It is unlawful to select employees for redundancy on grounds of sex, marital status or race under the Sex Discrimination Act 1975 and the Race Relations Act 1976. Furthermore, it is unlawful unjustifiably to select an employee for redundancy on grounds of 'disability' under the Disability Discrimination Act 1995.

Indirect discrimination relates to a condition or requirement which, although apparently neutral, can be discriminatory in effect (*see* Chapters 4 and 5). One notable example from case law concerns a decision to select part-timers first in a redundancy programme. All part-timers in the company were female. The EAT stated that this criterion had a disproportionate and adverse impact on women in the workforce and could not be justified objectively (*Clarke* v *Eley (IMI) Kynoch Ltd* [1982] IRLR 482). In *Whiffen* v *Milham Ford Girls School and another* [2001] IRLR 468, the Court of Appeal held that the selection of fixed-term employees first in a redundancy situation – irrespective of their aggregate length of service – was indirect sex discrimination.

In this case, it was also said that LIFO might be discriminatory because 'by reason of childbearing and other domestic commitments, fewer women than men might have long service'. It would be a matter for each tribunal to determine, on the facts, whether or not the use of LIFO is justifiable and non-discriminatory under discrimination law.

Alternative employment

There are various alternatives to redundancy (which are explored in more detail below in section 3.5: Employment policies and practices). One of these is the offer by the employer of alternative employment or re-engagement.

Where an employee is offered and accepts re-engagement on the same terms as previous employment, that person is not regarded as dismissed and there is no entitlement to redundancy pay.

If the terms offered by the employer (or an associated employer) are different from those in the previous contract, then a trial period of four consecutive weeks can be invoked (ERA, s 138(3)) when the old contract has ended. It is possible to extend a trial period for the purposes of retraining. This must be in the form of a written agreement between the employer and the employee (or their representative) (s 138(6)). This offer must be made before the previous employment ends, and the take-up of the new offer must be within four weeks of the end of the previous employment.

During the trial period, the employee may resign and be treated as dismissed (by the employer for redundancy under the old contract). If, however, the employee unreasonably refuses an offer of suitable alternative employment or unreasonably terminates the contract during the trial period, their entitlement to statutory redundancy pay is lost. Employment that could be considered as unsuitable would be that involving adverse changes in pay, changes in skill requirements, loss of status and requirements for travelling time.

Time off work

An employee who is under notice of dismissal because of redundancy (and who has two years' continuous service on the date on which the notice is due to expire) 'is entitled to be permitted by his employer to take reasonable time off during the employee's working hours before the end of his notice in order to (a) look for new employment, or (b) make arrangements for training for future employment' (ERA 1996, s 52(1)). If an employer unreasonably refuses and the employee is successful at tribunal, the maximum award payable is two-fifths of a week's pay for that employee.

Consultation

There are three aspects to redundancy consultation considered here: the duties upon an employer to consult trade unions and, in non-union organisations, employee representatives in relation to collective redundancies; and the situation relating to individual employees.

The nature of consultation is not explicitly outlined in the legislation. However, from case law, it is possible to discern the standards that might be adopted in considering complaints. In one case involving redundancies in the coal-mining industry, Glidewell LJ stated that 'fair consultation involves giving the body consulted a fair and proper opportunity to understand fully the matters about which it is being consulted and to express its view on those subjects, with the consultor thereafter considering those views properly and genuinely' (*R v British Coal Corporation and Secretary of State for Trade and Industry ex parte Price* [1994] IRLR 72). This guidance is relevant for consultation on both collective redundancies and individual cases.

As far as **collective redundancies** are concerned it is stated that 'where an employer is proposing to dismiss as redundant twenty or more employees at one establishment within a period of ninety days or less, the employer shall consult about the dismissals all the persons who are appropriate representatives of any of the employees who may be so dismissed' (TULRCA 1992, s 188(1)). This consultation 'shall begin in good time' (s 188(1A)). Where the employer is proposing to dismiss 100 or more, there should be at least 90 days' consultation; where between 20 and 99 employees are involved, the period should be at least 30 days. Such consultation should be 'undertaken by the employer with a view to reaching agreement with the appropriate representatives' (s 188(2)).

The purpose of the consultation should be to include discussion on avoiding the dismissals, reducing the numbers of employees to be dismissed and mitigating the consequences of the dismissals. Clearly, this is a signal to consider both a range of alternatives to redundancy and the consequences for individual members of staff. (The policies that employers might adopt are considered in more detail in section 3.5: Employment policies and practices.)

An obvious preliminary to genuine consultation is the disclosure of relevant information. The legislation requires that 'the employer shall disclose in writing to the [appropriate] representatives' (s 188(4)) the following:

- the reasons for his proposals;
- the numbers and descriptions of the employees whom it is proposed to dismiss;
- the total number of employees of any such description employed by the employer at the establishment in question;
- the proposed method of selecting the employees who may be dismissed;
- the proposed method of carrying out the dismissals 'with due regard to any agreed procedure including the period over which the dismissals are to take effect' (s 188(4)(e));

- the proposed method of calculating the amount of any redundancy payment which is in excess of the statutory scheme.

The employer is obliged to allow representatives access to relevant employees and also such accommodation and other facilities as may be appropriate.

The statutory duty to consult has been subject to amendment in recent years – to comply with the European Collective Redundancies Directive 1992 and the ECJ ruling (*EC Commission* v *UK* [1994] IRLR 392, 412) that consultation must be with representatives of employees rather than being restricted to trade union representatives (as had been the case in Britain since 1975). The Collective Redundancies and Transfer of Undertakings (Protection of Employment) (Amendment) Regulations 1995 widened the scope of representation to include non-union organisations; and the Collective Redundancies and Transfer of Undertakings (Protection of Employment) (Amendment) Regulations 1999 introduced further amendments. The Trade Union and Labour Relations Consolidation Act 1992 has been amended accordingly (for more detail *see* Chapter 14 on employee participation).

If an employer fails to consult, according to the statutory requirements, the employees are entitled to a protective award (TULRCA 1992, s 189). This will be an award of pay for the protective period which the tribunal considers just and equitable having regard to the seriousness of the employer's default (s 189(4)(b)). Detailed provisions are set out in ss 190–1. 'Special circumstances' for not consulting are permitted. However, this term is not defined. The employer must, nevertheless, 'take all such steps as are reasonably practicable in those circumstances' (s 188(7)).

The EAT, in *Middlesbrough Borough Council* v *Transport and General Workers' Union and another* (EAT 26/00) found that consultation in 1998 over avoiding redundancies was 'a sham'. It was not 'genuine consultation'.

The issue of **individual consultation rights** arises under the law on unfair dismissal (*see* Chapter 9). A person who is to be made redundant might allege before an employment tribunal that they have been unfairly dismissed. The reason for the dismissal (i.e. redundancy) is a fair reason. But the tribunal would need to consider whether the employer behaved 'reasonably' and whether the termination of employment had been conducted in a procedurally fair manner. Evidence of individual consultation would go a long way to establishing procedural fairness. This is of particular significance where there is no statutory duty to consult about collective redundancies. But it is still important in the context of these – an individual might have specific issues that they might wish to raise and discuss. In a leading case, the House of Lords asserted the importance of such consultation (*Polkey* v *AE Dayton Services Ltd* [1987] IRLR 503). A grievance about an individual grievance is covered by the minimum grievance procedure implied into contracts of employment under the Employment Act 2002.

Termination of employment

If an employee is sacked as part of a redundancy programme, then the law relating to unfair dismissal sets out the appropriate provisions (Employment Rights Act 1996, ss 94, 95, 98). There are three broad elements in the framework (*see also* Chapter 9) which have to be tested by an employment tribunal: the reason for the dismissal, the reasonableness of the dismissal decision, and procedural fairness.

The reason for the dismissal

Redundancy is a 'fair' reason; however, the tribunal would need to satisfy itself that no other reason was involved that was an unfair reason for dismissal and there was genuine redundancy.

The reasonableness of the decision to dismiss

The broad guidance on this is set out in ERA, s 94(4). This states that:

> the determination of the question whether the dismissal is fair or unfair (having regard to the reason shown by the employer) –
> (a) depends on whether in the circumstances (including the size and administrative resources of the employer's undertaking) the employer acted reasonably or unreasonably in treating it as a sufficient reason for dismissing the employee, and
> (b) shall be determined in accordance with equity and the substantial merits of the case.

In redundancy cases, reasonableness is considered principally in respect of three issues: whether there was a fair selection, whether there was proper consultation and whether alternatives to redundancy were considered.

Procedural fairness

Procedural issues concern how individuals are selected for redundancy, how any collective consultation takes place and how representations by individuals are dealt with. If an agreed procedure (for example, negotiated with union or employee representatives) is in place or there is a customary practice, then employers are advised to comply with them. If there is no established agreed procedure, then, procedural arrangements should be discussed with employee or union representatives. Where there are fewer than 20 redundancies, there should be individual consultation.

Pay

The right to redundancy payment is set out as follows: 'An employer shall pay a redundancy payment to any employee of his if the employee (a) is dismissed by the employer by reason of redundancy or (b) is eligible for a redundancy payment by reason of being laid off or kept on short-time' (ERA 1996, s 135(1)). Under European equal treatment law, it has been ruled by the ECJ that 'pay' (under Art 141 of the Treaty of Amsterdam) includes redundancy pay. Consequently, redundancy benefits must be provided to men and women on the same terms. This includes eligibility for redundancy payments, the calculation of payments and age limits on entitlements.

Exclusions to the right to redundancy payment arise in various circumstances. The first is where the employee is dismissed for gross misconduct during the obligatory notice period. Secondly, where an employee unreasonably refuses an offer of suitable alternative employment. Thirdly, when the employee is taking part in a strike (but not other forms of industrial action) before the employee is under the redundancy notice to terminate employment. Finally, redundancy payment is reduced by one-twelfth for each whole month in which the employee is over the age of 64 years.

The statutory redundancy payment scheme is calculated by taking account of the employee's age and length of service. The number of 'weeks' pay' will depend on the employee's age at the time of the redundancy. Employment before the age of 18 is not included (ERA 1996, s 162). Calculations are made as follows:

- one and a half week's pay for each year of service in which the employee was over the age of 41 years but below the normal retirement age or 65 (whichever is the lower);
- one week's pay for each year of service in which the employee was over 22 years of age and under 41 years; and
- half a week's pay for each year of service between the ages of 18 and 22 years.

In calculating the statutory entitlement, a week's pay cannot be more than £260. (This maximum was set in February 2003 and is periodically revised.) The maximum number of years of service that can be taken into account is 20. Redundancy pay (both statutory and contractual) is tax free up to a specified limit which varies from time to time.

Special provisions apply in respect of redundancy payments due from an insolvent employer. Payment may be claimed from the Department of Trade and Industry.

Exercise 3.3 **Some problems in managing redundancies**

Read these scenarios and decide on the following:

- *What legal issues do you think might be involved?*
- *What do you recommend that the employer do both in law and in practice?*

1 A small print shop, because of technological change, decided to make two print operators redundant. The owner/manager is planning to give them their notice in a letter.

2 Catherine Morgan is a personnel officer in a medium-sized non-union insurance company. Because of a business reorganisation, her employer wants to make one person redundant in the central administration department. Catherine tells the general manager that she has heard 'on the grapevine' that Michaela Johnson is pregnant and she suggests that she be dismissed. She is a moderate performer, whereas some of the staff with shorter service records are better at their jobs. Despite the fact that the company had used the 'last in first out' criterion to select people for redundancies in the recent past, the general manager agrees with Catherine's suggestion.

3 Because of a fall in sales, a medium-sized regional grocery chain are proposing redundancies. The managing director suggests that staff employed on temporary contracts should be dismissed. The personnel manager asks to discuss the proposal with him.

4 Because of technological change and reorganisation in a further education college's administration department, Trisha Wilson has been told that her post as course administrator will no longer exist. The college is proposing to dismiss two administrators as redundant. To date, Trisha has worked for a course leader and has had a reasonable amount of autonomy in the day-to-day organisation of her work. Now, she has been offered a new position as a member of the 'course support team'. This will involve carrying out a wider range of administrative and secretarial functions together with two other members of staff. It means greater functional flexibility. She, along with the other administrators, will have contact with course leaders – but it will be a pool of five rather than one. Her monthly pay and hours will remain the same, but she will be expected to schedule her working hours differently to provide greater cover. This will involve occasional work until 7 pm.

Feedback on this exercise is provided in the Appendix to this book.

3.5 Employment policies and practices

Although this section considers three discrete areas, in reality all three may interlock as change is implemented in employing organisations. When dealing with any of these areas, employers need to consider the following:

- decide to approach change *strategically*;
- define clearly the *business objectives* to be achieved;
- understand thoroughly the *human resource/employee relations implications* of change;
- recognise *the coping cycle* through which employees might go when confronted with change;
- appreciate and comply with the *legal standards and requirements* to be met;
- acknowledge the value of *consultation* and (if appropriate) collective bargaining to help manage change.

3.5.1 Variation

Best practice on contract variation is largely drawn from case law. The recommended approach comprises a number of steps:

1 Consider whether the change affects a term of the contract or might relate to lawful and reasonable instructions.
2 Give information about the proposed change to each affected individual employee.
3 Be prepared to discuss, consult and/or – if unionised – negotiate.
4 Try to obtain the employee's consent. This might involve making some concessions or offering *consideration*.
5 Be prepared to justify contractual changes against the organisation's operational requirements and business needs.
6 Anticipate the arguments that might be put at a court or tribunal – for example, in terms of the scale of the change and the issue of reasonableness.

3.5.2 Transfers

Practical steps to managing transfers include the following. Whilst initially, the steps to be taken will be more significant for the transferor organisation, there are consequences for the transferee (the employer that will receive the staff).

Identifying the staff to be transferred

The size of the group of staff is irrelevant. Even the transfer of one member of staff is covered by the TUPE Regulations. However, given the fluidity of the law (arising from ECJ decisions), an early decision on the applicability of the Regulations is advisable (particularly if second-generation contracting is involved).

Information gathering and dissemination

The Regulations (reg 10(2)) require a transferor employer to inform employee representatives on a range of matters. These include the timing of the transfer; the reasons for it; the 'legal, economic and social implications' of the transfer for the staff; whether various 'measures' will be taken in respect of the staff by either the transferor or the transferee employer. The measures could include business reorganisation, technical change and the possibility of redundancies. The information to be acquired should also include data on terms and conditions of employment for the affected employees. It may be that collective agreements are in force for these staff. Those agreements that will be transferred should be identified.

Consultation arrangements

Employers are under a statutory duty to consult employee representatives 'with a view to seeking their agreement' (reg 10(5)). Those which recognise trade unions for collective bargaining will, no doubt, involve these unions in the necessary consultation. Other employers must create alternative consultation arrangements (*see* Chapter 14).

Employee relations decisions

Various employee relations issues should be discussed between the two employing organisations. For example, although pensions are explicitly excluded under the Regulations (reg 7), some consideration might be given to alternative provision. There may be proposals to dismiss some staff where there is 'an economic, technical or organisational reason entailing changes in the workforce of either the transferor or the transferee' (reg 8). Also, both organisations should identify potential liability for employment complaints, e.g. employment tribunal applications, personal injury claims (reg 5).

Contract variations and harmonisation

The transferee employer may wish to plan for these outside 'the transfer period'. Such measures could involve the reconciliation of terms and conditions of employment between existing and acquired staff.

3.5.3 Managing redundancies

The CIPD Code of Practice on Redundancy identifies a number of key practical issues that employers need to take into consideration: the important context of human resource planning, consideration of alternatives to redundancy, the management of redundancies and the consequences for individual employees. We will look at each of these in turn.

The CIPD's view is that the development of **human resource planning** has advantages in helping secure 'the commitment of employees towards achieving their commercial objectives'. It helps focus on skill mix and the appropriate size of the workforce and helps consider relevant longer-term training, retraining and development issues. 'it will help to reduce the likelihood of compulsory redundancy by equipping employees with the necessary skills to meet the organisation's future requirements'.

The context of HRP may assist in decisions on how labour reductions are to be achieved and which alternatives to redundancy might be utilised. The Code states that 'as far as is consistent with operational efficiency and the competitiveness of the organisation, managers should seek to avoid declaring compulsory redundancies if possible by considering' various options. It is, however, acknowledged that some of these may also have disadvantages. The options suggested are:

- restrictions on recruitment of permanent staff;
- leaving vacancies unfilled permitting a gradual decrease in numbers by 'natural wastage';
- the termination, where practical, of the employment of temporary or contract staff, taking care to avoid sex or race discrimination;
- short-time working to cover temporary fluctuations in labour requirements;
- retraining and redeployment, where appropriate, of existing staff into internal vacancies which arise or are expected to arise;
- retirement of employees who are beyond the normal retirement age (provided, of course, that a non-discriminatory normal retirement age has been established);
- seeking applicants for early retirement or voluntary redundancy amongst existing staff before declaring compulsory redundancy.

As far as **the management of redundancies** is concerned, there are two related aspects: procedural issues and substantive issues. The *procedural issues* concern both collective and individual matters. They cover information disclosure, consultation and collective bargaining (*see* the statutory requirements outlined earlier). In anticipation of redundancies an organisation might negotiate a redundancy agreement with a trade union. The CIPD Code states that 'for managers, it provides a jointly agreed procedure for implementing redundancies and reduces the potential for conflict when they are declared', and 'for trade unions, it provides an opportunity to influence management policy'.

The *substantive issues* concerned in the management of redundancies relate to matters of pay, benefits and other contractual terms. As indicated earlier, the law provides statutory minimum redundancy pay. This may be enhanced by employers in respect of individual employees. Some examples of employer policies were reported an IRS survey (June/July 1998). Eighty-three per cent of the respondents (primarily large organisations) made payments in excess of the legal minimum. This can be achieved by exceeding the weekly pay maximum or that which sets a 20-year limit. It was reported that three-fifths of surveyed organisations took account of allowances when calculating entitlements: 'for example the Automobile Association includes London weighting, as well as shift and standby payments where they are major terms of employment'. In various other organisations such remuneration as holiday bonuses, season tickets, company cars, healthcare allowances and luncheon vouchers were included. Only 34 per cent of organisations took account of performance-related pay.

There was a two-year qualifying period for access to statutory redundancy pay. However, the IRS survey found that this was used by 46 per cent of the organisations; 26 per cent had no qualifying period, and 22 per cent set it at one year.

The **consequences for individual employees** of redundancy can be substantial. It is 'always a stressful personal experience which, although the employee may not recognise it, often requires support and guidance' (CIPD Code). Good employers would provide time off to look for work and/or make arrangements for training (irrespective of the statutory qualifying period). Also, they would provide practical assistance in finding alternative employment through contacts with other companies and organisations. Finally, 'subject to affordability, whenever possible employers should consider offering redundancy counselling either on a one-to-one or group basis' (CIPD Code). This may be undertaken through an external special agency.

Case study 3.1

The organisation

The college, which has charitable status, is a long-established private residential cookery, fashion and design teaching institution. It has a maximum capacity of 120 female students. There are 30 full and part-time employees consisting of lecturers, administrators, house and domestic staff. The eight full-time teaching staff include three senior staff: one designated director of studies and two heads of department. Although the senior staff had administrative and course organisation responsibilities, some three-quarters of their workload involved teaching. The heads of department, Penny Stimson and Ursula Dalton, were, respectively, specialists in cookery and fashion. Penny, was the longest serving member of the teaching staff (with 15 years' service), and Ursula had eight years' service.

The issue

Immediately prior to the commencement of the new teaching year, a staff meeting was called on Monday, 6 September. At this the chair of the Board of Governors announced that, following recommendations from the principal, the college must radically restructure its courses to meet changing circumstances. The restructuring would mean staff redundancies. There had been a drastic reduction in enrolments and the accountant's advice was that staff costs must be reduced. At the end of the meeting, a number of staff, including the three senior staff, were handed redundancy notices terminating their employment at the end of the autumn term on Friday, 3 December. These notices were dated Friday, 3 September – before the staff meeting had been held.

Throughout the autumn term the two heads of department tried unsuccessfully to negotiate a withdrawal of the redundancy notices. Failing that, they were seeking a satisfactory compensation sum. In late October, it was announced that the college would be closing in July, at the end of the teaching year. This was quickly followed, in early November, by a further announcement that the college was going to be 'saved' by a takeover which would be effective from Monday, 6 December. In fact, there was to be a merger with the neighbouring college. There was to be a review of the courses offered and a reorganisation and rationalisation of the structures of both colleges. It was made quite clear, however, that the contracts of existing staff who had been designated as redundant would still be terminated on Friday, 3 December.

In the absence of reinstatement or of a satisfactory compensation settlement, the two heads of department filed complaints to the employment tribunal alleging unfair dismissal.

The tribunal application and response

The **applications** from the two heads of department cited the following complaints about their dismissal:

- there was no actual redundancy because the applicants' teaching timetables continued to exist after their dismissals as did their administrative responsibilities;
- even if redundancy was found to exist, the dismissals were unfair because:
  - there was no prior warning of the impending redundancies nor any opportunity of consultation before the redundancy notices were served;
  - the selection process and criteria were unfair;
  - the sequence of events surrounding the dismissals pointed to the possibility that attempts were being made to reduce staffing levels prior to a takeover, which is automatically unfair under the Transfer of Undertakings (Protection of Employment) Regulations.

(More detailed supportive evidence was provided by the applicants.)

The **response from the employer**, resisting the application, made the following main points:

- the college had been advised in mid-August by its accountants that the financial situation was such that it should close immediately;
- on 24 August the Board of Governors made a number of decisions including:
  - a restructuring of staff, which would mean that there would no longer be heads of department; and
  - those teachers to be retained would have cross-curricular expertise;
- because the applicants were entitled to a full term's notice, there was no opportunity for any consultation prior to the issuing of the redundancy notices;
- the college had set out criteria for termination of employment in accordance with its needs and these were adhered to;
- there was no substance in the suggestion made with regard to reducing staffing in preparation for a takeover.

(The respondent also provided further particulars in support of the above arguments.)

Exercise 3.4

1 What further factual information, if any, do you think the tribunal would require in order to reach a decision?

2 What are the key legal issues arising in this case? What are their sources in statute and case law?

3 On the information provided, what do you think the tribunal's decision is most likely to be in relation to the allegation of unfair dismissal?

Feedback on this exercise is provided in the Appendix to this book.

Further reading

Chartered Institute of Personnel and Development (1995) *Code of Practice on Redundancy*. London: CIPD.

References

Carnall, C. (1990) *Managing Change in the Organisation*. London: Prentice Hall.

Cavalier, S. (1997) *Transfer Rights: TUPE in Perspective*. London: Institute of Employment Rights.

Central Statistical Office (1997) *Social Trends 27*. London: Stationery Office.

Chartered Institute of Personnel and Development (1995) *Code of Practice on Redundancy*. London: CIPD.

Cully, M. *et al.* (1998) *The 1998 Workplace Employee Relations Survey: First Findings*. London: DTI.

Cully, M. *et al.* (1999) *Britain at Work*. London: Routledge.

Deakin, S. and Morris, G. (1998) *Labour Law*. London: Butterworths.

Department of Trade and Industry (1998) 'Fairness at Work', Cm. 3968. London: Stationery Office.

Department of Trade and Industry (2001a) *TUPE 1981: Government proposals for reform – detailed background paper*. London: DTI Employment Relations Directorate.

Department of Trade and Industry (2001b) *TUPE 1981: Government proposals for reform – public consultation document*. London: DTI Employment Relations Directorate.

Institute for Public Policy Research (2001) *Building Better Partnerships*. London: IPPR.

Linden, T. (1992) 'Service Contracts and the Transfer Business', *Industrial Law Journal*, 21(4) December, 293–301.

Marginson, P. *et al.* (1995) 'Strategy, Structure and Control in the Changing Corporation: A Survey-based Investigation', *Human Resource Management Journal*, 5(2), 3–27.

Millward, N. *et al.* (1992) *Workplace Industrial Relations in Transition*. Aldershot: Dartmouth.

Millward, N. *et al.* (2000) *All Change at Work?* London: Routledge.

National Association of Citizens Advice Bureaux (1993) *Job Insecurity*. London: NACAB.

Sachdev, S. (2001) *Contracting Culture: from CCT to PPPs*. London: UNISON.

Torrington, D. and Hall, L. (1998) *Human Resource Management* (4th edn). Hemel Hempstead: Prentice Hall Europe.

PART TWO

Discrimination and equal opportunities

Introduction to Part Two

This Part explores the issues of equal opportunities and discrimination in employment. Principally, it will focus on sex, race and disability discrimination. Each chapter explores a specific area of discrimination. However, there are certain common themes that link all discriminatory treatment and the pursuit of equal opportunities.

Consequently, this Part Introduction is longer than usual in order to discuss the following common issues:

- the **concepts** of discrimination, equal opportunities and equal treatment;
- the general character of the **legal framework**;
- the nature of voluntary action taken by employers to develop **equal opportunities policies**.

THE CONCEPTS

Discrimination as a phenomenon occurs widely both within the employment relationship and within society at large. It has a number of related dimensions. Clearly, it is about the exercise of choice – for example, in recruitment and in promotions. Implicit in the exercise of this choice is the fact that action can be taken *in favour* of one person and *against* another. The issue that will concern us here is the grounds on which that discrimination or choice is made. So, for example, when a manager appoints a person to a post, the key question that has to be answered is: *what were the grounds for making that choice and rejecting other applicants*? Were the applicants considered against **objective criteria** for the position – i.e. experience, skills and qualifications? Or, was there evidence that **unlawful criteria** were used – e.g. avoiding the recruitment of pregnant women, Afro-Caribbean applicants or disabled persons?

The concept of discrimination, of course, encompasses wider patterns of social, economic and political behaviour whereby particular groups of people are stereotyped, victimised and discriminated against on the presumption that they possess certain characteristics. Various social and employment barriers can reinforce unfair discrimination and prevent a person achieving equal treatment. For example, the social role of caring for children which is, traditionally, ascribed to women has been found to be a considerable obstacle in the attainment of promotion, career progression and equal pay. In the subsequent chapters, we will return to and explore some of these wider issues.

As the law stands at present, **unlawful discrimination** does not encompass all grounds of what might be regarded as unfair discrimination. However, the statutory framework is becoming more wide-ranging. Discrimination and victimisation are now outlawed in employment on the following grounds: sex; marital status; pregnancy; gender reassignment; race; colour; nationality; ethnic origin; disability; religion and political opinion (in Northern Ireland only); trade union membership and non-membership; carrying out a role as a recognised trade union representative; carrying out a role as an employee representative under consultation law on redundancies, business transfers and health and safety; disclosing information about an employer's poor health and safety standards.

Discrimination in respect of age, homosexuality, dress and appearance have, occasionally, been addressed in specific cases, in the context of sex or race discrimination law, and some protections have been accorded. Other areas of potential discrimination concerning social origin, AIDS and HIV-positive status, political affiliation and religion (outside of Northern Ireland), and accent are not covered explicitly by any statutory prohibitions although occasionally they may feature in case law. In 2000, the European Union adopted two Directives which will amend and develop anti-discrimination law in respect of race, religion, sexuality, age and disability.

Anti-discrimination action and policies are invariably discussed in the context of **equal opportunities** and/or **equal treatment** policies. Equal opportunities, as a concept, derives from the United States and was imported into British civil rights and employment law in the 1970s. Less common in usage is the term originating from European Union discrimination law: equal treatment. Differentiating these two terms is difficult. In practice – in the thinking of managers, in the experience of working people and, usually, in the interpretation of the law – they have become synonymous. Superficially, *equal opportunities*, as a term, is attractive because it is aspirational. It seems to go beyond the present situation to consider access to improved conditions and circumstances, the provision of better standards and the encouragement of those who are discriminated against. In fact, however, the *equal treatment* law of the European Union has facilitated a considerable range of opportunities for women. In terms of outcomes, then, there may be little to suggest that either term is preferable.

Having said this, there is a fundamental problem in the concept of *equal opportunities* (and also *equal treatment*) that is common in both sex and race discrimination law: the issue of comparison. It has been described in these terms: 'The notion of equality requires a standard against which the position of different groups can be measured. The answer to the question: "Equal to what?" becomes "Equal to white males"; ultimately the white male is the underlying norm which must be mirrored and adhered to. The effect is that women are expected to conform to a world based on male values and black people to white values' (Fredman and Szyszczak, 1992: 216).

The issue of comparison, which is at the heart of British sex discrimination law, can create some bizarre legal gymnastics. For example, in considering the rights of pregnant women, the courts sought the nearest equivalent male comparator (in terms of absence from work) and produced *the sick man*. However, the ECJ in 1990, in the *Dekker* case, invoked the Equal Treatment Directive 1976 which prohibits any 'discrimination whatever on grounds of sex directly or indirectly'. It ruled that in this case, involving a pregnant job applicant, there was 'no absolute comparability'. The detrimental treatment of a woman because of pregnancy is always direct discrimination because such treatment can, by definition, only affect women. This thinking was followed through into the Pregnant Workers Directive 1992 (that is now part of British law in the Employment Rights Act 1996, s 99).

Fredman and Szyszczak also draw attention to the compounding of discriminatory treatment, where there is an interaction of discrimination on grounds of both sex and race. In their argument, they state that 'for black women, the status of being both a woman and a black is not regarded as additive, but synergistic' (1992: 215). Clearly this principle can be recognised in a growing number of situations where various grounds of unfair discrimination interact – particularly, the interactions of sex, race and disability discrimination.

THE LAW

The evolving framework of statute law has been enacted as a complement to **the common law of contract**. The contract of employment, as the instrument for regulating the employment relation (*see* Chapter 2) makes no explicit acknowlegement of equal treatment. To deal with this situation, the Equal Pay Act 1970 (s 1) enacted an equality clause that is deemed to exist within all contracts of employment.

Most of the present body of **statute law** to proscribe unfair discrimination and promote equal opportunities was enacted in the United Kingdom in the 1970s. The specific discriminatory treatment that was outlawed concerned sex, marital status (under the Sex Discrimination Act 1975 and the Equal Pay Act 1970), and race, colour, nationality and ethnic origin (under the Race Relations Act 1976).

Progressively, other areas of discrimination have been tackled. In Northern Ireland, religious and political discrimination was prohibited under 'fair employment' legislation. This was designed to overcome entrenched patterns of discrimination in the province, particularly against Catholics. As an addition to the framework of equal treatment rights, the European Union adopted the Pregnant Workers Directive 1992 which outlawed discrimination on the grounds of pregnancy and maternity. The British government widened the framework of rights for disabled persons through the Disability Discrimination Act 1995 and repealed the rarely enforced, weak and limited legislation that operated since 1944. In a creative interpretation of the 1976 Equal Treatment Directive, the ECJ has ruled that the dismissal of a transsexual came within the provision on discrimination on the grounds of sex and was discriminatory and unlawful (*P* v *S and Cornwall County Council* [1996] IRLR 347). The Sex Discrimination (Gender Reassignment) Regulations were implemented in 1999 to reinforce this protective framework in the sphere of employment. In April 2001, the Race Relations (Amendment) Act 2000 came into force, strengthening the obligations of public authorities – particularly to promote equal opportunities. By July 2003, the European Union Race Directive 2000 is to be transposed into UK law. This will be followed by the phased implementation of the Employment Directive 2000 in respect of sexual orientation and religion or belief (by December 2003) and in respect of age and disability (by December 2006).

The following action has been taken by the government to implement both the Race Discrimination Directive 2000 and also the Employment Directive 2000:

- The Race Relations Act 1976 (Amendment) Regulations 2002 have enacted the provisions of the Race Directive into the Race Relations Act 1976 with effect from July 2003.

■ The Employment Equality (Sexual Orientation) Regulations 2003 implement the relevant provisions of the Employment Directive from December 2003 (see chapter 4 for more detail).

■ The Employment Equality (Religion or Belief) Regulations 2003 implement the relevant provisions of the Employment Directive from December 2003 (see chapter 5 for more detail).

■ The Disability Discrimination Act 1995 (Amendment) Regulations 2003 implement the relevant provisions of the Employment Directive (see chapter 6 for more detail).

Although sex and race discrimination issues are covered in different statutes and the law is monitored and enforced by two different commissions, 'the structure and conceptual framework of the legislation have close parallels' (Fredman and Szyszczak, 1992: 214). To this extent, some employment lawyers have defined it as **a single body of law**. However, it has also been commented, with a great deal of justification, that Britain's framework of anti-discrimination law is incoherent and 'an incomplete patchwork' (Hepple *et al.*, 1997). Furthermore, the available remedies for aggrieved individuals are frequently inadequate. These views will be explored later.

Against this background of piecemeal enactment and, generally, weak enforcement, two developments, of potential significance, have resulted from recent government action: the incorporation of the 1950 European Convention on Human Rights into British law (discussed in Chapter 1) and the ratification of the Treaty of Amsterdam 1997.

The law of the European Union forms an important ingredient in the body of British anti-discrimination law in respect of sex. This derives from a number of sources: Art 141 of the Treaty of Rome, which asserts that 'men and women should receive equal pay for equal work'; from the Directives on Equal Pay and on Equal Treatment, and from the Pregnant Workers Directive. The Equal Treatment Directive has been particularly significant in the creation of a wider framework of protection against discrimination. It states that 'the principle of equal treatment shall mean that there shall be no discrimination whatsoever on grounds of sex either directly or indirectly by reference in particular to marital or family status' (Art 2.1). As mentioned above, this has been used to challenge discrimination, successfully, on the grounds of transsexual status and, unsuccessfully, on grounds of homosexuality.

The European Union has been slow to adopt effective measures to combat other forms of discrimination. There have been campaigns on race discrimination and xenophobia, and on age discrimination, but only in the past few years have new Directives been adopted on race, religion, sexuality, age and disability. These establish the 'principle of equal treatment' in the respective pieces of legislation.

One legal concept that is an important instrument of social policy for tackling discrimination is **positive action**. This contrasts with **positive discrimination** (or reverse discrimination or affirmative action). The detailed working of such law will be explored in the relevant chapters on sex and race discrimination. Here we will consider the nature of the two concepts. Both have individual and group dimensions, in that they are concerned with the position of individual job applicants or existing workers and with the wider patterns of discrimination in society.

Positive action is provided for in the legislation (SDA 1975, ss 47 and 48; RRA, ss 37 and 38). It is also commended in the statutory codes of practice published by the Equal Opportunities Commission and the Commission for Racial Equality. Largely, it is conceived as encouragement for underrepresented groups to apply for posts and promotion and to participate in training opportunities.

Positive discrimination contrasts with positive action. It is sometimes referred to as reverse discrimination to reflect the American practice of affirmative action. Essentially, it is preferential treatment on the grounds of sex or race. Under British discrimination law it is unlawful – following the direct discrimination provisions (SDA 1975, s 1(1)(a); RRA 1976, s 1(1)(a)).

However, two qualifications can be made about any theoretical, clear-cut distinction between the two concepts. First, it is said that preferential access to training and development opportunities may, in fact, be both positive action and reverse or positive discrimination – particularly if a course is 'rigidly confined' to the disadvantaged group (Pitt, 1992: 283). Secondly, in selection for a particular post, the outlawing of positive discrimination may not be altogether certain. As a general comment, Deakin and Morris (1998: 592) state that 'as part of an equal opportunities policy it is arguable that an employer may legitimately decide to employ or promote a woman, for example, who is found to be *equally well qualified* with a male applicant or colleague, with the aim of improving the balance of women and men in particular parts of its workforce.' Recent developments within the European Union have taken this issue on somewhat and are discussed in Chapter 4.

The arguments for and against positive discrimination are contentious. The key sets of arguments in the debate relate to the eradication of historic patterns of disadvantage, and to moral obligations and rights.

Eradication of historic patterns of disadvantage. This argument is founded on the view that historic patterns are still influential today in framing social attitudes and expectations towards women, members of various ethnic groups and disabled persons. As will be considered in the later chapters of Part Two, the various obstacles to equal opportunities have included male social dominance, the legacy of colonialism, slavery and historic racism, and the social marginalisation and the low expectations held of disabled persons. So, 'the point of positive discrimination is to give them the capacity and the confidence to decide their goals for themselves, to empower them, to remove their existential marginality and to assure them that no area of life is necessarily and inherently inaccessible to them' (Parekh, 1992: 270).

Moral obligations and rights: This argument derives, in part, from the moral standards and rights that underpin the political systems of liberal democratic societies which are evident in, for example, the European Convention on Human Rights 1950. It is suggested that this moral argument implies compensatory action for past systematic breaches of what are current standards of behaviour. Indeed, it is frequently compensatory action that is at the heart of current debates about the appropriateness of positive discrimination. Such action can take place on a number of levels.

First, at the level of the wider society, it can relate to the distribution of public funding and the initiation of policies designed to overcome inherited patterns of disadvantage. Examples include encouraging various public training and education courses for women and different ethnic groups; providing assistance with childcare; appointing people from disadvantaged groups to public office as both representatives of particular interests and as role models. The social purposes of such action would be covered by such phrases as 'social justice', the creation of greater social cohesion and the avoidance of social division, exclusion and marginalisation.

Secondly, at the level of the employing organisation, it can involve access to training opportunities, and, more controversially (and unlawfully, in Britain) can involve the use of quotas in recruitment and promotion. Associated with this is the situation whereby the individual receives preferential treatment in recruitment or promotion because of their designation as a member of a disadvantaged group.

The two major criticisms of compensatory action are that it is wrongly focused and that it is potentially divisive. One view is that it is previous generations that experienced the discrimination and, therefore, it is inappropriate to compensate people today. Another view is that, even if the influence of previous patterns of discrimination on contemporary policies are acknowledged, positive discrimination only benefits **some** members of the disadvantaged group. However, 'they have at least managed to get themselves into the position of being serious candidates for the desirable opportunity' (Pitt, 1992: 285). Thirdly, some commentators point to the 'backlash' effect, whereby reverse discrimination is seen as disadvantaging, for example, men and white workers on grounds that are not objectively justifiable.

The balance of argument is by no means clear-cut. It may be that the more defensible course of action is to pursue the eradication of unfair discrimination through the twin-track approach already extant in Britain of: (1) following the principles of equal treatment and equal opportunities and (2) giving emphasis to effective positive action programmes.

VOLUNTARY ACTION BY EMPLOYERS

Equal opportunities policies

Generally, employers are not required in law to have an **equal opportunities policy**. Nevertheless, the construction of the law provides strong encouragement for an employer to develop one. The Equal Opportunities Commission and the Commission for Racial Equality have published, after wide consultations, codes of practice. (Similarly, there is a code of practice in respect of disability discrimination.) These are made and approved by Parliament under the Sex Discrimination Act 1975 (s 56A), the Race Relations Act 1976 (s 47) and the Disability Discrimination Act 1995 (s 53). Failure to comply with any of these codes will not result in an employer being subject to legal proceedings. However, breach of the code might be used in evidence against an employer before a court or employment tribunal. This is important in the context of liability. An employer, under all three pieces of anti-discrimination legislation, is liable for anything done by another person (e.g. employee, contractor, manager) 'whether or not it was done with the employer's knowledge or approval' (SDA, s 41; RRA, s 32; DDA, s 58). The only defence for an employer is 'to prove that he took such steps as were reasonably practicable to prevent the employee from doing that [discriminatory] act or from doing in the course of his employment acts of that description'. Consequently, evidence of an effective equal opportunities policy may contribute to that defence.

Amendments in respect of race discrimination were implemented in 2001. They require specified public authorities to prepare a Race Equality Scheme. Guidance is given in a code of practice on the duty to promote race equality, published by the CRE, and effective from December 2001.

The approach of employers to equal opportunities has been extremely patchy. This can be seen by considering several issues: the nature and scope of equal opportunities policies, their incidence and the extent to which their implementation is monitored.

The **nature and scope** of equal opportunities policies vary widely. To be effective, such a policy should be structured around the following circular process: diagnosis of the existing situation, assessment of the information and of the likely courses of action to be taken, the setting of objectives, the planning of action to be taken, the implementation of policies and practices and monitoring and review of action taken.

Diagnosis involves, in particular, the collection of data on the existing workforce profile, an identification of barriers to equal opportunities, and the collation of information about complaints of unfair treatment. Fundamental to this process, however, is a consideration of the organisation's culture. Culture in this context embraces the values, history, traditions and practices that are accepted as normal within the organisation. Failure to address and eradicate a discriminatory culture will make any further equal opportunities action difficult, if not impossible, to achieve.

A few examples will illustrate the significance of organisational culture and the ways in which it can be reinforced by other personnel management practices. Recruitment practices whether for entry into the organisation or for promotion opportunities can be particularly powerful agents in reaffirming an existing culture. Even where there is a professional system for recruitment, prevailing attitudes and expectations can result in unfair discrimination. Such discrimination is compounded where there is word-of-mouth recruitment.

In a study of banking, Boyden and Paddison (1986) refer to what amounted to a 'two-tier recruitment practice' evident in the 1960s. Under this, 'men were seen as future managers and expected to study for the professional banking exams so vital for promotion in branches, while women were expected to work short term on routine work and to leave on marriage or soon after'. This approach to recruitment, informally based on sex, 'left a powerful legacy of attitudes and assumptions which even now are slow to change'. Clearly, historic discrimination continues to mould existing patterns of employment and create barriers to advancement.

Seniority of service is, also, significant in the banking example. As a criterion for advancement, it has, however, been both criticised and applauded. While it is disadvantageous to women because of their likely career breaks, it can be beneficial as a means of tackling race discrimination between different groups of male workers. In a survey of London Underground, Brooks (1975: 179) commented that seniority 'does not guarantee that members of minority groups are not discriminated against in promotion, but it makes such discrimination far more difficult and less likely to occur; it provides an objective criterion which can be easily measured, and it is an impersonal mechanism'.

Overlaying these kinds of recruitment practices can be wider, more diffuse cultural standards and practices. In an investigation for the Equal Opportunities Commission into British Rail, Diana Robbins (1986: 6) referred to 'the idea of the "Railway family"' as a significant factor in recruitment. 'In the past, when staff turnover was a serious and expensive problem, some family connection with an existing employee was believed to influence a recruit's staying power'. She adds that 'even the most recently drafted application form for rail jobs (at the time of writing) included a question about relatives working on the Railway, implying that a preference for such a connection still exists'. In terms of unfair discrimination, such a policy (although not an absolute criterion in recruitment and selection) would clearly tend to have an adverse effect on recruits from non-white ethnic groups.

Objective setting, action planning and implementation will together create the essential elements of the equal opportunities policy as a working document. Among the key issues to be considered in these areas are the following.

How does the equal opportunities policy relate to the organisation's wider objectives?

The debate on the relative significance of 'equal opportunities' as against 'the management of diversity' (which is explored later in this introduction) draws attention to the ways in which equal opportunities policies are frequently marginal to wider organisational objectives. The management of diversity, by contrast, is seen as integral to these. For example, in terms of human resource management, it is concerned with effective resourcing – using all the skills and capabilities of staff. In terms of product design and provision, knowledge of the diverse spectrum of customer needs can help business organisations meet these demands. In terms of marketing, a diverse workforce helps establish effective sales relationships with potential customers. Finally, in terms of public relations, a diverse organisation can achieve credibility within a wider society that is both multiracial and one where women play increasingly more significant roles. In this respect, diversity management and equal opportunities can make 'business sense'.

Is the scope of the policy to be restricted to areas of unfair discrimination prohibited by law?

An organisation may adopt a restricted scope for its equal opportunities policy. However, a more inclusive approach recognises that other forms of unfair discrimination can be damaging to employment relations.

Which barriers to equal opportunities are to be given priority for eradication?

Barriers to equal opportunities are both internal and external. The former encompasses lack of management commitment to equal opportunities; failure to invest in adequate training as part of positive-action programmes; and failure to monitor an equal opportunities policy effectively and use the data obtained to make appropriate amendments. External constraints include the lack of adequate childcare provision.

Which targets for positive action are to be set?

Within the context of British employment law, positive-action programmes are permissible to encourage underrepresented groups to apply for posts and to provide special training and development schemes for women (or men) or for different ethnic groups to help people compete more effectively in promotional or other job opportunities.

How can the commitment of line managers be assured?

Line managers have been identified, frequently, as an internal obstacle to the effective implementation of equal opportunities policies. The explanation for this can be found in looking at the role of such managers and their position within an organisation's structure. Clearly, there are tensions in defining priorities for action. Managers are, principally, required to carry out designated operational tasks to deliver a service or achieve production targets. Increasingly, they may have to manage budgets and operate within specified financial systems. Depending on the nature of the work, health and safety considerations might be significant requirements. Additionally, there are multiple pressures arising from delayering in organisations, the promotion of teamworking, and of the devolving of employee relations and human resource management responsibilities to line managers. This devolution has resulted in the acquisition of some potentially time-consuming tasks: for example, recruitment and selection of staff, the operation of performance appraisal schemes, and contributions to employee-involvement systems, like team briefing and quality circles.

Against this background, it is possible to see how equal opportunities (often perceived as a 'soft HRM' issue, peripheral to the organisation's 'real' work, and having no quantifiable tangible benefits) is ignored or complied with in a minimalist way. This marginalisation can be compounded by senior management's failure both to identify equal opportunities as an explicit core value and to ensure organisational compliance and effective monitoring. Such senior management commitment is essential on a continuing basis. It is vital in the context of organisational reorganisation and change. The contraction or abolition of central human resource functions can result in the dissolution of any coherent equal opportunities approach and the fragmentation of responsibility. One contribution to achieving an effective policy could be the inclusion of equal opportunities objectives in managers' own performance contracts.

How can the workforce be engaged in policy formulation, implementation and review?

According to the statutory codes of practice, it is expected that equal opportunities policies should be associated with the usual processes of managerial decision-making and also those involved in employee relations. However, the extent to which equal opportunities issues are a regular and integrated feature of employment relations is limited.

The first findings of the 1998 Workplace Employee Relations Survey (Cully *et al.*, 1998) reported, perhaps surprisingly, that 64 per cent of workplaces are covered by formal written equal opportunities policies. All the statutory grounds for unfair discrimination were overwhelmingly covered. In addition, the following were included: religion (84 per cent of cases) and age (67 per cent of cases). Half the workplaces without a formal written policy 'claimed to have an unwritten one or otherwise aimed at being an equal opportunity employer . . . Workplaces without a policy were predominantly small' (1998: 13).

Table A (derived from the responses of 1906 managers in organisations with 25 or more employees) shows 'unequivocally, that workplaces with a formal equal opportunities policy are much more likely to have a range of practices in place which aim to promote equal treatment'.

Dickens and Colling (1990), drawing on various research studies, point to the weakness of collective bargaining, to date, as an instrument for promoting and reinforcing equal opportunities policies. They identify three areas of *equality bargaining*:

Table A Equal treatment practices (per cent)

	Formal EO policy in workplace (%)	No policy (%)
Keep employee records with ethnic origin identified	48	13
Collect statistics on posts held by men and women	43	13
Monitor promotions by gender and ethnicity	23	2
Review selection procedures to identify indirect discrimination	35	5
Review the relative pay rates of different groups	17	15
Make adjustments to accommodate disabled employees	42	16
None of these	27	67

■ *benefits or arrangements* which are of particular interest or advantage to women. This would cover enhanced maternity, career break and parental leave provisions; flexibility of working time; pro-rata conditions for part-time employment;

■ *equality awareness* in the handling of commonplace bargaining issues (e.g. pay and other remuneration opportunities);

■ *an equality dimension* to the negotiation of change. This would cover the recognition of equal value considerations when reforming grading structures and sensitivity to unintentional discrimination in the introduction of appraisal schemes.

They concluded that the research 'found little extension of the bargaining agenda in the way indicated under the first of the three areas; little if any sensitivity on the part of most negotiators to equality implications in the handling of commonplace agenda items; and only very exceptionally any equality dimension to change'. Several factors were suggested as creating this state of affairs: 'negotiators who concentrate on improving bonus rates and premium pay rates at the expense of basic rates are often in practice enhancing male rather than female earnings'; the job segregation of women into comparatively lower-skilled occupations 'was perceived generally by negotiators interviewed as "natural" or objectively justifiable in terms of workers' preferences'; and, finally, because bargainers for both unions and employers are drawn from male-dominated groups, there is a marked tendency for the agenda priorities to be those of men.

What resource allocation is necessary to make the policy effective?

It is difficult to quantify the necessary resource allocation with any certainty. But there are obvious costs in terms of meetings, the time of employees and managers involved, the preparation of documentation, the delivery of training events and the provision of monitoring arrangements.

The implication of **monitoring and review** is illustrated in the comment of an employee-relations manager that an equal opportunities policy without monitoring 'is not a policy but a statement of wishful thinking and is likely to be as much use as a finance policy which makes no provisions for checking how much cash there is in the bank'. Despite this self-evident truth, many organisations still fail to set in place effective monitoring (*see* Table A above). There are two elements in a monitoring system: quantitive and qualitative. The first concerns the data that might need to be collected on the profile of the workforce by gender, race and grade which should help identify areas of vertical and horizontal segregation. This should be supplemented by continuing data from the recruitment and selection process and from promotions. The second element in monitoring concerns consultation and discussion, evaluations about how policies are working, and the modification and improvement of policies and practices.

In practice, it is rare to encounter such rigorous monitoring. Given the limitations of the legal framework in not imposing a general obligation on employers to monitor, this is not surprising. A recent critique of equality law, drafted by a group of distinguished lawyers, stated that 'this means that employers and enforcement agencies do not have the facts about any significant differences in the position of men and women and between white people and people from ethnic minorities. As a result, employers tend to react defensively to allegations of discrimination instead of taking the initiative towards achieving equal opportunities by means of equality programmes and targets' (Hepple *et al.*, 1997: 9). The authors advocate a general statutory obligation, modelled on that in the Northern Ireland 'fair employment' legislation. The Race Relations (Amendment) Act 2000 has provided some strengthening of the law on monitoring relating to public authorities' duties to promote equal opportunity (*see* Chapter 5).

Managing diversity

One consequence of the limitations of equal opportunities policies has been a growing interest in the concept of managing diversity. This is seen either as an evolutionary step in the development of equal opportunities or as a concept that individualises equal opportunities issues and distracts attention from the group basis of discrimination. It has emerged within the past decade in Britain. It is likely to be a durable concept because, in some ways, as indicated earlier, it relates to other strategic and fundamentally important management issues. Its significance has been recognised by the Chartered Institute of Personnel and Development with the publication of a position paper in December 1996.

In earlier literature (Kandola *et al.*, 1994), the concepts of *equal opportunities* and *managing diversity* were seen as opposed in some critical respects. The former was seen as restrictive, while the latter was advocated as a more inclusive and, above all, business-related idea. The publication of the CIPD paper marks some shift in opinion. The Chartered Institute suggests that the two concepts can be linked together. It defines them as 'complementary', 'interdependent' and 'not alternatives'.

Diversity management is defined as having a number of distinctive characteristics. First, it is perceived as providing a coherent approach which integrates both business and personal needs together with ethical standards, the impact of social trends affecting employment and legal requirements on equal treatment. The CIPD says that it is 'based on the concept that people should be valued as individuals for reasons related to business interests, as well as for moral and social reasons'.

Secondly, it provides a strategic approach to equal opportunities. So, it is associated with such strategic business and human resource issues as quality management, productivity and cost effectiveness, empowerment, performance management and continuous development. It has an explicit economic focus in respect of labour cost-effectiveness.

Thirdly, it is inclusive. It embraces all corporate policies and working practices and expects that they are tested against the criteria of diversity management. Such policies and practices should be assessed when they are being formulated, when they are implemented and when audit and review takes place.

Fourthly, the essential focus of diversity management is the individual employee. It is concerned with his/her characteristics, needs, aspirations and differences. It is not restricted to those areas of unlawful discrimination proscribed in statute. It is more wide-ranging. It is designed to take account of the vast range of differences evident within any workforce – whether these derive from gender, race, disability, religion, age, responsibilities for dependants, sexual orientation and so on. The success of the policy is, then, determined by the extent to which the interests of individuals are accommodated by corporate policies.

Finally, diversity management is management driven. It is line managers, team leaders and human resource managers who are responsible for establishing the ways in which both legislative requirements and individual needs result in corporate action.

By contrast, equal opportunities (in the context of management policy) differs from diversity management in a number of key aspects. First, it is limited in its coverage. It deals, usually, with discrimination defined as unfair by the legislators, which can lag behind public opinion about what is unacceptable discriminatory treatment. It is said that diversity management is capable of embracing these issues.

Secondly, equal opportunities is said to be characterised as emphasising group rather than individual concerns. Certainly, there is a focus on the group because the objective is to eradicate discrimination arising from stereotyping whereby individuals are presumed to have certain characteristics of others in the same group (e.g. all young women are going to have children and will consequently make unreliable employees). Such a focus does not, however, ignore consideration of the individual's circumstances and aspirations (e.g. access to training, fair consideration for promotional opportunities, access to childcare provision). Unlawful discrimination can only be tackled effectively by addressing both its individual and group dimensions.

Thirdly, equal opportunities as a concept, supported by the law, permits 'positive action'. This is designed to deal with historic patterns of discriminatory treatment against groups. Individuals from groups which are underrepresented in the workforce in the preceding 12 months are encouraged to apply for particular posts or promotional opportunities. Positive action has, however, been criticised by proponents of diversity management. These authors adduce a range of evidence from the United States to illustrate negative effects of positive action: i.e. the stigma of being a participant in a positive-action programme and the related perception that the person may be incompetent. It is debatable whether such culture-specific research drawn from the impact of American law can point to helpful conclusions about British experience. Interestingly, the CIPD position paper explicitly rules *in favour of* the contribution of positive action. It does this in the context of support for 'development training to help people reach levels of competence which let them release their true potential'.

The fourth difference between the concepts of diversity management and equal opportunities concerns the range of implementation weaknesses of the latter. These have been documented in various studies. For example, equal opportunities policies can be seen as, and can be, unrelated to business goals; they can appear unrelated to the day-to-day responsibilities of line managers; the only 'guardians' of the policy may be the personnel department; employers can adopt the policies as tokenism; there can be minimal compliance with the law on a piecemeal basis if and when a complaint arises.

So, the CIPD attempts, in its model, to synthesise the two concepts, which, as we have seen, have some divergent characteristics. It sees diversity management, in effect, as an evolutionary step in the implementation of equal opportunities. This is elaborated in the following terms. Managing diversity is a step beyond legal compliance. It is 'essentially a quality assurance approach'. It has three important functions: to identify 'hidden organisation barriers', to create an 'open' and an 'empowering' culture and to combat prejudice, stereotyping and unacceptable behaviour. Above all, it is 'a continuous process of improvement, not a once and for all initiative'.

CONCLUSION

It is against this background, then, that consideration will be given to certain key areas of discrimination. Sex discrimination and the wider interpretation embracing gender reassignment and homosexuality will be explored in Chapter 4. In Chapter 5, the complementary body of law on race discrimination will considered. Finally, the management of disability within a new and evolving legal framework is discussed in Chapter 6.

Further reading

Chartered Institute of Personnel and Development (1996) *Managing Diversity: an IPD Position Paper*. London: CIPD.

Commission for Racial Equality (1983) *Code of Practice for the Elimination of Racial Discrimination and the Promotion of Equality of Opportunity in Employment*. London: CRE.

Commission for Racial Equality (2002) *Code of Practice*. London: CRE.

Department for Education and Employment (1996) *Code of Practice for the Elimination of Discrimination in the Field of Employment against Disabled Persons or Persons Who Have Had a Disability*. London: DfEE.

Equal Opportunities Commission (1985) *Code of Practice for the Elimination of Discrimination on the Grounds of Sex and Marriage and the Promotion of Equal Opportunity in Employment*. Manchester: EOC.

Kandola, R. *et al.* (1998) *Diversity in Action: Managing the Mosaic*, 2nd edn. London: CIPD.

References

Boyden, T. and Paddison, L. (1986) 'Banking on Equal Opportunities', *Personnel Management*, September, 42–6.

Brooks, D. (1975) *Race and Labour in London Transport*. London: Oxford University Press.

Chartered Institute of Personnel and Development (1996) *Managing Diversity: an IPD Position Paper*. London: CIPD.

Commission for Racial Equality (1983) *Code of Practice for the Elimination of Racial Discrimination and the Promotion of Equality of Opportunity in Employment*. London: CRE.

Cully, M. *et al.* (1998) *The 1998 Workplace Employee Relations Survey – First Findings*. London: Department of Trade and Industry.

Deakin, S. and Morris, G. (1998) *Labour Law*. London: Butterworths.

Dickens, L. and Colling, T. (1990) 'Why equality won't appear on the bargaining agenda', *Personnel Management*, April, 48–53.

Equal Opportunities Commission (1985) *Code of Practice for the Elimination of Discrimination on the Grounds of Sex and Marriage and the Promotion of Equal Opportunity in Employment*. Manchester: EOC.

Equal Opportunities Commission (1991) *Equality Management: Women's Employment in the NHS*. Manchester: EOC.

Fredman, S. and Szyszczak, E. (1992) 'The Interaction of Race and Gender' in Hepple, B. and Szyszczak, E.M. (eds) *Discrimination: the Limits of the Law*. London: Mansell.

Hepple, B. *et al.* (1997) *Improving Equality Law: the Options*. London: Justice and the Runnymede Trust.

Kandola, R. *et al.* (1994) *Diversity in Action: Managing the Mosaic*. London: CIPD.

Parekh, B. (1992) 'A Case of Positive Discrimination' in Hepple, B. and Szyszczak, E.M. (eds) *Discrimination: the Limits of the Law*. London: Mansell.

Pitt, G. (1992) 'Can Reverse Discrimination Be Justified?' in Hepple, B. and Szyszczak, E.M. (eds) *Discrimination: the Limits of the Law*. London: Mansell.

Robbins, D. (1986) *Wanted Railman*. London: HMSO.

Sex discrimination in the workplace

This chapter considers the social and economic background to sex discrimination and explores the nature of such discrimination in employment. It outlines the essential legal framework and explores the policies and practices that should be adopted by employers. Having read it you should understand:

■ The origins of sex discrimination.

■ The key concepts in discrimination law: direct and indirect discrimination, the concept of justification, victimisation, the special provisions, the contribution of positive action, liability, the right of complaint and the legal procedures, the remedies available.

■ The steps that you could take to advise on the development of an equal opportunities policy for your organisation.

It is important to remember that this area of discriminatory practice should be considered in conjunction with race discrimination (Chapter 5) and disability discrimination (Chapter 6).

4.1   Structure of the chapter

This chapter comprises the following sections:

■ *Introduction*: The historic situation of women and changing perspectives.

■ *The context*: Participation in the labour market, women's pay, social trends and influences, and political approaches.

■ *The legal framework*: Grounds for unlawful discrimination, access to statutory rights, direct discrimination, indirect discrimination, equal pay, victimisation, positive action and positive discrimination, special provisions, liability, enforcement procedures and remedies.

- *Employment policies and practices*: Recruitment and selection, pay, working time, terms and conditions of employment, training and development, promotion and career progression, retirement and pensions and dismissal.

4.2 Introduction

4.2.1 Historic situation of women

Historically, predominant social attitudes have seen women's contribution to society outside the home as largely peripheral. Women were generally regarded as inferior and dependent upon men, having no separate legal identity. Blackstone, the eighteenth-century jurist, put the situation as follows: 'by marriage, the very being or legal existence of woman is suspended, or at least incorporated and consolidated into that of the husband, under whose wing, protection and cover she performs everything'. In the middle of the nineteenth century, a fictional lawyer in George Eliot's novel, *The Mill on the Floss*, commented, 'We don't ask what a woman does, we ask whom she belongs to'.

The overwhelming emphasis, then, was on the importance of male roles in society. It was not until the late nineteenth century that slow legislative progress started which began piecemeal improvements in both status and rights. It is this gradual process of legislative change that is continuing right up to the present day. Some of these key changes are outlined below.

First of all, on marriage, **a woman's property** and income became her husband's by law. In 1882, the Married Women's Property Act enacted the principle, revolutionary at the time, that married women should have the same rights over their property as unmarried women and that husbands and wives should have separate interests in their property. Wives were also enabled to carry on trade and business using their property.

Secondly, **government** and **political activity** were regarded as male preserves (in fact, largely the preserve of property-owning males). It was not until 1918 that certain women (over 30 years of age) were granted the vote in Parliamentary elections; and 1928 before they acquired it on equal terms, in respect of age, with men. The first woman to be elected to Parliament, who took up her seat, did this in 1919.

Thirdly, **education** was seen as essential for boys but not for girls. Various views – often eccentric by present-day standards – were used to justify this discriminatory attitude. In the mid-nineteenth century, 'educating girls was thought to damage their health as adolescence was the time their reproductive organs were growing and so . . . rest was essential. Schooling might damage this process by being too taxing. Experts predicted infertility or, at the very least, an inability to breastfeed' (Holdsworth, 1988: 41). Biologically, 'women were thought to have smaller brains and, it followed, less intellectual potential. It was also a common belief that women were behind men in evolution as their prime function, motherhood, kept them closer to nature. In short they were inferior' (Holdsworth, 1988: 42).

In 1870, compulsory education, up to the age of 14 years in elementary schools, was introduced. 'Such official thought as went into the education of working-class girls (and that does not appear to have been a great deal) concentrated on preparing them to be wives and mothers or taking work as domestic servants' (Holdsworth, 1988: 47). Cookery, hygiene, laundrywork and housewifery were all on the curriculum of elementary schools for girls, sometimes supplemented by infant-care lessons.

At university level, access was gradually available from the latter part of the nineteenth century. For example, in 1878, the University of London admitted women for the first time. Oxford permitted women to take degrees from 1920, Cambridge not until 1947. Girton College had been opened there in 1870, but was not recognised by the university.

Finally, full-time **work** and the 'breadwinner role' were ascribed to men. Women, on marriage, were generally expected to give up work and ultimately care full-time for their husband and children. 'Men lost face if they could not support their wives' (Holdsworth, 1988: 62). The two World Wars (1914–18 and 1939–45) did disturb the conventional views of men's and women's roles, both in society and in employment. However, it is generally agreed that any changes in the world of work were short-lived and the general expectation by employers, politicians, men and many women was that, after both wars, women would return to their 'proper' roles of being wives and mothers.

During these wars women took up employment in jobs which were previously thought unsuitable for them, such as ambulance drivers, stokers, tool setters, welders, carpenters and bus conductors. However, they had not established any rights to equal pay.

After World War II, however, one factor was different from the situation after World War I: immediately the economy began to grow and there were labour shortages. This was a primary influence in the subsequent developing participation of women in the labour market.

4.2.2 Changing perspectives

It would be a mistake to see the emergence of changing perspectives of women's role in society, politics, the economy and employment as a recent phenomenon. Questioning and challenging the inferior and dependent status ascribed to women has been evident in Britain for the past two centuries. One early writer who articulated the problems of women's status and advocated alternative views was Mary Wollstonecraft in *A Vindication of the Rights of Women* (1792). Her ideas influenced other women in the nineteenth century and, as we have seen, gradual action began to be taken through legislation. It was not, however, until the 1960s that a feminist critique of gender roles in society received more serious consideration among a wider audience. Even then, much entrenched sexism persisted as existing male-dominated power structures continued to be defended.

One of the fundamental objectives of the feminist movement was 'consciousness raising'. Essentially, this involved women appraising and understanding their social, economic and political roles and status together with the expectations that usually underpinned these. Invariably this diagnostic approach was restricted to women only. This deliberately fostered segregation and focus on 'women's issues' was controversial. On the one hand, it was argued that it facilitated more in-depth discussion by women of their concerns. On the other hand, it was contended that it would perpetuate the marginalisation of 'women's issues'. Given that the power structures necessary for affecting change (the political system, the judicial system, the trade union movement, etc.) were male dominated, attention should be focused on changing these and creating alliances with sympathetic men.

It was, perhaps, inevitable that the concept of a single feminist movement would not survive. The movement was characterised by diversity. The experiences, attitudes and values of the women involved would mean that the movement would be cross-cut by class differences, ethnic differences, different political perspectives, different employment experiences and different attitudes about tactical alliances with existing political structures.

There are, now, probably, three broad tendencies among feminists: radical, socialist and liberal feminists. Radical feminists tend to emphasise 'women-only' campaigning and the development of a woman's culture, freed from patriarchy (i.e. rule by men). Particular campaigning issues have concerned male violence towards women as well as the sexual exploitation of women. Socialist feminists tend to focus more widely on the issue of oppression and discrimination – not just of women. In this context, there can be dialogue and alliances with male supporters. The liberal feminists concentrate largely on political lobbying for legislative and administrative reforms for women. They seek to influence the decision-makers through the existing political channels. This categorisation, however, suffers from the danger of rigidity. Any person's attitudes to social and employment policies are likely to reflect a diversity of influences.

From the experience of the past 30 years, it possible to draw the following tentative conclusions. Structurally, male dominance persists in many aspects of our society: for example, in the political system, the judicial system, corporate and public service management, health care and education. Nevertheless, there is some evidence of slow, piecemeal change and there now exist (since the mid-1970s) legal mechanisms to challenge discriminatory practice. Similarly, in terms of treatment, progress has been slow in respect of, for example, equal pay, access to equal pension entitlements, employment protection in respect of pregnancy and maternity and the availability of childcare. However, political campaigning and the creative approach of European law and the ECJ have resulted in *some* landmark decisions. The agenda of political action now encompasses, as routine, many issues and concerns affecting women. Effectively, all these are small steps on a very long road to full equal treatment.

4.3 The context

The context within which sex discrimination law is developing comprises a number of key features. First, there continue to be marked changes in attitudes and aspirations among women towards their role in society at large and also their participation within the labour market. Secondly, as a result of employer drives for cost effectiveness, the nature of the labour market itself is changing. In terms of employment status and working time, it is becoming more flexible. It is frequently characterised as a 'dual labour market' with women predominating in *peripheral*, *marginal* or *atypical* work (*see* Chapter 2). Thirdly, and belatedly, political and legal steps have been taken, since the mid-1970s, to address unfair discrimination within the labour market and within society generally. While relatively weak legal redress has been provided for individual complainants, there has been even less serious attention focused on institutional patterns of discrimination against women (e.g. in the provision of childcare, in tackling low pay and equal pay and the barriers to training and promotional opportunities). Fourthly, action by employers to tackle discrimination has been fitful. Equal opportunities policies have scarcely dealt effectively with patterns of discrimination. While the newer concept of *diversity management* might provide equal opportunities with a strategic business edge, it is still questionable whether it will stimulate the commitment necessary to eradicate unlawful discrimination.

In this section, we will explore the following issues: participation in the labour market, social trends and political approaches of Britain and the European Union. Specific employment issues will be dealt with in the final section of this chapter.

4.3.1 Participation in the labour market

Management drives for flexibility and cost effectiveness have resulted in the development of a dual labour market in Britain, comprising full-time core workers and various peripheral workers, who are on other forms of employment status (*see* Chapter 2). Although this has always been a characteristic of British employment, it is now regarded as a much more clear-cut feature. In such a dual labour market, the range of employment status is wide.

Against this background, a significant trend in the labour market, which has accelerated in the past three decades, has been the growing *economic activity of women*. Approximately 90 per cent of the overall increase in the labour force (1971–90) is attributable to an increase in the number of women employed. In 1990, women accounted for 43 per cent of the labour force. By 2000, the proportion was 45 per cent – 12.5 million women in the labour market (Labour Force Survey 2000, *Labour Market Trends*, February 2001). This is the highest UK female employment rate recorded. Britain now has the third highest female employment of all EU member states after Denmark at 72 per cent and Sweden at 71 per cent. The EU average rate is 53 per cent.

This greater participation is driven by three factors: changing social attitudes, more facilitating economic conditions and the availability of legal standards through the British and European courts.

There are four important aspects to female participation:

1 the greater tendency for women to have peripheral employment;
2 higher economic activity in child-bearing and child-rearing years;
3 women with dependency responsibilities;
4 a tendency for women to be segregated into lower skilled, lower paid and lower status employment.

The first aspect is illustrated in Table 2.1 (p 58) by a broad profile of the workforce by sex and employment status (2001 UK data).

The second aspect of female participation in the labour market is evident in the Labour Force Survey statistics (Summer 2001) in Table 4.1 which provide data

Table 4.1 Female economic activity by age (per cent)

	1971	1991	2006
20–24 years	60.2	72.7	68.0
25–35 years	45.5	69.7	80.6

and projections of women's economic activity in various years, according to age cohort.

The third aspect concerns women with dependency responsibilities and married female workers. For example, in Spring 1997, 67 per cent of women with dependent children were economically active (as compared with 76 per cent for women without dependent children). Of such women, 55 per cent had a child under 5 years of age. The older the dependent children, the more likely it is that the mother will be economically active. So, if their children were of primary school age (between 5 and 10 years) then 71 per cent of women were economically active, and if between 11 and 15 years, then the figure rose to 78 per cent. The highest economic activity was 81 per cent for those with dependent children between 16 and 18 years (*Labour Market Trends*, March 1998). This Labour Force Survey also shows that over one-fifth of all women whose youngest child was under school age had been in employment prior to having their child and had not left employment after their child was born. Recent Labour Force Surveys reveal no significant changes to these patterns over the subsequent years.

The fourth aspect is evident in various studies of occupational segregation. The internal labour markets of organisations can be characterised by two forms of segregation: horizontal and vertical. These can, in practice, interlock with the core–periphery segregation, outlined earlier, and, as a consequence can exacerbate the discriminatory treatment of women.

Horizontal occupational segregation describes the situation where, for example, men and women in an organisation may work in different types of jobs – men's work and women's work. Workforce surveys, published by the Equal Opportunities Commission since the late 1980s, indicate heavy concentrations of women workers in relatively few occupations (EOC, 1990: 15). These are frequently those with a large demand for part-time labour. Examples include: clerical and related work; catering; cleaning; hairdressing; personal services; professional and related in education; welfare and health; retail selling; and, in manufacturing, repetitive assembly and product packaging. This occupational segregation reflects, in large part, stereotypical female responsibilities: caring, cleaning, cooking. Recent Labour Force Survey data (*Labour Market Trends*, March 1998) confirm that little has changed. Women form the majority of workers in three major occupational groups: clerical and secretarial (75 per cent); personal and protective services (66 per cent); and sales (62 per cent). These three groups account for over half of working women, but less than a fifth of working men.

Vertical occupational segregation describes the situation where men predominate in the higher graded posts in an organisation and women in the lower ones. In a broad survey of the phenomenon, the Hansard Society (1990) reported: 'For many women there is a glass ceiling blocking their aspirations, allowing them to see where they might go, but stopping them from arriving there. In any given occupation and in any given public office, the higher the rank, prestige or influ-ence, the smaller the proportion of women.'

The Labour Force Survey (Spring 2001) highlighted a 'glass ceiling' that was more or less penetrable depending on the sector concerned. Clearly, in those sectors where women predominate (like health, education and social care) there is a growing tendency for them to gain management positions (*see* Table 4.2).

Table 4.2 Proportion of female managers in selected managerial occupations (per cent)

	Female managers as a proportion of all managers (%)
Production managers	6
Financial institution managers	37
Advertising and PR managers	45
Personnel, training & IR managers	57
Office managers	66
Health & social services managers	73
All managers and senior officials	**30**

Source: Office for National Statistics: Labour Force Survey, Spring 2001.

4.3.2 Women's pay

Discrimination in women's pay (and benefits) has been long-standing. It has historically been related to occupational segregation. The skills, experience and tasks carried out in 'women's jobs' were rated less than those of men and so were rewarded less. Until 1970, when the Equal Pay Act was enacted, payment systems (whether negotiated with trade unions or not) could provide for explicit 'women's rates of pay'. Indeed, many collective agreements in manufacturing industry iden-tified the hierarchy of pay as follows: skilled grades, semi-skilled grades, unskilled grades and women's rates. The law prohibits such explicit statements of discrim-inatory practice. But, in some sectors 'women's rates' have 'gone underground'. Discriminatory pay continues to exist but is less easy to detect and eradicate.

A '**gender pay gap**' in earnings is still evident (*see* Table 4.3). It is, however, slowly closing. For example, in terms of full-time hourly earnings, the overall position over the past 15 years has been as follows. In 1987, women's gross hourly earnings were 73.4 per cent of the comparable male earnings. By 1996, they had risen to 79.9 per cent; and by 2001 to 81.6 per cent. (The pay gap is wider in respect of the gross weekly earnings of full-time employees. These earnings include additions to basic pay such as overtime, shift premia and incentive pay which are earned by a smaller proportion of women than of men.)

Other figures reveal different occupational gender pay gaps (Labour Force Survey, Spring 2001).

In addition to equal pay legislation, one other policy area is of considerable significance to the eradication of unequal pay. This is the issue of minimum pay. It was contended that the abolition of statutory Wages Councils in 1993 (which had the responsibility for setting minimum pay rates for particular sectors) would disproportionately disadvantage women workers. They predominated in the sec-

Table 4.3 The gender pay gap in the major occupational groups (per cent)

	Gender pay gap (%)
Managers and senior officials	23.7
Process, plant and machine operatives	21.6
Skilled trade	21.5
Elementary (unskilled occupations)	19.6
Associate professional and technical	18.7
Personal service	18.6
Administrative and secretarial	10.8
Professional occupations	10.2
Sales and customer service	9.7
All full-time employees	**18.4**

Source: *Labour Market Trends*.

tors and the grades covered by the Councils. The government enacted a statutory minimum wage (*see* Chapter 10). It is calculated that about two million workers (1.5 million of whom are women) benefit from this.

The labour market within which equal pay regulation in now operating has changed substantially since 1970. The greater flexibility of this labour market (*see also* Chapter 2) poses considerable difficulties for the effective elimination of 'the gender pay gap'. There are three problems: the process of pay determination, the substance of pay and the nature of the legislation itself. Heery (1995) explores these issues in the following way.

First of all, collective bargaining has ceased to be the predominant means for **determining pay**. Increasingly, pay has become linked more closely to the attributes of individual employees (for example, skills, competence or performance). This feature is linked with the devolution of pay decisions to line managers. While this contributes to the achievement of business performance targets in, for example, profit centres and other business units, the discretion accorded to managers will require careful guidance and monitoring. The degree to which reward determination is devolved is considerable. 'In a small but growing band of organisations individualisation has progressed, via cafeteria plans, to the point where employees can choose the form of their remuneration' (Heery, 1995: 12).

Secondly, there are a number of issues in respect of **the substance of pay**. There is a greater reliance on 'variable pay'. Consequently, a consolidated basic salary forms a smaller proportion of total remuneration. Furthermore, there is an increased use of pay systems that make earnings dependent on the performance of the enterprise, the work group or the individual employee's own performance. Finally, there has been 'a fairly widespread revision of pay structure to reflect more flexible forms of work and organisation. Examples include the adoption of flatter grade structures and broader pay bands which, *inter alia*, provide scope for the flexible deployment of employees without running into grade boundaries' (Heery, 1995: 12).

Thirdly, **the nature of the legislation** poses some difficulties in dealing with complaints deriving from this context of flexibility. Heery (1995: 12) puts the issue this way:

Equal pay law rests on the assumption that pay should be 'job-based'. It is predic-ated on a model of pay management in which jobs are tightly defined and analysed in terms of component factors in order that differences in pay will accurately reflect differences in job demands. The assumed outcome of pay management is a hierar-chy of grade rates based on analytical job evaluation . . . The legal preference seems to be for an integrated, organisation-wide approach to pay management, which is centrally authored, monitored and controlled.

This, clearly, creates tensions with trends in systems of pay determination and the bases on which the substance of pay is decided. Given that unequal pay has to be objectively justified, then, the careful defining of, for example, performance cri-teria is essential if employers are to have an acceptable defence.

4.3.3 Social trends and influences

The labour market trends outlined above reflect an ongoing feminisation of employment, which in turn is a response to a range of changing social attitudes held by women. The following are among the key changes in expectations that have been evident since World War II: that married women should be able to return to work; that women with childcare responsibilities should be able to return to work; that maternity leave career breaks will be relatively short; that women returners should be able to fulfil career aspirations; that parenting should be a joint female and male responsibility; and that employers should accom-modate, to some extent, the dependency responsibilities of their staff.

These expectations could be met by adaptations to employment practices. However, there remain many hostile and inhibiting attitudes – from both men and women. These can be demeaning and patronising, reinforcing specific stereo-types. For example, one British Rail manager was reported as saying 'I have a num-ber of ladies in my establishment and they are quite happy being routine booking clerks, travel centre clerks and that's not to say they don't do a good job. But they're possibly there because its basically pin money to them. So they do a good job by their pleasant personality and they get job satisfaction from it, but no way do they wish to go forward and take greater responsibility' (Robbins, 1986).

Other attitudes may reflect women's diffidence about their own status and their opportunities in employment. For example, Anna Pollert (1981) in a survey of women factory workers, reported that they saw themselves as having no right to a job, saw their pay as marginal to a man's, saw themselves as dependent on a man and saw marriage as an alternative to a job. Tina Boyden and Lorraine Paddison (1986) in a survey of non-manual workers in Barclay's Bank saw similar attitudes reflected:

> We recently asked a sample of male managers what they saw as the major factors inhibiting the progress of women in the bank and they replied that women lacked ambition and confidence, were reluctant to obtain professional qualifications, did not make long-term career plans and tended to put their husband and families first. More to the point, women staff, surveyed independently, also volunteered these reasons for women's lack of progress.

It is the fact and the legacy of these social attitudes that infuses employment practices and provides the underpinning of most discrimination claims in law.

Discriminatory attitudes can be difficult to eradicate because most are a result of *socialisation*. This is the process through which attitudes, values and standards of behaviour are inculcated and developed particularly within the family, within education, within religious organisations, within the workplace and within society at large.

Examples of this can be seen in a number of the early life-time choices made by girls and young women, which often determine ultimate employment and career opportunities. One EOC (1989) report commented how 'segregation begins at school' and 'continues into first jobs'. Markedly fewer female students choose maths and physics at A level than boys. They show a greater tendency to study English and modern languages, history, music and the visual arts and biology. 'As fewer girls take science examinations at school, this affects choice of degree subjects and the type of job obtained by graduates. Scientific and engineering work account for a fifth of graduates in all, but only one in ten female graduates' (EOC, 1989: 18).

4.3.4 Political approaches

Political approaches towards equal opportunities will reflect one of two broad sets of opinions. These are characterised as the **minimalist** and the **maximalist** views (Cunningham, 1992: 177).

The **minimalist view** centres on the the operation of free labour markets where everyone has the opportunity to compete. It stresses the importance of a society based upon merit and the removal of barriers to achievement: 'Policies are followed which are both colour and gender blind; positions are awarded on merit alone' (Cunningham, 1992: 177). It is defined as an approach concerned essentially with procedures. This view reflects the thinking of the 'new' right which gained influence within the Conservative Party. Some adherents to this view advocate the repeal of sex and race discrimination legislation and the abolition of both Commissions.

One 'new right' writer on 'free-market feminism' says that it 'denies that the anti-market measures advocated by modern feminism are either necessary for or effective in promoting equality of opportunity' (Conway, 1998: 43). He adds that 'these measures are both costly, ineffective and deprive women of the opportunity to be the primary carers of their children which many still appear to want to be'. The free market is proposed as 'the most effective instrument available to women for removing whatever residual obstacles remain to their enjoying equality of opportunity'. The writer provides the following illustration:

> By allowing employers to pay unequal wages for the same work to men and women and to engage in reverse discrimination in favour of women as well as ordinary sexual discrimination against them, a free market would provide women with enormous opportunity to display their abilities if discriminated against by some employers, by offering their services at lower rates than men. It would also allow women to set up female-only businesses in which those women who would prefer such a working environment could find space to explore their own potential, free from the pressure of men. It is likely that, in a free market, there would be a great plurality of different kinds of firm: some mixed, some male only, and some female

only. Between them, these firms would employ a variety of different policies in relation to the sexual composition of their workforce: some not practising any discrimination, others practising reverse discrimination in favour of one or other sex, and others old fashioned discrimination against one sex.

Such views did not, however, influence John Major, as Prime Minister. He clearly indicated his support for the principles of sex and race anti-discrimination law. The present leader of the Conservative opposition has continued these policy commitments.

The **maximalist view** is more comprehensive in its approach. It takes as its starting point a 'holistic' view of society, whereby the individual is seen not as an entity herself or himself (nor just as a factor of production in a market economy) but as part of a social group. So, the historical and social circumstances, which have created and reinforced stereotyping and prejudice, can be taken into account and addressed. This view encourages the adoption of positive action strategies to diagnose and dismantle historic barriers to equal opportunities. Government policy-makers will take a wider view of women's contribution to society and the economy and evaluate action on, for example, matrimonial rights, social security provision, childcare, low pay, working time, labour market flexibility, training and development and general access to services. This maximalist approach acknowledges a civil-rights dimension to equal opportunity and equal treatment.

If these two views are seen as the ends of a spectrum, then intermediate positions are possible. So, Cunningham identifies a 'liberal' position. This is described as following the minimalist view, though it is 'less extreme'. 'The liberal account recognises that society does restrict the opportunity of some disadvantaged groups and advocates positive action to counter this.' She adds, however, that it 'does not challenge the main institutions of oppression such as the family and existing income and status hierarchies of society'. It is largely piecemeal in its approach – dealing with individual issues and problems as they arise.

The present Labour government, in terms of legislation and policy, tends towards the development of a comprehensive range of policies to enhance women's contribution and status in society. These policies and legislative action have encompassed:

- proposals on a national childcare strategy;
- the working families tax credit;
- the enactment of the European Directive on parental leave and the promotion of a wider 'work-life' balance (*see* Chapter 13);
- encouragement, through the social security system, of single mothers to return to work;
- the enactment of the European Directive on part-time working and the encouragement of flexible working for parents with dependants (*see* Chapters 2 and 13);
- the adoption of a national minimum wage, overwhelmingly benefiting female workers (*see* Chapter 10);
- continuing commitment to the existing sex discrimination policies.

There are, nevertheless, special circumstances when government may not pursue equal opportunities for women in every situation. For example, in May 2002, following a two-year study, the Ministry of Defence announced that it will not be operationally effective to open up to women certain close-quarter combat roles which involve killing an enemy face to face. This is consistent with exemptions provided under the Sex Discrimination Act 1975 s 85(4) and the Equal Treatment Directive 1976 Article 2(2). At present, 73 per cent of roles in the Royal Navy; 70 per cent in the Army; and 96 per cent in the Royal Air Force are already open to women.

4.4 The legal framework

There are three broad principles underlying this framework of law:

1 comparison between men and women;
2 the European 'principle of equal treatment' which construes discrimination on grounds of sex more widely;
3 special circumstances permitting sex discrimination (e.g. pregnancy).

These will be explored, as appropriate, below.

4.4.1 Structure of discrimination law

It has been commented that Parliament's intention in sex discrimination law was to create a balance between '*proscription, prescription and permission*' (Sacks, 1992). The basic legal provisions and concepts of sex discrimination law are covered under the following headings: the grounds of unlawful discrimination, access to statutory rights, direct discrimination, indirect discrimination, equal pay, victimisation, positive action and positive discrimination, special provisions, liability, enforcement procedures and remedies.

4.4.2 Grounds of unlawful discrimination

In Britain, there are two major *complementary* pieces of legislation to deal with sex discrimination: the Equal Pay Act 1970 (as amended by the 1983 Equal Value Regulations); and the Sex Discrimination Act 1975 (as amended by the Sex Discrimination Act 1986 and the Sex Discrimination (Gender Reassignment) Regulations 1999). This domestic framework of legislation enacts in Britain various requirements in European law (under Art 141 of the Treaty of Rome, the Equal Pay Directive 1975 and the Equal Treatment Directive 1976). It continues to be profoundly influenced by rulings of the ECJ. In addition, from 1 December 2003, protection against discrimination on grounds of sexual orientation is enacted under the Employment Equality (Sexual Orientation) Regulations 2003. These implement provisions of the European Employment Directive 2000.

By way of introduction, we will look briefly at the essentials of the Equal Pay Act 1970, the Sex Discrimination Act 1975 and the Equal Treatment Directive 1976.

The Equal Pay Act 1970 and Regulations

This Act is concerned with sex discrimination, but not marital status, in respect of 'the terms of a contract'. It sets out a requirement that if the terms of a contract of employment do not include an equality clause, then 'they shall be deemed to include one' (s 1). These terms of the contract may be 'concerned with pay or not' (s 2). The Act is, then, very wide-ranging in scope. In fact, through case law, particularly the rulings of the ECJ, pay has been construed widely. Indeed, Art 141 (which asserts 'the principle that men and women should receive equal pay for equal work') states that 'pay means the ordinary basic or minimum wage or salary and any other consideration, whether in cash or in kind, which the worker receives, directly or indirectly, in respect of his employment from his employer'. It includes the following:

■ redundancy pay (*Hammersmith and Queen Charlotte's Special Health Authority* v *Cato* [1987] IRLR 483, EAT);

■ occupational pensions (*Bilka-Kaufhaus GmbH* v *Weber von Hartz* [1986] IRLR 317, ECJ; *Barber* v *Guardian Royal Exchange Group* [1990] IRLR 240, CA);

■ severance pay on retirement (*Kowalska* v *Freie und Hansestadt Hamburg*, 1992 C–33/89, ECJ);

■ sick pay (*Rinner-Kunn* v *FWW Special-Gebaudereinigung GmbH and Co* [1989] IRLR 493, ECJ);

■ paid leave (*Arbeiterwohlfahrt der Stadt Berlin* v *Botel* [1992] IRLR 423, ECJ).

This legislation requires an *actual* comparator. There are three bases for comparison: (1) like work, (2) work rated as equivalent and (3) work of equal value. These are in relation to people 'in the same employment'. This is defined as employment by the same employer (or an associated employer) at the same establishment; or at establishments in Great Britain (which includes the one where the complainant works) and 'at which common terms and conditions of employment are observed either generally or for employees of the relevant classes' (s 1(6)).

A woman is to be regarded as employed on **like work** with men in the same employment 'if, but only if, her work and theirs is of the same or a broadly similar nature and the difference (if any) between the things she does and the things they do are not of practical importance in relation to terms and conditions of employment'. In comparing her work and theirs, 'regard shall be had to the frequency or otherwise with which any such differences occur in practice as well as to the nature and extent of the differences' (EqPA, s 1(4)).

A woman is to be regarded as employed on **work rated as equivalent** with that of men in the same employment 'if, but only if, her job and their job have been given an equal value, in terms of the demand made on a worker under various headings (for instance, effort, skill, decision) on a study undertaken with a view to evaluating in those terms the jobs to be done by all or any of the employees in an undertaking or group of undertakings, or would have been given an equal value but for the evaluation being made on a system setting different values for men and women on the same demand under any heading' (s 1(5)).

The equal value provision was enacted under the Equal Pay (Amendment) Regulations 1983 and came into force on 1 January 1984. It allows a woman to claim equal pay with a man in the same employment provided her work is 'of equal value' to that of a man she has specified. In the absence of an existing evaluation system covering both jobs, 'equal value' is assessed by an *independent expert* appointed by the employment tribunal who examines and compares the two jobs in question in isolation using whatever factors the expert considers to be most relevant to those two jobs. If the expert assesses the two jobs to be of equal value in this abstract context then, assuming that the man is being paid more than the woman, discrimination is defined as occurring. The employer's defence is based on a 'genuine material factor' (*see* later section).

Unequal pay can arise as a result of either direct or indirect discrimination. It is noted in the Code of Practice on Equal Pay 1997 that unlawful discrimination in pay now occurs primarily because women and men tend to do different jobs or to have different work patterns. So, women receive lower pay because the tasks they perform have traditionally been undervalued compared to the tasks typically carried out by men and because pay systems have been geared to a male pattern of full-time permanent employment.

The Sex Discrimination Act 1975

The Act proscribes discrimination on grounds of sex (covering both women and men); and, for women, on grounds of marital status. It 'does not apply to benefits consisting of the payment of money when the provision of those benefits is regulated by the woman's contract of employment' (s 6(6)). So, it excludes 'terms'. These come under the Equal Pay Act. The Sex Discrimination Act is largely founded on comparison. The comparison must be such that 'the relevant circumstances in the one case are the same, or not materially different, in the other' (s 5(3)). It may involve a hypothetical comparator. Special provisions (*see* below) have, however, been enacted where sex is a qualification for a particular job (i.e. sex as a 'genuine occupational qualification'), and where a woman is pregnant and comparison is clearly unrealistic.

The Equal Treatment Directive 1976

The Directive asserts 'the principle of equal treatment' for men and women. This principle means that 'there shall be no discrimination whatsoever on grounds of sex either directly or indirectly by reference in particular to marital or family status' (Art 2.1). The ECJ has ruled that the elimination of discrimination based on sex is a 'fundamental right' and is 'one of the general principles of Community law' (*Defrenne* v *Sabena* 149/77 [1978]).

Until 1996, discrimination on grounds of sex under European law was construed in relation to the treatment of men and/or women. However, cases involving discrimination on grounds of sexuality began to enlarge the meaning of 'the principle of equal treatment'. In one case, involving discrimination on the grounds of gender reassignment (transsexual status), the ECJ ruled that such discrimination was contrary to the Directive (*P* v *S and Cornwall County Council* [1996] IRLR 347). In this case, the ECJ expressly stated that the scope of European law 'cannot be confined simply to discrimination based on the fact that a person is of one or other sex'.

However, applications relating to discrimination on the grounds of homosexuality have been unsuccessful. The *Grant* case related to a lesbian partner's access to concessionary travel benefits. The ECJ's decision overturned the Advocate-General's Opinion. It took the unequivocal view that the discrimination was not on the grounds of sex but of sexual orientation. It ruled that 'an employer is not required by Community law to treat the situation of a person who has a stable relationship with a partner of the same sex as equivalent to that of a person who is married to or has a stable relationship outside marriage with a partner of the opposite sex'.

When implemented in December 2003, the Employment Directive 2000 will prohibit direct and indirect discrimination in employment on the grounds of sexual orientation. The Directive does not cover discrimination in respect of access to goods, facilities and services. (See summary of the Employment Equality (Sexual Orientation) Regulations 2003 on p 180.)

4.4.3 Access to statutory rights

As indicated earlier, sex discrimination law constitutes part of a framework of civil rights available to citizens in various areas of social, economic and political activity. In the sphere of employment it is also widely available.

Two important preliminary points need to be made. The first is that while the Sex Discrimination Act 1975 refers to discrimination against women its provisions in s 1 and in relation to employment and other discrimination (Parts II and III) 'are to be read as applying equally to **the treatment of men**' (s 2(1)). Secondly, '**employment**' means 'employment under a contract of service or of apprenticeship or a contract personally to execute any work or labour' (EqPA, s 1(6)(a); SDA, s 82(1)).

The following persons, irrespective of age or any restrictions relating to hours worked or length of service, may bring complaints under the legislation within three months of the act complained of occurring.

Applicants for employment

Such persons are protected by the following provision:

> It is unlawful for a person, in relation to employment by him at an establishment in Great Britain, to discriminate against a woman –
> (a) in the arrangements he makes for the purpose of determining who should be offered that employment, or
> (b) in the terms on which he offers her that employment, or
> (c) by refusing or deliberately omitting to offer her that employment (SDA 1975, s 6(1)).

Employed people

The employed are protected as follows:

> It is unlawful for a person, in the case of a woman employed by him at an establishment in Great Britain, to discriminate against her –

(a) in the way he affords her access to opportunities for promotion, transfer or training, or to any other benefits, facilities or services, or by refusing or deliberately omitting to afford her access to them, or

(b) by dismissing her, or subjecting her to any other detriment (s 6(2)).

An exception to these rights is in relation to work done 'wholly or mainly' outside Great Britain (s 10).

The protection of **contract workers** 'applies to any work for a person ("the principal") which is available for doing by individuals ("contract workers") who are employed not by the principal himself but by another person who supplies them under a contract made with the principal' (s 9(1)). It is then stated that:

It is unlawful for the principal, in relation to work to which this section applies, to discriminate against a contract worker –
(a) in the terms on which he allows her to do that work, or
(b) by not allowing her to do it or continue to do it, or
(c) in the way he affords her access to any benefits, facilities or services or by refusing or deliberately omitting to afford her access to them, or
(d) by subjecting her to any other detriment (s 9(2)).

The self-employed

Self-employed persons may also be protected by the Sex Discrimination Act (and by extension, the Race Relations Act). The issue is whether they are employed under contracts 'personally to execute any work or labour' (s 82(1)). In one case (*Quinnen* v *Hovels* [1984] IRLR 227, EAT), a self-employed salesman of 'fancy goods' who had 'pitches' in various department stores recruited some temporary assistants to work for him on a commission basis. Although they were self-employed, nevertheless, the EAT ruled that they were protected by the SDA.

The Court of Appeal, later, ruled on the issue of '**dominant purpose**' in the contract (*Mirror Group Newspapers Ltd* v *Gunning* [1986] IRLR 27, CA). A single obligation to provide personal services in a contract was not seen as sufficient: 'one has to look at the agreement as a whole and provided that there is some obligation by one contracting party personally to execute any work or labour, one then has to decide whether that is the dominant purpose of the contract or whether the contract is properly to be regarded in essence as a contract for the personal execution of work or labour' (Balcombe LJ).

Exceptions

There are, of course, some exceptions. We will discuss special provisions relating to **pregnancy** and to '**genuine occupational qualifications**' below. There is no exemption for private households. This was removed in 1986 as contrary to the Equal Treatment Directive. However, there is a relevant provision under 'genuine occupational qualifications' (s 7(2)(ba)) (*see* later section).

Further exemptions include: acts done for the purpose of safeguarding national security (s 52); employment of ministers of religion (s 19). In addition, although 'the holding of the office of constable shall be treated as employment' (s 17(1)), certain forms of discrimination in respect of police officers are permitted. These exceptions include regulations governing height, uniform and equipment, or allowances in lieu of uniform and equipment (s 17(2)).

4.4.4 Direct discrimination

> A person discriminates against a woman in any circumstances relevant for the purposes of any provisions of this Act if on the ground of her sex he treats her less favourably than he treats or would treat a man (SDA, s 1(1)(a)).

The key test for determining direct discrimination is the '**but for**' test. It was outlined in the House of Lords judgment in *James* v *Eastleigh Borough Council* [1990] IRLR 288. Lord Goff stated that 'cases of direct discrimination under s 1(1)(a) can be considered by asking the simple question: would the complainant have received the same treatment from the defendant but for his or her sex?'

He added that:

> this simple test possesses the double virtue that, on the one hand, it embraces both the case where the treatment derives from the application of a gender based criterion and the case where it derives from the selection of the complainant because of his or her sex; and on the other hand, it avoids, in most cases at least, complicated questions related to concepts such as intention, motive, reason or purpose and the danger of confusion arising from the misuse of those elusive terms.

It is important, in this context, that the court or tribunal has to arrive at a view, on the facts, that the less favourable treatment was on the grounds of sex (even in part) and on no other grounds.

Motive and intentions are not relevant in cases of direct discrimination. No justification or defence is allowable. Lord Goff (in *R* v *Birminghan City Council ex parte EOC* [1989] IRLR 173) stated that 'the intention or motive of the defendant to discriminate . . . is not a necessary condition to liability; it is perfectly possible to envisage cases where the defendant had no such motive and yet did in fact discriminate on the grounds of sex'.

The concept of direct discrimination has provided the legal basis for tackling discrimination on the grounds of pregnancy (*see* later section of this chapter). In addition, it has been ruled that sexual harassment constitutes direct discrimination (*see* Chapter 7).

An important contrast with the Race Relations Act (s 1(2)) is the absence in sex discrimination legislation of the prohibition of segregation in employment as 'less favourable treatment'.

To comply with European law, the direct sex discrimination provisions were amended in 1999 to cover discrimination on the grounds of gender reassignment in employment and vocational training. It proscribes less favourable treatment on the grounds that a person 'intends to undergo, is undergoing or has undergone gender reassignment' (s 2A). Less favourable treatment can involve comparison of arrangements for sick absence and the absence for gender reassignment treatment.

4.4.5 **Indirect discrimination**

While the direct discrimination provisions cover clear and blatant unfair discrimination against women or men, those relating to indirect discrimination (SDA 1975, s 1(1)(b)) are designed to tackle the less obvious and unintentional discriminatory treatment that might arise in the course of employment. Welcoming the incorporation of the concept into the legal framework, Mary Redmond (1986: 476) said that 'the proscription of indirect discrimination represents a landmark in British anti-discrimination legislation. The continuing absence of women and of minority groups from important areas of employment is due, in large measure, to indirect discrimination.' However, she adds an important word of warning that 'the road to be travelled by a person alleging indirect discrimination is strewn with complexities'.

The long-standing provisions relating to indirect sex discrimination are as follows:

> A person discriminates against a woman in any circumstances relevant for the purposes of any provisions of this Act if . . . he applies to her a condition or requirement which he applies or would apply equally to a man but –
> (i) which is such that the proportion of women who can comply with it is considerably smaller than the proportion of men who can comply with it, and
> (ii) which he cannot show to be justifiable irrespective of the sex of the person to whom it is applied, and
> (iii) which is to her detriment because she cannot comply with it (SDA, s 1(1)(b)).

Since October 2001, in cases brought under the employment or vocational training provisions of the Sex Discrimination Act 1975, a new definition of indirect sex discrimination applies (the Sex Discrimination (Indirect Discrimination and Burden of Proof) Regulations 2001). This, using the language of the 1997 European Directive (on the burden of proof in cases of discrimination based on sex), refers to 'a provision, criterion or practice' which is such that 'it would be to the detriment of a considerably larger proportion of women than of men'. The term 'provision, criterion or practice' is not defined but it includes the existing terms, 'requirement or condition'. It is likely that it would cover informal practices in recruitment and during employment. The applicant must show that they have suffered a detriment and the employer has the opportunity to justify their behaviour.

The complexity in this area is evident as we consider answers to the questions in the following four-stage process. (It is important to remember that the case law referred to here draws on complaints concerning the earlier definition of indirect sex discrimination that related to a 'requirement or condition'.)

The provision, criterion or practice

The first question to be answered is: **Which provision, criterion or practice does the employer have that is applied equally regardless of sex?**

This part of the legislation refers to those rules, conditions and practices that although appearing neutral in their application can put a person at a disadvantage because of their sex (*see also* Chapter 5 on race discrimination). The Court of Appeal has ruled, in two race discrimination cases, that the requirement or condition must be an absolute bar (*Perera* v *Civil Service Commission and Department of Customs and Excise (No. 2)* [1983] IRLR 166; *Meer* v *London Borough of Tower Hamlets* [1988] IRLR 399).

Among the conditions or requirements which may be indirectly discriminatory are the following:

- *Age barriers in recruitment.* These may indirectly discriminate against women who have taken time out of employment to bring up children (*Price* v *Civil Service Commission* [1978] IRLR 3, EAT). The CIPD in its Statement on Age and Employment comments that 'the use of age, age bands, age guides and age-related criteria reduces objectivity in employment decision making. It increases the likelihood of poor quality and inappropriate decisions which are harmful to individuals, wasteful of people's skills and detract from organisational efficiency'.

- *Requirements on length of service.* These, again, can disadvantage women who have taken time out of employment to have and bring up children. There is clear general statistical evidence that women's continuity of service tends to be less then men's when compared at particular points. In the Labour Force Survey 1992, it was found that 24 per cent of women had been with their current employer for 12 months or less (compared with 42 per cent of men), and 37 per cent had been with this employer for two years or less (compared with 59 per cent of men). The differential impact of the two-year continuous service qualification for access to unfair dismissal rights was at the centre of a case concerning its compatibility with the principle of equal treatment (*R* v *Secretary of State for Employment ex parte Seymour-Smith and Perez* [1997] IRLR 315).

- *Mobility conditions.* These may indirectly discriminate against women who have family commitments and are less likely to be able to comply than a man.

- *Unsocial hours requirements.* Again, these can indirectly affect women because of family responsibilities. For example, in one case (*London Underground Ltd* v *Edwards (No. 2)* [1998] IRLR 364, CA), a female train operator, who was a single parent, was required to work a new roster or face dismissal. Prior to this (for five years) she had been able to organise a shift pattern which enabled her to work and care for her child. The new roster would have required her to work longer hours than previously. She complained of unfair dismissal.

- *Requirement to work full-time.* This may be indirectly discriminatory against women returners if the work can be undertaken on a part-time basis. (This issue is discussed more fully in Chapter 13 on dependency rights.)

- *Redundancy selection.* A criterion (e.g. the selection of part-timers first) might be indirectly discriminatory because of its differential adverse impact upon women.

Defining a smaller proportion

The second question is: **Is the requirement or condition such that a considerably smaller proportion of women/men can comply with it?**

There are three aspects to this: the pool of comparison, the proportion of women and the ability to comply.

The principal question to be determined is **the appropriate pool of comparison**. This is a matter of fact for the tribunal. Of course, a problem arises for an applicant who selects what they reasonably believe to be an appropriate pool and find that this is different from the tribunal's selection. The application may then fail. The pool may be the whole population or general labour market, employees in a particular workforce, or of a particular workplace. Statistical evidence may be provided to prove a case. General labour market statistics have been used in two high-profile cases involving general employment rights: access to unfair dismissal compensation and redundancy payments (*R v Secretary of State for Employment ex parte EOC* [1994] IRLR 176), and the lawfulness of the two-year qualifying period for unfair dismissal applications (*R v Secretary of State for Employment ex parte Seymour-Smith and Perez* [1997] IRLR 315).

The purpose of submitting these data is to establish **the proportion** of women or of men who are said to have been disadvantaged. The recent case referred to above (*London Underground Ltd v Edwards (No. 2)* [1998] IRLR 364, CA) throws interesting light on the way in which this issue might be considered. In this case, a new working roster was implemented which had a detrimental effect on Ms Edwards, a train operator. All 2023 male train operators complied with the new roster and Ms Edwards was the only one of just 21 female train operators who could not comply with it. The court acknowledged that the impact of the new requirement might be *statistically insignificant*. However, taking into account the fact that it is common knowledge that women are more likely than men to be single parents, caring for children, there was disproportionate impact.

Finally, the ability to comply with a condition or requirement was defined in the late 1970s as the ability to **comply in practice**. Mr Justice Phillips said (in *Price v Civil Service Commission* [1977] IRLR 291, EAT) that 'it should not be said that a person "can" do something merely because it is theoretically possible for him to do so; it is necessary to see whether he can do so in practice'. It has been ruled, also, that compliance or inability to comply must be at the time of the incident in question and not at some future date.

Establishing a detriment

The third question is: **Is it to the detriment of those unable to comply and is the person alleging detriment unable to comply?**

It is not enough to show that there is a discriminatory requirement or condition which disadvantages women in general. It must be shown that the effect was detrimental to the employment of the particular complainant at that time. In *Barclays Bank plc v Kapur* [1995] IRLR 87, the Court of Appeal that 'there has to be some physical or economic consequence as a result of discrimination to constitute a detriment in this context, which is material and substantial'. An unjustified sense of grievance cannot amount to a detriment. Examples of detriments can include the following: an application for employment was not considered, failure to hear of job vacancies because they were inadequately advertised, or receiving lower pay or less favourable benefits or working conditions.

Justification

The final question to be answered is: **Can the provision, criterion or practice be shown to be justifiable and not unlawful?**

The question of justification has been considered in various court and tribunal cases – up to the Court of Appeal. It is a question of fact for a tribunal to decide whether the circumstances of any particular case meet the prevailing standards of justification. In an early case (*Steel* v *UPW* [1978] ICR 181) Phillips J set the standard for determining the justification of a requirement or condition as 'necessary' for the employer to adopt 'rather than merely convenient' for him.

Bourn and Whitmore (1993: 79) comment that 'subsequent cases tended to weaken this standard'. They refer to various cases where the following standards have been used:

- 'reasonably necessary' (*Singh* v *Rowntree Mackintosh* [1979] ICR 554, EAT);
- 'right and proper in the circumstances' (*Panesar* v *Nestlé Co* [1980] ICR 144, CA);
- 'acceptable to right thinking people as sound and tolerable reasons for adopting the practice in question' (*Ojutiku* v *MSC* [1982] ICR 661, CA).

The authors concluded that 'this series of definitions showed a consistent tendency over time for the objective standards first enunciated by Phillips J . . . to be weakened by the addition of subjective elements'.

However, the construction of 'justification' was further elaborated in the Court of Appeal (*Hampson* v *Department of Education and Science* [1989] IRLR 69, CA) by the explicit acknowledgement of a balance that had to be struck between, on the one hand, the discriminatory effect of the condition or requirement and, on the other hand, 'the reasonable needs of the person who applies the condition'. This has been stated by Lord Keith as the 'appropriate' analysis, superseding that set out in the *Ojutiku* case. The ECJ has ruled that the objective standards of 'justification' require that the employer has a real need and that the discriminatory action is necessary and appropriate to achieve that end (*Bilka-Kaufhaus GmbH* v *Weber von Hartz* [1986] IRLR 317). It has affirmed the principle of proportionality.

In the *Edwards* case, mentioned above, the EAT ruled that London Underground Ltd had not established justification. It stated that it could easily have accommodated Ms Edwards without losing the objective of its business plan and reorganisation. It had been well aware of her misgivings and difficulties and had not addressed itself to them. She had been working for this employer for nearly ten years and there had been no complaints about her work performance. Her family demands were of a temporary nature. London Underground could have accommodated her reasonable demands.

4.4.6 Claims relating to equal pay

Earlier in this chapter the grounds were outlined under which unlawful pay discrimination might take place. One key issue which arises in equal pay applications is the **'material factor defence'** (s 1(3)). This enables an employer to argue that the pay structure is discriminatory not on the unlawful grounds of sex discrimination but on other objective grounds. It is a matter for the employer to convince the tribunal that these objective grounds are the true reasons for the differential treatment.

Examples of acceptable 'genuine material difference' have included:

- *market forces*: in a 'like work' case, one member of staff was recruited at a lower salary than a man some three months earlier (*Rainey* v *Greater Glasgow Health Board* [1987] IRLR 26, HL);
- *'red-circling' of pay*: in a 'like work' case, comparison was with a long-serving man who was transferred to this lighter work on protected pay because of age and infirmity – a practice that had operated for some 25 years (*Methven & Musiolik* v *Cow Industrial Polymers Ltd* [1980] IRLR 289, CA).

Examples of unacceptable 'genuine material difference' have included:

- *financial constraints*: where an employee was employed on a lower salary than men on 'like work' and after the financial constraints had ceased her pay was not increased. The Court of Appeal ruled against the employer (*Benveniste* v *University of Southampton* [1989] IRLR 122, CA);
- *an error* in determining pay in relation to qualifications (*McPherson* v *Rathgael Centre for Children and Young People and Northern Ireland Office* (*Training Schools Branch*) [1991] IRLR 206, CA);
- *part-time working* is not acceptable for paying a lower hourly rate than full-timers receive (*Jenkins* v *Kingsgate* (*Clothing Productions*) *Ltd* (*No. 2*) [1981] IRLR 388, EAT).

4.4.7 Victimisation

To show victimisation, three elements must be satisfied:

1 The victim must have taken a sex discrimination action, given evidence in a sex discrimination case or alleged that sex discrimination has taken place.
2 It must be demonstrated that the treatment of the victim has been less favourable than that of someone who has not been involved in a sex discrimination case (*Chief Constable of West Yorkshire* v *Khan* [2001] IRLR 830).
3 It must also be demonstrated that the less favourable treatment is a direct result of the involvement in the sex discrimination case (*Aziz* v *Trinity Street Taxis Ltd* [1988] ICR 534, CA).

In a recent case, the ECJ ruled that protection against action by an employer extended to circumstances after the end of the employment relationship. The case involved a refusal to provide a reference to an employment agency for a woman who had alleged that she had been dismissed because of pregnancy. Any retaliatory measures by an employer (whether in cases of dismissal or not) were unlawful. They could deter workers from pursuing claims and might seriously jeopardise the Equal Treatment Directive's aim (*Coote* v *Granada Hospitality Ltd* C–185/97, ECJ).

4.4.8 Positive action and positive discrimination

As discussed earlier, patterns of discrimination – on the grounds of sex and race – are deep-seated in history and in much already-established employment practice.

In any policy attempts to eradicate endemic unfair discrimination two concepts are frequently mentioned: *positive action* and *positive discrimination* (or *reverse discrimination* or *affirmative action*).

Positive action is provided for in the legislation (SDA 1975, ss 47 and 48). It is also commended in the statutory code of practice published by the Equal Opportunities Commission. In practice, the theoretical distinction between positive action and positive discrimination can be blurred. This can be seen by looking at evolving case law – in particular rulings of the ECJ. To consider this topic, it is possible to propose a four-fold categorisation of positive-action measures which develop from work of Pollert and Rees (1992: 3).

Access to employment

This is a particularly important dimension to equal opportunities – not only at the point of initial recruitment into an organisation but also in relation to career progression and promotion. (The latter is discussed below in respect of access to training.) The EOC Code of Practice identifies the importance of encouraging 'underrepresented' groups to apply for posts (EOC, 1985: paras 41–42; CRE, 1983: para 1.45). In this context, an organisation can set targets for the number of women to be recruited. (Quotas would be evidence of positive discrimination and unlawful under the Sex Discrimination Act.)

However, some legislative uncertainty have been created about the role of positive discrimination in a 'tie-break' situation in selection for a specific post – i.e. where a woman was equally qualified with a man. In 1995, the ECJ ruled, in a German case, that national rules which guarantee women absolute and unconditional priority for public sector appointments (where women are underrepresented) go beyond promoting equal opportunities and overstep the limits of the Equal Treatment directive (*Kalenke* v *Freie Hansestadt Bremen* [1995] IRLR 660). In a later German case, it was ruled that it was not contrary to the Directive for equally qualified women to be given preference for promotion where there are fewer women than men in the relevant post. This was subject to the proviso that the employer could take into account objective factors which were specific to an individual man and so tilted the balance in his favour (*Marschall* v *Nordrhein-Westfalen* [1998] IRLR 39).

In this case, a German comprehensive school teacher, Hellmutt Marschall, applied for promotion to a higher-grade teaching post. The civil service law of the federal state provides that where 'there are fewer women than men in the particular higher-grade post in the career bracket, women are to be given priority for promotion in the event of equal suitability, competence and professional performance, unless reasons specific to an individual (male) candidate tilt the balance in his favour'. He was informed that an equally qualified woman was to be appointed. He initiated legal proceedings in Germany.

The ECJ, in ruling on compliance with the principle of equal treatment, stated that the provision in the civil service law was compatible provided that:

- in each individual case there is a guarantee that the candidates will be subject to an objective assessment which takes account of all criteria;
- where one or more of those criteria tilts the balance in favour of a male candidate, the priority accorded to female candidates will be overridden; and
- such criteria are not discriminatory against female candidates.

As far as Britain is concerned, positive discrimination is still unlawful under the Sex Discrimination Act. 'The decision does not require member states – or employers – to discriminate in favour of women. Instead, it authorises such discrimination as a matter of Community law, subject to the proviso laid down by the Court' (EOR 77, January/February 1998).

Family-friendly measures

These 'seek to do no more than make it easier for women to carry the "double load" of paid work and domestic commitments' (e.g. career break schemes, flexible working time and assistance with childcare). 'They may certainly assist women to return to work and to remain in employment despite having children. However, they are not necessarily aimed at helping women to move up the organisation and any such effect would be a by-product of not losing seniority – a male biased criterion for promotion' (Pollert and Rees 1992: 3). The adoption of these measures would reflect the guidance of the statutory code (EOC, 1985: para 43).

The ECJ ruled, in a Dutch case in 2002, that a policy under which an employer provided women employees only with access to nursery places for their children, while denying male employees with children the same facility (except in an emergency) was not a breach of the Equal Treatment Directive (*Lommers* v *Minister van Landbouw, Natuurbeheer en Visseij* [2002] IRLR 430). Such a practice would be unlawful under the UK's Sex Discrimination Act 1975 (s 6(2)). However, the Treaty of Rome (as amended by the Treaty of Amsterdam) states that:

> with a view to ensuring full equality in practice between men and women in working life, the principle of equal treatment shall not prevent any Member State from maintaining or adopting measures providing for specific advantages in order to make it easier for the under-represented sex to pursue a vocational activity or to prevent or compensate for disadvantages in professional careers (Art 141(4)).

This amendment facilitates positive discrimination if a member state wishes to take such steps.

Access to training

The legislation specifically refers to provision of training (SDA 1975, ss 47–8; RRA 1976, ss 37–8). This is qualified by the requirement that the group has been under-represented in the preceding 12 months in particular work. Pollert and Rees (1992: 3) point to 'women's relative lack of access to training' and to its importance in terms of development and promotion opportunities. 'Women are less likely to have participated in higher education; while they go on to further education in substantial numbers, it tends to be for training in typically female work such as secretarial work and hairdressing. They are less likely to be sponsored by their employers for continuing training.' So, access to single-sex training can 'allow women to overcome earlier educational and training disadvantage and encourage them to move either up the management hierarchy or over into male dominated occupations'. Indeed, for these reasons, the provisions on access to training are more properly seen as positive, or reverse, discrimination. However, research shows that 'the law in this field is little known, misunderstood and minimally used' (Sacks, 1992: 380). Among the suggested reasons are the absence of a mandatory legal requirement, resource problems and lack of commitment by those in charge.

Organisational and cultural change

The previous three types of positive action have been by their very nature piecemeal. They may, in the context of effective equal opportunities policies, achieve some incremental change. However, this fourth type of positive action is strategic in focus and by implication should combine the other types. It 'involves a detailed examination of existing structures and practices which systematically yet invisibly sustain white, male power structures, sexual segregation and stereotyping. This is clearly the most difficult kind of measure to implement successfully and requires commitment across the entire organisation' (Pollert and Rees, 1992: 4).

4.4.9   Special provisions

Two sets of special provisions have been enacted under sex discrimination law: those relating to circumstances where sex is '**a genuine occupational qualification**' and those relating to **pregnant workers**.

Genuine occupational qualifications (GOQs)

There are several circumstances where a person's sex can be a genuine qualification for a job (SDA 1975, s 7):

- 'the essential nature of the job' requires a man or woman 'for reasons of **physiology** (excluding physical strength or stamina)' or 'for reasons of **authenticity**' in drama and other entertainment;
- 'the job needs to be held' by a man or woman 'to preserve **decency or privacy**'. This is because the job requires 'physical contact' or because the holder of the job might work in circumstances where members of the opposite sex 'are in a state of undress or are using sanitary facilities';
- 'the job is likely to involve the holder of the job doing his work, or living, in **a private home** and needs to be held by a man because objection might reasonably be taken to allowing a woman (i) the degree of physical or social contact with a person living in the home, or (ii) the knowledge of intimate details of such a person's life';
- **single-sex accommodation** where it is 'impractical' for the job holder to live elsewhere than in the employer's premises; 'the only such premises which are available' are for one sex and these 'are not equipped with separate sleeping accommodation . . . and sanitary facilities', and 'it is not reasonable to expect the employer either to equip those premises with such accommodation and facilities or to provide other premises';
- **single-sex establishments** which are 'a hospital, prison or other establishment for persons requiring special care, supervision and attention' and that 'it is reasonable, having regard to the essential character of the establishment or that part that the job should be held' by a person of a specified sex;

- 'the holder of the job provides individuals with **personal services** promoting their welfare or education, or similar personal services and those services can most effectively be provided' by a person of a specified sex;
- the job involves **work outside the United Kingdom** 'in a country whose law and customs are such that the duties could not, or could not effectively' be carried out by a person of a specified sex;
- 'the job is one of two to be held by a **married couple**'.

The amendments to the Sex Discrimination Act 1975, relating to gender reassignment, enacted specific GOQ provisions:

- It is a defence to a claim of less favourable treatment if an employer can show that being a man or a woman is a genuine occupational qualification for a particular job and that the treatment (which could include dismissal or redeployment) is reasonable in the circumstances (s 7A).
- GOQs apply where a postholder is required to undertake 'intimate physical searches pursuant to statutory powers' (s 7B(2)(a)).
- GOQs also cover circumstances where a postholder is working or living in a private home and 'objection might reasonably to taken' to allowing that person physical or social contact or allowing 'knowledge of intimate details of such a person's life' (s 7B(2)(b)).
- In relation to those intending to undergo or undergoing gender reassignment, GOQs allow an employer to take discriminatory action where issues of 'decency and privacy' arise in relation to accommodation and facilities shared with either sex and it is not reasonable to expect the employer to make adaptations or alternative arrangements (s 7B(2)(c)). Furthermore, discrimination is possible where a postholder 'provides vulnerable individuals with personal services promoting their welfare, or similar personal services, and in the reasonable view of the employer those services cannot be effectively provided by a person whilst that person is undergoing gender reassignment' (s 7B(2)(d)).

Pregnant workers

The specific rights relating to pregnancy and maternity are discussed in Chapter 13. Here the discussion focuses on the ways in which pregnancy has been viewed under the broad umbrella of sex discrimination law. Pregnancy was difficult to accommodate under British law because, as stated earlier, this was founded on the principle of comparison. Tribunals and courts sought the nearest male comparable with a pregnant woman. So, the 'sick man' comparator was born!

This view was founded on the following legal approach: that the detrimental treatment of a pregnant woman may be direct discrimination if the woman can show that a man in similar conditions (such as absence through illness) would be treated more favourably.

However, in 1990, the ECJ signalled a new legal direction, stating that there was 'no absolute comparability' (*Dekker* v *Stichting VJV-Centrum* C–177/88 [1990],

IRLR 27, ECJ). The detrimental treatment of a woman because of her pregnancy is always direct discrimination because, by definition, such treatment can only affect women. The ECJ, applying the Equal Treatment Directive 1976, stated that comparability was not involved. The Directive prohibits any 'discrimination whatever on grounds of sex directly or indirectly'. This approach differs from and overrides that of the Sex Discrimination Act 1975. This special situation was subsequently reaffirmed with the adoption of the Pregnant Workers Directive 1992.

4.4.10 Liability

There are important commonalities between the case law on race discrimination and that on sex discrimination. Liability clearly rests not just with the discriminator but also with the employer. The employer is vicariously liable for the behaviour of the employee, manager or supervisor. 'Anything done by a person in the course of his employment shall be treated for the purpose of this Act as done by his employer as well as by him, whether or not it was done with the employer's knowledge or approval' (s 41(1)). Furthermore, 'anything done by a person as agent for another person with the authority (whether express or implied, and whether precedent or subsequent) of that other person shall be treated for the purposes of this Act as done by that other person as well as by him' (s 41(2)). This would cover managers.

The law provides a defence for an employer in court or tribunal proceedings: 'it shall be a defence . . . to prove that he took such steps as were reasonably practicable to prevent the employee from doing that [discriminatory] act, or from doing in the course of his employment acts of that description' (s 41(3)).

In a race relations case (*Jones* v *Tower Boot Co Ltd* [1997] IRLR 68 CA) the Court of Appeal ruled that 'in the course of his employment' should be interpreted broadly in line with 'the natural meaning of those everyday words' (*see* Chapter 5). This construction will be applicable to sex discrimination cases.

4.4.11 Enforcement procedures

Time limit

Complaint to an employment tribunal should be made within three months of the act complained of. However, 'a court or tribunal may nevertheless consider any such complaint, claim or application which is out of time if, in all the circumstances of the case, it considers that it is just and equitable to do so' (SDA 1975, s 76(5)). The Sex Discrimination Act 1975 envisages two types of situation: a single act and an act that might extend over a period. Usually, a single act can easily be seen as being 'in time' or 'out of time'. Greater difficulties arise in relation to 'an act extending over a period' (s 67(6)(b)).

This was at issue in one case (*Cast* v *Croydon College* [1998] IRLR 318, CA). Ms Cast was a manager who on three separate occasions was refused her request to work part-time after maternity leave (between 1992 and 1993). The Court of Appeal ruled that, on the facts, there were several decisions by the college of which she was complaining. These indicated the existence of a discriminatory policy in relation to her post and herself. This extended up to the time she left employment. The court also proposed an alternative way of considering the matter if it was considered wrong to see this as 'an act extending over a period of time'. It would be appropriate to take the last refusal complained of as the basis of determining whether the application was 'in time'. In this specific case, there was 'a trivial over-run' of three days beyond the time limit and the application was allowed to proceed.

Burden of proof

In October 2001, the law was amended with the transposing into British law of the European Directive on the Burden of Proof in Sex Discrimination cases (SDA 1975, s 63A(2)). This applies to matters arising under Art 141 of the Treaty of Rome (equal pay) and the Directives on equal pay, equal treatment, health and safety of pregnant workers and parental leave. The Directive creates the following framework:

- the complainant must, first of all, establish a prima facie case (i.e. 'such facts from which it may be presumed that there has been direct or indirect discrimination');
- it will then be for the employer 'to prove that there has been no breach of the principle of equal treatment'.

Questionnaire

An applicant, under the Sex Discrimination Act, is allowed to serve a question-naire on an employer. Its purpose is to obtain information and documents in order to decide whether to start proceedings, to establish as far as possible the facts and to establish the reasons for the treatment (e.g. what criteria have been applied and to find out how others have been treated in similar circumstances). The replies are admissible in evidence and a refusal to reply without reasonable excuse allows the tribunal to draw adverse conclusions. An equivocal reply might also lead a tribunal to infer that there has been sex discrimination. With the permission of the tribunal, a supplementary questionnaire may be served on the employer to seek, for example, data on workforce make-up where documents are not already available. The Employment Act 2002 (s 42) will bring an Equal Pay Questionnaire into force during 2003.

Discovery (recovery in Scotland)

Employment tribunals have power to order inspection of documents, on an application from the complainant, where the evidence is relevant to the case and necessary either for disposing fairly of the action or matter or for saving costs. The employer may resist on the grounds that it is onerous (particularly, in terms of time and cost to prepare documentation).

4.4.12 Remedies

Where an employment tribunal upholds a complaint, it must then grant one or more of the following three available remedies:

- a **declaration**;
- an award of **compensation** payable by the employer to the complainant;
- a **recommendation** that, within a specified period of time, the employer does what the tribunal considers can be done to remove or lessen the harmful effect of the unlawful discrimination on the complainant.

In choosing which one or more of these three remedies to grant, the tribunal must decide which are 'just and equitable'. They are the only remedies available. Tribunals have no power to order an employer to appoint, promote, reinstate or re-engage a complainant in unlawful discrimination cases.

Declaration

A declaration is 'an order declaring the rights of the complainant and the [employer] in relation to the act to which the complainant relates' (SDA, s 65(1)(a)). A tribunal has a duty to make one. In itself, it can have little deterrent effect, unless the employer is concerned about adverse publicity. In practice, a declaration is usually accompanied by compensation and/or a recommendation.

Compensation

In practice, this is the remedy that complainants most frequently seek and, if successful, are awarded. Since November 1993, the upper limit has been removed as a result of a ruling in the ECJ (*Marshall* v *Southampton and South West Hampshire Area Health Authority (No. 2)* [1993] IRLR 445). The court reasoned that 'where financial compensation is the measure adopted in order to achieve the [1976 Equal Treatment Directive's] objective, it must be adequate, in that it must enable the loss and damage actually sustained as a result of the discriminatory dismissal (or other circumstances) to be made good in full in accordance with applicable national rules'. Compensation is awarded for **financial losses**, if any, and for **injury to feelings**.

Financial loss

This can comprise loss of earnings, past and projected; loss of fringe benefits (e.g. pension right, subsidised travel or company car); and expenses associated with the discrimination claim.

The assessment of compensation is based on the principle that the complainant must be put into the position they would have been in had the unlawful discrimination not happened. The objective is 'restitution' (*Alexander* v *Home Office* [1988] IRLR 190, CA). In an earlier case (*Coleman* v *Skyrail Oceanic Ltd* [1981] IRLR

398), the Court of Appeal had indicated that this objective was subject to four qualifications:

1 **Foreseeable damage**: compensation is for foreseeable damage arising directly from an unlawful act of discrimination.

2 **Mitigation of loss**: the complainant is obliged to take all 'reasonable' steps to minimise their losses resulting from the unlawful discrimination (e.g. seeking alternative employment, if dismissed).

3 **Behaviour**: the compensation award may be affected by the conduct, character and circumstances not merely of the employer but also of the complainant and so be reduced.

4 **Non-financial loss**: this is difficult to establish and in this respect tribunals have fairly wide discretion. The EAT recommended, in one case (*Ministry of Defence* v *Cannock and Others* [1994] IRLR 509) a 'due sense of proportion'. This 'involves looking at the individual components of any award and then looking at the total to make sure that the total award seems a sensible and just reflection of the chances which have been assessed'.

In *West Yorkshire Police* v *Vento* [2001] EAT 522/01, the EAT set aside an employment tribunal's calculation of future loss of earnings at £165 000 and a recalculation by a different employment tribunal was ordered. It took the view that Ms Vento did *not* have a 75 per cent chance of completing a full police career. (The Chief Constable submitted statistics which showed that only 9 per cent of female police officers who left the force between 1989 and 1999 served for more than 18 years; and no more than 50 per cent of *male* officers served up to retirement age.) Statistics are an important consideration in deciding such loss, although they are not the only consideration. (It might also be argued that historic figures, such as those provided, might understate the impact of changing social trends – e.g. the commitment of more women to develop careers.)

Injury to feelings

This refers to emotional harm and it is almost inevitable that compensation under this heading will arise in discrimination cases. In harassment cases it may be the **only** form of compensation because financial loss may not be experienced. The factors which can be taken into account include the conduct and character of all the parties involved; the age and vulnerability of the complainant may also be included.

It is not automatically awarded as part of compensation and has to be proved by the complainant. It was observed by the EAT that 'it will often be easy to prove in the sense that no tribunal will take much persuasion that the anger, distress and affront caused by the act of discrimination has injured the [complainant's] feelings. But it is not invariably so.'

The EAT has clarified the basis on which such awards are calculated (*ICTS (UK) Ltd* v *Tchoula* [2000] IRLR 643). Certain principles have been asserted. Such awards should bear broad general similarity to awards in personal injury cases. Also awards should be determined by reference to purchasing power or earnings. The EAT outlined two categories: higher and lower awards. A higher-level award is based on these factors:

- the applicant proving most of all of their complaint;
- evidence of a long-term campaign of discrimination;
- the consequences of the discrimination (e.g. stress, depression);
- a power relationship between the perpetrator and the victim;
- management's approach in dealing with a complaint through the grievance procedure.

An award for injury to feelings should include an element of aggravated damages where the employer has 'behaved in a high handed, malicious, insulting or oppressive manner' in discriminating against the complainant (*Alexander* v *Home Office*). Also, unsatisfactory replies to the discrimination questionnaire (*see* above) can be grounds for such damages. In one case, where replies were found to be 'misleading, inconsistent and untruthful' and the employer had disclosed 'irrelevant and misleading' documents while failing to disclose the relevant one, the tribunal awarded £1000 (*Webster* v *Ministry of Defence* 2628/91).

Interest

The ECJ, in the *Marshall* (*No. 2*) case, ruled that interest is '*an essential component of compensation*'. The tribunal has discretion to include the payment of interest – calculated as simple interest which accrues from day to day.

Recommendations

A tribunal's powers to make recommendations are limited to recommendations for action that will affect the individual complainant.

Examples of recommendations can include the following: that within six months all managers be trained in equal opportunities, that records of interviews be kept and questions should only relate to a job's requirements, that a person dismissed on grounds of discrimination should be provided with a factual reference on their abilities which should be agreed with the complainant, and that the perpetrator of harassment be moved to another post and should be suspended from duty until such a transfer was practical.

In *West Yorkshire Police* v *Vento* [2001] EAT 522/01, the EAT supported an employment tribunal recommendation that the Chief Constable send a written sex discrimination policy to Ms Vento. It also recommended, as good employment practice, that the Deputy Chief Constable interview the police officers about whose conduct she had complained and consider with them the relevant parts of the tribunal's decision. However, the EAT did not support the employment tribunal's recommendation that these officers should individually be invited to apologise to her. This case illustrates the wide discretion that a tribunal has in respect of recommendations.

If a respondent employer fails 'without reasonable justification' to comply with a recommendation, a tribunal may, if it thinks it just and equitable, increase the amount of compensation to be paid or, if no order for compensation has been made, it may make one.

***Draft* Employment Equality (Sexual Orientation) Regulations 2003**

Key provisions to be implemented on 1 December 2003. These enact parts of the Employment Directive 2000.

- **Sexual orientation**: This is defined as being an orientation towards persons of the same sex; the opposite sex; or both sexes. It does not include sexual practices and preferences (e.g. sado-masochism and paedophilia).
- **Employment**: Defined in similar terms to SDA, RRA and DDA. Applicants and employees are protected in terms similar to SDA 1975 s 6; RRA 1976 s 4; and DDA 1995 s 4. Contract workers are also protected (as in SDA s 9; and RRA s 7). (Specific occupational groups are also identified).
- **Direct discrimination**: This occurs where, because of a person's sexual orientation (or perception of this), another treats this person less favourably than s/he would treat others. This provision includes a person who refuses to carry out an employer's discriminatory instruction.
- **Indirect discrimination**: This occurs where an employer applies to an employee (or applicant) a 'provision, criterion or practice' which is applied equally to others. This puts a person of that sexual orientation at a particular disadvantage and the person, in question, suffers that disadvantage. The employer may be able objectively to justify the discriminatory treatment.
- **Victimisation**: Provides similar protection to that in the SDA 1975 s 4 and the RRA 1976 s 2.
- **Harassment**: This is defined as an unlawful act which 'violates the dignity' of a person; or creates 'an offensive environment' for him/her; or which 'should reasonably be considered' as having done these things.
- **Genuine occupational requirement**: Where a person's sexual orientation is such a requirement for a particular post, then, an employer may take it into account in appointing, promoting, transferring or training.
- **Liability of employers and principals**: An employer is vicariously liable for the acts of his employees. The provision is similar to SDA 1975 s 41; and RRA 1976 s 32.
- **Positive action**: This is permitted in certain circumstances.
- **Enforcement proceedings**: Complaint to employment tribunal within three months irrespective of a person's length of service. Complainant may serve questionnaire on the employer. The tribunal may make a declaration or recommendation or order unlimited compensation.
- **Burden of proof**: Once a person has made out a *prima facie* case, it is for the employer to prove that he did not commit the act of discrimination or harassment. This is similar to SDA 1975 s 63A.
- **Contracts and collective agreements**: Those with discriminatory provisions are void.

Figure 4.4

4.5 Employment policies and practices

The broad issue of equal opportunities policies was discussed in the Introduction to Part Two. Here we look at the details of what employers might do in practice. Considering the various **stages in the employment relationship** we will see how equal opportunities infuses them.

It is important to remember that both contracts of employment and collective agreements are subject to sex discrimination law. Discriminatory terms in **contracts of employment** are unlawful. An equality clause is deemed to be incorporated into these contracts (EqPA 1970, s 1). As for **collective agreements**, discriminatory terms are 'void' (SDA 1986, s 6). It is also important to consider employment policies in the context of positive action (ss 47 and 48).

4.5.1 Human resource strategy

Although this section considers a range of specific employment policies, it is important to remember that an employer may well consider a more strategic perspective to rooting out discrimination and promoting equal opportunities. Such an approach will inevitably require an assessment of organisational culture, an audit of institutional patterns of discrimination and consideration of the contribution that might be made by 'managing diversity' (see Introduction to Part Two).

4.5.2 Recruitment and selection

Discrimination is at the heart of the recruitment and selection process because choices have to be made about the suitability of a person. It is critical that such choices are made against objective criteria rather than reflecting stereotyping, prejudice and assumptions. There are several aspects of this process: recruitment policy, job and person specifications and selection criteria, advertising, application forms and interviews.

In considering **recruitment policy**, employers should, first of all, identify the existing profile of their workforce. This can reveal evidence of historic patterns of discrimination, producing both vertical and horizontal occupational segregation. So, an employer may decide whether any positive action is necessary. Part of this process is the establishment of targets for the recruitment of particular groups that are underrepresented in the workforce.

The **specifications and criteria** against which applicants are to be judged must avoid unlawful discrimination (unless the special provisions on *genuine occupational qualification* are invoked) and so must be objectively justifiable. There is, however, one potentially complicating factor. This is the extent to which 'acceptability criteria' are used as against 'suitability criteria'. The latter should more readily be defensible objectively (e.g. by reference to experience, skills, appropriate qualifications). 'Acceptability criteria' may be more difficult to defend and could be discriminatory. Such criteria are associated with 'fit' – among other factors, an applicant's compatibility with the organisation's culture.

The first step in the mechanics of the recruitment and selection process concerns **advertising**. It is unlawful direct discrimination to 'publish or cause to be published' a discriminatory advertisement (SDA 1975, s 38(1)). This covers internal and external publications. The advertisement must not 'indicate or be reasonably understood as indicating an intention by a person to do any act which is or might be unlawful' (s 38(1)). Job descriptions with 'a sexual connotation' (e.g. stewardess, salesgirl, postman, fireman) 'shall be taken to indicate an intention to discriminate, unless the advertisement contains an indication to the contrary' (s 38(3)). Exceptions should be covered by the 'genuine occupational qualification' provisions (s 7).

Advertising employment may, of course, be by 'word of mouth'. This could be indirectly discriminatory, particularly under the amended definition of such discrimination, which covers 'practices' – whether formal or informal. It can reinforce an existing gender profile in the workgroup if there is already marked gender segregation. It is suggested that men are more likely to mention job vacancies to other men and women more likely to mention them to women. However, given the cost of the recruitment process, there is a strong likelihood that, for certain jobs, employers will adopt this informal and relatively cost-effective method. Furthermore, managers may feel more certain of the reliability of potential employees recommended through this process. In one EOC investigation into British Rail (Robbins, 1986: 10) it was reported:

> There was general agreement that 'asking around' amongst existing staff was an obvious first resort when generating applicants. Most [managers] thought the advantages of this to the system were clear; people were more likely to stay given a family connection and existing staff could in some sense vouch for the new recruit: 'we usually go by the parents'.

The EOC in the statutory Code of Practice (1985: para 19c) recommends that 'the method should be avoided in a workforce predominantly of one sex, if in practice it prevents members of the opposite sex from applying'.

As far as **application forms** are concerned, some organisations ask for various categories of information – some of which is inappropriate at the recruitment stage. Such requests may make them liable to allegations of unfair discrimination. There are likely to be three different sets of information that organisations will require from applicants/employees:

1 Information to provide some indication of a person's competences and likely suitability for a particular job: primarily this will cover experience, skills and qualifications (if appropriate). This information is used principally for selection for interview and as an aid in interviews.

2 Information for monitoring purposes (i.e. to identify applicants/employees in terms of age, gender, ethnicity, etc. to help assess the effectiveness of equal opportunities policy).

3 Information about new employees in relation to their eligibility for certain benefits (e.g. participation in a pension scheme).

There should, ideally, be separate forms and processes for collecting such data. The EOC statutory code states that 'information necessary for personnel records can be collected after a job offer has been made' (1985: para 23c). The application form, then, would probably require name, address, phone number, previous work experience, educational qualifications, other skills and contact information for referees. It should not ask for age, sex, marital status or numbers of dependent children. In an EOC (1991) survey of health authority forms, 60 per cent asked for marital status, 50 per cent for an applicant's sex and 23 per cent for the number of children.

The CIPD, in its voluntary code on equal opportunities, comments that **the interview** 'as a predictive device is an extremely fallible instrument, highly susceptible to interviewer bias and stereotyped perceptions'. So, care must be taken to avoid questions which could be construed as discriminatory, to make decisions to offer employment that can be defended by structured decision-making, and to record the interview process (EOC Code, 1985: para 23c). It implies proper training for managers who interview.

4.5.3 Terms and conditions of employment

Most of these will come under the Equal Pay Act 1970, which is concerned with contractual terms 'whether concerned with pay or not' (s 1(2)). It is important to remember the wide construction given to 'pay' under equal pay law (*see* above). In some circumstances a contractual term can be ruled to be irrelevant. For example, the ECJ (*Brown v Rentokil* [1991] IRLR 31) ruled that a contractual provision (which stated that after 26 weeks' continuous sick absence an employee would be dismissed) could not override the principles of equal treatment law. The case in question concerned a pregnant woman who was absent for pregnancy-related illness. The ECJ ruled that although pregnancy is not comparable to a pathological condition, it is a period during which disorders and complications may arise that can cause a person to be incapable of work. Dismissal during pregnancy for absences due to such incapacity 'must therefore be regarded as essentially based on the fact of pregnancy'. Such a dismissal can only affect women and, therefore, constitutes direct discrimination on grounds of sex.

As far as equal pay is concerned, employers should audit payment systems to identify whether or not there is evidence of indirect pay discrimination. This may arise as a result of two factors. First, horizontal occupational segregation into 'men's jobs' and 'women's jobs' can result in differential pay and earnings opportunities. Secondly, the different work patterns of many women (involving career breaks, discontinuous work and part-time work) can lead to discrimination where, for example, certain benefits are available to those working full-time and/or are service-related. Where practices of this kind result in lower pay for women, then their use would have to be objectively justified in an equal pay claim.

So, the Equal Pay Code of Practice (1997) recommends the systematic review of pay (and benefits) practice by employers. This would involve the following stages:

- *Statistical analysis*: This would involve a breakdown of the pay of all employees by sex, job title, grade, performance rating, etc. This would help identify likely areas of complaint.
- *Causes of difference*: If there appears to be a gender difference in pay, then the components of a pay system should be analysed to test what is causing the difference.
- *Changing rules and practices*: Contractual terms and provisions of collective agreements which are the source of the discriminatory treatment should be changed.
- *The adoption of an equal pay system*: This may involve developing a plan for transferring employees to a new grade and extending the coverage of pay supplements and benefits to employees who have not received them in the past.
- *Monitoring the new system*.
- *Formal equal pay policy*: Drafting and publishing one.

4.5.4 **Working time**

The significance of working-time arrangements under discrimination law can arise in a number of ways: return to work after maternity leave, the consequences of working-time rescheduling, and hours qualifications providing access to benefits. The legal issues involved usually concern whether or not there is evidence of indirect sex discrimination and, if so, whether or not it can be justified.

The right of a woman to **return to work** after maternity leave may involve a requirement by the employer that she works full-time. A woman returning to work in such circumstances, however, may wish to work part-time or on some flexible working hours basis. Consideration of such a claim should be made using the fourfold test of indirect discrimination. So, the tribunal would need to be satisfied that there was a condition or requirement to work full-time, that a considerably smaller proportion of women could comply with it than men, that the employer could justify the condition or requirement and that the applicant had suffered a detriment because she could not comply with the requirement to work full-time (*Home Office* v *Holmes* [1984] IRLR 299, EAT).

Secondly, the **re-scheduling of working time** may also be indirectly discriminatory against women. A claim against a new shift pattern for London Underground train operators was considered earlier (*London Underground Ltd* v *Edwards (No. 2)* [1998] IRLR 364).

These first two issues should be seen in the context of strong support expressed by women (particularly those with dependency responsibilities) for non-traditional working-time arrangements. Surveys suggest greater preference by women, than men, for flexible working hours (variable start and finish times), for part-time employment, for job-share arrangements, for career break schemes and for occasional time off.

Finally, any qualifying condition on the number of **hours to be worked as a qualification** (for access to a benefit, for example) may, depending on the facts, be indirect discrimination and need to be justified. Hours qualifications restricting access to statutory rights were removed in 1995, following a successful complaint by the Equal Opportunities Commission before the House of Lords (*R* v *Secretary of State for Employment ex parte Equal Opportunities Commission and Another* [1994] IRLR 176).

4.5.5 **Training and development**

In the CIPD's voluntary code of practice on equal opportunities, it is observed that women 'are barred from some jobs because they lack the necessary training. Often this is because, through direct or indirect discrimination, they have been excluded from training schemes.' The law, as we have seen earlier, enables an employer to take positive action in the area of training (SDA 1975, s 6). The EOC's Statutory Code (1985: para 42) says that employers may wish to consider **'positive measures'** such as:

- training their own employees (male or female) for work which is traditionally the preserve of the other sex;
- positive encouragement for women to apply for management posts (acknowledging that special courses may be needed).

In recent years, surveys have shown that there are still distinct problems in the general provision of training for skill development, and training for career development. An EOC Report (1991) showed that young men were far more likely to receive job-related training than young women. Almost a third of men aged 16–19 years old, in full-time employment, said that they had had training recently, compared with one-fifth of women in the same age group. Among older workers, the Commission found that women part-timers were less likely to receive training than full-timers. The review concludes that the absence of a strategic approach to training is likely to result in a perpetuation of the status quo, with little likelihood that job segregation between the sexes and skill shortages will be tackled successfully. 'This is to the disadvantage of women who are under-represented in the higher echelons of organisations, where training and training decisions are traditionally concentrated.' So, these limitations on access to training are considerable barriers to women's career progression.

4.5.6 Promotion and career progression

There are four important constraints to women's career progression which have been evident in various surveys: access to training and development opportunities (which we have already discussed), attitudes, dependency and the significance of a maternity break in service.

As far as **attitudes** are concerned, this may, in part, be women's perceptions of themselves or male attitudes towards them. In one survey, by the Society of Telecom Executives, of 1000 female British Telecom managers, 68 per cent believed that they had to be better than men to get the same promotion, and 60 per cent believed that men were less likely to listen to them than to other men (reported in the *Financial Times*, 28 June 1988).

The probability that women will have some **break in service** from employment because of child-bearing and child-rearing is a considerable obstacle to career progression. Institutionalised barriers can exist, with promotion being directly linked to length of service. Robbins (1986: 19) reported how such a seniority rule applied in British Rail for staff in the wages grades. Applications were presented to the interviewing panel in order of seniority. At the time of her survey 95 per cent of 'waged staff' were male. So, 'strict adherence to the seniority rule can clearly cause particular problems for women attempting to break into employment areas previously reserved for men'.

Even without a seniority rule (explicit or implicit), a maternity break in service is a clear disadvantage, particularly because of the social pattern of a mother being a child's principal carer. So, women can experience a double detriment: **dependency** and **break in service**. The consequences have been widely reported. The EOC (1991: 22) survey into the NHS states that the assumption that men were interested in a career whereas women were not, was compounded by 'an acute lack of part-time work or other flexible working arrangements in senior positions to enable women to combine career and family responsibilities'.

Dependency is clearly a problem for women. In a survey of women in a hospital pharmacy, it is stated that 'the picture that emerges is of two distinct "types" – the male manager is more likely to be married and have children, the female manager is more likely to be single and childless' (Bevan *et al.*, 1989).

It is not suggested that generalisations are to be drawn from this survey evidence. It is merely presented to signal important patterns and instances of discriminatory treatment that may be diagnosed in other organisations.

4.5.7 Dress and appearance

Dress and appearance can be a contentious contractual issue. It can also have important implications for both sex and race discrimination (*see also* Chapter 5); and freedom of expression under the European Convention on Human Rights 1950 (*see* Chapter 1). An employer may specify certain rules expressly in the contract. These can cover uniforms, requirements on everyday clothing and standards of appearance (relating, for example, to hair length, grooming, the use of make-up, earrings and other jewellery). These requirements are governed by the implied contractual term of mutual trust and confidence. So, if an employer insists on unacceptable rules that undermine or demean an employee, then there is a repudiatory breach of the contract and the employee might resign claiming constructive dismissal.

A more likely legal remedy would be in respect of discrimination law. The leading case in this area involved a complaint that a woman shopworker was, unlike a male shopworker, not allowed to wear trousers (*Schmidt* v *Austicks Bookshops Ltd* [1977] IRLR 360, EAT). The EAT stated that the way to approach this issue was as follows: 'There were in force rules restricting wearing of apparel and governing appearance which applied to men and also applied to women although, obviously, women and men being different, the rules in the two cases are not the same.' Therefore, in so far as comparison was possible, the employer treated men and women alike by restricting the choice of dress in general. This approach, said the EAT, was more likely to lead to a 'sensible result' than an approach which examined the situation point by point and garment by garment.

This decision was reached before the direct discrimination 'but for' test was determined. Nevertheless, in a more recent case (*Smith* v *Safeway plc* [1996] IRLR 457) on acceptable hair length (which was different for men and women), the Court of Appeal upheld the approach in the *Schmidt* case. So, the current position appears to remain that employers may treat men and women differently according to social convention, provided the treatment was even-handed. But rules that might be per-ceived as too restrictive on one sex could, arguably, be less favourable treatment.

4.5.8 Retirement and pensions

In this area two significant cases, ultimately heard in the ECJ, established equal treatment. The first concerned differential **retirement ages** as between men and women (*Marshall* v *Southampton and SW Hampshire Area Health Authority* [1986] IRLR 140, ECJ). In this case a health authority had a compulsory retirement age for women (of 62 years). In contrast men retired at 65 years. (Such differential treatment was at the time permitted by the Sex Discrimination Act.) Ms Marshall challenged the rule as contrary to 'the principle of equal treatment'. She was successful. Ultimately, British sex discrimination law was amended to require employers to have harmonised retirement ages for men and women (at whatever retirement age is specified under company policy). As far as differential **pension ages** were concerned, these were ruled to be contrary to the principle in Art 119 of the Treaty of Rome (now Article 141) of equal pay for equal work (*Barber* v *Guardian Royal Exchange Assurance Group plc* [1990] IRLR 240, ECJ). This ruling was also enacted into British law (Social Security Act 1989).

4.5.9 Dismissal

The issue of dismissal law is covered in Chapter 9. It is sufficient to note here the importance for employers of ensuring that the reason or, if there is more than one, the principal reason for dismissal is a fair reason. Under the Sex Discrimination Act (s 6(2)), 'it is unlawful . . . to discriminate against [a woman] . . . by dismissing her' on the grounds of sex or marital status. Furthermore, it is unfair dismissal if the reason or principal reason is concerned with pregnancy or childbirth (ERA 1996, s 99). Dismissal encompasses redundancy and so also redundancy selection criteria.

4.6 Conclusion

It is just over thirty years since the first piece of sex discrimination legislation was enacted in Britain. What assessment can be made of the law's effectiveness in tackling this discrimination? Effectiveness can be judged by looking at the following issues: the eradication of discriminatory treatment, implementation of workplace equal opportunities policies, confidence of complainants in the law-enforcement process and adequacy of remedies.

First is **the extent to which discriminatory treatment has been eradicated**. This is impossible to quantify. On the positive side, there is a greater willingness (among both women and men) to challenge such behaviour. There is growing acknowledgement, widely in society, that that the traditional childcare role has to be shared with male partners and that employers must make some accommodation. There is a greater awareness of procedures to make complaints within the workplace and in the legal system. On the negative side, sexist attitudes and stereotypes persist. Equal pay is slow in coming. Women are predominant in the more disadvantaged parts of the flexible labour market. The glass ceiling in many organisations has not been broken.

Secondly, there is the question of the implementation of workplace **equal opportunities policies**. There is no statutory requirement upon employers to produce one. Consequently, their effectiveness is very problematic. Survey evidence (Workplace Employee Relations Survey (Cully *et al.*, 1998)) and anecdotal evidence suggest that they are seen as having no business relevance, line managers have little ownership of the policy objectives, committed staff are marginalised into units and committees and there is little if any effective monitoring and review. Nevertheless, they can provide a valuable tool for an organisation committed to rooting out discrimination. Furthermore, they can help, in tribunal proceedings, with an employer's defence by showing that he took such steps as are reasonably practicable to deal with discrimination.

The third issue is applicants' confidence in **the enforcement process**. Any evaluation of the tribunal process shows that there are considerable concerns: time delay in dealing with an application, the complexity of the law involved, the need for resources to advise and to help in case presentation and the burden of proof. In addition, there is the need for personal stamina to embark on the process and see it through to completion. Sex discrimination and equal pay applications can be particularly difficult for an individual lay person because of the detailed and complex body of law that is involved. It is not surprising, then, that the number of tribunal applications is still small (but, admittedly, growing). In 1977, ACAS conciliated 984 equal pay and 367 sex discrimination applications out of a total of almost 45 000. By 1997, the figures had risen to 2302 and 6587 respectively from an overall total of 107 495. In 2002, the figures were 2614 and 7525 respectively from a total of 165 093 claims. But it is important to note the valuable advisory role played by the EOC.

One factor that is likely to influence a person's attitude to the complaints process is the nature of the **likely outcome and the adequacy of the remedies**. Since 1994, the ceiling has been removed from compensation awards for sex discrimination. Potentially 'the sky's the limit', but the reality is much more sobering. Applying the structure to calculating awards, tribunals rarely grant compensation above £10 000. In the crude balance that applicants must make, they must weigh, on the one hand, the cost in terms of time, stress and resources to prepare and put forward a case against, on the other hand, the uncertainty of the outcome. The Equal Opportunities Review survey of compensation awards in 2001 (Equal Opportunities Review, 2002) reported that:

- only 10 per cent of sex discrimination awards exceeded £20 000;
- the median award in sex discrimination cases was £5125;
- the median award for injury to feelings was £2500.

It is, in this context, not surprising that, at the ACAS conciliation stage, the settlement and withdrawal rates are so high. ACAS showed that, of equal pay applications completed, 42 per cent were settled; 45 per cent were withdrawn; and 13 per cent went to employment tribunal. Of sex discrimination applications completed: 49 per cent were settled; 32 per cent were withdrawn; and 19 per cent went to employment tribunal. These figures are averaged over the three years 1999–2002 (ACAS Annual Reports).

Exercise 4.1 **Some discrimination problems**

*Read the following scenarios. As a personnel officer, consider what action you would advise. Taking account of **both** law and employment practice:*

- *What would be your reasons for the advice?*
- *What do you think might be the implications of adopting it?*

1 You are to interview some job applicants. The nature of the work involves some evening work and occasional weekend working. The applicants are both male and female. The manager of the section concerned has said to you that you are 'not to employ some woman who'll be off every time one of her kids has a runny nose'. How would you deal with this?

2 A woman you employed, six months ago, for a job is now pregnant and, as a consequence, has been off work with sickness for several weeks. Her absence is causing operational difficulties. Her manager wants to sack her. How would you deal with this?

3 Your organisation is to advertise a job. The manager of the department concerned wanted a keen, young person. He has stipulated in the advertisement that only people up to 27 years need apply. You have been asked to advise on whether or not there are any equal opportunities implications.

4 Your organisation is expanding and is advertising supervisory posts. The section manager says that the person specification must include a reference to 'commitment' to the organisation. He says this means having worked for the company on a full-time basis for a number of years, and being prepared to work hours as and when required. You have been asked to advise on the drafting of this specification.

5 A female full-time member of staff, with short service, is proposing to return from maternity leave and has asked her manager if it is possible to convert to part-time employment on a 75 per cent fractional contract. You have been asked for your advice.

Feedback on this exercise is provided in the Appendix to this book.

Further reading

Chartered Institute of Personnel and Development (1993) *Statement on Age and Employment*. London: CIPD.

Chartered Institute of Personnel and Development (1995) *Code on Equal Opportunities*. London: CIPD.

Chartered Institute of Personnel and Development (1996) *Managing Diversity: a Position Paper*. London: CIPD.

Equal Opportunities Commission (1997) *Code of Practice on Equal Pay*. Manchester: EOC.

References

Bourn, C. and Whitmore, J. (1993) *Race and Discrimination*, 2nd edn. London: Sweet & Maxwell.

Boyden, T. and Paddison, L. (1986) 'Banking on Equal Opportunities', *Personnel Management Journal*, September, 42–6.

Chartered Institute of Personnel and Development (1993) *Statement on Age and Employment*. London: CIPD.

Chartered Institute of Personnel and Development (1995) *Code on Equal Opportunities*. London: CIPD.

Chartered Institute of Personnel and Development (1996) *Managing Diversity: a Position Paper*. London: CIPD.

Commission for Racial Equality (1983) *Code of Practice for the Elimination of Racial Discrimination and the Promotion of Equality of Opportunity in Employment*. London: CRE.

Conway, D. (1998) *Free-Market Feminism*. London: Institute of Economic Affairs.

Cully, M. *et al.* (1998) *The 1998 Workplace Employee Relations Survey: First Findings*. London: DTI.

Cunningham, S. (1992) 'The Development of Equal Opportunities Theory and Practice in the European Community', *Policy and Politics*, 20(3).

Department of Trade and Industry (1998) 'Fairness at Work', Cm. 3968. London: Stationery Office.

Equal Opportunities Commission (1985) *Code of Practice for the Elimination of Discrimination on the Grounds of Sex and Marriage and the Promotion of Equality of Opportunity in Employment*. Manchester: EOC.

Equal Opportunities Commission (1989) *Women and Men in Britain 1989*. London: Stationery Office.

Equal Opportunities Commission (1990) *Women and Men in Britain 1990*. London: Stationery Office.

Equal Opportunities Review (2002) *Compensation Awards 2001*, August. London: Industrial Relations Services.

Hansard Society (1990) *Women at the top: the report of the commission on women at the top*. London: The Hansard Society.

Heery, E. (1995) 'Equality versus Flexibility' *Management and Strategy*, No. 59. Kingston upon Thames: Croner Publications.

Holdsworth, A. (1988) *Out of the Doll's House*. London: BBC Books.

Office for National Statistics (various years) *Labour Force Survey*. London: ONS.

Pollert, A. (1981) *Girls, Wires and Factory Lives*. London: Macmillan.

Pollert, A. and Rees, T. (1992) *Equal Opportunities and Positive Action in Britain: Three Case Studies*. Warwick Papers in Industrial Relations No. 42. Coventry: University of Warwick.

Redmond, M. (1986) 'Women and Minorities' in Lewis, R. (ed.) *Labour Law in Britain*. Oxford: Blackwell.

Robbins, D. (1986) *Wanted Railman*. London: HMSO.

Sacks, V. (1992) 'Tackling Discrimination Positively in Britain' in Hepple, B. and Szyszczak, E.M. *Discrimination: the Limits of the Law*. London: Mansell.

Race discrimination in the workplace

Learning objectives

This chapter considers the social and economic background to race discrimination and explores the nature of such discrimination in employment. It outlines the essential legal framework and explores the policies and practices that should be adopted by employers. Having read it you should understand:

- The origins of race discrimination.
- The key sociological concepts.
- The key concepts in discrimination law: direct and indirect discrimination, the concept of justification, victimisation, the special provisions, the contribution of positive action, liability, the right of complaint and the legal procedures and the remedies available.
- The steps that you could take to advise on the development of an equal opportunities policy for your organisation.

It is important to remember that this area of discriminatory practice should be considered in conjunction with sex discrimination (Chapter 4) and disability discrimination (Chapter 6).

5.1 Structure of the chapter

This chapter comprises the following sections:

- *Introduction*: The ethnic population profile of Britain; the concepts of race, ethnicity, colour; racism.
- *The context*: Social background, political approaches, labour-market participation.
- *The legal framework*: Grounds for unfair discrimination, areas of employment protection, direct discrimination, indirect discrimination, victimisation, genuine occupational qualification, positive action and positive discrimination, liability, enforcement, remedies and employing workers from overseas.

- *Employment policies and practices*: Recruitment and selection, pay and benefits, working time, training, development, promotion and transfers, dress codes and dismissal.
- *Case study 5.1*: Ye Olde Englishe Restaurants.

5.2 Introduction

Britain is a diverse society in terms of the ethnic and national origins of its citizens. It has become increasingly so since the middle of the nineteenth century. This ethnic diversity derives from a number of principal causes of migration. First, there is Britain's position in continental Europe, which itself has been characterised by religious and political persecution, ethnic cleansing and genocide, particularly from the late nineteenth century onwards. Secondly, there is Britain's former role as an imperial power, with colonies in all other continents and the perception of Britain as 'the mother country'. Thirdly, occasional severe shortages of both skilled and unskilled workers, particularly after World War II, encouraged immigration to Britain. Finally, a loose moral commitment in favour of protecting people whose human rights have been abused has existed as part of Britain's political culture.

Examples of significant 'waves' of immigration have included the following:

- those escaping from the famine in Ireland in the 1840s;
- Jews fleeing pogroms in Russia and eastern Europe in the late nineteenth and early twentieth centuries, and genocide in Nazi Germany after 1933;
- those encouraged in recruitment campaigns in the Caribbean in the 1950s and 1960s to take up employment, particularly in public transport and the National Health Service;
- East African Asians who were expelled from Kenya (1968) and Uganda (1972) as a result of 'Africanisation' policies.

Additionally, Britain, like most industrialised societies, has experienced other ad hoc migration: internally between England, Scotland, Wales and Northern Ireland, and also as a consequence of the 'free movement of labour' policy within the European Union.

In the past 40 years, increasingly stringent steps have been taken by both Conservative and Labour governments to regulate immigration.

5.2.1 Population profile of Britain

The 1991 Census reported the resident population of Britain by ethnic group (Table 5.1).

Obviously, this provides only a partial view of ethnic variety. The 'white' group is undifferentiated and so masks the incidence of various other ethnic groups. For example, it is estimated that 10 per cent of the population can trace their ancestry back to Ireland (Mason, 1995: 22); there are some 300 000 Jews in Britain.

Table 5.1 Britain's population by ethnic group

Ethnic group	Population (000s)
All groups	54 889
White	51 874
Other groups	3 015
Black Caribbean	500
Black African	212
Black other	178
Indian	840
Pakistani	477
Bangladeshi	163
Chinese	157
Other groups	488

In addition, various localities have populations where particular nationalities predominate. For example, some 30 000–40 000 Italians live in Bedfordshire, Hertfordshire and Buckinghamshire, having immigrated after World War II to work for the London Brick Company. Occasional concentrations of Turks, Greek Cypriots, Australians and (white) South Africans and Zimbabweans can be found in London and some other large cities.

The **regional location** of the three million people who are members of non-white ethnic groups are reported in the census data (Jones, 1996: 27): 97 per cent live in England, 2 per cent in Scotland and 1 per cent in Wales. Looking at the English regions, 54 per cent of people in these ethnic groups live in the South East, 14 per cent in the West Midlands, 9 per cent in the North West and 8 per cent in Yorkshire and Humberside. Taking each ethnic group in turn, the largest regional proportions of each group are reported as follows:

- *African-Caribbean*: 63 per cent live in the South East and 16 per cent in the West Midlands.

- *African Asian*: 63 per cent live in the South East, 12 per cent in the East Midlands and 10 per cent in the West Midlands.

- *Indian*: 47 per cent live in the South East, 21 per cent in the West Midlands and 8 per cent in the North West.

- *Pakistani*: 31 per cent live in the South East, 19 per cent in Yorkshire and Humberside, 18 per cent in the West Midlands and 18 per cent in the North West.

- *Bangladeshi*: 62 per cent live in the South East, 9 per cent in the West Midlands and 8 per cent in the North West.

- *Chinese*: 58 per cent live in the South East and 9 per cent in the North West.

One consequence of this historic immigration is that, both socially and in terms of employment, different languages, cultures and religions are evident in British society. Specific policy measures may need to be undertaken by governments and employers to accommodate such diversity. These will be discussed later, particularly in the section on employment policies and practices.

5.2.2   **The concepts**

To explore the issue of racial discrimination we need to consider the meaning of two key concepts: race and ethnicity; and, in addition, the issue of 'colour'. All are used in everyday language and also indicated in race relations legislation as characteristics of 'racial groups'.

Race

'Race' as a concept originally emerged in the late eighteenth century and led to the development of a 'race science', based on *biological* differences. It established a hierarchy of inferiority and superiority between races and was used to reinforce existing power structures (primarily, the domination of white people over other races). This 'science' enabled certain races to be defined as 'non-human' and, therefore, they could be enslaved, treated as a commodity and denied any basic human rights. In its extreme form, race science underpins Nazi ideology. In this, the northern European Aryan people are seen as supreme. By the end of World War II, this 'science' had become generally discredited. 'Race' has also been defined as a *sociological* concept. Again, it is seen as a form of categorisation, but as such it is imperfect. The implication is that people organise themselves and behave in certain ways according to racial origin. This, in itself, poses difficulties. Does this mean the following categories: European, African, Semitic, Chinese, etc.? Given that these are extremely broad categories, which themselves cover a wide degree of diversity, the sociological definition of 'race' is comparatively unhelpful. Its limited role, today, seems to be as one of numerous characteristics of a person, providing some reference points for considering social behaviour and relationships.

Ethnicity

Ethnicity, on the other hand, is a more useful term for helping to structure discussions on discrimination. Most academic commentators would 'stress some sort of cultural distinction as the mark of an ethnic grouping' (Mason, 1995: 12). Evidence of this distinctiveness can be seen in common descent (for example, Jews originating in Israel); common cultural heritage or traditions; common traditions relating to marriage and family life (e.g. the arrangement of marriages); possibly, common religion; probably, a common language; and such factors as dress (for example, the head-dress and veil worn by women in Islamic ethnic groups). At the heart of ethnicity is a sense of belongingness to a group and to certain 'roots' – with distinctions sometimes drawn, especially by first-generation immigrants, between 'natural' and 'adopted' home countries. The significance of these indicators of ethnicity will vary, often substantially, between different ethnic groups – with some of lesser importance than others.

In Britain, ethnicity has also been defined, conventionally, by skin colour. As a consequence, various European groups, for example, are not generally perceived as ethnic groups (e.g. Italians, Poles, Ukrainians) – but as white people. Indeed, 'white British people are apt to see ethnicity as an attribute only of others – something that distinguishes "them" from "us" ' (Mason, 1995: 14). This is a distortion of the concept and, in this text, ethnicity will be used to reflect any cultural distinctiveness.

In part, then, ethnicity is rooted in 'the self-definitions of members' (Mason, 1995: 12). Rather than being an entirely ascribed category, like race, ethnicity enables individuals to determine their belonging to an ethnic group. So, a person can have a range of different ethnic identities depending on the situation. A person might be a Hindu, **and** an Indian, **and** Kenyan, **and** British, depending upon the circumstances they are in and the treatment they receive at the hands of other people. As subsequent generations become established in the host society, individuals will probably manifest these *multi-ethnic* characteristics to a much greater extent. As a consequence, the term 'ethnic minority', as a description of identity, can be misleading and dangerously exclusive.

Colour

Colour, as a term, features in the legislation and, historically, has been used to differentiate between people (primarily between black and white people). Indeed, in most ethnic monitoring schemes, there can be, even today, an unsatisfactory confusion of racial, ethnic and colour categories. Mason (1995: 6) comments that characterising people by colour is 'of considerable importance because of the way in which the colours black and white were emotionally loaded concepts in the English language'. These colours are 'polar opposites'. Also, 'white' represents 'good, purity and virginity' whilst 'black' is 'the colour of death, evil and debasement'. Such contrasts can be seen as long-standing features of our language, literature and philosophy as well as being elements in racist political rhetoric. Colour can be useful as *one* characteristic of an ethnic group (or *racial group* under the legislation) but that is all. Otherwise, it provides a crude and unhelpful categorisation.

Underlying this discussion of concepts is the question of **acceptability**. This covers not just the issue of whether the concept provides a useful sociological tool, but also what is connoted by the language. There are varying views about **acceptable language**. This arises because words are powerful instruments for identifying, categorising, stereotyping and demeaning people. They carry with them connotations. From time to time, there are shifts in the use of acceptable language. For example, the word 'negro' has ceased to be used because it was associated with racism in the southern states of the USA and particularly with its corrupted and offensive form, 'nigger'. It was replaced, in the late 1960s, by the term 'black' – reflecting the growth of 'black consciousness' and the 'black power' political movements. In recent years, the term African-Caribbean (or, if appropriate, African-American) has become more acceptable, and has closer associations with ethnicity in a way that colour does not.

Finally, in respect of the concepts, it is important to note that a person's position in society may also be significantly influenced by their social class and gender (as we have seen in Chapter 4 on sex discrimination). So, the origin of deprivation or the existence of discriminatory treatment might not be attributable exclusively to a person's ethnic origin.

Racism

The legislation against race discrimination has been framed to tackle a particular *wrong* that has been an endemic feature of British society. The short-hand term to describe this *wrong* is 'racism'. It is a complex concept. It usually refers to behaviour and language which, intentionally or not, can have a number of results. It may be individually demeaning to the victim; it may isolate a particular group of people from participation in the wider society; it may lead to the harassment of a person; or it may provoke violence against an individual or group. As a consequence, it covers a wide range of behaviour from that which is sometimes described as 'low-level' racism (but none the less upsetting and offensive) to those extreme forms, involving violence and murder.

At the heart of much racism is a range of views which derive from the discredited 'race science'. In particular, members of other ethnic groups may be regarded as **biologically inferior**. This may be an unstated presumption and not an expressed opinion. Some racists are concerned with **cultural difference**. Other ethnic groups are seen as **incompatible with the dominant white ethnic group**. This can result in **the advocacy of segregation** (either formal or informal). Other racist views involve a failure (or unwillingness) to understand the perspectives of different ethnic groups and a readiness to judge their behaviour, customs and traditions solely by **the standards of the host society**. The highlighted words in this paragraph signify a fundamental element in racism whereby a crude dichotomy can be drawn: there is 'us' and 'them', an 'in-group' and an 'out-group', 'our (indigenous) people' and those who are 'alien'.

Finally, some racism has been characterised as **'institutional racism'**. This describes, for example, circumstances where the rules, qualifying conditions and systems of the host society may discriminate (sometimes unconsciously) against certain ethnic groups in respect of access to housing, education and training, welfare benefits or entry to jobs and professions. It may also encompass entrenched practices whereby certain ethnic groups are presumed, particularly but not exclusively by public authorities, to behave in a particular way or have particular charactistics. One example of this, in the wider society, is police attitudes to Afro-Caribbean teenage men. The Stephen Lawrence Inquiry Report defined institutional racism as:

> the collective failure of an organisation to provide an appropriate and professional service to people because of their colour, culture or ethnic origin. It can be seen or detected in processes, attitudes and behaviour which amount to discrimination through unwitting prejudice, ignorance, thoughtlessness and racist stereotyping which disadvantage minority ethnic people (Macpherson, 1999).

Expressions of racism

British society is not alone in producing evidence of racist behaviour. In most societies there is inter-ethnic intolerance and conflict. For example, the European Parliament published an extensive report of a Committee of Inquiry into Racism and Xenophobia (1991). This revealed instances in all member states. Furthermore, a poll (of 16 000 people in 15 European Union member states) from the EU's Eurostat statistical office (1997) reported widespread self-acknowledged racism. In Britain, 35 per cent said that they were 'not at all racist' (contrasting with 25 per cent in France, 32 per cent in Germany, 45 per cent in Ireland). When asked if they were 'very racist', the highest scores were 22 per cent in Belgium, 16 per cent in France and 14 per cent in Austria. Britain was middle-ranking with 8 per cent.

The nature, scale and expression of racism in any society is moulded by a number of key factors. The first is **the history and traditional values of the host country**. For example, Britain's relations with other nations and ethnic groups has been influenced by three elements in its history: its status as the leading slave-trading nation in the eighteenth century (transporting some two million slaves from Africa across the Atlantic between 1680 and 1786), its role as a major imperial power throughout the nineteenth and early twentieth centuries and its participation in wider European culture. Historically, racist views originated in notions of European racial superiority over the Africans who were regarded as 'an equivocal race between man and monkey' (quoted in Hiro, 1973: xii). Despite the abolition of slavery in Britain in 1834, racism was 'so ingrained in social thinking' that it 'seemed to leave the basic attitudes essentially unaltered' (Hiro, 1973: xii). Indeed, in the subsequent century or more of colonial rule these attitudes persisted. Hiro (1973: xviii) refers to an 'attitude of superiority blended with paternalistic concern that underlay the actions of those who administered the Empire'. Alongside this was the historic prejudice against Jews that is widely evident in European culture and supported, well into the twentieth century, in the teachings of Christian churches. As an ethnic group they are vilified as anti-Christ and conspirators against nation states; and, in the ideology of antisemites, the Aryan (or Caucasian) and the Jew were 'as far apart as humans and animals' (Boonstras *et al.*, 1993: 67).

The second factor is **the economic role of ethnic groups** in a society. Some members of the host society may see individuals from ethnic groups as positive contributors to a national economy, undertaking essential tasks within the professions and other skilled and unskilled work. However, the economic role of ethnic groups has, invariably, been perceived in negative terms. The Eurostat survey (1997) found that 80 per cent of respondents believed that ethnic minorities paid less in social security than they claimed; 63 per cent believed they increased unemployment; and 59 per cent said minorities abused the benefits system. These sentiments reflect long-established stereotyping and at times of economic dislocation can find powerful expression in the rhetoric of racist political parties. At the present time, concern about the high levels of unemployment in Germany (particularly in its eastern regions) is being directed against Turkish 'guest workers' (many of whom were recruited to work there from the 1960s onwards to contribute to the post-war regeneration of the economy). In France, high and persistent levels of unemployment have been a factor contributing to some electoral successes for the National Front.

Thirdly, there is **the perceived or actual power of ethnic groups**. This is usually associated with the economic role and status of ethnic groups. So, for example, the historic persecution of Jews was not merely rooted in ideological and religious stereotyping but also related to the perceived economic power they were said to exercise in the professions and banking.

Finally, **the political culture of the host country** is important to the extent that it promotes racism or is actively hostile to it. At one extreme, the entire structure of the Nazi state in Germany (1933–45) and the 'apartheid' regime in South Africa (1948–94) was organised for racist purposes. In some countries, ad hoc racist policies can be introduced for a specific purpose. One example is the 'Africanisation' policies adopted in Kenya and Uganda. These led to the expulsion of a predominantly commercial and professional class of Asian people of Indian origin to create employment opportunities for Africans.

In the present day, clear international standards are adopted by liberal democratic countries (e.g. European Union member states) to outlaw discrimination and oppression on the grounds of religion, ethnic origin and nationality (*see*, for example, the European Convention for the Protection of Human Rights and Fundamental Freedom, Arts 9 and 14). In Britain, race relations legislation is an attempt to translate these principles into wide-ranging civil rights. However, as we have seen from the foregoing discussion, entrenched racist views still find expression in these countries and require action not only on the political and legislative front but also within the workplace.

5.3 The context

5.3.1 The social background

Legislation introduced initially in 1965 to tackle racism was restricted to 'certain places of public resort' (e.g. hotels, restaurants, public houses, theatres, dance halls, swimming pools, public transport, etc.). In 1968, new legislation extended protection by outlawing direct (but not indirect) discrimination in employment. Eventually, the 1976 Act remedied this by providing provisions on indirect discrimination. Social and political commitment to enact legislation (however limited in scope it might be) was moulded by a number of influences: the experience of racism in British society, the conciousness-raising of the civil rights movement in the United States in the 1960s and the support of the government of the day.

The experience of racism was well documented in the reports of some important social investigations. In a survey of West Indians, Pakistanis, Indians and Cypriots, 35 per cent reported 'colour and racial prejudice in general' and 'unfriendliness to foreigners'; 26 per cent reported 'employment difficulties'. The proportion of West Indians reporting such discrimination was significantly higher – at 41 per cent and 32 per cent respectively (Daniel, 1968: 37).

Further investigations in employment showed that the principal answer for an employer refusing work to a person from a non-white ethnic group was the existence of a 'no coloureds' policy. The other key finding was that applicants were told that there were no vacancies but, nevertheless, the company continued to advertise (in 17 per cent of cases), or white men applying at the same time got jobs (in a further 17 per cent of cases) (Daniel, 1968: 73).

From interviews with employers' representatives and trade union officials, Daniel (1968: 89) drew three general conclusions.

> The first is that there was a high degree of generalization and stereotyping and little attempt to distinguish between different types of coloured people in terms of level of ability, personality or character, although some distinctions were drawn in terms of race or country of origin. The second is that . . . whether or not they themselves saw coloured immigrants in all the ways described, informants said or assumed that other people (their clients in the case of employment exchanges and bureaux; their members in the case of trade unions; their other employees, customers or clients in the case of employers) objected to coloured people for these reasons.

Indeed, in this context, the retail and distributive trades sector were

> the most resistant to the employment of coloured people . . . [and] most of them displaced responsibility on to customers or the public (109). The third and most important point, and this is partly a consequence of the first two, is that coloured immigrants had been and were being considered by employers, if at all, only where no suitable white English personnel were available.

In terms of promotion, there were even more difficulties. Non-white ethnic workers 'become less acceptable or unacceptable in jobs that imply authority over white subordinates, reciprocal relationships with white colleagues in other departments and other functions and contact with clients and the general public' (Daniel, 1968: 107).

From all the data analysed, it is not surprising that 'many of the coloured immigrants who were interviewed had been very disappointed and even bitter about their experience of life in Britain and of the white British people with whom they had come into contact' (Daniel, 1968: 83).

During the late 1950s and the 1960s, **the civil rights movement in the United States** was articulating opposition (primarily, in certain southern states) to segregation in public places and access to services, denial of voting rights, 'separate but equal' policies and refusal of entry to education institutions. In many respects, this represented the unfinished business of seeking full citizenship rights for the black Americans, a hundred years after the abolition of slavery and the American Civil War. One ingredient in the pursuit of these citizenship rights was the landmark Civil Rights Act 1964. The principle of providing such a non-discriminatory legislative framework was also seen as attractive in Britain as an instrument to achieve particular public policy objectives. Although Britain's race relations problems were not as entrenched as America's, nor characterised by the same degree of violence, it was clear to policy-makers that, given the experience of recent immigrants to Britain and prevailing social attitudes, preventive, as well as remedial, action was appropriate (*see* Fig. 5.1).

Mark Gilroy, 25, an Afro-Caribbean delivery worker, who worked for ten months with a Blackpool-based luxury kitchen company, was awarded £25 000 (of which £12 500 was for injury to feelings) by an employment tribunal in Liverpool in January 2001. He had endured a sustained campaign of racist abuse from workmates. He said that the two drivers refused to let him sleep with them in the comfortable compartment behind the cab of the 18-ton lorry which was fitted with twin bunk beds. The drivers had ordered him to bed down on cardboard in the trailer between cookers and parts. It was cold and dark. He was locked in and could not get out in an emergency. After one incident he was assaulted by one of the drivers. He ended up on sick leave and undergoing stress counselling.

Figure 5.1 The case of Mark Gilroy: No change there, then

5.3.2 Political approaches

As indicated in Chapter 4, political action against discrimination can be either 'minimalist' or 'maximalist'. In Britain, it is tending towards the latter position.

Comparing Britain with other member states of the European Union, Justice, the human rights group, comments (1996) that the Race Relations Act 1976 is 'unique' in having had legislation against discrimination on racial grounds on the statute book for some 30 years. Although all member states 'have written Constitutions that prohibit race discrimination in some way, detailed implementing legislation is often lacking. Where it does exist, it may be limited to acts committed by organs of the State' (1996: 28). A separate report (Forbes and Mead, 1992), reviewing the details of member state action, commented that 'in general, measures to combat discrimination are by no means comprehensive or uniformly effective, and in some cases are largely absent'.

This British race relations legislation has been characterised as flawed and could, according to the Commission for Racial Equality (1998), be improved and strengthened. The Race Relations (Amendment) Act 2000 and the accompanying statutory Code of Practice (2002) are attempts to rectify some of the shortcomings, particularly in respect of public authorities and the exercise of their functions. Furthermore, the criminal law on racially motivated harassment and violence has been improved (Crime and Disorder Act 1998); and the Crime and Security Act 2001 has created a new criminal offence of 'religiously aggravated harassment'. This covers the workplace as well as society in general. However, there remains some concern about the interaction of asylum and immigration law on attempts to improve race relations.

There has been change in European legislation. Until 2000, the EU took a generally minimalist approach to the problems of discrimination on grounds of race. In that year, the Council of Ministers adopted the Race Directive 2000. The wider Employment Directive 2000 was also adopted. This outlaws religious discrimination. The race and religion or belief provisions are implemented from 2003 (*see* section 5.4 on the legal framework).

5.3.3 Labour-market participation

Studies of the labour-market participation of different ethnic groups reveal several features: the existence of occupational segregation (both vertically and horizontally), a dual labour market in respect of employment status, some marked differences between non-white ethnic groups about their experiences of the labour market, differential levels of unemployment affecting different ethnic groups and the marked significance of gender as an additional basis for different practices and experiences.

The Labour Force Surveys (Jones, 1996: 91) show the following **overall participation rates** by ethnic group of people of working age (i.e. between 16 years and 59 years for women and 16 years and 64 years for men):

	All (%)	Male (%)	Female (%)
All origins	80	89	71
White	81	89	71
Total ethnic minority	70	81	57

Two aspects of these overall figures are worth comment. First, the age structure of non-white ethnic groups tends to be younger than that of the white population.

This, in part, explains their lower labour-market participation because of involvement in post-16 full-time education. In this, there are significant differences between ethnic groups. For example, 37 per cent of white young people are in such education, 43 per cent of African-Caribbean, 66 per cent of African Asian, and 77 per cent of Chinese (Jones, 1996: 45).

Secondly, the markedly lower female rate for non-white ethnic groups both reflects the age profile and also suggests that the difference may be a consequence of 'differences in culture concerning the role of women in home-making and child-rearing' (Jones, 1996: 64). 'African-Caribbean women have relatively high rates of economic activity whether or not they are married or cohabiting or have dependent children. Pakistani and Bangladeshi women have much lower rates of economic activity than women of other groups, and this is true of both married and unmarried women' (Jones, 1996: 64 and 92).

In terms of the **economic and employment status** of people of working age, two principal features are revealed in these Labour Force Survey data (Jones, 1996: 94–6). First, 'employee' is the predominant form of employment status (for 64 per cent of white people and 49 per cent of non-white ethnic groups). Between ethnic groups there are differences (e.g. 61 per cent for African-Caribbeans, 42 per cent for Chinese, 28 per cent for Pakistanis). Of these 'employees' about one-fifth, overall, are part-timers. There is, of course, a markedly greater tendency for women to work part-time. This is true, across ethnic groups, with the exception of Pakistani and Bangladeshi women (where there is a low incidence).

The second feature of employment status that is revealed is the variable incidence of 'self-employment' between different ethnic groups. A general growth in self-employment took place in the labour market in the 1980s. It covers 9 per cent of labour market participants and is a largely male activity. In terms of ethnic origin, there is a greater incidence among the following: Indian (at 13 per cent), African Asian (14 per cent) and Chinese (18 per cent).

The concentrations of ethnic groups in different **industries and sectors** does vary (Jones, 1996: 99). For example:

- 48 per cent of Pakistani, 35 per cent of Indian and 27 per cent of African Asian employees work in *manufacturing* (contrasting with 10 per cent of all employees);
- 18 per cent of African Asian employees work in *retail distribution* (as against 11 per cent of all employees);
- 41 per cent of Bangladeshi and 38 per cent of Chinese employees work in *hotel and catering* (in contrast with 4 per cent of all employees);
- 14 per cent of African, 13 per cent of African-Caribbean and 13 per cent of Chinese employees work in *hospitals and medical care institutions* (in contrast with 5 per cent of all employees).

The data on **occupation** or **job level** are presented on a gender basis. For men 'a complex pattern is developing' (Jones, 1996: 71), with some ethnic groups having similar or higher job levels than white male employees. So, for example, 27 per cent of all male employees were in the top (professional, managerial, employer) category. Some comparative figures on the basis of ethnic origin were 30 per cent Chinese, 27 per cent African Asian and 25 per cent Indian. One conclusion, from further analysis, was that 'it seems that men from certain minority groups had, by the end of the 1980s, penetrated successfully into certain professions, but to a much lesser extent into the senior management of large organisations' (Jones, 1996: 71).

Jones (1996: 72) defines 'the apparent polarisation within some of the minority groups, which have high proportions within the upper and lower categories'. So, for example, 28 per cent of Indians and 40 per cent of Chinese are in semi-skilled and unskilled manual jobs (compared with 19 per cent of all male workers). On the other hand, African-Caribbean, Pakistani and Bangladeshi male employees are most likely to be concentrated in skilled, semi-skilled and unskilled manual work at 68 per cent, 71 per cent and 75 per cent respectively.

As far as women are concerned, a long-standing finding in social surveys is reaffirmed: 'there is much less disparity between women employees of different ethnic groups than is the case for men' (Jones, 1996: 72). There are smaller proportions of women employees than of men in the top professional, managerial, employer category. However, Chinese, white and Indian women have the highest proportions at 16 per cent, 11 per cent and 10 per cent respectively (contrasting with the figure of 11 per cent for all employees). The largest proportion (around a half for all ethnic groups) is found in the 'other non-manual' category.

In terms of **unemployment**, white people 'remained much less prone to unemployment than ethnic minorities' (Jones, 1996: 116) at the end of the 1980s. Differential unemployment rates for people of working age in the Labour Force Survey (1988–90) are set out in Table 5.2.

Table 5.2 Unemployment by age (per cent)

All origins	8
White	7
Total ethnic minority	13
African-Caribbean	14
African Asian	9
Indian	11
Pakistani	22
Bangladeshi	24
Chinese	7
African	14
Other/Mixed	10

On an age basis, there were particularly high unemployment rates for those between 16 and 24 years in the Indian, Bangladeshi, African-Caribbean, African and Pakistani ethnic groups at 16, 19, 23, 27 and 30 per cent respectively (in contrast with a rate of 11 per cent for young persons of all origins) (Jones, 1996: 127). These results were further confirmed in the published figures of the 1991 Census.

There are many suggestions as to why unemployment differs between ethnic groups, often relating to occupational segregation:

- *The location of Pakistanis and Bangladeshis in lower-level jobs* which are more vulnerable to unemployment.

- *The shift from manufacturing to a service-based economy* has resulted in fewer unskilled and semi-skilled jobs and more administrative, professional and managerial posts. This has had a disproportionate effect on workers from ethnic groups who were initially employed in traditional industries. However, there is some suggestion that the expansion of the service sector may have resulted in a net employment advantage to non-white ethnic groups in general.

■ *Technological change* within companies has sometimes displaced more non-white than white workers. This is partially because of their concentration in lower-level jobs directly affected by redundancies caused by automation. Their disadvantage may be compounded by their comparatively shorter service and the use of LIFO (the 'last in first out' criterion) for redundancy selection. Furthermore, Newnham (1986) identifies stereotyping whereby members of non-white ethnic groups may not always be seen as having the mental attributes for retraining, only the physical attributes for unskilled manual jobs.

■ *Language difficulties*, in relation to both spoken and written English, account for some unemployment. Smith (1985) found that over 50 per cent of Asian men and women had a 'serious linguistic handicap' in that they could not sustain an interview in English. However, this language barrier does not exist for African-Caribbean people or the overwhelming majority of British-born African and Asian people.

■ *Exclusion from employment opportunities* as a result of straightforward racism also is a certain explanation of differential unemployment rates.

One dimension of race relations in the labour market is **the contribution of migrant workers**. Recent research (Glover *et al.*, 2001) has provided some useful data to inform discussion. The profile of these workers reveals the following characteristics:

■ They are 'very heterogeneous'.

■ There is 'no principal source country' of migration to the UK. The largest single identifiable group (around a quarter) is UK nationals – mostly returning emigrants and some who were born abroad. The next largest group (at around a third) comprises European Union nationals.

■ Migrants are 'highly concentrated – and increasingly so – in London. No only do over half of all migrants live in London and the South East but more than two-thirds of new migrants are settling there' (Glover *et al.*, 2001: 39).

■ There, education and skills levels are 'polarised' in that 'proportionately, there are both more highly educated people and more relatively unskilled' (Glover *et al.*, 2001: 30).

■ Migrants have 'mixed success in the labour market'. 'Overall migrants are less likely to be employed and more likely to be unemployed than natives. In addition, migrants are half as likely again as natives to be inactive, probably partly reflecting lower participation rates among women and partly reflecting the numbers of students' (Glover *et al.*, 2001: 31).

■ Levels of entrepreneurship and self-employment 'appear to be high among migrants'.

■ Language fluency is 'an important determinant of employment . . . the employment rate for ethnic minority migrants is 20 to 25 percentage points higher when they are fluent in English' (Glover *et al.*, 2001: 32).

EMPLOYMENT

Racism: racial discrimination may hinder people from getting employment.

Work experience: lack of work experience and a resulting lack of references in the UK may be a disincentive for employers.

Re-accreditation: qualifications from abroad may not be recognised in the UK, requiring people to requalify locally.

National Insurance numbers: employers may ask for these. Asylum seekers may have problems obtaining them.

Documentation checks: asylum seekers' papers may say that they are subject to detention and may not say that they have the right to work.

Gender: usually, only principal asylum applicants are granted the right to work. This may exclude many women from the workplace.

Paperwork: asylum seekers must obtain permission from the Immigration and Nationality Directorate [of the Home Office] or have restrictions removed from their documentation.

Status: for the first six months, asylum seekers are normally not entitled to work.

Language barriers: many arrivals speak little or no English. English spoken in other countries may have local differences.

Figure 5.2 Migrants: the cumulative barriers to employment

Source: Glover *et al*. (2001) 'Migration: an economic and social analysis' RDS Occasional Paper No. 67, London: Home Office.

- Supply-side barriers 'contribute to migrants' lower labour force participation rates' (Glover *et al.*, 2001: 35). The Audit Commission summarised the barriers as a progressive series of steps which could ultimately lead to employment (*see* Fig. 5.2).

5.3.4 Social issues

Social policies that will facilitate participation in the wider community are key to creating a wider context within which discrimination can be tackled and equal opportunities advanced. Many of these areas extend beyond employment (the brief of this book). However, because there are connections, it is important to identify them. They include the following:

- access to education and training opportunities;
- access to employment and career development opportunities;
- access to social and voluntary groups (political parties, trade unions, women's organisations, other clubs and societies – Round Table, sporting clubs);
- access to public appointments/elective office – political office in local government, magistracy, tribunal lay membership;

■ ability to have concerns seriously treated and their interests protected and taken into account.

We will now consider the legal framework that governs race discrimination in employment.

5.4 The legal framework

5.4.1 Grounds for unfair discrimination

The Race Relations Act outlaws direct and indirect discrimination on '**racial grounds**' (s 1(1)). This is defined as meaning 'any of the following grounds, namely colour, race, nationality or ethnic or national origin' (s 3(1)). The term 'racial grounds' has been interpreted to extend beyond the characteristics of a complainant. In 1984, Browne-Wilkinson J said that this phrase was capable of covering any reason for an action based on race (*see also* Fig. 5.3):

> We find it impossible to believe that Parliament intended that a person dismissed for refusing to obey an unlawful discriminatory instruction should be without a remedy . . . We therefore conclude that s 1(1)(a) covers all cases of discrimination on racial grounds whether the racial characteristics in question are those of the person treated less favourably or of some other person. The only question in each case is whether the unfavourable treatment afforded to the claimant was caused by racial considerations' (*Showboat Entertainment Centre Ltd* v *Owens* [1984] IRLR 7, EAT).

A '**racial group**' is defined by 'colour, race, nationality or ethnic or national origin' (s 3(1)). A person may be a member of several 'racial groups' simultaneously and these can be indicated in any complaint alleging discrimination, direct or indirect. The legislation provides no explicit protection against discrimination on the grounds of religion (*see* Fig. 5.4 p 207).

In a leading case (*Mandla* v *Dowell Lee* [1983] IRLR 209), which tested whether Sikhs qualified as a racial group, the House of Lords ruled that 'ethnic origin' was

---

In May 1999, three young cable-layers from Bradford who were friends won the first employment tribunal case to decide whether a white person can suffer racial discrimination by supporting black colleagues. Ninja (Iain Wilson), 24, Toffo, 24, and Parksy, 27, were white, Asian and African-Caribbean, respectively. In 1998, they were sent to Warwick, a predominantly white town, to lay TV cables for a Manchester-based company. On arrival, they were told they were 'too scruffy for our customers' by a senior manager. When they returned to their van to load up their gear, Iain Wilson was taken aside by a line manager. He was offered work and told that there was no problem with him – 'it's the other two'. He added, 'you know what I mean'. Iain Wilson refused and returned to Bradford with his colleagues. Toffo commented that 'the guys who sacked me and Parksy were sly. They thought they'd not be found out because Iain would have the same racist views as them.'

Figure 5.3 Three cable-layers

a wider concept than 'race', to be construed in 'broad, cultural historic sense' (Bourn and Whitmore, 1993: 57). To be an 'ethnic group', under the Act, a group must have certain essential characteristics:

- a long shared history, of which the group is conscious as distinguishing it from other groups and the memory of which keeps it alive;
- a cultural tradition, including family and social customs and manners (which may be associated with religious observance).

In addition, some of the following factors may be relevant in distinguishing the group:

- common geographical origin or descent from common ancestors;
- a common language (not necessarily restricted to the group);
- a common literature particular to that group;
- a common religion (different from that of neighbouring groups or from the general community);
- being a minority or being an oppressed or a dominant group within a large community.

In addition to these objective factors, self-designation is also a consideration: 'provided a person who joins the group feels himself or herself to be a member of it, and is accepted by other members, then he is, for the purposes of the Act a member' (Fraser LJ). This could extend coverage to converts, and those who marry into groups.

This test, deriving from the *Mandla* case, has been applied to define gypsies as an ethnic group (*Commission for Racial Equality* v *Dutton* [1989] IRLR 8, CA); and likewise, Jews and Sikhs. However, Muslims and Rastafarians have been unsuccessful in persuading the courts and tribunals that they were ethnic groups. They have been defined as religious groups (*Tariq* v *Young* 19.4.89 COIT, 24773/88; *Dawkins* v *Department of Environment* [1993] IRLR 284).

However, it has been possible to cover some religious discrimination where different racial groups (as opposed to ethnic groups) are being compared under the indirect discrimination provisions. In a recent case (*JH Walker Ltd* v *Hussein* [1996] IRLR 11), the employer introduced a rule for all workers prohibiting them from taking holidays during May and June each year. The Muslim religious day of Eid falls within this period. There were two racial groups in the relevant pool for comparison – almost half the workforce originating from the Indian sub-continent (the majority of whom were Muslim) and the remaining workforce being primarily Europeans. Consequently the number of the first group who could comply with the requirement to work in Eid was considerably smaller than the proportion of Europeans who could comply.

The Court of Session in Scotland considered the question of 'racial groups' with reference to 'national origin'. It held that there can be direct or indirect racial discrimination within Britain arising from a person's national origin as English or Scots. However, English and Scots are not racial groups defined by 'ethnic origin' (*BBC* v *Souster* [2000] IRLR 150, Court of Session).

***Draft* Employment Equality (Religion or Belief) Regulations 2003**

Key provisions to be implemented (except in Northern Ireland) on 1 December 2003. These enact parts of the Employment Directive 2000.

- **Religion or belief**: This is defined as being any religion, religious belief or similar philosophical belief. Courts and tribunals will define this in more detail, considering a number of factors (collective worship, clear belief system, profound belief affecting a person's way of life or view of the world).

- **Employment**: Defined in the similar terms to the SDA, RRA and DDA. Applicants and employees are protected in terms similar to SDA 1975 s 6; RRA 1976 s 4; and DDA 1995 s 4. Contract workers are also protected (as in SDA s 9; and RRA s 7). (Specific occupational groups are also identified).

- **Direct discrimination**: This occurs where, because of a person's religion or belief (or perception of this), another treats this person less favourably than s/he would treat others. This provision includes a person who refuses to carry out an employer's discriminatory instruction.

- **Indirect discrimination**: This occurs where an employer applies to an employee (or applicant) a 'provision, criterion or practice' which is applied equally to others. This puts a person of that religion or belief at a particular disadvantage and the person in question suffers that disadvantage. The employer may be able objectively to justify the discriminatory treatment.

- **Victimisation**: Provides similar protection to that in the SDA 1975 s 4 and the RRA 1976 s 2.

- **Harassment**: Defined as an unlawful act which 'violates the dignity' of a person; or creates 'an offensive environment' for him/her; or which 'should reasonably be considered' as having done these things.

- **Genuine occupational requirement**: Possessing a particular religion or belief may be a requirement for a specific post; or because an organisation has a particular religious ethos.

- **Liability of employers and principals**: An employer is vicariously liable for the acts of his employees. The provision is similar to SDA 1975 s 41; and RRA 1976 s 32.

- **Positive action**: This is permitted in certain circumstances.

- **Enforcement proceedings**: Complaint to employment tribunal within three months irrespective of a person's length of service. Complainant may serve questionnaire on the employer. The tribunal may make a declaration or recommendation or order unlimited compensation.

- **Burden of proof**: Once a person has made out a *prima facie* case, it is for the employer to prove that he did not commit the act of discrimination or harassment. This is similar to SDA 1975 s 63A.

- **Contracts and collective agreements**: Those with discriminatory provisions are void.

Figure 5.4

5.4.2   The areas of employment protection

Under the Race Relations Act, it is unlawful for an employer to discriminate against a person on racial grounds (s 4) at both the *application stage* and in *employment*. There is, however, no formal statutory protection for former employees. Nevertheless, a recent sex discrimination case dealt with victimisation arising from a retaliatory measure of not providing a reference (*Coote* v *Granada Hospitality Ltd* C–185/97, ECJ).

'**Employment**' for these purposes means 'employment under a contract of service or of apprenticeship or a contract personally to execute any work or labour and related expressions shall be construed accordingly' (RRA, s 78(1)). (This definition is broadly identical with that in the Equal Pay Act 1970, s 1(6); and the Sex Discrimination Act 1975, s 82(1).) The key issue is that there must be an actual or anticipated contract (agreement) between, on the one hand, the person alleged to be the employer and, on the other hand, either the employee or contractor.

Much of the case law relating to the interpretation of 'employment' is found under sex discrimination law (*see* Chapter 4). Such case law is accepted by the courts as applicable also to the interpretation of race discrimination law.

Such discrimination on racial grounds can arise in the following ways:

Applicants

- in arrangements made for deciding who shall be offered employment;
- in the terms on which employment is offered;
- by refusing or deliberately omitting to offer the person employment.

Employed people

Exempted are those who are employed in private households (RRA, s 4(3)). The principal areas of prohibited discrimination are:

- in the terms of employment provided;
- in the ways in which access is provided (or refused) to opportunities for promotion, transfer and training or any other benefits or services;
- by dismissing the person or subjecting him/her to any other detriment.

Agency workers and contract workers

Clearly, in this area there are three parties: the agency which supplies labour, the organisation which provides work (defined as 'the principal' in RRA, s 7), and the individual (the 'contract worker'). (The intricacies of such relationships are discussed more fully in Chapter 2.)

It is unlawful (RRA, s 7(2)) for the principal to discriminate on the following grounds:

- in the terms on which an organisation allows an individual to work for it; or
- by not allowing the individual to do the work or not do the work; or
- in the way the organisation affords access to any benefits, facilities or services or by refusing or deliberately omitting to afford access to them; or
- by subjecting the individual to any other detriment.

In a recent case it was ruled that the Act applied to concessionaires in a department store (*Harrods Ltd* v *Remick and Others* [1997] IRLR 9, EAT). In these instances, Harrods gave, refused or withdrew 'store approval' to concessionaire staff who complied with certain rules and requirements. The EAT found that the work done by the three complainants was work done 'for' Harrods as 'the principal' (s 7(1)). It was done in the Harrods store, for that company's benefit and under Harrods' control. The fact that the three individual workers also worked for their employers (i.e. Sheaffer Pens Ltd, Brigade International Ltd and Moyses

Stevens Ltd) did not prevent the work that they had done from being work 'for' Harrods within the meaning of s 7.

The Race Relations Act (s 14) explicitly forbids discrimination by an employment agency against a person as follows:

- in the terms on which the agency offers to provide any of its services; or
- by refusing or deliberately omitting to provide any of its services; or
- in the way it provides any of its services.

An 'employment agency' is defined as 'a person who, for profit or not, provides services for the purpose of finding employment for workers or supplying employers with workers' (s 78(1)).

Summarily dismissed employees

Whilst the Act (s 4) clearly protects employees and applicants for employment, it has been ruled by the Court of Appeal not to cover those who are summarily dismissed employees who allege discrimination in an internal appeal procedure (*Adekeye* v *Post Office* (*No. 2*) [1997] IRLR 105, CA). The ex-employee, subject to immediate dismissal, was seeking reinstatement and was not an applicant for employment. Thus such a person would be seeking the reversal of a decision to dismiss and would not be making a fresh application for employment.

There is, nevertheless, overall protection against dismissal (s 4(2)(c)) irrespective of length of service, hours worked or age. However, there is no express definition of 'dismissal' (unlike that provided in the Sex Discrimination Act, s 82(1A), which covers constructive dismissal and the expiry and non-renewal of a fixed-term contract. Nevertheless, from case law, the Race Relations Act provision is held to cover repudiatory breach of contract by an employer and the associated constructive dismissal (*Weathersfield Ltd t/a Van and Truck Rentals* v *Sargent* [1998] IRLR 14, EAT). It is, however, uncertain whether on the expiry of a fixed-term contract a person is an ex-employee and, therefore, unprotected.

So, in brief, the Race Relations Act protects applicants for jobs, employees, contract workers and self-employed people (provided the dominant purpose of the contract is the execution of personal work or labour) 'in relation to employment . . . at an establishment in Great Britain' (s 4(1), s 8). More specifically, civil servants are covered but the Act does not affect Civil Service Regulations restricting entry to Crown employment relating to national security (s 75). Police officers (who hold 'the office of constable') are for the purposes of the employment provisions (RRA, Part II) to be regarded as being in employment (s 16).

All workers are covered irrespective of their length of service, the number of hours they work each week or their age. Persons who object to instructions to discriminate and are themselves discriminated against are protected. It is unlawful to instruct or pressurise a person to act in a way prohibited by the Act (ss 30 and 31).

Race Relations (Amendment) Act 2000

This legislation, part of the response to the Stephen Lawrence Inquiry's concern about institutional racism, was implemented in May 2001. It 'mainsteams' race equality into the functions, culture and aims of public sector organisations. A

Council of Europe report defines 'mainstreaming' as 'the organisation, improvement and evaluation of policy processes, so that . . . equality perspective is incorporated in all policies at all levels and at all stages, by the actors normally involved in policy making'. So, the Act requires a more proactive approach to the tackling of discriminatory practice. It contrasts with the reactive, piecemeal and complaints-based approach that frequently arises under other discrimination law.

The Act places a general statutory duty on public authorities to promote equality of opportunity, eliminate unlawful racial discrimination and promote good race relations. It covers both service delivery and employment. It includes specific duties concerning the monitoring on grounds of ethnic origin and producing a race equality scheme. (These issues are considered in more detail below.)

The 2000 Act extends the duty placed on local authorities under the 1976 Act (s 71). It, therefore, includes government departments, local authorities, the police, NHS bodies, non-departmental public bodies, public sector schools and further and higher education bodies. Any public services provided under contract by private or voluntary organisations are also covered and subject to the duty. The public authority has the responsibility to ensure compliance with the statutory duty by the contracted service providers. Also, agencies that inspect or audit public authorities (e.g. the Commission for Health Improvement or Ofsted) are also bound by the duty to promote race equality. 'These agencies will need to consider how the new duty fits with their inspection or audit obligations' (Code of Practice: para 2.14).

5.4.3   Direct discrimination

This is defined in the legislation in the following terms:

> A person discriminates against another in any circumstances relevant for the purposes of any provision of this Act if . . . on racial grounds he treats that other less favourably than he treats or would treat other persons' (RRA, s 1(1)(a)).

Also, it is stated that 'for the purposes of this Act, segregating a person from other persons on racial grounds is treating him less favourably than they are treated' (s 1(2)).

In determining whether or not there is direct discrimination, it is unnecessary to show the intention of the employer to discriminate on racial grounds. If less favourable treatment is established, then the employer is liable. The issue of comparison is clearly there. The 'but for' test (*see* Chapter 4 on sex discrimination) can be used: 'would the complainant have received the same treatment from the defendant but for his or her [racial group]'? (*James* v *Eastleigh Borough Council* [1990] IRLR 288, HL). But the Act cautions that 'a comparison of the case of a person of a particular racial group under section 1(1) must be such that the relevant circumstances in the one case are the same, or not materially different, in the other' (s 3(4)). The correct comparators must be chosen. Stereotyping is clearly compatible with the 'but for' test. Essentially, the comparison must be between the treatment received by the complainant and the actual or hypothetical treatment of another person (who had all the characteristics of the complainant) apart from his/her racial group or attitude to race. By looking at the facts and then excluding racial issues, it is possible to decide whether the differential treatment is on racial grounds.

An individual must have received less favourable treatment than an actual or hypothetical comparator had received or would have received on racial grounds. The Court of Appeal has affirmed that if there is no actual comparator, then, an employment tribunal must construct a hypothetical one. Failure to do so is an error in law (*Balamoody* v *United Kingdom Central Council for Nursing, Midwifery and Health Visiting* [2002] IRLR 288). The less favourable treatment can involve restriction of choice (denial of training or promotion opportunities) or the imposition of a detriment (harassment).

The racial grounds underlying the less favourable treatment need not be the sole grounds for the less favourable treatment. There can be other non-racial grounds. Knox J has stated that:

> where an industrial tribunal finds that there are mixed motives for the doing of an act, one or some but not all of which constitute unlawful discrimination, it is highly desirable for there to be an assessment of the importance from the causative point of view of the unlawful motive or motives. If the industrial tribunal finds that the unlawful motive or motives were of sufficient weight in the decision-making process to be treated as a cause, not the sole cause but as a cause, of the act thus motivated, there will be unlawful discrimination (*Nagarajan* v *Agnew* [1994] IRLR 61, EAT).

In recent cases, courts have ruled on the 'reasonableness' of the treatment. In brief, the approach adopted suggests that unreasonable treatment (without more evidence) becomes discrimination on racial grounds merely because the person affected by this unreasonable treatment is from a specific ethnic group. So, for example, an employer might be an 'unreasonable employer' and treat specific categories of staff badly (irrespective of their ethnic origin). The appropriate comparison is not between the unreasonable employer and a reasonable employer. It should concern the comparative treatment of staff employed by the unreasonable employer.

Lord Morison put the situation this way:

> The requirement necessary is to establish less favourable treatment than that which would have been accorded by a reasonable employer in the circumstances, but of less favourable treatment than that which would have been accorded by the same employer in the same circumstances. It cannot be inferred, let alone presumed, only from the fact that an employer has acted unreasonably towards one employee, that he would have acted reasonably if he had been dealing with another employee in the same circumstances (cited by Browne-Wilkinson LJ in *Zafar* v *Glasgow City Council* [1998] IRLR 36, HL).

5.4.4 Indirect discrimination

This is defined in the legislation in the following terms:

> A person discriminates against another in any circumstances relevant for the purposes of any provision of this Act if . . . he applies to that other a requirement or condition which he applies or would apply equally to persons not of the same racial group as that other but
> (i) which is such that the proportion of persons of the same racial group as that other who can comply with it is considerably smaller than the proportion of persons not of that racial group who can comply with it; and

(ii)   which he cannot show to be justifiable irrespective of the colour, race, nationality or ethnic or national origins of the person to whom it is applied; and

(iii)   which is to the detriment of that other because he cannot comply with it (s 1(1)(b)).

The Race Directive 2000 provides a new definition of indirect discrimination as relating to any neutral 'provision, criterion or practice' (see p 166 in relation to sex discrimination). The Race Relations Act is amended from July 2003.

In Chapter 4 on sex discrimination, the key legal issues relating to indirect discrimination were discussed. They should be followed because of the links between the two bodies of discrimination law. In this section, we will draw attention briefly to certain examples of indirect race discrimination. As with direct discrimination (discussed above) there must be like-with-like comparison. It is also important to note that the issue of intention to discriminate here can be a consideration. In respect of indirect discrimination, the Race Relations Act says that 'no award of damages shall be made if the respondent proves that the requirement or condition in question was not applied with the intention of treating the claimant unfavourably on racial grounds' (s 57(3)) – although case law has mitigated this.

In the *Raval* case (*Raval* v *Department of Health and Social Security and Civil Service Commission* [1985] IRLR 370), various questions were proposed to help analyse claims of indirect discrimination. These were as follows:

1   Does the complainant (the employee) belong to the racial group in question?
2   Has the respondent employer applied a condition or requirement to the employee?
3   If so, when was the condition or requirement applied (the 'material time')?
4   Did the requirement or condition apply to other persons who were not of the same racial group as the employee?
5   If so, was the appropriate comparison made under s 3(4) of the Act?
6   Within which section of the community is the proportionate comparison made?
7   Is it found that the proportion of persons in the same racial group as the employee (who could comply with the condition or requirement at the material time) is considerably smaller than the proportion of persons **not** of that racial group who could comply with it?
8   Can the requirement or condition be shown by the employer to be justifiable?
9   Could the employee (at the 'material time') comply with the requirement or condition?
10   If not, was it to the employee's detriment that they could not do so?

The issues involved in this set of questions are discussed in the following sections.

Condition or requirement

These terms (which overlap in meaning) refer to those rules, conditions and practices that although appearing neutral in their applicant can put a person at a disadvantage because of their ethnic origin. They may be formally written down or they may be implied. The accepted view in the courts is that it is something which must be complied with and creates an 'absolute bar' (*Perera* v *Civil Service*

Commission (*No. 2*) [1983] IRLR 166, CA). So, preferences in personnel specifications are unlikely to be construed as conditions or requirements under race discrimination law. However, this may not be the case under sex discrimination law (*see* Chapter 4).

Examples of requirements or conditions relating to race discrimination can encompass language qualifications, dress and appearance, seniority of service or residential qualifications. The latter, for example, was the subject of a complaint (in *Hussein* v *Saints Complete House Furnishers* [1979] IRLR 337). In this case a job applicant was not considered because he lived in one of a specific group of postal districts in Liverpool. These had a high proportion of non-white residents. It was found by the tribunal that 50 per cent of the population in the specified postal districts were non-white. The figure for the rest of Merseyside was about 2 per cent. The tribunal found that the particular racial group was therefore disproportionately affected.

Comply in practice with the condition or requirement

There are several aspects to the issue of compliance. First, there is the question of the pool for comparison. This will, of course, vary from case to case. It can be a national pool, a regional or a local one. Furthermore, it could be all or part of a particular workforce. Secondly, the legislation requires comparison between proportions of each racial group (the complainant's and the comparator's). It refers to the issue of whether 'a considerably smaller proportion' of the complainant's racial group can comply. This implies the preparation of statistical data. This can be difficult for applicants if an over-elaborate approach is adopted.

The third issue is the meaning of 'can comply'. The House of Lords (in *Mandla* v *Dowell Lee* [1983] IRLR 209) affirmed that it means can comply in practice. The case involved a requirement for Sikhs not to wear a turban. Lord Fraser stated that 'in the context of section 1(1)(b)(i) of the 1976 Act, it must, in my opinion, have been intended by Parliament to be read not as meaning "can physically", so as to indicate a theoretical possibility, but as meaning "can in practice" or "can consistently with the customs and cultural conditions of the racial group"'.

Detriment

This arises where a rule or condition of employment adversely affects a person's chance of employment, promotion, training or access to benefits. It arises because a person cannot comply with the condition or requirement. A detriment can be caused in various ways: applications not being considered, failure to be recruited or promoted, failure to hear of vacancies, receiving lower rates of pay or less favourable benefits or working conditions, or dismissal.

Justification

This is considered by the same standards as those set out in Chapter 4. An employer must show a real need, which can be objectively justified, for the condition or requirement. It need not be on economic grounds. It can be for administrative efficiency or health and safety. The latter justification was put forward and accepted (in *Panesar* v *Nestlé Co Ltd* [1980] IRLR 64, CA). Here, a rule forbidding beards in a chocolate factory was justifiable on grounds of hygiene. This was despite the fact that the proportion of Sikhs would could comply was considerably smaller than the comparable proportion of non-Sikhs.

5.4.5 Victimisation

This is the third form of discrimination. Anyone involved in enforcing the Race Relations Act, by bringing proceedings, making allegations or giving information, is protected against victimisation (s 2). The issues relating to victimisation are discussed in Chapter 4 and are relevant to race discrimination law.

In *Chief Constable of West Yorkshire* v *Khan* [2001], the House of Lords considered the refusal to provide a reference for a police sergeant, who had lodged a race discrimination claim at an employment tribunal. It considered whether, consciously or not, he was subject to less favourable treatment. It ruled that the proper comparator was with an employee who had not brought legal proceedings against the Chief Constable and had requested a reference. In this case, the refusal was not that Sergeant Khan had brought proceedings. It was the employer's concern to protect their position in the race discrimination case which was still ongoing. Lord Hoffman suggested a practical test which might be helpful. Employers should ask: *would the request have been refused if the litigation had already concluded, whatever the outcome?* The House of Lords, unanimously, held that there was no victimisation.

5.4.6 Special provisions: 'genuine occupational qualification'

In certain circumstances, as under sex discrimination law, discrimination on 'racial grounds' is permissible in employment. Being a member of a racial group can be a 'genuine occupational qualification' (s 5) for a post. Essentially, there are two broad reasons provided: 'authenticity' and the most effective ways of providing 'personal services promoting the welfare' of a particular racial group. Examples of the former are acting and entertainment; modelling for clothes and in the production of works of art; the provision of food and drink in a particular setting like a Chinese restaurant. Examples of the latter cover counselling and other social welfare posts where specific knowledge of an ethnic group is required. Genuine occupational qualifications (GOQs) do not apply when filling vacancies where an employer already has a sufficient number of employees of the racial group in question whom it is reasonable to employ on those duties. The provisions of the Act (s 5) are:

> Being of a particular racial group is a genuine occupational qualification for a job only where
> (a) the job involves participation in a dramatic performance or other entertainment in a capacity for which a person of that racial group is required for reasons of authenticity; or
> (b) the job involves participation as an artist's or photographic model in the production of a work of art, visual image or sequence of visual images for which a person of that racial group is required for reasons of authenticity; or
> (c) the job involves working in a place where food or drink is (for payment or not) provided to and consumed by members of the public or a section of the

public in a particular setting for which, in that job, a person of that racial group is required for reasons of authenticity;

(d)   the holder of the job provides persons of that racial group with personal services promoting their welfare, and those services can most effectively be provided by the person of that racial group.

Employers' use of the GOQ provisions can be challenged and must be defended. In one notable case (*Tottenham Green Under Fives' Centre* v *Marshall* [1989] IRLR 147) involving recruitment of a nursery helper in a multi-ethnic nursery, the Employment Appeals Tribunal set out guidance on the application of the personal services GOQ:

- the particular racial group must be clearly, even narrowly, defined because it must be the same for the postholder and the recipient of the personal services;
- the postholder must be directly involved in the provision of the services. It is insufficient if they are merely directing others;
- if the postholder provides several personal services to the recipient, then provided one of these genuinely falls within the subsection, the defence is established;
- 'promoting the welfare' is a very wide expression and the meaning should be interpreted widely in the light of the facts of each case;
- the Act assumes that the personal services could be provided by others, but the question is whether they can be 'most effectively provided' by a person of that racial group.

The requirements on employers to defend the GOQ can bring to light trivial or false duties said to be covered by this section of the Act. These may be devices to introduce positive discrimination.

5.4.7   Positive action and positive discrimination

In the Introduction to Part Two of this book and in Chapter 4, the concepts of positive action and positive discrimination were explored. As far as discrimination on racial grounds is concerned, the same fundamental points apply. Positive discrimination is unlawful. Positive action, however, is permitted in the following contexts: access to facilities for training which help fit (members of particular racial group) for particular work, and encouraging people from a particular racial group 'to take advantage of opportunities' for doing that work (ss 37 and 38). This is subject to the following qualification (among others): that it 'reasonably appears' to the employer that, within the preceding 12 months, 'there were no persons of that group among those doing that work' in an area in Great Britain (Race Relations Act 1976, s 37). Furthermore, the Act allows the provision of facilities or services, in training, education or welfare, to meet the special needs of people from particular racial groups (e.g. classes in the English language) (s 35).

The CRE *Code of Practice* (1983) outlines further guidance on the use of positive action measures, principally in respect of advertising and training for posts (paras 1.44 and 1.45). Such measures are dependent, of course, on the collection and collation of monitoring data by employers. Because of substantial gaps here these statutory provisions are largely unenforced.

The CRE statutory *Code of Practice* (2002) to support the Race Relations (Amendment) Act 2000 recommends that where monitoring reveals under-representation among some racial groups, the public authority concerned 'could consider using "positive action"'. It does not require this. It draws attention to the provisions in the 1975 Act (ss 35, 37 and 38).

5.4.8 Liability

As in sex discrimination law, the vicarious liability of an employer is fundamentally important. The Race Relations Act 1976 (s 32(1)) states that 'anything done by a person in the course of his employment shall be treated for the purposes of this Act . . . as done by his employer as well as by him, whether or not it was done with the employer's knowledge or approval'. An employer, then, is directly liable for the discrimination and also vicariously liable for the discriminatory behaviour of, for example, managers, supervisors and other employees.

In *Jones* v *Tower Boot Co Ltd* [1997] IRLR 68, the Court of Appeal clarified the meaning of 'in the course of employment'. It was stated that these words should be interpreted broadly, in line with 'the natural meaning of those everyday words'. However:

> this is not to say that when it comes to applying them to the infinite variety of circumstances which is liable to occur in particular instances – within or without the workplace, in or out of uniform, in or out of rest breaks – all laymen would necessarily agree as to the result . . . The application of the phrase will be a question of fact for each [employment] tribunal to resolve in the light of the circumstances presented to it, with a mind unclouded by any parallels sought to be drawn from the law of vicarious liability in tort.

The Court of Appeal, then, signalled a clearer framework for the consideration of vicarious liability in this context by directing tribunals to consider the facts and come to a view as experienced, intelligent lay people. It disposed of the use of restrictive tort law in these circumstances.

Because of the interlocking of the parallel provisions of sex and race discrimination law, this ruling on interpretation is applicable to liability in sex discrimination cases.

The employer's defence against liability is 'to prove that he took such steps as were reasonably practicable to prevent the employee from doing that act, or from doing in the course of his employment acts of that description' (s 32(3)). Evidence of such 'steps' would be the adoption, implementation and monitoring of an equal opportunities policy. This should be communicated effectively throughout the workforce. Workforce rules prohibiting discriminatory treatment must be enforced.

Individual employees are also liable for unlawful discriminatory acts for which their employer is liable (s 32(2)). This is so, whether or not the employer has a defence (s 32(3)). In *Crofton* v *Yeboah* [2002] CA (a case involving a senior council employee who 'knowingly' aided unlawful discrimination), the Court of Appeal confirmed that employees can be personally liable for acts of unlawful discrimination against colleagues and can be so liable even where the employer itself is not found to have acted unlawfully.

5.4.9 **Enforcement**

A person alleging race discrimination in employment must, as a general rule, present their individual complaint to an employment tribunal within three months of the alleged incident(s) of discrimination. Complaints from members of the armed forces are subject to a six-month time limit to allow for a reference to internal procedures (Armed Forces Act 1996).

The tribunal may hear a complaint which is out of time 'if, in all the circumstances of the case, it considers that it is just and equitable to do so' (RRA 1976, s 68(6)). Factors that might be considered by a tribunal in exercising this discretion are the experience and knowledge of the applicant, the time when a succession of incidents 'crystallised' into a discriminatory complaint or whether an applicant has been given erroneous advice.

There are three principal aspects to enforcement: the questionnaire, discovery and the burden of proof.

For a person alleging discrimination, a **questionnaire** procedure is in force. This would help the person to decide whether to institute proceedings, and, if so, to formulate and present a case in the most effective way (s 65(1)). Essentially, there are two sets of issues:

- forms by which the complainant may question the respondent on his reasons for doing any relevant act, or on any matter which is or may be relevant;
- forms by which the respondent may reply to any questions.

The Race Relations (Questions and Replies) Order 1977 sets out the relevant questions. A respondent employer is asked if the treatment is accurately described or not; how, in the employer's view, it varied; whether or not the employer accepts that the treatment was unlawful discrimination; what were the reasons for the treatment; and 'how far considerations of colour, race, nationality (including citizenship) or ethnic or national origins' affected the employee's treatment. The employer is provided with an opportunity to respond. A completed questionnaire may be used in evidence before a tribunal.

A tribunal may order the completion of another questionnaire. An employer's failure to respond may not result in their being struck out. However, tribunals can and do draw adverse inferences from such behaviour.

A tribunal may also order **discovery** or inspection of documents. This can be as a result of the application of either the aggrieved employee or the employer or because the tribunal requires the information. The aim is to provide further information about the grounds of the case upon which the parties rely and any further relevant facts. If a tribunal is satisfied that sight of such documents is necessary for dealing fairly with the complaint, then the fact that they are confidential is irrelevant. An employer's failure to comply with a discovery order may result in the striking out of the application or of the respondent's notice of appearance.

The burden of proving discrimination on racial grounds (under s 1(1)(a)) rests on the applicant. It is for the applicant to establish the case on the balance of probabilities. This poses considerable difficulties for the complainant in respect of producing direct factual evidence. This clearly makes the questionnaire and the use of discovery important. As Lord Browne-Wilkinson has commented, 'those who discriminate on the grounds of race or gender do not in general advertise their prejudices: indeed, they may not even be aware of them' (*Zafar* v *Glasgow City Council* [1998] IRLR 36, HL).

In *King* v *Great Britain-China Centre* [1991] IRLR 513, CA guidance was formulated on this. It was acknowledged that it can be appropriate to draw inferences from the primary facts. These inferences can include any inferences that it is 'just and equitable' to draw (RRA, s 65(2)(b)) from an 'evasive or equivocal' reply to a questionnaire. So, at the end of the hearing, a tribunal has to determine its decision based on the primary facts and such inferences that it considers proper to draw from those facts. Issues of credibility and probability will also be considered.

From July 2003, amendments to the Race Relations Act deriving from the Race Directive 2000 enable a complainant to establish a prima facie case. The onus is then on the respondent employer to prove that it did not commit a discriminatory act.

The duties on public authorities in respect of employment, under the Race Relations (Amendment) Act 2000, are enforced in a different way. The *general* duty to promote race equality and eliminate unlawful racial discrimination is enforceable through judicial review in the High Court. The enforcement of the *specific* duties is with the CRE. It can use its powers to investigate and issue a compliance notice if it is satisfied that a person has failed (or is failing) to meet a specific duty. This is enforceable through the County Court or the Sheriff Court in Scotland. Where the public authority fails to obey the order of the court it will be in contempt of court.

5.4.10 Remedies

As under sex discrimination law, where an employment tribunal finds an individual applicant's complaint 'well founded' (RRA, s 56(1)), then, it must grant one or more of the following three available remedies:

- a **declaration**;
- an award of **compensation** payable by the employer to the complainant;
- a **recommendation**.

A **declaration** order states the rights of the applicant and the respondent in relation to the discrimination allegation (s 56(1)(a)).

An order can be made requiring **compensation**. The compensatory principle is that, as best that money can do it, the complainant must be put into the position they would have been but for the unlawful discrimination. Since 1993, there has been no limit on the amount of compensation that can be awarded. It is important to note that 'no award of damages shall be made if the respondent proves that the requirement or condition in question was not applied with the intention of treating the claimant unfavourably on racial grounds' (s 57(3)).

Compensation can include:

- *loss of earnings* to the date of the hearing (reduced by any pay actually earned);
- *loss of future earnings*: this may involve the financial consequences of being deprived of promotional opportunities. If the applicant has been dismissed, then some consideration of the likelihood of future employment will be made;
- *loss of the value of pension entitlements, and of other benefits*;

- *injury to feelings*: it is a matter for the tribunal to decide on the facts the degree to which feelings were hurt by the discrimination. In one recent race discrimination case (*Armitage and Others* v *Johnson* [1997] IRLR 162) certain principles were outlined: awards should be just to both parties – so they are compensatory to the complainant without being punishing to the respondent employer; they should not be too low and so reduce respect for anti-discrimination legislation; they should bear some broad general similarity with personal injury awards; the award must have some realistic relationship to purchasing power; such awards must have the respect of the general public;
- *aggravated damages*: these may be part of the compensation for injury to feelings. The employer's conduct may be sufficiently intentional as to aggravate hurt feelings. For example, in one case (*Qureshi* v *Victoria University of Manchester and Another*, 21.11.97, 01359/93), the sum of £8000 was awarded in aggravated damages. This was to take account, among other issues, of the employer's lack of interest or understanding of equal opportunities policies, an inadequate and hostile response to the raising of such issues and a brusque and critical attitude in dealings with the complainant.

A **recommendation** is that, within a specified period of time, the employer undertakes what the tribunal considers can be done to remove or lessen the harmful effect of the unlawful discrimination on the complainant (s 56(1)(c)). If an employer fails 'without reasonable justification' (s 56(4)) to comply with a recommendation, a tribunal may, 'if it thinks it just and equitable to do so', award (additional) compensation.

5.4.11 Employing workers from overseas

An ancilliary, but important related issue to race discrimination is the employment of overseas nationals in the United Kingdom. There are three broad sets of provisions in the law: for those who have free movement, for those subject to immigration control and need no work permit, and for those who do require a work permit. (This framework of law is complex and, therefore, to resolve any problems appropriate advice should be sought at the time from the Department for Education and Skills and the Home Office.)

Free movement

The right to free movement is conferred on nationals of the states of the European Economic Area (EEA) (i.e. European Union, Iceland, Liechstenstein and Norway). They have the right to accept offers of employment in the UK and to stay here for the purposes of seeking employment. They may be required to leave the UK (subject to appeal) if they have not found a job after six months, unless they are continuing to look for work and have genuine chances of being employed (*R* v *Immigration Appeal Tribunal ex parte Antonissen* [1991] ECR 1–745). This framework is supplemented by a European Union Directive (68/360) which gives the right to come to the UK on the production of a valid identity card or passport issued by another EEA state. With appropriate confirmation of employment they can acquire a residence permit. EEA migrant workers may be denied access to 'employment in the public service'.

A 'worker', in this context, is a person who for a given period does work for and under the direction of another in return for remuneration. Such work should be, according to rulings in various cases, 'effective and genuine' and not on such a small scale as to be 'purely marginal and ancilliary'. The term 'worker' is construed widely and can cover part-timers, temporary and casual staff, trainees, job seekers and those between jobs.

Furthermore, free movement is available to citizens of independent Commonwealth countries who have the 'right of abode' in the UK. They are 'free to live in and to come and go into and from the United Kingdom without let or hindrance' (Immigration Act 1971, s 1(1)). They are also free to take any employment they choose. British citizenship, and hence the right of abode, may be acquired by birth or adoption, descent, registration or naturalisation. British nationals without the right of abode will need a work permit.

Immigration control

There are certain categories of foreign nationals who are subject to immigration control but need **no work permit** to be able to work legally in the UK. Among this group are working holiday-makers, au pairs, exchange students, postgraduate doctors and dentists, seasonal farmworkers, asylum seekers and posted workers.

Work permits for other foreign nationals may be **full**. These are issued to named individuals for specific posts with particular employers for a period of up to four years (with possible extension allowed). The posts must require a recognised degree-level or equivalent professional qualification, senior executive or administrative skills, or must be for highly qualified technicians with specialised or rare skills. Full work permits are not, therefore, issued for jobs at manual, craft, clerical, secretarial or similar levels or for resident domestic work (childminders or housekeepers). Foreign nationals with full work permits are expected to be on equivalent pay and conditions to British employees, and to have an adequate command of English and normally at least two years of relevant experience at the level of the post. The application for the work permit must be made by the employer. **Other permits** for foreign nationals can be granted for up to 12 months for work experience or for up to three years for approved training. Specialist work permits may also be issued to top-class entertainers and sportspeople from abroad. Overall, the Home Office reported that 100 000 work permits were issued in 2000.

It is **a criminal offence** for an employer to employ workers who live in the United Kingdom illegally and they may be fined up to £5000 for breaches (Asylum and Immigration Act 1996, s 8). This provision came into force on 27 January 1997 and covers employees who start work on or after that date. There are no accurate figures on the extent of illegal working. However, the Home Office calculated that in 1996 (the final year before the new legislation was implemented) there were some 10 000 illegal workers in the country.

There is **a defence for an employer** under statute. The employer must see and retain a copy of an orginal specified document. This includes the following: a document issued by a previous employer, the Inland Revenue, the Benefits Agency, the Contributions Agency or the Employment Service (or their Northern Ireland equivalents) containing the National Insurance number of the person named in it; a passport describing the holder as a British citizen or as having the right of abode in, or entitlement to readmission to, the United Kingdom; a certification of registration or naturalisation as a British citizen; a birth certificate issued in the UK or the Republic of Ireland; a work permit or other approval to take employment issued by the DfES or, in Northern Ireland, the Training and Employment Agency.

Concern has been expressed by employers and trade unions about one possible consequence of this criminal liability: damage to race relations. However, careful inquiries by employers at the point of recruitment will become more essential because of the twin liabilities: criminal action for employing illegal workers; civil liability for race discrimination.

5.5 Employment policies and practices

The broad issues relating to equal opportunities policies were discussed in the introductory section of Part Two. Here we will look at what employers might do in practical terms. Some of the material outlined below is drawn from the CRE *Code of Practice* (1983) and from the *Code of Practice* (2002).

The two mechanisms that regulate employment (i.e. the contract of employment and collective agreements) are governed by the Race Relations Act 1976. It is unlawful for an employer to discriminate against an employee 'in the terms of employment which he affords him' (RRA 1976, s 4(2)(a)). So, any terms of a contract of employment which are discriminatory can be the subject of complaint. By extension, the provisions of a collective agreement which become terms of a contract of employment could also be unlawfully discriminatory.

5.5.1 Human resource strategy

Although this section considers a range of specific employment policies, it is important to remember that an employer may well consider a more strategic perspective to tackling discrimination and promoting equal opportunities. Such an approach, inevitably, requires an assessment of organisational culture, an audit of institutional patterns of discrimination and consideration of the contibution that might be made by 'managing diversity' (see Introduction to Part Two).

A more strategic approach is particularly important for public authorities given the new duties under the Race Relations (Amendment) Act 2000. Nevertheless, it should be attractive to private-sector employers. For example, in a survey of 140 leading private and public-sector organisations (including Barclays, BT, Cadbury Schweppes, the Cabinet Office, the Inland Revenue and Procter & Gamble) 71 per cent of the private-sector organisations saw a direct link between good diversity policies and improved business performance. The comparable figure for the public sector was 87 per cent. The business benefits included: better recruitment, increased retention, improved understanding of markets and communities, an enhanced repution and cost savings (Schneider-Ross, 2002).

However, despite these benefits, other evidence shows that a strategic focus is still missing in many employing organisations. The Industrial Society (now the Work Foundation) reported that only 45 per cent of organisations had a strategy in place for achieving diversity in the workplace. Yet, two-thirds saw diversity as a current high priority; and three-quarters expected the issue to become even more important over the next couple of years (Industrial Society, 2001).

Following the full implementation of the Race Relations (Amendment) Act 2000, it is expected that clearer strategic approaches will be evident in the public sector. The Act requires public authorities to publish a 'race equality scheme' (RES) covering policy, service delivery and employment practices. 'An RES is effectively a strategy and a timetabled and realistic action plan. It should summarise a public authority's approach to race equality and its corporate aims. It should say how the authority plans to carry out each part of the specific duty – in other words, its arrangements for:

- Assessing, consulting on and monitoring its functions and policies for any adverse impact on promoting race equality;
- Publishing the results;
- Making sure the public have access to its services; and
- Training staff.' (Home Office guidance).

Strongly associated with this required action is the duty on public authorities to monitor by reference to racial groups the following (RR(A)A 2000, s 5(2)): the numbers of staff in post; applicants for employment, training and promotion from each such group. For those public organisations with 150 or more full-time staff, there is a duty to monitor the number of staff who: receive training; benefit or suffer detriment as a rsult of its performance assessment procedures; are involved in grievance procedures; cease employment. The monitoring results are to be published annually.

5.5.2 Recruitment and selection

There are several aspects to recruitment and selection to be considered. The first is the nature of an employer's **overall recruitment policy**. Several questions need to be answered:

- Has there been *monitoring* of the existing workforce profile to identify whether or not there is evidence of vertical or horizontal segregation of staff on racial grounds?
- What forms of *positive action* can be undertaken to encourage applicants from different ethnic groups? This can include the use of *targets*.
- Is it appropriate to use *genuine occupational qualification* provisions?

Targets are one the most controversial issues in respect of recruitment strategy. Unlike quotas, which would be evidence of positive discrimination, targets are permissible under discrimination law. The government has set diversity targets for several public-sector organisations. For example, in 1999, the Home Office published targets for recruitment, retention and progression of ethnic minority employees in the police service, the fire service, the probation service and the prison service. The rationale for these targets included the need to reflect the local circumstances of the service concerned. It was expected that targets were part of a ten-year programme to achieve changes which needed to be periodically reviewed (Home Office, 1999).

Secondly, there is the question of **advertising**. 'Employers should not confine advertisements unjustifiably to those areas or publications which would exclude or disproportionately reduce the numbers of applicants of a particular racial group' (Code, para 1.6a). Likewise, 'in order to avoid indirect discrimination it is recommended that employers should not confine recruitment unjustifiably to those agencies, job centres, careers offices and schools which because of their particular source of applicants, provide only or mainly applicants of a particular racial group' (para 1.9). In this context 'word of mouth' recruitment might reinforce an existing ethnic profile of the workforce. So, wider advertising is recommended.

Thirdly, **selection criteria and tests** need to be examined to ensure they are related to job requirements and not unlawfully discriminatory. Criteria like English language qualifications and proficiency should be justified; recognition of equivalent overseas qualifications should be accepted after appropriate investigation. On selection tests, the Code states that those 'which contain irrelevant questions or exercises on matters which may be unfamiliar to racial minority applicants should not be used (for example, general knowledge questions on matters more likely to be familiar to indigenous applicants)'. Furthermore, 'they should be checked to ensure that they are related to the job's requirements' (para 1.13).

Fourthly, as far as **the selection process** is concerned,

staff responsible for short-listing, interviewing and selecting candidates should be:
- clearly informed of selection criteria and of the need for their consistent application;
- given guidance or training on the effects which generalised assumptions and prejudices about race can have on selection decisions;
- made aware of the possible misunderstandings that can occur in interviews between persons of different cultural backgrounds (para 1.14).

Part of the early sifting of applicants concerns whether or not a person is permitted to work in the United Kingdom. To avoid allegations of discrimination on racial grounds it is recommended by both the Home Office and the CRE that such investigations of eligibility to work are consistent across all applicants and not used just with those whose names sound foreign.

Two interpersonal factors that can enter the selection process, particularly at the interview stage, are body language and cross-cultural communication. Clearly, there can be difficulties in both verbal and non-verbal communication between people of different ethnic origin. First, an applicant might have limited proficiency in the English language and may not fully understand subtleties of expression, technical language, jargon and idioms. Secondly, 'ethnocentrism' on the part of the interviewer can involve the interpretation of another person's behaviour/communication in terms of his/her own cultural framework. Frequently, this is done unconsciously. Thirdly, an applicant may have pronounciation difficulties.

As far as body language is concerned, this is an important form of non-verbal communication and its meaning can differ between cultures. One complicating factor can be that all people from a particular ethnic group may not identify with particular body language. They may have internalised that of the host society. One example is the use of eyes. Whereas in Britain to look a person in the eyes is to show respect and integrity, in African-Caribbean culture it is likely to indicate insolence. Among south Asian cultures, looking away from authority (e.g. a manager) rather than directly at it tends to show deference and respect.

5.5.3 **Pay and benefits**

It would be discriminatory to pay members of a particular racial group lower rates of pay than another racial group for the same job. This could constitute direct discrimination. It is also possible that access to earnings opportunities and benefits that were dependent on a particular condition or requirement could be indirectly discriminatory. Such conditions might include a specific educational qualification, length of service, etc.

5.5.4 **Working time**

Two specific aspects of working time that relate to different ethnic groups are the question of special leave for religious observance; and extended leave arrangements to visit families abroad. As far as the first is concerned, it is important to remember that discrimination on grounds of religion is not expressly covered by the Race Relations Act. However, it can be a factor in specific claims if a specific group of people can be defined as a 'racial group'. For example, in one case, a refusal to allow a Muslim employee to attend mosque on Friday afternoons was ruled as indirect discrimination which the employer could not justify (*Yassin* v *Northwest Homecare Ltd* [1994] *Equal Opportunities Review Case Digest 19*). The CRE Code recommends that 'employers should consider whether it is reasonably practicable to vary or adapt [work] requirements to enable such needs to be met' (para 1.24). In another case, restrictions on the taking of leave during May and June were ruled by the tribunal as indirectly discriminatory against Muslims who wished to take time off for the religious festival of Eid (at the end of Ramadan) (*JH Walker Ltd* v *Hussein* [1996] IRLR 11).

In the second set of cases, the code says that 'many employers have policies which allow annual leave entitlements to be accumulated, or extra unpaid leave to be taken to meet these circumstances. Employers should take care to apply such policies consistently and without unlawful discrimination' (para 1.21).

The Employment Directive 2000 covers discrimination on the groups of religion or belief (*see also* p 207). It will affect the question of leave. The government indicated, in a consultation document, that:

> the legislation will not require employers automatically to grant all requests for leave for religious observance. But they must avoid both direct discrimination (for example, by refusing individual requests for leave simply because of the employee's religion or belief) and indirect discrimination – i.e. applying rules on leave which particularly disadvantage some groups in comparison with others and which cannot be objectively justified (para 13.8, DTI 2001, *Towards Equality and Diversity*).

5.5.5 **Training and development, promotion and transfers**

To avoid indirect discrimination, the Code makes the following recommendations:

■ Staff responsible for selecting employees for transfer to other jobs should be instructed to apply selection criteria without lawful discrimination.

■ Industry or company agreements and arrangements of custom and practice on job transfers should be examined and amended if they are found to contain requirements or conditions which appear to be indirectly discriminatory.

- Staff responsible for selecting employees for training, whether induction, promotion or skill training should be instructed not to discriminate on racial grounds.

- Selection criteria for training opportunities should be examined to ensure that they are not indirectly discriminatory (para 1.16).

In addition, the Code recommends other training measures in the context of improving workplace communication and encouraging people to compete for promotional opportunities (paras 1.26–1.27). Such measures should include training:

- in English language and in communication skills;

- for managers and supervisors in the background and culture of racial minority groups.

Supplementing this is an emerging interest by some employers in mentoring as a means of supporting certain employees in their career development. Initiatives have arisen in the context of evidence which reveals differential experience of ethnic groups in the labour market, those with qualifications at A level and above finding greater difficulty in access to employment and to promotion. Mentoring schemes can support undergraduates during studies and entry to work. In-company schemes can assist the development of graduate trainees and other staff to work towards promotion within the organisation.

5.5.6 Dress codes

There can be two related aspects to these in respect of racial discrimination: cultural practices and religious observance. Some workplace rules on dress and appearance might be indirectly discriminatory and therefore must be justified. The issues for employers, based on the facts of each individual case, are as follows (using the structure set out earlier in the section on indirect discrimination):

- Is the complainant a member of a protected 'racial group' (RRA, s 3)? Such examples would be Jews and Sikhs.

- Has a condition or requirement been imposed? Evidence of such an absolute bar would be, for example, if disciplinary action would be instituted for non-compliance.

- Can the employee comply in practice? So, for example, in the *Mandla* case the complainant could not comply with the 'no-turban' rule because he was required under his religion to wear such head-dress.

- Is the proportion of the complainant's racial group which can comply with the condition or requirement considerably smaller than the proportion of people **not** of that group who can comply?

- Has the complainant suffered some detriment because of non-compliance? This would normally be refusal of employment or disciplinary action (including possible dismissal) for breaking the rules.

Consideration then turns to 'justification'. Here a balance is considered between, on the one hand, the 'discriminatory effect' of the condition or requirement and, on the other hand, the 'reasonable needs' of the employer and whether or not the employer could achieve operational objectives by some other way. Issues that have been put forward as justifications include: hygiene, health and safety (in cases involving Sikhs wearing hard-hats), corporate image (involving Muslim women and their requirement to wear trousers). (Under the Employment Act 1989, s 11, Sikhs are exempt from any statutory requirement to wear safety helmets on construction sites.)

The Employment Directive 2000 (to be implemented by December 2003) covers discrimination on the groups of religion or belief. It will affect the question of dress. The government has indicated, in a consultation document, that 'the directive does not require employers to put specific arrangements in place on any of these fronts'. (These also included matters of diet and religious observance.) 'However', it added, 'employers will need to avoid having rules which discriminate directly or indirectly against staff on the ground of religion or belief.' It is proposed to provide detailed guidance (para 13.9, DTI 2001, *Towards Equality and Diversity*).

5.5.7 Dismissal

Dismissal can arise in several circumstances. First, dismissal of an employee can be unlawful discrimination (Race Relations Act 1976, s 4(2)(c)) and may result (irrespective of the length of service, hours worked or age of the individual) in an allegation of unfair dismissal to an employment tribunal. Secondly, it may be that an employer does not renew a fixed-term contract and the employee believes that this is on racial grounds (*see* the legal framework above and the section in Chapter 2 on fixed-term contracts). Thirdly, an employee may resign as a result of the discriminatory treatment by an employer (particularly if this involves victimisation or harassment). This repudiatory breach of the contract of employment could be the basis of a constructive dismissal claim (*see also* Chapter 7). Finally, the dismissal of the perpetrator of discrimination (another employee, a supervisor or a manager) could be evidence that the employer was taking 'such steps as were reasonably practicable' to prevent discrimination (RRA 1976, s 32(3)). Clearly, in any of these cases before an employment tribunal, the appropriate tests of fairness will be considered unless it is established that the reason for the dismissal is an 'automatically unfair' reason (*see* Chapter 9).

Case study 5.1

The company

A restaurant chain specialises in themed restaurants with a so-called 'traditional English ambience'. It has 12 restaurants (mostly in the south and south-west of England). It generally caters for parties which pre-book for celebrations and workplace functions.

The workforce

Nationally, it employs about 50 permanent staff and a large number of temporary workers (provided by employment agencies). The permanent staff include managerial and administrative staff, head waiters and chefs. The bulk of the staff who wait on tables and those working in the kitchen are agency workers. All staff are white.

On one occasion, a young black woman was taken on as a serving wench. The agencies are given clear specifications on the types of staff required. Two of the cleaners (provided by a contract cleaning firm) are Asian.

The issues

Rosemary Smythe had been employed full-time as assistant manager at the Bath restaurant for under one month. It was her first job after having qualified in hotel and catering management. She was sacked for refusing to obey an instruction from the company's general manager at head office. The circumstances leading up to her dismissal were as follows.

A customer, a tutor from a local higher education college, asked to book a private party for 100 people. She mentioned that some party members preferred vegetarian meals. (These could be provided as part of the menu.) In the course of casual conversation she said that a number of the students were from overseas and she was hoping to give them an example of typical English hospitality.

Rosemary asked the manager of the restaurant, who was in the back office, about the feasibility of such a booking. She was told to refuse this private party and say that the restaurant could only accommodate 50 and could not undertake special dietary requirements. On being told this, the customer said she could restrict the group by using a 'first come first served' basis. Rosemary explained the situation to the manager. He said that they had had a group from this college before and didn't want them back. He added, 'You know what the restaurant's policy is about blacks, don't you?' She said, 'No'. 'Well just go and say that we can't accommodate them', the manager replied.

Rosemary was uncomfortable about the situation. Nevertheless, she explained to the customer about the difficulty of accommodating such a large group on that night. The tutor proposed an alternative evening. Again, Rosemary spoke to the manager and began a (sometimes heated) discussion with him about the company policy. The manager said that 'there were too many coloured people in the restaurant the night before and it is not to happen again. It ruins the theme.' Some of this argument was overheard by the customer. In particular, she heard Rosemary say 'So am I supposed to tell this customer that only white people can use this restaurant?', and the reply was 'Yes'. Although the customer did not hear it, Rosemary refused and, shortly after the overheated altercation, the manager himself came out of the office and told the customer he was refusing the booking. He denied that the company was racist and said that the customer had misunderstood what was being said. He added that they had had many mixed-race groups of customers in the past.

After the customer had left, rather disgruntled, the manager told Rosemary that he would not have her flouting company policy. He said that she had only been there a few weeks and if she didn't like it she could leave.

Later that afternoon, Rosemary was looking through the recent diary of bookings. One had scribbled next to it 'do not re-book'. In pencil was added 'Asians'. She challenged the manager about this. He repeated that 'there were too many coloured people in the restaurant the night before and it is not to happen again'. He said that 'do not re-book' may be used by the company because insufficient numbers of the expected customers in a party turn up, because there has been 'trouble', or because too many under-age people were trying to enter the party. However, Rosemary noticed that on several occasions when insufficient people turned up 'DNR' was not put against their booking. Where it was used, it tended to be in relation to parties containing a number of black and Asian people.

Rosemary told the manager that this policy put her in a difficult position. The manager said, 'Well, you know what to do. I'll tell head office that you're not suited to working here.' He told her not to return to work the following day. She didn't and instead went to the Citizens Advice Bureau, asking about the possibility of claiming unfair dismissal.

1 Would Rosemary have a case before an employment tribunal? What are the reasons for your answer?
2 Do you think that there is any action that the Commission for Racial Equality might take against the company? If so, what?

Feedback on this exercise is provided in the Appendix to this book.

Further reading

Commission for Racial Equality (1983) *Code of Practice for the Elimination of Racial Discrimination and the Promotion of Equality of Opportunity in Employment.* London: CRE.
Commission for Racial Equality (2002) *Code of Practice.* London: CRE

References

Advisory Conciliation and Arbitration Service (various years) *Annual Report.* London: ACAS.
Audit Commission (2000) *Another Country – implementing dispersal under the Immigration and Asylum Act 1999.* London: Audit Commission.
Boonstras, J. *et al.* (eds) (1993) *Antisemitism: a History Portrayed.* Amsterdam: Anne Frank Foundation.
Bourn, C. and Whitmore, J. (1993) *Race and Sex Discrimination*, 2nd edn. London: Sweet & Maxwell.
Commission for Racial Equality (1998) *Reform of the Race Relations Act 1976.* London: CRE.
Daniel, W.W. (1968) *Racial Discrimination in England.* Harmondsworth: Penguin Books.
Department of Trade and Industry (2001) *Towards Equality and Diversity: implementing the Employment and Race Directives (a consultation document).* London: DTI.
European Parliament (1991) *Report of Committee of Inquiry into Racism and Xenophobia.* Brussels: European Parliament.
Forbes, I. and Mead, G. (1992) *Measure for Measure: a Comparative Analysis of Measures to Combat Racial Discrimination in the Member Countries of the European Community*, Research Series No. 1. London: Department of Employment.
Glover, S. *et al.* (2001) *Migration: an economic and social analysis.* London: The Home Office.
Hiro, D. (1973) *Black British, White British.* Harmondsworth: Penguin Books.
The Home Office (1999) *Race Equality, the Home Secretary's Employment Targets.* London: The Home Office.
The Industrial Society (now the Work Foundation) (2001) *Managing best practice: valuing diversity.* London: The Work Foundation.
Jones, T. (1996) *Britain's Ethnic Minorities.* London: Policy Studies Institute.
Justice (1996) *The Union Divided: Race Discrimination and Third Country Nationals in the European Union.* London: Justice.
Macpherson, Sir William (1999) 'The Stephen Lawrence Inquiry Report', Cm. 4262–1. London: Stationery Office.
Mason, D. (1995) *Race and Ethnicity in Modern Britain.* Oxford: Oxford University Press.
Newnham, A. (1986) *Employment, Unemployment and Black People.* London: Runnymede Research Report.
Schneider-Ross (2002) *The Business of Diversity. How organisations in the public and private sectors are integrating equality and diversity to enhance business performance.* London: Schneider-Ross.
Smith, D. (1985) *Unemployment and Racial Minorities.* London: Policy Studies Institute.

CHAPTER 6

Disability discrimination in the workplace

This chapter considers the social and economic background to disability discrimination and explores the nature of such discrimination in employment. It outlines the essential legal framework and considers the policies and practices that should be adopted by employers. Having read it you should understand:

- The nature of disability discrimination.
- The social and employment contexts in which it arises.
- The key concepts of discrimination law: the coverage of the legislation, the meaning of disability, the meaning of discrimination, the duty to make reasonable adjustments, liability, enforcement procedures and the remedies available.
- The steps that you could take to advise on the development of an equal opportunities policy for your organisation.

This area of discriminatory practice should be considered in conjunction with sex discrimination (Chapter 4) and race discrimination (Chapter 5).

6.1 Structure of the chapter

This chapter comprises the following sections:

- *Introduction.*
- *The context*: Defining disability, the social context, incidence, labour-market context, technological developments, political and legal developments and social welfare support.
- *The legal framework*: The coverage of the legislation, the meaning of disability, the meaning of discrimination, the duty to make reasonable adjustments, liability, the burden of proof, enforcement procedures, remedies and the role of the Disability Rights Commission.

■ *Employment policies and practices*: The approach to managing disability discrimination, the Act's effect on contracts and agreements and the *Code of Practice* (1996).

6.2   Introduction

The enactment of the Disability Discrimination Act 1995 was the latest legislative attempt to provide a framework of civil rights for a substantial group of people who had experienced discriminatory treatment within employment and in society at large. The employment provisions were implemented in December 1996. Those relating to access to goods, services and facilities were implemented in October 1999. The legislation replaced the previous Disabled Persons (Employment) Acts 1944 and 1958. It abolishes the previous quota scheme and provides, for the first time, a framework of rights which can be enforced at an employment tribunal.

6.3   The context

In this section we will consider several issues:

■ what the term 'disability' means;

■ the social context of disability (in terms of both attitudes and social infrastructure);

■ the incidence of disability;

■ data on the experience of disabled people in the labour market and in employment;

■ the nature of technological changes which provide assistance for disabled persons;

■ the political and legal context in which the Disability Discrimination Act 1995 (DDA) was enacted;

■ the degree of social welfare support.

6.3.1   Defining disability

There are two distinct approaches to defining disability: the 'medical model' and the 'social model'. The traditional definition (the 'medical model') is that used by the World Health Organisation (Wood, 1991). This categorised the following:

■ Impairment: any loss or abnormality of psychological, physiological or anatomical structure or function.

■ Disability: any restriction or lack of ability (resulting from an impairment) to perform an activity in the manner or within the range considered normal for a human being.

■ Handicap: a disadvantage for a given individual, resulting from an impairment or a disability, that limits or prevents the fulfilment of a role (depending on age, sex and social and cultural factors) for that individual.

This 'medical model' concentrates on dysfunction and on how to make the person well or on the aids necessary for the person to function 'normally'. So, the amputee is fitted with an artificial limb. The implication is that people with functional limitations need to adapt to fit into society.

The 'social model' sees disability as 'resting in society rather than in any factor inherent in disabled people' (Massie, 1994). This is not to deny the medical aspects of disability, which may be considerable. It acknowledges that the impact of disability frequently depends on the 'context in which someone lives' (Massie, 1994). Against this background, Disabled People's International has adopted the following definitions:

■ Impairment: the functional limitation within the individual caused by physical, mental or sensory impairment.

■ Disability: the loss or limitation of opportunities to take part in the normal life of the community on an equal level with others due to physical or social barriers.

This social model allows people to have an impairment without having a disability. It is social factors that translate the impairment into a disability. So, if the physical and attitudinal barriers that exist within society are reduced, then, so is the disability. Individuals will still have the physical or mental impairment and the consequent pain and emotions but their ability to participate in society will be enhanced. The importance of the second model is that it focuses attention on the individual's interface with the environment and not on the individual's impairment. Thus, people are seen as individuals – and not as 'the disabled' – with effort being put into addressing any social and physical barriers that exist. It helps move away from the notion that 'disability' equates with 'inability'.

The most common problems affecting people with a disability (Twomey, 2001) were:

■ Musculo-skeletal (relating to arms, legs, neck, back, hands and feet) – affecting 36 per cent.

■ Chest or breathing problems – 13 per cent.

■ Heart, blood pressure and circulatory conditions – 11 per cent.

■ Mental illness – 8 per cent.

6.3.2 The social context

The social context of disabled people has two relevant dimensions which affect their day-to-day living and employment opportunities: prevailing *attitudes* within society, and the character of *social infrastructure*. We will look at each of these in turn.

In terms of *attitudes*, disabled people are frequently subject to stereotyping and preconceptions about the nature of their disability. First of all, there is the ever-present tendency to regard 'the disabled' as an undifferentiated group. In reality, the spectrum of impairment is extremely wide. Consequently, the impact of an impairment on a person's ability to carry out day-to-day activities, to live independently, to travel and so on varies very significantly from person to person. This may seem an obvious statement but it is surprising how it is still forgotten in the whole range of social activities and in the employment arena.

Secondly, disabled people can be treated with suspicion, apprehension, ridicule and pity. Thirdly, social attitudes frequently fail to consider the situation of a disabled person from that person's perspective. For example, expressions are used such as 'confined to a wheelchair' when, in fact, the wheelchair may liberate the user by providing mobility. Someone might be described as suffering from a particular condition when that person does not regard the condition as a disability but a normal part of their life. There can be a failure to allow the disabled person to take the initiative in deciding the adjustments and assistance that they want or do not want. One survey found that employers tended to hold inaccurate or exaggerated beliefs about the restrictions that impairments place on employment (Honey *et al.*, 1993). Many of the prevailing social attitudes reflect the traditional medical model of disability where the focus is on the individual's condition and care and welfare.

A final comment on attitudes (evident in all areas of discrimination) is the pernicious and deterrent effect that stereotyping, prejudice and insulting behaviour has on the self-esteem of disabled people. This creates a further psychological obstacle that needs to be overcome in order that they may become active participants in society and employment. This has been described as the 'discouraged worker' syndrome – whereby people withdraw from the labour market after repeated rejection and lack of opportunities. They tend to devalue their own potential.

In respect of *social infrastructure*, people with impairments face difficulties associated with public transport and building design. These, inevitably, can cause access problems in relation to training, employment, the purchase of goods and services, entertainment. Access problems in one area can exacerbate access in others. For example, difficulties in acquiring education and training, which may be caused in part by transport problems, can obstruct entry into the labour market and employment. The ability to lead a constructive and rewarding life is inhibited.

Attitudes and social infrastructure issues are linked in providing five obstacles to the entry of disabled people into employment. Weiss (1974: 457) identified five:

1 physical and vocational problems during rehabilitation and training;
2 barriers created by architectural design and transport systems;
3 resistance by employers to hiring disabled persons;
4 self-doubt as a result of previous prejudice;
5 overcoming ill-focused and often unnecessary medical tests.

6.3.3 Disability and the labour market

In the Labour Force Survey (Summer 2000), it is calculated that some 6.8 million people of working age (i.e. between 16 years and 59 years for women and between

16 years and 64 years for men) are classified as disabled in the UK, 3.6 million of whom are men and 3.2 million are women. In aggregate, 19 per cent of the working age population has a current long-term disability, using the broad definition of the Disability Discrimination Act 1995 (Twomey, 2001).

Various other findings were reported:

- *Age relationship*: The incidence of long-term disability or health problems is age related. For example, 10 per cent of those between 16 and 19 years have a disability; and 21 per cent of those between 45 and 49 years do.

- *Economic activity*: This is the proportion of people in work or actively looking for work. Among disabled people this is 52 per cent in contrast to 86 per cent for non-disabled people. The highest economic activity rate for disabled people is 71 per cent for men between 25 and 34 years (contrasting with 97 per cent for non-disabled men). One-third of economically inactive disabled people say that they would like to work.

- *Employment rate*: 3.2 million disabled people were in employment – an employment rate of 47 per cent.

- *Unemployment*: The unemployment rate for disabled people is twice that for non-disabled people – 10 per cent as against 5 per cent. This disparity increases with age. Unemployment rates also vary according to a person's type of disability. The highest unemployment rates were 31 per cent for people with learning difficulties and 23 per cent for those with some kind of mental illness. The lowest was for those with heart, blood pressure and circulation problems – at 5 per cent.

- *Employment status*: Disabled people are slightly more likely to be employed part-time than non-disabled people (i.e. 29 per cent of the disabled working population, in contrast to 23 per cent of the non-disabled working population).

- *Lower socio-economic groups*: 45 per cent of employed disabled people people are in the three lower occupational groups – skilled manual, partly skilled and unskilled. This compared with 39 per cent of people without a disability.

The experience of disabled people in the labour market and in employment is reflected in the preceding statistics. More detailed surveys have elaborated upon this experience. Scope (formerly the Spastics Society) carried out two studies (one in 1986 and one in 1989/90, when unemployment had fallen). These both entailed submitting two almost identical applications for secretarial vacancies – one from a disabled person and another from an able-bodied person. In 1986, the able-bodied person was 1.6 times more likely to receive a positive response than the disabled applicant (1.5 times in 1989/90) (Graham *et al.*, 1990). A variety of reasons for rejecting the disabled applicant were given in the rejection letters. In some cases there was evidence of personal discrimination as the applicant was informed that the job was too demanding and, therefore, unsuitable for a disabled person. Other employers used the physical barrier of stairs as the basis of their refusal to offer an interview, despite knowing only the general nature of the applicant's impairment.

6.3.4 The employment context

The employment context of disability discrimination can be considered by outlining the results of three investigations which cover a three-year period: a 1993 survey by the Institute of Manpower Studies of employers' attitudes towards the employment of people with disability, a 1995 Kingston University Business School survey which coincided with the enactment of the Disability Discrimination Act (Pidduck, 1995) and a 1997 survey by Equal Opportunities Review of the steps being taken to ensure compliance. These data are supplemented by some more recent findings (CIPD, 2001).

Institute of Manpower Studies Survey 1993

This surveyed employers' attitudes towards the employment of people with disabilities (Honey *et al.*, 1993). The random sample comprised 1116 employers and included a sub-sample of 199 'good practice' employers. Among the key findings were the following.

Policy

■ 54 per cent of employers had no policy concerning the employment of disabled people; only 26 per cent had a written policy and these tended to be large employers with wider anti-discrimination policies.

Recruitment

■ One-fifth of all employers (mainly larger ones) actively sought to recruit people with disabilities.

■ Just over half of employers (57 per cent) knowingly employed someone with a disability.

■ Most (79 per cent) who did not employ disabled people said that this was because nobody had applied or was known to have applied.

Experience of employing disabled people

■ A quarter of those who employed somebody with a disability had actually experienced problems. These were reported as:

	%
Job/low productivity	24
Attitude to work/temperament	16
Mobility	14
Access to facilities	12
Manual labour	11
Safety	10
Absence/timekeeping	10

■ Only 29 per cent of employers saw some benefit in employing people with disabilities.

Accommodating disabled people

■ Half the organisations that employed people with disabilities had taken some action to accommodate them. Of these 61 per cent provided special equipment, 49 per cent modified premises, 23 per cent reorganised work, 23 per cent raised staff awareness and 14 per cent provided special training.

■ Less than 2 per cent of the survey respondents had considered and rejected making accommodations. Their reasons were cost, practicality and unwillingness.

■ 43 per cent of those surveyed thought there would be extra costs in employing disabled persons, and 24 per cent that there would not be. The larger employers were more likely to anticipate that there would be additional costs.

■ Employers were reluctant to attach maximum or average price tags to accommodating someone with a disability. The circumstances and what was reasonable were often mentioned, as was the fact that other employees and customers could benefit from expenditure.

Advice

■ Only 31 per cent of employers had sought external help and advice, with the most likely being large companies and those with a policy.

Overall, the larger employers were more likely to employ people with disabilities, to have a written policy, to have realistic perceptions of the costs and problems involved, to use the disability 'two ticks' symbol, to seek to recruit and accommodate disabled persons and to look for external help and advice. Employers who adopted one of these initiatives were more likely to have adopted others. On the whole, smaller organisations did not appear to have taken on board the legal, moral and good practice reasons for employing people with disabilities.

Those employers who did not employ anyone with a disability were more likely to perceive physical and safety problems and to anticipate costly accommodations. They tended to hold stereotyped and exaggerated views of 'wheelchairbound' applicants bringing a range of difficulties relating to the type or level of work, and to safety and to the premises.

The Kingston Business School Survey 1995

This smaller survey was of 57 large organisations, predominantly in the service sector (about two-thirds private and the remainder public sector) in London and the south-east of England (Pidduck, 1995). It coincided with the Disability Discrimination Act receiving the Royal Assent. The questionnaire was completed primarily by human resource practitioners. The key findings were as follows:

Policy

■ Just over a quarter of employers were 'good practice' employers (i.e. members of the Employers' Forum on disability or users of the Employment Service 'two ticks' symbol).

■ Two-thirds of organisations had written policies relating to people with disabilities. In the overwhelming majority of cases, these were part of general anti-discrimination policies. But few organisations had a well-developed and clearly defined policy towards people with disabilities.

Advice and information

■ Knowledge of the DDA was greatest amongst the larger, 'good practice' and public-sector employers. The main sources of information were the Employers' Forum on Disability and the Department of Employment. Other employers obtained their information from a much wider range of sources (including the national and professional press, employment law publishers, the Institute of Personnel and Development).

Accommodating disabled people

■ Four-fifths of employers employed someone with a disability – although the precise numbers in organisations were unavailable (often as a result of defective records).

■ Respondents were asked what initiatives they had taken or were proposing:

– developing a specific disability policy: 71 per cent of good practice employers had done this or had it under consideration (as against 54 per cent of other employers);

– reviewing adjustments (i.e. special equipment, modifying premises, reorganising work, etc.): around 80 per cent of good practice companies had done this or had it under consideration (in contrast to 60 per cent of other companies).

The low levels of response in respect of certain training and recruitment are attributable, in part, to the outsourcing of these functions.

■ Initiatives to review adjustments were often prompted by the needs of a particular employee and therefore were reactive rather than the consequence of a strategic or long-term policy decision.

■ The range of initiatives encompassed close liaison with disability groups, counselling for those who become disabled, awareness training for staff, minicom recruitment lines and the ring-fencing of jobs for disabled recruits.

■ The main impetus for initiatives had come from general policy reviews which were part of wider equal opportunities policies. In some cases, the consideration of disability issues within an organisation might include customers, clients and students.

From her survey, Pidduck (1995) suggests that employers' perceptions and their associated behaviours can be categorised into one of five groups. First, there are those who are ignorant of employment legislation or who deliberately disregard it. Secondly, there are those who adopt an approach of minimal compliance. They will treat disability discrimination in the same way as sex and race discrimination. They generally have sufficient knowledge of the law to avoid being seen to be directly discriminating but they have little understanding of the nature of indirect discrimination. Thirdly, there are those whose position is one of neutral reactivity. This group has the potential to comply, with not just the letter but also the spirit of the law. However, they need direction and encouragement. It is contended that the incidence of these three categories is generally found among small to medium-sized employers. Given the statutory exemption of small organisations (DDA 1995, s 7), the legal incentive to achieve good practice is not available. Such organisations are reported to employ some ten million working people.

The fourth group of employers is a group of medium to large organisations (in both public and private ownership). Some of these may be defined as 'good practice' employers. They have started to review their policies and to implement changes. They have seen the wider business reasons for accommodating those with disabilities. They had investigated the best course of action in anticipation of all of the provisions of the Disability Discrimination Act.

Finally, there is a positive and proactive group, typified by medium to very large organisations (many in the public sector) which are often members of the Employers Forum on Disability. They are well informed and have and continue to take a wide range of initiatives to facilitate the recruitment and retention of people with disabilities. The impetus for their initiatives has both a moral and business foundation dating back to before the 1995 Act. The Act would provide an added stimulus to their activities. They have developed a strategy and a clear policy. Their activities have extended beyond their own organisations into the wider community and specialist networks.

This evidence from the employment context of disability discrimination confirms what has been expected from anecdotal evidence. It shows that considerable difficulties lie ahead in terms of compliance with the law.

The Equal Opportunities Review survey 1997

This reviewed employer compliance – mostly in over 200 medium and large-sized organisations. Of the sample 73 per cent employed over 1000 employees. The key findings were as follows:

Policy

- 87 per cent of respondents had a written policy on the employment of disabled people, and 10 per cent were planning to introduce a policy.

- 96 per cent of respondents had allocated responsibility for compliance with the Act. Of these, 56 per cent had allocated it to human resource officers and 19 per cent to equal opportunities staff.

- Of those with a written policy, 52 per cent had not made any changes to the policy in preparation for the Act; 31 per cent had already made changes; and 17 per cent were in the process of making changes.

- 72 per cent of organisations had not yet carried out an audit or survey to establish the proportion of employees who were disabled within the meaning of the Act.

Training and guidance

- Nearly half the organisations had provided written guidance for managers on the Act.

- 69 per cent of organisations provided training for HR managers on the Act, but only 28 per cent had provided such training for line managers.

Cornell University survey

An alarmist scenario often suggested by managers involves concern about the scale of any adjustments that need to be made for disabled employees. This is despite the 'reasonableness' provision in the Act. Interestingly, in a survey of over 800 human resource managers, undertaken by Cornell University and the Chartered Institute of Personnel and Development (2001), it was found that four-fifths viewed adapting their procedures and workplaces to comply with the 1995 Act to be 'easy'. Among the adjustments commonly made were the following:

- Flexibility in the application of HR policies   83 per cent
- Making existing facilities accessible   77
- Acquiring or modifying equipment/devices   68
- Parking or transportation adjustments   58
- Restructuring jobs and working hours   57
- Redeployment into vacant positions   46

Less common adjustments were:

- Providing qualified readers or interpreters   38 per cent
- Changing supervisory methods   36

According to the survey, the biggest challenge facing HR professionals was changing the attitude of fellow workers. Thirty-six per cent said that this was 'difficult' or 'very difficult'.

6.3.5 Technological context

The issue of adjustments that can be made to assist disabled people is central to the 1995 Act. The nature of these adjustments is discussed later in section 6.4 on the legal framework. However, it is important to note, in this context, the significance of technological developments. The following are among the facilities that are available to assist in the employment of disabled people: large-print software, special computer equipment and software packages, a Braille transcription service, special telephone aids, electrically powered wheelchairs, minicom. It is important to note that in many cases all that is required are 'low-tech' adjustments (e.g. a special chair, raised or lowered working surfaces, special grips for tools, additional lighting).

6.3.6 The political and historical background

Next, we turn to the political and legal context in which the Disability Discrimination Act 1995 was enacted. To that date, there had been little progress in protecting disabled people from discrimination and facilitating full social and economic participation. Among the key statutes and regulations which were passed by Parliament were the following.

1 *Chronically Sick and Disabled Persons Act 1970*: This requires local authorities to provide disabled people with information and assistance.

2 *Companies (Directors' Report, Employment of Disabled Persons) Regulations 1980*: These require companies with more than 250 employees to include a statement in the annual directors' report describing the policy for giving full and fair consideration to disabled persons applying for jobs, for continuing the employment of and providing training for employees who become disabled, and for the training, career development and promotion of disabled employees.

3 *Police and Criminal Evidence Act 1984*: This contains specific requirements for criminal cases involving persons with mental disability.

4 *Representation of the People Act 1985*: This makes provision to allow access for disabled people to polling stations.

5 *Building Regulations 1987*: These require all new buildings (including factories, shops and offices) to take account of the needs of disabled people.

In addition to these were the Disabled Persons (Employment) Acts 1944 and 1958 (now repealed under the DDA). The 1944 Act was seen as a significant major piece of legislation enacted towards the end of World War II, when it was expected that it would go some way to assisting demobilised members of the armed forces. It introduced a registration scheme for disabled people, a quota scheme in employment and reserve occupations. The quota scheme required employers with 20 or more employees to have at least 3 per cent of their workforce as registered disabled persons (RDPs). It was unlawful to engage an able-bodied person or to dismiss an RDP without reasonable cause if the quota was, or would fall below, 3 per cent. Only the positions of passenger electric lift attendant and car park attendant were ever designated as occupations only to be carried out by RDPs.

The number of people registering gradually fell to approximately 1 per cent of the working population according to the Department of Employment in 1995. There were several reasons for this. Individuals perceived no benefit in registering. Indeed, the myth developed that it was impossible to dismiss an RDP so employers were reluctant to recruit one and consequently registering became counterproductive. Many individuals did not want to be labelled as disabled, preferring to seek and retain employment on their own abilities. Lastly, the majority of disabled services were available to all, regardless of registration status. So it conferred little additional advantage.

There were three other reasons for the poor compliance. First, a lack of awareness among employers about the quota scheme. Secondly, it had become common practice, since the 1970s, for employers to apply successfully for exemption certificates from the 3 per cent quota. Finally, there was low enforcement of the Act. There have been ten prosecutions for quota offences, of which eight were successful. The last was in 1975. The average fine was £62, and the maximum remained at its original level of £100.

European involvement in disabled persons' rights was, until recently (*see* below), largely confined to Action Programmes (in 1974, 1988 and 1992) with minimal legislative intervention. For example, in 1988, the HELIOS programme was introduced to promote social and economic integration and independent living. (This is an acronym for: Handicapped people in the European Community Living Independently in an Open Society.) This followed a Recommendation which had been adopted two years earlier.

In 1986, a Council Recommendation (which is non-binding) on the Employment of Disabled Persons in the European Community was approved. Its objective is 'to promote fair opportunities for disabled people in the field of vocational training and employment'. It related to access to, and retention in, employment and training; protection from unfair dismissal; and opportunities for promotion. It asks the governments of member states to take steps to eliminate discrimination and to take positive action.

It is against this background of weak and unco-ordinated legislation, then, that campaigning in Britain was taking place to strengthen significantly the civil and employment rights of disabled people. The campaigning was undertaken not just by pressure groups representing disabled people but also by other bodies like the Law Society and various trade unions. It also encompassed (from 1982) direct attempts at legislation by numerous backbench MPs proposing private member's Bills. The Conservative government remained opposed to legislation until 1994 when consultation took place on possible legislation. The proposals put forward owed much to the experience of the Americans with their Disabilities Act 1990 and little to European experience. Eventually, after many years of campaigning and 15 failed private member's Bills, the Disability Discrimination Act gained Royal Assent on 8 November 1995. The Act gives people with disabilities greater rights of access to goods, facilities, services, premises, education, public transport and employment.

6.3.7   The developing political and legislative context

There are three issues in the political and legislative context: individual applications; the removal of the small firms exclusion; and the European Employment Directive 2000.

Individual applications

Following the implementation of the Disability Discrimination Act 1995, one potentially significant provision was the right of individual employees to complain about infringements of their rights at an employment tribunal. ACAS reports an increasing number of complaints (*Annual Report 2001/02*). In 2001/02, 5057 cases were received. This was an increase of 14 per cent over the previous year. In the two previous years the increases were 23 per cent (2000/01) and 22 per cent (1999/00). Most cases are settled or withdrawn. Annually, about 20 per cent of cases which are completed proceed to employment tribunal.

Removal of the small firms exemption

The Labour government, elected in 1997, was committed 'to secure comprehensive, enforceable civil rights for disabled people'. The original exclusion of employees working for companies with fewer than 20 staff was amended and the threshold was reduced to 15. From October 2004, this exclusion will be abolished, extending rights to some 400 000 disabled employees.

European Employment Directive 2000

The disability discrimination provisions are to be implemented by 2 December 2006. Apart from the rescission of the small firms exemption, the government has indicated a number of changes to be made to the Disability Discrimination Act 1995 to ensure compliance with European law (*Towards Equality and Diversity*, Cabinet Office, 2001). Among the measures indicated are the following – some of which derive from the Directive and some from the government's own initiative:

- *Occupational exemptions*: These are to be ended. They include barristers and their pupils, partners in business partnerships, police officers, fire-fighters and employees on board ships and aeroplanes.

- *Duty to make reasonable adjustments*: The Directive requires member states to introduce a specific duty to make 'reasonable accommodations' for disabled people. The government takes the view that 'this is similar to the reasonable adjustments duty . . . We therefore have no plans to change the DDA's general approach to adjustments in the field of employment' (Cabinet Office, 2001: para 14.9).

- *Indirect discrimination*: Currently there is no prohibition under the 1995 Act against indirect discrimination. The duty to make reasonable adjustments is seen as the route to tackling discriminatory practices. Under the Directive, there will be a new definition similar to that already in force in respect of sex discrimination (*see* Chapter 4). Such indirect discrimination could be justified if the treatment could be objectively justified as appropriate and necessary. This would be in addition to the duty to make reasonable adjustments.

- *Pay*: There is to be consultation about indirect discrimination (which is currently permitted) in respect of performance-related pay, occupational pensions and group insurance schemes.

- *Harassment*: This is outlawed as unlawful discrimination. It is conduct which violates a person's dignity or creates an offensive, hostile, degrading, humiliating environment.

- *Duty on public authorities*: This is not part of the Directive. It is intended that public authorities should be under a duty to promote equality of opportunity for disabled people. It will widen the scope of the 1995 Act to cover most functions of public authorities not already covered by that Act.

6.3.8 Social welfare support

Although the government had not, until 1995, provided any general framework of disability law, there were in place various forms of social welfare support. These comprised schemes and services to assist disabled people and to promote their social integration. In the context of implementing the employment provisions of the 1995 Act, they can be of help.

Examples of these schemes and services include placement, assessment and counselling, access to work, the 'two ticks' and supported employment.

Disability Service Teams

Until April 1999, these were known as PACTs (Placement, Assessment and Counselling Teams). These are staffed by *Disablement Employment Advisers*. There are 70 teams across the country. They are designed to provide a coherent employment and advisory service for employers and for people with disabilities. These are usually an employer's first contact for information about government schemes. Their three principal aims are: to help overcome obstacles to employment, to enable disabled people to compete on an equal basis, and to encourage employers to recruit and retain disabled people by offering practical help.

Access to Work Scheme

This provides a range of employment support services. Full or partial paid assistance can include: a communicator for people who are deaf or have a hearing impairment; a part-time reader or assistance for a blind employee; a support worker for someone who needs practical help at work or getting to work; equipment or adaptations to suit individual needs; and alterations to premises for a disabled employee.

The 'Two Ticks' Scheme

This was introduced in 1990 by the Department of Employment as part of a voluntarist, rather than legislative, approach to tackling disability discrimination. It is an indication that an employer is working towards standards of good practice. Employers may use the symbol if they undertake five commitments:

1 To interview all disabled applicants who meet the minimum criteria for a job vacancy and consider them on their abilities.
2 To make every effort when employees become disabled to ensure they stay in employment.
3 To ask disabled employees at least once a year what can be done to make sure they can develop and use their abilities.
4 To ensure that key employees develop the awareness of disability needed to make these commitments work.
5 To review these commitments and what has been achieved annually, to plan ways to improve and to inform all employees about progress and future plans.

The Supported Employment Programme

This comprises sheltered workshops, the sheltered placement scheme and Remploy Ltd. Advice and information on these are available from Disablement Employment Advisers.

6.4 The legal framework

The employment provisions of the Disability Discrimination Act 1995 came into force in December 1996. The provisions on access to goods, services and facilities were implemented in October 1999.

A statutory code of practice 'on the elimination of discrimination in the field of employment' was prepared by the Secretary of State and approved by Parliament in 1996. This can be used in evidence before an employment tribunal or court (DDA, s 53(5)). In addition, there are two sets of regulations: the Disability Discrimination (Meaning of Disability) Regulations 1996 and the Disability Discrimination (Employment) Regulations 1996. Also, statutory Guidance on 'matters to be taken into account in determining questions relating to the definition of disability' was approved by Parliament primarily to assist courts and tribunals.

There are several key provisions in the Act which will be considered: the coverage of the legislation, the meaning of disability, the meaning of discrimination, the duty to make reasonable adjustments, liability, enforcement procedures, remedies and the role of the Disability Rights Commission.

6.4.1   The coverage of the legislation

The Act prohibits discrimination against disabled persons (of either sex and any age). Those protected are people who have a disability (*see* below), and those have been disabled.

Initially, the Act did not apply to employers with fewer than 20 employees. However, from 1 December 1998 this threshold was reduced to 15 employees. An employer which is part of a larger group is covered if other employers in the group are associated and the total number of employees exceeds 15. The exemption covering employees of small organisations will be abolished in October 2004.

Those on the Register of Disabled Persons both on 12 January 1995 and when the Act came into force are deemed disabled under the new legislation. Contract workers are protected from discrimination under s 12 of the Act.

6.4.2   The meaning of disability

A person has a disability for the purposes of this Act if he has a physical or mental impairment which has a substantial and long-term adverse effect on his ability to carry out normal day-to-day activities (s 1(1)).

Several issues arise in this section which will be looked at in more detail.

Physical or mental impairment

There are several important aspects to this.

The Act does not define physical impairment.

Mental impairment 'includes an impairment resulting from or consisting of a mental illness only if the illness is a clinically well-recognised illness' (DDA, Sch 1, para 1), recognised 'by a respected body of medical opinion' (Guidance on the Definition of Disability, para 14). Tribunal cases have accepted bulimia nervosa and depression as mental impairments.

In *Morgan* v *Staffordshire University* [2002] IRLR 190, the Employment Appeals Tribunal provided guidance on whether in particular cases there was evidence that mental impairment could be established. It ruled that medical notes referring to terms like anxiety, stress and depression are not proof of a mental impairment within the meaning of the DDA. Proof should be established under the following possible headings:

- Of a mental illness specifically mentioned in the WHO's International Classification of Diseases.

- Of a mental illness specifically mentioned in a publication that has a wide professional acceptance by peers in the area.

- The illness is recognised by a respected body of medical opinion.

- There is a substantial and specific body of medical evidence of a mental impairment which neither results from nor consists of a mental illness.

Impairment controlled by medication, appliances or prostheses is regarded as an impairment to the extent that the individual would be disabled without the medication, etc. (but this does not apply to eyesight corrected by spectacles).

Severe disfigurement is to be treated as disablement except where it has been deliberately self-inflicted. So, the Meaning of Disability Regulations explicitly rule out as impairments tattoos and 'piercing of the body for decorative or other non-medical purposes, including any object attached through the piercing for such purposes' (reg 5).

Progressive conditions (e.g. multiple sclerosis, AIDS, cancer) that will result in serious disability are treated as a disability although they are not yet in such an advanced state as to impair normal day-to-day activities.

Addictions are covered if they arise originally as a result of the administration of medically prescribed drugs or other medical treatment, but addiction to alcohol, nicotine or any other substance is not an impairment under the Act (Meaning of Disability Regulations, reg 3). However, according to the Guidance on the Definition of Disability, 'it is not necessary to consider how an impairment was caused, even if the cause is a consequence of a condition which is excluded. For example, liver disease as a result of alcohol dependency would count as an impairment' (para 11).

Various other conditions are explicitly ruled as not being impairments under the Act: a tendency to set fires, a tendency to steal, a tendency to physical or sexual abuse of other persons, exhibitionism and voyeurism (Meaning of Disability Regulations, reg 4(1)).

In *College of Ripon and York St John* v *Hobbs* [2002] IRLR 185, the EAT ruled that in determining that a physical impairment existed within the meaning of the Act it was not necessary for a tribunal to know precisely what underlying disease or trauma caused the impairment. Evidence of the effects of the impairment was sufficient.

Substantial adverse effect

The Guidance on the Definition of Disability describes 'a substantial effect' as one which is 'more than minor or trivial' (para A1). It states that it 'reflects the general understanding of "disability" as a limitation going beyond the normal differences of ability which may exist among people'. An assessment of whether the effect was substantial would include the time taken to carry out the activity, the way in which the activity is carried out, the cumulative effects of an impairment and environmental factors (paras A2–A10).

In *Foster* v *Hampshire Fire and Rescue Service*, 23.6.98, EAT, 1303/97, a sufferer from asthma and migraine was ruled as not being a 'disabled person' because, although she had a physical impairment which had a long-term adverse effect on her mobility, the effect was not substantial. In reaching its view, on the facts, account had been taken of the applicant's own evidence, her GP's factual medical report describing her condition and the medication prescribed and the opinion of the fire service's occupational health physician.

In *Leonard* v *Southern Derbyshire Chamber of Commerce* [2001] IRLR 19, the EAT ruled that a tribunal must focus on what an applicant could not do rather than what they could do. It also stated that the employment tribunal had erred in taking into account the applicant's performance before the tribunal, saying that this 'cannot readily be regarded as an entirely reliable guide to the individual's ability to perform day-to-day activities'.

Long-term effect

An impairment will be regarded as long term if it has lasted for at least 12 months or is reasonably expected to last for at least 12 months or the rest of the person's life (Sch 1, para 2(1)).

'Where an impairment ceases to have a substantial adverse effect on a person's ability to carry out normal day-to-day activities, it is to be treated as continuing to have that effect if that effect is likely to recur' (Sch 1, para 2(2)). So, according to the Guidance on the Definition of Disability, conditions such as epilepsy can be included as are those like rheumatoid arthritis where there might be periods of remission (paras B3–B5). However, 'the condition known as seasonal allergic rhinitis shall be treated as not amounting to an impairment' (Meaning of Disability Regulations, reg 4(2)).

In a case involving a person with multiple sclerosis, a consultant neurologist had stated that it was not possible to provide an accurate prognosis for any individual with MS because of the variable nature of the condition. In the circumstances, the EAT stated that:

> it is not enough simply to establish that he has a progressive condition and that it has or has had an effect on his ability to carry out normal day-to-day activities. The claimant must go on and show that it is more likely than not that at some stage in the future he will have an impairment which will have a substantial adverse effect on his ability to carry out normal day-to-day activities. How the claimant does this is up to him. In some cases, it may be possible to produce medical evidence of his likely prognosis. In other cases, it may be possible to discharge the onus of proof by statistical evidence (*Mowat-Brown* v *University of Surrey* [2002] IRLR 235).

Normal day-to-day activities

An impairment is to be taken to affect the ability of the person concerned only if it affects one of the following:

- mobility;
- manual dexterity;
- physical co-ordination;
- continence;
- ability to lift, carry or otherwise move everyday objects;

- speech, hearing or eyesight;
- memory or ability to concentrate, learn or understand;
- perception of the risk of physical danger (Sch 1, para 4(1)).

When the Act refers to an adverse effect on an ability to carry out 'normal day-to-day' activities what is meant is what is normal for most people, not what is normal for the individual concerned. So, clearly, the legislation links the definition of 'disability' to day-to-day activities and not to work-related activities. Detailed guidance is provided in section C of the Guidance on the Definition of Disability.

6.4.3 The meaning of discrimination

For the purposes of the employment provisions of the Act, 'an employer discriminates against a disabled person if:

(a) for a reason which relates to the disabled person's disability, he treats him less favourably than he treats or would treat others to whom that reason does not apply; and

(b) he cannot show that the treatment in question is justified (DDA, s 5(1)).

The issue of **comparison** is central to finding discrimination. So, inevitably, tribunals have to decide on what is an appropriate comparator whether actual or hypothetical. The *Code of Practice* (1996) states that:

a disabled person may not be able to point to other people who were actually treated more favourably. However, it is still 'less favourable treatment' if the employer would give better treatment to someone else to whom the reason for the treatment of the disabled person did not apply. This comparison can also be made with other disabled people, not just non-disabled people. For example, an employer might be discriminating by treating a person with a mental illness less favourably than he treats or would treat a physically disabled person (para 4.3).

In *Clark v TGD Ltd t/a Novacold* [1999] IRLR 318, the Court of Appeal ruled on the three-stage approach to be used in determining less favourable treatment. This was used by the EAT in *Cosgrove v Caesar and Howie* [2001] IRLR 653:

- What was the material reason for the applicant's treatment? In this case the applicant, Ms Cosgrove, a legal secretary, had been absent from work for a year with depression. The material reason for her dismissal was her absence on medical grounds.
- Did the material reason relate to the person's disability? The reason for her dismissal did relate to her disability.
- Would the employer have dismissed another employee to whom that material reason did not apply? The employment tribunal had used as a comparator another employee who had been absent from work for one year. The EAT stated that this was the wrong comparator. The correct comparator was *not* somebody who had been absent from work and therefore the treatment was discriminatory.

As a result of this approach, an employer must consider reasonable adjustments (*see* below) where an employee has been absent from work for a long period. Unless reasonable adjustments are considered, the discriminatory treatment of a disabled person will not be justified.

Discriminatory advertisements are also covered (s 11). 'The tribunal hearing the complaint shall assume, unless the contrary is shown, that the employer's reason for refusing to offer, or deliberately not offering, the employment to the complainant was related to the complainant's disability' (s 11(2)).

There is one important exception to the protection given by s 5. The Disability Discrimination (Employment) Regulations 1996 provide a justification for pay discrimination. This differential treatment is taken to be justified 'if it results from applying to the disabled person a term or practice – (a) under which the amount of a person's pay is wholly or partly dependent on that person's performance; and (b) which is applied to all of the employer's employees or to all of a class of his employees which includes the disabled person but which is not defined by reference to any disability' (reg 3.1). Such payment schemes or practices 'are not to be taken to place that disabled person at a substantial disadvantage of the kind mentioned in section 6(1) of the Act' (reg 3.2).

Specific protection against **victimisation** is also covered by the Act (s 55). So, in relation to employment, this is defined as follows. It involves the employer treating an employee less favourably than they treat or would treat other persons whose circumstances are the same as the employee's; and, furthermore, the employer does so for one of the following reasons:

- because the employee has brought proceedings under the Act; or
- because the employee has given evidence or information in connection with such proceedings brought by any person; or
- because the employee has 'otherwise done anything under this Act in relation to' the employer; or
- because the employee has alleged that the employer or another person has contravened the Act; or
- because the employer 'believes or suspects that [the employee] has done or intends to do' any of the above things.

The person who is alleging victimisation does not have to be disabled. The protection 'does not apply to treatment of a person because of an allegation made by him if the allegation was false and not made in good faith' (s 55(4)).

The Act does not expressly refer to 'harassment', although the *Code of Practice* (1996) states that 'harassing a disabled person on account of disability will almost always amount to a "detriment" under the Act' (para 6.22). Indeed, it could be said that harassment of a disabled or non-disabled person is likely to be a repudiatory breach of the contract of employment (*see* Chapter 7).

6.4.4 The duty to make reasonable adjustments

The duty

In discussing the meaning of discrimination above, it was said that an employer also discriminates against a disabled person if they fail to comply with the duty to make adjustments and 'cannot show that his failure to comply with that duty is justified' (s 5(2)).

Knowledge of the impairment

Clearly, one precondition of this duty is that the employer is informed that a particular person is disabled. 'If the employer does not know and could not reasonably be expected to know' about a person's disability, then no duty is imposed (s 6(6)).

The *Code of Practice* (1996) offers two important pieces of guidance in this area. The first concerns the degree of caution necessary before other staff are notified about an individual's disability (para 4.60). The second is the acknowledgement that 'the Act does not prevent a disabled person keeping a disability confidential from an employer'. This is likely to remove from the employer the duty to make a reasonable adjustment (para 4.61).

In *Callaghan* v *Glasgow City Council* [2001] IRLR 724, EAT the judge stated that:

> given that the discriminatory act related to treatment, that is to say, how the employer treats the employee, knowledge of disability is not necessarily an essential element . . . the fact that the employer did not know the disability exists might affect the justification but does not preclude it . . . What matters therefore is to analyse the treatment meted out by the employer.

Adjustments

The duty of an employer to make adjustments is set out in the following terms:

> Where –
> (a) any arrangements made by or on behalf of an employer or
> (b) any physical feature of premises occupied by the employer,
> place the disabled person concerned at a substantial disadvantage in comparison with persons who are not disabled, it is the duty of the employer to take such steps as it is reasonable, in all the circumstances of the case, for him to have to take in order to prevent the arrangements or feature having that effect (s 6(1)).

'Arrangements' relate to the following:

- 'arrangements for determining to whom employment should be offered';
- 'any term, condition or arrangements on which employment, promotion, a transfer, training or any other benefit is offered or afforded' (s 6(2)).

This section does not refer to dismissal. However, the EAT has held that a duty does arise where a disabled person is dismissed. The provision 'any arrangements on which employment . . . is . . . afforded' was construed as being broad enough to cover dismissal (*Morse* v *Wiltshire County Council*, 1.5.98, EAT, 1279/97).

The Act provides *examples* of the types of adjustments that can be made by an employer (s 6(3)). Obviously, they are not exhaustive. These can be grouped as follows:

Buildings

■ adjustments to premises.

Equipment

■ providing or modifying equipment.

Preparation for work

■ providing training;
■ modifying instructions or reference manuals;
■ modifying procedures for testing or assessment.

Work organisation

■ allocating some of a disabled person's duties to another person;
■ transferring a disabled person to fill an existing vacancy;
■ assigning a person to a different place of work;
■ providing a reader or interpreter;
■ providing supervision.

Working time

■ altering a person's working hours;
■ permitting absence for rehabilitation, assessment or treatment.

A key word relating to this duty is 'reasonable'. The Act specifies a range of factors that should be taken into account in deciding whether or not it would be 'reasonable in all the circumstances of the case' for an employer to make specific adjustments (s 6(4)). These are set out as follows:

■ the extent to which making the adjustment would prevent the 'substantial disadvantage';
■ the extent to which it is practicable for the employer to make the adjustment;
■ the financial and other costs incurred by the employer in making the adjustment and the extent to which it would disrupt any of the employer's activities;
■ the extent of the employer's financial and other resources;
■ the availability to the employer of financial or other assistance (e.g. from public funds) to help make the adjustment.

It is possible for an employer to make more than one adjustment for a particular disabled person (*Code of Practice*, para 4.33). The duty placed on an employer to make reasonable adjustments does not 'require an employer to treat a disabled person more favourably than he treats or would treat others' (s 6(7)).

Justification

An employer may be able to show justification for not making a reasonable adjustment and thereby treating the employee less favourably. This issue was considered by the Court of Appeal in *Jones* v *the Post Office* [2001] IRLR 384. The

Act states that the less favourable treatment of the employee 'is justified if, but only if, the reason for it is both material to the circumstances of the particular case and substantial' (s 5(3)). The Court of Appeal ruled:

- That the rights under the Act had to be considered in the context of the employer's duties to other employees and to the general public. In this case, there was risk because the applicant's medical condition might affect his standard of driving when delivering mail.
- In this case, it was appropriate for the employer to undertake a properly conducted risk assessment. The employment tribunal was not entitled to substitute its own appraisal of the medical evidence to challenge a proper assessment of risk.
- 'Material' concerns the 'quality' of the connection which must exist between the employer's reason for discriminating against the individual (i.e. by stating that it was not possible to make a reasonable adjustment).
- 'Substantial' means that the reason given by the employer for the discriminatory treatment must have some real weight and be of substance.
- If an employer failed to consider a further request by the employee to consider making a reasonable adjustment when the employee put forward new evidence, then, the discriminatory treatment may not be justified.

6.4.5 Liability

The liability provisions of the DDA mirror those in the sex and race discrimination legislation, namely: the liability of the employer, the vicarious liability of the employer for the acts of employees and other persons and the meaning of 'in the course of employment'. The detailed provisions are as follows:

> Anything done by a person in the course of his employment shall be treated for the purposes of this Act as also done by his employer, whether or not it was done with the employer's knowledge or approval (s 58(1)).

Furthermore, 'anything done by a person as agent for another person with the authority of that person shall be treated for the purposes of this Act as also done by that person' (s 58(2)). This applies whether or not the authority was 'express or implied' or 'given before or after the act in question was done' (s 58(3)).
Finally, employers can have a defence:

> In proceedings under this Act against any person in respect of an act alleged to have been done by an employee of his, it shall be a defence for that person to prove that he took such steps as were reasonably practicable to prevent the employee from – (a) doing that act; or (b) doing, in the course of his employment, acts of that description (s 58(5)).

There are some potential difficulties here if the employer is invoking health and safety reasons as a defence. In *Smith* v *Carpets International UK plc*, 11.9.97, 1800507/97 a tribunal found that it was justified on health and safety grounds for an employer to exclude an epileptic, who was reported as having had seizures, from work in a warehouse (because of the significant amount of heavy machinery and forklift truck activity). A risk assessment had been made and it was concluded that no adjustments could be made to warehouse work. The use of such a defence, however, requires an employer to carry out a proper investigation for a 'justification' argument to be taken seriously.

6.4.6 Burden of proof

The onus of proof is on the applicant. It applies in this way:

- The applicant identifies what they believe to be the reason for their treatment. This must be linked to their disability.
- The applicant shows that other people to whom that reason does not (or would not) apply have been (or would have been) treated more favourably than the applicant has been.
- The tribunal looks to the employer for an explanation of the reason for the applicant's treatment.
- If the employer is unable to provide an explantaion (or puts forward an explanation that does not relate to the applicant's disability but is unconvincing) the tribunal is entitled (although not obliged) to infer that the reason for the applicant's treatment was the one that related to the applicant's disability.

When the provisions of the Employment Directive 2000 are implemented, a complainant will need to make out a prima facie case of discrimination. The onus is, then, on the employer to show that the conduct was not unlawful.

6.4.7 Enforcement procedures

Complaints under Part II of the Act are made to an employment tribunal (s 8) about discrimination by an employer or an employer's failure to make a reasonable adjustment. As with other tribunal applications, ACAS is under a statutory duty to conciliate and promote a settlement (Sch 3, para 1).

It is possible, under specific circumstances, for compromise agreements to be made as an alternative to the making of a tribunal complaint (s 9(2)–(4)). These circumstances are if:

- an ACAS conciliation officer has acted under the Act on the matter, or if the following conditions apply –
  - the disabled person must have received independent legal advice from a qualified lawyer about the terms and effects of the agreement, particularly its effect on his ability to complain to a tribunal;
  - the adviser must have an insurance policy covering any loss arising from the advice; and
  - the agreement must be in writing, relate to the complaint, identify the adviser and say that these conditions are satisfied.

6.4.8 Remedies

If an employment tribunal finds that a complaint is 'well founded', then 'it shall take such of the following steps as it considers just and equitable' (s 8(2)). These steps are:

- **declaration** of the rights of the complainant (the employee) and of the respondent (the employer) in respect of the complaint;

- **compensation** to be paid by the employer to the employee;

- **recommending action** to be taken by the employer within a specified period. This would be 'action appearing to the tribunal to be reasonable, in all the circumstances of the case, for the purpose of obviating or reducing the adverse effect on the complainant of any matter to which the complaint relates' (s 8(2)(c)).

Compensation payments can include past loss of earnings, estimated future loss of earnings, loss of enhanced or accrued pension rights, and injury to feelings. Deductions can be made for social security payments such as the Disability Living Allowance. Compensation for injury to feelings may be ordered whether or not compensation is paid under any other head (s 8(4)). Furthermore, an employer may be required to pay aggravated damages because of the way in which the employee was treated. According to the Equal Opportunities Review survey of compensation (August 2002), the highest median award of compensation for disability discrimination in 2001 was £7218, an increase of 39 per cent over the previous year's figure. The median figure for injury to feelings was £3000 (2001).

6.4.9 The Disability Rights Commission

The Disability Discrimination Act 1995 provided for the establishment of the National Disability Council. This did not have the same enforcement powers as the Commissions on Equal Opportunities and Racial Equality (*see* Chapters 4 and 5). The Labour government, elected in 1997, implemented its commitment to abolish the NDC and replace it with a more powerful Disability Rights Commission (DRC).

The DRC was established in April 2000 under the Disability Rights Commission Act 1999. It comprises 15 members, 10 of whom have a disability. These have been recruited for the particular expertise that they can bring to the work of the Commission. In addition there are commissioners with a business interest and a trade union interest. The role of the DRC includes the following:

- to work towards the elimination of discrimination against disabled persons;

- providing, as appropriate, material assistance to a complainant where, because of the effects of a person's impairment, it would be unreasonable to expect the individual to put a complaint without support;

- the power to carry out formal investigations where it believes an unlawful act of discrimination has been committed and to publish its findings;

- the ability to commission or carry out research on disability within employment;

- to review the working of the DDA;

- to encourage good practice in the treatment of disabled people;

- the power to issue non-discrimination notices where it believes a person is committing or has committed an unlawful act of discrimination – requiring the person to stop the discrimination;

- where a person continues to commit acts of unlawful discrimination, the DRC may apply for an injunction.

6.4.10 Managing long-term sick absence

An additional complicating issue can arise in disability discrimination complaints alleging unfair dismissal. This concerns the implications of long-term sick absence. The Employment Rights Act 1996 enacts several 'fair reasons' for dismissal. Among these is the issue of an employee's 'capability' which is defined as encompassing 'health or any other physical or mental quality' (s 98(3)(a)). A dismissal on such grounds must conform to the standards of substantive and procedural fairness (*see* Chapter 9). However, in such cases, it is now clear that consideration must be given to the question of whether the decision to dismiss constitutes discrimination against a person who has disability (within the meaning of the DDA). Furthermore, the relevant circumstances of the case require consideration of the employer's compliance or not with the duty to make reasonable adjustments (*see* the *Cosgrove* case above).

6.5 Employment policies and practices

There are three aspects to employers' policies and practices that we will consider: the recommended approach to managing disability discrimination; the Act's effect on contracts and agreements; and the practical steps advocated in the Code of Practice 1996.

6.5.1 Management approach

The 1996 *Code of Practice* ('for the elimination of discrimination in the field of employment against disabled persons or persons who have had a disability') initially, provides **general guidance** to help avoid discrimination. First, employers should be flexible. 'There may be several ways to avoid discrimination in any one situation . . . Many ways of avoiding discrimination will cost little or nothing' (para 3.1). Secondly, it suggests that employers do not make assumptions. 'It will probably be helpful to talk to each disabled person about what the real effects of the disability might be or what might help' (para 3.2). Thirdly, employers should consider whether or not expert advice is necessary on the extent of a disabled person's capabilities (para 3.3). Fourthly, 'when planning for change it could be cost-effective to consider the needs of a range of possible future disabled employees and applicants' (para 3.4). Finally, the existence of an equal opportunities policy (supported by effective monitoring) is likely to count in an employer's favour before a tribunal (para 3.5).

In addition, it is important to consider action against disability discrimination in the context of wider equal opportunities or managing diversity policies and to incorporate it, as far as possible, into existing systems. It is also the case that the existence and effective operation of an equal opportunities policy can be a defence against liability for discrimination. The employer can argue before a tribunal that he took reasonable steps to prevent discriminatory behaviour.

6.5.2 Implications for contracts and agreements

The Act also has legal significance for contracts of employment and 'other agreements' (including collective agreements with trade unions and workforce agreements with employee representatives). As outlined in Chapter 1 both of these are important instruments for regulating the employment relationship. The DDA makes it clear that 'any term in a contract of employment or other agreement is void so far as it purports to – (a) require a person to contravene any provision of, or made under [the employment provisions]; (b) exclude or limit the operation of any provision of [the employment provisions]; or prevent any person from presenting a complaint to an [employment] tribunal' (s 9(1)).

6.5.3 Practical steps: the 1996 *Code of Practice*

Campaigners against disability discrimination have identified four main barriers to employment for disabled people:

1 *Lack of credibility*: Potential employees have to convince recruitment officers and line managers of their skills and abilities to complete the tasks required. This can be difficult for a disabled person if that person is rejected prior to interview, or if the focus of the selection process is on what they cannot do rather than on identifying potential.

2 *Anxiety over taking risks*: Employers do not seem to be prepared to take the risk of employing disabled persons. The perceived risks often relate to the cost of adaptations, the belief that they will have greater sick absence, the likelihood that they are accident prone, the perceived attitudes and possible hostility of existing staff.

3 *Lack of imagination*: Many employers may not know of the ways in which technology can be used to enable full and active participation in work.

4 *Lack of appropriate access*: The majority of disabled people have no additional access requirements and need no additional equipment. For those that do, some government grants are available to adapt premises and extend appropriate facilities. Generally, the individual's impairment will have little or no bearing upon the capacity to realise their employment potential.

It is against this background that the 1996 *Code of Practice* provides specific guidance on policies and practices. We will look at these under the following headings: management systems, recruitment and selection, terms and conditions of service, promotion and transfer, training, occupational pension scheme, and termination of employment.

Management systems

The principal systems involved are, first of all, communication channels. 'Employers should communicate to their employees and agents any policy they may have on disability matters and any other policies which have elements relevant to disabled employees (such as health, absenteeism and equal opportunities)'. Furthermore, employers 'should provide guidance on non-discriminatory practices for all employees' (para 4.56). Secondly, employers should have a monitoring system to 'ensure as far as possible that these policies and practices are implemented' (para 4.56). Thirdly, an employer should have in place systems to ensure that requests for adjustments can be received, properly considered and, if granted, implemented. The implementation of adjustments may involved specific communication with and explanation to fellow workers.

Recruitment and selection

Included in the *Code of Practice* is the following guidance. First, it states that 'the inclusion of unnecessary or marginal requirements in **a job specification** can lead to discrimination' (para 5.3). Likewise, 'blanket exclusions' can be discriminatory. An employer can stiplulate 'essential health requirements', but 'may need to justify doing so and . . . show that it would not be reasonable for him to have to waive them in any individual case' (para 5.5). Secondly, the *Code* presents guidance on **advertisements**: these include every form of advertisement or notice, whether to the public or not (DDA, s 11(3)). This would include internal advertisements. Advertisements could be provided in 'alternative formats' (e.g. Braille). Thirdly, as far as **application forms** are concerned the Act does not prevent employers including a question on whether or not a person is disabled. 'Employers can also ask whether the individual might need an adjustment and what it might be' (para 5.11).

As far as **selection** is concerned, there are several important factors to be taken into account. First, there must be no discrimination against applicants who are disabled. This, however, is qualified by the fact that the employer knows (or could reasonably be expected to know) that a person is disabled. In **shortlisting** for interview the advice is as follows:

> if an employer knows that an applicant has a disability and is likely to be at a substantial disadvantage because of the employer's arrangements or premises, the employer should consider whether there is any reasonable adjustment which would bring the disabled person within the field of applicants to be considered even though he would not otherwise be within that field because of that disadvantage. If the employer could only make this judgement with more information it would be discriminatory for him not to put the disabled person on the shortlist for interview if that is how he would normally seek additional information about candidates (para 5.14).

Employers should encourage applicants 'to indicate any relevant effects of a disability and to suggest adjustments to help overcome any disadvantage the disability may cause' (para 5.15). Various reasonable adjustments for the interview are outlined (para 5.17). As far as the job is concerned, for which the applicant has applied, an employer can ask **questions** about a person's disability 'if it is or may be relevant to a person's ability to do the job – after a reasonable adjustment, if necessary' (para 5.20). An employer can insist on a disabled person having a **medical examination**, if it is standard practice for all applicants/new employees (para 5.23). The code of practice also provides some important guidance on the potential discriminatory effects of selection and aptitude **tests** and on the level of entry qualifications specified (paras 5.21–22).

A critical question asked by those selecting new employees is 'what if a disabled person just isn't **the right person for the job**?' The *Code* states that:

> an employer must not discriminate against a disabled candidate, but there is no requirement (aside from reasonable adjustment) to treat a disabled person more favourably than he treats or would treat others. An employer will have to assess an applicant's merits as they would be if any reasonable adjustments required under the Act had been made. If, after allowing for those adjustments, a disabled person would not be the best person for the job the employer would not have to recruit that person (para 5.26).

Terms and conditions of service

'Terms and conditions of service should not discriminate against a disabled person' (para 5.27). It is open to an employer to adjust terms and conditions for a disabled person (e.g. the scheduling of working time). However, an employer can offer a disabled person a less favourable contract. 'Such a contract may be justified if there is a material and substantial reason and there is no reasonable adjustment which can be made to remove that reason' (para 5.28). Performance-related pay is still permissible. It would be 'justified so long as the scheme applied equally to all employees or all of a particular class of employees' (para 5.29).

The *Code* also draws attention to the avoidance of discrimination in the provision of benefits. The provision of these is also subject to the duty to make reasonable adjustment. 'Benefits might include canteens, meal vouchers, social clubs and other recreational activities, dedicated car parking spaces, discounts on products, bonuses, share options, hairdressing, clothes allowances, financial services, healthcare, medical assistance/insurance, transport to work, company car, education assistance, workplace nurseries and rights to special leave' (para 6.7).

Promotion and transfer

Employers must not discriminate in assessing a disabled person's suitability for promotion or transfer 'in the practical arrangements necessary to enable the promotion or transfer to take place, in the operation of the appraisal, selection and promotion or transfer process, or in the new job itself – and may have to make a reasonable adjustment' (para 6.4).

Training

Employers must not discriminate in selection for training and must make any necessary reasonable adjustments (para 6.6).

Occupational pension schemes

A non-discrimination rule is inserted into every occupational pension scheme (DDA, s 17). The trustees or managers of the scheme are prohibited from doing (or omitting to do) anything to members or non-members of schemes that would be unlawful discrimination. 'Less favourable treatment for a reason relating to a disability can be justified only if the reason is material and substantial' (para 6.10). An example suggested would be where 'a disabled person's health or health prognosis is such that the cost of providing benefits under a pension scheme is substantially greater than it would be for a person without the disability' (para 6.11).

Termination of employment

The *Code of Practice* emphasises the importance of retaining disabled persons in employment. 'An employer must not discriminate against an employee who becomes disabled or has a disability which worsens'. It adds that 'the issue of retention might also arise when an employee has a stable impairment but the nature of his employment changes' (para 6.19). In these circumstances, the employer must consider 'any reasonable adjustment that would resolve the difficulty'. Furthermore, 'the employer may also need to consult the disabled person at appropriate stages about what his needs are and what effect the disability might have on future employment, for example, where the employee has a progressive condition' (para 6.20).

Should termination of employment arise, the *Code* states that 'dismissal – including compulsory early retirement – of a disabled person relating to the disability would need to be justified and the reason for it would have to be one which could not be removed by any reasonable adjustment' (para 6.21).

Exercise 6.1 **Some discrimination problems**

1   A small packaging and dispatch company employing up to 25 full and part-time staff handles DIY products such as nuts and bolts. The company recently withdrew a verbal offer of employment to Sarah, a young woman, when she mentioned, after the interview, that she had a history of mental illness and suffered from panic attacks. She has now written to the company claiming disability discrimination.

   Advise on the situation and outline any action that it should take.

2   Jo, one of the marketing executives at a pharmaceutical company, has recently informed you that she has been diagnosed with AIDS. She is currently working full-time but absences are resulting in major work problems with which senior management are becoming exasperated. They wish her to take medical retirement with a generous financial settlement. She does not wish to go.

   Advise the company on the situation.

3   Jason has recently applied for promotion to sales representative with a large multi-national electronics company. This position provides a company car and involves considerable travel throughout the Greater London area. He has experience and skills comparable with those of the successful external candidate. However, a factor that the selection panel took into account in reaching its decision was Jason's health. He has a spinal problem which causes pain if he has to sit for long periods. It gives him a stooped appearance and also limits his mobility. Although he has a driving licence, he does not currently own a car. He travels to work in a colleague's car.

   You are a union representative. He has asked you for advice.

   Feedback on this exercise is provided in the Appendix to this book.

Further reading

Department for Education and Skills (1996) *Code of Practice for the Elimination of Discrimination in the Field of Employment against Disabled Persons or Persons Who Have Had a Disability*. London: DfES.

References

Advisory Conciliation and Arbitration Service (2002) *Annual Report 2001–02*. London: ACAS.

Cabinet Office (2001) *Towards Equality and Diversity*. London: Cabinet Office.

Chartered Institute of Personnel and Development (2001) *Adapting to Disability*. London: CIPD.

Equal Opportunities Review (1997) *Implementing the DDA: an EOR survey of employers*, January/February, 20–6, and March/April, 18–25. London: Industrial Relations Services.

Equal Opportunities Review (2002) *Compensation Awards 2001*, August. London: Industrial Relations Services.

Graham, P., Jordan, A. and Lamb, B. (1990) *An Equal Chance? or No Chance? – a Study of Discrimination against Disabled People in the Labour Market*. London: SCOPE.

Honey, S., Meager, N. and Williams, M. (1993) *Employers' Attitudes Towards People with Disabilities*. Brighton: Institute of Manpower Studies.

Massie, B. (1994) *Disabled People and Social Justice*. London: Institute for Public Policy Research.

Pidduck, J. (1995) (unpublished) *The Implications of the Disability Discrimination Act for People with Disabilities*. Kingston upon Thames: Kingston University Business School.

RADAR (1993) *Disability and Discrimination in Employment*. London: RADAR.

Twomey, B. (2001) *Disability and the labour market: results from Summer Labour Force Survey*. London: Labour Market Trends.

Weiss, S. (1974) 'Equal Employment and the Disabled; a proposal', *Columbia Journal of Social Problems*, 10.

Wood, P. (1991) *International Classification of Impairments, Disabilities and Handicaps*. Geneva: World Health Organisation.

PART THREE

Regulating performance and conduct

Introduction to Part Three

In Part Three, there are two broad sets of often interlocking factors that have promoted or influenced the legal regulation of conduct. The first is social attitudes about acceptable workplace behaviour and fair procedures. The second relates to the economic objectives of employers.

In the early 1970s there was a concerted attempt to enact legal standards in respect of workplace discipline. These were designed to minimise arbitrary treatment of employees, to establish some consensus on acceptable behaviour, to promote consistency of treatment and to encourage improvement as a first step, rather than inflict punishment. The conduct of both employees and employers is, consequently, regulated through the standards set in unfair dismissal law. Fair procedures were specified. This body of law is now deeply entrenched in employment protection.

Although this legislation was largely driven by principles of social justice, the economic interests of employers are not excluded. For example, among the fair reasons for dismissal are those concerning employee capability and redundancy. In addition, the category of 'some other substantial reason' includes other business reasons for terminating contracts of employment (e.g. to introduce contractual changes). Furthermore, there are explicit economic, technical and organisational reasons for dismissal set out in the Transfer of Employment (Protection of Employment) Regulations 1981. Employers, then, should be able to achieve their business objectives. The proviso is that they operate fair procedures.

Shifting social expectations and changing standards of acceptability have, in recent years, raised the profile of one specific type of conduct: harassment or bullying. There is no coherent body of law governing such behaviour, although within present law attempts are made to provide aggrieved persons with some redress.

The legal instruments used are:

- discrimination legislation;
- a Recommendation and a Code of Practice published by the European Community;
- the law of contract with allegations of repudiatory breach of the contract and resulting in constructive dismissal complaints;
- the criminal law relating to 'stalking'.

The connections between these two areas (discipline and harassment) will be obvious. Disciplinary action, including dismissal, can constitute one of the 'steps that are reasonably practicable' (*see* Chapters 4–6 on discrimination law) that an employer can take to deal with a perpetrator.

Standards and procedures relating to workplace conduct are far from resolved. Periodically, attempts are made to enact more coherent legislation on the dignity of men and women at work.

A further set of issues that are increasingly being woven into the whole area of workplace conduct are privacy, 'whistleblowing', and data control. Legal guidance is developing on appropriate standards of behaviour.

Harassment and bullying at work

This chapter considers the wide range of behaviour that constitutes harassment and bullying at work. Having read it, you should understand:

- The meaning of 'harassment' and 'bullying'.
- The context in which it can develop and the principal sociological explanations for the origin and exhibition of such behaviour.
- The ways in which employers can tackle it.
- The ways in which it can be dealt with through contract law and through discrimination law.

7.1 Structure of the chapter

This chapter comprises the following sections:

- *Introduction*: Defining harassment and bullying.
- *The context*: Power relations, cultural factors, the characteristics of the workplace, the nature of the parties involved and possible consequences.
- *The legal framework*: The contract of employment, standards of acceptable treatment, direct discrimination and detriments, dismissal, liability for the harassment, action against the perpetrator and possible remedies in law for the victim.
- *Employment policies and practices*: Defining harassment and bullying, approach to allegations, managerial roles and responsibilities, informal procedures and counselling, grievance procedures, training, communications, disciplinary action, consultation with unions, monitoring.

7.2   Introduction

Workplace bullying and harassment have, historically, been a feature of working life. However, only since the mid-1980s have they become high-profile issues of public concern. Generally, they are considered in the context of equal opportunities policies and anti-discrimination strategies like the management of diversity. Press reports have revealed individuals targeted for harassment because of gender, race, ethnic origin, nationality, religion, political affiliation and sexuality. The range of behaviour that constitutes harassment covers a very wide spectrum and, in its extreme form, can be a crime.

7.2.1   Growing concern about harassment

The reasons why harassment has become a focal issue in employment relations are complex. First, the standards of acceptable behaviour, in society at large, are changing and are being articulated more clearly. This, inevitably, has an impact in employment – given the greater feminisation of the labour market, the growing multi-ethnic composition of workforces and greater acceptance of different sexual orientation. The expectations of these social groups are being imported into employment.

Secondly, some employers have begun to recognise the economically damaging consequences of tensions, conflict and victimisation that can arise from harassment and bullying as well as the likely adverse effect on corporate image. Thirdly, coherent employer responses to the problems of harassment (through the adoption of workplace policies and procedures) have been encouraged by the publication of various codes of practice and statements. For example, in 1991 the European Community published a code on the dignity of men and women at work. Also, in 1992, the Chartered Institute of Personnel and Development issued a statement on bullying to guide managers.

Fourthly, more effective legal remedies have become available since the *Porcelli* case in 1986. This concerned allegations of sexual harassment. The definition of sexual harassment as 'direct sex discrimination', accepted in this case, stimulated more serious consideration of both sexual harassment and, increasingly, other forms of harassment (*Porcelli* v *Strathclyde Regional Council* [1986] IRLR 134, Court of Session). Furthermore, the later removal of the ceiling on compensation in discrimination cases has concentrated the minds of many employers.

Finally, wider social concerns about the extreme manifestations of harassment (particularly racial and sexual) have been reflected in, for example, the Protection from Harassment Act 1997 and legislation on racial harassment and violence (Crime and Disorder Act 1998).

7.2.2   Definitions

Before we consider the context in which harassment and bullying arises we must try to define the terms. The distinction between harassment and bullying can be largely theoretical. The behaviour under each definition can, to a large extent, be the same. The element that differentiates the two terms is the grounds which prompts the behaviour. So, whilst harassment may be initiated purely for interpersonal reasons, it is normally for 'social' reasons. It is related to the victim's membership of a 'social group' and so concerns gender, sexuality, race, nationality, ethnic origin, religion, political affiliation, etc. The intention of the perpetrator is invariably to demean the victim. Bullying is more likely to be interpersonal. It may not necessarily relate to, for example, the victim's sex or race. Where it exists, it is likely (but not exclusively) to be part of a management style that is aggressive, overbearing, heavily critical, 'nit-picking', demeaning and intimidatory. It is invariably an abuse of power.

There are three principal elements in a definition of harassment and bullying:

1 Harassment concerns *behaviour*: this may be verbal or written, or involve gestures, looks or physical contact.

2 It is behaviour that is *unwanted* and viewed as unreasonable and offensive by the recipient.

3 The behaviour may be one act of *unacceptable* conduct or be persistent misconduct.

The incidence of harassment is difficult to measure. By its very nature, complaints may not be made for fear or humiliation, or because of denial. Furthermore, the legal processes may be daunting and the remedies uncertain and, perhaps, limited. Nevertheless, some surveys have attempted to quantify the most widespread form of harassment – that against women on grounds of sex. It is calculated, from various surveys, that over half of working women experience sexual harassment (Collier, 1995: 7). In certain heavily male-dominated workplaces, the incidence was considerably higher. The numbers of men reporting sexual harassment is usually below 25 per cent. Such surveys are of limited broad-brush value. They do not report on whether the employer is actively taking steps to tackle the problems, and they provide no perspective on the relative seriousness of incidents of harassment, nor do they indicate whether the problem is persistent.

7.3 The context

The origins of stereotyping, prejudice and discriminatory treatment have been explored in Chapter 4 on sex discrimination and Chapter 5 on race discrimination. The discussion here should be seen, in part, as a development of the issues raised earlier.

Many people – not least the victims – are frequently perplexed about the reasons for harassment. Why does it happen? Is there something 'wrong' with the victim? Is the perpetrator mentally ill? These are some of the questions that are, invariably, raised in respect of any specific incident.

From sociology, it is possible to construct a theoretical framework that attempts to explore the context of such behaviour. This involves looking at five areas: power relations, cultural factors, the characteristics of the workplace, the nature of the parties involved and the possible consequences.

7.3.1 **Power relations**

A key characteristic of social relationships is 'power' – whether it is formally or informally designated. Any social relationship involves a balance of power between the parties and the possible exercise of power by one person (or group of persons) over another. Clearly, those with power in any area of social life (e.g. the workplace, the police service, the criminal justice system, the medical profession, trade unions, etc.) will probably be reluctant to relinquish their power and the status and authority it confers.

Feminist social analysis has usefully contributed to our understanding of power relations by signalling their possible gender basis. Traditionally, in most aspects of social life, power structures have tended to be male dominated and so operated, predominantly, in the interests of men. It is also argued that, furthermore, these men tend to be white. Consequently, there is likely to be both a sex and a race bias within many organisations. In a society that is increasingly redefining the role and contribution of women and also acknowledging its multi-ethnic character tensions will, then, inevitably arise as existing power structures and relations are challenged. We have already discussed the workplace issues of vertical occupational segregation (in Chapter 4).

It is said by many commentators that all harassment is about power. Collier (1995: 27) argues from her experience as a counsellor and from a study of the literature that the common assumption that sexual harassment is about flirtation or about sex is incorrect. It too is about power. With some occasional exceptions, this is probably true.

7.3.2 **Cultural factors**

'Culture' refers to the values, the norms or standards and the traditions that exist in society at large or within particular groups in society. Clearly, tensions will exist when one group in society has different expectations and values from another. Culture is also a feature of workplace organisations where likewise traditions, values and standards exist. To illustrate the significance of culture, a workplace example can be taken from a recent report on the police service. One officer commented: 'Sexual harassment has always been an acceptable part of the police environment and any worthwhile female officer can deal with it herself and give as good as she gets' (Home Office, 1993).

This statement reflects a number of things. First, that the standards of 'acceptable' behaviour are determined by male police officers. Secondly, that this behaviour is in-built – it has 'always' been so. Thirdly, that the appropriate response is not to challenge the norms (the standards of behaviour) but to accept and 'give as good as you get'. Finally, there is no acknowledgement that the victim might be upset and need support. The implication is that a traditionally 'male' response is the only appropriate one in order to demonstrate that you are a 'worthwhile' officer – i.e. individual retaliation in kind.

This example illustrates the concept of a 'male reality' which involves a belief system whereby men and what men think and do constitute 'the norm' (Wise and Stanley, 1987: 81). As we saw in the earlier chapter on sex discrimination, this reality had and continues to have a profound effect on the ways in which work is organised and rewarded and on the extent to which non-work life is accommodated (to only a limited extent) by employers. Harassment is a weapon designed to preserve this 'reality'. It is designed to make people conform or quit. One further dimension of this 'reality' deserves comment. It is a heterosexual 'male reality'. This 'compulsory heterosexuality' (Collier, 1995: 36) is the foundation for much homophobia and hostility to transsexuals.

The question of 'difference' in values, norms and traditions that has been outlined above reflects the wider sociological concept of 'other'. This refers to the people who are not 'one of us'. They are 'one of them' or 'you people' or 'them'. They are an 'out' group. Invariably, such an 'out' group will be stereotyped. The wish to isolate yourself from the 'other' group can take various forms: special clubs and organisations; formal rules and informal practices to regulate entry into, for example, employment, or particular organisations or educational institutions. In extreme forms it can manifest itself in the development of racial ghettos, apartheid and 'ethnic cleansing'.

Harassment (in its varied forms), then, clearly plays its part in dealing with the 'other' group. It can be used to bring individuals into line and force them to comply with the prevailing cultural norms and standards. It can be used to exclude them from access to various opportunities by threats or the fear of intimidation. So, for example, sexual harassment 'plays an important role in society: maintaining a status quo' (Collier, 1995: 33).

7.3.3 The characteristics of the workplace

The social factors outlined above are reflected in any workplace. There will be a range of power relations. The culture of the organisation will reveal particular values, attitudes, norms and traditional practices. Various groups within the workforce may be marginalised and regarded as an 'other' or 'out' group. Essentially, there are three likely categories of perpetrators of harassment: managers/supervisors; individual fellow workers; and workgroups. These perpetrators, in their various ways, wish to preserve the existing situation. So, harassment may be used as a means of discouraging applications for promotion and breaking through 'the glass ceiling'. Also, various practices might be used to make working life sufficiently uncomfortable for individuals to leave.

Evidence from various tribunal cases and from research indicates that harassment can be particularly fierce where a 'different' person breaks through into a workgroup. So, some of the worst examples of sexual harassment have occurred in traditionally male-dominated employment: City of London financial institutions, the construction industry, the railways, the police service and the armed services. In these circumstances, the few women who are 'pioneers' have frequently been targeted. The nature of the harassment can and does cover the entire spectrum of possible behaviour.

So, for employers who wish to pursue effective anti-discrimination policies there are two equally important principal questions:

■ Are there appropriate procedures for dealing with individual complaints?

■ Does the culture of the organisation need changing?

The ability of employers to effect such changes is explored later, in section 7.5 on employment policies and practices and in Case study 7.1 (*see* below).

7.3.4 **The parties involved**

In harassment cases, there are two *principal* parties: the victim and the perpetrator(s). (The employer also is an associated 'party' because the employer is, in law, vicariously liable for the behaviour of the perpetrator.) Several questions need to be considered.

First of all, what is the nature of the relationship between the two principal parties? This can be a peer relationship or a power relationship. In the former, one work colleague is harassing another. In the second case, a more senior person is harassing a subordinate. This abuse of power is generally regarded as aggravating the offence. The victim is more vulnerable.

Secondly, is the harassment perpetrated by an individual or by a group? It is arguable that group harassment also aggravates an offence. Thirdly, what is the motivation for the harassment? It might be 'social' or 'personal'. In the former case, it is likely to concern power relations and/or the preservation of the existing culture. If it is 'personal', then, clearly, it could be an isolated incident. (For example, it might be a work colleague who stalks a fellow worker for sexual purposes.) In practice, of course, it is rare for this theoretical distinction to be maintained. Instances of harassment can well contain both aspects. Of course, as stated above, the most significant party is the recipient or victim. The victim defines 'harassment'. Strictly speaking, the motivation of the perpetrator is irrelevant. However, it is a factor when an employer considers how to deal with an allegation.

7.3.5 **Possible consequences**

For victims, there are four possible consequences deriving from incidents of harassment: action to tackle it, deliberate submission by the individual, denial of its occurrence and escape. Any of these consequences may be accompanied by symptoms of physical or mental illness and behaviour changes (for example, migraine, raised blood pressure, loss of appetite, inability to sleep, panic attacks, depression, increased consumption of tobacco or alcohol, becoming withdrawn).

Action, in the first instance, needs to be taken by the victim to report the incident to their employer. It is then incumbent on the employer to respond positively to investigate the complaint and take remedial action. As we will see later, the law now sets clear expectations upon how an employer should behave in these circumstances.

A victim may decide to submit rather than face the difficulties of making a complaint. The victim may isolate themselves from the harassment as far as practical; or behave in ways that the group wants. So, a person might be sufficiently discouraged from applying for training courses, or may keep out of the way of the work group at lunch breaks or tolerate or engage in sexist, racist or homophobic banter.

Linked with these tactics, to some extent, is denial – whereby the victim does not explicitly accept that they are being victimised and tries to ignore the harassment or attribute it to other motives. Finally, escape is often the most likely outcome. The victim resigns or is moved, by the organisation, to another job away from the perpetrator. As a solution, this does not tackle the fundamental source of the problem.

The consequence for an employer is described in the CIPD's *Statement on Harassment at Work* in the following terms:

> No employer should underestimate the damage, tension and conflict within the workplace which harassment creates. The result is not just poor morale but higher labour turnover, reduced productivity, lower efficiency and divided teams. Although the effects may be difficult to quantify, they will eventually show through in the performance of the organisation.

7.4   The legal framework

We will look at a number of legal themes: the contract of employment, European equal treatment legislation, direct discrimination and detriments, dismissal, liability for the harassment, action against the perpetrator, and possible remedies in law for the victim.

7.4.1   The contract of employment

Implied terms of the contract of employment are central to the issue of bullying and harassment. These are mutual trust and confidence and the duty to take reasonable care of the employee (*see also* Chapter 2). An employer told of bullying or harassing behaviour against an employee (by a supervisor, manager or fellow worker) has a duty to deal with the grievance promptly and properly. There may be concerns about the employee's health, safety and welfare. Failure to deal with the issue seriously is likely to be a repudiatory breach of the contract of employment. In such circumstances, the victim can resign and claim constructive dismissal. In their complaint, the employee might be alleging not only a breach of the contract but an infringement of discrimination law (*see* Fig. 7.1).

Soon after Ms Miles joined the double glazing department of Enterprise Glass, she began to be harassed by Mr Peake, the other employee in the department. He repeatedly made remarks of a suggestive or sexual kind which Ms Miles found offensive. Her initial complaint to Mr Cooper, a manager and director of the company, was met with the response that she should not worry. He said that it was just Mr Peake's way of encouraging her to settle in. The harassment continued and Ms Miles made a formal complaint to Mr Cooper. He said that he needed positive evidence that harassment was occurring. She taped a converstaion with Mr Peake. This satisfied Mr Cooper that she was telling the truth. In response he moved her temporarily to another department.

After a couple of weeks, pressure of work in the double glazing department was such that Ms Miles was moved back there again. At the same time, Mr Cooper told Mr Peake that the harassment must stop or he would be given a formal written warning which could lead to a second formal warning and eventual dismissal.

Shortly afterwards, Mr Peake was promoted to supervisor and began harassing Ms Miles again. She complained again to Mr Cooper. He said he was too busy to deal with the matter and that she should ignore Mr Peake's comments. The ill-feeling between Ms Miles and Mr Peake grew. Ms Miles could stand it no longer and resigned.

Figure 7.1   The case of Ms Miles

Source: Summarised from Employment Appeals Tribunal case 538/89.

7.4.2   **European equal treatment legislation**

In Britain, at the present time, there is no general statutory prohibition of harassment at work. However, a legal framework has evolved since the mid-1980s, through anti-discrimination case law, following a ruling in the Scottish Court of Session (*Strathclyde Regional Council* v *Porcelli* [1986] IRLR 134) on sexual harassment. This leading case has been followed by subsequent claims relating to **both** sexual and racial harassment allegations (under the appropriate legislation). In 1991, a contribution to this developing legal framework came from the European Community which adopted a Recommendation and a Code of Practice on 'the protection of the dignity of men and women at work'.

National courts of EU member states 'are bound to take Recommendations into consideration in order to decide disputes submitted to them, in particular where they clarify the interpretation of national provisions adopted in order to implement them or where they are designed to supplement Community measures' (*Grimaldi* v *Fonds des Maladies Professionelles* [1990] IRLR 400).

Given that (a) action against sexual harassment can now be taken under the Sex Discrimination Act 1975, (b) this legislation enacts the Equal Treatment Directive 1976 into British law and (c) the Recommendation concerning the dignity of men and women at work is in support of the principle of equal treatment, it is right that courts and tribunals in Britain use the European Recommendation and code of practice in considering sexual harassment claims.

Article 1 of the Recommendation sets the standard by which conduct is to be judged and refers to consequential disadvantages that a person might suffer.

> It is recommended that the Member State take action to promote awareness that conduct of a sexual nature, or other conduct based on sex affecting the dignity of women and men at work, including conduct of superiors and colleagues, is unacceptable if –
> (a) such conduct is unwanted, unreasonable and offensive to the recipient;
> (b) a person's rejection of or submission to such conduct on the part of employers or workers (including superiors or colleagues) is used explicitly or implicitly as a basis for a decision which affects that person's access to vocational training, access to employment, continued employment, promotion, salary or other employment decisions; and/or
> (c) such conduct creates an intimidating, hostile or humiliating work environment for the recipient; and that such conduct may, in certain circumstances, be contrary to the principle of equal treatment within the meaning of Articles 3, 4 and 5 of Directive 76/207/EEC.

This provision, then, creates a standard of acceptability that is determined by the victim. It is a subjective and uncertain standard. In the following discussion, we will consider how this standard has been used and developed.

The Race Directive 2000 and parts of the Employment Directive 2000 have provided some clarity in the definition of harassment. Amendments to the Race Relations Act 1976 and to the Disability Discrimination Act 1995 define harassment as behaviour which intentionally 'violates the dignity' of the individual person or 'creates an intimidating, hostile, degrading, humiliating or offensive environment' which will amount to harassment. It also encompasses behaviour which 'could reasonably be considered' as having these effects. Similar provisions are enacted in respect of harassment on the grounds of religion or belief (*draft* Employment

Equality (Religion or Belief) Regulations 2003) and sexual orientation (*draft* Employment Equality (Sexual Orientation) Regulations 2003). All these provisions are implemented into law in Britain at various dates during 2003. By 2005, a revised European Directive on Equal Treatment is to be implemented in member states. This encompasses formal provisions defining sexual harassment and outlawing it.

7.4.3   Direct discrimination and detriments

Case law on harassment (under the Sex Discrimination Act 1975 and the Race Relations Act 1976) has elaborated the legal framework. The Court of Session judgment in the *Porcelli* case outlined the issues to be considered. The principal consideration, reflecting the direct discrimination provisions, is whether it can be established that a person **on the grounds of their sex** has been treated **less favourably** than a person of the opposite sex and so has sustained a **detriment**.

In this case, Mrs Porcelli, a school science laboratory technician, complained that two male colleagues in the same department were harassing her with a view to making her apply for a transfer, which she did. The harassment took the form of persistent personal insults, obscene language, suggestive remarks and unwanted physical contact. The employer argued that the perpetrators would have behaved in the same way towards a male colleague whom they disliked. The court rejected this view, asserting that a man would not have been subject to such harassment which was of a particular sexual nature. It stated that there was unlawful direct sex discrimination and that Mrs Porcelli had suffered a detriment for which she was entitled to be compensated.

The *Porcelli* case involved a deliberate campaign. Now it is accepted that single incidents of unacceptable behaviour are sufficient to constitute a detriment – for example, an act of gross indecency (*Bracebridge Engineering Ltd* v *Darby* [1990] IRLR 3, EAT) and an offensive sexual remark (*Insitu Cleaning Company* v *Heads* [1995] IRLR 4, EAT). Such cases are in line with the subjective standard that the behaviour is 'unwanted, unreasonable and offensive to the recipient'.

However, there are some cases where it is clear that the court or tribunal introduces either its own standards of acceptability or what are, arguably, more objective standards. The Court of Appeal (in *de Souza* v *Automobile Association* [1986] IRLR 103) stated that 'racially to insult a coloured employee is not enough by itself even if that insult caused him or her distress; before that employee can be said to have been subjected to some "other detriment" the court or tribunal must find that by reason of the act or acts complained of a reasonable worker would or might take the view that he had thereby been disadvantaged in the circumstances on which he had thereafter to work'. So, distress is not automatically a detriment. However, this case seems to be out of line with more recent cases and the broad approach normally taken to the interpretation of "detriment".

In two other EAT cases, it was insufficient for the victims to complain about the perpetrator's alleged behaviour. Their own general attitudes to sexual behaviour and appropriate clothing were subject to cross-examination at the tribunals (*Snowball* v *Gardner Merchant Ltd* [1987] IRLR 397; *Wileman* v *Minilec Engineering Ltd* [1988] IRLR 144). The former case gives a tribunal chair discretion to admit such evidence if appropriate to establish whether or not a detriment has been sustained. In the second case, the EAT determined that the complainant had suffered no more than 'minor irritation' as a consequence of four years' alleged harassment by a director. So, the tribunal could take account of the way a person dressed at work. (In this case the complainant had worn scant and provocative clothing.)

Finally, a more recent case (*Stewart v Cleveland Guest Engineering Ltd* [1994] IRLR 440) illustrates the wider problems of trying to combat harassment through equal treatment law. Reflecting sex discrimination law (as indicated above in the *Porcelli* case), the issues to be considered are comparative treatment and disparate or neutral impact. The *Stewart* case illustrates these problem areas and, particularly, the choice of the right comparators.

The facts of the case are these: Miss Stewart was employed as an inspector in an engineering company. She was required as part of her responsibilities to visit the factory floor where a large number of calendars displaying nude women were on view. She complained to the works manager that she found these offensive and asked for them to be removed. Initially, he refused, saying that the complaint was trivial. Eventually, after Miss Stewart's trade union raised the issue, he ordered the calendars to be removed. It became known that Miss Stewart had made the initial complaint. When a deputation of women employees told management that they did not share her view about the calendars, she resigned, on the grounds that the employer could not protect her from embarassment and distress. A tribunal found that she had been constructively dismissed on the grounds that the employer was in breach of the duty of mutual trust and confidence. It found her dismissal unfair; but found no sex discrimination. The tribunal took the view that 'the display itself was neutral. A man might well find this sort of display as offensive as the applicant did.' So, it was concluded that she had not succeeded in establishing that she had been treated less favourably than a man would have been treated. The EAT upheld the tribunal decision on the narrow ground that it was not perverse.

The problems arising from this case are as follows:

■ Where behaviour might be equally offensive to both sexes, the exploration of comparison is inappropriate.

■ If, however, comparison is accepted, it might be argued that explicit sexual imagery is particularly offensive to women and that 'the psychological detriment to which they are subjected cannot, in this type of case, be equated with the offence felt by men' (Deakin and Morris, 1998: 605).

■ It might also be argued that the more appropriate comparison might have been the reaction of men to a display of pictures of nude men.

Whilst discrimination law has been interpreted as a means of taking action against sexual and racial harassment, it is an imperfect instrument. It has required, as we have seen, consideration of comparative treatment. Complaints invariably arise from subjectively determined standards of acceptability. Wider evidence on a complainant's 'lifestyle' can be used to challenge whether or not they genuinely regarded particular behaviour as 'unwanted, unreasonable and offensive'. Tribunals and courts can, on the evidence they have heard, substitute their view as to whether a complainant sustained a detriment or, alternatively, minor irritation or distress.

There are views that 'harassment should be seen as a free-standing employment wrong' (Deakin and Morris, 1998: 605). Certainly, as discussed earlier in this chapter, there are many grounds for harassment – some of which do not fit comfortably into the framework of equal treatment or race discrimination law. Any advance in protection is likely to derive from three, at present uncertain, routes: the interpretation of European equal treatment law, claims for repudiatory breach of a contract of employment and further legislative action within the European Union and within Britain.

A recent case involving the harassment of a person intending to undergo gender re-assignment (*Chessington World of Adventures* v *Reed* [1997] IRLR 556) signalled two important legal implications. First, no comparison is necessary under European equal treatment law; secondly, the 'principle of equal treatment' covers any discrimination on grounds of sex (*see also* Chapter 4).

7.4.4 Dismissal

Dismissal in respect of harassment can arise in three sets of circumstances:

1 Where a victim of sexual or racial harassment is sacked for failing to comply with the demands of the harasser.
2 Where the victim resigns because of the conduct of the harasser and the employer's failure to act.
3 Where the harasser is dismissed.

The first set of circumstances is covered by the normal unfair dismissal process; and a right to complain is not qualified by length of service, because it is related to the law on unfair discrimination. Proof needs to be established that the victim was dismissed within the meaning of 'dismissal' (ERA, s 95). The employer must show that the reason for the dismissal was for a specified 'fair' reason or for 'some other substantial reason' (ERA, s 98). The applicant will, however, contend that the reason or the principal reason was harassment (as direct discrimination).

The second set of circumstances arises by 'reason of the employer's conduct' (ERA, s 95(1)(c)). So, the employee terminates the contract of employment with or without notice. The employer's conduct is said to constitute a fundamental, that is repudiatory, breach of the contract of employment. This means that the employer has indicated that they do not wish to be bound by the essential terms of the contract. In sexual and racial harassment cases the essential term will be the implied mutual duty to maintain trust and confidence in the employment relationship. The complainant must show that there was not a long time-lapse between the alleged harassment and the resignation. The last of a series of apparently minor incidents can be said to justify resignation (*Lewis* v *Motorworld Garages Ltd* [1985] IRLR 465).

The third set of circumstances where dismissal might relate to harassment allegations is when an employer decides to sack the perpetrator. In this situation there should be explicit disciplinary rules against harassment, and it is important that the disciplinary procedures recommended in the ACAS statutory code be complied with. Where the perpetrator denies the allegation, the 'Burchell principles' (relating to misconduct) apply: the employer must have a genuine belief in the employee's guilt based on reasonable grounds following a reasonable investigation (*British Home Stores Ltd* v *Burchell* [1978] IRLR 379) (*see also* Chapter 9 on dismissal). Furthermore, determining the issue of 'reasonableness in the circumstances', the tribunal could be satisfied that the decision to dismiss was within 'the range of reasonable responses' open to an employer.

Raymondo Jones, whose mother was white and father was black, worked for the Tower Boot Company as a machine operative for one month until he resigned. During that time he was subjected to a number of incidents of racial harassment from work colleagues. One employee burnt his arm with a hot screwdriver; metal bolts were thrown at his head; his legs were whipped with a piece of welt; someone stuck a notice on his back bearing the words: 'Chipmonks are go'; and he was called names such as 'chimp', 'monkey' and 'baboon'.

Figure 7.2 The case of Raymondo Jones

7.4.5 Liability for the harassment

The issues affecting an employer's vicarious liability, in law, for harassment are those described in respect of sex discrimination, race discrimination and disability discrimination (*see* Chapters 4–6). Principally, these are whether the harassment took place 'in the course of employment' (SDA, s 41(1); RRA, s 32(1); DDA, s 58(1)), and whether the employer 'took such steps as were reasonably practicable' (SDA, s 41(3); RRA, s 32(3); DDA, s 58(5)) to deal with the harassment.

In an important racial harassment case (Fig. 7.2), the Court of Appeal has ruled on the provision concerning 'in the course of employment' (*Jones* v *Tower Boot Co Ltd* [1997] IRLR 68). It said that these words should be interpreted broadly in line with 'the natural meaning of those everyday words'.

By clearly defining 'in the course of employment', the court's decision means that employers will not be able to avoid legal liability for both the racial and sexual harassment of their employees by other employees by saying that it was not part of the perpetrator's job to harass and, therefore, the harassment was outside 'the course of employment'.

As indicated earlier, employers can have a defence against such allegations if they can show that they took such steps as were reasonably practicable to deal with incidents of harassment. The existence of effective equal opportunities policies and ancilliary policies against harassment would make a significant contribution towards an employer's defence.

A similar approach to liability is adopted in relation to harassment on the grounds of sexual orientation and religion or belief.

7.4.6 Harassment by third parties

Inevitably, discussion has focused on the employer–employee relationship. However, in the course of employment, employees may have dealings with contractors, suppliers or customers. An employer is liable for the treatment of employees during these contacts. As we saw earlier in this chapter, the Court of Appeal determined that the phrase 'in the course of employment' should be construed in a way that is commonly understood in everyday language (the *Tower Boot* case). Management are responsible for raising the issue with the third party. Such action could be used as evidence of taking 'reasonable steps' (*see* Fig. 7.3).

7.4.7 Action against the perpetrator

There are three broad courses of action that might be taken against the perpetrator of harassment: disciplinary action and dismissal, criminal proceedings and civil proceedings.

Freda Burton and Sonia Rhule were employed as waitresses at a private police social function. Both were African-Caribbean. They were subject to racial harassment during and after Bernard Manning's act . He made a number of very offensive racist and sexist remarks to the women as they were clearing tables. They were very upset by the remarks, the consequential banter from the predominantly male gathering and sexual harassment by some guests. They brought claims of racial discrimination against their employer because of the racial harassment they had experienced.

On the question of liabilty, the EAT held that the employer was liable for the harassment committed by the third party (Manning). It could have protected the women. It failed to instruct managers to watch the situation and withdraw the waitresses when it became unpleasant. It was established that the employer had control over the circumstances in which the harassment happened. The women were successful in their complaint.

Figure 7.3   Harassment by Bernard Manning

Source: Summarised from *Burton and Rhule* v *de Vere Hotels* [1996] IRLR 596.

Disciplinary action and dismissal

These can be invoked for the perpetrator's breach of workplace disciplinary rules. Many such rules specify that harassment is viewed as gross misconduct and, therefore, may result in dismissal. Furthermore, a harasser would be in breach of implied contractual terms (principally, mutual trust and confidence) and so, liable to disciplinary action. Any dismissal must comply with the appropriate standards of fairness. So, there must be a fair reason for the dismissal (i.e. misconduct); the decision to dismiss for that reason must be reasonable in all the circumstances of the case; and the dismissal must have been handled in a procedurally fair manner (*see* Chapter 9 on dismissal).

Criminal proceedings

These have always been possible against harassers. In such cases, the offending behaviour must be reported to the police who would investigate the complaint and, in turn, send the papers to the Crown Prosecution Service (CPS). The CPS would decide whether or not there were sufficient grounds for prosecution.

In the wide spectrum of harassment, some behaviour may be assault, grievous bodily harm, or acts of indecency, and prosecution may take place in the criminal courts. In 1997, additional legislation came into force: the Protection from Harassment Act 1997, the so-called 'anti-stalking' legislation. This has implications for harassment at work.

It creates two criminal offences:

- pursuing a course of conduct which amounts to harassment of another person, which the offender knows or ought to know amounts to harassment;
- pursuing a course of conduct which the offender knows or ought to know causes another person to fear that *violence* will be used against them.

A 'course of conduct' refers to conduct on at least two occasions (s 7(3)). 'Harassment' expressly includes 'alarming the person or causing the person distress' (s 7(2)). 'Conduct' includes speech (s 7(3)).

For the harassment offence, the offender does not have to intend to cause harassment. The prosecution has to prove only that the course of conduct occurred in circumstances where 'a reasonable person in possession of the same information would think the course of conduct amounted to harassment of the other' (s 1(2)). An offender, if guilty, can be fined up to £5000 and sentenced to a maximum prison sentence of six months. A court can also make a restraining order, limited in time or until further notice, to protect the victim.

Likewise for the more serious 'fear of violence' offence, the prosecution does not have to prove intention on the part of the offender. It is sufficient that the offender ought to have known that the course of conduct in question would have that effect. An offender guilty of this offence is liable to a prison sentence of up to five years or a fine or both. Again a restraining order can be made.

Civil proceedings

These are also extended under the Protection from Harassment Act 1997. Where there is 'actual or apprehended' harassment then the victim of the 'course of conduct' may be awarded damages (for anxiety and any financial loss resulting from the harassment) and an injunction. A warrant can be sought for breach of the injunction, without reasonable excuse.

7.4.8 Possible remedies in law for the victim

The outcomes under employment law, on discrimination and breach of contract, are the usual remedies for successful applicants (*see also* Chapters 4–6 on discrimination and Chapter 9 on dismissal).

Resignation (for breach of contract) and constructive dismissal claim

In successful cases the possible remedies are:

- compensation;
- an order for reinstatement or re-engagement (with which the employer may refuse to comply).

Discrimination claim

In successful cases the possible remedies are:

- compensation, which is unlimited (*see* Fig. 7.4);
- payment for injury to feelings;
- a declaration;
- an order for reinstatement or re-engagement (with which the employer may refuse to comply) if dismissal by the employer is involved in the harassment.

Mrs Fowles worked for a transport company for three years. During that time she was subject to sexual harassment and general bullying from the company directors. Both directors made offensive comments, sexual innuendos and sexual contact. The managing director was the main instigator of the behaviour. When she was attempting to contact her union representative about the harassment, she was dismissed.

The employment tribunal made awards against the two directors personally and no additional award against the company. The tribunal observed that, in reality, the directors were in control. She received loss of earnings and awards for injury to feelings of £5000 and £2500 from each of the directors.

Figure 7.4   Compensation against individual harassers

Source: Summarised from case no. 1701754/01.

7.5   Employment policies and practices

The policies and practices of employers for dealing with allegations of harassment at work will be influenced by four factors deriving from the law: their liability under anti-discrimination law, the requirement under this law to take such steps as are reasonably practical to deal with harassment, the consequences of repudiatory breaches of contracts of employment and their liability under discrimination law to pay unlimited compensation to a complainant.

As a consequence, various large companies have drafted harassment policies, often as adjuncts to the corporate equal opportunities policy. It is important to remember that the legal requirements cover all employers without exception. So, small and medium-sized enterprises have the same obligations. The 'reasonable steps' that they must take are the same in principle – although, obviously, in a different organisation context.

7.5.1   Defining harassment and bullying

It is not necessary or desirable to restrict the definition of 'harassment' to that deriving from discrimination law. It may be of a sexual or racial nature or it may be directed towards people because of their age, their sexuality, a disability, either physical or mental, or some other characteristic. Acts against property as well as a person may constitute harassment.

Some organisations extend their policy so that it explicitly covers work performance and may, arguably, be construed as an anti-bullying policy. So, harassment is defined as any repeated and unwanted verbal or physical advances, leering, ridicule, embarrassing or derogatory remarks made by an employee to another in the workplace which are offensive to the person involved which cause that person to feel threatened, humiliated, patronised or harassed or which interfere with the person's job performance, undermine job security or create a threatening or intimidating work environment. It encompasses various forms of electronic communications: text messages; e-mail messages; and internet sites.

7.5.2 Who might be possible victims?

It is clearly impossible to identify the full range of possible victims of harassment. However, common sense, experience and knowledge of previous tribunal cases might suggest to employers both certain categories of people who might be vulnerable; and also certain situations where harassment might be attempted – particularly, but not necessarily, in respect of power relationships.

The Equal Opportunities Commission research (*see* analysis of employment tribunal cases on the EOC website, www.eoc.org.uk), in respect of sexual harassment has pointed to people who were most likely to be victims. These were: women who were divorced or separated; a young woman who has been in a job for less than a year; a woman who is working in a non-traditional job (i.e. in a male-dominated work group); someone in a low-paid job (e.g. carer, shopworker, factory worker and/or who works shifts); or a lesbian or homosexual man.

7.5.3 Approach to allegations of harassment and bullying

The approach to harassment at work will reflect the corporate culture and signal (to all staff and managers) the seriousness with which the issue is treated. A key issue is whether it should be corrective rather than punitive with the broad aim to encourage improvement in conduct. This reflects the approach recommended by ACAS to disciplinary action in its *Code of Practice* on disciplinary procedures (ACAS, 2000: para 8). Of course, there may be serious incidents of harassment when only a punitive approach is appropriate.

In dealing with specific allegations the importance of confidentiality and sensitivity is strongly recommended. In the investigatory process, the career and reputation of either party should not be unjustly affected. This is an essential warning against pre-judging matters and in favour of objectivity.

Some policies advocate confronting harassers and 'warning them off'. This could involve a direct approach (verbally or in writing) to the harasser by the victim stating that the behaviour is unacceptable and should stop. A colleague might be used if direct confrontation is too difficult or embarrassing. The use of this approach can be difficult. Much will depend on the circumstances: for example, the employment relationship between the harasser and victim, and the confidence of the victim.

Underlying many policies is a preference for resolving issues as soon as possible. Invariably at the start informal approaches are advocated (unless the issue is too serious). Generally, escalation of the issue through the grievance and disciplinary procedures is discouraged.

7.5.4 Managerial roles and responsibilities

Policies to tackle harassment at work should contribute to the nature of corporate culture – and particularly the values that are seen as important. Against this background, senior management commitment is essential to ensure that policies are properly formulated, implemented and monitored. Obviously, the prevention of harassment should be the primary objective. This involves setting clear standards of acceptable behaviour. Where incidents do occur then line (or operational) managers or supervisors have the responsibility to deal promptly and effectively with complaints. Evidence of effective managerial action in dealing with harassment can be cited at a tribunal as evidence of an employer taking 'such steps as are reasonably practical' for dealing with harassment relating to discrimination law. Managerial action or inaction is critical to the issue of employer liability and the likelihood of an employer being required to pay unlimited compensation. Senior management have a responsibility for ensuring that operational managers and supervisors are equipped to respond appropriately (*see* the discussion on training below).

7.5.5 Informal procedures and counselling

The general predisposition towards a corrective approach and against the procedural escalation of complaints leads most large companies to favour an informal initial step, often linked to counselling. Counsellors or harassment advisers are invariably drawn from existing employees (attempting to reflect the organisation's gender and ethnic profile). It is a client-led approach, whereby the complainant drives the issue as far as they wish.

The counsellor should:

- listen to what has happened;
- help and support the person to deal with the emotions that arise;
- draw attention to whatever formal or informal action is available;
- assist in filing a grievance, as necessary, and if required by the victim;
- assist in informing management, if desired;
- support the employee through the grievance procedure.

Clearly, the role is one of facilitation.

This role could also be played by the personnel department, by nursing and medical staff and the employer's occupational health service, or by equal opportunities officers. Line managers can be the recipient of complaints (unless, of course, the complaint is against this manager). All these groups could be acceptable for hearing initial complaints, subject to appropriate training and briefing.

The outcome of this initial stage should be the identification of certain factual information. A record might include answers to the following questions: When did the harassment start? What happened? Were there any witnesses? Were there any threats of reprisals? What did the complainant do?

7.5.6 Role of grievance procedure

Following this informal process, it might be appropriate, in the circumstances, to lodge a formal grievance against the harasser. This will probably depend on whether the harassment is persistent or serious.

7.5.7 Training

There are several areas where training is essential to support an effective anti-harassment policy. The participants in the complaints procedures (counsellors, managers and supervisors) need to be equipped with appropriate listening and diagnostic skills. This should be associated with awareness training and an understanding of the contribution the policy makes to wider corporate objectives.

7.5.8 Communications

Associated with training, the policy and procedures need to be communicated (verbally and in writing) to all staff – at induction into the organisation and reinforced subsequently.

7.5.9 Role of disciplinary action

The disciplinary process can contribute to anti-harassment policies in a number of ways: the setting of standards, the nature of the disciplinary process and defining the penalties to be used.

First, the disciplinary rules should set clear **standards of acceptable conduct**. Harassment is invariably defined as gross misconduct. Harassment by a supervisor or manager will probably be seen as an aggravating factor. The disciplinary rules should also state that victimisation or threats of retaliation against a complainant will be regarded as a serious offence.

Secondly, the disciplinary procedure used against the alleged harasser will be the normal one, which should conform to the **standards of procedural fairness** prescribed in the ACAS *Code of Practice*. The investigation stage is particularly important and evidence drawn out in the informal/counselling stage will be relevant. It may be appropriate to suspend the harasser on full pay pending the investigation.

Thirdly, there is the imposition of **penalties**. An employer may aim to deal with harassment by corrective rather than punitive measures. However, sanctions are particularly important when corrective measures have failed or when the harassment is so serious that punishment is the right outcome. Disciplinary penalties deal not merely with the consequences of a specific complaint. They send a signal to the wider workforce that the anti-harassment policy will be enforced. Consequently, they should reinforce acceptable standards of practice.

The most serious penalties that can be used are dismissal or a disciplinary transfer. The purpose of the first is clearly to punish the harasser. The second involves punishment but enables the harasser to remain in employment. Clearly, every effort should be made to move the harasser and not the victim, unless it is the victim's wish to move. If an employer is using either of these sanctions, then they might be liable for an unfair dismissal claim or an allegation of breach of contract (for the disciplinary transfer).

Finally, disciplinary action can reinforce the confidentiality necessary to make harassment procedures work effectively. Breaches can be dealt with. Such confidentiality is important for both the victim and the alleged harasser.

7.5.10 Consultation with trade unions

In those organisations where trade unions are recognised for collective bargaining and consultation, it is helpful to discuss the formulation, implementation and monitoring with the union(s). It can lend more credibility to the policy and, probably, ensure more effective enforcement. It is recommended in the equal opportunities codes that unions have an important contribution to make in eradicating discrimination (CRE Code: para 3.16; EOC Code: paras 6–8). These codes provide an over-arching framework for policies on harassment. So, by logical extension, union involvement is desirable, if not essential.

7.5.11 Monitoring

It is commonplace to say that policies need to be monitored to ensure effectiveness. The evidence of equal opportunities policies is that, frequently, they are not. In respect of harassment three sources of information are important: that which comes from specific cases (where the circumstances and outcomes are recorded); information from exit interviews; and informal records of incidents that are not formally raised. For a harassment policy to have credibility, then, there should be periodic review either by management or jointly with unions.

7.6 Conclusions

The law on harassment at work, at present, can be complex and uncertain and also patchy in its coverage. It derives, as we have seen, from creative case law in respect of discrimination law and implied contractual terms. European law, as it develops in the next few years, should create a firmer legal base for dealing with the issue.

Case study 7.1

The organisation

Moneybrokers act as independent intermediaries between two financial institutions, usually banks, assisting them in buying or selling money products on the wholesale money market. This market is not located in any one place as participants communicate through a global network of telecommunications and computer links. A moneybroker acts like an auctioneer between the client and other market participants, communicating bid and offer prices at high speeds. Millions of pounds can be transacted in a matter of seconds.

The moneybrokers

The brokers in broking houses and banks, as in the money market generally, are predominantly white men. There are few female brokers (mostly in junior grades), and about 1 per cent are of non-white ethnic origin. (Overall, women are concentrated in non-management grades.)

Brokers work in teams in extremely pressurised and cramped conditions with up to 50 people in one small area. When the market is busy, it is a frenzied, noisy environment with brokers shouting prices at each other and at clients. They work long hours (nine per day plus evening entertainment). They rarely sustain their career beyond 45 years of age. Where they do, they usually move into management but retire at 55 years.

The issue

This close team environment breeds familiarity, friendships and, because there are few women, a 'laddish' culture. Brokers both talk openly and joke about their latest sexual conquests and physical attributes. Cartoons and pornographic pictures are adapted to depict fellow staff and are circulated. Everyone has a nickname which can usually be related to their physique, religion, race or personality. Pin-ups of

▶

women and some nudes are displayed in the dealing rooms. Women, who are in the back-office area, commonly hear sexual remarks and innuendos.

The motivation for this behaviour is varied. It can be to have 'fun'. So, 'bad' language, playing pranks and jokes on colleagues are seen as part of everyday life. Sometimes the pressure of the job leads to loss of tempers, to the use of foul and abusive language and to what could be perceived as crude behaviour among the brokers – particularly when a deal goes wrong. (This is not intentionally offensive. If it is so, it is only meant to be short-lived and is soon forgiven.) On other occasions, the purpose is to vent anger at subordinates or to teach them not to repeat mistakes and to 'toughen' junior staff to make them better brokers. Sometimes unruly behaviour can be triggered by a broker after a 'boozy' client lunch.

The situation is compounded by the fact that departmental managers are brokers promoted because of their broking expertise. However, they have had no management or discrimination awareness training. The overwhelming majority have not read the company's equal opportunities policy. So, if someone reacts badly the usual view is that they can't handle pressure. Indeed 80 per cent or more of the managers do not consider foul language, verbal abuse when tempers fray or 'exclusion from a group on grounds of sex or race' as forms of harassment. They are seen as typical of the working environment. Nevertheless, just over 40 per cent of managers have received complaints about harassment. The personnel department has recorded seven complaints in the past five years. In only one case did the dismissal of a broker result. The company is concerned that someone may claim racial or sexual harassment at an employment tribunal.

Company policies

An equal opportunities and harassment policy was adopted in 1990. This was incorporated into employees' contracts in 1993 and staff have to acknowledge in writing their acceptance of their terms and conditions of employment. The company undertakes to do everything possible to prevent harassment of any kind and to deal with all complaints in a serious, sensitive and speedy fashion. It is stated in the policy that 'boisterous' behaviour is a normal part of the broking environment. However, the policy differentiates between this and harassment, which is where someone is made to feel 'demeaned or threatened'. The policy covers behaviour during working time, client entertainment or at other events.

Supervisors and managers are responsible for implementing the policy and for reporting harassment even before a complaint is made. They are expected to seek advice from the personnel manager in all instances. The procedure provides for a thorough investigation within five working days. They are required to remind staff of the standard of behaviour that is expected. Perpetrators of harassment will be dealt with under the normal disciplinary procedure. Action can involve (subject to appeal) transfer, demotion or summary dismissal.

Exercise 7.1

1 What recommendations would you make to the company about ways of minimising workplace harassment by tackling the culture of the organisation?

2 What obstacles might impede the implementation of your recommendations? How might you overcome these obstacles?

Feedback on this exercise is provided in the Appendix to this book.

Further reading

Advisory Conciliation and Arbitration Service (2000) *Code of Practice: Disciplinary and Grievance Procedures*. London: ACAS.

Chartered Institute of Personnel and Development (1992) *Statement on Harassment at Work*. London: CIPD.

European Community (1991) Recommendation on the protection of the dignity of men and women at work (91/131/EEC).

European Community (1991) *Code of Practice on Protecting the Dignity of Men and Women at Work*. Luxembourg: EC.

References

Collier, R. (1995) *Combating Sexual Harassment in the Workplace*. Buckingham: Open University Press.

Deakin, S. and Morris, G. (1998) *Labour Law*. London: Butterworths.

Home Office, Police Department (1993) *Aspects of Sex Discrimination within the Police Service*. London: Home Office.

Wise, S. and Stanley, L. (1987) *Georgie Porgie: Sexual Harassment in Everyday Life*. London: Pandora Press.

Information, privacy and surveillance

Having read this chapter you should be able to:

■ Understand the outline framework of law governing information collection, storage and disclosure; privacy; and surveillance in the workplace.

■ Understand the rights of individual employees and the remedies available to them.

■ Recommend policies and practices that might be adopted by an employer to comply with the legislation.

8.1 Structure of chapter

This chapter comprises the following sections:

■ *Introduction*: The significance of a developing area of legislation, including compatibility with the European Convention on Human Rights.

■ *The context*: Technological change; social values and human rights; economic and security considerations.

■ *The legal framework*: Data Protection Act 1998 – the principles, the parties involved, defining data, processing data, the role of the Information Commissioner, enforcement action; privacy and surveillance; 'whistleblowing' and public interest disclosure legislation.

■ *Employment policies and practices*: The implications of the data protection Codes of Practice.

8.2   Introduction

Over the past twenty years or so, concern has grown about the acquisition, strorage and use of information relating to individual working people. Examples have occurred of some employers blacklisting some job applicants because of their trade union membership (Hollingsworth and Norton-Taylor, 1988; Hollingsworth and Tremayne, 1989). Such concerns can extend to complaints of victimisation and less favourable treatment being meted out to individuals. Alongside these anxieties, technological developments have created opportunities for more extensive surveillance of staff in the work environment – perhaps with concern about the potential for disciplinary action. So, within the workplace, an important issue is about the boundaries of privacy. This has been given added impetus by the incorporation, through the Human Rights Act 1998, of the European Convention on Human Rights and Fundamental Freedoms 1950. This enshrines, under Article 8, a right of privacy – albeit a qualified right (*see* Chapter 1).

This chapter aims to explore these essential issues: the protection of individual workers from the misuse of data about themselves; the issue of privacy in the workplace; and those rights of working people (not explored elsewhere in the text) to disclose information about their employer for specific 'public interest' purposes. As an area of law it is complex. Several Acts of Parliament are relevant and, arguably, cut across each other in certain respects. Consequently, the purpose is to set out the essentials that should guide a human resource practitioner.

8.3   The context

The issues of data protection, privacy and surveillance are, obviously, a matter of wide social concern affecting all walks of life in addition to the workplace. Our focus in this chapter is primarily on issues affecting employment relations. However, it is worth reflecting briefly on the wider context.

There are three broad factors involved: the ever-evolving capacity of technology to monitor, store and process information; the economic interests of employers; and social values, about privacy and about security. Consequently, tensions and conflicts of interest inevitably arise – particularly between economic and security interests and social values. The issue in each workplace is how to reconcile the tensions. In the wider society the question is how to strike a balance that is appropriate in a liberal democratic society. Some of the contextual issues are considered below.

8.3.1   Technological developments

It is a commonplace to say that the speed of technological change is considerable. The size and capacity of computers for storing and processing data have developed radically in the past thirty years. Alongside this there have been many innovations in surveillance technology. Some sound as though they should feature in James Bond films. Nevertheless, they are real. For example, 'window bouncers' can, without breaking and entering premises, aim a laser beam at a window to pick up vibrations of sounds inside. These are then translated, amplified and listened to. Secondly, 'keystroke logging' is available. This allows other people to read messages that an individual types by means of incorporation into software packages. It intercepts keystrokes to record what is typed and sends the information to the eavesdropper. Thirdly, in motor vehicles, devices can record or transmit information on the location of the vehicle, the distance it has travelled and information on the driver's driving habits. Finally, swipe cards on entrances to buildings can be read to track all the movements of an employee within the premises. So rapid is the pace of change, it has led commentators to observe that it is difficult for the law to keep up with it.

8.3.2 Social values and human rights

This technological change is taking place, in liberal democracies, against a background of growing concern about the issue of human rights and, within that framework, privacy. This is outlined, but not defined, in the European Convention on Human Rights and Fundamental Freedoms 1950. Article 8 states that 'everyone has the right to respect for his private and family life, his home and his correspondence'. But this does not define privacy. It refers to 'private life' and case law has shown that this can exist in the workplace as well as at home. It refers to 'correspondence', which embraces electronic communications as well as letters. It is not suggested that personal 'correspondence' at work is automatically excluded from the provisions of the Convention. There is an assumption behind the Article that some balance will be recognised by employers and working people and will be implemented. (*See* later section in this chapter.)

Implicit, perhaps, in this notion of privacy is the concept of 'dignity'. A person who is subject to intrusion and surveillance is in an undignified position. In this context, it is interesting to quote an American judge, who in that jurisdiction some thirty years ago, put the situation in this way:

> The [constant filming by CCTV] is not only personally repugnant to employees but it has such an inhibiting effect as to prevent the employees from performing their work with confidence and ease. Every employee has occasion to pause in the course of his work, to take a breather, to scratch his head, to yawn, or otherwise be himself without affecting his work. An employee, with reason, would hesitate at all times to so behave if his every action is being recorded on TV. To have workers constantly televised is . . . reminiscent of the era depicted by Charlie Chaplin in 'Modern Times' and constitutes . . . an affront to the dignity of man. (US judge in case: *Re Electronics Instrument Company and International Union of Electrical Workers* (1965) LA563.)

In the UK, the general public attitude to privacy can be ambivalent. Much depends on the context and the prevailing political climate. For example, in July 2002, in an ICM Research survey published in the *Guardian*, 72 per cent said that 'giving up some privacy is necessary to fight terrorism and crime'. In a time of actual terrorist threats this might be understandable. The degree of privacy that should be sacrificed was not, however, explored. Two other statistics reflected more general concern about the preservation of privacy. Only 26 per cent agreed that 'the government can be trusted to keep our personal information secure'; and 66 per cent agreed with the statement that 'I am worried about the security of my personal information travelling on the internet and email' (*Guardian*, 7 September 2002).

The potential for invading privacy is considerable. For example, there is a continuing blurring of the distinction between work and private/home life as more working people are 'home based'. Equipment like cars, mobile phones and computers may be used for both work and personal life. In other areas there is the potential for the intrusive testing of individuals, including medical/genetic testing, and testing for alcohol or drugs and the consequent use of these data by employers.

Clearly, there are issues of balance to be struck here – between the need to intrude into an individual's privacy and the individual's right to protect that privacy. Indeed, the right under Article 8 of the Convention is not absolute. It is a qualified right. There can be circumstances in which it can be 'interfered with'. Among those reasons are public safety, the prevention of crime and the economic well-being of the country.

In the workplace, the economic well-being of an employer's business is also a factor to be considered. The Information Commissioner in the preamble to the draft Code of Practice on Monitoring at Work (*see* section 8.5) comments that 'monitoring is a recognised component of the employer–worker relationship. Most employers will make some checks on the quantity and quality of work produced by workers. Workers will generally expect this. Some employers may carry out monitoring to safeguard workers as well as to protect their own interests or those of their customers' (Section 2). However, it is suggested by the Commissioner that 'continuous video or audio monitoring is particularly intrusive for workers. The two combined are even more intrusive. The circumstances in which continuous monitoring is justified are likely to be rare, for example in particularly hazardous environments such as refineries or nuclear power-stations or where security is at risk.' In addition the Commissioner sets out the principle of 'proportionality'. There should be '[a] presumption that workers are entitled to keep their private lives private and that employers should not intrude into this unless they face a real risk to which the intrusion is a proportionate response'.

8.3.3 Economic and security considerations

The balance that should be struck between privacy and economic and security considerations will depend on the circumstances of the business. Similarly, the processing, recording, storage and use of data is again dependent on the circumstances. Among the factors that might justify an employer taking particular courses of action (through monitoring or collecting data) are the following:

- to preserve confidentiality of business transactions;
- to ensure secrecy in research and development activities;
- to ensure the security of plant, equipment and staff – e.g. from attempted criminal or terrorist action;
- to protect staff from harassment and violence;
- to ensure that staff are suitably qualified and complying with accepted standards;
- to vet job applicants where the issue of client or public protection is essential.

8.4 The legal framework

8.4.1 The Data Protection Act 1998

The European Data Protection Directive 1995 was transposed into UK law through the Data Protection Act 1998. The Act came into force on 1 March 2000, repealing the Data Protection Act 1984. The new legislation contained transitional provisions. The first and most extensive phase was completed on 23 October 2001. The second phase will be completed on 23 October 2007. Effectively, the legislation is virtually fully implemented. The second transitional phase covers some manual files. However, from October 2001, all processing of automated or manual data must fully comply with the provisions of the 1998 Act.

The data protection principles

The Data Protection Act 1998 sets out eight principles with which an organisation must comply (*see* Fig. 8.1). They govern how any personal data (including sensitive personal data) must be processed. All data controllers are under a duty to comply with the Principles.

Who are the parties involved?

There are several parties or 'roles' referred to in the legislation: the data subject; the data controller; the data processor; the recipient; and a third party.

- *The data subject*: This is the living individual (whether or not a UK resident or national) who is the subject of the data. In the employment context, the subject is most likely to be a 'worker'. However, this term is more wide-ranging

---

- Principle 1: personal data must be processed fairly and lawfully.
- Principle 2: personal data must be obtained only for one or more specified and lawful purposes and must not be processed in a way that is incompatible with that purpose or those purposes.
- Principle 3: personal data must be adequate, relevant and not excessive.
- Principle 4: personal data must be accurate and, where necessary kept up to date.
- Principle 5: personal data must not be kept for longer than is necessary for their purpose.
- Principle 6: personal data must be processed in accordance with the rights of the data subjects.
- Principle 7: appropriate technical and organisational measures must be taken against unauthorised or unlawful processing and against accidental loss, destruction or damage to personal data.
- Principle 8: personal data must not be transferred to a country or territory outside the European Economic Area unless that country or territory ensures an adequate level of protection of the rights and freedoms of data subjects in relation to processing of personal data.

Figure 8.1 The data protection principles

Source: Data Protection Act 1998, Sch 1.

than that used elsewhere in other employment legislation. As defined in the *Employment Practices Data Protection* Code of Practice (issued for consultation in December 2001), the term covers any individual who applies to work, does work or did work for an employer. Essentially, the term covers current and previous job applicants (successful or not); employees (current and previous); and the range of agency, casual and contract workers who may not be defined, under law, as an 'employee' but as a 'worker' (*see* Chapter 2). A data subject *cannot* be a company or an incorporated or unincorporated body.

- *The data controller*: This is a 'person' (i.e. a legal 'person'). It encompasses organisations, companies, incorporated and unincorporated bodies. This 'person' decides the purposes for which personal data are to be processed; and the ways in which they are to be processed. In doing this, the person may act jointly with others. So, employers are likely to be data controllers for the purposes of the legislation. Data controllers should be registered with the Office of the Information Commissioner. They must abide by the data protection principles (*see* Fig. 8.1); and observe the rights of data subjects.

- *The data processor*: This is the legal person who acts on behalf of the data controller. It can be an agency or contractor but not an employee of the data controller. The controller retains full responsibility for the actions of the processor.

- *The recipient*: This is the person to whom the information is disclosed. This terms encompasses employees or agents of the data controller; and any data processor and its employees or agents.

- *A third party*: This refers to any other person apart from those outlined above.

Which data are covered?

In the legislation, *data* is described as information. This information can be:

- Processed by means of equipment operating automatically in response to instructions given for that purpose. (It also includes information that is recorded with a view to processing.) The term 'automated systems' covers all types of computers including mainframe, hand-held and laptop computers and organisers. In addition it includes microfiche and microfilm, audio and video systems.

- Manual data that are part of a relevant filing system or recorded to become part of such a system.

- Accessible records which would include, for example, health records.

The legislation also defines '*personal data*'. Personal data must relate to a 'living individual' who is capable of being identified. They are data which are in the possession of the data controller or likely to come into its possession. They include 'any expression of opinion about the individual and any indication of the intentions of the data controller or any other person in respect of that individual'. So, for example, a job applicant will have data recorded about them arising from the sifting process and an interview. The data will be held by the 'data controller' (i.e. the employer). The data are likely to include a view (i.e. 'an expression of opinion') about suitability for the post. Further guidance on this is provided in

- Details of a worker's salary and bank account on an organisation's computer system or in a manual filing system.
- E-mail messages about incidents involving named workers.
- A supervisor's or manager's notebook containing sections on several named individuals.
- A supervisor's or manager's notebook containing information on only one individual but where it is intended to put the information on the worker's file.

Figure 8.2 Personal data in the workplace

the Code of Practice (*see also* Fig. 8.2). Guidance from the Information Commissioner indicates that knowledge of the individual's 'identity' does not have to rely on possession of their name and address. For example, CCTV tapes may be sufficent to match the image of an individual with the person, a description of them or a photograph. Although not necessarily an easy process, 'anonymisation' of personal data is advised where person identifiers are not necessary for the processing of particular information.

'*Sensitive personal data*' comprises information on the 'data subject' covering their racial or ethnic origin, political opinions, religious or similar beliefs, union membership, physical or mental health, sex life, criminal offences or alleged offences or other legal proceedings.

What is 'processing'?

The term 'processing' in the legislation means the following:

- obtaining, recording or holding information or data;
- carrying out any operation or set of operations on the information or data, including organising, adapting or altering them;
- retrieving, consulting or using the information or data;
- disclosing the information or data by transmitting, disseminating or otherwise making them available; or
- aligning, combining, blocking, erasing or destroying the information or data.

The rights of 'data subjects'

Under the Data Protection Act 1998, the following rights exist for data subjects:

- *The right of subject access* (ss 7–8): An individual who has made a written request to a data controller (and paid any appropriate fee, if charged) is entitled to be told whether the data controller (or someone on its behalf) is processing that individual's personal data. If this is so, the data subject is entitled to a description of the personal data; the purposes for which they are being processed and those to whom the data are or may be disclosed. The individual is also entitled to have a copy of all information which constitutes their personal data. This information should be in intelligible form. If producing information involves a disproportionate effort, then, some other form can be agreed. The data controller must comply quickly and within 40 days of receiving the request.

- *The right to prevent processing causing damage or distress* (s 10): An individual who believes that a data controller is processing personal data that cause (or are likely to cause) substantial unwarranted damage or distress may send a 'data subject notice' to the data controller requiring it to stop processing the information within a reasonable time. The data subject must specify their reasons for believing substantial unwarranted damage or distress will be caused. The data controller should within 21 days state in writing whether it is complying with the notice in full or in part or not at all. (In certain circumstances – for example, where the data controller has to comply with a legal obligation – the individual is not entitled to serve a 'data subject notice'.) An individual may seek a court order to require a data controller to comply with the notice. An individual also may ask the Information Commissioner to make an 'assessment' (*see* discussion below).

- *Rights relating to automated decision-making* (s 12): An individual may require the data controller, in writing, to ensure that no decision significantly affecting them is based solely on the processing by automatic means of personal data. This provision covers any evaluation of the individual's performance at work, reliability and conduct. However, certain exceptions to the right are indicated.

- *The right to compensation* (s 13): An individual who suffers damage or damage and distress as a result of the data controller breaching the Data Protection Act is entitled to compensation. The data controller may have a defence if it can establish that it took such care as was reasonably required in all the circumstances to comply with the requirement concerned.

- *The right to rectify, block, erase or destroy inaccurate data* (ss 12A and 14): In circumstances where data are inaccurate, the data subject may apply to a court for an order to rectify, block, erase or destroy inaccurate data relating to them. The court may order the data controller to notify third parties to whom the data have been disclosed of the action to be taken.

The role of the Information Commissioner

Formerly, the Information Commissioner was known as the Data Protection Commissioner. The title of the office was changed in 2000. The Commissioner has several principal functions. First, the Commissioner is empowered to take enforcement action against 'data controllers' who are in breach of the data protection principles (*see* Fig. 8.1). In respect of enforcing data protection in the workplace, the Commissioner has issued the *Employment Practices Data Protection* Code of Practice. This encompasses various 'benchmarks' that will guide enforcement action (*see* section 8.5 on employment policies and practices). Secondly, a 'data subject' may complain to the Commissioner that the data protection principles are not being complied with in a particular case. The Commissioner may investigate by initiating an assessment (DPA 1998, s 42). Thirdly, the Commission is under a statutory duty (DPA 1998, s 51) to promote and disseminate good practice – which includes the preparation of codes of practice. Fourthly, the Commissioner must maintain a register of data controllers who are required to notify their data processing.

Enforcement action

This comprises the serving of an Information Notice and an Enforcement Notice by the Information Commissioner; and also requests by data subjects for an assessment.

- *The Enforcement Notice*: This is served on a data controller (e.g. an employer). It requires the data controller to stop processing any personal data or any specified personal data; or processing it in a specified manner. The Commissioner, in deciding whether to serve the notice, must consider whether damage or distress has been caused (or is likely to be caused) to the person in question (i.e. the 'data subject'). If the data controller appeals to the Information Tribunal, then, the enforcement notice is suspended (DPA 1998, s 48).

- *A request for an assessment*: This may be made by a person (a 'data subject') who is, or believes, themselves to be directly affected by the processing of personal data. Essentially, the request is for the Information Commissioner to assess whether it is likely or unlikely that the processing has been or is being carried out in compliance with the Act.

- *The Information Notice*: This is served by the Commissioner on a 'data controller'. It specifies the information required, within a given period of time, in order to respond to a request for an assessment; or to decide whether the data protection principles have been complied with. Appeal can be made to the Information Tribunal (DPA 1998, s 48).

- *Appeals*: Appeals from the Information Tribunal on points of law are possible to the High Court in England and Wales; the Court of Session in Scotland; and the High Court in Northern Ireland.

- *Compliance with a notice*: Non-compliance is an offence (DPA 1998, s 47). The defence is that the person exercised due diligence to comply with the notice.

8.4.2 Privacy and surveillance

The issue of privacy and surveillance covers 'personal data' and 'sensitive personal data' under the Data Protection Act 1998 (as outlined above). It also covers the surveillance of working people. The Data Protection Act 1998 applies to monitoring where data is recorded. The process of interception of electronic communications is covered by the Human Rights Act 1998; the Regulation of Investigatory Powers Act 2000; and the Telecommunications (Lawful Business Practice) (Interception of Communications) Regulations 2000. Such electronic communications are, for example, telephone calls, fax transmissions, e-mails, internet access.

Clearly, privacy is an important workplace issue. Employers need to consider carefully the degree of surveillance and the justification for it. Also, they need to inform those who are subject to surveillance that it is taking place – unless there are very strong reasons why this is not done. The issue of proportionality arises. Intrusion into an employee's privacy should be in proportion to the benefits (economic and otherwise) that an employer is likely to obtain from the monitoring.

Human Rights Act 1998

This legislation incorporates the European Convention on Human Rights and Fundamental Freedoms 1950 into the law of the United Kingdom (*see also* Chapter 1). Article 8 of the Convention confers the following right: 'everyone has the right to respect for his private and family life, his home and his correspondence'. This is often referred to, in shorthand, as the 'right of privacy'. It is a qualified and not an absolute right. The second part of Article 8 states that:

> there shall be no interference by a public authority with the exercise of this right except such as is in accordance with the law and is necessary in a democratic society in the interests of national security, public safety or the economic well-being of the country, for the prevention of disorder or crime, for the protection of health or morals, or for the protection of the rights and freedoms of others.

Clearly, such 'interference' with the 'right of privacy' by public authorities would cover circumstances where, for example, the safety of vulnerable individuals was at risk. As stated in Chapter 1, such interference must:

■ be provided for in law (e.g. through some other piece of legislation);

■ fulfil a pressing social need (e.g. protecting people from harassment);

■ pursue a legitimate aim (e.g. preventing criminal behaviour);

■ be proportionate to the aim being pursued (i.e. not excessive).

Case law relating to Article 8 has been limited and, generally, pre-dates the incorporation of the Convention into UK law. So, the reported cases principally concern rulings of the European Court of Human Rights in Strasbourg (*see* Fig. 8.3).

Regulation of Investigatory Powers Act 2000

This legislation covers a range of situations. Monitoring in the workplace is only one of these. It creates a criminal offence. It is unlawful for 'a person intentionally and without lawful authority to intercept, at any place in the United Kingdom, a communication in the course of its transmission by means of (a) a public postal service; or (b) a public telecommunications system' (RIPA 2000, s 1). A 'public telecommunications system' is defined as a 'system that, without itself being a public system, is attached, directly, to a public system'. This, then, would cover a workplace e-mail system but not a self-standing intranet.

The Act establishes the principle that interception needs the express or implied consent of the sender and recipient. The Telecommunications (Lawful Business Practice) (Interception of Communications) Regulations 2001 give employers authority to make interceptions for certain specified purposes. So, an interception may take place, without consent, in the course of lawful business practice:

■ To monitor or keep a record of communications in the following circumstances:
  – To establish the existence of facts relevant to the business. For example, this can involve an organisation keeping records of transactions.
  – To ascertain compliance with regulatory practices. An example would be checking whether workers selling financial services are giving customers the advice and guidance prescribed under financial services regulations.

The background and circumstances

Alison Halford was Assistant Chief Constable with the Merseyside Police. She was engaged in a sex discrimination allegation against the police concerning promotion (which was eventually settled). She was supplied with an additional phone in her office which was designated for her private use and she was assured that she could use the phone for her discrimination claim. Her petition to the European Court of Justice (ECJ) was that calls she had made from her office were intercepted by the police in order to gather information for use against her in the sex discrimination proceedings.

What is 'private life'?

In the *Halford* case, it was held that 'private life' can encompass the workplace. This reflected the earlier view in *Niemietz* v *Germany* [1992] 16 EHRR 97. Here the Court stated that 'it would be too restrictive to limit the notion to an "inner circle" in which the individual may live his own personal life as he chooses and to exclude therefrom entirely the outside world not encompassed within that circle. Respect for private life must also comprise to a certain degree the right to establish and develop relationships with other human beings.' The Court added that 'there appears to be no reason of principle why this understanding of the notion of "private life" should be taken to exclude activities of a professional or business nature since it is, after all, in the course of their working lives that the majority of people have a significant, if not the greatest, opportunity of developing relationships with the outside world'.

What is 'correspondence'?

This includes communication by letter or by other, including electronic, means. Phone calls (and other communications) by an employee at work *may* be covered by the notions of 'private life' and 'correspondence'.

The outcome

The bugging of private telephone calls made to an office telephone could constitute a violation of the right to respect for private life. An employee would have had 'a reasonable expectation of privacy' for phone calls if no warning had been given to them (as a user of the system) that the the calls would be liable to interception. The Court rejected the argument that an employer was free to monitor calls made by an employee on phones which it had provided.

Figure 8.3 The case of Alison Halford

Source: *Halford* v *United Kingdom* [1997] IRLR 471.

- To ascertain or demonstrate standards that are or ought to be achieved by the persons using the system in the course of their duties (e.g. monitoring for quality control; or supervising staff undergoing training in, for example, call centres).

- In the interests of national security.

- For the purpose of preventing or detecting crime (e.g. theft or fraud).

- For the purpose of investigating or detecting unauthorised use of the telecommunication system (e.g. to ensure that confidential information sent by e-mail uses encryption).

- To ensure the effective operation of the system (e.g. protecting a system from viruses).

■ To monitor, but not to record, communications to determine whether they are relevant to the business.

■ To monitor a communication to a confidential and anonymous helpline providing free counselling or support.

These interceptions are authorised only if the controller of the system has made 'all reasonable efforts' to inform users that their communications may be intercepted.

8.4.3 Whistleblowing and public interest disclosure legislation

Under the contract of employment (*see* Chapter 2), all employees are under an implied duty of confidentiality. This prevents them making unauthorised disclosures of confidential information. Such an obligation may be express and it may extend beyond the period of employment through a restrictive covenant. Breach of the duty of confidentiality may be regarded as gross misconduct and result in summary dismissal. However, there may be circumstances when an employee believes that it is 'in the public interest' to disclosure information of various forms of wrongdoing. In fact, there are two conflicting aspects to the 'public interest' in this area. First, there is public interest in the preservation of confidence. Secondly, there is public interest in receiving information about matters of genuine public concern (e.g. fraud, ill-treatment of patients in a hospital, illegal price fixing). This tension has been reflected in various court cases. Furthermore, genuine whistleblowers who had ethical and not malicious reasons for disclosing information were vulnerable to dismissal and the likelihood that further employment opportunities would be unavailable. It was against this background that, following campaigning, the Public Interest Disclosure Act 1998 was enacted.

This Act (now Part IVA of the Employment Rights Act 1996) is designed to protect workers, who make certain disclosures, from detrimental treatment by their employer; and to protect employees from unfair dismissal. The legislation defines 'qualifying disclosures' and 'protected disclosures'.

What is a 'qualifying' disclosure?

This is a disclosure of information which the worker reasonably believes tends to show some malpractice – whether this is currently happening, has happened or is likely to happen in the future. Specifically, the legislation refers to:

- a criminal offence;
- the breach of a legal obligation;
- a miscarriage of justice;
- a danger to the health and safety of any individual;
- damage to the environment;
- deliberate covering up of information tending to show any of the above matters.

It does not matter that after the matter has been considered, the worker's belief is found not to be correct. However, the worker must show that, at the time of the disclosure, it was reasonable to hold the particular belief that the information and allegation was substantially true; and that the worker acted in good faith and did not act for personal gain. Disclosures in breach of the Official Secrets Act 1989 are excluded.

What is a 'protected' disclosure?

A 'qualifying' disclosure will be a 'protected' disclosure where it is made either directly to the employer or through internal procedures authorised by the employer. Furthermore, disclosure to a person prescribed by the Secretary of State may be 'protected'. This is conditional on the worker making the disclosure in good faith; and reasonably believing that the information and any allegation are substantially true. A further condition is that the worker reasonably believes that the matter is the responsibility of the 'prescribed person'. For example, a matter relating to health and safety is the responsibility of the Health and Safety Executive. Other 'prescribed persons' include the Building Societies Commission, the Audit Commission for England and Wales, the Inland Revenue, Customs and Excise, the Environment Agency, the Serious Fraud Office, the Financial Services Agency, the Occupational Pensions Regulatory Authority.

A qualifying disclosure will also be a protected disclosure if it is made to a legal adviser in the course of obtaining legal advice.

An employment tribunal application

This can be made where a worker suffers a detriment for making a protected disclosure. The tribunal will decide whether the worker acted reasonably in all the circumstances (*see* Fig. 8.4). In particular it will take into account:

- The identity of the person to whom the disclosure was made (e.g. an appropriate professional body).
- The seriousness of the relevant failure.
- Whether the relevant failure is continuing or is likely to occur again.
- Whether the disclosure breaches the employer's duty of confidentiality to others (e.g. clients).
- What action has been (or might reasonably be expected to have been) taken if a disclosure was made previously to the employer or a prescribed person.
- Whether the worker complied with any internal procedures approved by the employer if a disclosure was made previously to the employer.

An employee, irrespective of length of service or age, may claim unfair dismissal.

'Gagging' clauses

These are void (ERA 1996, s 43J). So, a term of a contract of employment cannot stop a worker disclosing information covered by the 'protected disclosure' provisions.

8.5 Employment policies and practices

In this section, we will look at the implications of the three areas mentioned in this chapter – concentrating, principally, on the implications of the Data Protection Act 1998. This is an evolving area of law, and advice on good employment practice

The applicant: Bryan Bladon had 20 years' experience as a nurse. In June 1999, he joined ALM Medical Services Ltd at one of its private nursing homes. From mid-August 1999 to 2 September, when the matron was on sick leave, he temporarily 'acted up'.

His concerns: On 19 August he phoned Mr Sinclair, PA to the Managing Director, Dr Matta. He was concerned about a number of matters relating to the management of the home and the welfare and care of patients. These included poor drug records, staffing levels, patient neglect and a wound to a resident. He was asked to put his concerns in writing which he did by fax. (This was a 'protected disclosure'.) Mr Sinclair said that he would deal with the issue on return from holiday. By 31 August, Mr Bladon saw further deterioration in patient care. He decided to take further action. He phoned the Social Services Inspectorate (although this was not a 'prescribed person').

The inspection: On 1 September 1999, the SSI and an inspector from the health authority's nursing home inspectorate carried out an inspection. On 8 September, the inspectors wrote to Dr and Mrs Matta saying that four of the six concerns raised by Mr Bladon were 'substantiated in whole or in part'. These should be investigated and addressed by the company.

Disciplinary action against Mr Bladon: On 9 September he was summoned to a disciplinary hearing without prior warning about what was to be discussed. He was given a written warning on 10 September by Dr Matta. It was claimed in the letter that Mr Bladon's own alleged lack of professional care was partly responsible for problems; and that they were motivated by poor relations he had with colleagues. He was denied any internal right of appeal.

Dismissal of Mr Bladon: On 16 September he was summarily dismissed. It was said that in carrying out his professional duties, he fell below the standards expected of him.

Application to an employment tribunal: Mr Bladon complained that he had been subject to a detriment (the written disciplinary warning); and also had been unfairly dismissed because he had made 'protected disclosures'.

The tribunal's consideration: It was appropriate for Mr Bladon to raise his concerns with Mr Sinclair. Mr Bladon had a 'reasonable belief' that the information disclosed was covered by the 'qualifying disclosure' provisions. The disclosure was made in good faith because of his concern about his professional responsibilities and, in particular, about patient welfare. His disclosure to the inspectorate was reasonable since this was the appropriate body. It was reasonable for Mr Bladon to raise the issue with the inspectors and not await Mr Sinclair's return. Furthermore, in the absence of a whistle-blowing policy and of any indication that the company would investigate his concerns, it was again reasonable for him to go to the inspectorate. The tribunal accepted that the respondent employer (in particular Dr Matta) had 'acted in a demeaning, insensitive, unprofessional, unreasonable and arrogant way' that had left Mr Bladon feeling 'belittled, professionally slurred, isolated and unable to respond in an effective way'. The employer had 'manufactured' or 'fabricated' a disciplinary situation; failed to follow its own procedures; and made no attempt to investigate Mr Bladon's concerns.

The tribunal's decision: The tribunal ruled that he was subject to a detriment (both the written warning and being deprived of an opportunity to appeal). He was also found to have been dismissed unfairly.

Financial award: Mr Bladon was awarded £5500 compensation for net losses to the date of the hearing; £7500 for future losses; and £10 000 of aggravated damages (taking account also of injury to feelings) for the detrimental treatment he suffered. Total compensation was £23 000.

Figure 8.4 *Bladon v ALM Medical Services*

Source: Summarised from *Bladon v ALM Medical Services Ltd*, employment tribunal case 2405845/99.

is developing. The legislation imposes substantial requirements on employers (including on the work of human resources departments). Consequently, this section focuses principally on the *Employment Practices Data Protection* Code of Practice published by the Information Commissioner.

8.5.1 The Data Protection Act: the *Employment Practices Data Protection* Code

This Code provides practical guidance for employers (as 'data controllers') in a complex area. Employment policies and practices will be moulded by the Codes of Practice. Students reading this section might usefully cross-refer to other chapters in the textbook (as indicated).

The Code of Practice comprises four parts:

- Part 1: recruitment and selection (published)
- Part 2: employment records (published)
- Part 3: monitoring at work (published in draft for consultation)
- Part 4: medical information (awaited)

The Code is organised around benchmarks, notes and examples and checklists and action points. Employers are not under a legal obligation to comply with the Code. However, since it provides evidence of the Commissioner's recommendations about compliance with the Data Protection Act and the 'benchmarks' will be used in evidence in enforcement proceedings by the Commissioner, employers ignoring its provisions would be making a mistake.

The Commissioner draws attention to the fact that:

> data protection compliance is a multidisciplinary matter. For example, a company's IT staff may be primarily responsible for keeping computerised personal data secure, whilst a human resources department may be responsible for ensuring that the information requested on a job application form is not excessive, irrelevant or inadequate. All workers, including line managers, have a part to play in securing compliance (Code of Practice, Part 1).

Managing data protection: General benchmarks, reflecting the data protection principles, are set out. These include defining organisational responsibilities; and assessing the nature of information already in existence and considering whether it is relevant. In terms of employment relations, it is also recommended that the employer should 'consult trade unions or other workers' representatives, if any, or workers themselves over the development and implementation of employment practices and procedures that involve the processing of workers' data'. Although such consultation is not a legal duty, it is recommended as good employment practice.

Part 1: Recruitment and selection

This part of the Code of Practice was published in early 2002.

In this area, a balance is to be struck between, on the one hand, the needs of employers to have an effective recruitment and selection process and, on the other hand, the right of the job applicant to respect for his/her private life (under

Art 8 of the European Convention on Human Rights). 'Benchmarks' are set out in the Code to help achieve the balance. These are considered under the various stages in the recruitment and selection process. (It might be helpful to consider Part 1 of the Code also in the context of Chapters 4–6 on sex, race and disability discrimination in the workplace.)

Advertising

The benchmarks are as follows:

- Inform individuals responding to job advertisements of the name of the organisation to which they will be providing their information and how it will be used unless this is self-evident.

- Recruitment agencies, used on behalf of an employer, must identify themselves and explain how the personal data they receive will be used and disclosed unless this is self-evident.

- On receiving identifiable particulars of applicants from an agency, ensure, as soon as possible, that the applicants are aware of the name of the organisation now holding the information.

Applications

The benchmarks are as follows:

- State on any application form to whom the information is being provided and how it will be used if this is not self-evident.

- Only ask for reasonable data that are relevant to recruitment decision-making.

- Only request information about an applicant's criminal convictions if that information can be justified in terms of the role offered. (It should be made clear where certain jobs are covered by the Exceptions Order to the Rehabilitation of Offenders Act 1974; and that otherwise spent convictions do not have to be declared.)

- Explain any checks that might be undertaken to verify the information provided in the application form including the nature of the additional sources from which information may be gathered.

- If sensitive data are collected, ensure that a sensitive data condition is satisfied.

- Provide a secure method for sending applications.

Verification of applicant's details

The benchmarks are as follows:

- Explain to applicants as early as is reasonably practicable in the recruitment process the nature of the verification process and the methods used to carry it out.

- If it is necessary to secure the release of documents or information from a third party, obtain a signed consent form from the applicant unless consent to their release has been indicated in some other way.

- Give the applicant an opportunity to make representations should any of the checks produce discrepancies.

Shortlisting

The benchmarks are as follows:

■ Be consistent in the way personal data are used in the process of shortlisting candidates for a particular position.

■ Inform applicants if an automated shortlisting system will be used as the sole basis for making a decision. Make provisions to consider representations from applicants about this and to take these into account before making the final decision.

■ Ensure that tests based on the interpretation of scientific evidence, such as psychological tests and handwriting analysis, are only used and interpreted by those who have received appropriate training.

It is noted by the Information Commissioner in the Code of Practice that 'it is beyond the scope of the Code to set down general rules as to how shortlisting and selection testing should be carried out. This should be primarily a matter of good employment practice.' It is acknowledged, however, that there is a potential for the breach of discrimination law (*see* Chapters 4–6). It is added that 'the Information Commissioner's concern is more with ensuring that the selection criteria are applied in a way that is consistent and fair to applicants rather than that the criteria are, in themselves, fair'.

Interviews

The benchmarks are as follows:

■ Ensure that personal data, which are recorded and retained following an interview, can be justified as relevant to, and necessary for, the recruitment process itself, or for defending the process against challenge.

The Information Commissioner notes that:

> this Code is not concerned with setting out how interviews should be conducted. This should be primarily a matter of good employment practice. However, the collection of personal data at interview, their recording, storage and use are likely to represent processing which falls within the scope of the Act. This means that, for example, applicants will normally be entitled to have access to interview notes about them which are retained as part of the record of the interview.

Pre-employment vetting

The benchmarks are as follows:

■ Only use vetting where there are particular and significant risks to the employer, clients, customers or others, and where there is no less intrusive and reasonably practicable alternative.

■ Only carry out pre-employment vetting on an applicant at an appropriate point in the recruitment process. Comprehensive vetting should only be conducted on a successful applicant.

■ Make it clear early in the recruitment process that vetting will take place and how it will be conducted.

- Only use vetting as a means of obtaining specific information, not as a means of general intelligence gathering. Ensure that the extent and nature of information sought is justified.

- Only seek information from sources where it is likely that relevant information will be revealed. Only approach the applicant's family or close associates in exceptional cases.

- Do not place reliance on information collected from possibly unreliable sources. Allow the applicant to make representations regarding information that will affect the decision to finally appoint.

- Where information is collected about a third party, e.g. the applicant's partner, ensure that so far as practicable that the third party is made aware of this.

- If it is necessary to secure the release of documents or information from a third party, obtain a signed consent form from the applicant.

The Information Commissioner notes that:

> checks should be proportionate to the risks faced by an employer and should be likely to reveal information that would have a significant bearing on the employment decision. The risks are likely to involve aspects of the security of the employer or of others. They could range from the risk of breaches of national security or the risk of employing unsuitable individuals to work with children through to the risk of theft or the disclosure of trade secrets or other commercially confidential information.

A further note adds that:

> as a general rule, do not routinely vet all applicants; do not subject all shortlisted applicants to more than basic written checks and the taking up of references – e.g. against the list of persons considered unsuitable to work with children under the Protection of Children Act 1999. Do not require all shortlisted applicants to obtain a disclosure from the Criminal Records Bureau.

Retention of recruitment records

The benchmarks are as follows:

- Establish and adhere to retention periods for recruitment records that are based on a clear business need.

- Destroy information obtained by a vetting exercise as soon as possible or in any case within six months. A record of the result of vetting or verification can be retained.

- Consider carefully which information contained on an application form is to be transferred to the worker's employment record. Delete information irrelevant to ongoing employment.

- Delete information about criminal convictions collected in the course of the recruitment process once it has been verified through a Criminal Records Bureau disclosure unless in exceptional circumstances the information is clearly relevant to the ongoing employment relationship.

- Advise unsuccessful applicants that there is an intention to keep their names on file for future vacancies (if appropriate) and give them the opportunity to have their details removed form the file.

- Ensure that personal data obtained during the recruitment process are securely stored or are destroyed.

The Information Commissioner notes that:

> employers must consider carefully the justification, if any, for retaining recruitment records once the recruitment process has been completed. Retention of recruitment records may be necessary for the organisation to defend itself against discrimination claims or other legal actions arising from recruitment. However, the possibility that an individual may bring a legal action does not automatically justify the indefinite retention of all records relating to workers. A policy based on risk-analysis principles should be established.

It is further noted that 'recruitment agencies have some legal obligations to retain records under the Employment Agencies Act 1973'.

Part 2: Employment records

This part of the *Employment Practices Data Protection* Code of Practice was published by the Information Commissioner in the Summer of 2002. The following benchmarks are included.

Collecting and keeping employment records

The benchmarks are as follows:

- Ensure that newly appointed workers are aware of the nature and source of any information kept about them, how it will be used and to whom it will be disclosed.

- Inform new workers and remind existing workers about their rights under the Act, including their right of access to the information kept about them.

- Ensure that there is a clear and foreseeable need for any information collected about workers and that the information collected actually meets that need.

- Provide each worker annually with a copy of information that may be subject to change, e.g. personal details such as home address, or allow workers to view this information online. Ask workers to check their records for accuracy and ensure any necessary amendments are made to bring records up to date.

- Incorporate accuracy, consistency and validity checks.

Security

The benchmarks are as follows:

- Apply security standards that take account of the risks of unauthorised access to, accidental loss or destruction of, or damage to employment records.

- Institute a system of secure cabinets, access controls and passwords to ensure that staff can only gain access to employment records where they have a legitimate business need to do so.

- Use the audit trail capabilities of automated systems to track who accesses and amends personal data.

- Take steps to ensure the reliability of staff who have access to workers' records. Remember this is not just just a matter of carrying out background checks. It also involves training and ensuring that workers understand their responsibilities for confidential or sensitive information. Place confidentiality clauses in their contracts of employment.

- Ensure, if employment records are taken off-site (for example, on laptop computers), that this is controlled. Make sure that only the necessary information is taken and that there are security rules for staff to follow.

- Take account of the risks of transmitting confidential worker information by fax or e-mail. Only transmit such information between locations if a secure network or comparable arrangements are in place. In the case of e-mail, deploy some technical means of ensuring security such as encryption.

Sickness and accident records

The benchmarks are as follows:

- Keep sickness and accident records separately from absence records. Do not use sickness or accident records for a particular purpose when records of absence could be used instead. (An example could include the circumstances when benefit is being calculated. All that is required is the period of absence and not the nature of the sickness.)

- Ensure that the holding and use of sickness and accident records satisfy a sensitive data condition.

- Only disclose information from sickness or accident records about a worker's illness, medical condition or injury when there is a legal obligation to do so; where it is necessary for legal proceedings; or where the worker has given explicit consent to the disclosure.

- Do not make the sickness, accident or absence records of individual workers available to other workers, other than to provide managers with information about those who work for them in so far as this is necessary for them to carry out their managerial roles.

(*See also* Chapter 6, Disability discrimination in the workplace.)

Equal opportunities monitoring

The benchmarks are as follows:

- Information about a worker's ethnic origin, disability or religion is sensitive personal data. Ensure that equal opportunities monitoring of these characteristics satisfies a sensitive data condition.

- Only use information that identifies individual workers where this is necessary to carry out meaningful equal opportunities monitoring. Where practicable, keep the information collected in an anonymised form.

- Ensure questions are designed so that the personal information collected through them is accurate and not excessive.

The Information Commissioner notes that 'the sensitive data conditions should mean that most equal opportunities monitoring can take place without the need to obtain a worker's consent'. It is also noted that employers 'should take account of the advice of relevant bodies before designing, distributing, collating and evaluating an equal opportunities monitoring initiative and incorporating it into procedures'. Furthermore, 'public sector employers will also need to take into account the requirements of the Race Relations 1976 (Statutory Duties) Order 2001 and the Race Relations (Amendment) Act 2000'. Advice is obtainable from the EOC, the CRE and the DRC.

(*See also* Chapters 4–6 on sex, race and disability discrimination at work.)

Workers' access to information about themselves

The benchmarks are as follows:

- Establish a system that enables it to recognise a data subject access request and locate all the information about a worker in order to be able to respond promptly (and within 40 calendar days).
- Check the identity of anyone making a subject access request to ensure that information is only given to the person entitled to it.
- Provide the worker with a hard copy of the information kept, making clear any codes used and the sources of the information.
- Make a judgement as to what information it is reasonable to withhold concerning the identities of third parties, using the guidelines given in the Code.
- Inform managers and other relevant people in the organisation of the nature of information relating to them that will be released to individuals who make subject access requests.
- Ensure that on request, promptly and in any event within 40 calendar days, workers are provided with a statement of how any automated decision-making process, to which they are subject, is used and how it works.
- When purchasing a computerised system ensure that the system that you will use to take automated decisions about workers provides the information needed to enable you to respond fully to requests for information about how the system works.

References

The benchmarks are as follows:

Where references are given by the organisation:

- Set out a clear company policy stating who can give corporate references, in what circumstances, and the policy that applies to the granting of access to them. Make anyone who is likely to become a referee aware of this policy.
- Do not provide confidential references about a worker unless you are sure that this is the worker's wish.
- Establish, at the time a worker's employment ends, whether or not the worker wishes references to be provided to future employers or to others.

Where references are received:

- When responding to a request from a worker to see his/her own reference, and the reference enables a third party to be identified, make a judgement as to what information to withhold, using the guidelines in the code.

(*See also* Chapter 2, Regulating the employment relationship.)

Disclosure requests

The benchmarks are as follows:

- Establish a disclosure policy to tell staff, who are likely to receive requests for information about workers, how to respond and to where they should refer requests that fall outside the policy rules.
- Ensure that disclosure decisions that are not covered by clear policy rules are only taken by staff who are familiar with the Act and the Code of Practice and who are able to give the decision proper consideration.
- Unless you are under a legal obligation to do so, only disclose information about a worker where you conclude that in all the circumstances it is fair to do so. Bear in mind that the duty of fairness is owed primarily to the worker. Where possible take account of the worker's views. Only disclose confidential information if the worker has clearly agreed.
- Where a disclosure is requested in an emergency, make a careful decision as to whether to disclose, taking into account the nature of the information being requested and the likely impact on the worker of not providing it.
- Make staff aware that those seeking information sometimes use deception to gain access to it. Ensure that they check the legitimacy of any request and the identity and authority of the person making it.
- Ensure that if you intend to disclose sensitive personal data, a sensitive data condition is satisfied.
- Where the disclosure would involve a transfer of information about a worker to a country outside the EEA, ensure that there is a proper basis for making the transfer.
- Inform the worker when a non-regular disclosure is to be made following a request from, for example, the Inland Revenue or a local authority housing benefits department. (An exception to this would be where the employer is prevented from doing so in law or where this would constitute a 'tip-off' in criminal or tax investigations.) The information that is disclosed might be challenged by the worker and so they should be given an opportunity to check its accuracy.
- Keep a record of non-regular disclosures. Regularly check and review this record to sensure that the requirements of the Act are being satisfied.

Mergers and acquisitions

The benchmarks are as follows:

- Ensure, wherever practicable, that information handed over to another organisation in connection with a prospective acquisition or merger is anonymised.

- Only hand over personal information prior to the final merger or acquisition decision after securing assurances that it will be used solely for the evaluation of assets and liabilities; that it will be treated in confidence and will not be disclosed to other parties; and it will be destroyed or returned after use.

- Advise workers wherever practicable if their employment records are to be disclosed to another organisation before an acquisition or merger takes place. If the acquisition or merger proceeds, make sure workers are aware of the extent to which their records are to be transferred to the new employer.

- Ensure that if you intend to disclose sensitive personal data, a sensitive data condition is satisfied.

- Where a merger or acquisition involves a transfer of information about a worker to a country outside the EEA, ensure that there is a proper basis for making the transfer.

- New employers should ensure that the records they hold as a result of a merger or acquisition do not include excessive information and are accurate and relevant.

(*See also* Chapter 3, Managing change in the employment relationship.)

Discipline, grievance and dismissal

The benchmarks are as follows:

- Remember that the Data Protection Act applies to personal data processed in relation to discipline, grievance and dismissal proceedings. The Information Commissioner comments that 'records used in the course of disciplinary and grievance proceedings must be accurate and sufficiently detailed to support any conclusions that are drawn from them'. These records must be kept secure. The Commissioner also notes that 'records of allegations about workers that have been investigated and found to be without substance should not normally be retained once an investigation has been completed'. However, there can be exceptions. These are where:

    > for its own protection, the employer has to keep a limited record that an allegation was received and investigated, for example, where the allegation related to abuse and the worker is employed to work with children or other vulnerable individuals. There may also be a case for keeping records of unsubstantiated allegations of bullying or abuse of workers by a colleague, provided that it is made clear in the record what is an unsubstantiated allegation and what has been established as fact.

- Do not access or use information you keep about workers merely because it might have some relevance to a disciplinary or grievance investigation if access or use would be either:

    – incompatible with the purpose(s) you obtained the information for; or

    – disproportionate to the seriousness of the matter under investigation.

    To illustrate this benchmark, the Information Commissioner provides two examples of the inappropriate use of information:

For example, a worker in a business that issues credit cards might also be a holder of one of the business's cards. The business should not access information it obtains about the worker because he or she is a card-holder for use in connection with disciplinary or grievance investigations arising from his or her employment. Similarly, an employer might store e-mail messages for a limited period to ensure the security of its communications system. It must not access stored, personal messages sent by or to workers for incompatible purposes such as checking whether workers have been making adverse comments about their managers.

■ Ensure that there are clear procedures on how 'spent' disciplinary warnings are handled. The Information Commissioner comments that the term 'spent' or 'expire' should be clarified: 'For example, is the warning removed from the record or is it simply disregarded in determining a future disciplinary penalty? Put in place arrangements, such as a diary system, to ensure that the procedure is put into practice and that where the procedure provides for warnings to be removed or deleted that this is actually done.'

■ Ensure that, when employment is terminated, the reason for this is accurately recorded and that the record reflects properly what the worker has been told about the termination. The Information Commissioner notes the importance of considerations of accuracy. 'For example, where a worker has been allowed to resign but, because he or she has been left with little choice, the employer has recorded "dismissed". Particular care should be taken in distinguishing resignation from dismissal.'

(*See also* Chapter 9, Discipline and dismissal.)

Retention of records

The benchmarks are as follows:

■ Establish and adhere to standard retention times for categories of information held on the records of workers and former workers. Base the retention times on business need, taking into account relevant professional guidelines.

■ Anonymise any data about workers and former workers where practicable.

■ If the holding of any information on criminal convictions of workers is justified, ensure that the information is deleted once the conviction is 'spent' under the Rehabilitation of Offenders Act 1974. The Information Commissioner comments that 'in exceptional circumstances which involve jobs covered by the Exceptions Order to this Act, there might be a business need that justifies the continued retention of "spent" convictions'.

■ Ensure that records which are to be disposed of are securely and effectively destroyed.

Part 3: Monitoring at work

This part of the Code of Practice is at the time of writing (November 2002) in draft form. See website of Information Commission for developments.

Monitoring communications

The benchmarks are as follows:

- *General*: Establish a policy on the use of electronic communications and inform the workforce (*see* Fig. 8.5).

- Ensure that where monitoring involves the interception of a communication it is not outlawed by the Regulation of Investigatory Powers Act 2000.

- Make an 'impact assessment' to determine what, if any, monitoring of electronic communications is justified by the benefits. Limit the scope of monitoring to what is strictly required to deliver those benefits. Such benefits can include efforts to detect viruses, the abuse of passwords, detection of harassing e-mails.

- *Telephone monitoring*: Ensure that workers and those making calls to (or receiving calls from) workers are aware of any monitoring and the purpose behind it 'unless this is obvious'.

- Ensure that workers are aware of the extent to which you receive information about the use of telephone lines in their homes, or mobile phones provided for their personal use, for which the business pays partly or fully. Do not make use of information about personal calls for monitoring.

To satisfy data protection requirements a policy for the use of electronic communications should:

- Set out clearly to workers the circumstances in which they may or may not use for private communications the employer's telephone systems (including mobile phones, the e-mail system and internet access).

- Make clear the extent and type of private use that is allowed – e.g. restrictions on overseas phone call or limits on the size and/or type of e-mail attachments that they can send or receive.

- In the case of internet access, specify clearly any restrictions on material that can be viewed or copied. A simple ban on 'offensive material' is unlikely to be sufficiently clear for workers to know what is and is not allowed. Employers should at least give examples of the sort of material that is considered offensive, for example, material containing racist terminology or images of nudity.

- Advise workers what personal information they are allowed to include in particular types of communication and the alternatives that should be used, e.g. communications with a company doctor should be sent only by internal mail rather than by e-mail.

- Lay down clear rules regarding the personal use of the employer's communication equipment when used from home or away from the workplace, e.g. the use of facilities that enable external dialling into company networks.

- Explain the purposes for which any monitoring is conducted, the extent of the monitoring and the means used.

- Outline how the policy is enforced and the penalties which exist for a breach of policy.

There may, of course be other matters that an employer also wants to address in its policy.

Figure 8.5   Policy for the use of electronic communications

Source: Extract from draft *Code of Practice on Monitoring at Work*, published by the Information Commissioner, 2002.

- *E-mail and internet access monitoring*: Ensure workers and those sending e-mails to workers are aware of any monitoring and the purpose for it.

- If it is necessary to check the e-mail accounts of workers in their absence, make sure that they are aware that this will happen.

- Inform workers of the extent to which information about their internet access and e-mails is retained in the system and for how long.

- In reviewing the results of any monitoring take account of the possibility of unintentional access of websites by workers.

Video and audio monitoring

The benchmarks are as follows:

- Carry out an 'impact assessment' to determine what, if any, video and audio monitoring is justified by the benefits. Limit the scope of monitoring to what is strictly necessary to deliver these benefits. So, for example, the monitoring may be targeted at areas of security and safety risk; or where the workers' expectations of privacy may be low (e.g. in public areas like the sales areas of supermarkets).

- Give workers a clear notification that video or audio monitoring is being carried out and where and why it is being carried out.

- Ensure that people other than workers, such as visitors or customers, who may inadvertently be captured by monitoring, are made aware of its operation and why it is being carried out.

Covert monitoring

The benchmarks are as follows:

- Only use covert monitoring where there are grounds for suspecting that criminal activity is taking place and the employer concludes that notifying workers about the monitoring would prejudice an investigation.

- In the case of public authorities, ensure that the monitoring is carried out in accordance with an authorisation granted under the provisions of Part II of the Regulation of Investigatory Powers Act 2000. In private-sector businesses ensure that covert monitoring is not carried out unless it has been authorised at a senior level.

- Ensure that any covert audio or video monitoring is strictly targeted at obtaining evidence within a set timeframe. So, the Information Commissioner notes that 'if covert monitoring is to be deployed as part of a particular investigation, its deployment should cease once the investigation has been completed'.

- Do not use covert audio or video monitoring in areas where it would be especially intrusive such as toilets or offices allocated for workers' individual use. The Information Commissioner comments that 'in exceptional circumstances, such monitoring could be justified', giving the example of drug-dealing on the employers' premises. 'Any monitoring is likely to take place under the direction of the police.'

- If a private investigator is employed to collect information on workers covertly, make sure that there is a contract in place that requires them to collect the information in a way that satisfies the employer's obligations under the Data Protection Act 1998.

- Ensure that information obtained through covert monitoring is used only for the prevention or detection of the criminal activity or the apprehension or prosecution of offenders to which the monitoring was directed. Disregard and, where feasible, delete other information collected in the course of monitoring unless it reveals information that no reasonable employer could be expected to ignore.

In-vehicle monitoring

The benchmarks are as follows:

- Make an 'impact assessment' in order to determine what, if any, monitoring of vehicles used by workers is justified by the benefits. Limit the scope of monitoring to what is strictly necessary to deliver these benefits.

- Set out a policy that states what use can be made of vehicles provided by, or on behalf of, the employer and any conditions attached to use.

- If intending to undertake covert in-vehicle monitoring ensure the benchmarks on covert monitoring are taken into account.

Monitoring information about workers' private lives

This occurs where employers use information held by third parties (e.g. credit reference information, electoral registration) to monitor workers. It can also cover employers' monitoring their own workers' information (e.g. banks monitoring workers' bank accounts). The benchmarks are as follows:

- Carry out an 'impact assessment' to determine what, if any, monitoring of workers' private information is justified by the benefits. Limit the scope of monitoring to what is strictly necessary to deliver these benefits.

- Tell workers what information sources are to be used to carry out checks on them and why the checks are to be carried out.

- Ensure that if workers are monitored through the use of information held by a credit reference agency, the agency is aware of the use to which the information is put. Do not use a facility provided to conduct credit checks on customers to monitor or vet workers.

- Avoid monitoring workers through information you have as a result of a different relationship with them. For example, a bank may be an employer of a worker and that worker may be a customer of their employer's bank. The Information Commissioner comments that:

> a bank must not routinely monitor the bank accounts of all workers. If monitoring can be justified, it must be targeted at particular individuals and particular information that poses a risk. In this case, monitoring to detect serious indebtedness of the most senior workers might be justified on the basis of avoiding potential public embarrassment to the bank. This would not, however, justify examining the details of payments made by these workers unless criminal activity was suspected.

- Ensure that staff carrying out this type of monitoring are properly trained to do so. Put in place rules preventing the disclosure or inappropriate use of information obtained in connection with the monitoring. The Information Commissioner comments that employers should 'consider placing confidentiality clauses in the contracts of employment of staff'.

- Avoid retaining all the information obtained in connection with the monitoring. Merely record that a check has taken place and the result of this.

Part 4

At the time of writing, Part 4 of the Code of Practice on medical information is awaited.

8.5.2 Privacy and surveillance

The possible action that employers might take in respect of privacy and surveillance can, currently, be drawn from the previous section on the implementation of the Data Protection Act.

8.5.3 Whistleblowing

The pressure group, Public Concern at Work (PCAW), which worked towards the enactment of whistleblowing legislation, recommends the adoption by employers of a whistleblowing policy. PCAW states that 'the purpose of a whistleblowing policy is primarily to deter and detect wrongdoing. It is not meant to replace any other procedure already in place; it is a separate and additional channel of communication'. (See also ACAS Code of Practice on *Disciplinary and Grievance Procedures*, 2000: para 47.) Such a policy, explicitly backed by senior management, sends a clear signal to staff about expectations, standards and procedures for dealing with claims of wrongdoing. Notification of external routes (e.g. to inspectorates, etc.) should provide further assurance to staff that honesty and transparency are central to the operation of the employer's business.

The key provisions of a whistleblowing policy are as follows:

- Making it clear that it is safe and acceptable for workers to raise a concern they have about misconduct or malpractice within the organisation.

- Indicating the proper way in which concerns may be raised outside the organisation if this is necessary.

- Where a worker raises a concern about a specified malpractice, making every effort to respond (and demonstrate that it has responded).

- Where a protected disclosure has been made, taking all reasonable steps to try and ensure that no colleague, manager or other person under its control victimises the whistleblower.

- Anything that might be seen as an attempt to suppress evidence of wrongdoing is inadvisable. Reasonable suspicion of a 'cover-up' would itself provide a basis for a 'protected disclosure'.

8.6 Conclusion

This is a complex area in which the law is evolving, technology is rapidly changing and social values about acceptable disclosure of information and about privacy are shifting. In this context, the law sets certain principles and requirements and guidance on procedures – sometimes imperfectly. An important concern must be whether the framework of law can deal satisfactorily with these changes and developments. It is probable that there will be test cases concerning the acceptability of certain forms of surveillance and covert monitoring, the definition of privacy, the degrees of access to certain data. There is likely to be a lengthy process towards some consensus on standards of lawful and good practice in these areas.

Further reading

Office of the Information Commissioner: *Annual Reports*.

References

Advisory Conciliation and Arbitration Service (2000) *Code of Practice: Disciplinary and Grievance Procedures*. London: ACAS.

Hollingsworth, M. and Norton-Taylor, R. (1988) *Blacklist: the inside story of political vetting*. London: The Hogarth Press.

Hollingsworth, M. and Tremayne, C. (1989) *The Economic League: the silent McCarthyism*. London: National Council for Civil Liberties.

Office of the Information Commissioner (2002) *Employment Practices Data Protection* Code of Practice. London: Office of the Information Commissioner.

Discipline and dismissal

Learning objectives

Having read this chapter you should be able to:

- Understand the nature and purpose of disciplinary procedures.
- Recommend the steps that employers should take in relation to workforce discipline.
- Understand the legal standards which govern the disciplinary process.
- Understand the legal processes available to employees.
- Know the remedies available, in law, for successful applicants.

9.1 Structure of the chapter

This chapter comprises the following sections:

- *Introduction*: Significance of law on discipline and dismissal.
- *The context*: The nature of the employment relationship, the common law of contract, social perceptions of standards of good practice, political action to enact standards and current assessments about the nature and effectiveness of the law.
- *The legal framework*: The nature and purpose of discipline at work; circumstances in which contracts of employment end, fair and unfair dismissal, procedure for redress and remedies.
- *Employment policies and practices*: Discipline at work: expectations and norms, the reason for dismissal, reasonableness in the circumstances and proper compliance with the standards of procedural fairness.

9.2 Introduction

Over the past thirty years, workplace discipline and dismissal from employment have become the subject of increasing regulation by statute law and judicial decision. Complaints alleging unfair dismissal have, year after year, constituted the largest proportion of employment rights applications to industrial (now employment) tribunals. In 2001–2, the Advisory Conciliation and Arbitration Service received 165 000 tribunal applications for conciliation. Of these, 52 000 (31 per cent of the total) were unfair dismissal claims.

In some ways, it is surprising that there should be such a volume of complaints given the qualifying period restricting access. (This was, between 1985 and 1999, two years' continuous service by an employee.) It is also surprising given the ceiling on compensation awards (which was raised substantially in 1999) and the inability of the tribunal to enforce reinstatement or re-engagement for successful applicants. Furthermore, it is surprising given the, often tortuous, process of lodging a complaint and presenting a claim at a court-like tribunal hearing. Indeed, such evidence as we have about non-applicants who believe that they have been unfairly dismissed suggests that the fifty thousand-odd applicants are merely the tip of the iceberg.

The impact of this legal framework on employers has been experienced principally through the introduction and operation of disciplinary procedures. These should conform to the practical guidance set out in the *Code of Practice: Disciplinary and Grievance Procedures* 2000 (published by the Advisory Conciliation and Arbitration Service). It is customary for decisions on discipline and dismissal to be taken by line managers. Indeed, the ACAS Code stipulates certain recommendations about the appropriate status of line management (paras 9(vii) and 15). Personnel/human resources officers will be responsible for advice on company practice, legal standards and other standards of good practice.

The legal framework relating to discipline and termination of employment extends into many facets of employment and, consequently, other bodies of law (which have been covered in other chapters of this book). The principal examples are as follows:

- disciplinary action might be construed as victimisation, harassment or a 'detriment' under discrimination law;
- dismissal which is found, by a tribunal, to be for a discriminatory reason (whether entirely or in part) is automatically unfair.

Such discriminatory action encompasses the following grounds (among others): sex, marital status, pregnancy, race, trade union membership, representing fellow workers in consultation procedures, raising health and safety grievances.

Furthermore, it is important to remember that, in a minority of dismissal cases, the termination of employment by the employer is not for a disciplinary reason. It could be to do with ill-health retirement or redundancy. Such employees are, nevertheless, entitled to challenge their dismissal as unfair before a tribunal.

Finally, political concern about the inadequate use of in-company disciplinary procedures has resulted in the enactment of a minimum statutory procedure for dismissal and discipline (Employment Act 2002, Sch 2). This procedure is statutorily implied into all contracts of employment from late 2003.

9.3   The context

The context in which the regulation of discipline at work and dismissal has developed and continues to develop is explored under five headings: the nature of the employment relationship, the common law of contract, social perceptions of standards of good practice, political action to enact standards, and current assessments about the nature and effectiveness of the law.

9.3.1   The nature of the employment relationship

The nature of **the employment relationship** was explored in Chapter 2. It was characterised as a power relationship between the employer and an employee – with an imbalance of power usually favouring the employer. It was shown how an employee was potentially vulnerable to arbitrary, unfair and discriminatory treatment by an employer. Some commentators, describing the situation just before the enactment of unfair dismissal legislation in 1971, contended that in certain sectors of employment the workplace situation did not appear to have moved on much since the beginning of the nineteenth century where 'the legal regime in a factory could be fairly described as that of a private legislative kingdom in which the employer was sovereign, judge, jury and executioner' (Clark, 1970).

Even in recent times, after the enactment of protective legislation, the National Association of Citizens' Advice Bureaux (1993) has reported abuse by employers of employees who have not completed the statutory qualifying period:

- A Bureau in Hampshire reported of a client who was dismissed a few days prior to completing two years' service. One week before receiving her notice, she had been promoted and received a salary increase. She then informed her employer that she was pregnant and was dismissed.

- A Bureau in Essex reported of a client who had been employed for 18 months during which time she had endured appalling working conditions, including poor health and safety provisions. She worked a ten-and-a-half-hour day and Saturday mornings. She was then asked to increase her hours. When she refused to do so, she was dismissed.

- A Bureau in Gloucestershire reported of a client who had been employed for three years as a specialist printer. She worked for ten hours per week. She arrived at work one day to find a 'new team' in place. Her employer claimed that the new team was prepared to do the work for less pay, but the client and her colleagues had not been given the opportunity to negotiate on their pay rises.

Clearly, dismissal exposes an employee not just to loss of job but potentially to loss of income, loss of status and loss of reputation. In these circumstances, it was regarded as imperative that widely recognised standards of natural justice (fair treatment) were established to determine whether or not an employee had been unfairly treated.

9.3.2 The common law of contract

It might be thought that **the common of law of contract** could have protected an employee from abuse by an employer. There are some protections but these are limited. The situation at common law has been described as follows: 'as long as proper contractual notice of termination was given, an employer was legally entitled to dismiss an employee for whatever reason he wished. There was no obligation on the employer to reveal his reason for dismissal to the employee, much less to justify it' (Anderman, 1986: 416). An employee dismissed in circumstances where his honesty was questioned and who, as a consequence, found it difficult to obtain other employment, might only have available an action for defamation – which would be costly, complex and uncertain. An employee dismissed on grounds that could be construed as victimisation or discriminatory would have had no special protection. Certainly, the common law, emphasising freedom of contract, did not proscribe discriminatory treatment.

So, as Anderman commented about the general situation prevailing until the early 1970s: 'even if the employer dismissed an employee without notice or with inadequate notice, the only remedy open to the employee was that of claiming wrongful dismissal in the ordinary courts – a course of action for which the only remedy was damages generally limited to pay for the notice period' (1986: 416).

Wrongful dismissal involves a right, which still exists, to make a claim in the High Court or a County Court usually on the grounds that the terms of the contract relating to termination have not been complied with – for example, shorter notice having been given than is stipulated. The employee is effectively seeking pay that is due. The court would not 'grant an order or even a declaration against a defendant [employer] guilty of wrongful dismissal' (Wedderburn, 1986).

9.3.3 Social standards

It was against this background that **social policy concern**, in Britain, about employee protection was recorded. Three publications reflected the need for commonly accepted standards and a widespread dissatisfaction with the situation. The first was a report by the International Labour Organisation (1962). This found that in most of the 68 countries investigated there were provisions by statute or otherwise for protection from unjust or arbitrary dismissal. Subsequent to this report, the ILO published, in 1963, a Recommendation (No. 119) on Termination of Employment to which the British government subscribed in 1964. The underlying principle of this is that 'termination of employment should not take place unless there is a valid reason . . . connected with the capacity or conduct of the worker or based on the operational requirements of the undertaking, establishment or service'. The reasons for dismissal which were identified as not valid cover most of those now in force in British employment law. The Recommendation also proposed, among other things, appeals against termination, notice periods and criteria for selecting workers for redundancy.

The second publication was on dismissal procedures. It was a report of the National Joint Advisory Council for the (then) Ministry of Labour (1967). This drew unfavourable comparisons between Britain and other industrialised countries in terms of procedural arrangements for contesting arbitrary dismissal. It reported wide discrepancies in practice within British industry and, where there was some protection, heavy reliance upon voluntary measures.

> It appears, therefore, that formal dismissal procedures are general in the public sector of employment and fairly widespread in large firms, especially those employing 2000 or more. These usually provide for the decision on dismissal to be taken at a level higher than that of the immediate supervisor; for the personnel department to play a part (often advisory) in the decision-making process; and for the employee to have an opportunity to appeal. Appeal is normally to a higher level of management . . . [However,] there remain a very large number of firms, including the vast majority of smaller firms, which have no formal dismissal procedure . . . [So,] some employees – particularly those employed by small firms in the less highly organised sectors of employment – may well have no effective means of redress against arbitrary dismissal, whether through the courts, through a disputes procedure or through a procedure within the firm. It is difficult, however, to ascertain the extent of this problem' (Ministry of Labour, 1967: paras 71–3).

Finally came the influential report of the Royal Commission on Trade Unions and Employers' Associations 1965–1968 (the Donovan Report). The Commission (which comprised employers, trade unionists and independent members) reported that 'there is a very general feeling, shared by employers as well as trade unions, that the present situation is unsatisfactory and it was reflected in the submissions of many who gave evidence to us' (para 525), and stated that 'we share in full the belief that the present situation is unsatisfactory' (para 526).

In a further comment the Royal Commission outlined, vividly, the consequences of dismissal for employees. This still has many echoes today in terms of social policy, so it is worth quoting:

> In practice there is usually no comparison between the consequences for an employer if an employee terminated the contract of employment and those which will ensue for an employee if he is dismissed. In reality people build much of their lives around their jobs. Their incomes and prospects for the future are inevitably founded in the expectation that their jobs will continue. For workers in many situations dismissal is a disaster. For some workers it may make inevitable the breaking up of a community and the uprooting of homes and families. Others, and particularly older workers, may be faced with the greatest difficulty in getting work at all. The statutory provision for redundancy goes some way to recognise what is really at stake for an employee when his job is involved, but it is no less at stake if he is being dismissed for alleged incompetence or for misconduct than if he is being dismissed for redundancy. To this it is no answer that good employers will dismiss employees only if they have no alternative. Not all employers are good employers. Even if the employer's intentions are good, is it certain that his subordinates' intentions are always good? And even when all concerned in management act in good faith, are they always necessarily right? Should their view of the case automatically prevail over the employee's? (para 526).

Underlying much of this public discussion was a concept of 'job property rights' – the notion that a job is of material importance to an employee (particularly as service entitlements accrue and they acquire more experience at it). Arbitrary sacking undermines these property rights. In comparison with an employer's property rights, an employee's were, under common law, ill protected.

9.3.4 Political action

Political action then followed, with the enactment of unfair dismissal law in 1971. This legislation signalled 'a radical departure from common law principles' (Anderman, 1986: 416). It was passed by a Conservative government. However, there was a broad political consensus about the basic objectives and principles of the law. Its objectives were, on the one hand, to provide protection and fair treatment for employees; and, on the other hand, to improve the management of staff and minimise conflict in employment relations. As a consequence of this, irrespective of whether there was a Labour or Conservative government in power in the following decades, the legislation (apart from some details of application) has been preserved. It must be remembered, however, that access to unfair dismissal rights did not (and still does not) cover all working people. Consequently, there remains a large pool of people in the labour market whose only imperfect legal redress is that of wrongful dismissal.

Although the Conservative governments (1979–97) did not fundamentally change the framework of the law, they did take certain steps to restrict its application. First, the qualifying period of continuous service for applicants (of six months since 1974) was extended to one year in 1980 and then to two years in 1985. Secondly, certain procedural hurdles were introduced in the tribunal process to filter out some complaints. Notable among these was the need to lodge a deposit with the tribunal if an applicant wanted to proceed to a hearing after being ruled against at a pre-hearing review.

However, European law, in rulings from the European Court of Justice, had the effect of enhancing some wide-ranging protections. In 1994, the ceilings on compensation in sex discrimination cases was removed as being contrary to European equal treatment law. This removal was also extended to compensation in race discrimination cases. In 1995, restriction on access to unfair dismissal rights for employees, depending on the number of hours they worked, was rescinded on the grounds that it was indirectly discriminatory against women.

Since 1997, the Labour government has initiated a number of key changes. The first is the adoption, from 2001, of an arbitration option (initially in unfair dismissal cases) as an alternative to a tribunal hearing (Trade Union and Labour Relations Consolidation Act 1992, s 212A). The government hopes that this 'will create a change of culture so that individuals who have been dismissed unfairly are more likely to get their jobs back' (DTI, 1998: *Fairness at Work*, para 3.4). Secondly, access to unfair dismissal rights is less restrictive. From June 1999, the qualifying period of service was reduced to one year. Finally, the ceiling on compensation for successful unfair dismissal cases was raised initially to £50 000 and is raised annually in line with inflation. It was set, in February 2003, at £53 500.

9.3.5 Assessing the law's effectiveness

The present-day context of unfair dismissal law can be summarised by reviewing **current assessments about the nature and effectiveness of this law**. This can be viewed from two perspectives: that of the employee and that of the employer.

For employees

There are several issues to be considered from the viewpoint of employees. On the positive side, the law provides standards of treatment which have in the past 30 years become more widely understood by employers and applied in employment relations, particularly in larger organisations. The existence of the law and the adverse publicity accorded to certain cases have, arguably, made many employers more circumspect about arbitrary treatment. Furthermore, the law has established procedural requirements for the handling of disciplinary matters and minimising arbitrary treatment.

On the negative side, access to legal remedies does not cover all working people. This is restricted to 'employees' (ERA 1996, s 94(1)). As we have seen in Chapter 2, certain legal tests need to be used to consider whether a person can be so defined as having a contract of employment. Furthermore, certain employees are excluded: those who have less than the necessary qualifying service with an employer at the effective date of termination (ERA 1996, s 108(1)), those who who have exceeded the upper age limit (ERA 1996, s 109(1)). Continuing evidence of employee vulnerability was found in a report of the National Association of Citizens' Advice Bureaux: 'dismissals frequently have nothing to do with employees' failure to perform their jobs adequately. CAB clients are losing their livelihood, and incurring all the problems that that entails, purely because their employer wants to prevent them from attaining employment protection' (NACAB, 1993: 1).

There is, however, some movement in political policy and judicial interpretation in the direction of 'universality'. Also, the upper age limit is being challenged at employment tribunal level as indirect sex discrimination. At present, no clear policy outcome has been decided on this.

The Employment Relations Act 1999 (s 23) provides for the extension of access to statutory employment right to 'workers'. Although, to date, this has not been implemented, the government has issued a consultation paper on the mattter (DTI 2001b).

Further drawbacks for employees have been the complexity in the operation of the complaint process. In one study of the tribunal process, some key findings illustrate this. First, it was found that 'the difference between the tribunals and the ordinary courts are differences of degree not kind . . . The legal member of the tribunal emerges as first among equals, a reflection of the court-like nature of the system which gives primacy to legal considerations' (Dickens *et al.*, 1985). Secondly, 'although the informal model of tribunals was found to have a continuing validity, the majority of self-represented applicants thought they failed to get their case across at their hearing and the majority of both chairpersons and lay members thought self-representation should not be encouraged' (Dickens *et al.*, 1985). Given the development and complexity of employment law, it is unlikely, and unrealistic to presume, that tribunal hearings will be freed from technicality and legal terminology. Nevertheless, the promotion of arbitration measures might help minimise the worst excesses of legalism.

A final drawback for employees has been the inadequacy of the remedies available. The principal effective remedy is compensation. The current median levels of actual compensation are below £5000. The remedies of reinstatement and re-engagement are, largely, ineffective. One survey found that tribunals 'pay a lot of attention to the employers' views regarding the acceptability and practicability of re-employment and rarely award the remedy in the face of employer opposition' (Dickens *et al.*, 1985). There is no evidence to suggest that, at the present time, the situation is different.

For employers

There are, likewise, several issues to be considered from the employers' viewpoint. One purpose of the legislation on unfair dismissal and discipline at work was to help improve the management of people at work. Indeed, the ACAS Code of Practice (2000) captures this in its rationale for disciplinary rules and procedures. These 'are necessary for promoting orderly employment relations as well as fairness and consistency in the treatment of individuals' (para 1).

There is some evidence, over the past 30 years, of greater management efficiency in the handling of discipline and dismissals – particularly in larger organisations. In part, this is due to the almost universal existence of disciplinary procedures. It is reported that, nowadays, 91 per cent of establishments have such a procedure – the larger the establishment the greater the incidence (Cully *et al.*, 1999: 77). Even in smaller organisations (those employing between 25 and 49 staff) 88 per cent have such procedures. However, the incidence of such procedures falls to 72 per cent in organisations with between 10 and 19 employees.

The main incentive for adopting such a procedure is the statutory provision that non-compliance with recommendations in the ACAS Code can be used in evidence against an employer in a tribunal hearing (TULRCA 1992, s 207). Indeed, recent research has shown that tribunal decisions which went against employers invariably did so as a result of procedural irregularity (Earnshaw *et al.*, 1998: i). Among the shortcomings reported were failures to give the dismissed employees an opportunity to defend themselves; not making them aware of the evidence or allegation against them; not holding a disciplinary hearing; or insufficient investigation.

A further insight into disciplinary practice was reported in the Workplace Employee Relations Survey: 'just 3 per cent of all workplaces do not allow employees to be accompanied by a third party in actions taken to discipline or dismiss them' (Cully *et al.*, 1998: 14). This finding was before the enactment of the statutory right to be accompanied (ERA 1999, s 10).

In terms of management decision-making on discipline and dismissals, it is clear that, increasingly, this is not exercised without the benefit of consultation with an HR/personnel management specialist. As early as 1978, one report stated that 'the impression that came through from our discussions with managers was that, as a whole, the employment legislation of recent years had increased the workload, the range of activities and the influence of the personnel function . . . there had been some tendency for the importance of the personnel function to grow following the legislation' (Daniel and Stilgoe, 1978: 41).

This trend became more clear-cut as the following decade passed. By the 1990 Workplace Industrial Relations Survey the network of management advice was becoming more complex. It was reported that 'when personnel managers sought advice from outside their organisation they were very much more likely to turn to the legal profession or to state agencies such as ACAS than they were at the beginning of the decade' (Millward *et al.*, 1992: 357). Confirming the trend to greater juridification, it was stated that 'the law had come to exercise a more significant role than ever before in the day-to-day conduct of employment relationships' (1992: 357).

Despite the procedural and employee relations improvements that have taken place, there are still evident problems. One indicator of this is the extent to which small and medium-sized employers are respondents in employment tribunal cases. Forty-four per cent of unfair dismissal claims originate in organisations employing under 25 employees; and 70 per cent in organisations with under 100 (DTI, 2002). There is also evidence from the Survey of Employment Tribunal Applications 1998 (DTI 2002) that in-company procedures are not fully used. Only 32 per cent of applicants and 58 per cent of employers reported that they were fully used. However, further analysis showed that 'procedures were most likely to be followed (all or part of the way) in unfair dismissal cases' (DTI, 2001: 22).

9.4　The legal framework

9.4.1　Introduction

There are two interlocking aspects to the legal framework: the provisions relating to **disciplinary action short of dismissal**; and those relating to **dismissal**. Normally, it is only in respect of the latter that an employee (if they meet the qualifying requirements) may complain to an employment tribunal. Other disciplinary decisions are rarely scrutinised by courts and tribunals. However, in certain specific circumstances they might be. Disciplinary action might be seen as victimisation or a 'detriment' under discrimination law. The withholding of 'wages' (under the ERA 1996, Part II) might be imposed as a disciplinary sanction. If this is done without contractual authority then a complaint might be made at the employment tribunal. Aside from discrimination law, warnings would not be the subject of a tribunal complaint. However, a pattern of warnings might be considered at tribunal if it was preliminary to dismissal (for poor performance or persistent misconduct). The more unusual disciplinary penalties (demotion, disciplinary transfer or suspension and fining) should be expressly provided for in an employee's contract of employment. If they are imposed without contractual authority, then an action for breach of contract in the High Court or County Court might be taken.

We will, in this section, explore the following areas:

- the nature and purpose of discipline at work;
- circumstances in which contracts of employment end;
- fair and unfair dismissal;
- procedure for redress;
- remedies.

9.4.2 The nature and purpose of discipline at work

A workplace disciplinary framework comprises two operational elements: rules and procedures. These need to be formulated in the context of an organisation's disciplinary policy.

Disciplinary policy

The ACAS Code of Practice emphasises the importance in the formulation of this policy of both management and employee involvement and also of consent. It is this policy that will provide the rules and the disciplinary procedures to be used. Since all workplaces are different (in terms of size, the products made or the services delivered, the technology used, the ways in which work is organised, the qualifications of the workforce), the rules and procedures need to be tailored to these different circumstances. In practice, however, employee involvement in formulating or revising disciplinary procedures is rare (Earnshaw *et al.*, 1998).

Disciplinary rules

In the light of the diversity of organisational circumstances:

> it is unlikely that any set of disciplinary rules can cover all circumstances that may arise. However, it is usual that rules would cover issues such as misconduct, substandard performance (where not covered by a separate capability procedure), harassment or victimisation, misuse of company facilities including computer facilities (e.g. e-mail and the Internet) poor timekeeping and unauthorised absences (ACAS *Code of Practice*: para 5).

It is added that 'rules should not be so general as to be meaningless'.

As a consequence, rules might cover the following matters: attendance at work; compliance with safety standards, theft of company property, confidentiality when dealing with customers/clients, harassment of fellow workers, drink and drug abuse, behaviour outside work, and a possible catch-all requirement relating to behaviour that might bring the company into disrepute.

Clearly, employees need to be informed about rules and the consequence of breaking them – 'in particular they should be given a clear indication of the type of conduct, often referred to as gross misconduct, which may warrant summary dismissal (i.e. dismissal without notice)' (para 7).

Disciplinary procedures

'Disciplinary procedures should not be viewed primarily as a means of imposing sanctions. Rather they should be seen as a way of helping and encouraging improvement amongst workers whose conduct or standard of work is unsatisfactory' (ACAS *Code of Practice*: para 8).

This objective sets a valuable guiding principle. Improvement in the conduct and performance of employees should be encouraged. Certainly, where unfair dismissal was alleged at tribunal, consideration would be given to the steps that an employer had taken: warnings, advice and guidance and training if necessary. A 'reasonable employer' would be expected to make such arrangements. Of course, in certain circumstances, sanctions might be the only appropriate course of action – usually cases defined as 'gross misconduct' (e.g. theft, drunkenness, assault, refusal to obey a lawful and reasonable instruction).

ACAS sets out a number of specifications for disciplinary procedures (*see* Fig. 9.1).

Good disciplinary procedures should:

- Be in writing
- Specify to whom they apply
- Be non-discriminatory
- Provide for matters to be dealt with without undue delay
- Indicate the disciplinary actions which may be taken
- Specify the levels of management which have the authority to take the various forms of disciplinary action
- Provide for workers to be informed of the complaints against them and where possible all relevant evidence before any hearing
- Provide workers with an opportunity to state their case before decisions are reached
- Provide workers with the right to be accompanied
- Ensure that, except for gross misconduct, no worker is dismissed for a first breach of discipline
- Ensure that disciplinary action is not taken until the case has been carefully investigated
- Ensure that workers are given an explanation for any penalty imposed
- Provide a right of appeal normally to a more senior manager and specify the procedure to be followed

---

Figure 9.1 Good disciplinary procedures

Source: ACAS Code of Practice, *Disciplinary and Grievance Procedures*, 2000: para 9.

The specifications in Fig. 9.1 embody the concept of 'procedural fairness'. This is a significant element in unfair dismissal claims. Failure by an employer to comply with the provisions in the ACAS Code (which should be incorporated in the organisation's own disciplinary procedure) is likely to result in a dismissal being ruled unfair. (This issue is discussed in more detail below.) This 'procedural fairness' reflects the two principal rules of 'natural justice'. The first is against partiality (that no one should be judge in his own cause). The second provides the opportunity for a person to state their own case and to know and also be able to challenge the other side's case. Clearly, knowing the allegation, having a full investigation, being given the opportunity to make representations and having the right to appeal, all should ensure compliance with 'natural justice'.

The practical operation of disciplinary procedures will be considered further in section 9.5: Employment policies and practices.

Disciplinary penalties

There is a hierarchy of disciplinary penalties in terms of severity. Minor infringements of workplace rules may be dealt with by an **informal oral (or verbal) warning**. More serious matters might result in a **formal oral (or verbal) warning**.

Further misconduct might lead to **formal written warning** and, subsequently, to a **final written warning**. Where disciplinary action is used, it is usual to progress through these different sanctions. However, if an employer regards a first offence as serious enough for a final warning but not serious enough for dismissal, then such a warning might be used as the first penalty. Warnings should indicate the likely consequences of a further breach of disciplinary rules. In the case of a final warning, this might be dismissal.

Some disciplinary procedures provide for other penalties short of dismissal: **demotion**, **disciplinary transfer** or **suspension** or **fining**. These are permissible. However, there should be contractual authority for imposing them. It would be good practice for these contractual terms to be explained to all employees at induction.

Dismissal is the most severe disciplinary penalty reserved for the most serious misconduct – whether this is a single act of 'gross misconduct' or persistent minor misconduct. Dismissal can take one of two forms: with due notice (i.e. what the individual employee is entitled to), or instant or summary dismissal (without notice). It is possible for an employer to provide pay in lieu of any notice. In such cases, the termination date is the last day of work.

> When deciding whether a disciplinary penalty is appropriate and what form it should take it is important to bear in mind the need to act reasonably in all circumstances. Factors which might be relevant include, the extent to which standards have been breached, precedent, the worker's general record, position, length of service and special circumstances which might make it appropriate to adjust the severity of the penalty (ACAS *Code of Practice*: para 16).

9.4.3 Circumstances in which contracts of employment end

There are several circumstances in which a contract of employment might end. The first is **resignation by the employee**. This may be for the simple reason that the employee has obtained another job and leaving the employer is reasonably amicable. However, the resignation might be because the employee can no longer tolerate the behaviour of the employer. The employee feels forced to resign. In these circumstances, there might the possibility of a constructive dismissal claim at an employment tribunal. The issue here would be whether the employer by their behaviour was repudiating the contract of employment – i.e. indicating that they were not bound by one of its essential terms. (As we see elsewhere in this book, this can cover, for example, the non-payment of wages, harassment or a persistent failure to comply with health and safety standards.)

The second set of circumstances relate to **dismissal by the employer**. Dismissal can be with notice. This can be the minimum which is due under statute (ERA 1996, s 86) or that which is due under the contract of employment if it is longer than the statutory minimum. Failure by an employer to provide due notice can lead to a claim for *wrongful dismissal*. Alternatively, the dismissal can be without notice. This is usually in cases of 'gross misconduct' as determined by the employer by reference to workplace rules. The reason for dismissal does, of course, vary. As we shall see below, statute law provides for fair and unfair reasons (ERA 1996, s 98). A sacked employee may then (assuming they are eligible) challenge the reason for the dismissal at a tribunal as part of the complaint against the ex-employer.

Finally, termination of a contract of employment can be a result of **frustration**. This is where, as a result of some unforeseen event it is not possible for the contract to be carried out. It covers employee ill-health and these are the circumstances we will discuss here. (It also covers death or imprisonment.) Courts are cautious of accepting frustration in respect of ill-health cases because it can save employers from having to answer an unfair dismissal claim. It is for the employer to prove frustration of contract.

If the employee is still able to perform the contract or will be able to do so in the foreseeable future, then, the contract cannot be 'frustrated'. Absence through ill-health for a long period of time does not automatically mean that there is frustration. In the (former) National Industrial Relations Court (NIRC), the issues to be considered were identified as: the terms of the contract, how long the employment was likely to last in the absence of sickness, the nature of the employment and the length of the employee's service (*Marshall* v *Harland and Wolff Ltd* [1972] IRLR 90, NIRC). In this case, the employer did not prove frustration. There was no medical evidence that Mr Marshall was permanently incapacitated and would never be able to resume work.

A few years later, the EAT (in *Egg Stores* v *Leibovici* [1976] IRLR 376) added to the list of considerations. These included: the nature of the job; the nature, length and effect of the illness; the need for the employer to get the employee's work done. A further consideration was added by the EAT in 1990 (*Williams* v *Watsons Luxury Coaches Ltd* [1990] IRLR 164). Here the employee had been hurt in an accident at work, causing long-term sick absence and eventual dismissal. It was stated by the tribunal that 'the party alleging frustration [i.e. the employer] should not be allowed to rely upon the frustrating event, if that event was caused by that party, or at least where it was caused by its fault'.

The caution about using frustration still remains. It is preferable for an employer to dismiss within the context of statutory fair dismissal provisions, arguing that the dismissal was on grounds of the employee's long-term incapability. The employer needs to demonstrate reasonableness in the circumstances. This is the critical issue (*see* section 9.4.7 on reasonableness).

9.4.4 Fair and unfair dismissal

The statutory framework relating to dismissal is concerned with two dimensions: substantive fairness; and procedural fairness. **Substantive fairness** concerns the reason for an employee's dismissal. This will involve consideration of whether or not the reason, or principal reason, given by the employer is the true reason; and whether this reason is a fair reason in law (ERA 1996, s 98). It also involves assessment of whether in the circumstances of the case it was reasonable for the employer to dismiss for that reason. **Procedural fairness** concerns the way in which the disciplinary process leading to the decision to dismiss was handled. Failures to comply with the ACAS Code of Practice can be used in evidence against the employer (TULRCA 1992, s 207). In brief, then, there are three statutory tests of 'fairness' which have to be considered by employment tribunals:

- the reason for dismissal;
- the reasonableness of that decision to dismiss in all the circumstances;
- the fairness of the procedures used.

We will look at these issues in more detail.

9.4.5 Fair reasons for dismissal

In deciding whether or not a dismissal is fair or unfair, the employer has to show the reason (or principal reason) for the dismissal. The employer then has to show that it is 'fair' reason or it is 'some other substantial reason of a kind such as to justify the dismissal of an employee holding the position which the employee held' (ERA 1996, s 98(1)(b)).

There are four specified categories of 'fair' reasons: capability and qualifications; conduct; redundancy; and a statutory bar. There may also be 'some of other substantial reason' for dismissal. We will look at these in more detail. The reasonableness of dismissing a person for these reasons will be explored in the next section.

Capability and qualifications

This is where a reason 'relates to the **capability or qualifications** of the employee for performing work of the kind which he was employed by the employer to do' (ERA 1996, s 98(2)(a)).

Capability

An employee's capability is 'assessed by reference to skill, aptitude, health or any other physical or mental quality' (ERA 1996, s 98(3)(a)). Such a reason can be related to either disciplinary or non-disciplinary matters. For example, poor performance or substandard work is likely to be a relevant disciplinary matter, while dismissal on the grounds of ill-health is not. Care would also need to be taken to ensure that other related statutory rights (under the Disability Discrimination Act 1995) are not infringed.

Qualifications

An employee's qualifications include 'any degree, diploma or other academic, technical or professional qualification relevant to the position which is held' (ERA 1996, s 98(3)(b)). The reason for dismissal might concern the failure to acquire an appropriate qualification. Misrepresentation of qualifications would probably be construed as gross misconduct.

Conduct

A second fair reason for dismissal is where it 'relates to the **conduct** of the employee' (ERA 1996, s 98(2)(b)). This concerns any behaviour by an employee. The expectations in any workplace are likely to be prescribed in the disciplinary rules. Misconduct is a wide spectrum of unacceptable behaviour ranging from minor infringements (like lateness or unauthorised absence) to behaviour which is criminal (e.g. assault, theft, reckless disregard of safety standards). Earnshaw *et al.* (1998: i) reported that in their survey of employment tribunal applications, conduct was the most common reason for dismissal.

Redundancy

A third reason is where the employee is **redundant** (ERA 1996, s 98(2)(c). *See* Chapter 3.

Contravening a statutory duty or restriction

A fourth reason is where 'the employee could not continue to work in the position which he held without **contravention** (either on his part or on that of his employer) **of a duty or restriction** imposed by or under an enactment' (ERA 1996, s 98(2)(d)). This covers such circumstances as where, for example, an employee loses their driving licence and consequently can no longer drive for an employer. If this is the employee's principal responsibility then the employer might dismiss.

Some other substantial reason

This category concerns 'other reasons' which must be 'substantial'. First, it could encompass the termination of a contract on grounds of 'business need' when an employer wishes to introduce changing working practices which an employee is resisting (*see* Chapter 3). Secondly, it will cover the 'economic, technical and organisational' reasons for dismissal in a transfer of undertakings situation (TUPE Regulations, reg 8) (*see* Chapter 3). Finally, it could cover the dismissal of an employee who was convicted of a criminal offence outside work. It may be felt that the nature of the offence was so serious as to make continued employment impossible. Often an important consideration is whether an offence committed outside of work can breach the implied duty of trust under the contract of employment. The ACAS *Code of Practice* recommends that criminal charges or convictions outside of employment 'should not be treated as automatic reasons for dismissal. The main consideration should be whether the offence is one that makes workers unsuitable for their type of work' (para 26).

9.4.6 Unfair reasons for dismissal

In other chapters in this book, various unfair reasons for dismissal have been outlined. In fact these statutory protections usually extend beyond dismissal to encompass 'any other detriment'. This term includes 'action short of dismissal' (i.e. other disciplinary action). Complaints about infringements of these statutory rights are not restricted by the length of service of the applicant. The key protections are summarised here:

Sex

It is unlawful for an employer to discriminate against an employee by dismissing them or subjecting them to any other detriment (SDA 1975, s 6(2)). This protection extends equally to women and men, and, under case law, the European 'principle of equal treatment' includes transsexuals. Because discrimination on grounds of pregnancy is direct sex discrimination, the protection also extends to pregnant women. In addition, a range of specific protections for pregnant workers are provided in the ERA 1996, s 99 (*see* Chapters 4 and 13).

Race

It is similarly unlawful for an employer to discriminate against an employee by dismissing them or subjecting them to any other detriment (RRA 1976, s 4(2)) (*see* Chapter 5).

Disability

It is similarly unlawful for an employer to discriminate against an employee by dismissing them or subjecting them to any other detriment (DDA 1995, s 4(2)) (*see* Chapter 6).

Redundancy

Whilst redundancy is a fair reason for dismissal (ERA 1996, s 98(2)), the criteria for selecting people for redundancy must be objective and not based on unfair discrimination (e.g. sex, pregnancy, race, disability). If this were shown to be the case, then the redundancy dismissal would be found to be unfair. Provisions on these matters are also found as follows:

- trade union membership (TULRCA 1992, s 152);
- representation responsibilities (ERA 1996, s 103);
- health and safety action/responsibilities (ERA 1996, s 100);
- trustees of occupational pension schemes (ERA 1996, s 102);
- transfer situations (TUPE 1981, reg 8);
- working time rights (WTR 1998, reg 32);
- national minimum wage rights (NMW Act 1998, s 25).

Assertion of a statutory right

An employee who is dismissed for asserting a statutory right shall be regarded as unfairly dismissed if the reason (or, if more than one, the principal reason) for the dismissal is:

- that the employee brought proceedings (at a tribunal) against the employer to enforce 'a relevant statutory right'; or
- that the employee alleged that the employer had infringed a right of theirs which is 'a relevant statutory right' (ERA 1996, s 104).

'A relevant statutory right' is defined as:

- any right in the ERA 1996 'for which the remedy for its infringement is by way of a complaint or reference to an employment tribunal'; and
- certain rights conferred under the TULRCA 1992.

It is 'immaterial' whether or not the employee has the right or whether or not the right has been infringed. But, 'the claim to the right and that it has been infringed must be made in good faith' (ERA 1996, s 104(2)).

Shop workers and betting shop workers

Such workers who refuse Sunday work have a right not to be dismissed because of their refusal (ERA 1996, s 101).

Working time cases

The 1998 Working Time Regulations provide protection (reg 32) against dismissal for those employees where the reason or principal reason for their dismissal was:

- a refusal to comply with a requirement by the employer which was in contravention of the regulations;
- a refusal to forgo a right conferred on the employee by the Regulations;
- a failure to sign a workforce agreement; or 'to enter into, or agree to vary or extend, any other agreement with his employer'.

National minimum wage

An employee is regarded as unfairly dismissed if the reason or principal reason for the dismissal was:

- any action taken to enforce the right;
- because the employer was prosecuted as a result of action taken by the employee;
- because 'the employee qualifies, or will or might qualify for the national minimum wage or for a particular rate of national minimum wage' (NMW Act, s 25).

9.4.7 Reasonableness in the circumstances

Once an employer has satisfied the requirement that the dismissal is for a fair reason (ERA 1996, s 98(1)–(3)), then the next issue to be considered is 'whether the dismissal is fair or unfair (having regard to the reason shown by the employer)' (ERA 1996, s 98(4)).

Deciding this question of fairness depends on a number of factors. These are set out in the Act in the following way. Whether a dismissal is fair 'depends on whether in the circumstances (including the size and administrative resources of the employer's undertaking) the employer acted reasonably or unreasonably in treating it as a sufficient reason for dismissing the employee'. Also, the question of fairness 'shall be determined in accordance with equity and the substantial merits of the case'. This reinforces the importance of seeing each individual dismissal case being considered, against the specified standards, on its own facts and circumstances.

The EAT has ruled that it is possible for different employers to take different courses of action in respect of the same employee in the same set of circumstances. It identified that there was 'a range of reasonable responses' to particular conduct or standards of performance. So, if a tribunal finds that an employer's decision to dismiss is within that range of reasonable responses, then, it should find a dismissal fair.

We will look at a number of elements in the concept of reasonableness: previous warnings; reasonable belief in misconduct cases; different treatment for different employees; evidence from informants; criminal convictions unconnected with work; capability and ill-health.

Previous warnings

The EAT has ruled on the relevance of an employee's disciplinary record (*Auguste Noel Ltd* v *Curtis* [1990] IRLR 326). Warnings for unconnected disciplinary offences (concerning conduct) could be taken into account despite the fact. The nature and timing of such warnings could be considered by employers.

Different treatment for different employees

In a disciplinary case involving more than one employee committing the same offence, it is possible that whereas one might be dismissed another might continue in employment. The EAT has ruled (*London Borough of Harrow* v *Cunningham* [1996] IRLR 256) that differential treatment can be within the range of reasonable responses of an employer. The employer can take into account disciplinary records – which may be clean for one person and contain warnings for the other.

Reasonable belief in misconduct cases

The EAT has ruled (*British Home Stores* v *Burchell* [1978] IRLR 379) that, in misconduct cases, the following tests apply. First, a tribunal must decide whether an employer had established a reasonable belief in the employee's guilt. Secondly, it must be shown that there were reasonable grounds to sustain this belief. Thirdly, the employer must have carried out as much investigation into the matter as was reasonable in all the circumstances.

Evidence from informants

In misconduct cases, evidence from an informant can be used. The EAT (*Linfood Cash and Carry Ltd* v *Thomson and Another* [1989] IRLR 235) has provided guidance on how this might be approached and suggests that steps be taken to preserve anonymity where required:

- there should be a written statement setting out the information from the informer, noting any circumstantial evidence and reasons why the evidence might be fabricated;

- investigations should take place;

- if the informant refuses to attend a disciplinary hearing, they should be interviewed by an appropriate manager;

- the written statement should be provided to the employee who is alleged to have committed the offence;

- full notes should be taken of the proceedings.

Criminal convictions unconnected with work

In some cases, a decision to dismiss for a criminal offence outside work can be fair. One example is the decision to dismiss a schoolteacher convicted of an act of gross indecency with an adult in a public lavatory. This is likely to be regarded as fair (assuming the disciplinary action is conducted fairly) given the position of responsibility of the teacher and the vulnerability of school children. In contrast, dismissals relating to the possession of certain drugs, especially cannabis, can be fair or unfair. Factors that might be involved are the extent to which the ex-employee is an habitual user, the nature of the work that the employee undertakes and their position within the organisation.

Capability and ill-health

Reasonableness in this area involves a number of matters: consultation, the use of medical evidence, consideration of alternative employment and consideration of the duty to make reasonable adjustments.

Consultation with the employee

'Discussions and consultation will often bring to light facts and circumstances of which the employers were unaware, and which would throw new light on the problem . . . only one thing is certain and that is that if the employee is not consulted and given an opportunity to state his case, an injustice may be done' (Phillips J in *East Lindsey District Council* v *Daubney* [1977] ICR 566, EAT).

Medical evidence

This needs to be available. The decision of an employer to dismiss is an employment question determined in the light of available medical evidence. The employer should seek medical advice from the employee's general practitioner or occupational health doctor (or, as appropriate, a specialist). If the employee does not consent to the employer having access to medical evidence, then the employer must act on the facts available.

Alternative employment

An employer should explore the possibility of alternative employment, but is not obliged to create a job.

The duty to make reasonable adjustments

Since 1996, the Disability Discrimination Act 1995 has added to the considerations that employers must undertake (*see* Chapter 6).

9.4.8 Procedural fairness

Procedural fairness is determined by the ACAS *Code of Practice* on disciplinary procedures. As indicated elsewhere, breach of the code can be used in evidence against an employer before a tribunal. It is possible for a tribunal or court to find that procedural defects are significant enough to make a dismissal unfair – even if on the substantive issues the employer had good grounds to dismiss. Indeed, in one survey of unfair dismissal applications to employment tribunals, it was found that 'where the employer lost, the reason related almost without exception to procedural shortcomings' (Earnshaw *et al.*, 1998: i). Compliance with procedural requirements is, consequently, most important. Some of the key rulings and guidance are set out below in respect of: natural justice, omission of a stage in the disciplinary procedure, appeal and representation.

Natural justice

In *Byrne* v *BOC Ltd* [1992] IRLR 505 the EAT found that a manager was too involved in a case where there was an allegation of misconduct to be able to deal with an appeal fairly. He was, in effect, 'a judge in his own cause'. He had investigated the matter and, having taken advice from the personnel department, decided on the appropriate level of punishment as well as having been the person who instigated the original hearing. His involvement amounted to a breach of natural justice, making the dismissal unfair.

Omission of a stage

In one case (*Sartor* v *P&O European Ferries (Felixstowe Ltd)* [1992] IRLR 271), the stage at which an employee should have been informed of the allegation prior to a disciplinary hearing was omitted. The Court of Appeal ruled that procedural defects which might result in an unfair dismissal could be rectified by an opportunity of a rehearing appeal.

Appeal

The ACAS *Code of Practice* recommends this (paras 9 (xiv) and 27–31) – even in small organisations: 'The opportunity to appeal against a disciplinary decision is essential to natural justice'. It adds that 'workers may choose to raise appeals on a number of grounds which could include the perceived unfairness of the judgement, the severity of the penalty, new evidence coming to light or procedural irregularities' (para 27). Good practice is that appeals are dealt with 'as promptly as possible' (para 28).

A question that frequently arises is the appropriateness of the individual who hears the appeal. Usually, this is a senior manager who has not been previously involved in the disciplinary procedure. 'In small organisations it may not be possible to find such an individual and in these circumstances the person dealing with the appeal should act as impartially as possible' (para 29). It is commented in the ACAS Code that 'independent arbitration is sometimes an appropriate means of resolving disciplinary issues and where the parties concerned agree it may constitute the appeals stage of procedure' (para 29).

Representation

The Employment Relations Act 1999 created a legal right for workers to be accompanied by a fellow worker or trade union representative of their choice during disciplinary procedures (*see* Fig. 9.2).

What is the right? For a worker to be accompanied in certain disciplinary hearings. They should make a 'reasonable request' to the employer to be accompanied (paras 50 and 56).

Who is the companion? The worker can choose from one of the following:

- A fellow worker.
- A full-time official employed by a trade union (irrespective of whether or not the particular union is recognised by the employer).
- A lay union official who has been certified in writing by the union 'as having experience of, or as having received training in, acting as a worker's companion' at disciplinary hearings (paras 57 and 60).

Which disciplinary hearings? 'It would not generally be good practice for the worker to be accompanied' at an informal interview or counselling session (para 53). It might be appropriate at the investigative stage where disciplinary action is contemplated. In particular, the statutory right to be accompanied applies to the following situations (para 54):

- Where a formal warning is given (i.e. a warning that is recorded).
- Where some other disciplinary action is undertaken (e.g. suspension without pay, demotion or dismissal).
- Where a warning or some other disciplinary action is confirmed.

The disciplinary hearing: 'The chosen companion has a statutory right to address the hearing but no statutory right to answer questions on the worker's behalf.' That said, the companion should 'with the agreement of the employer, be allowed to participate as fully as possible in the hearing' (para 64).

Infringements of the right: 'If an employer fails to allow a worker to be accompanied at a disciplinary . . . hearing or fails to re-arrange a hearing to a reasonable date proposed by the worker when a companion cannot attend on the date originally proposed, the worker may present a complaint to an employment tribunal' (para 65).

Remedy: 'If the tribunal finds in favour of the worker the employer may be liable to pay compensation of up to two weeks pay as defined in statute' (under ERA 1996) (para 65).

Broadly similar provisions are available, under the statutory right to be accompanied, in relation to grievances concerning legal duties of the employer to a worker – under the terms of the contract or under statute law (para 55).

Figure 9.2 The statutory right to be accompanied

Source: Summarised from ACAS *Code of Practice on Disciplinary and Grievance Procedures* (2000).

Misconduct cases: Scenarios

Read the following scenarios. Decide on the following in relation to each:

■ *What is the reason for the dismissal? Is it a 'fair' reason?*

■ *Consider whether or not the employer's decision to dismiss for that reason was reasonable in the circumstances. What specific circumstances would you expect a 'reasonable employer' to take into consideration?*

■ *How well did the disciplinary procedure measure up to recommended standards of procedural fairness?*

9.1.1 The supermarket manager: persistent misconduct?

John Smith, aged 27 years, is an assistant manager at the Dorchester branch of a supermarket. He has been employed in this post since November 1999. He was regarded as a good worker, but he began to have some attendance problems for which he received informal verbal warnings. He was required to take the days of absence as part of his annual leave. On Monday, 15 April 2002, the store manager spoke to him about the overall pattern of his attendance:

■ Monday, 11 February 2002: 60 minutes late because of clock failure;

■ Friday, 23 February 2002: absent one day because his wife was sick;

■ Monday, 11 and Tuesday, 12 March 2002: absent two days because both his wife and child were sick;

■ Friday, 23 March 2002: 30 minutes late because he overslept;

■ Thursday, 12 April 2002: absent one day because his child was sick.

John Smith said that his wife had been suffering from stress because of a recent court case that he had been involved in and because of the family's financial difficulties. He explained his absences and lateness as arising from the need to care for his three-year-old child.

The store manager asked him to ensure that the situation improved; otherwise he would be reported to the district manager. He was given a formal written warning. For a while the situation did improve.

But, he was 60 minutes late on Friday, 31 May because his car broke down. The situation then deteriorated again:

■ Monday, 8 July 2002: 45 minutes late because he overslept;

■ Monday, 15 July 2002: 60 minutes late because of clock failure;

■ Wednesday, 17 July 2002: absent for one day because he had an appointment at the council offices.

On Monday, 22 July, the store manager (who had been away on two weeks' holiday) asked for an explanation of his poor attendance. He asked why he had not notified the temporary store manager of his absence for an appointment at the council offices. John Smith said that it was an appointment at short notice. The lateness was because of his child keeping him awake during the night.

A formal disciplinary hearing was held on Monday, 29 July before the district manager. John Smith chose not to be represented. He restated his reasons for his poor attendance. The district manager found them to be unsatisfactory. He said that he was in a responsible position and the company relied on him on occasions to open the store – particularly since longer opening hours were implemented. He dismissed him with one month's pay in lieu of notice.

9.1.2 The bakery shift manager: gross misconduct?
Alistair McDougal was employed by a bakery for 19 years. The bakery, where he worked as a shift manager, had introduced a system to reduce stock losses, under which staff who wished to buy the bakery's products had to make immediate payment and obtain a ticket recording the purchase. McDougal was found leaving work with a loaf for which he had not paid. The company investigated this matter at a disciplinary inquiry carried out by the general manager. McDougal admitted that he had taken the bread but said that he had intended to pay for it the next day. In the general manager's view, there had been no such intention to pay and Alistair McDougal was dismissed. On appeal, in accordance with the company's procedure, the dismissal was upheld.

Feedback on this exercise is provided in the Appendix to this book.

9.4.9 Procedures for redress

The procedures for a person to obtain redress for unfair dismissal involve the following:

Deciding entitlement to complain

The right to complain about unfair dismissal is available to '**employees**' (*see* Chapter 2). The employee must have **the required continuous service** with the employer in question. For certain allegations (relating to discrimination law) no qualifying service is required (*see* Chapters 4–6). Furthermore, the employee must not be above the age of 65 years or **the normal retiring age** for that employment if this is below 65 years. Finally, the employee must have been **dismissed** by the employer.

Application to the employment tribunal

An applicant who alleges unfair dismissal has to complete **the appropriate form** (obtainable from tribunal offices, job centres and Citizens' Advice Bureaux). This should be sent to the tribunal office **within three months** of the effective date of the dismissal. It is possible for a tribunal to allow applications to be considered after the three months 'where it is satisfied that it was not reasonably practicable for the complaint to be presented' (ERA 1996, s 111(2)). Among other information, this form requires the person to summarise the basis of their complaint.

The employer's response

Having received a copy of the complaint, the employer must return their response **within 14 days**. If the employer does not contest an application, a tribunal can proceed without a full hearing.

The Advisory Conciliation and Arbitration Service

ACAS has two contributions to this process. First, it is under a statutory duty to offer **conciliation** for each complaint lodged with the employment tribunal with a view to promoting a settlement (TULRCA 1992, s 211). The outcome may be a **settlement** of the issue (with the employer paying a sum to the dismissed employee). As a consequence, the matter does not proceed to a hearing at the employment tribunal. Generally, the terms of the settlement will be recorded. Reflecting the pattern of recent years, 49 per cent of unfair dismissal cases are settled by ACAS (*Annual Report 2001/02*). Alternatively, the applicant may **withdraw** their complaint. This happens in 27 per cent of unfair dismissal cases. In 23 per cent of cases, the matter progresses to **a tribunal hearing**.

The second contribution of ACAS is to offer the option of **arbitration** to the parties. They may decline, in which case the matter can proceed to the employment tribunal. This scheme came into effect in 2001. It is restricted to non-discrimination unfair dismissal cases. The arbitrator's decision will be **final and binding**. The complaint may not then progress to a tribunal hearing (*see* Fig. 9.3). The arbitration process is intended to be 'confidential, relatively fast, cost-efficient, non-legalistic and informal' (ACAS, 2001b: 2). The scheme is not intended to deal with complex legal issues.

Compromise agreements

It is possible for the employer and the ex-employee to reach a compromise agreement. This would be a **settlement of the unfair dismissal claim** and an agreement by the ex-employee not to proceed with the tribunal application. Normally, such agreements to preclude the exercise of statutory rights would be void (ERA 1996, s 203(1)). However, special provision is made for 'compromise agreements', provided they meet certain conditions (ERA 1996, s 203(3)–(4)). These conditions are:

- the agreement must be in writing;
- it must relate to the particular complaint;
- the ex-employee must have received independent legal advice on 'the terms and effect of the proposed agreement' and 'in particular, its effect on his ability to pursue his rights before an employment tribunal';
- the adviser can be a qualified lawyer, a trade union officer, employee or member who has been certified in writing by the union as competent and authorised to give advice, or an advice-centre worker who is certified and authorised to give advice;
- the adviser must have in force indemnity insurance;
- the agreement must identify the legal adviser; and
- 'the agreement must state that the conditions regulating compromise agreements under this Act are satisfied'.

Preliminary hearing

The employment tribunal can hold a preliminary hearing to resolve **jurisdictional issues**. It will decide whether or not a party is entitled to bring or contest a matter. Each party can submit representations in writing and advance oral arguments before the tribunal.

Who can use the scheme? An ex-employee who has a right to submit an unfair dismissal claim to an employment tribunal. The former employer must also agree to go to arbitration. The decision to enter the scheme is entirely voluntary.

The arbitration agreement: This is signed by both parties under the auspices of an ACAS conciliation officer or an independent legal adviser. Both parties agree that they will forgo the right to a public hearing and the right to cross-examine witnesses. Once the agreement is signed, the unfair dismissal claim can no longer be heard by an employment tribunal.

Is there a right of appeal? Both parties accept in making the arbitration agreement that the decision of the arbitrator is final and binding. So, there is no appeal to an employment tribunal or to the Employment Appeals Tribunal. Only in very exceptional circumstances (where there is an allegation of 'serious irregularity') can there be a complaint about the conduct of the proceedings by the arbitrator.

The arbitrator: On receipt of a valid arbitration agreement, ACAS will appoint an arbitrator from its panel. The parties have no choice of arbitrator.

The hearing: The parties give the arbitrator a statement of their case before the hearing. The hearing is informal and the arbitrator will question the parties on their evidence and give them opportunities to outline their arguments. There is no cross-examination as at an employment tribunal. An inquisitorial rather than adversarial approach will be adopted by the arbitrator. There is no formal legal procedure – for example, the taking of oaths. Legally qualified people may attend the hearing but they have no special standing. The hearing is private and the award is confidential.

The arbitrator's terms of reference: In deciding whether the dismissal was fair or unfair, the arbitrator shall:

■ Have regard to general principles of fairness and good conduct in employment relations instead of applying legal tests or rules (arising from case law). This means that, for example, the arbitrator would draw on the ACAS *Code of Practice on Discipline and Grievance Procedures* (2000) and the advisory handbook, *Discipline and Grievances at Work* (2001).

■ Apply European Community law as appropriate.

The arbitrator shall not decide the case by substituting what he or she would have done for the actions taken by the employer.

The award: The arbitrator will decide whether the dismissal was fair or unfair. If it is determined to be unfair, reinstatement, re-engagement or compensation may be awarded. These decisions are made in a similar way to those made by employment tribunals.

The award is binding and enforceable in the courts.

Figure 9.3   The ACAS scheme for unfair dismissal arbitration

Source: ACAS arbitration scheme for the resolution of unfair dismissal disputes (ACAS, 2001b).

Pre-hearing review

A tribunal will consider the application and the response together with written representations and documents and oral argument. It will not hear details of the evidence. The tribunal can decide that the ex-employee's claim or the employer's defence has no **reasonable prospect of success**. If the party wishes to continue the proceedings, then the tribunal may order that party to pay up to £500 deposit (set in 2001) as a condition of being permitted to do so. This has to be paid within 21 days. There is also a liability of paying up to £10 000 (also set in 2001) towards the costs of the successful party. So, for example, an ex-employee who is advised that their unfair dismissal claim is weak may progress to a full employment tribunal hearing but on the condition that the deposit is paid and at the risk that they might be liable for the employer's costs up to the limit of £10 000.

Full tribunal hearing

The application is heard by **a tribunal of three persons**: a qualified lawyer who chairs and two lay members. Historically, one of the lay members is drawn from an employers' panel and one from an employees' panel. However, the Lord Chancellor in recent years has initiated a wider recruitment and selection exercise to encourage individual applications from experienced members of the public.

Normally, the applicant goes first. The applicant may make a statement, be questioned by the employer's representative and the tribunal and may call witnesses. The approach should be **inquisitorial** rather than adversarial.

The **evidence** before the tribunal can comprise written reasons for the dismissal, the employer's written response form, further particulars of the employer's reasons for the dismissal, and various relevant documents concerning employment. The tribunal has power to order an employer to provide more information and may order a witness summons. It can require a written answer to any question to help clarify matters and progress the proceedings.

The **possible outcomes** of a tribunal hearing are: the rejection of the application, or a ruling that the dismissal was fair, or, if the dismissal is ruled to be unfair, an award of compensation and, possibly, an order for the employer to re-engage or reinstate the ex-employee.

Earnshaw *et al.* (1998: i) reported, from a survey of tribunal claims from three particular sectors, that 58 per cent of dismissal claims were decided in favour of the employer; and 42 per cent in favour of the applicant. The reported situation, overall, is that in half of the cases that go to a full employment tribunal hearing, the applicant is successful. (There are variations between jurisdictions. For example, most hearings into sex and race discrimination find against the applicant.) The remedy that is granted is almost always financial compensation. Reinstatement is ordered very rarely – in only 0.3 per cent of hearings (DTI, 2001a).

Before we discuss the remedies that are available to unfairly dismissed ex-employees, there is one other matter to be considered: the issue of interim relief.

Interim relief

This is a form of interim re-employment pending the determination of a complaint at a full tribunal hearing or until it is otherwise settled. It is provided for in statute law in respect of particular complaints. It arises where an employee complains of unfair dismissal by their employer and the reason or principal reason for the dismissal relates to rights of trade union membership (TULRCA 1992, s 152), health and safety responsibilities and representation rights (ERA 1996, s 100), being a pension trustee (ERA 1996, s 102), a workforce representative (under the Working Time Regulations 1998, Sch 1), or being an employee representative or candidate for election in respect of collective redundancies and transfers of undertakings (ERA 1996, s 103).

The dismissed employee may apply to the employment tribunal for an order for interim relief. Such an application must be made before the end of seven days immediately after the effective date of dismissal (ERA 1996, s 128). In the case of trade union membership complaints, there must also be 'a certificate in writing signed by an authorised official of the independent trade union' (TULRCA 1992, s 161). This should state that on the date of dismissal the employee was or proposed to become a member of the union and that 'there appear to be reasonable grounds for supposing that the reason for his dismissal (or, if more than one, the principal reason) was one alleged in the complaint' (s 161(3)(b)). The tribunal shall determine the application for interim relief 'as soon as practicable after receiving the application' (TULRCA 1992, s 162; ERA 1996, s 128(3)).

In such a hearing the tribunal must be satisfied that the applicant was dismissed for the reason stated. It must ask the employer whether or not they will reinstate or re-engage the ex-employee. If the employer agrees to reinstate or re-engage, an order is made accordingly. If the employee refuses the re-engagement offer because the terms are unacceptable and the tribunal takes the view that the refusal is reasonable, then it must make 'an order for continuation of the contract of employment' (TULRCA 1992, ss 163–4; ERA 1996, ss 129–30). Such an order will be in force until the date the complaint is settled or determined by the tribunal.

The order is that:

the contract of employment will continue in force –
(a) for the purposes of pay or any other benefit derived from employment, seniority, pension rights and other similar matters, and
(b) for the purposes of determining for any purpose the period for which the employee has been continuously employed from the date of its termination (whether before or after the making of the order) until the determination or settlement of the complaint (TULRCA 1992, s 164; ERA 1996, s 130).

9.4.10 The remedies

There are two remedies available to an applicant who successfully claims unfair dismissal: an order for reinstatement or for re-engagement; and a compensation award.

In deciding whether or not to make an order for reinstatement or an order for re-engagement, the tribunal has to approach the matter as follows (ERA 1996, s 116). First, it considers a reinstatement order. It will take into account whether the ex-employee wishes to be reinstated, whether it is practical for the employer to comply with the order and whether the applicant caused or contributed to their own dismissal. If it decides not to make the reinstatement order, then it will consider the feasibility of a re-engagement order. Again, it will take account of any wish of the ex-employee about the order to be made, the practicality for the employer concerned of complying with the order, and whether the applicant caused or contributed to their own dismissal. Practicality for an employer does not include taking account of the fact that a permanent employee has been engaged to replace the dismissed employee (ERA 1996, s 116(4)).

Reinstatement

This refers to the circumstances in which a person is taken back into his previous job, as if they had not been dismissed (ERA 1996, ss 113–14). In making such an order the tribunal shall specify:

- any amount payable to the employee in respect of any benefit which the employee might have had but for the dismissal. This includes arrears of pay for the period between the dismissal date to the date of reinstatement. It includes any improvements to terms and conditions the employee might have had if they had not been dismissed (e.g. a pay increase);
- any rights and privileges, including seniority and pension rights, which must be restored to the employee;
- the date by which the order must be complied with.

Re-engagement

This means that the person is employed in another job on terms and conditions not less favourable than those that would have applied if they had not been dismissed. The order is 'on such terms as the tribunal may decide'. It covers engagement by 'the employer or by a successor of the employer or by an associated employer'. The employment must be 'comparable to that from which he was dismissed or other suitable employment' (ERA 1996, ss 113 and 115).

The re-engagement order shall specify:

- the identity of the employer;
- the nature of the employment;
- the remuneration for the employment;
- any amount payable by the employer in respect of any benefit which the complainant might reasonably be expected to have had but for the dismissal (between the date of the dismissal and the date of the re-engagement). This includes arrears of pay;
- any rights and privileges (including seniority and pension rights) which must be restored to the employee;
- the date by which the order must be complied with.

If an order is made for reinstatement or re-engagement and the employer fails to comply with it, the employer will be liable to pay additional compensation (ERA 1996, s 117).

Compensation

Where a tribunal makes an award of compensation for unfair dismissal (excluding redundancy cases) it consists of **a basic award** (ERA 1996, s 119) and **a compensatory award** (ERA 1996, s 123). There is also the possibility of **an additional award** (ERA 1996, s 117(3)).

Basic award

The calculation of this takes account of:

- the employee's period of continuous employment, which ended on the effective date of termination;

■ allowing appropriate amounts of money as follows:

- one-and-a-half week's pay for each year of employment in which the employee was not below the age of 41 years;

- one week's pay for each year of employment in which the employee was below the age of 41 years but not below the age of 22 years; and

- half a week's pay for each year of employment in which the employee was below the age of 22 years.

There are additional points to be considered in this framework. First, the maximum amount of a week's pay that can be taken into account is £260 per week (as of 1 February 2003). (This figure is reviewed periodically by the Secretary of State.) Secondly, where 20 years' employment has been calculated, then no account shall be taken of any earlier year. Thirdly, where the effective date of the dismissal is after the employee's sixty-fourth birthday, the amount of the basic award is reduced according to a formula (ERA 1996, s 119(4)–(5)).

It is possible for a tribunal to reduce a basic award in certain circumstances: where an ex-employee 'unreasonably refused' an offer of reinstatement (ERA 1996, s 122(1)); or because of 'any conduct of the complainant before the dismissal' (ERA 1996, s 122(2)). The amount of the deduction shall be such as the tribunal decides is 'just and equitable'. The tribunal cannot reduce the basic award because the ex-employee has not mitigated their loss by trying to find other employment.

Compensatory award

This is likely to be the largest element in a package of compensation. The amount of the compensatory award is 'such amount as the tribunal considers just and equitable in all the circumstances having regard to the loss sustained by the complainant in consequence of the dismissal in so far as that loss is attributable to action taken by the employer' (ERA 1996, s 123(1)).

Such an award is, however, subject to a limit. This is £53 500 (February 2003) and is subject to periodic review. (This ceiling will be varied upwards significantly under the Employment Relations Act 1999.) There is an expectation that the person will mitigate their loss by trying to find other employment and not unreasonably refusing reinstatement or re-engagement. This award might also be reduced if the tribunal finds that the dismissal 'was to any extent caused or contributed to by any action of the complainant' (ERA 1996, s 123(6)). The amount of the reduction will be what the tribunal considers is 'just and equitable'.

The 'loss' referred to includes: any **expenses** reasonably incurred by the ex-employee as a result of the dismissal (i.e. in seeking employment but not in obtaining legal advice for applying to the tribunal) and loss of **any benefit** 'which he might reasonably be expected to have had but for the dismissal' (ERA 1996, s 123(2)(b)). This can include a pay increase which was payable after the dismissal.

Five main heads of compensation have been identified in case law (*Norton Tool Co Ltd* v *Tewson* [1973] 1 All ER 183):

1 Immediate loss of earnings (i.e. between the date of dismissal and the date of the hearing).

2 Future loss of earnings. This can involve consideration of the personal qualities of the individual (including age, health, skill) and the current state of the labour market.

3 Loss arising from the manner of the dismissal.

4 Loss of statutory rights (i.e. compensation for being unable to comply with a statutory qualifying period).

5 Loss of pension rights (added in *Tidman* v *Aveling Marshall Ltd* [1977] IRLR 218).

In a recent case (*Whelan and Another t/a Cheers Off Licence* v *Richardson* [1998] IRLR 114), the EAT set out guidance on the approach to be used when assessing loss of earnings. The elements are that:

- The assessment should be based on facts available at the date of the assessment hearing.

- If the ex-employee has been unemployed between the date of dismissal and the assessment date, they will recover their net loss of earnings based on the pre-dismissal rate. This is subject to the duty on the ex-employee to mitigate their loss.

- Where the ex-employee takes new permanent employment with smaller earnings than they earned prior to dismissal, the ex-employee will be compensated on the basis of the full loss up to the date on which the new employment commenced. Thereafter, they will receive compensation for partial loss. This will be the difference between the earnings prior to dismissal and the earnings in the new permanent employment.

- If the ex-employee takes new employment which is for a limited period only, they will be able to claim compensation to the assessment date (or the date when permanent employment is obtained, whichever is the sooner). Account will be taken of the earnings received from the temporary employment.

- At the point when the ex-employee obtains permanent new employment which pays the same as or more than they received prior to dismissal, the loss attributable to the dismissal ceases. If they subsequently lose the new employment, the loss attributable to the first employer is not revived. The chain of causation is broken.

An additional award

If a tribunal has made an order for reinstatement or for re-engagement of the complainant and the employer does not comply with the order, then, an additional award of compensation may be made. If the unfair dismissal does not involve discrimination on grounds of union membership or breaches of discrimination law, the award is between 13 and 26 weeks' pay (ERA 1996, s 117(5)(b)).

9.5 Employment policies and practices

In this section, we will review the ways in which discipline at work should be managed to conform to good practice standards. It relies substantially on the advice given by ACAS in its handbook *Discipline and Grievances at Work* (2001a). We will look at five aspects:

- expectations and norms;
- identification of the reason for dismissal;
- reasonableness in the circumstances;
- whether there was proper compliance with the standards of procedural fairness;
- available disciplinary sanctions.

9.5.1 The context: expectations and norms

Workplace discipline operates in each organisation in the context of that organisation's culture. This reflects the standards and behaviour expected of managers and staff. These standards will concern acceptable levels of both performance and conduct by staff. These will also be reflected in the psychological contract (*see* Chapter 2) between the employer and each employee. Workplace culture is not always a positive influence on standards of behaviour. We have seen earlier (in respect of harassment) how workplace culture can inhibit good employment practice by tolerating bullying, sexism and racism.

In those organisations which adopt good employment practice there will be a high degree of consistency in the implementation of these standards. They will be adhered to. Managers will be expected to ensure compliance of performance standards through performance appraisal. Any necessary remedial action (through additional training and counselling) will be initiated. Failure to adhere to standards of behaviour will be dealt with through disciplinary procedures.

9.5.2 Handling discipline and dismissal

Where there is an apparent breach of rules a first step is for a manager of supervisor to decide whether disciplinary action is the most appropriate course of action for this breach. Initially, the manager or supervisor, having gathered all the relevant facts, will need to decide whether or not to take action of any kind; if action is required, then whether it is counselling or arranging a disciplinary interview.

Counselling is an attempt to correct a situation and prevent it from getting worse without using the disciplinary procedure. 'In many cases the right word at the right time and in the right way may be all that is needed, and will often be a more satisfactory way of dealing with a breach of rules, or poor performance than a formal hearing. Additional training, coaching and advice may be needed, and both manager and worker should be aware that formal processes will start if there is no improvement or any improvement fails to be maintained' (ACAS, 2001a: 24).

The circumstances in which counselling might arise are where an employee may be having family problems which result in unacceptable patterns of attendance (*see* Exercise 9.1). It may also be appropriate with more serious examples of misconduct, where, for example, an employee has a drink problem. Counselling is, however, usually used in the early stages of misconduct. Persistent misconduct and a failure by the employee to benefit from counselling are likely to lead to disciplinary action. In some cases, an employer might find that a twin-track approach is the right course of action. So, for example, counselling (e.g. to tackle an alcohol problem) might be initiated and disciplinary sanctions imposed (e.g. a final written warning) as a constraint upon an employee's behaviour.

A **disciplinary interview** is usually required where a matter is serious. A serious matter might be one incident of serious or gross misconduct or, alternatively, it might involve a pattern of minor misconduct.

We will now look at the steps necessary for the achievement of good practice in discipline handling. Earlier in this chapter, the tests used by tribunals to determine whether or not a dismissal was fair were outlined. It is important to recap because they provide essential guidance in the handling of all disciplinary action – whether or not that disciplinary action leads to dismissal or some other sanction. These tests provide a template against which to judge employer behaviour. In brief, they are:

- identifying the *reason* for the dismissal;
- deciding whether the employer behaved *reasonably in all the circumstances* of the case;
- establishing whether there was proper compliance with the standards of *procedural fairness*.

Reason for the dismissal: breach of rules and standards

Caution is necessary when an employer is establishing the reason for a dismissal. Some cases are not clear-cut and several reasons may be appropriate, with one being the principal reason. It is important that none of the reasons might be ruled 'automatically unfair' (i.e. concerning discriminatory treatment). All should be 'fair reasons' (in accordance with ERA 1996, s 98): capability, misconduct, redundancy, a statutory bar or some other substantial reason. This raises several practical issues for employers. They should have in place defined standards against which to assess both conduct and performance.

- *Poor performance*: Recommended practice for performance standards is that these should be SMARTA (i.e. specific, measurable, achievable, realistic, timely and agreed). All cases of poor performance should be investigated. This should help identify the employee's explanation and whether there is any lack of skill that could be remedied by training or coaching. If necessary, consideration might be given to some suitable alternative employment. If appropriate, continued poor performance after a number of warnings might result in dismissal.
- *Misconduct*: For standards of conduct, disciplinary rules are set. 'Rules will normally cover issues such as absence, timekeeping and holiday arrangements, health and safety, use of the organisation's equipment and facilities, misconduct, sub-standard performance, and discrimination, bullying and harassment' (ACAS, 2001a: 13). It is advisable that employers tailor rules to their own organisation's circumstances. They may be specific (stating that theft of company property is a sacking offence) or they may be more general in character (requiring an employee not to bring the company into disrepute). However, as the *Code of Practice* states, 'rules should not be so general as to be meaningless' (para 5). The overall aim should be to formulate rules 'necessary

for the efficient and safe performance of work and for the maintenance of satisfactory relations within the workforce and between employees and management' (para 5). Rules should be non-discriminatory. Some organisations can take a more stringent approach to certain offences than other organisations and should make clear the seriousness with which they view breaches of specific rules. For example, smoking in a chemical factory would be an instant dismissal offence. In an office, it would probably result in a verbal warning.

It is particularly important that rules relating to gross misconduct are clearly formulated. Gross misconduct is generally seen as misconduct serious enough to destroy the employment contract between the employer and the employee and make any further working relationship and trust impossible. It is normally restricted to very serious offences – for example, physical violence, theft or fraud – but may be determined by the nature of the business or other circumstances.

Rules should be in writing and have been properly communicated to all employees to avoid misunderstanding. Particularly important ones should be reinforced at induction. 'Special attention should be paid to ensure that rules are understood by any workers with little experience of working life (for instance young people or those returning to work after a lengthy break) and by workers whose English or reading ability is limited' (ACAS, 2001a: 14).

Rules should also be reviewed from time to time to ensure that existing ones are still appropriate and to decide whether or not new ones need creating. The responsibility for formulating disciplinary rules is management's. However, it is recommended in the *Code of Practice* that recognised trade unions and/or employees might be involved in discussions on the drafting of rules (para 4).

Finally, it is important to note that an employee has a right to request a written statement for the reason of the dismissal (ERA 1996, s 92). This is admissible in any tribunal proceedings.

Reasonableness in the circumstances

As outlined above, this can be a difficult area to grapple with. An employment tribunal will be reviewing the behaviour of the employer and considering whether or not the decision to dismiss, for the reason given, was within the range of reasonable employers. So, the standard for testing an employer's behaviour is not clear-cut. Much will depend on the facts given to the tribunal, the extent to which a convincing case is made out by the employer and the views formed by individual members of the tribunal. It is important to remember that if the reason (or principal reason) for the dismissal is found to be an 'automatically unfair' reason, then no consideration is given to reasonableness. The dismissal will be ruled as unfair.

It is important to remember that 'reasonableness' does not apply just to dismissal cases. The *Code of Practice* states that 'when determining the disciplinary action to be taken the supervisor or manager should bear in mind the need to satisfy the test of reasonableness in all the circumstances. So far as possible, account should be taken of the employee's record and any other relevant factors' (ACAS, 2001a: para 16).

The key issues, in relation to 'reasonableness', that an employer needs to consider can include the following (depending on the particular case):

- whether the employer has adopted the basic approach to workplace discipline recommended in the ACAS *Code of Practice* that 'disciplinary procedures should not be viewed primarily as a means of imposing sanctions. Rather they should be seen as a way of helping and encouraging improvement among workers whose conduct or standard of work is unsatisfactory' (para 8);
- whether an employee dismissed for failing to achieve the required standards of performance has been appraised and reviewed and been provided with appropriate training and counselling;
- whether an employee dismissed for minor misconduct has been persistently below the required standard and has been given appropriate warnings and opportunities to improve their conduct;
- whether, in all cases, account has been taken of an employee's length of service and disciplinary record;
- whether account has been taken of an extenuating circumstance that might explain an employee's misconduct or poor performance;
- ensuring that, except for gross misconduct, no employee is dismissed for a first breach of discipline (*Code of Practice*: para 9xi);
- ensuring that in ordinary misconduct cases, there is no evidence of erratic enforcement of standards.

Procedural fairness

An employer may have a good defensible reason for disciplining or dismissing an employee. However, failure to comply with the recommended procedural standards can result in a dismissal being ruled as unfair. As outlined above, ACAS sets out a number of specifications for disciplinary procedures (*Code of Practice*: para 9). We will revisit these and develop some of the issues.

Disciplinary procedures should be *in writing* and *specify to whom they apply*. This provides certainty and should go some way towards consistency of practice. They should also provide for *matters to be dealt with quickly*. If there is an infringement of performance standards or an example of misconduct, then prompt action is advisable. It reinforces standards and sets an example for the rest of the workforce. It could, if necessary, be used by an employer as a defence. For example, in a case involving sexual or racial harassment, prompt action against a perpetrator would form part of the evidence that the employer took 'such steps as are reasonably practicable' to deal with the abusive behaviour (*see* Chapters 4 and 5).

Authority levels need to be outlined. This will include clarifying who has authority to take the various forms of disciplinary action, i.e. managers who have the power to dismiss (normally not supervisors) and those who are involved in hearing appeals.

A reasonable employer will ensure that there has been *a careful investigation* of the circumstances of a disciplinary allegation. Such investigation might involve specialist functions (e.g. auditors). A decision on the scope and nature of the investigation depends on the circumstances of each case. In misconduct cases, an employer, having formed 'a reasonable belief' that the misconduct has taken place, can, after an investigation which sustains that belief, dismiss an employee.

The handling of this stage is critical to an employer's possible success in defending an unfair dismissal allegation. It is also essential in assuring that the standards of natural justice are adhered to in respect of the employee's treatment. Clearly, the employee must be *informed of the complaints* against them. If this is not fully explained, at this stage, there could be a serious procedural defect. In addition, the employee must be given an opportunity to state their case before any disciplinary decision is reached. Depending on the complexity of the disciplinary issue in question, the hearing may take some time to complete. It is better to take time at this stage and explore an allegation in detail than to be procedurally sloppy. The statutory *right to be accompanied* by a trade union representative or by a fellow employee of their choice should be complied with (*see* above). If the facility is refused, that should be recorded.

A special provision, under the *Code of Practice*, is outlined for disciplinary action against workplace trade union officials: 'Disciplinary action against a trade union official can lead to a serious dispute if it is seen as an attack on the union's functions. Although normal disciplinary standards should apply to their conduct as workers, if disciplinary action is contemplated then the case should be discussed with a senior trade union representative or full-time official' (para 26).

Finally, an employee should be given *an explanation for any penalty* imposed and told of *the right of appeal*. This avoids confusion and demonstrates compliance with the principles of procedural fairness.

Under the Employment Act 2002, a standard dismissal and discipline procedure is implied into all contracts of employment. This sets statutory minimum procedural requirements. The implementation date is likely to be late 2003. Many existing disciplinary procedures exceed these requirements (*see* Fig. 9.4). However, those employers with no procedures – particularly small organisations – should ensure compliance with this minimum procedural standard.

Disciplinary sanctions

A range of disciplinary sanctions are referred to in the *Code of Practice*. Selection of the appropriate one is dependent on the factors mentioned above. Essentially, there are four broad considerations that will determine appropriateness:

1 Is the breach of rules and standards a 'first offence'?
2 How seriously does the employer view the breach?
3 Are there any mitigating circumstances put forward by the employee?
4 What is the state of the employee's disciplinary record?

The usual sanctions are: informal oral (or verbal) warning, formal oral (or verbal) warning, formal written warning and a final written warning.

- **Informal oral warning**: This can be given by immediate supervisors to encourage improvement in performance or to discourage further minor misconduct (e.g. lateness) (*Code of Practice*: para 15).

- **Implementation**: late 2003.
- **Who is covered?** Employees. There is no small employer exemption.
- **What is provided?** A minimum set of procedural steps. They are implied into each contract of employment. There is a 'modified' procedure where dismissal for gross misconduct has already taken place.
- **General requirements**: No unreasonable delay; timing and location of meetings should be reasonable; employer and employee should have opportunities to present their cases; employee may use the statutory right to be accompanied (ERA 1999, s 10) (*see* Fig. 9.2).
- **The standard dismissal and disciplinary procedure**:
  - *Information*: Employer must tell employee in writing of the allegation or issue (this could cover misconduct, poor performance, sick absence, individual redundancy).
  - *Meeting*: Employee invited to a meeting after a reasonable opportunity to consider a response. They should take 'all reasonable steps' to attend the meeting. This should take place before disciplinary action is taken – except in the case of suspension.
  - *Decision*: Employer should inform employee of this and of right to appeal.
- **Appeal process**:
  - *Notification*: Employee must inform the employer of intention to appeal.
  - *Meeting*: Employee is invited to a meeting. They should take 'all reasonable steps' to attend the meeting.
  - *Implementing disciplinary action*: The appeal hearing need not take place before the dismissal or disciplinary action takes effect.
  - *Final decision*: Employer should inform employee of this.
- **The modified dismissal and discipline procedure**:
  - *When applicable?* When an employee has already been dismissed for gross misconduct – whether rightly or wrongly.
  - *Information*: Employer must tell employee of alleged misconduct which led to dismissal and of the right of appeal.
  - *Appeal*: If required, employee is invited to a meeting. They should take 'all reasonable steps' to attend the meeting.
  - *Final decision*: Employer should inform employee of this.
- **Failure to comply with statutory procedure**: This can result, as appropriate, in a decrease or increase in a compensation award at employment tribunal. So, if an employer fails to permit an appeal, compensation can be increased by between 10 and 50 per cent.

Figure 9.4 Standard dismissal and disciplinary procedure

Source: Employment Act 2002, Sch 2.

- **Formal oral warning**: This could be used, again by an immediate supervisor, where there is a recurrence of minor misconduct or poor performance. Such a warning should be recorded and the employee told of the recording. It is recommended that oral warnings are disregarded for disciplinary purposes after a period of time – for example, six months.

- **Formal written warning**: This can be the next step where there is persistent misconduct or poor performance. It might be considered that a 'first offence' is serious enough for such a sanction. One example might be taking a day's leave without permission. Such a warning might be in a letter or memo given to the employee concerned from the appropriate manager. It might set out expectations of future behaviour and possibly a review period. It is recommended that a written warning is disregarded for disciplinary purposes after a period of time – for example, twelve months.

■ **Final written warning**: This is the most serious warning. Usually, it is written to indicate that a further breach of disciplinary rules might result in dismissal. It can remain on a person's disciplinary record for any length of time. Normally, this is for between one and two years, depending on management's view of the seriousness of the breaches of disciplinary rules. It can be used where there are persistent breaches. It is also possible to use it for a first offence. Depending on all the circumstances, examples might include drunkenness at work, a first incident of harassment, minor assault on a work colleague.

Other disciplinary penalties (short of dismissal)

Other sanctions are: suspension without pay, loss of increment, transfer and demotion. These must only be used where they are allowed for by an express or implied condition of the contract of employment. If there is no contractual authority, then the employee might sue for breach of contract.

Disciplinary suspension without pay/loss of increment is different from the suspension that may be implemented before a disciplinary hearing. That should be with pay. At that stage the employer has not decided on whether the employee did or did not commit the disciplinary offence. The suspension referred to here is a punishment. ACAS advice is that: Special consideration should be given before imposing disciplinary suspension without pay. It must be allowed for in the worker's contract of employment, and no suspension should exceed the maximum period set out in the contract. It must not be unreasonably prolonged, since it would then be open to the worker to take action for breach of contract or resign and claim constructive dismissal (ACAS, 2001a: 120).

Disciplinary transfer or demotion: Implementing such action without contractual authority is likely to be a repudiatory breach of contract.

Dismissal

The final disciplinary sanctions considered here are dismissal with notice and dismissal without notice. As indicated above, the three tests will be used by an employment tribunal to determine whether or not the dismissal was fair.

Dismissal with notice: The notice given should be that to which the individual is entitled under their contract of employment. This should conform with the statutory minimum (ERA 1996, s 86) or be above it. It is possible for the employer to give pay in lieu of notice.

Dismissal without notice: 'Employers should give all workers a clear indication of the type of misconduct which, in the light of the requirements of the employer's business, will warrant dismissal without the normal period of notice or pay in lieu of notice. So far as possible the types of offences which fall into this category "gross misconduct" should be clearly specified in the rules, although such a list cannot normally be exhaustive' (ACAS, 2001a: 35).

Exercise 9.2	**Discipline at work: Scenarios**

Read these scenarios and decide on the following:

- *What legal issues do you think might be involved?*
- *What would you recommend that the employer did **both** in law and in practice?*

1 George McDonald was suspended without pay for five days for being drunk at work on one occasion. He decides that he wants to complain to an employment tribunal about the deduction. Can he?

2 Wendy Bryson has been late for work three times in the past fortnight. Her supervisor, having given her informal oral warnings on each occasion, tells her that more formal action will be taken next time. She says that she cannot help being late. She has just found out that she is pregnant and is suffering from 'morning sickness'.

3 Gary Wilson has just been found taking an unused computer disk from work.

4 Jason, one of your van drivers, has been disqualified from driving for two weeks for exceeding the speed limit. He was driving down the motorway at 102 miles per hour. Prior to this he had a clean licence.

5 You learn that Simon, one of your technicians, has been sent to prison for seven days for deliberately not paying a court fine (imposed for a motoring offence, which he still strongly denies). His manager believes that he should be sacked immediately.

6 Karen has been employed as a catering assistant for 12 months. One morning in the canteen she told her friend that her partner had just been diagnosed as HIV positive. This was overheard by another member of staff who told the supervisor that Karen 'had AIDS'. Some other staff expressed strong concern about dangers from cuts and the handling of food. The supervisor, anxious to avoid disruption and unpleasantness in a small team of 12, contacted her manager and said that she thought that Karen should be sacked. The manager agreed and she was sacked instantly.

Feedback on this exercise is provided in the Appendix to this book.

Further reading

Advisory Conciliation and Arbitration Service (2000) *Code of Practice: Disciplinary and Grievance Procedures*. London: ACAS.

Advisory Conciliation and Arbitration Service (2001a) *Discipline and Grievances at Work: the ACAS Advisory Handbook*. London: ACAS.

Advisory Conciliation and Arbitration Service (2001b) *The ACAS arbitration scheme for the resolution of unfair dismissal disputes*. London: ACAS.

References

Advisory Conciliation and Arbitration Service (2000) *Code of Practice: Disciplinary and Grievance Procedures*. London: ACAS.

Advisory Conciliation and Arbitration Service (2001a) *Discipline and Grievances at Work: the ACAS Advisory Handbook*. London: ACAS.

Advisory Conciliation and Arbitration Service (2001b) *The ACAS arbitration scheme for the resolution of unfair dismissal disputes*. London: ACAS.

Advisory Conciliation and Arbitration Service (2002) *Annual Report 2001–02*. London: ACAS.

Anderman, S. (1986) 'Unfair dismissals and redundancy' in Lewis, R. (ed.) *Labour Law*. Oxford: Blackwell.

Clark, G. de N. (1970) *Remedies for Unfair Dismissal: Proposals for Legislation*. PEP Broadsheet 518. London: Policy Studies Institute.

Cully, M. *et al.* (1998) *The 1998 Workplace Employee Relations Survey: First Findings*. London: DTI.

Cully, M. *et al.* (1999) *Britain at Work: The 1998 Workplace Employee Relations Survey*. London: Routledge.

Daniel, W.W. and Stilgoe, G. (1978) *The Impact of Employment Protection Laws*. London: Policy Studies Institute.

Department of Trade and Industry (1998) *Fairness At Work*, Cm. 3968. London: Stationery Office.

Department of Trade and Industry (2001a) *Dispute Resolution in Britain: a background paper*. London: DTI.

Department of Trade and Industry (2001b) *Consultation on Employment Status*. London: DTI.

Department of Trade and Industry (2002) *Findings from the 1998 survey of employment tribunal applications*. London: DTI.

Dickens, L. *et al.* (1985) *Dismissed: a Study of Unfair Dismissal and the Industrial Tribunal System*. Oxford: Blackwell.

Earnshaw, J. *et al.* (1998) *Industrial Tribunals, Workplace Disciplinary Procedures and Employment Practice*. London: DTI.

Millward, N. *et al.* (1992) *Workplace Industrial Relations in Transition*. Aldershot: Dartmouth.

Ministry of Labour (1967) *Dismissal Procedures: report of the National Advisory Council on dismissal procedures*. London: HMSO.

National Association of Citizens' Advice Bureaux (1993) *Job Insecurity*. London: NACAB.

Royal Commission on Trade Unions and Employers Associations (1968) *Final Report*, Cmnd. 3623. London: Her Majesty's Stationery Office (Donovan Report).

Wedderburn, Lord (1986) *The Worker and the Law*. Harmondsworth: Penguin Books.

Terms and conditions of employment

Introduction to Part Four

There are several overarching themes in the chapters in Part Four. Taken together they provide an important overview of the scale and nature of employment protection at the present time. They are:

- the creation of a minimum employment contract;
- the extended coverage of employment protection to workers and the gradual erosion of qualifying periods of employment;
- constraints on the detailed provisions of collective agreements;
- new regulatory procedures in the workplace;
- the extending boundaries of health and safety;
- the reconciling of work and non-work life;
- the contribution of European law.

A minimum employment contract: There is now clear evidence of the wide scope of such a minimum contract (*see also* Chapter 2). In aggregate, we see minimum standards provided for:

- the level of pay (through equal-pay legislation and the national minimum wage);
- the length of the working week;
- the pattern of working undertaken by shift workers and night workers;
- the level of paid holiday entitlement;
- the standards of health and safety to be applied in particular workplaces;
- arrangements for various forms of dependency leave from employment (both paid and unpaid);
- statutory minimum notice periods.

Employers are obliged to comply with statutory minima. However, they may provide conditions of employment above these. For example, although there is a right to four weeks' paid leave, employees can be (and often are) awarded more. Also, although there is a right to unpaid parental leave, this does not preclude an employer from paying average earnings. Furthermore, many rates of pay are clearly in excess of the National Minimum Wage.

The extended coverage of employment protection: This has two dimensions. There is a clear political move to extend rights to '**workers**' – those who have an employment relationship but may not be defined strictly as employees with a contract of employment. The National Minimum Wage Act 1998 and the Working Time Regulations 1998 explicitly cover this wider group of working people. In doing so, they reflect the views of the British government, which favours wider protection, as well as the objectives of European Union social policy. The Employment Relations Act 1999, s 23 provides for the extension of statutory rights to 'workers'. In mid-2002, the government began consultation on the implementation of this section. The other aspect of extended coverage is the gradual erosion of **qualifying periods of employment**. Most of the rights covered in this section are available to working people irrespective of length of service. Where such qualifying conditions are introduced, they are relatively short (e.g. six months of continuous employment for requests to be made for flexible working).

Collective agreements: As we have seen earlier, contracts of employment can incorporate terms of collective agreements. Many of the minimum standards described above already form the basic ingredients of negotiations between unions and employers. They, then, become provisions of collective agreements and, as a consequence, have become contractual as between an individual employee and the employer. When legislation prescribes minimum terms and conditions, it is, in effect, introducing **constraints on the detailed provisions of collective agreements**. This approach is already in being. Discrimination law, in particular, prohibits terms of collective agreements that would be discriminatory. They would be ruled as void (*see* Chapters 4–6). So, in essence, collective bargaining is operating in an increasingly circumscribed framework. However, although this is the case, there are still many opportunities for negotiation of enhancements above the statutory minima and for deciding on workplace procedures to ensure compliance with the law (*see* next paragraph). Voluntarism, then, still has a place but, arguably, within specified limits.

The creation of new regulatory procedures in the workplace: These are put in place to implement statutory standards. Examples of these include the following:

- implementing the specific requirements for night working and for risk assessment;
- putting in place specified procedures for individual employees who wish to work in excess of the maximum working week;
- making arrangements for workplace regulation of health and safety;
- setting up procedures for the negotiation of workforce agreements to implement provisions of the Working Time Regulations 1998.

The extending boundaries of health and safety: Although, traditionally, health and safety has been thought of as a narrow issue relating to such issues as operating machinery, its defined scope has increased significantly in the past 30 years. Indeed, the legitimate boundaries of health and safety have been the subject of much controversy in recent years. This reached a high point in the European Court of Justice case concerning whether the Working Time Directive 1993 was a health and safety measure or not. As we will see in this part of the book health and safety now not only encompasses the physical conditions of work, the technology used and operational systems, but also covers the patterns of and length of working time and, also, specific protections for child-bearing and breastfeeding women.

Reconciling work and non-work life. A significant driving influence has been the growing feminisation of the labour market. Increasingly, however, there is a discernible recognition that dependency (whether as a result of caring for children or adult relatives) is an issue which can affect both men and women. The Parental Leave Directive 1996 goes some way to providing minimum rights in this area. Again, it is also an area where, voluntarily, employers may introduce enhanced provisions, including paid paternity leave and dependency leave.

European law: Much of the employment protection outlined in this section derives from European law through, in particular, Directives on Safety and Health 1989, Pregnant Workers 1992, Working Time 1993, and Parental Leave 1996. In the case of health and safety, the new more extensive provisions were grafted on to already existing British law. In the other instances, new entitlements and obligations were created. The one significant home-grown piece of legislation is the National Minimum Wage Act 1998. While this does not implement European law, it reflects principles in the Community Charter of the Fundamental Social Rights of Workers 1989 on 'fair remuneration' and an 'equitable wage'.

10 Pay regulation

Having read this chapter, you should be able to:

- Understand the social policies that influence pay determination.
- Understand the legal regulation governing pay deduction.
- Understand the statutory framework governing the national minimum wage.

10.1 Structure of the chapter

This chapter comprises the following sections:

- *Introduction*: The growth of legal regulation of pay.
- *The context*: Economic issues, political action, social welfare issues, social policy – 'fair' pay and status differences, sex and race discrimination, minimum pay.
- *Legal provisions*: Definitions: wages and pay; common law of contract and pay; information about pay; methods of payment; overpayment; pay deduction; fines: disciplinary action; shortages and losses in retail employment; pay and sex discrimination; statutory national minimum wage.
- *Employment policies and practices*: Contracts of employment and collective agreements; information and records.

10.2 Introduction

Over the past 30 years, pay has been the subject of growing legal regulation by Parliament. The most notable examples are the enactment of equal pay legislation, a statutory framework on lawful and unlawful pay deduction, and the introduction of a statutory national minimum wage. Prior to the 1970s, however, pay was primarily regulated through the common law of contract – particularly as concerns the employer's duty to pay wages. This duty is obviously still important, but it has, clearly, been affected by the expanding body of statute law. This statute law has concerned itself not merely with the **transaction** (i.e. the paying and receiving of wages that are due). It has increasingly focused on the **level of pay**. This is reflected both in the legal framework governing equal pay (as between men and women) and in that relating to the statutory national minimum wage.

10.3 The context

The context within which the law on remuneration has been developed has been characterised by two broad sets of factors:

- the primacy, given by policy-makers, to **economic determinants** of pay and the view that it should reflect the free play of market forces;
- the view that pay levels should be influenced by **standards of social justice**.

Much legislation involves a blend of these economic and social justice issues. We will look at each in turn.

10.3.1 Economic issues

Much of the legislation concerns 'pay' or 'wages'. (These terms are defined below in section 9.4: The legal framework.) It must be remembered, however, that there are certain elements in the wider package of 'remuneration' that a person might acquire from employment. Remuneration will cover a range of other benefits (a bonus, a company car, private health insurance, a non-contributory pension scheme). So, in an individual case, it is necessary to confirm that the correct terminology is used.

The importance of pay to employees

Pay is one of the rewards of employment. It is important as an *extrinsic reward* for work done. It provides purchasing power for goods and services; helps a person maintain or improve their standard of living; and may also provide an indication of social status. But, it must be remembered that employees may also derive *intrinsic reward* from work: recognition, power and status and self-esteem. Individuals will differ in the significance they attach to these rewards or sources of satisfaction. Generally, however, it can be said that they are not solely motivated to maximise their income.

The importance of pay for employers

Three basic objectives are usually suggested as to the importance of pay for employers: recruitment, retention and motivation. As far as **recruitment** is concerned, comparative starting salaries with competitor organisations will probably influence their ability to recruit staff. Reputations for being a good employer with relatively high pay can be important. **Retention** can be achieved by payments above the market rate, and by lengthy salary scales with high maximum levels for experienced and competent employees. Other retention measures include loyalty bonuses and share options. Finally, **motivation** may be influenced through cash inducements to change attitudes and/or improve or modify performance. Harmonisation of pay and conditions and the creation of single status employment (*see* below) are suggested as contributors to this.

Payment systems

A wide variety of payment systems exists. They can fit into one of three categories:

1 *Time-based pay*: Pay is usually related to hours, weeks or months or work. Such systems focus on grade rates. They are found in the more bureaucratic organisations where the pattern of work is relatively stable and easy to define.

2 *Output-based pay*: Some measure is used to assess an employee's performance. It encompasses quantified measures such as volume or value output, and more subjective assessment such as appraisal.

3 *Skill-based pay*: This relates pay to the skill, experience and competence possessed by an employee. This is most commonly used for technical and 'knowledge' workers. It is intended to raise the quality and flexibility of the workforce. It is appropriate when the pace of change is rapid so that new ideas, methods and technology are being introduced regularly.

Payments under these systems may be fixed (e.g. basic weekly wage). Rates should only be changed by agreement (either upwards or down). Alternatively, payments may vary according to the amount of time an employee attends work or the time of day attended. So for example, longer attendance can result in overtime pay; and night and shift working in special premium rates. Much output-based pay can be variable (e.g. piecework, profit sharing and performance-related pay).

10.3.2 Political policy: the 'free play' of the market?

Under a pure 'free-market' model employers would have freedom to select the payment system to be adopted and the levels of pay to be provided. Furthermore, they would be able to select whether or not to pay 'wages' for work done under the employment relationship and which (if any) benefits to provide. Such freedom does exist to a large extent. However, there are certain constraints that affect employers' decision-making. The principal way in which the free market is modified concerns the extent to which the concept of 'fairness' enters into pay determination. Historically, this has been introduced principally by trade unions through the collective bargaining process. In more recent times it is being asserted through the legislative concepts of equal pay and the national minimum wage. These social factors in pay determination are explored below.

The Conservative governments (1979–97) pursued policies to give greater emphasis to the economic determinants of pay. Pay was expected to be related to the economic circumstances of particular employers and the economic performance and contribution of individual employees. It adopted the following action in pursuit of these policies:

- it rescinded the Fair Wages Resolution;
- it abolished Wages Councils;
- it did not accept 'comparability' as an argument in public-sector pay determination;
- it introduced competitive tendering and market testing in many public services;
- it weakened trade union bargaining power;
- it sought to 'decollectivise' employee relations;
- it supported the de-recognition of unions;
- it promoted performance-related pay.

Some of these free-market policies are discussed more fully below. They were modified by social policies introduced by the Labour government after 1997.

10.3.3 Social welfare factors

Before turning to those social policy objectives, it is important to note the importance of the interlocking of pay and access to certain in-work social security benefits. The interplay between these can create a 'poverty trap' where, in simple terms, a person loses certain in-work benefits as pay increases. So, there is little effect on available disposable income and in-work poverty can be entrenched.

The Low Pay Commission (LPC) (1998: 31) has described how the relationship between pay levels and social security benefits have operated in the recent past. For at least the last 20 years, workers on median earnings and those in the highest decile have seen a much more rapid increase in earnings than the lowest-paid workers. Earnings growth is outlined in Table 10.1.

The LPC follows through the implications of this. 'The widening distribution of earnings has led to a substantial degree of in-work poverty, particularly among families with young children and a consequential increase in dependence on in-work social security benefits' (1998: 32). So, expenditure on Family Credit (and the predecessor Family Income Supplement) rose, in cash terms, from nearly £200 million in 1987/8 to £2000 million in 1996/7. About three-quarters of a million families received Family Credit; and Housing Benefit and Council Tax Benefit are each payable to almost a quarter of a million working families and single people.

Table 10.1 Earnings growth 1983–97

1983 = 100	
1997 figures:	
Highest decile	145
Median decile	131
Lowest decile	121

Source: New Earning Survey data.

10.3.4 **Social policy**

It is against the background of economic determinism and the social-welfare poverty trap that new standards in relation to levels of pay are being created by legislative action. Social policy in respect of remuneration has a number of aspects. Some of these directly relate to government policy and others have evolved in managerial policy approaches. The issues involved are:

- 'fair' pay;
- status differences in remuneration between manual and non-manual workers;
- pay levels and sex or race discrimination;
- minimum pay;
- new social objectives.

We will look at each of these in turn.

Fair pay

In the issue of minimum pay there is some concept of 'fairness'. There is an expectation of a fair reward for the work undertaken. The notion of fairness also extends to comparative pay. Although this is theoretically distinct from minimum pay, there can, in practice, be clear links. In 1891, the House of Commons adopted the Fair Wages Resolution. This required that employers engaged on government contracts should pay their workers at least the wage level generally recognised for the sector or locality concerned. This Resolution was revised in 1946. It was ultimately rescinded in 1983 as part of the Conservative government's free-market economic policy. It has not been revived, presumably because the national minimum wage has, arguably, now created a more wide-ranging basis for fair pay.

Status-based pay

This refers to the traditional status distinction between manual (or 'blue-collar') and non-manual (or 'white-collar') workers. Historically, there was a clear dichotomy between these broad groups. This was reflected in the following terms and conditions of employment. Manual workers worked longer hours, had fewer holidays, no provision of sick pay nor of pensions and had less job security. Frequently, they were subject to one week's notice to terminate their contracts of employment. As far as pay was concerned, this was on a weekly basis (in manufacturing industry, it was often output-related and, therefore, weekly earnings fluctuated). Sometimes pay was on a daily basis, depending on the availability of work. Such casual workforces existed in, for example, the docks prior to 1947. Hourly rates of pay were, invariably, lower than the equivalent rates paid to 'white-collar' staff. During the 1960s and 1970s, however, changes began to take place to these status distinctions.

This is an area of social policy where political and legal action has had a more indirect contribution. Many of the initiatives towards single-status treatment and the harmonisation of conditions of employment have been taken by employers for reasons related to the management of their organisations.

Discrimination and pay

It is common to focus on discrimination-based pay under the provisions of the Equal Pay Act 1970, where direct comparisons are made in particular organisations between men's pay and women's pay. (This has been discussed in Chapter 4.) However, it is important to note that, in general levels of pay, discrimination is evident. This is seen in earnings distribution figures. Such discriminatory treatment is evident in respect of sex and ethnic origin.

As far as women are concerned, the LPC reports that they 'have generally experienced higher earnings growth than men since the introduction of the Equal Pay Act, but remain disproportionately lower paid' (1998: 36). In an analysis of the low paid (those earning below £3.50 per hour), the LPC shows the predominance of women in this group. It reports that 43 per cent of this group are part-time women workers and 23 per cent full-time women workers. Further analysis of working women shows that lone parents (who are predominantly female) 'tend be more affected by low pay than female workers and workers in general' (1998: 41). Finally, two-thirds of homeworkers who describe themselves as 'employed' are women. The LPC states that 'most homeworkers we met painted a vivid picture of low pay and in some instances outright exploitation' (1998: 42). To illustrate this, the LPC reports one survey from the National Group on Homeworking (across nine geographical areas and seven industries) which showed an average wage of £1.60 per hour (1998: 43).

As far as **ethnic origin** is concerned, the LPC says that 'reliable data on ethnic minorities are difficult to obtain' (1998: 38). It cites, with some qualifications, the information contained in Table 10.2.

The data in Table 10.2 are qualified in the following ways. First of all, the finding that ethnic minority women earn more than white women may be flawed because 'the data omit a good deal of homeworking which occurs, especially in the clothing and hosiery industries, among ethnic minority women' (1998: 38). Secondly, it has been suggested that the differences in earnings were related more to occupational status and level of qualification than to ethnic origin.

Table 10.2   Mean weekly earnings: full-time workers by ethnic group

	Men	Women
	(£ per week)	
White	336	244
All ethnic minorities	296	259
Chinese	336*	287
African Asian	335	254
Caribbean	306	267
Indian	287	252
Pakistani	227	181*
Bangladeshi	191	181*

* These are less reliable data due to the small size of the sample.

Minimum pay

Policies to set minimum pay levels in Britain can be considered under two broad headings: the system of Wages Councils, and the development of a statutory national minimum wage.

Wages Councils

For almost 100 years, the issue of minimum levels of pay have been part of the political agenda in Britain. However, the form of the minimum rates was on a sector/industry basis rather than as a national rate. In many respects, politicians in the early years of the twentieth century saw the enactment of machinery to implement statutory minima as a way of compensating for the limited coverage of free collective bargaining and the difficulties of developing trade union organisation in particular sectors of the economy.

The form of statutory pay determination adopted was the Wages Council. (Initially, these were called 'trade boards' in the originating 1909 legislation. The name was changed in 1945.) The long-term aim of these bodies was to have themselves replaced by full-blown collective bargaining. 'This original aim of providing "surrogate" collective agreements for those too weak to engage in collective bargaining remained uppermost until 1979' (LPC, 1998: 203). At their peak, in 1953, there were 66 Wages Councils covering some 3.5 million workers. The major sectors covered were retail distribution, catering and hotels, clothing, laundries and road haulage.

The political climate changed in 1979 with the election of a Conservative government committed to free-market economics. One significant dimension of its policy was to question and remove those social policies said to interfere with market forces. Action on Wages Councils took place in two stages. First, in 1986, their remit was reduced. For example, they were excluded from considering the pay of workers under 21 years; and they could only set a single minimum rate, a single hourly overtime rate and a maximum accommodation charge offset (against pay). They were also required to consider the impact on jobs of the rate set. The second action was to abolish the Councils completely (apart from those covering agricultural workers, which still remain in being). This took place in 1993. Twenty-six Wages Councils in Great Britain and nine in Northern Ireland were abolished. In aggregate, they covered 2.6 million workers. Some 90 per cent of the total number of workers were covered by the largest Councils – for clothing, retail and hotels and catering.

The enforcement of the Wages Orders made by Wages Councils was by the Wages Inspectorate. They carried out inspections and dealt with complaints. They were empowered to initiate prosecutions. Between 1979 and 1992, the annual average number of completed prosecutions was seven. 'Inspectorate policy was to achieve compliance through advice and persuasion rather than legal action' (LPC, 1998: 207). In 1992, it was found that 4 per cent of workers investigated were underpaid.

Towards a national minimum wage

Political commitment towards a national minimum wage (NMW) is of recent origin. The Labour Party and the trade union movement historically preferred a minimum wage system that was limited to those areas where collective bargaining could not be achieved. This would be in the context of a wider policy commitment of encouragement for collective bargaining. However, the decimation of the Wages Council system under free-market Conservatism resulted in a reappraisal. During the 1990s, a commitment to an NMW was accepted by the Labour Party in opposition. Originally, the rate was to be determined on a formula basis – half the median male earnings. However, after 1996, the Party developed the approach which has now been broadly adopted by the Labour government. The essential elements of this were:

- the establishment of a low pay commission involving employers, unions and independent members;
- consultation with employers and employees;
- the responsibility of the commission to set the national minimum wage;
- consideration being given to economic circumstances.

So, in July 1997, shortly after election, the Labour government appointed the Low Pay Commission, comprising employer, union and academic representatives. It surveyed research evidence and undertook extensive consultation. 'We undertook a substantial programme of visits to over sixty cities, towns and villages through-out the UK, where we heard directly from small firms, rural businesses, local outlets of national companies, low-paid workers, the unemployed and some operating on the fringes of the formal economy' (LPC, 1998: 1). Its principal recommenda-tions involved defining the 'wage', considering training and development issues, choosing the rate and addressing implementation and enforcement issues. In making its recommendations, the LPC was instructed to have regard to the wider economic and social implications; the likely effect on the level of employment and inflation; the impact on the competitiveness of business, particularly the small firms sector; and the potential costs to industry and to the Exchequer.

New social objectives

The LPC (1998: 35) reported that 'some groups of workers are more likely to be low paid than others. They include the following: women, young people, ethnic minorities, people with disabilities, part-time workers, lone parents, temporary and seasonal workers and homeworkers.'

From its consultation process, the LPC identified a number of 'emerging themes' (1998: 28). Among them were the following:

- Both employers and workers recognise that a National Minimum Wage could bring business benefits. It could halt competition based on a damaging down-ward spiral of wages made possible by state subsidies to low-paid workers. It could reduce staff turnover and enhance productivity.
- Employers and workers overwhelmingly advocate a simple structure for the National Minimum Wage that can be easily understood, managed and enforced.
- Some businesses are facing great difficulties and are genuinely concerned about a National Minimum Wage which is set too high.
- Although the incidence of low pay varies within and between regions, it is prevalent throughout the UK and therefore a National Minimum Wage has relevance for all.

- Pay varies considerably within and between business sectors and this will shape the impact of the National Minimum Wage.
- Many low-paid people feel undervalued, exploited and powerless to break out of the poverty trap.
- A lack of affordable childcare causes significant barriers to work for many parents.
- Further reform of the tax and benefits system is required so that increased earnings from a National Minimum Wage are not offset by significant cuts in benefits.
- Employers and workers generally support a training rate for the National Minimum Wage, but there is greater uncertainty about age-related rates.
- The informal economy poses a threat to reputable businesses and their staff: workers might not feel able to enforce their rights to the National Minimum Wage, and disreputable employers might seek to evade the legislation.

Although there are clear standards of social justice inherent in the concept of a statutory national minimum wage, the government has reflected, in legislation, the importance of recognising economic implications. 'In considering what recommendations to include in their report, the Low Pay Commission . . . shall have regard to the effect of this Act on the economy of the United Kingdom as a whole and on competitiveness' (NMW Act 1998, s 7(5)(a)). The national minimum wage covers around 1.5 million workers, 70 per cent of whom are women.

10.4 The legal framework

In this section, we will consider a number of legal issues under three broad areas:

- Definitions of wages and pay.
- The regulation of the pay transaction, covering the common law of contract and pay, information about pay, methods of payment, overpayment, pay deduction, the use of fines as disciplinary action, the issue of shortages and losses in retail employment.
- The principle of social justice influencing levels of pay, particularly in respect of the statutory national minimum wage.

10.4.1 Definitions

Two terms occur in legal action in this area. Both have been defined by statute and subsequent case law. In dealing with any issues concerning specific statutes, it is essential to take the definition in that statute as the starting point. The particular definitions are: **wages** in relation to unauthorised deductions, **wage** in relation to the national minimum wage, and **pay** under equal pay law.

Wages

These are defined for the purpose of **unauthorised deductions** under the Employment Rights Act 1996. 'Wages' are any sum payable to 'a worker in connection with his employment' (s 27). The term includes:

- 'any fee, bonus, commission, holiday pay or other emolument referable to his employment, whether payable under his contract or otherwise';
- statutory sick pay;
- statutory maternity pay;
- a guarantee payment (under ERA 1996, s 28);
- any payment for time off (under ERA 1996, Part VI and TULRCA 1992, s 169);
- remuneration on suspension on medical grounds (ERA 1996, s 64) and on suspension on maternity grounds (ERA 1996, s 68);
- any sum payable relating to a reinstatement or re-engagement order (ERA 1996, s 113);
- any sum payable in pursuance of an order for the continuation of a contract of employment (ERA 1996, s 130; TULRCA 1992, s 164);
- remuneration under a protective award (TULRCA 1992, s 189);
- non-contractual bonus (ERA 1996, s 27(3)).

Excluded are loans, an advance on wages, expenses, pension, allowance or gratuity in connection with retirement or loss of office, redundancy payment, and 'any payment to the worker otherwise than in his capacity as a worker' (ERA 1996, s 27(2)(e)).

Wage

Under the statutory national minimum wage legislation a 'wage' is 'such single **hourly** rate as the Secretary of State may from time to time prescribe' (National Minimum Wage Act 1998, s 1(3)).

Pay

Pay under the Equal Pay Act 1970 has been increasingly moulded by decisions of the European Court of Justice interpreting Art 141 of the amended Treaty of Rome 1957 which defines pay as 'the ordinary basic or minimum wage or salary and any other consideration, whether in cash or in kind, which the worker receives directly or indirectly in respect of his employment from his employer'. As discussed in Chapter 4, the law on equal pay encompasses not only basic pay but also redundancy pay, occupational pensions, incremental pay systems, sick pay and paid leave.

10.4.2 Regulating the pay transaction

The common law of contract and pay

A contract of employment is supported by 'consideration' (something of value by which one party obtains the promise of the other party). Wages clearly can constitute consideration. The employee promises to work for the employer and this agreement is underpinned by the employer's commitment to pay wages. If there is no consideration, there can be no legally enforceable contract.

Wages, although the most common, are, however, only one form of consideration. There can be a valid contract of employment even if no wages are set. The consideration may be entirely based on commission or the chance to earn tips from customers. Furthermore, the employee might be on a remuneration system which is entirely output based. In these instances, there can be an implied term of the contract of employment that the employer will provide the employee with a reasonable amount of work.

Information about pay

Among the first, albeit limited, statutory interventions concerning pay were the requirements placed upon employers to disclose information to individual employees about their pay. Currently, there are two aspects to this:

- *The statement of initial employment particulars* (ERA 1996, s 1): An employer is required to give information about the scale or rate of remuneration or the method of calculating remuneration, and the intervals at which it is paid (i.e. weekly, monthly or at other specified intervals). There must be associated information about hours of work. Information on other forms of pay must also be given: holiday pay and sick pay.

- *The itemised pay statement* (ERA 1996, s 8): This shall consist of the gross amount of wages or salary; the amounts of any variable and any fixed deductions (s 9) and the purposes for which they are made; the net amount of wages or salary payable; and where different parts of the net amount are paid in different ways, the amount and method of payment of each part-payment.

Methods of payment

Nowadays, the principal method of paying wages is through cashless means (credit transfer to an employee's bank account). For many workers in the flexible labour market, cash may still be important. Since 1986, the law has improved the opportunities for employers to use cashless means. Any existing employee (manual worker or non-manual worker) who is paid in cash can be asked to accept non-cash pay. Once an employee has agreed, then the decision cannot be revoked.

Pay deduction

The Employment Rights Act 1996 includes a 'right not to suffer unauthorised deductions' (s 13). An employer may only make deductions from an individual's wages if the deduction is authorised. There are three sources of authority:

1 A deduction may be required or authorised by **an Act of Parliament**. So, for example, an employer is required to deduct Income Tax and National Insurance contributions.

2 The deduction may be authorised by a relevant provision in the employee's own **contract of employment**. For example, this could involve the deduction

of pension contributions, or the possibility of imposing a fine under the disciplinary procedure, or a deduction for cash shortfalls and stock deficiencies in retail employment (*see* below).

3 The worker has previously given **specific consent in writing** for a specific deduction (e.g. the payroll deduction of trade union contributions or the repayment of a loan).

A deduction is defined in this way: 'where the total amount of wages paid on any occasion by an employer to a worker employed by him is less than the total amount of the wages properly payable by him to the worker on that occasion (after deductions), the amount of the deficiency shall be treated . . . as a deduction made by the employer from the worker's wages' (ERA 1996, s 13(3)).

Overpayment

An employer is not prevented from making deductions in respect of overpayment of wages or an overpayment of expenses (ERA 1996, s 14). Several issues can arise in this area:

- *Does the employee dispute whether or not there has been overpayment?* If so, the issue could be raised in the county court.

- *Was the overpayment a consequence of an error in law?* If so, it is not generally recoverable. However, if the employee knew of the error and it would be inequitable to allow the money to be retained, then recovery is possible.

- *Was the overpayment as a result of a mistake made by the employer?* The general position is that the employer can recover this money provided that he can prove that the mistake was one of fact. However, there are a number of issues that may need to be considered which may make this difficult (outlined by the Court of Appeal in *Avon County Council* v *Howlett* [1983] IRLR 171). These provide a defence for the employee. The first is whether or not the employer led the employee to believe that they were entitled to the money that was overpaid. Secondly, the employee genuinely believed that they were entitled to the money and spent it. Thirdly, the overpayment was not the fault of the employee.

Participation in industrial action

Where a worker takes part in a strike or other industrial action, the employer can make an appropriate deduction from the worker's wages (ERA 1996, s 14(5)). *See also* Chapter 15.

Fines for disciplinary action

An employer may only impose fines on an employee where these are provided for under the contract of employment or, in exceptional cases, by statute (ERA 1996, s 14(2)). They are likely to be included in the sanctions available to the employer under the disciplinary procedure. Subject to this authorisation, they are permitted deductions.

Cash shortages and stock deficiencies in retail employment

This statutory provision is restricted to 'retail employment'. This 'means employment involving (whether or not on a regular basis) the carrying out by the worker of retail transactions directly with members of the public or with fellow workers or other individuals in their personal capacities' or the collection by the worker of amounts payable in connection with retail transactions (ERA 1996, s 17(2)). 'Retail transaction' refers to 'the sale or supply of goods or the supply of services (including financial services)' (s 17(3)).

There are several key steps in the process authorising such deductions:

- the deduction must be for cash shortage or stock deficiency;
- the worker must be notified in writing of the total liability (ERA 1996, s 20(1)(a));
- the demand for payment must be in writing (ERA 1996, s 20(2));
- the deduction limit is set at 10 per cent of gross wages due on any given day (ERA 1996, s 18(1));
- deductions of up to 10 per cent can be made on successive pay days;
- the 10 per cent rule does not apply to the final pay day;
- the rule can be used within 12 months of the shortage being established (ERA 1996, s 20(2)).

10.4.3 Statutory national minimum wage

Policies promoting social justice in employment have had an impact in two areas of pay determination: where pay rates are subject to sex discrimination, and where levels of pay are regarded as exploitative. The first of these areas has been discussed already in Chapter 4 in relation to *equal pay*. The second will be the focus of this section and we will explore the new provisions on the *statutory minimum wage*.

A national rate

The national minimum wage (NMW) applies to workers regardless of where they live or work or the sector they are employed in or the size of the company in which they work. However, there is a facility within the Act for different rates to be determined for different age groups and according to whether a worker is a trainee. Increases in the NMW rates are not automatically linked to prices or earnings. The government considers uprating periodically in the light of advice from the Low Pay Commission and the economic circumstances of the time. Changes are brought into force by regulations laid before Parliament (*see* Table 10.3).

Who is covered?

There is wide coverage (NMWA, s 1(2)). Those qualifying are workers who work ordinarily in the UK and who are over the school leaving age. The Act covers the whole United Kingdom including Northern Ireland. Those covered are as follows.

Table 10.3 National minimum wage rates since 1999

	National rate for 22 years and above	Rate for 18–21 years
April 1999	£3.60	£3.00
June 2000	£3.60	£3.20
October 2000	£3.70	£3.20
October 2001	£4.10	£3.50
October 2002	£4.20	£3.60
October 2003	£4.50	£3.80

Workers: a worker is defined as an individual who works under either a contract of employment or '*any other contract . . . whereby the individual undertakes to do or perform personally any work or services for another party to the contract whose status is not by virtue of the contract that of a client or customer of any profession or business undertaking carried on by the individual*'. This definition is in the same terms as that in the ERA 1996, s 230(3).

The Act, then, covers any part-time workers, temporary workers, agency workers (NMWA, s 34), and homeworkers (s 35). Although this coverage of the Act appears comprehensive, there is a reserve power (s 41) enabling the Secretary of State to propose additional Regulations extending the Act to a specific description of workers. Whilst it cannot be used to include a category that is specifically excluded under the Act, it could be used to respond to developments in the flexible labour market. The Act also covers Crown employees (s 36).

This coverage is regardless of:

- the region, sector, size of business or occupation in which a worker works;
- who a person's employer is;
- the worker's length of service;
- the number of hours a worker works each week;
- the worker's pattern of work;
- whether a worker is paid by time or by output.

There is a provision (s 3) empowering the Secretary of State to exclude any age group at or below 25 years from the NMW. Those aged 26 years and above can be excluded for specific reasons (e.g. participation in training schemes).

Those who are implicitly or explicitly excluded are:

- the genuinely self-employed (independent contractors);
- officeholders, such as police officers and prison officers;
- company directors who are not also employees of the company;
- serving members of the armed forces and reservists who are covered by the armed forces pay review body;
- volunteers;

- 'voluntary workers' who work for charitable organisations and may only receive expenses or subsistence payments (s 44);

- offshore workers;

- those on work experience who are **not** trainees working under contracts of employment;

- family members who simply help out on an informal basis unless there is a contract of employment;

- prisoners in custody, including those on remand, working under prison rules (s 45);

- sharefishermen and women (s 43);

- schoolchildren.

The employer

The National Minimum Wage Act makes clear the obligation upon a worker's employer to pay remuneration which is not less than the NMW in any pay reference period. 'Employer' is defined (s 54(5)) 'in relation to an employee or worker' as 'the person by whom the employee or worker is (or, where the employment has ceased, was) employed'. The definition is the same as that in the ERA 1996, s 230(4).

The NMW Act also covers the situation of 'superior employers' (s 48). 'Where (a) the immediate employer of a worker is himself in the employment of some other person and (b) the worker is employed on the premises of that other person, that other person shall be deemed for the purposes of this Act to be the employer of the worker jointly with the immediate employer.' Examples of such relationships can occur in the construction industry.

If a worker is employed by different employers on separate but parallel contracts, then each employer is responsible for ensuring compliance with the NMW Act.

Calculating hourly rates

The National Minimum Wage Regulations 1999 (implemented on 1 April 1999) prescribe how to calculate a worker's hourly rate of remuneration for the purposes of determining if it is at or above the NMW. For some workers, the calculation is likely to be straightforward. However, difficulties are likely to arise where a person is paid by output or works on irregular patterns. The NMW Act provides for a 'pay reference period' (s 1(4)) for which a worker must be paid at least the national minimum wage (*see* Fig. 10.1).

In defining the 'wage', the LPC (1998: 51) makes the following point:

> in general, low-paid workers receive few, if any additions to basic pay. In some business sectors, however, variable payments of a business-specific nature, premia and benefits may form a significant part of a low-paid worker's wage. The definition of earnings that may count towards the National Minimum Wage is designed to be simple and fair, easily enforceable and consistent with the needs of business and the low paid.

■ **A nightwatchman**: Mr Wright worked between 5pm and 7am seven nights a week. He received wages of £210 per week. He was expected to respond if intruders set off an alarm. Otherwise, he was allowed to read or watch television or sleep when on the premises. Sleeping facilities were provided. He claimed entitlement to the NMW for each hour that he was on the premises. The Employment Appeal Tribunal ruled that where a worker was required to be on the employer's premises to carry out his duties over a specific number of hours, then, *all* the hours were eligible for the NMW. It noted a distinction with the situation where the employer allowed a worker time off to sleep (reg 15(1)).

Source: *Wright* v *Scottbridge Construction Ltd* [2001] IRLR 589.

■ **Nurse 'bank' administrator**: The Court of Appeal upholding decisions of the employment tribunal and the EAT, ruled on the eligibility for the NMW of nurses who spent the night at home, answered phone calls requesting 'bank' nurses and allocated nurses. They were ruled to be working for the full shift and entitled to be paid the NMW for each hour of the shift. The Court saw no difference between a worker in an office waiting for phone calls and a nurse in this case. To suggest that there were different rules for homeworkers was 'misconceived'.

Source: *British Nursing Association* v *Inland Revenue (National Minimum Wage Compliance Team)* [2002] IRLR 480.

Figure 10.1 NMW and atypical work patterns

It continues that:

> in whatever way workers' pay is defined or whatever hours they work, only their 'standard' pay shall count towards the National Minimum Wage. Hence incentive payments, such as commission, tips and gratuities paid via the payroll and piece rate, should count. In contrast, allowances and premium payments which are provided for non-standard work or hours, as well as all benefits with the exception of accommodation, should not count towards compliance. A worker should be entitled to the National Minimum Wage for each hour of actual working time, averaged over the worker's normal pay reference period up to a maximum of one month.

The proposed deduction for accommodation is suggested by the Commission at the maximum figure of £20 per week (LPC, 1998: 60).

Collective agreements and contractual terms

The Act makes it clear that 'any provision in any agreement (whether a worker's contract or not) is void in so far as it purports (a) to exclude or limit the operation of any provision of this Act; or (b) to preclude a person from bringing proceedings under this Act before an employment tribunal' (NMWA 1998, s 49(1)). The exceptions to this are in relation to conciliated complaints (under the Employment Tribunals Act 1996, s 18) and in respect of compromise agreements (ETA 1996, s 18(1)(dd); NMWA 1998, ss 3–11).

Enforcement: civil proceedings

There are three principal aspects to the civil enforcement process: record-keeping, underpayment and the role of inspectors. The NMW Act also provides for action on criminal offences (*see* next section).

First, considerable emphasis has been put on **the need for an employer to keep records**. Failure to do so is a criminal offence (s 31). Regulations relating to the nature of such records will be made. These regulations may 'make different provision for different cases or for different descriptions of person' (s 51(1)(a)).

A worker has the right to require their employer to produce 'relevant records' for establishing whether or not the worker has been paid at least the NMW, and to inspect and copy those records (s 10). There are three important provisions in the exercise of this right:

1 The worker must have reasonable grounds for believing that they are being paid less than the national minimum wage.

2 The worker must give the employer a written 'production notice' requesting the production of any relevant records relating to a particular period. This notice should indicate whether the worker wishes to be accompanied.

3 The employer can determine where the inspection takes place, having given the worker 'reasonable' notice of the place and time. Having received the 'production notice', the employer must produce the relevant records within 14 days; although a later time can be agreed, during those 14 days, between the employer and the worker in question.

The failure of an employer to produce 'relevant records' at a specified place and time or to allow inspection and copying of them by the worker entitles them to complain to an employment tribunal within three months of the production deadline (s 11). Such a case may be heard by a tribunal chairman sitting alone.

If it is established that the employer prevented access to the 'relevant records', then, two (and no other) remedies are available and must be granted:

■ a declaration;

■ an award to the worker of 80 times the national minimum wage in force when the award is made. This would be £336 where the NMW is £4.20. This award cannot be varied.

The second aspect to the enforcement process is **the issue of underpayment**. A worker, still in employment, who has been underpaid has a right to claim the difference between what has been paid (if anything) and the prevailing NMW. The worker may complain to an employment tribunal (under ERA 1996, s 23(1)(a) alleging unauthorised deduction of wages). Alternatively, the worker may bring an action for breach of contract in the county court. A former worker can allege breach of contract at an employment tribunal in relation to the termination of their employment. Workers who successfully complain to an employment tribunal are entitled to recover the amount of the underpayment but no interest. Those who go to the county court are entitled to interest also.

The normal burden of proof is reversed in national minimum wage under-payment cases before both employment tribunals and the county court. So, the presumption will be that the worker was paid below the NMW and that qualifies for the NMW. It will be for the employer, if the claim or status of the applicant is disputed, to show that the worker was paid the NMW or is not a worker covered by the protection (i.e. is genuinely self-employed).

- 79 000 queries received at the helpline during the year.
- Since 1999, the helpline has responded to more than 275 000 enquiries and handled over 7500 complaints.
- The majority of complaints received are from adult workers aged between 22 and 60 years.
- Complaints were again received in equal numbers from male and female workers. 'The Inland Revenue have not yet been able to establish why complaints are received in equal number from men and women when the expected ratio would be weighted towards female workers, who tend to work in lower paid sectors' (p. 14).
- Each sector attracting complaints is in similar ratios to earlier years. The sectors producing the most complaints are: hospitality, market services, retail, production/construction, hairdressing.
- The highest incidence of complaints came from Yorkshire and Humberside and from the North West of England.

- 16 compliance teams investigate all complaints about non-payment of the minimum wage. (During the year, the government increased the number of teams from 14.)
- 36 per cent of employers investigated by compliance officers were found not to be paying the minimum wage – an increase of 6 per cent on the previous year.

- Over £5 million in wage arrears was identified by the compliance teams – an increase of almost £2 million on the previous year.
- The average arrears per worker is growing. In 1999 it was just over £200. In 2002, it is just on £500 (*see also* Fig. 10.3).

Figure 10.2   Trends in the *National Minimum Wage Annual Report 2001/02*

Source: Extracted from *National Minimum Wage Annual Report 2001/02*, published by Inland Revenue and Department of Trade and Industry.

The third aspect of the enforcement process is the role of **inspectors** (NMWA 1998, s 13). The Inland Revenue was appointed as the enforcement body in 1998 (*see* Fig. 10.2). The powers of inspectors include the following:

- *The serving of an enforcement notice upon an employer* (NMWA, s 19). This will require both the payment of the NMW to the worker or worker concerned and any arrears. Such a notice is a warning to the employer. It is likely to have been preceded by informal discussions. The employer can appeal to an employment tribunal within four weeks of receiving the notice. Such an appeal can be heard by a tribunal chairman sitting alone. A tribunal may rescind or amend an enforcement notice. To succeed in a complaint an employer needs to show that, for example, the workers concerned were genuinely self-employed, or that the workers had not been underpaid or that the amount of the alleged arrears was wrong.
- *Making a complaint to an employment tribunal* (NMWA, s 20). If an enforcement notice is not complied with, the enforcement officer may, on behalf of the workers concerned, complain that the employer has made an unauthorised deduction. The officer must be satisfied that the employer has a case to answer. This will involve scrutiny of the evidence and an interview with the employer. A complaint by an enforcement officer does not take away the rights of individual workers to complain.

- In Wales, a homeworker assembling crackers complained about non-payment of the NMW. The employer initially thought that homeworkers were not 'workers' under the legislation. After the compliance officer explained the position, he accepted that they were and contacted the National Group of Homeworkers to assist him in drawing up a fair estimate agreement. *Over £8600 in wage arrears was identified for this worker.*

- In Northern Ireland, a worker complained that, while employed as a night sitter in a residential home, she did not receive the NMW. The compliance officer visited the employer. He agreed payment of arrears. He suggested they had used a similar payment practice to that of a local health trust. The compliance officer later visited the health trust concerned. *Arrears totalling £25 000 benefiting almost 100 workers were identified.*

- In the South-East of England, a compliance officer investigated a failure to pay the NMW to an 81-year-old worker who was employed as a car polisher. The company was unaware of its liability to pay pensioners the NMW. *It promptly paid arrears of £3000.*

- In Yorkshire, a worker complained that he and his colleagues were not being paid the NMW. All were residential officers at a university who lived on campus. Although provided with free accommodation, they were not paid a wage. Accommodation provided does count towards the minimum wage (up to a maximum of £22.75 per week*). In this case, it did not equate to the minimum wage for every hour worked which the workers were entitled to. *Arrears totalling £137 000 were identified for 27 workers.*

* This rate for the accommodation offset was set on 1 October 2001.

Figure 10.3 Some successful cases

Source: Extracted from *National Minimum Wage Annual Report 2001/02*, published by Inland Revenue and Department of Trade and Industry.

- *Taking other civil proceedings* (NMWA, s 20). This would be an alternative route through the county court.

- *The serving of a penalty notice* (NMWA, s 21). Where an employer fails to comply with an enforcement notice, then, a penalty notice may be served setting out the nature of the non-compliance and indicating a fine that must be paid within four weeks after the receiving of the penalty notice. The fine increases the longer the employer takes to comply. The amount of the fine is twice the hourly rate of the NMW (currently in force) for each worker who is underpaid on each day of non-compliance. A penalty notice is not enforceable while the appeal process on an enforcement notice is still in train. Furthermore, a penalty notice can itself be appealed against to an employment tribunal and so cannot be enforced until an employer's appeal has been decided upon. Again, a tribunal may rescind or amend such a notice.

- *Access to records* (NMWA, s 14). In order to be effective in ensuring compliance, inspectors are provided with certain powers in respect of an employer's records. They can require production of these. They have a right to examine and copy them and to have them explained. They have a right to require additional information to be produced. They can enter an employer's premises 'at all reasonable times' in order to exercise any of these powers. (The disclosure and exchange of such information by an inspector is restricted to matters relating to the enforcement of the national minimum wage (NMWA, s 15).)

Enforcement: criminal action

An employer commits a criminal offence (NMWA, s 31) who:

- 'refuses or wilfully neglects to remunerate the worker for any pay reference period at a rate which is at least equal to the national minimum wage' (NMWA, s 31(1));
- fails to keep records in accordance with any Regulations made under NMWA, s 9;
- 'knowingly causes or allows to be made' in a record 'any entry which he knows to be false in a material particular' (NMWA, s 31(3));
- 'produces or furnishes or knowingly causes or allows to be produced, any records or information which he knows to be false in a material particular' (NMWA, s 31(4));
- 'intentionally delays or obstructs an officer' seeking to enforce the Act (NMWA, s 31(5));
- 'refuses or neglects to answer any question, furnish any information or produce any document when required to do so' (NMWA, s 31(6)).

An employer's defence in respect of the refusal or wilful neglect to pay the NMW or of keeping required records is 'to prove that he exercised all due diligence and took all reasonable precautions to secure that the provisions of this Act and of any relevant regulations made under it, were complied with by himself and by any person under his control' (NMWA, s 31(8)).

The prosecutor in these cases can be enforcement officers (whether they have a legal qualification or not). All these offences are triable without a jury. So, they can be heard in a magistrates' court or a court of summary jurisdiction in Northern Ireland. Conviction will be determined against the criminal standard of proof – that the evidence shows beyond reasonable doubt that the offence was committed. The maximum fine is set at level 5 (currently £5000). Government expects such action to be very rare.

Victimisation

Workers are protected from victimisation – i.e. being 'subjected to any detriment' (NMWA, s 23). The circumstances attracting such protection are where:

- a worker asserts in good faith their right to the NMW, right of access to records and right to recover the difference between what (if anything) they have been paid and the NMW;
- as a result of asserting such rights, the employer was prosecuted for an offence under the NMWA 1998;
- the individual worker qualifies, or will or might qualify for the NMW or for a particular, higher rate of the NMW.

A complaint in relation to victimisation can be made to an employment tribunal within three months of the alleged detriment being implemented (NMWA, s 24). The employer must show the reason for the act or omission.

If a tribunal finds that victimisation has taken place, it must make a declaration and it may award compensation. If the complainant was not an employee (i.e. party to a contract of employment) and the detriment was the termination of the employment relationship, the amount of compensation awarded must not exceed the amount that the worker would have received if they had been an employee who had been unfairly dismissed. But, in any other case, the amount of compensation awarded is not limited. It is the amount that the tribunal considers just and equitable.

Unfair dismissal

Unfair dismissal protection is extended (NMWA, s 25). This extension relates only to employees (as do other unfair dismissal rights). It is applicable from the first day of employment and is not subject to an upper age limit. An employee will be regarded as unfairly dismissed if the reason or the principal reason for the dismissal (or selection for redundancy) is that:

- the worker asserted in good faith a right to the NMW, right of access to records and right to recover the difference between what (if anything) they have been paid and the NMW;
- as a result of asserting such rights, the employer was prosecuted for an offence under the NMWA 1998;
- the individual worker qualifies, or will or might qualify, for the NMW or for a particular, higher rate of the NMW.

Agricultural workers

The NMW sets the floor below which the pay of agricultural workers must not fall. The Agricultural Wages Boards (for England, Scotland, Wales and Northern Ireland) still retain powers to set other minimum conditions. Enforcement of the minimum wage in agriculture is undertaken by the specific departments and agencies responsible for agriculture in England and Wales, Scotland and Northern Ireland.

10.5   Employment policies and practices

There are several practical issues that employers need to consider in respect of the law and the administration of pay: contracts of employment and collective agreements; special agreements; information and records.

10.5.1   Contracts of employment and collective agreements

The starting point for any complaints about employment rights concerning pay will, inevitably, be the contract of employment. This will, as appropriate, encompass any terms of a collective agreement with a trade union that is incorporated into the contract. An employer must appreciate the importance of operating within the contract of employment, particularly in respect of pay. There are various potential repudiatory breaches of the contract of employment that can arise and could result in constructive dismissal claims. These are:

- not paying wages due to a person for work undertaken;
- making deductions from wages without authorisation;
- varying pay without the consent of the individual employee (or, if appropriate, the union);
- arbitrarily deducting overpayment of wages without consulting the employee concerned.

The contract of employment is, then, a source of entitlements to particular remuneration. Furthermore, it can be the source of authority for certain pay deductions (e.g. in the retail trade, for pensions, for disciplinary fines). (*See* Chapters 2 and 3 where the significance of the contract of employment is discussed.)

10.5.2 Special agreements

Certain money that an employer wishes to recover from an employee might not be subject to contractual terms. A special agreement may be made. This should be in writing and should clearly cover all relevant requirements and expectations. It should be made in advance of the expenditure being incurred. Examples of such ancillary agreements could be:

- an undertaking to return company property on termination of employment. If that is not done, permission to deduct the replacement value from the employee's final pay;
- an agreement by the employee to repay expenditure on expensive training courses if the employee leaves an organisation within a specified period of time (e.g. 12 months);
- an agreement on the repayment of a loan during employment and on termination of employment.

10.5.3 Information and records

As we saw above, there already exist rights relating to the provision of information to employees. (The law does not explicitly mention 'workers' in this respect.) Such rights to information relate to:

- **the Statement of Initial Employment Particulars** (ERA 1996, s 1): employees are to be told the scale or rate of remuneration or the method of calculating it, and the intervals at which it is paid (weekly, monthly or otherwise). A linked information requirement concerns hours of work. Taking these together, then, an employee can calculate their hourly rate of pay;

- **a written itemised pay statement and a statement of fixed deductions** (ERA, ss 8–9): this must contain the following information:
  - the gross amount of wages or salary;
  - the amounts of any variable and fixed deductions from gross pay and the reasons for them;
  - the net amount of wages or salary payable; and
  - where different parts of the net amount are paid in different ways, the amount and method of payment of each part-payment.

New information requirements are introduced under the **National Minimum Wage Act** 1998. A critical part of the process for enforcing the NMW is the availability of adequate records. Failure to maintain them is a criminal offence (NMWA 1998, s 31).

Exercise 10.1 | **Pay regulation: Scenarios**

Read the following scenarios and decide whether or not the worker concerned is subject to any infringement of their statutory rights.

10.1.1 National minimum wage

1. Darren is aged 17 years and works for six hours on a Saturday afternoon in a burger bar. His employer pays him £2.25 per hour.

2. Sara is aged 19 years and delivers a free newspaper for five hours a week at weekends. She is paid £3.00 per hour.

3. Sharon, aged 26 years, works as a waitress on a permanent part-time contract. Her basic pay is £2.50 per hour. Tips are paid through the till. Her hours and additional remuneration over a four-week period are as follows:

   Week 1: 12 hours
   Tips (through till) £12; tips (direct) £3

   Week 2: 6 hours
   Tips (through till) £6; tips (direct) £3

   Week 3: 8 hours
   Tips (through till) £10; tips (direct) £4

   Week 4: 14 hours
   Tips (through till) £21; tips (direct) £4

4. Hassan, aged 30 years, is a waiter who has been supplied to the Parkside Hotel by an agency. (He also works on a casual basis in the restaurant of a separate employer in between engagements at the hotel.) His basic pay from the hotel is £2.50 per hour. Because he is a cousin of the owner, he is provided with free accommodation, although he has to pay for food and heating. His hours and additional remuneration for a four-week period of work for the hotel were as follows:

   Week 1: 12 hours
   Tips (through till) £7; tips (direct) £3

   Week 2: 6 hours
   Tips (through till) £6; tips (direct) £4

   Week 3: 8 hours
   Tips (through till) £6; tips (direct) £3

   Week 4: 14 hours
   Tips (through till) £11; tips (direct) £5

5   Siobhan has worked as a cleaner for one specific cleaning company for the past two years. She is aged 20 years. She has been paid £2.70 per hour. Just before her twenty-first birthday, her supervisor says that she is sacked. He says they do not need her anymore.

6   Fiona, aged 29 years, has just started work in a small 'open all hours' shop. It employs fewer than 20 staff – all of whom work on some form of part-time contract. She believes that she has been wrongly paid because her hourly wages over the past month average £2.90 per hour. She calculated that she should have received an hourly rate in line with the NMW. She has been given a handwritten piece of paper stating the hours she worked, her gross pay, the deductions made for tax and National Insurance and her net pay. She asks the owner of the shop if she can check his pay records to make sure that she has not been underpaid. He refuses.

10.1.2 Pay deduction

7   Warren had a loan agreement with his employer. It stipulated that when he left employment, payments would continue until the debt was paid off. His contract of employment was terminated and the employer did not pay his final wages of £278.50, saying it was to cover the outstanding loan payments.

8   Bill normally worked shifts and, under a collective agreement, he received a shift allowance. During a temporary stoppage in production he was not required to work shifts and the allowance was not paid. He claimed that this was unlawful deduction.

9   Jehan has been overpaid by £250 in one month's pay cheque because of an administrative error. His normal gross pay is £1200 per month. He had heard rumours that the union had negotiated a pay increase and so he decides to spend the money on a new tumble-drier. The company asks him to repay the overpayment immediately.

10 Winston was a van driver. He was given a document with details of the vehicle insurance policy under which he would be liable for the excess for damage caused during personal use of the van. Private mileage was also limited. Further provisions covered charges for private phone calls made from the van. The amount of £305 was deducted from his final wages; £155 of this was for the cost of repairs for damage during private use, although he had agreed to repair the van himself; £150 was a provisional deduction for both private phone calls and excess private mileage. He claimed the deduction was unlawful.

11 Helena works at a small café. Her boss deducted £16 from her weekly pay of £150 because of a shortfall in the till. Her boyfriend Andreas says that he cannot do that.

Feedback on these exercises is provided in Appendix 1.

References

Department of Trade and Industry and Inland Revenue (2002) *National Minimum Wage Annual Report 2001/02*. London: DTI.

Low Pay Commission (1998) *First Report: The National Minimum Wage*, Cm. 3976. London: Stationery Office.

CHAPTER 11

Regulation of working time

This chapter considers the extent to which working time has been and is regulated through both voluntary measures and legal regulation. Having read this chapter you should be able to:

■ Understand the historic role of voluntary regulation.

■ Understand the piecemeal growth of legal regulation of working time in Britain.

■ Understand the essential purposes and provisions of the new European law on working time regulation.

■ Advise your organisation on the implications of the Working Time Regulations.

11.1 Structure of the chapter

This chapter comprises the following sections:

■ *Introduction*: The scope of working time and its regulation.

■ *The context*: The role of voluntary regulation, the long hours culture, social policy objectives, economic considerations, and the impact of the Working Time Regulations 1998.

■ *The legal framework*: Piecemeal regulation of working time, and the 1998 Working Time Regulations.

■ *Employment policies and practices*: A strategic approach to implementation, a checklist of action to be taken, and some problem scenarios.

11.2 Introduction

The regulation of working time can and does cover various issues:

- the **number of hours** worked by an individual worker in a specified time period (e.g. the basic or standard working week);
- arrangements of **'non-work' time** (e.g. rest periods, rest days and holidays);
- the **scheduling** and availability of working time (e.g. night work, Sunday working and part-time working);
- the **quality of work** (e.g. the adaptation of work to the worker).

In the course of this chapter we will consider all of these issues.

Working time is measured and parcelled in various ways and, so, it is important to outline the commonly used definitions. The following are the standard terms that occur frequently in working time arrangements, collective agreements and the law.

The basic working week

This is the number of hours per week that a full-time employee is expected to work. It will usually be an express term of the contract of employment and should be stated in the written statement of employment particulars (ERA 1996, s 1). For full-time workers this is usually specified as a number of hours above 30 per week. There is no statutory provision on the length of the basic working week. It will depend on either management decision or the provisions of a collective agreement.

Overtime

This refers to the number of hours per week performed in excess of the employing organisation's basic working week. In law, there is no specific ceiling on overtime. However, the regulations on an average maximum working week of 48 hours certainly have a bearing on overtime arrangements (WTR 1998, reg 4).

Shift work

The Working Time Directive 1994 defines this as follows: 'shift work shall mean any method of organising work in shifts whereby workers succeed each other at the same work stations according to a certain pattern, including a rotating pattern and which may be continuous or discontinuous, entailing the need for workers to work at different times over a given period of days or weeks' (Art 2.5).

The Labour Force Survey (1997) reports that some 3.5 million working people are shift workers (of whom 2.1 million are men). Of these, 286 000 people are on night shifts; 429 200 work sometimes night and sometimes days; and 537 300 are on three-shift working.

Annualised hours schemes

Under these schemes, the total number of hours to be worked each year are aggregated and then scheduled to be worked according to variations in customer demand for a product or service. This may result in variations in the length of working days at different times of the year. It is estimated that around 9 per cent of the workforce (two million people) are covered by such arrangements. The largest proportion (15.8 per cent) was found in professional occupations; 10.3 per cent were plant and machine operatives, and 9 per cent were in craft and related occupations. The lowest incidence was among managers and administrators at 6.6 per cent (Department of Employment, 1994).

Weekend working

This is usually regarded as any working on a Saturday or Sunday: 52 per cent of men and 36 per cent of women work at least one day at the weekend.

Part-time working

This describes the situation where an employee works a number of hours less than the employing organisation's basic working week. It can cover any number of hours per week/month that are just short of the basic. At the other end of the spectrum, it may include people who work as little as two hours per week. In official statistics it is usually specified as working up to 30 hours per week. Around a quarter of the working population works part-time.

Job share

This is a situation where a full-time job is split, usually between two employees, and they work on pro rata conditions of employment. It developed in the mid-1980s and is evident in a minority of organisations (less than 20 per cent). ACAS reported that its introduction 'was greatest in industries which employ mainly white collar staff such as public administration and banking' (ACAS, 1988: 21). The Labour Force Survey 2000 recorded that one per cent of employees were job sharers.

Flexible hours

Flexible hours of employment can vary from day to day, week to week, or month to month. In some instances the employee instigates the flexible working by deciding their arrival and departure time around a 'core time'. In other instances, the employer will set the pattern of working (e.g. term-time working).

Zero-hours contracts

These are a development of flexible working, instigated by employers. There are three possible broad categories of such contracts:

1 where an employee attends the employer's premises but is only regarded as 'working' when their services are required by a customer or client;
2 where the employee is 'on call' (by telephone at home) at specified times, should the employer require their services;
3 where an employee is part of a 'bank' of potential workers and either the employer will contact the employee to see if the worker wants work or, alternatively, the employee might contact the employer to see if work is available.

The government calculates that there are some 200 000 people in the United Kingdom on these contracts (DTI, 'Fairness at Work' White Paper, 1998: para 3.14).

11.3 The context

The employment context contains a number of elements: the historic predominance of voluntary regulation; a developing long-hours culture; attempts to achieve various social purposes; and concern about economic consequences.

11.3.1 The historic use of voluntary measures

For most of the twentieth century, in Britain, working time was generally regulated through collective agreements negotiated between employers (on an industry-wide or single-employer basis) and trade unions. Such agreements set the standard working week. They would also cover, if appropriate to working patterns in the sector, shift working arrangements and premium rates of pay for such shift working and for overtime working.

Given that collective agreements have generally been presumed to be legally unenforceable (*see* Chapter 14), such voluntary standards would usually be enforceable through their incorporation into the contracts of employment of individual employees (*see* Chapter 2). Non-compliance by an employer would be a breach of contract.

Generally, this regulation of working time concerned the standard working week of manual workers in unionised sectors. In practice, there was periodically concerted action by unions. They used a pace-setting national deal to set a new maximum basic working week. Invariably, this was the national agreement covering some one million workers in the engineering industry. As a consequence of a deal, pressure would then be exerted on employers in other sectors to provide comparative treatment. Usually, such campaigning was successful. The following key dates show the reductions in the basic working week for manual workers in engineering. They also reflect the general reduction taking place through British industry:

1920s	48 hours
1947	44 hours
1960	42 hours
1965	40 hours
1979	39 hours

After 1979, there was an unsuccessful campaign to achieve a 35-hour basic working week in engineering. By 1989, national bargaining in this industry was terminated by the employer federation. Likewise, other multi-employer (or industry-wide) bargaining diminished in importance. The general political climate favoured decollectivisation and the membership of unions and the extent of union recognition decreased in importance. Consequently, this co-ordinated voluntary approach has ceased to be a feature of British employee relations.

The voluntary approach has some limited success. However, this was only in respect of the level of the basic working week. Restrictions on overtime levels were rare and, generally, shift-working arrangements were agreed at company level.

11.3.2 A growing long-hours culture

The Labour Force Survey shows that nearly 4 million employee (16 per cent of the total workforce) now work over 48 hours per week. This compares with 3.3 million (15 per cent) in the early 1990s. This increase follows a period of long-term decline.

The increase is notwithstanding the fact that between 1988 and 1998 the basic average standard hours fell for both men and women. For men the drop was from 40.2 hours to 39.3 hours; and for women, from 37.4 hours to 36.8 hours. The actual increase in hours resulted from increases in paid and unpaid overtime. Drawing international comparisons can be difficult – particularly in view of the high incidence of part-time working in the UK. Comparing *full-time* male employees, statistics show that 22 per cent in the UK work long hours compared with 11 per cent across other EU member states.

In an extensive review of research literature and some new research (Kodz *et al.*, 2002), the following results were reported of those most likely to work long hours:

- 11 per cent if UK employees;
- men more likely than women;
- men with children are slightly *more* likely than those without;
- women with children are *less* likely than those without;
- people between 30 and 49 years;
- managers, professional and operative and assembly workers. (Over two-thirds of these managerial and professional workers are neither paid overtime nor given time off in lieu. In contrast well over half of craft and skilled, service, operative and assembly workers are compensated in some way for extra hours.)

The incidence of long hours is higher in the private sector than in the public sector; and greater among workers in construction, transport, communication, agriculture, forestry and fishing.

The research review and the new in-depth case studies (Kodz *et al.*, 2002) found that the major reason for long-hours working, particularly when it is unpaid, is the volume of work. Factors which were seen to be associated with increasing volumes of work were: new organisational initiatives (e.g. de-layering, project-based working and a greater emphasis on customer focus); staff shortages; IT and e-mail overload. Research also suggests that an organisational culture of 'presenteeism' (and hence long hours), indicating employee commitment, can put pressure on an individual employee. 'Overall, the research findings show that many people woking long hours do so for a combination of reasons which can be difficult to disentangle, especially in an organisation or part of an organisation where a long hours culture is perceived or is known to prevail' (Kodz *et al.*, 2002).

An ancilliary but important issue, linked with long working hours, is the question of paid holiday entitlement. Until the implementation of the Working Time Regulations, Britain was the only country in the EU where workers had no legal rights to paid annual leave. The matter traditionally was dealt with through collective bargaining where that existed. Otherwise, it was at management's discretion. Consequently, there were nearly 2.5 million workers who received no paid annual leave (most of this group constituted part-time workers of whom 1.4 million were women), 4.1 million received fewer than three weeks of paid holiday and 5.9 million received fewer than four weeks (Labour Force Survey, Autumn 1995).

11.3.3 Social issues

There are two broad social policy issues which relate to long hours and the regulation of working time: the *health, safety and welfare* of employees (*see also* Chapter 12); the impact on *family life* and *work-life balance* (*see also* Chapter 13). Both issues are policy concerns for the EU and the present British government.

The originating 1993 Directive was, primarily, conceived of as a **health and safety** measure, augmenting those Directives adopted under the 1989 Social Action Programme. The present British government, unlike its predecessor Conservative government, firmly sees working time regulation as a health and safety matter. This conforms to the view of the ECJ which in 1996 rejected the Conservative government's challenge to the legality of the Working Time Directive. Essentially, the health and safety dimension of the regulations concerns three elements: maximum working time, patterns of breaks and leave from working time and job design.

In terms of health and safety, Kodz *et al.* (2002) comment that the research literature shows 'clear grounds for concern' about the adverse effect of long hours working and the frequency of health and safety incidents. However, they note that because this research focuses on specific occupations (e.g. long-distance road haulage, the medical professions) it is not possible to draw more general conclusions. In terms of employee health, they refer to the considerable body of research looking at the impact of work patterns. (Most of this focuses on unsocial-hours working or shift patterns rather than the specific aspect of long hours.) The cumulative research evidence shows that there are *associations* between long-hours working and mental health and cardio-vascular problems (author's italics).

The issue of **work-life balance** is explored in more detail in Chapter 13. Here it is sufficient to note both the political impetus to change and the social consequences of long hours. The government, in its Consultation Document (DTI, 1997) on the proposed legislation, commented that 'the "long hours" culture has historically not only created barriers to work for women with caring responsibilities, but also prevented many men from taking an active role in their children's upbringing' (para 10). The consequences for family life were revealed in research which found that a quarter of all fathers were working over 50 hours per week and almost 10 per cent were working more than 60 hours per week (Ferri and Smith, 1996).

11.3.4 Economic considerations

While the achievement of social objectives is important, there are also economic factors that should be taken into account. Essentially, there are two sets of arguments. On the one hand, there are those which see the long hours culture having an adverse economic effect on output and productivity. On the other hand, there are those which see compliance with the legislation as costly – increasing unit labour costs and administration. The issue of economic impact is far from clear-cut. As the research data show, there are many variables that have to be taken into account in what can be a complex picture.

The effects on work performance

The research review by Kodz *et al.* (2002) shows that long-hours working, especially when coupled with sleep disruption, causes deterioration in the performance of tasks. This is because it has detrimental effects on, for example, error rates, pace of work and social behaviour. However, it is commented that 'there is no conclusive evidence that long hours working leads to lower levels of overall work or organisational performance'. If it does, 'it is difficult to establish the working time duration thresholds at which any such effects set in, especially as this is likely to vary significantly according to individual characteristics'.

In terms of productivity, the research review states that 'it is not possible to establish conclusively whether long hours working has beneficial, detrimental or neutral overall effects'. It adds that there is some recent evidence suggesting that reductions in long hours might be a factor associated with increases in employment or productivity. However, 'it is difficult to isolate the impact of reducing working hours per se, since reductions in long hours working are typically accompanied by other developments such as changes in work organisation, new capital investment etc.'

Costs of compliance

This is also a difficult area for which to produce precise calculations. Estimations of costs are often influenced by political views. Attempts were made to estimate the cost of compliance with the Regulations (Annex C in the DTI Consultation Document, 1997) (*see* Table 11.1 below). However, these have been acknowledged as a possible overestimate because it is assumed in these figures that all workers affected by the Directive are earning the average hourly rate of £8.32 (as at April 1995). Indeed, a substantial proportion of people who benefit from the Regulations are part-time workers on relatively low wages. Furthermore, the Consultation Document's statistics do not take into consideration the cost savings arising from reduced ill-health and accidents.

Table 11.1 Estimated costs to employers

	Workers affected (millions)	Costs with options/ derogations (£billion)
Maximum weekly hours (48)	2.7	0.1
Minimum daily and weekly rest periods	2.1	1.0
Maximum night work hours (48)	0.2	0.1
Health assessments for night workers	1.5	0.05
Minimum paid leave	1.8	0.5
Total		£1.8 billion

Recent research into the cost of regulation (after the implementation of the Working Time Regulations (Neathy and Arrowsmith, 2001) showed that during the first stage of their research (within six months of implementation of the Regulations) there was considerable concern amongst employers about the costs and bureaucratic burden associated with the new record-keeping requirements. However, the follow-up study (12 months later) found that, once established, these systems were seen as less of a problem and, in some cases, to have positive operational benefits.

11.4   The legal framework

The current legal framework on working time regulation is considered under two headings:

- the piecemeal legal requirements that have developed in recent years in both statutory and case law covering different occupations, or categories of workers;
- the details of the 1998 Working Time Regulations and the amendments.

11.4.1   Piecemeal legal regulation

The piecemeal regulation covers the following: those working in certain specific occupations; children and young people; those protected by sex discrimination law and by disability discrimination law; and those alleging overwork as a breach of contract.

Specific occupations

Working time is regulated for drivers of public-service vehicles and certain commercial vehicles. Monitoring (where required) is undertaken through the use of the tachograph. The Transport Act 1968 was enacted to protect the public against risks which arise in cases where the drivers of motor vehicles are suffering from fatigue. The working hours of underground miners were regulated by the Mines and Quarries Act 1954. Recent legislation for those who work 'in and around shops' and betting shop workers did not affect the amount of work undertaken, but provided workers with a choice whether to work on Sundays and protection from victimisation if the employer subjected them to a detriment in the exercise of this choice (Employment Rights Act 1996, Part IV).

Children and young people

Children under the age of 13 years are prohibited from working, except with special permits (for example, for a role in drama and entertainment). Between the ages of 13 and 15 years, they may not be employed in any industrial undertaking. They may not be employed in shops, offices or factories during school hours or for more than two hours on school days and Sundays. Furthermore, they may not be employed on nightwork (i.e. between 7 pm and 7 am) (Children and Young

Persons Acts 1933 and 1963). This legislation is modified by a model by-law issued to local authorities in April 1997. Further rights concerning adolescent workers (those between 15 and 18 years) are incorporated into the Working Time Regulations 1998.

Sex discrimination law

There are have been two developments here: the repeal of the restrictions on night work undertaken by women (Sex Discrimination Act 1986); and the extent to which full-time work can be a condition of employment. This second area has arisen in case law relating to women returning to work after maternity leave and concerns indirect sex discrimination (Sex Discrimination Act 1975, s 1(1)(b)) and the question of whether or not an employer can 'justify' the requirement to work full-time in the individual case (*see* Chapter 4).

Disability Discrimination Act 1995

This places a duty upon an employer to make a reasonable adjustment to accommodate a disabled person (s 6(1)). One possible adjustment is an alteration to a person's working hours. 'This could include allowing the disabled person to work flexible hours to enable additional breaks to overcome fatigue arising from the disability, or changing the disabled person's hours to fit with the availability of a carer' (*Code of Practice*, 1996: para 4.20).

Breach of contract

Breaches of two implied terms in the contract of employment – an employer's duty to take reasonable care of an employee and the duty of mutual trust and confidence – can be invoked in circumstances where the employee is alleging physical or mental injury as a result of long working hours (*see* Chapters 2 and 12).

11.4.2 The Working Time Regulations 1998

These Regulations implement, under the European Communities Act 1972, two Directives: that on working time (1993/104/EC) and provisions of that relating to the protection of young workers (1994/33/EC). The new Regulations were effective from 1 October 1998. They were amended in 1999 in respect of record-keeping and unmeasured working time. In addition, the Council of the European Union has adopted amending Directives to cover occupational groups who were exempted from the original 1993 Directive.

11.4.3 Working people with entitlements

The Regulations apply to workers over the minimum school-leaving age. This includes 'employees' who work under a contract of employment and those who work under other forms of contract. Some special provisions apply to 'young workers' (i.e. those over the minimum school-leaving age but under 18 years). Those who are genuinely self-employed are excluded. In cases where there is some ambiguity about employment status, the facts and circumstances will be considered by the court and tribunal. In one case, the EAT held that labour-only subcontractors were 'workers' for the purposes of the Regulations. On the facts of the case, the workers concerned had a contract of personal service – despite a limited power to delegate work. They were found not to be engaged in their own business undertaking and there was the necessary mutuality of obligations (*Byrne Brothers (Formwork) Ltd.* v *Baird and others*, EAT 542/01).

Certain groups were excluded from the 1993 Directive. The EU has adopted amending Directives which will cover these workers as follows:

- **Road transport**: From August 2003, *non-mobile workers* are covered by the full provisions of the Working Time Directive 1993. This amends the situation where the ECJ ruled, in October 2001, that all workers in road transport, including office workers, were excluded from the 1993 Directive (*Bowden and others* v *Tuffnells Parcels Express Ltd*, ECJ C–133/00). Also from August 2003, *mobile workers* are entitled to paid annual leave, a 48-hour maximum working week and health checks for night workers. In addition, the Road Transport Directive sets out detailed working time for drivers covered by European drivers legislation. It is to be implemented by March 2005.

- **Rail transport**: From August 2003, a Social Partner Agreement incorporated into the amending Directive extends the 1993 Directive in full to both *mobile* and *non-mobile rail workers*. It provides derogations from the entitlements to daily rest, rest breaks, weekly rest and the night work provisions for rail workers whose activities are intermittent, whose hours of work are spent on trains and whose activities are linked to rail transport timetables and ensuring the continuity and regularity of rail traffic.

- **Air transport**: From August 2003, the 1993 Directive is extended in full to *non-mobile workers*. *Mobile workers* are entitled to paid annual leave, a 48-hour maximum working week, health checks for night workers and adequate rest. A Social Partners' Aviation Directive, covering civil aviation, is implemented from December 2003. It limits the annual working time of airborne personnel to 2000 hours, covers some elements of standby time and restricts flying time to 900 hours. It also requires 'appropriate' health and safety protection for all mobile personnel and contains provisions for a monthly and yearly number of rest days.

- **Sea transport**: From August 2003, the 1993 Directive is extended in full to *non-mobile workers*. The Seafarers' Directive agreed by the Social Partners, implemented in 2002, is based on ILO Convention 180. It provides a maximum working week of 72 hours and 14 hours rest in any 24-hour period; *or* a minimum weekly rest requirement of 77 hours and 10 hours in any 24-hour period. It also provides for 4 weeks paid annual leave and health assessments for night workers.

- **Junior Doctors**: The provisions of the Working Time Regulations apply in full. However, the implementation of the 48-hour maximum working week is phased over a possible 12-year period. An initial 4-year implementation period is followed by a transitional period of 5 years with weekly working limits of 58 hours for three years and 56 hours for the next two years. Member states with particular operational difficulties can seek an additional 3-year period. Initial implementation is by 1 August 2004. Full implementation is by 1 August 2012 at the latest.

In addition to these amendments, there are specific extensions of the 1993 Working Time Directive to workers engaged in inland waterway and lake transport, seafishing and working offshore.

11.4.4 The employer

Where there is a contract of employment, the employer is usually clear. If a worker is an agency worker, then the 'employer' will depend on the particular contractual arrangements (*see* Chapter 2). The Department of Trade and Industry (1998) in guidance on the Regulations adds that 'in the absence of a contract between the worker and either the agency or agency's client, the employer is deemed to be whoever is responsible for paying the worker or, if neither is responsible, whichever of them in fact pays the worker' (para 1.2.2).

11.4.5 Defining 'working time'

The Regulations, following the 1993 Directive, divide 'time' into 'working time' and rest and annual leave time. 'Working time' is any period when a worker is 'working, at his employer's disposal and carrying out his activity or duties' and 'any additional period which is to be treated as working time for the purpose of these Regulations under a relevant agreement'. In relation to a young worker, it also includes any time spent on training under a combined work/training scheme or an in-plant work-experience scheme (reg 2.1).

For most working people this definition is clear-cut. However, there will be uncertainties in respect of workers who are 'on call' or who are on zero-hours arrangements. How much time is to be designated as 'working time'? To help resolve the issue of what is 'working time' and what is not, the Regulations permit the negotiation of a 'relevant agreement' between the employer and an individual employee. Such an agreement might be derived from a collective agreement with an independent trade union or by a 'workforce agreement' (more details on these below). A relevant agreement must be in writing and legally binding.

In 2000, the ECJ ruled, in a Spanish case, on the status of 'on-call' time (*Sindicato de Medicos de Asistencia Publics (SIMAP)* v *Conselleria de Sanidad y Consumo de la Generalidad Valenciana*, C–303/98). It involved doctors employed in primary health care teams. The ruling was that 'on-call' time is 'working time' when a worker is required to be at their place of work. When a worker is away from the workplace when 'on-call' and free to take part in other activities, then 'on-call' time is not 'working time'.

11.4.6 Some key working-time provisions

Weekly working hours limits

Working time including overtime is limited to an average of 48 hours per week over a standard averaging period of 17 weeks (reg 4). This period can be extended to 26 weeks in certain circumstances (e.g. security and surveillance work), or up to 52 weeks by an agreement between an employer and their workforce (reg 23). Furthermore, individuals can voluntarily agree to disapply the weekly working hours limit (reg 5). In calculating a person's average working time, certain periods are neutral in effect – i.e. when the person is sick, on maternity leave or on holiday.

In *Barber* v *RJB Mining (UK) Ltd* [1999] IRLR 308, the workers concerned had worked more than the maximum average hours permitted in the initial reference period. They worked under protest and, in the High Court, sought a declaration of their rights and an injunction restraining the employer from requiring them to work additional hours beyond the maximum. It was ruled that reg 4(1) is 'a manadatory requirement which must apply to all contracts of employment'. It was noted that this 'will have the effect of making it clear that [the employees] are entitled, if they so choose, to refuse to continue working until the average working hours come within the specified time limit'. The reasoning in this case could also be applied to the maximum length of night work (reg 6).

The individual 'opt-out'

An individual worker may agree to work in excess of 48 hours per week. The worker should sign a simple opt-out agreement. This can be terminated. If a period of notice is part of the agreement, then it should be of up to three months. If no notice is specified, the worker should give a minimum of seven days' notice. An employer cannot force a worker to sign an 'opt-out' agreement – by, for example, threatening dismissal, overlooking for promotion or cutting pay.

The United Kingdom is the only EU member state to have used this provision. By November 2003, the European Commission is required to prepare a report reviewing this individual 'opt-out' and put proposals to the Council of Ministers for it to decide on the action to be taken.

Weekly rest periods

Adult workers are entitled to an uninterrupted rest period of not less than 24 hours in each seven-day period. Young workers are entitled to a rest period of not less than 48 hours during each seven-day period (reg 11). Derogations are possible (*see* below).

Daily rest periods

Adult workers are entitled to a daily rest per day of not less than 11 consecutive hours and young workers to a period of not less than 12 consecutive hours (reg 10). Derogations are possible (*see* below).

Rest breaks

Adult workers are entitled to a minimum 20-minute rest break if their working day is longer than 6 hours. Young workers are entitled to a minimum 30-minute rest break if they work for longer than 4.5 hours (reg 12). Derogations are possible (*see* below).

Night work

Night workers are subject to a limit of an average shift of 8 hours in each 24-hour period. This is averaged over a 17-week period but can be extended by derogations (*see* below). Night-time is defined as a period of at least 7 hours' duration between 11 pm and 6 am (or midnight and 5 am if there is a relevant agreement). A night worker is one who works at 'night time' 'as a normal course' (i.e. on a majority of working days) (reg 6).

Night workers whose work involves special hazards or heavy physical or mental strain are subject to an 8-hour actual working time in any 24-hour period.

Adult night workers are entitled to a health assessment (and a young worker to a health and capacities assessment) before being required to perform night work and periodically thereafter (reg 7).

A young worker can be required by his employer to undertake work (which has the effect of breaching his daily rest and rest-break entitlements) when there is no adult worker available to perform the work and when this work is caused by either 'an occurrence due to unusual and unforeseeable circumstances beyond the employer's control' or 'exceptional events, the consequences of which could not have been avoided despite the exercise of all due care by the employer'. The work must also be 'of a temporary nature' and 'must be performed immediately' (reg 27).

Opt-outs from the Young Workers Directive 1994 relating to their situation on night work and working time will be removed.

11.4.7 Paid annual leave

For the first time a right to paid holiday has been introduced into British employment law. Workers are entitled to four weeks' minimum paid annual leave. The entitlement is available to part-time and temporary workers (reg 13). Initially, the entitlement did not arise until a 13-week qualifying period had been completed. The principle of a qualifying period was challenged in the ECJ (*BECTU* v *Secretary of State for Trade and Industry*, C–173/99). In 2001, the Court ruled that a qualifying period was not compatible with the 1993 Directive. A worker's entitlement accrues from the first day of employment. The EU Charter of Fundamental Rights was also relied on. This asserts the unqualified right of every worker to annual paid leave (Art 8). From October 2001, the British government amended the Working Time Regulations.

The entitlement is for a worker to accrue from the first day of employment one-twelfth of the annual leave entitlement each month. Any week in which a worker has a contractual relationship with an employer – for all or for part of the week – will count. So, for example, a part-time worker who works for five hours each week will, on completion of thirteen weeks (65 hours of work), be entitled to paid leave. In this case, the worker will be entitled to be away from work for a minimum of four weeks – i.e. 20 working hours. The worker is entitled to be paid for that number of hours.

Workers who work irregular hours are entitled to be away from work for the statutory minimum number of weeks. The number of hours for which they are entitled to receive payment might create problems. However, the law permits an averaging process (*see* below). Overtime hours are not normally included in the calculations unless, contractually, a worker is bound to work some overtime hours.

A worker is to be paid for their annual leave according to the Employment Rights Act 1996 (ss 221–4). A normal week's pay is:

- in the case of a worker with regular hours what that worker would earn for a normal working week;

- in the case of a worker whose normal working hours vary from week to week, it is the average hourly rate of pay received multiplied by an average of the worker's normal weekly working hours over the previous 12 weeks;

- in the case of a worker with no normal working hours, it is the average pay received over the previous 12 weeks.

The entitlement cannot be 'bought out' by payment in lieu. However, there is entitlement to pay in lieu where employment ends during a leave year. No derogations apply to this entitlement. Public holidays can count towards the minimum paid-leave entitlement.

Leave years will normally start on a date set by agreement between the employer and the worker concerned (or a trade union). If there is no such agreement, then it will begin on either:

- 1 October, if the worker started work with the employer on or before 1 October 1998. Each subsequent leave year will start on the anniversary of that date; or

- the date the worker started the employment, if the worker starts work with the employer after 1 October 1998. Each subsequent leave year will start on the anniversary of the date on which the worker started.

There have been a number of cases in respect of paid annual leave:

- *Entitlement to holiday pay*: The EAT ruled, in respect of workers who had been absent from work on long-term sickness, that they were entitled to claim holiday pay attributable to the period they were absent from work. They continue to accrue holiday entitlement as long as they are employed. There is no requirement under the Regulations that work has to be undertaken (*Kigass Aero Components Ltd* v *Brown* [2002] IRLR 312).

- *Casual workers and holiday*: The EAT ruled that a casual waitress was not entitled to paid annual leave because she had no overarching contract of employment or contract for services for the periods she worked – i.e. every week for a 13-week period (*Voteforce Associates* v *Quinn*, EAT 1186/00). Although the qualifying period has now been removed, the issue of entitlement to paid leave for casual workers continues to be complex (*see also* Chapter 2). Each case has to be considered on its own facts.

11.4.8 Implementing the Regulations

The implementation of the Regulations will, understandably, differ between organisations. Going back to first principles, it will be remembered that the scheduling of working time is likely to be determined by a number of interrelated factors: customer demand and expectations, the nature of the product or service being provided and the technology in use. The crafting of the Regulations is not designed to impede employers. On the contrary, the government's intention has been (as mentioned in the introduction) to accommodate two sets of apparently conflicting objectives: minimum protection for employees under health and safety law, on the one hand, and business operational flexibility, on the other.

Any organisation, whatever its size, would be well advised to undertake both some fact-finding of its existing practices, as well as some benchmarking of these against the Regulations. In this way, discrepancies can be defined. Furthermore, this exercise will enable an employer, in a more strategic way, to manage compliance with the Regulations. Essentially, the issue under consideration here is the means by which an employer can, constructively, use the derogations and individual voluntary agreements.

The term 'derogation' is, to some extent, a novelty in British employment relations. It means a specified 'waiver', but, if a derogation exists, there is expected to be some equivalent compensation in return.

Broadly, there are three derogations available in the Regulations: 'the unmeasured working-time derogation'; that relating to 'specified circumstances'; and the more general concept of derogation through the use of jointly negotiated agreements in the workplace. The government made it clear, in the *Consultation Document* (DTI, 1997), that a derogation 'should never . . . be confused with provisions disapplying the Working Time directive or all the Regulations applying to workers in general' (para 137). To this extent it is procedurally different from the individual voluntary agreements which are designed to disapply the weekly maximum working time provision.

The '**unmeasured working time derogation**' (reg 20) waives certain Regulations for those whose work, because of its '*specific characteristics*', cannot be measured or determined. It refers particularly to managing executives and/or other persons with autonomous decision-taking powers, family workers or workers officiating at religious ceremonies. This derogation relates to the maximum working week; to night work; and to weekly, daily and rest-break provisions. The government believes that there is compensatory protection for these workers in the general body of UK law (including health and safety at work legislation and the common law duty of care owed by employers under the contract of employment.

Secondly, there are **derogations for certain 'specified circumstances'** (reg 19) in relation to rests and breaks and night work but not the maximum working week. There are five categories of circumstances set out. The first relates to certain security and surveillance activities. The second concerns activities involving the need for continuity of service or production. The third is where there is a foreseeable surge of business activity. The fourth is where unusual and unforeseeable circumstances arise (including accidents). The fifth is 'where the worker's activities are such that his place of work and place of residence are distant from one another or his different places of work are distant from one another' (reg 21a). On this last one, there may well be some definitional problem relating to 'distant'.

The range of organisations that might potentially be affected by 'the specified circumstances' derogation is considerable. It may not concern the delivery of their core service or product, but it may affect indirect or ancillary labour, or the work of contractors on site. Should the use of this derogation be challenged, then the facts of the specific case would be considered in relation to the Regulations.

Regulation 24 establishes the principle of 'equivalent periods of compensatory rest'. If this is not possible 'for objective reasons', then the worker is 'afforded appropriate protection'. The nature of this 'protection' is not defined. This 'specified circumstances' derogation clearly expects equivalent compensation as a central principle. This, theoretically, ensures achievement of the health and safety purposes of the Directive and appropriate operational flexibility for employers.

Flexibility is enhanced by the third use of derogations through negotiated agreements. Employers and working people can agree an alternative way of achieving the purposes of the Directive and of achieving its specific requirements. This reflects the concept of 'social partnership' (between employers and workers) that is embedded in European processes. The Regulations provide two routes:

- collective agreements negotiated with independent trade unions; or
- in non-unionised organisations, workforce agreements negotiated with workforce representatives (or with the workforce as a whole).

A conceptual distinction is clearly drawn between 'collective agreements' and 'workforce agreements'. We will look at each in turn.

Collective agreements

The regulatory role of 'collective agreements' in British employment relations is well established. It is already subject to a statutory legal framework (TULRCA 1992, ss 178–9). Furthermore, the (express or implied) 'incorporation' of provisions of a collective agreement into the terms of individual contracts of employment is an accepted process under contract law (*see* Chapters 2 and 14). The Regulations state (reg 23) that a collective agreement may 'modify or exclude the application' of the following Regulations for 'particular workers or groups of workers':

- averaging period for working time (regs 4; 23b): this can be extended 'for objective or technical reasons or reasons concerning the organisation of work' to a period not exceeding 52 weeks;
- length of night work (regs 6(1); 23b);
- night work involving 'special hazards or heavy physical or mental strain' (reg 6(7));
- daily rest (reg 10);
- weekly rest (reg 11);
- rest breaks (reg 12).

Such modifications or exclusions as are negotiated on rest periods and night work are subject to the principle of 'compensatory rest' or other 'appropriate protection' as discussed above (reg 24).

Workforce agreements

'Workforce agreements' are able to achieve these same modifications and exclusions. However, there are certain specific requirements applicable to such agreements. A workforce agreement can only be made between an employer and a workforce (or part of a workforce) whose terms and conditions are **not** set by collective bargaining. To have the status of a 'workforce agreement' the following conditions and requirements must be satisfied (Working Time Regulations 1998, Sch 1):

- it must be in writing;
- it must specify the date of application to the workers concerned;
- before signature 'all those workers to whom it is to apply must be provided by the employer with copies of the text of the agreement and with guidance';
- it must be signed by either a majority of the relevant workforce; or the representative (or a majority of the representatives) of the relevant workforce;
- it should have an expiry date no later than five years after the commencement date, when it can be renewed or replaced.

Although it is not made explicit in the Regulations or the *Consultation Document*, it is presumed that the government wishes a 'workforce agreement' to have an equivalent legal role to a collective agreement: presumed not to be a legally enforceable agreement unless specified by the parties, and capable of incorporation into individual contracts of employment. Furthermore, the Regulations are silent on whether or not the employer alone determines the 'relevant workforce' to be covered by the workforce agreement.

We have seen above how the averaging period for the maximum working week might be extended through agreement with an independent trade union or members of a relevant workforce or their representatives. In addition, in respect of weekly working time limits, there is the facility for an employer to agree '**an individual voluntary agreement**' to disapply this limit. Such an agreement:

- must be in writing;
- may be for an indefinite or for a specific duration;
- may be terminated at any time by the worker with due notice.

11.4.9 Records

The employer must maintain appropriate records for inspection by 'an enforcing authority' (i.e. the Health and Safety Executive inspector or a local authority environmental health officer). The records required cover the maximum working week, night-work patterns and the assessment of night workers. Records must be kept for two years.

11.4.10 Enforcement

There are two routes to enforcement. **Individual entitlements** (e.g. rest periods, rest breaks and paid leave), in common with other employment rights, are enforceable through application to an employment tribunal within three months of the alleged infringement – although the tribunal has discretion to extend this period if it considers that 'it was not reasonably practicable' for the case to be presented (reg 30). Complaints about infringements of entitlements can be made irrespective of a worker's length of service. As is generally the case with employment rights applications, ACAS has a statutory duty to conciliate and attempt to achieve a settlement (reg 33 and Employment Tribunals Act 1996, s 18(1)).

Where an employment tribunal finds a complaint well founded, it 'shall make a declaration to that effect' and 'may make an award of compensation to be paid by the employer to the worker'. The amount of compensation shall be such as the tribunal considers 'just and equitable in all the circumstances' having regard to 'the employer's default in refusing to permit the worker to exercise his right' and 'any loss sustained by the worker which is attributable to the matters complained of' (reg 30).

Limits (e.g. the weekly working-time and night-work limits) will be enforced by the appropriate health and safety authorities (the Health and Safety Executive (HSE), or local authority environmental health officers) (reg 28). (The role and powers of the HSE and its inspectors are discussed in Chapter 12.)

In brief (as reported in the DTI guidance (2000)), the HSE is responsible for enforcing the working time limits where they apply in factories, building sites, mines, farms, fairgrounds, quarries, chemical plants, nuclear installations, schools and hospitals. Local authority environmental health officers are responsible for retailing, offices, hotels and catering, sports, leisure and consumer services.

The powers of inspectors provided in the Health and Safety at Work Act 1974 apply to the enforcement of the Working Time Regulations 1998. A person guilty of an offence (HASWA 1974, s 33(1)) shall be liable to prosecution and on conviction in a magistrates' court to a fine not exceeding the statutory maximum (currently £20 000). If the conviction is on indictment, the fine is not limited.

In summary, enforcement is as follows.

By application to an employment tribunal:

- daily rest for adult workers;
- daily rest for young workers;
- weekly rest for adult workers;
- weekly rest for young workers;
- in-work rest breaks for adult workers;
- in-work rest breaks for young workers;
- paid annual leave.

By HSE inspectors and local authority EHOs:

- weekly working-time limit of 48 hours;
- night-work limit;
- health assessment for night workers.

11.4.11 Are the Working Time Regulations working?

Initial reviews of the legislation suggests a patchy impact. Case study research (Neathy and Arrowsmith, 2001) in 20 organisations undertaken over the 18-month period after the implementation of the Working Time Regulations 1998 reported a number of findings. Also, the Trades Union Congress (2002) published a report on the long hours culture; and AMICUS, the engineering and electrical trade union has initiated a complaint to the European Commission, alleging that the 1993 Directive has not been fully implemented. The Commission is considering (May 2002) infringement proceedings in the ECJ. The research finding and comments are summarised below:

- **Impact of the Regulations**: Ten of the 20 case study organisations surveyed by Neathy and Arrowsmith (2001) indicated that the Regulations had 'marginal or no impact'. Where there was an impact, it included a review of working practices which could involve taking a more strategic approach to the organisation of working time. The TUC commented that the impact of the Working Time Regulations was 'small scale' and also 'one off', arguing that there has been little or no reduction in the numbers of workers working over 48 hours per week in the past three years.

- **Areas of uncertainty**: All but one case study organisation faced some difficulties interpreting provisions of the Regulations. These included:

  - *Defining working time*: In particular, this concerned travelling time and on-call time (*see* earlier section).

  - *Unmeasured working time*: There were differences of opinion about whether the amendment (Working Time Regulations 1999) had clarified this area. AMICUS in its complaint is concerned that there is no obligation on employers to keep records of time worked voluntarily above normal working time, particularly for this group of workers.

  - *Casual workers*: This was particularly a problem for 'as and when' casuals and their continuity of service and their entitlement to paid annual leave (*see also* Chapter 2).

  - *Staff with more than one job*: The DTI guide (2000: 26) suggests finding out this information from individuals and considering, if approporiate, an 'opt-out' to disapply the 48-hour maximum. 'If a worker does not tell an employer about other employment and the employer has no reason to suspect that the worker has another job, it is extremely unlikely that the employer would be found not to have complied.'

The researchers also found significant misinterpretation by employers. Key areas involved the application of individual opt-outs from the 48-hour maximum working week and the definition of workforce agreements.

- **The 48-hour maximum working week**: The survey data in this area can appear conflicting. There are several issues involved: whether or not the employer has introduced the facility of the individual 'opt-out' (to be operated as and when required); the proportion of that employer's workforce covered by individual 'opt-outs'; the actual use of the 'opt-out' to exceed the 48-hour maximum; and the use of the alternative mechanism – varying the reference period through a collective or workforce agreement.

  The TUC quotes one survey which reported that 47 per cent of companies have used opt-outs for *some* groups of workers. This rose to 71 per cent in the case of larger companies with between 500 and 5000 employees. In 15 out of the 20 organisations surveyed by Neathy and Arrowsmith (2001), the *proportion of the workforce* regularly exceeding the limit was small. The principal method used was to encourage workers to sign forms opting out of the 48-hour limit. One-third of employers had signed a collective or workforce agreement to vary the reference period. A similar proportion had changed working practices to reduce the hours worked by individual workers. These included revised shift arrangements and increases in staffing.

- **Holidays**: This was the least problematic aspect of the Regulations for the case study organisations (Neathy and Arrowsmith, 2001). Only two had annual leave entitlement that was below four weeks. The main issue was the provision of leave for casual workers. Also, the cost implications of the definition of 'holiday pay' was important for four organisations.

- **Night work**: The most significant part of the Regulations for most of the organisations with night workers was the health assessment requirements. In practice, these assessments, once implemented, had not led to workers being moved away from night work. A part of AMICUS's complaint is the exclusion of overtime hours on night shift from the count of 'normal hours'.

- **Collective and workforce agreements**: Five organisations with recognised unions used the flexibilities provided through collective agreements. Three non-union establishments used workforce agreements – although the involvement of employee representatives took the form of consultation rather than negotiation.

- **Enforcing 'entitlements'**: Part of AMICUS's complaint concerns the lack of obligation on employers to enforce workers' rights to rest breaks and holidays. Because they are described as 'entitlements' workers can choose whether or not to take them. This contrasts with the provisions on weekly working time and night working. Here there is a specific obligation on an employer to take all reasonable steps to ensure compliance with the appropriate limits.

11.5 Employment policies and practices

11.5.1 A strategic approach to implementation

Because of the traditional way of determining working time (through collective bargaining or unilateral employer decision), the Regulations will have a disproportionate impact on British employee relations compared with that on those in other member states. Employers might be tempted to respond to the Regulations in a piecemeal way. However, given their wide-ranging implications, a more strategic approach might be advisable. There are six broad considerations for employers, which encompass corporate strategy, operational practice, the use of internal and/or external professional resources of advice and information, employee relations policy, and the contribution of personnel administration. These involve:

- *Identifying which members of their workforce are covered by the various provisions*: This would involve paying attention to specific grades of staff who might be covered by derogations, whether or not any workers are 'young workers', and those who work on particular working-time patterns (shift working and night work).

■ *Identifying the impact of the Regulations upon existing contractual terms and (where relevant) collective agreements*: This would involve considering whether or not the new legislation would limit existing contractual terms (e.g. the number of working hours undertaken each week by an employee) or whether it would require the introduction of new contractual rights (paid holiday entitlement) to comply with the law.

■ *Considering the ways in which, for operational reasons, the organisation might wish to utilise the opportunities available within the Regulations through derogations*: There are three ways to introduce flexibilities: 'collective agreements', 'work-force agreements' and 'an individual voluntary agreement'.

For all employers, the 48-hour maximum working week can be disapplied by agreement with the individual employee (reg 5).

For employers which recognise trade unions, the Regulations state (reg 23) that a collective agreement may 'modify or exclude the application' of various Regulations for 'particular workers or groups of workers'. These are the averaging period for working time (regs 4; 23b), the length of night work (regs 6(1); 23b), night work involving 'special hazards of heavy physical or mental strain' (reg 6(7)), daily rest (reg 10), weekly rest (reg 11) and rest breaks (reg 12).

For non-union workforces, workforce agreements are able to achieve these same modifications and exclusions. There are certain specific requirements applicable to such an agreement. It can only be made between an employer and a workforce (or part of a workforce) whose terms and conditions are **not** set by collective bargaining. To have the status of a 'workforce agreement' the following conditions and requirements must be satisfied (Working Time Regulations 1998, Sch 1, para 1) (*see* above).

Workforce agreements are new to British employee relations and employers need to be aware of the requirements and practical steps involved in setting up the representative machinery. These are set out as follows (Sch 1, para 3):

– the number of representatives to be elected is determined by the employer;

– candidates for election are relevant members of the workforce or part of a workforce;

– no worker who is eligible to be a candidate is unreasonably excluded from standing for election;

– all relevant members of the workforce are entitled to vote for a representative;

– the election is conducted so far as to secure that 'so far as is reasonably practicable those voting do so in secret' and that 'the votes given at the election are fairly and accurately counted' (para 3f).

■ *Using, as appropriate, professional resources (particularly those competent on health and safety assessments) to diagnose workers' suitability for night work and shift work*: The issues of risk assessment and the role of occupational health services are discussed later in this book (*see* Chapter 12).

■ *Deciding whether, procedurally, to use workforce or collective agreements, or agreements with individual workers to comply with the requirements*: Individual employers need to weigh up the balance of advantages for their own organisations to determine which of the mechanisms to use.

■ *Deciding on the likely use of individual voluntary agreements to disapply the 48-hour maximum working week*: Individual employers need to consider the operational advantages of such agreements, to be aware of possible allegations of unlawful pressure to force employees to sign such agreements and to consider the operational implications that might arise if such an agreement is not secured or if it is brought to an end by the employee.

■ *Deciding on whether the staff (full-time, part-time, temporary, etc.) currently employed (as well as new starters) are already receiving the minimum paid annual leave entitlement*: A worker is entitled to a *minimum* of four weeks' paid leave.

■ *Deciding on appropriate record systems (probably using and adapting existing personnel information systems)*: The records required cover the maximum working week, night-work patterns, and the assessment of night workers. The DTI has set out guidance (DTI, 2000) on this. In respect of **the maximum working week**, it is for the employer to determine the records to be kept. The employer may be able to use existing records maintained for other purposes, such as the payment of wages.

As far as **night working and health assessments** are concerned, it is for the employer to decide on the records to be kept. They need to be able to 'show who is a night worker, when they had an assessment and the result of the assessment' (para 4.5).

The likely impact of the Regulations is considered in the following section in two ways. First, the suggested checklist might help human resource practitioners consider, in a structured way, the likely impact of the new Regulations on their organisation. Finally, the scenarios in Exercise 11.1 will help with the exploration of the practical application.

11.6 A checklist for action

1 What is the profile of the workforce in terms of:
   - employment status (i.e. full-time, part-time, temporary, etc.)?
   - working pattern (e.g. shift and night working, annual hours arrangements)?
   - age (adult and young workers)?

2 Do existing arrangements comply with the standards set in the Regulations? Where an independent trade union is recognised for the staff in question, then would it be more constructive to undergo this diagnosis jointly?

3 Is any use to be made of 'individual voluntary agreements' to disapply the 48-hour working week average?

4 Is there any working time which cannot be 'measured, predetermined or fixed by the employer'? Is it, therefore, appropriate to invoke the derogation?

5 If trade unions are not recognised for particular groups of staff, what use might be made of 'workforce agreements' to achieve some flexibility in the implementation of the Regulations?

6 Is more detailed advice necessary on specific matters from, for example, the Department of Trade and Industry, the Advisory Conciliation and Arbitration Service, the Health and Safety Executive or any relevant employers' association?

7 If necessary, does the organisation have its own (or access to) specialist health and safety/occupational services to assist in the preparation of health and safety assessments?

8 What administrative arrangements need to be made to create (and maintain for two years) the necessary records; and can these records be integrated into existing computerised personnel records? Employers will need to hold records on the following to enable the competent authorities to monitor compliance (reg 8). These cover:

- a worker's average working time including overtime (reg 4.1);
- the details of individual voluntary agreements to disapply the 48-hour working week maximum (reg 5);
- the operation of night work (reg 6);
- health and safety assessments (reg 7).

9 What are the likely implementation costs for the organisation – in respect of changed terms and conditions of employment, record keeping, and the provision/funding of health and safety assessments?

Exercise 11.1 | **Some scenarios**

1 A small, non-unionised print shop employing some 19 people occasionally has a rush order requiring 70-hour weeks. How can the employer deal with **the 48-hour maximum average week**?

2 A call centre has traditionally defined **'work'** as the period when a worker is dealing with a customer on the telephone. Sometimes staff have attended their place of employment for eight hours but only received six hours' pay. Can this now be challenged at an employment tribunal? How should working time be defined?

3 Jez, a freezer engineer is based at home. He is 'on call' (through a mobile phone) to a supermarket chain in a specific region. He is only paid by the supermarket for specific tasks he carries out for it, as and when required. Is he **a 'worker'** protected by the Working Time Regulations?

4 A manager tells his personnel officer that he cannot have temporary staff and part-timers taking **holidays**. It would be disruptive. The whole point of employing them was that they would be 'flexible'. Can he, lawfully, do this?

5 A large non-unionised international hotel employs, on **night work**, a night manager and a night team of eight staff in its front office between the hours of 11 pm and 8 am. Each member of staff works an average of 45 hours per week (over five days). The night team comprises the assistant night manager, a cashier, two receptionists and four porters.

The length of the shift is important. There needs to be a short overlap between the day shift and the night shift to deal with any outstanding problems. In the morning, the concierge department shift does not begin until 8 am. This means that all luggage of the guests arriving or departing in the morning before 8 am is dealt with by the night staff. Furthermore, daytime reception staff start their shift at 7 am. The one-hour overlap between the two shifts is used for hand-over. Are these arrangements still permissible under the new Working Time Regulations?

6 Ronke, a worker in a medium-sized company, tells her employer that she wants to terminate (in eight days' time) **an individual voluntary agreement** to disapply the 48-hour maximum working week limit. It has been in force for several months after the implementation of the Working Time Regulations. No notice period is indicated for the termination of this agreement. The employer says that it is not convenient and asks what her reasons are. She refuses to say and insists on ending the agreement. The employer does not say he will sack her immediately. However, he implies that he might be looking for staff to replace her who will agree to disapply the limit.

7 Staff in the in-house grounds maintenance department of a local authority work the following **annual pattern of working time**: 45 hours per week (April–September inclusive) and 33 hours per week (October–March inclusive). There are occasions, particularly in the summer months, when overtime can increase the working hours of some staff to between 55 and 60 hours per week. Hearing about the Working Time Regulations, but unaware of all the implications, the manager asks the personnel officer about the impact on the 1999 rotas.

8 Maggie, a waitress, has been employed by a catering company on an 'as required' basis for some 15 months. Generally, this means that she works four of five evenings a week. A friend told her that she should be entitled to some paid holiday. When she spoke to her manager, she said that she was entitled to nothing. What is her situation?

Feedback on this exercises is provided in the Appendix to this book.

Further reading

Department of Trade and Industry (2000) *Your guide to the working time regulations.* London: DTI.

Hall, M., Lister, R. and Sisson, K. (1998) *The New Law on Working Time.* London: Eclipse Group; Coventry: University of Warwick.

Kodz, J. *et al.* (2002) *A review of the research literature, analysis of survey data and cross-national organisational case studie*s, Employment Relations Research Series No. 16. London: DTI.

Neathy, F. and Arrowsmith, J. (2001) *Implementation of the Working Time Regulations,* Employment Relations Research Series No. 11. London: DTI.

References

Advisory Conciliation and Arbitration Service (1988) *Labour Flexibility in Britain: the ACAS 1987 Survey.* London: ACAS.

Department for Education and Skills (1996) *Code of Practice for the Elimination of Discrimination in the Field of Employment against Disabled Persons or Persons Who Have Had a Disability.* London: DfES.

Department of Trade and Industry (1997) *Measures to Implement Provisions of the EC Directive on the Organisation of Working: A Consultation Document.* London: DTI.

Department of Trade and Industry (1998) 'Fairness at Work'. White Paper, Cm. 3968. London: Stationery Office.

Department of Trade and Industry (2000) *Your guide to the working time regulations*. London: DTI.

Ferri, E. and Smith, K. (1996) *Parenting in the 1990s*. London: Joseph Rowntree Foundation and Family Policy Studies Centre.

Kodz, J. *et al.* (2002) *A review of the research literature, analysis of survey data and cross-national organisational case studies*, Employment Relations Research Series No. 16. London: DTI.

Neathy, F. and Arrowsmith, J. (2001) *Implementation of the Working Time Regulations*, Employment Relations Research Series No. 11. London: DTI.

Office for National Statistics (1997) *Labour Force Survey*. London: ONS.

Trades Union Congress (2002) *UK's Long Hours Culture*. London: TUC.

The principal focus of this chapter is upon the management of health and safety. Having read it you should be able to:

■ Appreciate the range of influences affecting the achievement of good health and safety standards and practice.

■ Understand the legal framework governing health and safety at work.

■ Understand the role of management in the achievement of good health and safety practice.

12.1 Structure of the chapter

This chapter comprises the following sections:

■ *Introduction*: The management of health and safety; the concepts of health, safety and welfare; the history of health and safety regulation; the present legal framework.

■ *The context*: The economics of safety; technology and ergonomic factors; work-related stress; the incidence of major accidents; and the European dimension.

■ *The legal framework*: Common law duties – tort, contract, liability, employer's defences; statute law – Health and Safety at Work Act 1974; Regulations – Management of Health and Safety at Work 1999, Display Screen Equipment 1992; the rights of employees; consultation and representation rights.

■ *Employment policies and practices*: Creating a safety culture; company safety policy; consultation and representation; occupational health; and employee assistance programmes.

12.2 Introduction

The **management of health and safety** at work involves dealing with a wide range of factors: the nature of the technology used and related ergonomic considerations; the nature of the products and materials used; the ways in which work is organised and carried out; the scheduling of working time; the appropriateness of staffing levels; the nature of reward systems; and the relevance of training and development for staff. All these factors have health and safety implications.

As a consequence, the sources of **information** necessary to consider the nature and extent of risk at work are likely to be drawn from various academic disciplines: physics, chemistry, biology, engineering, medicine, etc. Furthermore, financial considerations are also important: in respect of injuries and accidents and also the implementation of health and safety standards. This, in turn, requires knowledge of relevant details of the legal framework affecting work in the organisation. Clearly, then, health and safety management is an integrative area – involving the interlocking of many specialisms. The expertise necessary for effective health and safety management may need to be gathered from a wide range of sources. Consequently, one important characteristic of anyone involved in such management is an ability to diagnose potentially complex situations and know when and how to draw on appropriate expertise.

Additionally, it is important to remember that health and safety standards and good practice are implemented in an **employee relations context**. Standards and practice can control how employees behave, how they are paid, staffing levels and the conditions under which they work. So, the management of health and safety needs to be linked with strategic and day-to-day decision-making processes within organisations, as well as with specialist functions (finance, HRM and safety) and also with employee relations processes.

There are two other ancillary issues. First, to what extent is there a need for management to provide support systems (training, communications, etc.)? Secondly, is there a need for management to provide special resources (safety officer, occupational health, counsellors)? The answers to these questions are likely to depend on the size of the organisation and the nature of work undertaken (and the associated risks). These services can be provided in-house or bought-in on a consultancy basis.

12.2.1 The concepts

'Health', 'safety' and 'welfare' are frequently used in ways that gloss over the differences between them. Indeed, the terms are not defined in the Health and Safety at Work Act 1974 nor in the European Framework Directive 1989. It is helpful to attempt definitions and draw distinctions.

Health

The International Labour Organisation defines 'health' in relation to work as 'not merely the absence of disease or infirmity; it also includes the physical and mental elements affecting health which are directly related to safety and hygiene at work' (Convention 155 concerning Occupational Safety and Health and the Working Environment). In this context issues concerning workplace stress, exposure to toxic fumes and substances are relevant, as likely to create hazards to a person's health. The implication of these is that the person might sustain some illness or medical condition from which he or she might recover.

Safety

'Safety' is concerned with protection from risk of injury, disease or death. It concerns preventative steps that can be taken and protections that might be implemented. These can include, among others, working practices, the scheduling of working time, training, staffing levels, protective clothing and the physical guarding of machinery. Clearly, there are substantial links with the concept of 'health' and it is not surprising that the two terms are invariably linked.

Welfare

'Welfare' is a term rarely used in discussions. Yet it is explicitly part of the general duties placed on an employer (HASAWA 1974, s 2(1)). It is frequently defined as a state of well-being – the state of being well, healthy and contented. Again, it interlocks with the other concepts. By adopting protective and preventative measures, it is anticipated that employees' welfare will be taken into account. Generally, managers see welfare as being concerned with a range of issues: minimising stress at work, helping employees reconcile the competing demands on their time (e.g. work and care for children or a disabled relative), the evidence of concern for employees who are suffering personal problems (e.g. bereavement, financial or domestic difficulties), and support for employees who may have drug and alcohol problems.

The World Health Organisation (an agency of the United Nations) speaks of 'a state of complete physical, mental and social well-being that does not consist only in the absence of illness or infirmity'. So, it rightly links all three concepts together into a creative whole.

History of health and safety regulation

In Britain health and safety regulation has a long history – stretching back to the early years of the nineteenth century. However, such legislation was generally piecemeal (concerning specific industries or particular groups of workers) and was, in some respects, regarded as ineffective in promoting standards. Indeed, such standards as existed were understandably much lower than those in present-day legislation. By the 1960s, there were two *principal* pieces of legislation in force: the Factories Act 1961 and the Offices, Shops and Railway Premises Act 1963. In addition, there were 11 other Acts of Parliament and 500 sets of Regulations dealing with health and safety. Yet despite this, the law's coverage was still patchy and enforcement arrangements were fragmented. Following the Robens Report in 1972, a new statutory framework was enacted with bipartisan support in Parliament: the Health and Safety at Work Act 1974. This extended statutory protection to some additional seven million working people.

Legal framework governing health and safety at work today

The present legal framework has a number of facets and is explored later. At this stage, it is important to note that both civil and criminal law can be involved. **Civil law** involves liability for the tort of negligence and suing for damages for injuries caused. It may also involve repudiatory breach of a contract of employment because of the behaviour of the employer and a consequent claim for constructive dismissal. **Criminal law** involves the prosecution of an employer (usually by the Health and Safety Executive) for breaches of health and safety standards. If successful, this might result in a fine or, in exceptional cases, imprisonment. The present legal framework owes much to the expansion of European law – particularly since the late 1980s.

12.3 The context

Within the past fifteen years or so, the issue of health and safety has become a matter of some public attention. The reasons have been various. Technological change has resulted in concern about new risks (e.g. repetitive strain injury). Intensification of work and the culture of long working hours has made stress an issue of much discussion and debate. Alcohol and drug abuse in society at large has raised implications about people's fitness for work. AIDS and HIV status are health issues that employers have to take into account. Associated with these trends has been published evidence about the cost and adverse economic effect of accidents, injuries and ill-health.

Lastly, but by no means least, a series of appalling and well-publicised accidents focused public concern on corporate responsibility for the safety of their own staff and also the public at large. These tragedies brought into focus not just the effectiveness of management arrangements for providing safe systems of work but also such issues as post-traumatic stress (affecting staff, the emergency services and the general public). Whether the publicity generated by these incidents has produced greater safety consciousness is highly questionable.

The Health and Safety Executive records the pattern of accidents and injuries (*see also* Fig. 12.1). Since 1985/6, the number of fatal workplace accidents (to employees, the self-employed and the public) has fluctuated but the long-run trend shows a reduction in fatalities. However, significant annual 'blips' can arise

---

- Fatalities: 162 employees; and 58 self-employed workers (1999/2000).
- Non-fatal injuries: 164 033 employees; and 1395 self-employed workers.
- Rates of fatal and non-fatal injury are higher in men than women.
- Rates of fatal injury are highest for older, male workers.
- The rate of less serious injury is higher in young men than in older men.
- Workers in the first few months with their employer have the highest rate of injury.

Figure 12.1 Workplace death and injury: some statistics

Source: Health and Safety Commission (2001), *Health and Safety Statistics 2000/01*.

if there are major tragedies. Statistics for 2001–2 indicate a decrease of 15 per cent in the the number of deaths – 249, compared with 292 (2000–1). (Among these, 79 fatalities were in construction and 39 in agriculture.) The rate of fatal injury dropped from 1.03 to 0.88 per 100 000 workers in the same period.

The number of non-fatal major injuries to employees has, likewise, fluctuated. The long-run trend suggests some discernible fall, as does the number of 'over three-day' injuries to employees. These have fluctuated between 167 000 and 132 000 (Annual Reports of the Health and Safety Commission). However, it is important to note that there is evidence of considerable under-reporting. Recent annual Labour Force Surveys show that 60 per cent of reportable injuries to employees are not reported. The figure for the self-employed is over 90 per cent.

In this section, we will focus on five of the broad issues mentioned above: the economics of health and safety, technology and ergonomic factors, work-related stress, the lessons that can be learned from the major accidents and the European dimension. (The welfare issues that became matters of public interest will be discussed in the context of employee assistance programmes in section 12.5 on employment policies and practices.)

12.3.1 The economics of health and safety

There are three ways of considering this issue. First, by reviewing the general economic consequences of accidents, injury and ill-health; secondly, the cost of compliance with safety standards through risk assessments and modifications to existing equipment and working practices; thirdly, the associated cost of resourcing various ancillary functions (e.g. training, communications, consultation and specialist services).

On the **general economic consequences**, the Chartered Institute of Personnel and Development (1996a) quotes statistics which illustrate the overall economic costs. For example, the CBI has shown that sickness absence accounts for 3.5 per cent of working time at a cost to employers of at least £13 billion a year. In the UK, inefficiencies arising from stress cost up to 10 per cent of gross national product – a cost of £3.7 billion. An EU survey found that illness accounts for 24.3 per cent of absence in member states (compared with only 0.8 per cent for industrial action). The TUC reported that in 2002 members of affiliated unions were awarded a total of £321 million in damages for work-related injury or ill-health.

The implications of these global figures can be difficult to comprehend. However, at the level of the individual, it can be viewed in this way. The work-related injury or illness of an employee can have a number of possible direct and immediate economic consequences for the employer: work not completed and productivity reduced; the payment of sickness benefit; the need to recruit and train replacement staff; time spent investigating the injury, reporting it and meeting the HSE (if appropriate); the cost of legal proceedings and the payment of possible damages. This individual injury will probably result in other indirect economic costs borne by the employer and the general public through the taxation system: the cost of medical care and social security benefits. Against this background, public concern about injury and sick absence (and the causes of the problems) has grown in recent years.

The principal way of tackling this problem is by the achievement of good health and safety standards at work. This, however, is also associated with the specific issue of **the cost of compliance** with safety standards and resourcing supporting functions. Indeed, as we will see later, there is tension built into the Health and Safety at Work Act 1974 between, on the one hand, compliance with relevant safety standards and, on the other hand, the cost, time and trouble to be taken to adopt certain standards. The recurrent phrase in the general duties imposed on employers is 'so far as is reasonably practicable' (HASAWA, s 2). This invites discussion about what is reasonable and enables an employer to take into account the cost of risk elimination or minimisation.

In one report, the Health and Safety Executive (HSE) has approached this issue from the opposite direction by considering the cost of non-compliance. In 1989, its Accident Prevention Advisory Unit began a series of five case studies with organisations from various sectors. 'The aim was to develop a methodology to accurately identify the full cost of accidents, to publish the methodology and results and thereby provide an incentive for all organisations to take the management of health and safety more seriously' (HSE, 1993: 1). The costs of accidental loss identified in each of the case studies were regarded by the management as 'significant'. In each case, 'considerable sums of money were involved' (HSE, 1993: 16). For example, the loss sustained by a hospital represented 5 per cent of its annual running costs, that of a transport company was 1.8 per cent, and that of a construction site was 8.5 per cent of the tender price. The HSE accepts that it was not possible to say how representative of their sectors these organisations were. Nevertheless, it advocates its costings methodology, saying that it 'has been shown to work in a cross-section of industry and (with a minimum of adaptation) should prove workable in industry in general' (1993: 16).

12.3.2 **Technology and ergonomic factors**

Ergonomics is a key factor in the effective management of health and safety at work. It is the study of the relation between an individual person and their occupation, equipment and environment. In particular, it concerns the application of anatomical, physiological and psychological knowledge to problems that arise. So, it is a multi-disciplinary science that draws on a wide range of knowledge from biology to physics and engineering. The aim of ergonomics is to understand human physical and psychological characteristics and to use this knowledge to create equipment, jobs and working environments that enable people to work as effectively and safely as possible. Additionally, ergonomic principles are not only important for employers considering work organisation and job design. They are vital for any designer or manufacturer of the equipment and products used.

There are over 400 000 people with musculoskeletal (mainly upper limb) disorders claiming disablement benefit (Health and Safety Commission, 2001: 128). Such disorders arise because a person's job puts too great a demand on certain muscles and joints and provides insufficient opportunities for rest and recovery. Generally, a number of risk factors, acting together, cause such disorders: the degree of force applied in the work, the frequency and duration of the work and a worker's posture in carrying out the work.

Force is concerned with the degree of muscular effort required in carrying out the task. If too much is used, it can damage muscles and tendons. If a job is repetitive, the cumulative effect of repeated applications of force could cause injury. So, striking a keyboard does not require much force and, in itself, is not dangerous.

However, it is the repetition that can create health problems. In extreme cases repetition can cause various WRULDs: for example, tenosynovitis (tenderness, swelling, severe pain and difficulty in using the hand), or carpal tunnel syndrome (tingling, pain, numbness and loss of grip). Consequently, this highly repetitive movement requires a risk assessment of the way in which the work is carried out and the equipment used as well as breaks for rest and recovery to minimise risk. Requiring staff to work hard for long periods is clearly unsafe. The final factor is posture. The physical layout of the workstation may force staff to adopt an awkward or uncomfortable posture for long periods. A certain amount of muscular effort is required to hold the body in an awkward position. So, a keyboard that is too high can affect the wrists, forearms and shoulders, causing pain and stiffness after several hours. This can result in the related problems of frequent headaches and tiredness.

These disorders that can arise from the regular use of VDUs clearly show the necessity of adopting an integrative approach to the assessment of risk and the adoption of preventative and protective measures. The factors to be considered embrace the ergonomics of the workstation, medical conditions to which the employee might be susceptible, work organisation and job design and employee relations considerations. The interlocking of all these factors has been illustrated by one example. Obviously, the same broad approach can be adopted in considering other workplace risks.

12.3.3 Work-related stress

Work-related stress has been regarded, by many observers and participants in the labour market, as both a consequence of working conditions (such as noise, dust, extremes of temperature) and a by-product of the various managerial policies adopted since the early 1980s:

- business process re-engineering, 'market testing' and competitive tendering;
- de-layering, downsizing and fears of job insecurity;
- work intensification to increase labour productivity;
- greater surveillance and monitoring of staff;
- the expansion of the flexible labour market;
- tensions in the reconciliation of work and non-work (particularly family) life.

It has been identifed as a feature of working life for professionals (e.g. teachers, junior hospital doctors and nurses); staff in the emergency services (i.e. the police, fire and ambulance services); manual workers; transport staff; and managers in public and private-sector employment.

'Stress' is, however, a general term that can be misused. It is suggested in the scientific literature that a person can experience anxiety in two possible ways: through *physical hazards* at work (e.g. the danger of fire or explosion, the threat of violence, the danger of injury from equipment) or from *psycho-social hazards*. This latter set of hazards has been described by the International Labour Organisation as involving the interaction of job content, work organisation and management, together with environmental and organisational conditions together with an employee's competences.

The context of work

- *Organisation function and culture*: poor task environment and lack of definition of objectives; poor problem-solving environment; poor development environment; poor communications; non-supportive culture.
- *Role in organisation*: role ambiguity; role conflict; high responsibility.
- *Career development*: career uncertainty; career stagnation; poor status or status incongruity; poor pay; job insecurity and redundancy; low social value to the work.
- *Interpersonal relationships at work*: social or physical isolation; poor relationships with superiors; interpersonal conflict and violence; lack of social support.
- *Home/work interface*: conflicting demands of work and home; low social or practical support at home; dual career problems.

The content of work

- *Task design*: ill-defined work; high uncertainty in work; lack of variety or short workcycles; fragmented or meaningless work; underutilisation of skill; continual exposure to client/customer groups.
- *Workload/work pace (quantitative and qualitative)*: lack of control over pacing; work overload or underload; high levels of pacing or time pressure.
- *Work schedule*: shiftworking; inflexible work schedule; unpredictable work hours; long or unsocial hours.
- *Decision latitude/control*: low participation in decision-making; lack of control over work; little decision-making in work.

Figure 12.2 Psycho-social stressors

Source: Cox (1993). Reproduced with permission.

The psycho-social stressors have been categorised as shown in Fig. 12.2 (Cox, 1993).

As a result of stress a person may exhibit various reactions:

- **adverse health conditions**: increased heart rate, heart disease, high blood pressure, thyroid disorders, ulcers, panic attacks, depression, headaches, blurred vision, aching neck and shoulders;
- **behavioural consequences**: irritability, anxiety, insomnia, poor concentration, (increased) consumption of alcohol, tobacco and other drugs.

A person's response to the different types of pressure will, of course, vary.

So widespread has been the public concern and discussion about stress that action on various levels has begun to be taken. In 2002, the HSE published guidance. In this, it clearly asserted the duty of employers:

> Ill health resulting from stress caused at work has to be treated the same as ill health due to other physical causes present in the workplace. This means that employers do have a legal duty to take reasonable care to ensure that health is not placed at risk through excessive and sustained levels of stress arising from the way people deal with each other at their work or from the day-to-day demands placed on their workforce. Employers should bear stress in mind when assessing possible health hazards in their workplaces, keeping an eye out for developing problems and being prepared to act if harm to health seems likely. In other words, stress should be treated like any other health hazard.

In addition, challenges to stressful working conditions have been lodged in the courts. (Two such cases are considered later.) It has become clearly accepted that the employer's common law duty of care to employees covers both physical and mental health and safety. Finally, the better employers have begun to address some of the sources of stress or provided support through counselling and employee assistance programmes.

12.3.4   The incidence of major accidents

There are many different perspectives held about health and safety regulation by employers, employees and the general public. Outside of high-risk industries, employers often regard it as a cost and a constraint on operational effectiveness. Workers can, likewise, regard it as a constraint to the carrying out of work, and they may even see it as imposing restrictions on earnings opportunities. The assertion from employers and working people that 'we are all concerned about health and safety' is not always borne out by the evidence. Occasionally, shocking major accidents occur which demonstrate this. What is revealed, in the large organisations concerned, is the absence of a safety culture and a failure to comply with some very basic health and safety requirements. To illustrate this we will recall, briefly, the details of some of these accidents that have occurred in recent years (Fig. 12.3).

The issues that have arisen from these cases are various: management failures to provide safe systems of work; a preparedness to take operational short-cuts which compromise safety; a failure to monitor the implementation of appropriate safety standards; and poor communication and consultation with employees about the implementation of safety standards and procedures. Furthermore, there arises the issue of liability (both civil and criminal) in law for negligence (*see* section 12.4).

12.3.5   The European dimension

It is generally acknowledged that 'the most significant influence on the architecture of law on health and safety in Britain during the last twenty five years has been the European Union' (Walters and James, 1998: 18). This has arisen from the EU's 'rapid and wide-ranging legislative activity' (James, 1993: 140), particularly since 1988. In 1988, the Commission proposed a substantial third action programme. Furthermore, the Community Charter of the Fundamental Social Rights of Workers stated that:

> every worker must enjoy satisfactory health and safety conditions in his working environment. Appropriate measures must be taken in order to achieve further harmonisation of conditions in this area while maintaining the improvements made. These measures shall take account, in particular, of the need for the training, information, consultation and balanced participation of workers as regards the risks incurred and the steps taken to eliminate or reduce them (para 19).

The legislative base for this shift in emphasis was the Single European Act 1987, which enacted amendments into the Treaty of Rome. The Council of the European Union can, by 'qualified majority voting', adopt Directives, setting out minimum requirements for gradual implementation. The availability of QMV has been 'a crucial factor influencing the speed of recent developments, both directly and

Herald of Free Enterprise

A roll-on/roll-off ferry which set sail with her bow doors open and sank on 6 March 1987 in shallow waters outside Zeebrugge, killing 150 passengers and 38 crew. In the accident report it was stated by Mr Justice Sheen that: 'All concerned in management, from the members of the board of Directors down to the junior superintendents, were guilty of fault in that all must be regarded as sharing responsibility of the failure of management'.

Kings Cross fire

In the early evening of 18 November 1987, discarded smoker's materials had probably set alight highly inflammable rubbish that had been allowed to accumulate in the running tracks of an escalator. The inspector placed responsibility for the disaster with the management of London Regional Transport and its operating company, London Underground. The investigation of the disaster shows an operational system littered with confusion and misinterpretation resulting from a lack of communication and consultation. Within 20 minutes of the start of the fire, 31 people were killed and many were injured.

Piper Alpha

On 6 July 1988, following two initial explosions, a fire swept through the Piper Alpha production platform in the North Sea, 120 miles from Aberdeen – 167 people died. Investigations showed the need for risk assessment and also for communication and consultation. The accident is reported to have cost £2 billion, including £746 million in direct insurance payouts (HSE, 1993: 1).

Clapham rail crash

On 12 December 1988 a crowded commuter train travelling into London ran head-on into the rear of a stationary train. The commuter train toppled towards an adjoining line and struck a third oncoming train – 35 people died and nearly 500 were injured, 69 seriously. The cause of the accident was faulty signal rewiring which was not checked by a supervisor. The blame was placed on British Rail's management for allowing stress through long working hours to build up to a point where safety was compromised. The electrician involved had worked seven days a week for the 13 weeks immediately before committing the fatal error.

Paddington train crash

In October 1999, 31 people were killed in a crash at Ladbroke Grove when a Thames Train passenger train passed through a red signal (SN109) and hit a Great Western one speeding to Paddington station. The Health and Safety Executive reported, in 2000, that SN109 had been passed at danger seven times in the five years before the crash. A public inquiry, set up under Lord Cullen, was told that Great Western had written to Railtrack three times to demand action over the signal which was said to be difficult to see. Reporting on poor management, the Cullen Report (2001) commented on 'a serious and persistent failure' of Railtrack to consider the siting of signals; and its failure to deal with an earlier passing of the same signal at danger (in 1998) 'in a prompt, proactive and effective manner'. The safety culture at Thames Trains in regard to training was reported as 'slack and less than adequate' and there were 'significant failures in communication within the organisation'. The Thames Train driver, Michael Hodder, 31, who was killed, had only recently qualified as a driver and 'there were significant shortcomings in his training'.

In May 2002, the Crown Prosecution Service, after taking specialist legal advice on corporate manslaughter, raised the possibility of manslaughter charges against Railtrack executives.

Figure 12.3 Major disasters

indirectly' (James, 1993: 144). Removing a requirement for unanimity has helped overcome obstructionist tactics by some member states.

The legislative product of the post-1988 changes has been significant. It has included the 1989 framework Directive on health and safety (including risk assessment and the management of health and safety) together with a pack of specific measures (e.g. on the use of display screen equipment, manual handling, personal protective equipment). Some of these will be explored in more detail in the following section. Most of these measures have been transposed into UK law as regulations under the Health and Safety at Work Act 1974.

One more debatable outcome from European social policy has been the changing and widening perception of health and safety at work. We have seen (Chapter 11) how the regulation of working time has been defined as a health and safety issue. The concept of working environment is susceptible to various interpretations. It could, narrowly, mean work as carried out by the worker concerned. It could, on the other hand, cover the wide range of working conditions which might have an impact on a worker's health and safety. This could include the volume of work, a worker's control over the pacing of work, the duration of working time and its scheduling as well as the physical conditions of employment. Gradually, it can be argued, this wider perception is gaining some acceptance. Indeed, the 1989 Directive on the safety and health of workers in its obligations on employers (Art 6) provides evidence of this.

12.4 The legal framework

12.4.1 Introduction: a diversity of legal action

The legal framework governing health, safety and welfare is extremely wide ranging and diverse in terms of the proceedings that can be initiated. It embraces both civil and criminal law and can be used against employees as well as employers and individual managers. It also covers contractors and suppliers. It draws on the common law of contract, statute law and regulations approved by Parliament. In part, it includes provisions deriving from European Directives. In brief, it covers the following legal issues.

Civil law

This covers the:

- liability of employer for breach of the contractual duty of care;
- liability of employer for the tort of negligence;
- liability of employee for contributory negligence;
- dismissal of employee for breach of safety rules;
- constructive dismissal for employer's repudiatory breach of the contract of employment.

Criminal law

This concerns:

- criminal prosecution of an employer
- corporate manslaughter (*see* Fig. 12.4).

Simon Jones, 24, a student on casual work, started a labouring job for Euromin, a Dutch-owned firm, at Shoreham Docks, Sussex on 24 April 1998. It was provided through a Brighton employment agency, Personnel Selection. His job involved unloading cobblestones from a ship. He was given no training for it; and provided with no safety equipment. He worked in the hold of the ship hooking bags of cobbles on to chains. The chains had been welded into the crane's open grab. Within two hours of starting work he was dead. His head was crushed and partially severed by a two-tonne crane grab, which had been brought too low over the hold and accidentally closed on his head.

The question of prosecution for manslaughter was considered by the Crown Prosecution Service (CPS). It took the view that there was no realistic prospect of a conviction. However, in March 2000, the High Court ordered the CPS to reconsider. This was the first successful judicial review of a decision not to prosecute for manslaughter over a workplace death. In November 2001, the prosecution of Euromin and of the general manager opened at the Old Bailey.

It was alleged that the system of work was not safe. The principal defects were:

■ The welding of the hook attached to the grab was dangerous and done for reasons of speed and economy.

■ Instructions in the cab, which stated that no one should be in the grab's area when it is operating, were ignored.

■ The 'hatchman' responsible for communication between the crane operator and the hold was not experienced and was a Polish speaker with little knowledge of English.

On a majority verdict, the jury cleared the general manager of manslaughter. However, the company was found guilty of two breaches of health and safety regulations and fined £50 000 and ordered to pay £20 000 costs.

Footnote: Corporate manslaughter cases rarely come before the courts. It is an evolving body of law which is being considered by government. It involves the unlawful killing of one person by another. Criminal liability of employers has been very difficult to establish. Prosecutors have to prove beyond reasonable doubt – the criminal standard of proof – that the individuals responsible for the death were 'the directing mind and will' and had the necessary 'guilty mind' (*mens rea*). The first successful prosecution did not occur until 1994. This involved OLL Ltd which ran an activity centre. Four young people, on a canoeing trip organised by the company, drowned in Lyme Bay, Dorset. The conviction of OLL Ltd was possible because it was a small organisation. It was clear that its managing director was the embodiment of the company. He was jailed for three years for the manslaughter.

Figure 12.4 The case of Simon Jones

Source: www.simonjones.org.uk

One way of illustrating the diversity of law involved in health and safety is to take a simple, yet serious, workplace accident and consider the legal consequences that *might* result (*see* Fig. 12.5).

The range of legal action briefly outlined here will now be discussed in more detail under the following headings: the common law, statute law, rights of employees and consultation and representation.

12.4.2 The common law

There are two aspects of the common law relevant to health and safety at work: the tort (i.e. a civil wrong) of negligence, and the implied contractual duty of care owed by an employer to an employee.

The incident: *a machine operator loses a finger on an unguarded machine.*

1 Under **civil law**, the employer appears to have neglected to meet the common law duty to take reasonable care of the employee. So, it is possible for the employee to sue the employer (for damages) for this **negligence** in the county court. However, in his defence, the employer might be able to say that the employee contributed to the injury by deliberately removing the guard – in breach of workplace rules. The court would need to decide, on the facts, whether or not there was **contributory negligence**. If this is established, then, any damages awarded could be reduced by up to 100 per cent – depending on the extent to which it was decided that the employee did contribute to the injury.

2 The employer might, also, feel that if the employee broke workplace rules, then **disciplinary action** should be taken against them. Obviously, the disciplinary procedure would need to be followed fully (in accordance with the ACAS *Code on Disciplinary Procedures*, 2000). The outcome of the disciplinary process could include a warning or even dismissal. If the employee was dismissed, depending on the circumstances, they might lodge a claim for unfair dismissal before an employment tribunal. Whether the employee would be successful would depend on the facts and circumstances of the case.

3 In the area of civil law, one further additional course of action is possible. The injury sustained by the employee might be entirely the fault of the employer. Furthermore, it might be the latest in a series of injuries that the employee has sustained in this employer's employment. Clearly, the employer is failing to comply with the implied contractual term to take reasonable care of the employee. In these circumstances, the employee could view the employer's behaviour as **a fundamental (i.e. repudiatory) breach of the contract of employment**. An employee can accept the employer's repudiation of the contract and resign. Depending on the circumstances the employee could claim unfair constructive dismissal before an employment tribunal.

4 **Criminal law** might also be used. This would involve the **prosecution** of the employer, by the Health and Safety Executive (under the Health and Safety at Work Act 1974) in the magistrates' court or the Crown Court (depending on the seriousness of the accident). Given that physical injury was sustained in an accident, criminal proceedings are probable. Such criminal action would bring in evidence of the employer's failure to provide a safe system of work (including the way health and safety was managed) under the Health and Safety at Work Act 1974, and regulations relating to the guarding of machinery that were not complied with. The most likely outcome would be a fine – although, in very serious cases, imprisonment is possible. (It is important to note that individual employees cannot prosecute their employer.) A successful prosecution could help an individual's subsequent claim for compensation for the injury and also for proving a repudiatory breach of the contract of employment.

Figure 12.5 The unguarded machine

Specific references to legislation are covered in more detail later in the chapter.

The tort of negligence

An employer is under a duty to take 'reasonable care' for the health and safety of each individual employee at work. Effectively, this comprises the provision of a safe place of work, safe plant and equipment and competent and safe fellow employees. What is regarded as 'reasonable' will depend on such matters as the scale of the risk; whether risk is, from the facts available to the employer, reasonably foreseeable; the seriousness of the consequences for the employee if the risk was not dealt with and the employee was injured; and the cost and practicality of preventing the risk.

An employer will, then, breach this duty if they fail to prevent reasonably fore-seeable risks. A breach of this duty (i.e. the employer's neglect) usually provides the basis of personal injury claims. In this context both physical and/or mental health are relevant. So, if an employee suffers from a recognised psychiatric illness or condition and it can be proved on the balance of probabilities (the relevant standard of proof in civil matters) that the illness was caused by the defendant employer's breach of duty, then that employer is liable.

One well-publicised case relating to work-related stress was that involving a social services officer who alleged a failure by his employer to deal with excessive workload (*Walker* v *Northumberland County Council* [1995] IRLR 35, HC). In this case, Mr Walker alleged that his employer failed in a number of respects. First, the county council had not responded to his requests to restructure the depart-ment to provide more field officers to deal with increasing case work (particularly in respect of child abuse cases). Secondly, after he had suffered a nervous break-down and subsequently returned to work, promises of assistance from a seconded member of staff and weekly visits by his boss were not delivered upon. Thirdly, during his four-month absence, a substantial volume of paperwork had built up. Fourthly, the number of pending childcare cases continued to grow at a consider-able rate. Ultimately, within a few months he had a second nervous breakdown and was dismissed by the council on grounds of permanent ill-health. He claimed damages against the council for breach of its common law duty of care in failing to take reasonable steps to avoid exposing him to a workload that endangered his health.

He was successful at the High Court (and the matter was not taken on appeal to the Court of Appeal). The duty of care owed to Mr Walker was ruled as encom-passing the prevention of foreseeable psychiatric illness. An out-of-court settlement of £175 000 was agreed in 1996.

In 2002, the House of Lords made a landmark judgment in repect of tortious liability. It ruled on a test case (*Fairchild* v *Glenhaven Funeral Services Ltd* [2002] HL) and several related cases which concerned liability for mesothelioma. The Court of Appeal has, previously, held that where a claimant suffered (or might suffer) mesothelioma as a result of exposure in the course of employment with more than one employer to asbestos dust, then, that claimant could not recover dam-ages from any of the employers. This was because it could not be established, on the balance of probabilities, when the claimant inhaled the fibre which led to the development of mesothelioma. However, the House of Lords overturned this ruling. The defendant employers should be regarded as jointly and severally liable for the wrong.

Repudiatory breach of contract

The second aspect of common law relevant to health and safety issues concerns the implied contractual term: the employer's duty of care to the individual employee. Failure to meet this duty may be a repudiatory breach of the contract. If the employee accepts the breach, they can resign and claim unfair constructive dis-missal at an employment tribunal. Alternatively, they might remain in employment but seek remedies in either the High Court or the county court. These remedies may include a declaration of contractual rights, damages and an injunction which could prevent an anticipatory breach of contract.

One recent case, again involving work-related stress, has put in focus a number of contractual issues (*Johnstone* v *Bloomsbury Health Authority* [1991] IRLR 118, CA). Dr Johnstone was a senior house officer in obstetrics at University College Hospital. Under the express terms of his contract of employment, he was required to work 40 hours per week and to be on call, at the employer's discretion, for up to a further 48 hours. So, contractually, he could be required to work 88 hours a week. He alleged that from February 1989 onwards the health authority had required him to work excessive hours (sometimes over 100 in a week). He claimed that the deprivation of sleep and rest damaged his health and put his patients at risk. He said that, as a consequence, he suffered from stress, depression, lethargy, physical sickness and exhaustion. He was successful in his claim and reached an out-of-court settlement of £5600.

The Court of Appeal ruled that it would be a breach of contract if an employer used an express discretionary power (i.e. to call upon a doctor to work additional hours if required) in breach of the implied contractual duty to take reasonable care for the employee's health and safety. So the additional hours requirement had to be exercised in conformity with the overall duty of care. If so many additional hours would damage an employee's health and this was reasonably foreseeable then it was a breach of the duty.

The Court also agreed that the Unfair Contract Terms Act 1977 applied to this case. So, following this case, any contractual term which effectively excludes or restricts an employer's liability for the death or personal injury (physical or psychological) of an employee may be ruled as void under this Act.

Liability and vicarious liability

The issue of liability for breach of health and safety law covers both common law and the duties under statute law (which are outlined in more detail below).

Under common law, as we have seen, an employer is liable for breaches of duty (i.e. the tort of negligence) which are 'in the course of employment'. The issue of vicarious liability can also arise. This can occur, for example, where an employee injures a fellow worker or a customer or a contractor. The injured person may sue the employer for the injury because the employer is vicariously liable for the 'acts and omissions' of their employees. In practical terms, it is advantageous to the injured person because of the significantly better financial and insurance position of the employing organisation. It also acknowledges the employer's ultimate responsibility for the organisation of the work in question and for the deployment and training of staff.

A point of uncertainty that can arise in such cases is the meaning of 'in the course of employment'. This has been defined in a particularly wide way under discrimination law (*Jones* v *Tower Boot* [1997] IRLR 68, CA: *see* Chapter 5). Among the issues under health and safety law are:

- whether or not the employee is carrying out tasks wrongly;
- whether the work was performed by the employee negligently;
- whether the acts are outside working hours;
- whether the employee was travelling to or from work;
- whether the employee behaved violently (e.g. towards a customer or fellow worker).

Clearly, courts will need to consider the facts and circumstances of each case to establish liability.

An employer's defences

In such common law claims an employer might have defences available to him. There are two principal ones that may be possible. The first is described as '*volenti non fit injuria*'. Translated from Latin, this means 'no wrong is done to one who consents'. For this defence to be effective in health and safety matters, the employer would need to establish that the employee not only knew of the risk and continued working but also consented freely to work. This might be difficult for the employer to prove because the employee might have been ordered to work or, alternatively, the employee needed to work in such a way to carry out the duties. The view of academic lawyers is that *volenti* 'rarely succeeds' in industrial injury and employment cases (Smith and Thomas, 2000: 734).

As to liability for breaches of statutory duty, 'the position is even clearer, for it has been held that *volenti* does not apply **at all** to an action for breach of a statutory duty laid upon the employer by the relevant legislation' (Smith and Thomas, 2000: 735). The authors added: 'the principal reason being that it would be contrary to public policy to allow an employee by agreement or consent to "contract out" of his statutory protection'.

The second defence relates to **contributory negligence**. This can arise when an employee disobeys a safety instruction given by the employer or is reckless and, consequently, sustains an injury. This applies to all cases involving breaches of statutory duty as well as common law actions. An employee's statutory duties are set out below.

12.4.3 Statute law

Following the recommendations of the Robens Report 1972, a broad political consensus resulted in the enactment of the Health and Safety at Work Act 1974. This had a number of purposes (both explicit and implicit):

- to extend the coverage of health and safety protection to a wider range of working people;
- to provide a legislative vehicle for rationalising existing health and safety law;
- to impose general duties upon all employers;
- to permit the exercise of discretion and flexibility in implementation by qualifying the duties by the phrase 'as far as is reasonably practicable';
- to encourage self-regulation by employers and workforce representatives;
- to ensure that relevant information is available to employers and employees, as appropriate;
- to provide clear enforcement procedures and create specific enforcement agencies (the Health and Safety Executive and, as appropriate, local authorities);
- to establish a tripartite body, Health and Safety Commission, comprising employers, unions and certain independent people, to review and advise the Secretary of State on health and safety policy.

The key provisions of this Act are outlined below.

Who is covered?

The Act covers all employers and every aspect of work. It brought into legal protection some seven million additional working people. The Act applies to the Crown (s 48). It covers an employer's responsibilities to contractors and to the general public. Domestic servants in a private household are exempt (s 51).

What is the nature of the Act?

The Act is described as 'enabling' legislation. To promote health and safety standards in the workplace, regulations can be proposed to Parliament, under the authority of the Act. The Act sets 'general' duties. The regulations are more precise, setting detailed prescriptions. So, for example, in recent years the following have been approved by Parliament: the Reporting of Injuries, Diseases and Dangerous Occurrences Regulations 1995; the Control of Substances Hazardous to Health Regulations 1999; the Noise at Work Regulations 1989; and Health and Safety (Display Screen Equipment) Regulations 1992. From these examples, it is clear that regulations can cover the *procedures* to be adopted in the management of health and safety as well as the *standards of practice* in the workplace.

What are the general duties?

The general duties exist in respect of employers, employees and self-employed persons, and of designers, manufacturers, importers and suppliers.

'It shall be the duty of every **employer** to ensure, so far as is reasonably practicable, the health, safety and welfare at work of all his employees' (HASAWA 1974, s 2(1)). Several comments can be made about this basic duty. First, it is qualified by the phrase 'as far as is reasonably practicable'. In the earlier discussion on the context in which health and safety law has developed, it was noted that, invariably, there can be a balance to be struck between risk reduction/minimisation and the cost involved. Secondly, it is important to remember that the duty relates to welfare, as well as health and safety. This is an all-encompassing duty and should result in appropriate employer policies. Thirdly, this duty is extended to other particular matters. These cover:

(a) the provision and maintenance of plant and systems of work that are, so far as is reasonably practicable, safe and without risks to health;

(b) arrangements for ensuring, so far as is reasonably practicable, safety and absence of risks to health in connection with the use, handling, storage and transport of articles and substances;

(c) the provision of such information, instruction, training and supervision as is necessary to ensure, so far as is reasonably practicable, the health and safety at work of his employees;

(d) so far as is reasonably practicable as regards any place of work under the employer's control, the maintenance of it in a condition that is safe and without risks to health and the provision and maintenance of means of access to and egress from it that are safe and without such risks;

(e) the provision and maintenance of a working environment for his employees that is, so far as is reasonably practicable, safe, without risks to health, and adequate as regards facilities and arrangements for their welfare at work (HASAWA 1974, s 2(2)).

An employer, in aiming to comply with health and safety duties, may not impose any levy upon an employee (s 9).

These duties to employees are, also, extended to cover responsibilities to non-employees. 'It shall be the duty of every employer to conduct his undertaking in such a way as to ensure, so far as is reasonably practicable, that persons not in his employment who may be affected thereby are not thereby exposed to risks to their health or safety' (s 3(1)). A parallel duty is imposed upon self-employed persons towards non-employees (s 3(2)). Furthermore, there are general duties placed upon 'persons concerned with premises to persons other than their employees' (s 4).

In interpreting this duty (s 3), the Court of Appeal (*R* v *Board of Trustees of the Science Museum* [1993] IRLR 853) adopted a purposive approach and emphasised the 'risk' of harm as opposed to evidence that actual harm had been sustained. This approach differs from the common law approach which requires evidence of actual harm for damages to be awarded.

These general duties on employers, outlined above, are supplemented by further ones, designed to promote self-regulation. First, 'it shall be the duty of every employer to prepare and as often as may be appropriate revise **a written statement of his general policy** with respect to the health and safety at work of his employees and the organisation and arrangements for the time being in force for carrying out that policy, and to bring the statement and any revision of it to the notice of all his employees' (s 2(3)). (Those employing fewer than five employees are exempt from this requirement.)

Secondly, there are provisions on **safety representatives** and on the establishment of a **safety committee** (s 2(4)–(7)). These roles and functions are discussed in more detail below. They are created within the context of the following general duty on an employer 'to consult any such representatives with a view to the making and maintenance of arrangements which will enable him and his employees to co-operate effectively in promoting and developing measures to ensure the health and safety at work of employees and in checking the effectiveness of such measures' (s 2(6)).

Thirdly, as we shall see later in this chapter, there are supplementary duties arising from the Management of Health and Safety at Work Regulations 1999 particularly in respect of risk assessment, health surveillance of employees, and the protection of pregnant and young workers.

General duties are also imposed upon **employees**. However, these do not absolve the employer from the primary responsibility for health and safety at work:

> It shall be the duty of every employee while at work (a) to take reasonable care for the health and safety of himself and other persons who may be affected by his acts or omissions at work; and as regards any duty or requirement imposed on his employer or any other person by or under any of the relevant statutory provisions, to co-operate with him so far as is necessary to enable that duty or requirement to be performed or complied with (s 7).

These duties on employees are supplemented by those in the Management of Health and Safety at Work Regulations 1999: to use equipment, materials and procedures provided by the employer in the way that they are trained to do so; and to report any health and safety problems to their employer.

An ancillary duty affects a wide range of people (including employees): 'No person shall intentionally or recklessly interfere with or misuse anything provided in the interests of health, safety, or welfare in pursuance of any of the relevant statutory provisions' (s 8).

Finally, in respect of general duties, **designers, manufacturers, importers and suppliers** of 'any article for use at work' must, as far as is reasonably practicable, ensure that the article is designed and constructed so as to be safe when properly used; must carry out testing and examination; must ensure that information is available about the article, its testing and its use; must carry out research to minimise any risks; and must ensure safe installation (s 6).

What is the machinery for enforcing health and safety standards?

Three levels are provided for:

1 safety representatives and safety committees at workplace level (discussed later);

2 the Health and Safety Executive, which manages health and safety inspectors;

3 the Health and Safety Commission.

In terms of the day-to-day management of health and safety at work, the statutory role of health and safety inspectors (HSIs) is significant. These are set out as follows:

Entering premises

(a) at any reasonable time (or, in a situation which in his opinion is or may be dangerous, at any time) to enter any premises which he has reason to believe it is necessary for him to enter . . . ;

(b) to take with him a constable if he has reasonable cause to apprehend any serious obstruction in the execution of his duty;

(c) . . . to take with him any person duly authorised by his [the inspector's] enforcing authority; and any equipment or materials required . . .

Investigation

(d) to make such examination and investigation as may in any circumstances be necessary . . . ;

(e) as regards any premises which he has power to enter, to direct that those premises or any part of them, or anything therein, shall be left undisturbed . . . for as long as is reasonably necessary for the purpose of any examination or investigation . . . ;

(f) to take such measurements and photographs and make such recordings as he considers necessary . . . ;

(g) to take samples of any articles or substances found in any premises which he has power to enter, and of the atmosphere in or in the vicinity of any such premises . . .

Action on substances or equipment

(h) [if] an article or substance . . . appears to him to have caused or to be likely to cause danger to health and safety, to cause it to be dismantled or subjected to any process or test . . . or . . . unless [it] is in the circumstances necessary [destroyed] . . . ;

(i)   in the case of any [such] article or substance . . . to take possession of it and detain it for so long as is necessary for all or any of the following purposes, namely (i) to examine it . . . ; (ii) to ensure that it is not tampered with before his examination of it is completed; (iii) to ensure that it is available for use as evidence in any proceedings for an offence . . .

Obtaining information

(j)   to require any person whom he has reasonable cause to believe to be able to give any information relevant to any examination or investigation under paragraph (d) above to answer (in the absence of persons other than a person nominated by him to be present and any persons whom the inspector may allow to be present) such questions as the inspector thinks fit to ask and to sign a declaration of the truth of his answers;

(k)   to require the production of, inspect, and take copies of, or of any entry in, any books or documents . . .

Requiring assistance

(l)   to require any person to afford him such facilities and assistance with respect to any matters or things within that person's control or in relation to which that person has responsibilities as are necessary to enable the inspector to exercise any of the powers conferred on him by this section (HASAWA 1974, s 20(2)).

What powers does the HSE have?

Inspectors may issue an improvement notice (HASAWA 1974, s 21) or a prohibition notice (s 22). An **improvement notice** requires a person (usually an employer) to remedy a contravention of statutory provisions within a specified time period (normally 21 days). Appeal is possible to an employment tribunal within 21 days and this suspends the notice (s 24). A **prohibition notice** is issued to prevent a person carrying on activities where there is or may be a 'risk of serious personal injury'. Such a notice can have immediate effect. Again, appeal is possible to an employment tribunal. However, appeal does not rescind the notice. This can only be done by the tribunal after the hearing (s 24). In 2000/1, 11 058 enforcement notices were issued by the Health and Safety Executive. Improvement notices accounted for 60 per cent of these total notices. Ninety-seven per cent of prohibition notices were immediate prohibitions on the use of equipment or systems of work (HSC, 2001: 71).

Furthermore, the HSE may bring **criminal proceedings** in the courts for offences under the relevant statutory provisions. An inspector is authorised (s 39) to prosecute in magistrates' courts in England and Wales. In all other proceedings, the consent of the Director of Public Prosecutions is required (*see* Fig. 12.4 above). Contrary to the usual rules in criminal proceedings, it is for the defendant to prove what was reasonably practicable. Specific provision on the onus of proof is set out in the Act (s 40).

As far as penalties are concerned, the maximum fine in the magistrates' court is £20 000; in the higher courts it is unlimited. The power of imprisonment of up to two years is also available in certain circumstances. Section 33 sets out the details of the offences and the maximum penalties. The number of 'informations' laid before courts about breaches of health and safety regulations was 2077 in

2000/01. Convictions were secured in 72 per cent of cases. The average fine was £6250 (HSC, 2001: 73–4).

Who is liable for infringements of health and safety standards?

As we have outlined above, **an employer** is liable for complying with the general duties 'as far as is reasonably practicable' and for compliance with relevant statutory provisions (ss 2–4). It is, also, possible for individual **directors and managers** to be personally liable for offences:

> Where an offence under any of the relevant statutory provisions committed by a body corporate is proved to have been committed with the consent or connivance of, or to have been attributable to any neglect on the part of, any director, manager, secretary or other similar officer of the body corporate or a person who is purporting to act in any such capacity, he as well as the body corporate shall be guilty of that offence and shall be liable to be proceeded against and punished accordingly (s 37(1)).

The issue of liability in circumstances where an organisation employs contractors was clarified in a recent case. The Court of Appeal (*R* v *Associated Octel Ltd* [1994] IRLR 540) interpreting the duty under HASAWA, s 3(1), established the liability of an employer for injuries caused to **non-employees employed by independent contractors** – whether or not the employer had actual control over how the work was carried out. Liability is subject to the defence of 'as far as is reasonably practicable'. In this case a contractor's employee was badly burned in a flash fire that resulted from an explosion. This occurred when a lamp (which was not a safety lamp) broke and ignited acetone vapour within the tank he was cleaning. The court found that the cleaning and maintainance of the chorine tank did form part of Octel's 'undertaking' and that it was reasonably practicable for Octel to give the contractor instructions on carrying out the work and on the safety measures to be adopted. Each case would, of course, be considered on its own facts.

An employee is liable for failing to take reasonable care of their health and safety and that of other people, and for failing to co-operate with the employer in the implementation of health and safety standards (s 7). In practice, it is unlikely that an employee would have criminal proceeding taken against them unless the safety breach was so serious and, perhaps, involved recklessness or deliberate misuse of equipment etc. (s 8). Usually, a breach of safety rules by an employee would be dealt with through the internal disciplinary procedure.

Safety representatives are not legally liable for carrying out their function or for not carrying out their function. In the Safety Representatives and Safety Committees Regulations 1977 (reg 4.1) it is made clear that 'no function given to a safety representative by this paragraph shall be construed as imposing any duty on him'. In guidance to the Regulations, the HSE states that 'a safety representative by accepting, agreeing with or not objecting to a course of action taken by the employer to deal with a health or safety hazard, does not take upon himself any legal responsibility for that course of action'. Furthermore, it is stated that the HSC has directed that the HSE 'shall not institute criminal proceedings against any safety representative for any act or omission by him in respect of the performance of functions assigned to him by the Regulations' (Guidance Note 11).

12.4.4 Some key regulations

What is the role of regulations?

As stated earlier, the Health and Safety at Work Act 1974 was constructed as legislation to be supplemented by specific regulations (s 15). Regulations that have been prepared and approved over the past 30 years fall into two broad categories:

- those which set **standards** for dealing with specific hazards at work (e.g. noise, manual handling operations, eye protection);
- those which set **procedural requirements** for all employers (e.g. relating to the management of health and safety and information disclosure, and to the role and functions of safety representatives).

The range of regulations is considerable. The relevance of regulations to particular employers, obviously, varies. The incidence of certain workplace hazards (e.g. the use of visual display units) across industries can be extensive. Others have a much more industry-specific application. The regulations relating to procedures are generally of broad application. For illustrative purposes we will consider two sets of regulations: the Management of Health and Safety at Work Regulations 1999; and the Health and Safety (Display Screen Equipment) Regulations 1992. Other key regulations are briefly outlined in Fig. 12.6.

Management of Health and Safety at Work Regulations 1999

These implement requirements of the European Safety and Health Directive 1989. They apply to all employers in respect of their own employees and 'persons not in his employment arising out of or in connection with the conduct by him of his undertaking' (MHSW Regs, reg 3) (*see* above reference to the issue of liability in the *Octel* case). They set out ways in which risk and health and safety can be managed systematically. There are several key provisions.

Risk assessment

The first step must be to make 'suitable and sufficient assessment' of risks in the workplace (MHSW Regs, reg 3). The assessment must look at the way work is actually done (which may sometimes be different from the way the employer expects it to be done). It must enable the employer to identify and prioritise significant risks and decide on appropriate action. Appropriate action can involve a number of considerations:

- whether the risk can be eliminated completely – for example, by not using a specific substance or by re-designing the way in which work is carried out;
- whether the hazard can be tackled at source – for example, isolating noisy machinery in an acoustic booth rather than providing ear-protection;
- whether work should be adapted to the individual worker and not the other way – so avoiding monotonous work and work at a pre-determined rate;
- making sure that all workers (including part-timers, temporary staff and trainees) are informed in 'comprehensible' form (MHSW Regs, reg 10) of safety standards and expectations about how work is to be carried out.

Particular attention must be paid to the risks to which pregnant and breast-feeding women workers are exposed (MHSW Regs, reg 16). These can include physical hazards (such as noise, vibration, radiation, physical effort, etc.), and biological and chemical hazards. Where there is a problem, the employer should try to eliminate the risk. If this cannot be done, the employer must consider altering working conditions or working hours or offering suitable alternative work. If this is not possible, the woman concerned must be given paid leave for as long as necessary to protect the health and safety of both herself and her child.

Furthermore, the employer must assess particular risks for young people, taking into account their inexperience, lack of awareness of potential risks and immaturity. Where the risks cannot be adequately controlled, young people should not be employed for that work (e.g. where the work is beyond their physical or psychological capacity; or work which involves exposure to harmful agents or radiation; or presents a risk to health from extreme cold or heat, noise or vibration). If children under the minimum school-leaving age are employed, then parents must be given details of the risk assessment and control measures (Health and Safety (Young Persons) Regulations 1997 which implement certain provisions of the Young Workers Directive 1994). (*See* Exercise 12.1 below.)

Health and safety arrangements

These follow from risk assessment and require effective planning, organisation, control of health and safety, review; and should also include health surveillance arrangements (MHSW Regs, reg 5).

Health surveillance

Where appropriate, the MHSW Regulations require the employer to provide 'such health surveillance as is appropriate' of their workforce (reg 6). Central to this is monitoring. This can be carried out on various levels. For example, supervisors could be trained to check people's hands if they work with a substance which can cause skin rashes; whereas occupational health staff could undertake specific medical tests and examinations.

Competent persons

One or more such persons shall be appointed by an employer 'to assist him in undertaking the measures he needs to take to comply with the requirements and prohibitions imposed upon him by or under the relevant statutory provisions' (MHSW Regs, reg 7). Such a person must have sufficient training and experience or knowledge and other qualities to enable the function to be carried out. The person appointed must have:

- a good understanding of the principles of risk assessment and prevention;
- a knowledge of the employer's business and the work carried out by employees;
- awareness of the limitations of their own ability and when other expertise may be required.

Serious or imminent danger

Employers must plan in advance for foreseeable emergencies such as fire, a bomb scare, the release of toxic fumes, etc. Arrangements may involve a full evacuation of the work premises. In such an event, there should be sufficient trained designated people to supervise the evacuation. Staff who are required to enter a hazardous area (e.g. to close down a process) should be specially trained (MHSW Regs, reg 8).

Employees' duties

An employee must 'use any machinery, equipment, dangerous substance, transport equipment, means of production or safety device provided to him by the employer in accordance both with any training . . . and instructions' (MHSW Regs, reg 14). Additionally, an employee must inform the employer of situations which they reasonably thought 'represented a serious and immediate danger to health and safety'; or of shortcomings in the employer's arrangements for health and safety protection.

Exercise 12.1	**Assessing the risks?**

In small groups, discuss the working conditions of any number of the following and decide on the risks that you think they might encounter and the steps that the employer might take to deal with them:

- Call-centre worker
- Bus driver
- Nurse in an Accident and Emergency Department
- Social worker
- School teacher
- Traffic warden
- Solicitor
- Prison officer
- Pharmacist in a retail chemist

For guidance on risk assessment see *Five steps to risk assessment* (1998), available from the Health and Safety Executive website, www. hse.gov.uk.

Health and Safety (Display Screen Equipment) Regulations 1992

These Regulations implement the European Display Screen Equipment Directive. They cover most types of display screen equipment. Excepted pieces of equipment are, for example, screens in drivers' cabs and on other means of transport, portable systems not in prolonged use, cash registers, calculators or other equipment with a small data display. The ECJ ruled that the term 'graphic display screen' in the Directive must be interpreted to include screens that display film recordings in analogue or digital form. So the employer of a film cutter had to plan into her daily work breaks and changes in activity (*Dietrich* v *Westdeutscher Rundfunk* [2000] case C–11/99).

The Regulations apply to the whole **workstation**. This covers:

- the display screen equipment (DSE) and software, including keyboards and other inputting devices;
- optional accessories added to the DSE;
- disk drive, telephone, modem, printer, document holder, work chart, desk or other equipment;
- the immediate work environment around the DSE.

The following minimum requirements applicable to workstation use must be satisfied:

- **display screen**: well-defined characters of adequate size, stable image, easily adjustable brightness and contrast, easily tilting and swivelling screen, no reflective glare;
- **keyboard**: tiltable and separate from the screen, sufficient space in front of keyboard, matt surface, easy to use, adequately contrasted symbols on keys;
- **work surface**: sufficiently large and low-reflecting surface, allows a flexible arrangement of equipment, adequate space;
- **work chair**: stable, allows user easy movement and comfortable position, adjustable height (seat), adjustable height and tilt (seat back), footrests available on request;
- **space**: designed to allow operator to change positions;
- **lighting**: satisfactory lighting conditions, appropriate contrast between screen and background, prevention of glare through positioning of artificial lighting;
- **reflections**: positioning must prevent sources of light, such as windows, from causing distracting reflections on the screen;
- **noise**: must not distract attention or disturb speech;
- **heat**: must not produce excess heat causing discomfort;
- **radiation**: reduced to negligible levels in respect of user's safety, except for the visible part of the electromagnetic spectrum;
- **humidity**: establishment and maintenance of an adequate level;
- **software and systems**: software must be suitable for the task, easy to use and adaptable to the level of user's knowledge, no quantitive or qualitative checking facility may be used without user's knowledge, principles of software ergomonics must be applied.

The regulations only apply to '**users**' of display screen equipment. A user is a person who 'habitually uses display screen equipment as a significant part of his normal work'. Considerations in deciding whether or not a person would be a user are: whether DSE work is an essential part of a job, how long a person spends at any one time on the machine, etc.

There are four health and safety protection issues. First, there is the question of **daily work routine**. This could involve periodic breaks or job rotation (i.e. the carrying out of tasks that do not involve the similar use of hands and arms). In general guidance, the HSE suggests that breaks should be taken before the onset of fatigue and before productivity starts to fall. They should be included as part of working time. Short and frequent breaks are better than occasional longer breaks. Where possible, 'users' should have some discretion and individual control over how they do their jobs and when they take breaks.

Secondly, there is the question of **risk assessment**. As indicated in the Management of Health and Safety at Work Regulations 1999, this process should be systematic and comprehensive. The likely risks are: postural problems mainly caused by workstation design; visual problems such as sore eyes, headaches caused by glare, poor lighting, etc.; and stress and fatigue caused by workstation design, workload intensity, etc. These risks can result in work-related upper-limb disorders (repetitive strain injury).

Any risk must be reduced as quickly as possible. This could be done fairly simply, by, for example, repositioning or renewing equipment or providing the worker with some control over the tasks. The risk assessment should be reviewed where there is a significant change to the workstation, in the workforce or its capabilities or where new risks are established. As far as teleworkers are concerned, the risks must be assessed regardless of whether the workstation is provided partly or wholly by the employer.

Thirdly, there are matters relating to **eyesight**. Users are entitled to a full eye and eyesight test by a qualified optician or medical practitioner. The employer's liability for the cost of 'corrective appliances', usually spectacles, only applies to 'special' appliances required for DSE use or to special modifications to the users' normal spectacles required for DSE work.

Fourthly, the **information** and **training** provided should be tailored to the work the user does. Users must be provided with adequate health and safety training in the use of the workstation. Information must relate to all aspects of the workstation, daily work routine and eyesight requirements.

See Fig. 12.6 for an outline of other key regulations.

12.4.5 Rights of employees

Protection from detriments

Supplementing the duties that an employer owes to employees (under HASAWA and under common law) there are statutory protections 'from suffering detriments in employment' (EPA 1996, s 44); and parallel protection against unfair dismissal (ERA 1996, s 100). 'Detriment' has previously been outlined in relation to other employment rights. Essentially, it is construed as putting a person at a disadvantage. It includes disciplinary warnings and dismissal, temporary transfers to other work and suspensions from work, refusals to grant a pay rise or allocate overtime to an employee, and overlooking an employee for promotion. In this context it is stated that 'an employee has the right not to be subjected to any detriment by any act, or any deliberate failure to act, by his employer done on the ground that' they exercised certain statutory rights (ERA 1996, s 44(1)).

There are five circumstances covered by the protection:

- **'Competent persons' (appointed under MHSW Regulations 1999):** who, 'having been designated by the employer to carry out activities in connection with preventing or reducing risks to health and safety at work', 'carried out (or proposed to carry out) any such activities' (ERA 1996, s 44(1)(a)).

Noise at Work Regulations 1989: Implemented from January 1990, they cover workers and the self-employed. They impose duties on employers to prevent damage to workers' hearing; and parallel duties for designers, manufacturers, importers and suppliers. Daily personal noise exposure levels for workers is specified. These must be assessed. Action must be taken by employers to reduce unacceptable noise exposure levels.

Manual Handling Operations Regulations 1992: As far as reasonably practicable, employers are to avoid manual handling operations (e.g. lifting, pushing, pulling, carrying or moving) and consider whether such operations are necessary or could be achieved in a different way, or be automated or mechanised. A suitable assessment of the operations should be carried out in consultation with employees. Risk should be reduced to the lowest level practicable. Attention should be paid to workers who have been pregnant and those with health problems. Weight limits are specified.

Workplace (Health, Safety and Welfare) Regulations 1992: Implemented from 1996, they cover a wide range of workplaces (but excluding extractive industries, construction sites and outdoor agricultural and forestry workplaces). They have provisions on, for example, workplace temperatures, rest facilities, lighting, ventilation, cleanliness, space and workstations. There is an accompanying approved code of practice.

Provision and Use of Work Equipment Regulations 1992: Implemented from 1997, they cover all workers (including those off-shore) and the self-employed. The employers' duty is to ensure the suitability of work equipment for its purpose (by design, construction or adaptation). They must take account of likely risks (e.g. a wet or flammable atmosphere). Work equipment must be effectively maintained. All persons who use or supervise the use of work equipment must have received adequate information and health and safety training.

Personal Protective Equipment at Work Regulations 1992: These cover workers and the self-employed. Employers must provide suitable personal protective equipment for workers who may be exposed to health and safety risks. There must be a risk assessment; and equipment must be properly maintained.

Control of Substances Hazardous to Health Regulations (CoSHH) 1999: The COSHH Regulations were originally implemented in 1995. New ones came into force in 1999. These cover, among other matters, employers' duties, prohibitions relating to certain substances, risk assessment, the prevention and control of exposure to substances hazardous to health, and monitoring exposure and health surveillance.

Reporting of Injuries, Diseases and Dangerous Occurrences Regulations (RIDDOR) 1995: The original 1985 Regulations were modified in 1995 and implemented in 1996. They specify notification procedures (to the HSE or the local authority, as appropriate) for injuries, dangerous occurrences, work-related diseases (such as arsenic or lead poisoning) and for deaths of employees; and stipulate records to be kept by employers.

Figure 12.6   Some other key regulations

- **Safety representatives or safety committee members**: where an employee performed or proposed to perform the functions of this role.
- **Election of safety representatives**: where, under the 1996 Health and Safety (Consultation with Employees) Regulations, an employee took part or proposed to take part in consultation with the employer or in an election of safety representatives.
- **Informing the employer of hazards**: where, 'being an employee at a place where (i) there was no such representative or safety committee, or (ii) there was such a representative or safety committee but it was not reasonably practicable for the employee to raise the matter by those means, he brought to his

employer's attention, by reasonable means, circumstances connected with his work which he reasonably believed were harmful or potentially harmful to health or safety' (ERA 1996, s 44(1)(c)). It is expected that the employee would raise their complaint through the organisation's grievance procedure. This would be regarded as 'reasonable means' – whereas a direct complaint, in the first instance, to a director or an external body, like the HSE, would not be. Furthermore, the employee must show 'reasonable belief'. In an unfair dismissal case, the EAT provided the following guidance (*Kerr* v *Nathan's Wastesavers Ltd*, EAT, 91/95). An employee must show: that they did in fact believe that the circumstances were harmful, or potentially harmful, to health and safety; that they had in mind reasonable grounds to sustain that belief; that those grounds were based on all the relevant circumstances of the case.

■ **Leaving the workplace in 'serious and imminent' risk**: this may be a one-off incident or a continuing set of circumstances. Protection against detriment relates to 'circumstances of danger which the employee reasonably believed to be serious and imminent and which he could not reasonably have been expected to avert, he left (or proposed to leave) or (while the danger persisted) refused to return to his place of work or any dangerous part of his place of work' (ERA 1996, s 44(1)(d)). Such protection also concerns 'circumstances of danger which the employee reasonably believed to be serious and imminent' where 'he took (or proposed to take) appropriate steps to protect himself or other persons from the danger' (ERA 1996, s 44(1)(e)). Again, the issue of 'reasonable belief' arises. One aspect of this is the extent to which 'objective' evidence is required for the employee to sustain the 'subjective' belief that there is a 'serious and imminent danger'. It appears that there is no absolute obligation upon the employee to acquire such evidence – although clearly it can help (*see* Fig. 12.7).

The question of whether the steps which the employee 'took or proposed to take were appropriate is to be judged by reference to all the circumstances including, in particular, his knowledge and the facilities and advice available to him at the time' (ERA 1996, s 44(2)). Furthermore, if an employer can show that what the employee did was 'so negligent' that 'a reasonable employer' would have taken action against such an employee, then 'an employee is not to be regarded as having been subjected to a detriment' (ERA 1996, s 44(3)). To this extent, an employer has a defence.

A van driver refused to drive what he said was a defective vehicle and was dismissed. His employer had assured him that the vehicle was in a safe condition. Although he had obtained no expert evidence, it was provided before the tribunal where it was stated that the vehicle would have failed its MOT test and would have been ruled as unroadworthy. The tribunal commented that the assurance about the vehicle's safety given by the company was 'so informal and so undetailed that [he] was still entitled to hold his belief notwithstanding the fact that others had driven the van in the meantime'. The dismissal was ruled to be unfair.

Figure 12.7 The case of the van driver

Source: *Rawlings* v *Barraclough t/a Independent Delivery Services Ltd*, 2.5.95, COIT, 15595/95.

Complaint to employment tribunal

An employee who believes that they have suffered such a detriment may complain to an employment tribunal. There are no qualifying conditions. The rights cover all 'employees' irrespective of age, hours of work or length of service. The complaint must be lodged within three months of the unfair dismissal or the detrimental treatment complained of. The tribunal has discretion to extend this three-month period in respect of both allegations of unfair dismissal and other detrimental treatment. Where a detrimental act continues over a period, the date of the act means the last day of that period.

If an employee successfully complains of detrimental treatment (short of dismissal), then the employment tribunal must make a declaration to that effect and may award the employee compensation (which is unlimited) which it regards as 'just and equitable' in all the circumstances. This will involve consideration of any loss sustained by the employee and any injury to feelings. The employee has a duty to mitigate their loss. The compensation might be reduced because of the behaviour of the employee in contributing to the circumstances.

If the detrimental treatment is dismissal and the claim is successful, then, an ex-employee may be awarded compensation or an order for re-engagement or reinstatement can be made. The basic and compensatory awards are calculated in the normal way (*see* Chapter 9).

If the person is dismissed for undertaking their duties as a safety representative, member of a safety committee or as a 'designated employee', then additional remedies are available. The first is interim relief (ERA 1996, s 128). A claim for this must be made to the employment tribunal within seven days immediately following the effective date of termination of employment. If it appears to the tribunal that the employee is 'likely' (ERA 1996, s 129(1)) to establish that the reason for the dismissal is one prohibited under ERA 1996, s 100, and the employer is willing, then, it may order the reinstatement or re-engagement of the employee pending the final determination of the case at a hearing or settlement (e.g. through ACAS conciliation). Re-engagement means re-employment on terms that are 'not less favourable' than those that would have applied had the employee not been dismissed (ERA 1996, s 129(3)(b)). The employee may 'reasonably' refuse re-engagement (ERA 1996, s 128(8)(a)).

If no agreement is reached on reinstatement or re-engagement, the tribunal must make an order for the continuation of the contract of employment from the date of termination until the date of determination or settlement of the complaint. Unreasonable refusal of re-engagement by an employee will result in the tribunal making no order to continue the contract of employment (ERA 1996, s 129(8)(b)). An order to continue the contract of employment is 'an order that the contract of employment continue in force . . . for the purposes of pay and any other benefit derived from employment, seniority, pension rights and other similar matters' and for the purposes of determining the employee's continuity of employment (ERA 1996, s 130(1)).

The second additional remedies are monetary: a minimum basic award, and a special award of compensation.

In addition to the rights granted to employees in general and to safety representatives and 'designated persons', there is also special health and safety protection accorded to pregnant workers (MHSW Regs, reg 16).

12.4.6 **Consultation and representation**

The use of workforce representation (through the establishment of safety representatives and safety committees) was seen as central to the 'self-regulation' model for implementing effective health and safety standards, but in the period between the mid-1970s and 1996, Britain had a flawed system of representation. The 1977 Safety Representatives and Safety Committees Regulations were restricted to union-recognised health and safety representatives. As unionisation diminished in the following two decades, employees in the rapidly expanding non-union sector were without any legally enforceable rights of representation. This was clearly at variance with the 1989 Directive on Safety and Health. Article 11 outlined the responsibilities of 'workers' representatives' – with no distinction between unionised and non-unionised organisations. In 1996, the Health and Safety (Consultation with Employees) Regulations were approved by Parliament. These complement the 1977 Regulations. Together they create a general framework of representation rights. There are also separate regulations governing staff employed off-shore in the oil industry – the Offshore Safety (Safety Representatives and Safety Committees) Regulations 1989.

So, there are now four routes to health and safety representation and consultation:

1   through recognised trade union representatives (under the 1977 Regulations);
2   through non-union employee representatives (under the 1996 Regulations);
3   direct with the relevant workforce (under the 1996 Regulations);
4   through representatives off-shore (under the 1989 Regulations).

There are several issues in this legal framework that we will consider:

- the functions of safety representatives;
- information disclosure;
- the election/appointment of safety representatives;
- protections against detriments.

The functions of union safety representatives (the 1977 Regulations)

- to represent employees in consultation with the employer (1977 Regs, reg 4);
- to investigate potential hazards and dangerous occurrences at the workplace and examine the causes of accidents at the workplace;
- to investigate complaints by any employee they represent relating to the employee's health and safety or welfare at work;
- to make representations to the employer on general matters arising out of investigations;
- to make representations to the employer on general matters affecting the health, safety or welfare of the employees at the workplace;
- to carry out inspections in a number of circumstances (1977 Regs, regs 5, 6 and 7) (e.g. where there has been no inspection for the past three months; where there has been 'a substantial change in the conditions of work'; where there has been 'a notifiable accident or dangerous occurrence in a workplace

or a notifiable disease has been contracted'; where the employer has 'any document relevant to the workplace and to the employees');

■ to represent the employees they were appointed to represent in consultation at the workplace with inspectors of the HSE and of any other enforcing authority;

■ to attend meetings of safety committees where they attend in their capacity as a safety representative in connection with any of the functions set out above.

The functions of non-union representatives (the 1996 Regulations)

■ to make representations to the employer on potential hazards and dangerous occurrences at the workplace which affect, or could affect, the employees they represent (1996 Regs, reg 6);

■ to make representations to the employer on general matters affecting the health and safety at work of the employees they represent and, in particular, on such matters consulted about with the employer (*see* 1996 Regs, reg 3 below);

■ to represent the employees they represent in consultation at the workplace with inspectors.

These functions are exercised in the context of 'the duty of the employer to consult' provisions (1996 Regs, reg 3). The employer 'shall consult in good time' (with either the workforce directly or with representatives) particularly regarding:

■ the introduction of any measure at the workplace which may substantially affect the health and safety of those employees;

■ arrangements for nominating 'competent persons' (under the MHSW Regs, reg 7);

■ any health and safety information they are required to provide to those employees by or under the relevant statutory provisions;

■ the planning and organisation of any health and safety training they are required to provide to those employees by or under the relevant statutory provisions;

■ the health and safety consequences for those employees of the introduction (including the planning thereof) of new technologies into the workplace.

The 1996 Regulations are silent about inspections – though they could be implied from some of the provisions.

Disclosure of information

Obviously, consultation and representation can only be effective if information is adequate. The 1977 Regulations for union safety representatives specify:

■ 'Safety representatives shall for the performance of their functions . . . if they have given the employer reasonable notice, be entitled to inspect and take copies of any document relevant to the workplace or the employees the safety representatives represent which the employer is required to keep . . . except a document consisting of or relating to any health record of an identifiable individual' (reg 7.1);

■ an employer shall make available to safety representatives the information, within the employer's knowledge, necessary to enable the employer to fulfil their functions **except** information which 'would be against the interests of national security'; the disclosure of which would infringe some statutory provision; information which relates to an individual (unless that person has consented to disclosure); or information which would, if disclosed, cause 'substantial injury to the employer's undertaking'; or 'any information obtained by the employer for the purpose of bringing, prosecuting or defending any legal proceedings' (reg 7.2).

The 1996 Regulations provide a general duty to provide information (reg 5) to either employees directly or with their representatives 'as is necessary to enable them to participate fully and effectively in the consultation' and for representatives 'in the carrying out of their functions under these Regulations'. The exceptions set out in the 1977 Regulations (reg 7.2) are restated.

This information disclosure is in the context of the general duty on the employer 'to provide such information . . . as is necessary to ensure, as far as is reasonably practicable, the health and safety at work of his employees' (HASAWA, s 2(2)(c)) which is supplemented by the Health and Safety Information for Employees Regulations 1989 concerning approved posters and leaflets.

The election/appointment of safety representatives

This is provided for in the two sets of regulations. Under the 1977 Regulations, a recognised independent trade union may appoint safety representatives from among the employees 'in all cases where one or more employees are employed by an employer by whom it is is recognised' (reg 3.1). The person 'so far as is reasonably practicable' shall 'either have been employed by his employer throughout the preceding two years or have had at least two years experience in similar employment' (reg 3.4). The 1996 Regulations merely describe 'representatives of employee safety'. Such a person will have been elected from a group of employees 'to represent that group for the purposes of . . . consultation' (reg 4.1b).

A safety committee

This should be established by an employer 'having the function of keeping under review the measures taken to ensure the health and safety at work of his employees and such other functions as may be prescribed' (HASAWA, s 2(7)). Under the accompanying 1977 Regulations, two union-recognised safety representatives are needed to request a committee (reg 9). The 1996 Regulations have no parallel provision. Under these, consultation can be directly with the workforce, with one representative or with more than one representative (reg 4). The creation of a safety committee is subject to management discretion.

Protection against detriments

To help ensure the credibility and independence (from undue employer influence) of workforce safety representatives, certain protections against detriments (which might be imposed by employers) are provided for. These have been outlined above in the context of the general protections for employees.

By way of conclusion, this Robens 'self-regulation' model has, however, been characterised as having weaknesses.

> The model on which the Robens assumptions were based never could be generalised to employment across the economy as a whole. For its application was crucially dependent on two factors. First, the presence of sufficient expertise and commitment on the part of employers. Secondly, the existence of institutions of workforce representation that could act to both encourage and support the self-regulatory approach advocated. As a result the Robens model was most relevant to health and safety of men in stable full-time employment in large enterprises where there were well established channels of communication between the representatives of workers and their management, such as those typically associated with large establishments in the manufacturing or extractive industries (Walters and James, 1998: 27).

Given the labour market and organisational changes that have taken place in recent years – the growth of atypical employment and smaller more devolved organisations – the authors argue that 'the model on which Robens pinned its hopes is even less relevant today'. This conclusion may overstate the situation but only to some slight extent. Clearly, there is some need to review the provisions in the Representation Regulations. Also, there is a need to ensure more comprehensive coverage of representation arrangements and harmonisation and consistency between the 1977 Regulations and those approved in 1996.

12.5   Employment policies and practices

> The promotion of safety and health at work is first and foremost a matter of efficient management. But it is not a management prerogative. In this context more than most, real progress is impossible without the full co-operation and commitment of all employees. How can this be encouraged? We believe that work people must be able to participate fully in the making and monitoring of arrangements for safety and health in their place of work (Robens Report, 1972: 18).

The Chartered Institute of Personnel and Development elaborates the business case in these terms: 'effective management of the health and welfare of people at work: contributes to performance improvement and increases competitive advantage; reduces unacceptable losses associated with ill-health and injuries; and lowers absenteeism, improves morale and reduces litigation costs' (CIPD, 1996a).

These quotations encompass the essential issues that underlie employment policies and practices on health and safety. On the one hand there are issues of operational efficiency and cost effectiveness. On the other hand are issues of compliance with safety standards and minimising or eliminating risk. A company that has created a safety culture will have developed procedures and practices to try and reconcile these divergent issues. Part of its procedures will involve communication and consultation with the workforce. It will support its pursuit of high safety standards by training and possibly by having available specialist resources like occupational health and appropriate counselling.

A structured approach to health and safety management involves, then, consideration of five principal areas:

1 the creation of a safety culture;
2 the formulation and implementation of safety policies;
3 arrangements for workforce safety consultation and communication;
4 the contribution of an occupational health service; and
5 the availability of an employee assistance programme.

We will consider each of these in turn.

12.5.1 Creating a safety culture

A safety culture within an organisation would demonstrate a high degree of safety consciousness throughout. Safety would be perceived as a dimension of most, if not all, activities. Safety standards would be integrated into work operations, job design, working-time scheduling and reward systems. Appropriate training would be given to managers and employees. There would be regular and genuine consultation (backed by information disclosure). Standards would be enforced through inspections and other monitoring.

Of course, this is not typical. But, in certain industries, such as nuclear power, coal-mining, chemicals, some sectors of engineering, air transport and the railways, health and safety is regarded as a central management issue – not just operationally but also in the employee relations system. Two factors encourage this: the nature of the hazards that exist and the serious consequences that might follow from an accident, and, in many instances, the presence of strong workplace trade unionism. Clearly, policies are developed which are concerned with not merely minimising risks but also setting and implementing standards in an integrated manner – i.e. linked to work organisation, payment systems and staffing levels, etc. (although the incidence of major accidents, mentioned earlier, shows that implementation difficulties can occur).

In industry at large, several factors, already mentioned, limit the achievement of such a culture: management and workforce perceptions about the seriousness of risks within their workplace; the balance between risk minimisation or elimination, on the one hand, and the associated economic costs, on the other; the conflicts of interests and expectations between employees and their employer; and the contribution of the workforce consultation to the achievement of safety standards.

In written statements, of course, both employers and employees assert their commitment to good health and safety standards. In practice, however, it is clearly an area where conflicting interests can and do exist. From a trade union perspective, safety can be seen as a negotiating issue. This does not imply the 'selling' of safety standards for greater remuneration. It relates, rather, to the recurrent phrase in the Health and Safety at Work Act 1974 (s 2) where employers are required to achieve various general duties **'as far as reasonably practicable'**.

This phrase, inevitably brings into focus the issues of 'what is reasonable?' and 'what is practicable?' Employers and working people will have some different perspectives on these questions (particularly the first).

A balance has, then, to be reached between a person's exposure to a particular risk, on the one hand and, on the other, the cost and practicality of eliminating that risk, in whole or in part. This central conflict of expectations and interests is at the heart of much health and safety regulation. In many respects, it reflects the conflicts of interest endemic to the employment relationship (*see* Chapter 2).

This makes health and safety at work a theme in employment relations and particularly an issue for consultation. An organisation promoting a safety culture will fully recognise this. The management of health and safety at work will not be viewed as an isolated function of management but as an integral part of the way in which employees are organised, deployed and rewarded. The following issues, for example, clearly have a safety dimension:

- the staffing levels for particular jobs;
- the workload of employees;
- policies on 'work-life balance';
- policies on harassment at work;
- policies on substance abuse;
- the pace of production lines;
- incentive bonus schemes and other productivity arrangements;
- decisions made by management (or in negotiation with trade unions) on systems of work.

Experience over the past 30 years suggests that the presence of safety representation has been beneficial in contrast to situations where management acted alone. One study found that 'joint consultative committees, with all employee representatives appointed by unions, significantly reduce workplace injuries relative to those establishments where the management alone determine health and safety arrangements' (Reilly *et al.*, 1995: 273).

So, it is against these elements of a safety culture that the following issues are explored: safety policy, arrangements for workforce safety consultation and communication, the contribution of an occupational health service, and the availability of an employee assistance programme.

12.5.2 A safety policy

Employers (except those with fewer than five employees) are under a statutory duty (HASAWA, s 2(3)) to prepare and update a written safety policy. This should outline the organisation and arrangements in force for implementing health and safety standards. Employees should be informed about the policy. Guidance on the details of such policies has been issued by the HSE. In any prosecutions for breaches of health and safety regulations, the issue of whether or not an employer has adopted a safety policy can be used in evidence. Since the implementation of the MHSW Regulations (originally in 1992 and later in 1999), additional matters have to be included in these policies. The following provisions are recommended:

- A statement of the organisation's **commitment** to good health and safety practice. This can be phrased in terms which emphasise not merely management efficiency, but also the human resource management objectives of valuing staff. Consequently, it might also draw attention to commitments to reduce accidents, injuries and work-related sick absence, and to promote employee welfare. It could, consequently, be linked to the organisation's overall mission statement (if one exists).

- An explanation of the **possible risks** and of the preventative measures in place (including those for dealing with emergencies).

- An outline of the **procedures for implementing, monitoring and reviewing** health and safety standards. This can cover consultation with safety representatives and also periodic formal in-company inspections and 'spot checks'.

- A commitment to the provision and funding of appropriate **training** and an indication of how statutory obligations will be complied with.

- A commitment to the dissemination of relevant **information** to employees and other interested people (contractors, customers, the public).

- A commitment to maintain adequate **recording** of risk assessments, accidents, injuries and dangerous occurrences.

- A statement of the ultimate **responsibility of the chief executive** and board of directors (or equivalent people) for compliance with legal standards.

- A statement of the **responsibilities of managers and supervisors** for the implementation and monitoring of safety standards.

- An outline of the roles of **specialist and advisory functions** (e.g. safety officers, occupational health staff, medical advisers and nurses).

- An indication of those people who are designated as '**competent persons**' and of their role and function in helping to implement safety policy.

- A statement of the functions of trade union or employee **safety representatives**.

- An outline of the **consultation arrangements** with trade union or employee safety representatives.

- A procedure for employees to raise health and safety **grievances** and issues.

- A statement of the rights and responsibilities of **individual employees**.

12.5.3 Safety consultation and communication

The legal obligations governing consultation and representation were outlined and discussed earlier. Such arrangements were seen as central to the 'self-regulation' model advocated in the Robens Report. In this section we will explore the contribution that such representatives can make to health and safety management.

The incidence of workplace representation was researched in the 1998 Workplace Employee Relations Survey (Cully *et al.*, 1999: 96). It reported that 39 per cent of workplaces operated joint health and safety committees; 29 per cent consulted safety representatives; 30 per cent consulted directly; and 2 per cent reported no consultation about health and safety. Committees were more common in unionised workplaces: 47 per cent reported these as against 27 per cent in non-union workplaces.

A starting point for consideration for any employer must be the current employee relations context. Is the organisation unionised or not? Is there a mixture of unionised and non-unionised employees? What are existing arrangements for consultation, representation and communication? Answers to these questions are likely to suggest an approach to the structuring of health and safety representation. The critical duty imposed on an employer is to consult – with either union or employee representatives (HASAWA, s 2(6); HSCE Regs 1996, reg 3). The detailed arrangements by which an employer complies with this duty are subject to some flexibility – provided that the principles set out in law are met.

The following consequential questions need to be addressed in order to create an effective representation and consultation system:

- Is the company creating a safety committee (unionised and non-unionised)?
- What information is to be provided?
- What inspection and monitoring arrangements are to be established?
- What facilities/training are to be available to the representatives? (1977 Regulations, reg 4.2b; 1996 Regulations, reg 7);
- What time off is to be granted? (1977 Regulations, reg 4.2a; 1996 Regulations, reg 7).

12.5.4 Occupational health service

An occupational health service (OHS) resourced by an employer is likely to have access to a wide range of occupational health practitioners including physicians, hygienists, psychologists, ergonomic experts and occupational health nurses. These may be employees or used on a consultancy basis. Such a service will help an employer comply with the duties under health and safety law. It may, indeed, extend beyond the legal obligations to pioneer standards of good practice. Obviously, an OHS is more likely to be provided by larger organisations. It is, however, possible for smaller ones to subscribe to a group service, covering a number of employers. It is estimated that about half of employees are covered by an OHS. An OHS will have three broad, related functions which concern both the physical and psychological health of staff: prevention of ill-health, treatment of ill-health and promotion of health and welfare – with the HSE viewing *prevention* as much the most important.

Prevention will cover pre-employment assessment of an individual's suitability for particular tasks by means of a pre-employment questionnaire and/or a medical examination. Also, it will be achieved by regular surveillance of particular risks and hazards associated with the workplace. This would involve periodic reviews of materials, processes and procedures; periodic health reviews of staff, and monitoring the effectiveness of personal protection measures. Finally, the OHS would be responsible for the training and supervision of first-aid personnel. **Treatment** would cover the medical treatment by OHS staff of minor illnesses and accidents. **Monitoring** would encompass the monitoring and support of sick employees and pregnant workers; the recording of accidents, sickness and absence; compliance with the organisation's notification duties under the 1995 RIDDOR Regulations; and monitoring of work-related stress. **Health promotion**

could include the provision of counselling and treatment (e.g. in relation to stress, harassment, drug and alcohol abuse), guidance for an employer on redesigning the work environment, general feedback to improve work practices, referral to specialists for treatment and professional advice and the promotion of health education programmes.

12.5.5 Employee assistance programmes and counselling

These programmes are an important aspect of the promotion of employee welfare. The term originates from the USA. It implies a consistent and co-ordinated approach to dealing with problems experienced by employees:

> The role of EAPs has broadened over the years. Some now offer advice on how companies can change their work practices to alleviate stress, while others provide information services to help people solve their problems involving, for example, childcare or state benefits. They may have started by caring for the casualties of stress, but now they are used to help organisations prevent such instances from occurring in the first place (Midgley, 1997: 39).

The EAP may be resourced by professionally qualified specialists employed by the company (as well as specially trained employees). They may also rely on the use of appropriately qualified external consultants. Some companies in the UK have established such programmes. In other instances there may use ad hoc counselling.

Many work-related and non-work factors can, and do, have an impact upon an employee's attendance at work and their performance whilst there. These factors cover, for example, personal traumas like death within the immediate family; divorce; the diagnosis of a serious, possibly incurable, illness; harassment at work or within the family; or having to deal with a traumatic situation in the course of employment. The consequences, in terms of employee behaviour, can, for example, be evidence of post-traumatic stress, other stress symptoms, a too heavy reliance on alcohol or drug abuse.

Given the duties in law placed upon an employer, counselling and assistance is essential. This can be illustrated by looking at three issues: drug and alcohol abuse, AIDS and HIV status and the response to stress at work.

Drug, alcohol and other substance abuse

This can be a significant problem for employers. For example, 28 per cent of men in employment and 11 per cent of women drink more than the medically recommended 'sensible' limits of 21 units of alcohol (for men) and 14 units (for women) (Goddard, 1991). More specifically, one study of an engineering firm discovered that almost 21 per cent of accidents were alcohol related (Beaumont and Allsop, 1983). It has been estimated that problem drinkers take up to four times as many days off work as other workers, resulting in a total of some 8–14 million days excess absence per year across the workforce as a whole. The cost to industry of this absence, it has been calculated, is likely to exceed £700 million annually (Joeman, 1991: 669).

ACAS, in guidance on drug and alcohol abuse, states that 'consideration should be given to introducing measures to help workers, regardless of status or seniority, who are suffering from alcohol or drug abuse, or from stress. The aim should be to identify workers affected and encourage them to seek help and treatment. Employers should consider whether it is appropriate to treat the problem as a medical rather than a disciplinary matter' (2001: 43). This implies a twin-track approach: counselling within a disciplinary framework. But, obviously, disciplinary action alone might be the right course of action.

The legal obligations that will influence the course of action to be taken are as follows:

- the employer's duty to ensure the health, safety and welfare of all employees (HASAWA 1974, s 2(1));
- the contractual duty of care to an employee;
- the statutory duty upon an employee to take reasonable care (HASAWA, s 7);
- a possible contractual term permitting an employer to test and search an employee;
- the duty owed by an employer to other employees who may be exposed to risk as a consequence of an employee under the influence of drink or drugs (HASAWA, s 3(1));
- the duty owed by an employer, to third parties (customers, suppliers or the general public);
- a specific statutory duty (e.g. the Transport and Works Act 1992 covering railway workers, whereby it is a criminal offence for an employee to be unfit through drink or drugs – as is the employer if they do not exercise 'all due diligence' to prevent an offence being committed);
- the possibility of a criminal offence being committed by an employer or manager who knowingly permits a person to supply or use a controlled drug on work premises (Misuse of Drugs Act 1971, s 8);
- the legal framework on fair and unfair dismissal (the relevant issues are discussed in Chapter 9).

An employer, therefore, has obligations to meet but also opportunities (and duties) to take appropriate action to deal with these matters. The roles of disciplinary action and counselling were reviewed in one survey by Industrial Relations Services (Employment Trends, issues s 17–19, 1992). This showed that employers' formal policies on alcohol usually interlocked with disciplinary procedures. Different circumstances involving alcohol would be treated as follows. One-off incidents of drunkenness, perhaps involving bad behaviour, would be regarded as (gross) misconduct and be dealt with as a disciplinary matter by means of a warning or even dismissal. Drinking that resulted in deteriorating work performance and/or inappropriate behaviour are more likely to be handled by counselling or referral for medical treatment. However, problem drinkers who do not respond to counselling and treatment, or refuse it, may be subject to disciplinary action. Similar actions could also be adopted in relation to employees who are drug users. (The CIPD in 1996 published a guide, *Substance Abuse at Work*.)

AIDS and HIV status

These issues have become employment matters since the first reported cases of AIDS in 1981. Clearly, there can be counselling and support for an individual employee who is diagnosed as HIV positive or who has AIDS. There are issues about continued employment until this may have to be terminated on medical grounds. Furthermore, there may be related matters concerning the behaviour of fellow workers (particularly if harassment is involved). The employer may also need to consider what educational steps are appropriate to overcome ill-informed opinions, as well as what training is needed in procedures and precautions to protect specific staff (e.g. healthcare staff and first-aiders). Behaviour towards staff with AIDS and HIV-positive status is governed by the duties imposed under health and safety law and also the obligations in the contract of employment. Furthermore, under the Disability Discrimination Act 1995 (*see* Chapter 6), such progressive conditions (which will result in serious disability) are treated as a disability, although not in an advanced state as to impair normal day-to-day activities (DDA, Sch 1, para 8).

Stress at work

The reported extent of stress is considerable. The TUC in a survey of safety representatives reported that 66 per cent found stress to be the principal concern across almost all industrial sectors. Heavy workloads were cited by 74 per cent of those surveyed as the main cause of stress; and 53 per cent mentioned cuts in staff (TUC, 2000). A 1994 survey of managers by Ashridge Management Centre found that 77 per cent of the 400 managers surveyed said that work was a source of stress; 63 per cent said that it conflicted with their personal life; almost 50 per cent said that they had fears about job insecurity and career opportunities.

In discussing the legal framework earlier, we looked at the rather imperfect way in which allegations of severe workplace stress might result in both action against an employer and a successful claim for damages. The use of employee assistance programmes and counselling might go some way towards helping the employee manage stress and remain in productive employment. It may also prevent the occurrence of a breach of contract claim for negligence, or it may provide an employer with some defence that he did attempt to ensure the health and welfare of the employee and meet the duty of care.

It might also be that the sources of an employee's stress are of general application to other employees too. If this is so, it suggests that counselling alone may not be sufficient. An employer could reasonably be expected to take more fundamental action in the context of the general duty to ensure the health, safety and welfare of all employees (HASAWA, s 2). This can be seen in the context of those work factors that have been associated with psychological stress:

- the nature of the job (e.g. workload, travel, general working conditions, whether potentially stressful situations might be an expected part of the job, the degree of control a person has over the carrying out of tasks);
- a person's role within the organisation (and whether there is role conflict or ambiguity);

- the quality of working relationships (including with fellow workers and power relationships with managers);

- career issues (job insecurity, whether a person is underpromoted or overpromoted);

- the structure, climate and culture of the organisation (whether or not this facilitates mutual respect; whether or not the employer has reasonable expectations of employees).

Clearly, the action needed to deal with these sources of stress can be focused on the individual employee and, as appropriate, organisationally and operationally focused. Job design, organisational structure and culture, workloads, the scheduling of working time, the management of change, the management of redundancies, etc. are among the key areas that can have some impact on stress. In addition, it is important to recognise that circumstances that are stressful to one person may not be so for another.

There are, nevertheless, certain characteristics of jobs that, by their nature, require employees to deal with potentially very stressful situations. This is particularly true of the emergency and healthcare services. In these services, an employer's duty of care is to train and support (through counselling and advice) employees to handle stressful situations – even to the extent of dealing with post-traumatic stress.

Violence at work

The Health and Safety Executive's definition of work-related violence is 'any incident in which a person is abused, threatened or assaulted in circumstances relating to their work'. Verbal abuse and threats are the most common. Physical attacks are comparatively rare. According to the British Crime Survey (BCS), there are 1.3 million incidents of work-related violence (Home Office, 2001). Around 50 000 assaults resulted in the victim seeing a doctor. Around 5000 incidents resulted in broken bones. The majority of victims were upset by their experience, suffering a range of symptoms such as anger, fear and sleeping difficulties.

The occupations at highest risk are public transport workers, nurses and teachers. Other vulnerable workers are social workers, probation officers, the police, bar staff and security guards. BCS research suggests, however, that the estimated risk of a worker being assaulted is relatively low. In 1999, 2.5 per cent of working adults had been the victim of at least one incident at work; 1.2 per cent had been physically assaulted by a member of the public while they were working; and 1.4 per cent had been threatened. Nevertheless, 17 per cent of workers who had some form of contact with members of the public in their work were very or fairly worried about being threatened.

For employers, the consequences of violence against their staff can be: poor morale, high absenteeism, recruitment and staff turnover problems and poor corporate image. The BSC estimates that 3.3 million work hours were lost because of violence at work in 1997. In terms of economic cost, it is calculated, by the BCS, that the direct cost of work-related violence to society (in England and Wales) is £62 million per year. This takes account of medical costs and time taken off work. If account is taken also of compensation to victims, then, the figure could rise to £230 million.

Obviously, under health and safety legislation and the common law of contract employers have duties towards their staff. The issue for employers is: what to do to minimise the risk of violence to staff? The Health and Safety Commission initiated a three-year programme in March 2000 to tackle violence. This set a target of reducing the level of work-related violence by 10 per cent by 2003. The HSC suggests a four-stage process for the 'effective management of violence'. The first stage is diagnostic – finding out whether or not a problem exists. This involves a risk assessment. Part of this process is consultation with the staff, supervisors and managers concerned to ascertain their perception of likely risk. Another aspect is the keeping of records of incidents.

The second stage involves deciding on the action to be taken; and then, as a third stage, implementing it. This can involve some appropriate restructuring of the work environment and the design of the job. For example, the use of screens between customers and staff may exacerbate tension and aggressive behaviour. Action can also involve provision of training and information to staff and managers. Research evidence shows that only 18 per cent of workers say that they have received formal training in their current job about how to deal with violent or threatening behaviour. Seventy-two per cent had received neither formal training nor informal advice. Even amongst high-risk groups the level of training provision did not exceed 50 per cent – with the exception of security and protective services where 71 per cent received training.

The fourth stage is checking and monitoring action taken. This, of course, should be linked to established safety checking mechanisms and the work of safety representatives and safety committees.

Case study 12.1 The VDU operators: a safety grievance

The following case study encourages you to draw upon material in the Regulations that have been outlined earlier – particularly the Management of Health and Safety at Work Regulations 1999 and the Health and Safety (Display Screen Equipment) Regulations 1992. Also, you will need to consider the 1977 and the 1996 regulations on safety representation and consultation. The primary issue is how the employer can ensure compliance and how standards can be monitored.

Helen McDonald is one of eight VDU operators who work in the Central Administrative Services Department at the head office of a food processing company, based in Leeds. She has worked there for six months in the department's open-plan office. She spends 75–95 per cent of her working time on the VDU.

She has complained, on four occasions, to her supervisor about headaches arising from her work. The supervisor has been generally unsympathetic. Helen has just returned from two days' self-certified sick absence as a result of a severe migraine attack.

At lunchtime on her first day back she is chatting to Wendy Saunders. She is a safety committee representative at head office. (Although the company is non-union, Wendy is one of a group of clerical and administrative staff who are trying to obtain recognition from the company for the APEX Partnership, the white-collar section of the GMB Union.)

Helen tells Wendy that she is very unhappy about the working conditions for VDU operators. She mentions her headaches and the pains that some other staff get. She feels that management should do something about it.

| Exercise 12.2 | **The VDU operators: a safety grievance** |

This exercise is in two phases for syndicate groups.

1 Carry out a diagnostic task by listing the issues that you think arise under the following categories:
   - operational issues for the company;
   - job design;
   - health and safety requirements;
   - employee relations.

2 Students are allocated to one of two syndicates: 'an employer group' and 'an employee group'. Consider the following questions:
   - What are your objectives in resolving the grievance in terms of health and safety standards, and in terms of employee relations?
   - What would be your preferred outcome for resolving the grievance?
   - What constraints might exist to limit your achievement of this preferred outcome?

Feedback on this exercise is provided in the Appendix to this book.

12.6   Conclusion

The pervasiveness of health and safety issues throughout the employment relationship is clear from the text of this chapter. It is a continually evolving area. New hazards arise. For example, repetitive strain injury has become a more widespread hazard because of technological change, the adverse effects of passive smoking have become workplace issues for employers to tackle and violence by customers against workers (whether transport staff, police officers, hospital staff or social workers) has been more clearly established as a responsibility of employers.

In addition, the health and safety implications of existing working practices and arrangements are increasingly being seen as more significant. So, for example, the scheduling and amount of working time are ruled to be health and safety matters (*see* Chapter 11). Certainly, the contribution of the EU in driving health and safety standards has more clearly demonstrated connections with a wide range of work-related issues. Two extracts from the general obligations on employers (in the 1989 Directive on the safety and health of workers) illustrate the sweep of this.

Elaborating the 'general principles of prevention', the Directive sets out the importance of 'adapting the work to the individual, especially as regards the design of workplaces, the choice of work equipment and the choice of working and production methods, with a view, in particular, to alleviating monotonous work and work at a predetermined work-rate and to reducing their effect on health' (Art 6.2d). In respect of technical change, the Directive obliges employers to 'ensure that the planning and introduction of new technologies are the subject of consultation with the workers and/or their representatives as regards the consequences of the choice of equipment, the working conditions and the working environment for the safety and health of workers' (Art 6.3c).

Further reading

Health and Safety Commission, *Annual Reports*.

Health and Safety Executive website for specific guidance on workplace hazards and safety procedures: www.hse.gov.uk.

References

Advisory Conciliation and Arbitration Service (2000) *Code of Practice: Disciplinary and Grievance Procedures*. London: ACAS.

Advisory Conciliation and Arbitration Service (2001) *Discipline and Grievances at Work: the Advisory Handbook*. London: ACAS.

Beaumont, P. and Allsop, S. (1983) 'Beverage Report', *Occupational Safety and Work*, 13(10).

Chartered Institute of Personnel and Development (1996a) *Occupational Health and Organisational Effectiveness*. CIPD Key Facts. September. London: CIPD.

Chartered Institute of Personnel and Development (1996b) *Substance Abuse at Work*. London: CIPD.

Cox, T. (1993) 'Stress research and stress management: putting theory to work', Contract Research Report 61. HSE.

Cully, M. *et al.* (1999) *Britain at Work*. London: Routledge.

Goddard, E. (1991) *Drinking in England and Wales in the Late 1980s*. OPCS (Social Survey Division). London: Stationery Office.

Health and Safety Commission (2001) *Health and Safety Statistics 2000/01*. London: HSC.

Health and Safety Executive (1993) *The Costs of Accidents at Work*. London: HMSO.

Health and Safety Executive (2002) *Work-related Stress*. London: HSE.

The Home Office (2001) *Violence at Work: new findings from the 2000 British Crime Survey*. London: Home Office and HSE.

James, P. (1993) *The European Community: a positive force for UK health and safety law?* London: Institute of Employment Rights.

Joeman, L. (1991) 'Alcohol at Work: the Cost to Employers', *Employment Gazette*, December, 669.

Midgley, S. (1997) 'Pressure', *People Management*, July, 39.

Reilly, B., Paci, P. and Holl, P. (1995) 'Unions, Safety Committees and Workplace Injuries', *British Journal of Industrial Relations*, 33.

Robens, Committee of Inquiry, The (1972) *Report of the Committee on Safety and Health at Work*. London: HMSO.

Smith, I. and Thomas, G. (2000) *Smith and Wood's Industrial Law*. London: Butterworths.

Trades Union Congress (2000) *Focus on Health and Safety*. London: TUC.

Walters, D. and James, P. (1998) *Robens Revisited: the Case for a Review of Occupational Health and Safety Legislation*. London: Institute of Employment Rights.

CHAPTER 13

Work-life balance, parental and dependency rights

Learning objectives

Having read this chapter you should:

- Understand the increasing significance of family and dependency responsibilities for working people.
- Understand the steps that employers might take voluntarily to assist employees reconcile the demands of work and family life.
- Understand the legal obligations placed upon employers.

13.1 Structure of the chapter

This chapter comprises the following sections:

- *Introduction*: The range of dependency responsibilities.
- *The context*: Labour market and social trends, work-life balance and political initiatives.
- *The legal framework*: Pregnancy and maternity; maternity leave entitlements; the status of the contract of employment; returning to work; requesting flexible working; parental, paternity, adoption and dependency leave; detrimental treatment and unfair dismissal; statutory pay.
- *Employment policies and practices*: Workplace culture; facilitating work-life balance; leave entitlements; flexible working time; place of work; facilities; and communication and consultation about work-life balance.

13.2 Introduction

This chapter considers employment protection in a number of different situations: pregnancy, parenting and dependency. Statutory rights in this area have been fragmented and partial but are developing. Gaps in statutory protections are sometimes compensated for by contractual rights granted by certain employers. There are five related driving forces for developing entitlements in these areas:

- The implementation of the principle of equal treatment under European law.
- The acknowledgement under sex discrimination law of the special situation of pregnant workers.
- The growing feminisation of the labour market.
- Concern among male workers with dependency needs about their ability to utilise statutory rights.
- The promotion by the EU and, particularly, by the British government of the concept of 'work-life balance' for people with parental responsibilities.

13.3 The context

Parental and dependency arrangements are developing against the background of change in the following areas: the labour market, social attitudes and trends and political initiatives.

13.3.1 Labour market and social trends

Type of household and family

Within the past 30 years there has been a significant shift in the type of household and family in which people have lived. By contrasting official government statistics for 1961 and 1992 (*Social Trends* 24), clear trends are revealed in particular households. For example, there are increasing numbers of the following:

- people living alone;
- married couples with no children; and
- lone parents with dependent children.

The proportion of people aged 75 years and over has almost doubled since 1971 – from 4 per cent of households to 7 per cent (2000). In addition, over the past 30 years, household size has declined from an average of 2.91 persons (1971) to 2.48 (1991) and to 2.30 (2000) (ONS, 2001).

Overlaid on to this social trend are the three interrelated labour market trends: feminisation, the expansion of flexible employment status and the greater propensity for women with dependent children to work (*see* Chapter 3).

Family diversity

A profile of households is provided periodically by the General Household Survey. The 2000 data are summarised in Table 13.1.

Table 13.1 Households in Great Britain 2000

Types of household	Percentage
Married couple with dependent children	18
Married couple with no children or non-dependent children	30
Cohabiting couple with dependent children	3
Cohabiting couple with no children or non-dependent children	5
Lone parent with dependent children	7
Lone parent with non-dependent children only	2
One person only	32
Other	3
Total	**100**

Source: Office for National Statistics, 2001.

It is now more accurate to see the 'nuclear family' (of mother, father and children) as one of a number of arrangements in society. In practice, there is great diversity. This reflects changing social attitudes to cohabitation, marriage, divorce and second marriages; greater social mobility of young people; different religious values and practices; and different ethnic and cultural patterns. So, it is questionable whether there is such a universal social phenomenon as a 'typical' family.

A number of characteristics of families can be considered in more detail – particularly, family size and family structure. Official statistics show considerable differences in **family size** between ethnic groups. When measured in terms of size of household, the average figures are: white 2.5 persons, African-Caribbean 2.6 persons; Indian 3.8 persons, and Pakistani/Bangladeshi 4.8. These averages, of course, conceal some significant variations. For example, only 2 per cent of white families have six or more persons, in contrast to 41 per cent of Pakistani/Bangladeshi families.

To some extent differences in family size can be a consequence of a greater number of children, or the presence of more adults than would be found in 'white' households. So, some of the variations may be a consequence of social, religious or cultural obligations to elderly parents and other relatives. Other explanations can be found in the relatively youthful age profile of certain ethnic groups.

Sociologists have logged the changes that have taken place in **British family structure** over the past two centuries or more. Young and Willmott (1973) identify three phases of change. They accept that although the boundaries between the stages are 'somewhat arbitrary, the rough and ready division seems to us useful'. In the first stage, the pre-industrial, 'the family was usually the unit of production. For the most part, men, women and children worked together in home and field'. The second stage was that of 'disruption' by the new economic order that arose with the Industrial Revolution as people became wage-earners. In the third stage, which began during the twentieth century, 'the unity of the family has been restored around its functions as the unit not of production but of consumption'.

This present-day 'third-stage' family is said to have three main characteristics. The first is that 'the couple and their children are very much centred on the home, especially when the children are young. They can be so much together, and share so much together because they spend so much time together in the same space. Life has . . . become "privatised".' The second characteristic is that 'the extended family (consisting of relatives of several different degrees to some extent sharing a common life) counts for less and the immediate, or nuclear, family for more'. Finally, 'the most vital characteristic' is that 'the roles of the sexes have become less segregated' (Young and Willmott, 1973).

However, these characteristics of the contemporary British family have, as we have seen, been subject to the impact of a number of important social and employment-related changes. First, time spent at home (as discussed below) can be limited in the context of heavy work demands. Secondly, patterns of immigration in the post-war years have introduced different family characteristics. Finally, there has been a growth in one-parent families.

Most South Asian family systems have traditionally seen the interests of individual parents and children as subordinate to those of the wider group of kin. This wider group can be important in respect to economic and property matters and also marriage and domestic matters. Migrants to a new society may attempt to maintain such structures when confronted by an uncertain and hostile environment. However, the feasibility of maintaining these in the long term might be difficult because of various external pressures. Examples of these include immigration controls separating family members, the influence of cultural patterns in the host society, particularly on second-generation family members, and the small size and isolation of housing units.

The structure of African-Caribbean 'family units' differs from both the indigenous British model and the South Asian model. In terms of size, African-Caribbean 'family units' are similar to British ones, but among those with dependent children, 23 per cent consist of female lone parents with children. This contrasts with 6 per cent of white families, and 7 per cent of Indian and Pakistani/Bangladeshi families (Labour Force Surveys 1988–90).

It is, obviously, dangerous to sketch broad trends without some qualification. The principal qualification that perhaps should be made is that the white, Asian and African-Caribbean models that have been outlined will be cross-cut (within the ethnic groups concerned) by different religious values, different attitudes to cultural practices (e.g. arranged marriages), different perspectives on divorce, cohabitation and single parenting, differences in the availability of support networks to help with caring and different views on women's social roles as carers, as participants in the labour market and as employees with career prospects.

13.3.2 Work-life balance

Considerable tension can exist between the demands of employment and an employee's dependency responsibilities. This has prompted some discussion of the issue of *work-life balance*. 'Demographic changes, a more diverse workforce, business imperatives and government policy have all been driving work-life balance up the agenda' (Kodz *et al.*, 2002). This issue is the focus of 'an important public policy debate in Britain' which has grown in 'a remarkably brief period of time' (Taylor, 2002b: 6).

In this section we will look at the findings of various research projects and attempt, in conclusion, to define the concept of 'work-life balance'. The principal issues are:

- workplace culture;
- characteristics of the work context;
- employees' expectations about work;
- the caring demands confronting employees;
- expectations of employers and work colleagues;
- managing patterns of work;
- business benefits and disadvantages;
- defining 'work-life balance';
- achieving work-life balance.

Workplace culture

The *Baseline Study, Work-Life Balance 2000* (Hogarth *et al.*, 2001) found that, overall (in a survey of 2500 workplaces and 7500 people in employment) around 62 per cent of employers and 80 per cent of employees agreed with the statement that: 'everyone should be able to balance their work and home lives in the way they want'. This optimistic starting point was, inevitably, qualified. Employers almost always held to the view that 'the employer's first responsibility has to be to ensure that the organisation meets its goals'. Forty-three per cent of employers thought that work-life balance policies and practices were unfair to some staff; and 26 per cent of employees thought they were unfair to people like them. Developing this issue, the survey found that employers who had adopted work-life balance practices were more likely to have positive attitudes to the concept. These employers were also just as likely to agree that an employer's first responsibility was to ensure the achievement of organisational goals. They did not seem to regard achieving business goals and work-life balance as contradictory aims.

In one case-study-based survey of companies which were promoting work-life balance, some of the tensions between business operational demands and work-life balance became apparent. The cultures of 'working hard' and of 'constant availability, instant response' were 'ubiquitous' (Kodz *et al.*, 2002). Where there are entrenched traditions of 'presenteeism' and working long hours, then, staff with dependency needs found it difficult to take appropriate time off. It is clear that attitudes of managers and colleagues created adverse pressure, which was reinforced by the perceived impact on career prospects. These cultural pressures were also found in other research data drawing on the experience of employees in a social services department and an NHS Trust who, outside work, were informal carers of adults (Phillips *et al.*, 2002). Here, it was found that the 'long hours' culture combined with a belief that people need to be 'seen to be coping' helped create a climate which inhibited carers from asking for help. (Some of these issues are elaborated in the following subsection.)

Another report (Reeves, 2002), drawing on research from the Equal Opportunities Commission, highlighted a further aspect of workplace culture. It is still being defined by what are described as 'dinosaur dads' – an earlier generation of corporate men who were supported by stay-at-home wives. 'A new and important divide in the workplace is the one between fathers in their fifties and those in their thirties. Most of the former group have wives who stayed at home to raise their kids, at least in the pre-school years. Most of the latter group have wives or partners who work.'

Characteristics of the work context

Specific characteristics of the work context were elaborated in a research project funded by the Economic and Social Research Council (ESRC), the *Future of Work* programme. This reported that 'the most dramatic decline in job satisfaction during the 1990s occurred because of the hours people are now required to work and the amount of work that they must accomplish' (Taylor, 2002a: 10). In 1992, 35 per cent of men and 51 per cent of women were reported as stating that they were completely or very satisfied with the number of hours they worked. By 2000, these figures had fallen to 20 per cent and 29 per cent respectively. Secondly, the research looked at the management by working people of the competing demands facing them. 'As many as 27 per cent of employees surveyed in 2000 said they found they had less time available to carry out their family responsibilities than they would have liked. This compares with 21 per cent who thought so eight years earlier' (Taylor, 2002b: 11).

Employees' expectations about work

Work-life balance is influenced by the *expectations* that working people have about work. Theoretically, these may be distinguished as *psychological* (*see* Chapter 2 on the psychological contract); and *material* (i.e. concerning pay and benefits). Seventy per cent of men and 50 per cent of women said that the main reason they worked was to 'earn money for necessities' (as reported in Taylor, 2002b: 12). While general data are interesting and useful, it is important to remember the significance of the individual basis of work-life balance. Each individual brings to the employment relationship differing expectations and financial needs. These depend, for example, on age, lifestyle, number of dependants, housing requirements, commitment to their work, career expectations. 'The principle at stake here is that work should be healthy and should leave time and energy to pursue interests outside work' (Kodz *et al.*, 2002).

The caring demands confronting employees

These demands are seen primarily as falling upon women workers who have dependent children. Women workers are often characterised as working a 'double shift' (employment and domestic/dependency responsibilities). Generally, this is true. However, it is important to recognise two other related developments reported in research findings: the pressures of reconciling work and caring can also be experienced by men; and caring for elderly people is a growing phenomenon. Furthermore, as commented by Reeves (2002), 'to achieve gender equality we have to recognise that equality at work and equality at home are inescapably intertwined . . . Until there is a redistribution of unpaid work towards men, women will never be able to achieve full parity in the labour market.'

Men as carers

In one survey of (mostly male) managers it was found that eight out of ten felt that they had sacrificed something important at home for the sake of their career.

A quarter said that they missed their children growing up, and a similar number regretted putting work before family. Asked which one thing they would change to improve the balance between work and non-work life, 23 per cent said working fewer hours, 18 per cent said changing company culture, and 12 per cent said working flexible working hours (*Management Today*, June 1998).

In a recent survey (Reeves, 2002), the employment consequences for men of dependency was explored. It was pointed out that 59 per cent of mothers with pre-school children who are either married or cohabiting are also in employment. As a consequence there is more evidence of men taking some responsibility for childcare and for domestic tasks. But, fathers are nervous of taking paternity leave or asking for time off or for flexible working to help them manage their childcare responsibilities. There is a fear of appearing uncommitted or less masculine in front of colleagues.

Caring for dependent elderly adults

Phillips, quoting the Department of Health notes that 2.7 million people combine work with informal care for another adult. It has been commented in one research project (Phillips *et al.*, 2002) that, 'as the population ages and the pool of people who have traditionally provided care is shrinking and changing, there is an urgent need for employers to understand what actually works for carers if they are to adequately address their recruitment and retention problems and have sustainable workforces'. This research (carried out in a social services department and an NHS Trust) found that informal carers were most commonly caring for mothers, followed by mothers-in-law or fathers. Two out of five said that they were the primary carer. Two out of three spent under ten hours a week helping the recipient of care – mostly by shopping and transport, giving emotional support and checking on the person. Few carers provided very 'heavy' personal or physical care.

Expectations of employers and work colleagues

In one research project of good practice employers, despite efforts by the organisations to promote work-life balance (Kodz *et al.*, 2002), the take-up rate was 'relatively low'. A number of factors deterred employees. The main concern was the perceived impact on their career prospects. Other factors were unsupportive attitudes of senior managers, line managers and colleagues; lack of knowledge of what was available; the expectation that the individual should identify solutions for themselves; and the likelihood of reduced earnings. The responses of work colleagues could be negative. Particularly, colleagues could feel that they were 'left at work to carry the can' and were subject to pressure to stay at work and deliver targets.

In a separate research project (concerning those caring for elderly people) (Phillips *et al.*, 2002), it was reported that working carers tended to take steps that did not identify them publicly as in need of help – e.g. taking annual leave if time off was needed. This was despite the existence of dependency leave policies in the organisations in question (a social services department and an NHS Trust). These carers were highly committed to their jobs but inflexible work schedules and the pressures of the job made juggling the competing responsibilities difficult.

Managing patterns of work

The *Baseline Study* (Hogarth *et al.*, 2001) found that there was 'substantial demand' for flexible working-time arrangements from employees. More men wanted flexitime, compressed hours and annualised hours than women. Women were more likely than men to want term-time working or reduced hours. Where employed full-time before maternity leave, the majority of women on their return to work switched to part-time work.

Research (Kodz *et al.*, 2002) in six organisations which were promoting work-life balance policies found that employees were interested in flexibility and/or reduced hours. The largest proportion wanted more flexibility. The demand came not just from those with caring responsibilities but also from other sub-groups (e.g. those with long journeys to work, those who regularly work long hours and older employees). Participants in the survey were 'unanimous' in the view that all employees and not just those with children or other caring responsibilities should have access to work-life balance policies.

Kodz *et al.* (2002) suggest that individual workers and managers often need support on how to adapt successfully to a different pattern of work and how to deal with unexpected problems. Managers, the researchers say, need to learn how to manage teams working a range of working patterns and how to ensure that workloads are suitable and deadlines are met.

Business benefits and disadvantages

The *Baseline Study* (Hogarth *et al.*, 2001) reported 'a consensus' amongst employers that work-life balance practices improved certain aspects of work. In particular, reference was made to the quality of work relations and staff motivation and commitment – mentioned by 72 per cent of workplaces. In a survey of organisations promoting work-life balance (Kodz *et al.*, 2002), it was reported that human resource practitioners 'were generally convinced of the business benefits of their approach'. In coming to this view, they used indices such as improved employee morale, commitment and performance; and reduced casual absence and staff turnover. Against this, the *Baseline Survey* (Hogarth *et al.*, 2001) found that 51 per cent of workplaces reported that work-life balance practices had increased managerial workloads.

Overall, the *Baseline Survey* (Hogarth *et al.*, 2001) found the main advantage of such policies and practices was having happier staff – mentioned by 43 per cent. The main disadvantage (referred to by 10 per cent of employers) was staff shortages. Reeves (2002) commented that research showed that fathers who were hands-on at home were happier at work. Involved fathers were also more likely to have the 'emotional intelligence' considered essential for modern management.

Defining work-life balance

Despite the high profile of work-life balance, it is still a concept which is 'ill-defined' (Felstead and Jewson *et al.*, 2002: 54). In part this is because the notion of 'work-life balance' was born out of 'family-friendly policies'. Consequently, 'the gender dimension' (Taylor, 2002b: 6) was exclusively concentrated upon. The principal concern was how working parents and, in particular, mothers were able to reconcile paid employment and childcare. However, 'work-life balance' extends the concerns to encompass also dealing with family emergencies and the care of elderly and other dependent relatives. But even with this extension, the concept remains narrow. So, two important qualifications need to be made. First, work-life balance is not just a gender issue, it is a policy issue for all employees. Secondly, it is not just about caring for dependent children. It is an issue for all employees. It acknowledges that 'in reality life and work over-lap and interact' (Taylor, 2002b: 6). It accepts that the experience of work for different working people varies; and that the expectations that working people bring to employment also differ (*see* Fig. 13.1).

'Work-life balance'
A concept that seeks to facilitate a balance for each individual worker between the requirements of the employer, the individual's own expectations about work (both psychological and material), and the individual's concern to fulfil their requirements and expectations in non-work life. It can be facilitated by a variety of employment policies and practices about how, when and where work is performed. These may be required in law or may be initiated voluntarily by the employer.

Figure 13.1 Defining 'work-life balance'

Achieving work-life balance

As suggested in the above discussion, 'work-life balance' can be achieved through a compendium of policies and practices (concerned with leave entitlements, flexibility of working term and flexible policies on the location of work). However, these measures must be seen in the context of a necessary cultural shift within organisations. (The employment policy implications are discussed in section 13.5.) At political level, various proposals have been widely advocated as steps to ease the tension. Policy initiatives are discussed in the next section.

13.3.3 Political initiatives

The government has, in the White Paper, 'Fairness at Work' (DTI, 1998), in its consultation document *Supporting Families* (Home Office, 1998) and in its National Childcare Strategy, signalled commitment to 'family-friendly policies'. It is clear that the government is attempting to promote a cultural change as far as family-friendly employment policies are concerned. Many of the measures are connected to its general advocacy of the work ethic and the elimination of a dependency culture where certain categories of people become unduly reliant on social security benefits.

The White Paper stated that:

> many successful modern companies, both large and small, have . . . adopted a culture and practices in support of the family. To the mutual benefit of the employee and the business, they allow flexibility over hours and working from home allowing parents to spend more time with their children. They provide time off for family crises. Some provide childcare facilities or fund employees' use of nurseries. They know how important it is to retain staff in whom they have invested and

on whom they depend. The Government wishes to support and reinforce such a family-friendly culture in business. In future it will become increasingly important to enable employees to balance satisfactorily family responsibilities and work, and children to benefit from parental care (para 5.3).

These themes are elaborated in *Supporting Families*, where the benefits of family-friendly policies are outlined as follows:

- **Benefits for carers**: Such policies extend 'choice for both mothers and fathers by giving them the chance to spend more time at home as well as supporting their children financially'. They also 'allow carers of sick, disabled or elderly relatives to combine their highly valued social role with involvement in the labour market'.
- **Benefits for children**: 'Working parents can give their children a higher standard of living and provide role models for adult employment.'
- **Benefits for business**: 'Businesses with family-friendly employment policies can benefit through easier and cheaper recruitment, reduced sick leave and absenteeism and enhanced employee loyalty with improved retention rates.'
- **Benefits for the economy**: Such policies 'can help boost the economy':
  - by increasing the number of people, including skilled people, in the labour market, and increasing the numbers returning to education and training;
  - by enhancing financial independence especially in women, both immediately, as they benefit from a higher standard of living and after retirement as a result of building up a better pension entitlement;
  - by increasing the sustainable level of employment and improving productivity leading to an increase in overall living standards.
- **Benefits for society**: 'Family-friendly employment policies may bring wider social benefits through more stable families; fewer broken relationships between parents; children who are better supported in their education; reduced delinquent behaviour and criminality among young people; and a better quality of life for sick and disabled relatives' (para 3.19).

The policy measures outlined by the government included a National Childcare Strategy designed to encourage businesses to provide access to good quality childcare and develop policies of flexible working; encouraging working from home by raising its status; the Working Families Tax Credit to give financial support to working families; implementation of the Parental Leave Directive 1996; enhanced maternity leave and an extended right to maternity pay.

In addition, the government drew attention to the interlocking objectives of two other sets of measures: the Working Time Regulations 1998 designed to tackle excessive working time and the 'long hours culture'; and the National Minimum Wage Act 1998 which 'will help support working families'. Furthermore, it anticipated that the implementation of the Part-Time Work Directive 1996 would 'remove discrimination against part-time workers and increase access to part-time work'. The government added that 'this will mean better quality part-time jobs and more choice, which will help parents, women and men, to combine work with family life' (*Fairness at Work*, para 5.5).

This 'parent-focused' approach of earlier government policy and legislative initiatives has, to some extent, now been encompassed under a broader policy umbrella which includes a wider range of working people. In Spring 2000, the government launched its Work-Life Balance Campaign. This aimed to raise employers' awareness of the business benefits of introducing policies and practices which help working people achieve a better balance between work and the rest of their lives.

There is, nevertheless, still considerable government focus on the implications of work for childcare and dependency. A Work and Parents Taskforce (comprising employers of varying sizes, family interest groups and trade unionists), set up in 2001, reported late that year. The government broadly welcomed its report as recommending 'a cautious compromise which goes with the grain of good practice':

> We believe the taskforce has carried out a piece of work that will be regarded as historic in bringing about a transformation in the culture of the workplace. A culture in which it becomes accepted in all sectors and at all levels that it is normal for both men and women to work flexibly at some stages in their lives. A culture in which handling requests for flexible work becomes an essential business tool for success (government response to the recommendations from the Work and Parents Taskforce, November 2001).

A consequence of these reports and discussions has been the enactment of various measures:

- enhancements to maternity leave and statutory maternity pay;
- the introduction of paternity leave and statutory paternity pay;
- enhancements to adoptive leave and the introduction of statutory adoptive pay;
- enhancements to the entitlement to parental leave;
- a right to request flexible working.

These are outlined more fully in section 13.4. Whether the measures will form the basis of a credible 'work-life balance' approach or remain a loose set of statutory rights remains to be seen. In January 2003, the Government published a paper setting out its strategy (HM Treasury/DTI 2003).

13.4 The legal framework

Within the legal framework governing parenting, dependency and work-life balance, there are various provisions: those relating to pregnancy, leave entitlements, entitlements to statutory pay, other terms and conditions, the return to work, return to the same or an equivalent position, unfair dismissal and the right to request flexible working. This framework is evolving as a result of case law, UK statute law and European Directives. We will look at each of these areas in turn.

13.4.1 **Pregnancy**

No comparator

It is a fundamental principle of UK law that no person should suffer less favourable treatment of any kind on account of their sex (*see* Chapter 4). While this embraces a woman's rights during pregnancy, the law relating to maternity is based on a more specific notion that a pregnant women is in a special class all of her own. Because of her pregnancy she should have special rights and protection which stem from, but go beyond, the principle of equal treatment for men and women (*Dekker v Stichtung VJV-Centrum* [1990] IRLR 27).

The starting point is the Equal Treatment Directive 1976, which guarantees the right to the same terms and conditions for men and women without discrimination on the grounds of sex (Art 5). The Pregnant Workers Directive goes a step further and protects a woman's employment rights from the beginning of her pregnancy to the end of the period of maternity leave (except in circumstances unrelated to the employee's pregnancy). Both Directives have been transposed into British law. The first is implemented through the Sex Discrimination Act 1975. Provisions of the second Directive are in the Employment Rights Act 1996 (Part VIII). The maternity provisions in the Employment Rights Act are minimum rights which can always be extended by contract. An employee may pick and choose from her contractual and statutory rights and develop a 'composite' package consisting of the most favourable provisions of each.

Discriminatory treatment

Dismissal of a pregnant employee because of pregnancy is direct sex discrimination. Likewise is a refusal to recruit a pregnant applicant. As a defence against an employment tribunal claim, the employer would need to show that the woman's pregancy was not the reason or, if there was more than one reason, the principal reason for her treatment.

Pregnancy and sickness

Dismissal of a pregnant worker for sick absence bearing no relation to pregnancy is not discriminatory provided a man would be subject to the same policy (*Handles-og Kontorfunkionaererernes Forbund i Danmark v Dansk Arbejdsgiverforening* [1991] IRLR 31, ECJ). If the dismissal during the pregnancy was attributable to the pregnancy, then, it would be discriminatory on the ground of sex. In the event of illness arising from pregnancy after the end of the maternity leave period, this would be subject to comparison with a male worker's absence to determine whether or not 'less favourable treatment' had occurred (*Brown v Rentokil Ltd* [1998] IRLR 445, ECJ).

Health and safety issues

The Pregnant Workers Directive also concerns itself with 'the safety and health of pregnant workers and workers who have recently given birth or are breastfeeding'. These provisions are in the Management of Health and Safety at Work

Regulations 1999 (regs 16 and 18). Where a pregnant or breast-feeding woman is exposed to physical, biological or chemical hazards, the employer should try to eliminate the risk. If this cannot be done, the employer must consider altering the working conditions or working hours or offering suitable alternative work. If this is not possible, the woman concerned must be given paid leave for as long as necessary to protect the health and safety of both herself and the child.

13.4.2 Maternity leave entitlements

Antenatal care

A pregnant employee has the right not to be unreasonably refused time off during her working hours to attend a medical appointment (ERA 1996, s 55(1)). Appointments can include those for relaxation and parentcraft classes. She is entitled to be paid for this time at the appropriate hourly rate (ERA 1996, s 56(1)). Except for the first appointment she must, if requested, produce a certificate from a registered medical practitioner, midwife or health visitor confirming any appointment. The employee is protected against dismissal or selection for redundancy if she exercises this right.

Maternity leave

Two complementary forms of maternity leave are provided for in legislation (the Maternity and Parental Leave (Amendment) Regulations 2002) (*see also* Fig. 13.2):

- *Ordinary Maternity Leave (OML)*, the shorter basic entitlement. All female employees, regardless of length of service, are entitled to 26 weeks of maternity leave (ERA 1996, ss 71 and 73).

- *Additional Maternity Leave (AML)*, the longer service-related right. An employee who has been continuously employed for 26 weeks on the fifteenth week before the expected week of childbirth is entitled to an extended period of 26 weeks after the beginning of the week of childbirth. This is dependent on the employee notifying the employer of her intention to return to work (ERA 1996, s 79). This starts when OML ends.

In addition, there is *Compulsory Maternity Leave*. This is a period of not less than two weeks starting at the birth of the child. It falls within OML.

13.4.3 The status of the contract of employment

Ordinary maternity leave

Terms and conditions of employment

The employee is 'entitled to the benefit of the terms and conditions of employment which would have applied if she had not been absent; is bound by any obligations arising under those terms and conditions; is entitled to return from leave to the job in which she was employed before her absence' (ERA 1996, s 71(4)). The phrase 'terms and conditions' includes 'matters connected with an employee's

Week minus 15
- Employee must notify employer of intention to take leave by this week.
- Woman qualifies for statutory maternity pay and also AML if she has 26 weeks' continuous service with her employer.

Week minus 11
- OML may start having given employer notice stating she is pregnant, when the baby is expected and the start date of maternity leave. The start date is determined by the woman. Within 28 days of the notice, the employer must write to the employee setting out the expected return date.
- Notice need not be in writing unless the employer requires it. Employer may require certificate from registered doctor or midwife.
- There are exceptions for premature births when notification should be given as soon as reasonably practicable after the event.

Week zero: expected week of childbirth
Compulsory maternity leave starts and expires after two weeks.

Week plus 15
- OML ends (if it started at week minus 11) and, if the woman is eligible, AML begins.
- If the woman wishes to return from OML prior to this date, she must give at least 28 days' notice of her return to her employer.

Week plus 41
- AML ends (if OML started at week minus 11). However, an employee might additionally take a period of up to four weeks parental leave.
- If a woman wishes to return from AML prior to this date, she must give at least 28 days' notice of her return to her employer.
- An employee who has AML and wishes to return at the end of OML should notify the employer at least 28 days prior to the end of OML.

Figure 13.2 Notice requirements for maternity leave from 6 April 2003

employment whether or not they arise under her contract of employment'. However, it 'does not include terms and conditions about remuneration' (i.e. wages or salary) (ERA 1996, s 71(5)). Pay is replaced by statutory maternity pay (SMP) unless the contract of employment states otherwise – i.e. there is some agreement with the employer for the payment of normal wages.

Benefits

The employee continues to be entitled to benefits in kind (such as private medical or permanent health insurance) whether or not these are contractual. She will continue to accrue both contractual and statutory minimum paid holiday entitlement and other benefits that depend on length of service. Pension rights will continue during paid maternity leave – they are suspended. If, during the employee's absence on maternity leave, the employer anticipates any changes to the contract of employment (favourable or otherwise), then, he should consult her about the changes and allow her to comment on them.

There may be some difficulty in deciding whether a particular benefit constitutes remuneration or a benefit in kind. The determining factor appears to be whether a particular benefit has market value. In *Adcock and Others* v *H. Flude & Co (Hinckley) Ltd*, unreported, 29.1.98, Case 521/97, the EAT held that a system of holiday credits which were calculated as a proportion of pay amounted to deferred remuneration rather than a benefit in kind. In *Gillespie* v *Northern Health and Social Services Board* [1996] IRLR 214 a woman who was still in an employment relationship but on maternity leave was entitled to the benefit of a back-dated pay rise awarded during the maternity period. Pension contributions are not remuneration, nor is the right to a performance assessment, even though such assessment may result in a financial benefit and failure to maintain these entitlements during the period of leave may constitute discrimination (*Caisse Nationale d'Assurance Vieillesse de Travailleurs Salariés* v *Thibault* [1998] IRLR 399).

Continuous employment

The employee continues to be employed during OML. This period counts towards her continuous employment. This is important for the purposes of calculating entitlement to other statutory employment rights. It also counts for assessing seniority of service, pension rights and other length of service payments such as pay increments under her contract of employment.

Additional maternity leave

Contractual rights

The contract of employment continues throughout AML unless either party expressly ends it or it expires. Essentially, the employee is, during this period, released from the obligation to work. However, it has been ruled (in a parental leave case that is applicable to the circumstances of maternity leave) that an employee 'is entitled during the period of leave to the benefit of the employer's implied obligation . . . of trust and confidence and to any terms and conditions of . . . employment relating to notice of the termination of the employment contract by the employer; compensation in the event of redundancy or disciplinary and grievance procedures'.

Furthermore, the employee 'is bound, during that period, by the implied obligation to the employer of good faith and any terms and conditions of . . . employment relating to notice of the termination of the employment contract by her; the disclosure of confidential information; the acceptance of gifts or other benefits; or the employee's participation in any other business' (*Lewen* v *Denda* [2000] IRLR 67, ECJ).

Other terms and conditions

The continuation of these is a matter for negotiation and agreement between the employer and employee (or the employee's representatives).

Continuous employment

The employee continues to be employed during her AML. This counts towards her period of continuous employment in determining entitlement to other statutory employment rights. Unlike the situation in respect of OML, the AML period does not have to be counted in any assessment relating to seniority of service, pension rights and other payments based on length of service. Whether or not this happens depends on agreements between the employer and the individual employee.

If there is no contractual agreement acknowledging AML as continuous employment, then, the normal situation would apply. This means that the period of employment before the start of AML will be joined with the period of employment after the woman's return to work. This will determine her continuity of employment.

13.4.4 Returning to work

Ordinary maternity leave

A woman on OML will return to work automatically at the end of the 26-week period. She may not return to work at any time during the first two weeks after childbirth. Nor can she be forced to return against her wishes before the expiry of her leave. If she wishes to return prior to the expiry of OML she must give the employer 28 days' notice of her date of return.

She is entitled to return to the job in which she was employed before her absence with her seniority of service, her pension rights and similar rights as they would have been had she not been absent. Terms and conditions would be no less favourable than they would have been had she not been absent. 'Job' 'in relation to an employee means the nature of the work which he is employed to do in accordance with his contract and the capacity and place in which he is so employed' (ERA 1996, s 235).

Additional maternity leave

A woman on AML has an express right to return (ERA 1996, s 79). She is entitled to return to the job in which she was employed before her absence. If this is not reasonably practicable, the employer might provide 'another job which is both suitable for her and appropriate for her to do in the cirumstances' (Maternity and Parental Leave Regulations 1999, reg 18). She is entitled to return on terms and conditions in respect of remuneration that are not less favourable than those which would have applied to her had she not been absent from work at any time since the start of the leave (reg 18(5)).

Her seniority, pension and similar rights would be as they would have been had her employment prior to AML been continuous with her employment following her return (reg 18(5)). If she was paid during AML then her pension rights will have continued to accrue. She is entitled to terms and conditions of employment no less favourable than those which would have applied had she not been absent from work.

Part-time work

It could be that the employee will want to return to work on a part-time basis. She has no express right to do so. However, an employer's refusal may lead to a claim of indirect sex discrimination (*see* Chapter 4). The employer would have to show an objective reason to justify full-time working as a requirement and the refusal to permit part-time working (*Briggs* v *NE Education and Library Board* [1990] IRLR 181, NICA; *British Telecommunications plc* v *Roberts and Longstaffe* [1996] IRLR 601).

13.4.5 **Requesting flexible working**

Under the Employment Act 2002, s 47, employers are, from April 2003, under a legal duty to consider applications for flexible working from employees of either sex who are parents of children under six years of age or of disabled children under 18 years. A disabled child is one who is entitled to a disability living allowance. A 'qualifying employee' must be the biological parent, guardian, adopter or foster carer of the child; or married to this person and living with the child; or the partner of this person and living with the child. A partner is a person of a different or same sex who is in 'an enduring family relationship but is not a blood relative'.

An employee (but not an agency worker), with 26 weeks' continuous employment, can apply to the employer for a change to their terms and conditions of employment which relate to:

- the hours of work;
- the times they are required to work;
- where they are required to work – at the employer's premises or at home; and
- other aspects of terms and conditions of employment specified by the Secretary of State.

The changes can cover such working patterns as annualised hours, compressed hours, flexitime, homeworking, job-sharing, self-rostering, shift working, staggered hours and term-time working. However, applications for a change in working pattern will not always require a significant alteration.

If agreed, the change will be permanent. It is not envisaged that the employee has a right to revert back to their former work pattern should their childcare arrangements change. However, the employer might be willing to agree a further variation.

The employer should hold a meeting with the employee within 28 days of the application being made. A response will be given to the employee within 14 days of the meeting. If the decision is to refuse the application, the employer should give sufficient explanation of why the business grounds for refusal apply in the circumstances. The only grounds on which an employer may refuse the application are as follows:

- the burden of additional costs;
- the detrimental effect on the ability to meet customer demand;
- the inability to reorganise work among existing staff;
- the inability to recruit additional staff;
- a detrimental impact on quality;
- a detrimental impact on performance;
- insufficiency of work during the periods the employee proposes to work;
- planned structural changes; and
- other grounds which may be specified in regulations.

An employee has a right of appeal against the employer's refusal and the right to be accompanied in both the first meeting and at the appeal. The accompanying person is as provided under the Employment Relations Act 1999, s 10 (*see also* the ACAS *Code of Practice on Disciplinary and Grievance Procedures*, 2000, section 3). Complaints may be presented to an employment tribunal or, as an alternative, to binding arbitration provided by ACAS. If an employer refuses an application, the employee may not, under statute law, make another request for the next 12 months. However, the employee may broach the subject with the employer and the employer might voluntarily agree to a change.

Detailed provisions are in the Flexible Working (Eligibility, Complaints and Remedies) Regulations 2002; and the Flexible Working (Procedural Requirements) Regulations 2002.

13.4.6 Parental, paternity, adoption and dependency leave

Parental leave

Parental leave rights derive from the European Parental Leave Directive 1996. This was transposed into British law through the Maternity and Parental Leave etc. Regulations 1999. The purpose of the Directive is to lay down 'minimum requirements designed to facilitate the reconciliation of parental and professional responsibilities for working parents' (clause 1.1). The Regulations have the following provisions:

- Leave of 13 weeks for both men and women when they have a child or adopt a child to enable them to take care of that child. For parents of disabled children the period is 18 weeks. A disabled child is defined as one in receipt of the disability living allowance.

- Leave can be taken at any time up to the child's fifth birthday. (The Directive provides the entitlement up to the child's eight birthday.) Originally, the right applied to parents of children born on or after 15 December 1999. However, following a legal challenge by the Trades Union Congress, the right was extended to parents of children born or placed for adoption between 15 December 1994 and 14 December 1999. For parents of adopted children, the leave entitlement is available until the fifth anniversary of the adoption of the child or the child's eighteenth birthday – whichever is earlier.

- A mother who qualifies can take parental leave immediately after maternity leave, provided notice is given and other requirements on the taking of such leave are met (e.g. the amount of time she is permitted to take).

- The leave is non-transferable.

- The leave must be taken in blocks of one week and a total of four weeks' leave is permitted in one year. (It is possible that an employer could negotiate, through a workforce agreement, more flexible and improved arrangements.) However, for parents of disabled children, leave may be taken in blocks of one day.

- The leave is unpaid. However, the employer may agree to payment – possibly under a collective or workforce agreement – as a contractual right.

- The right is subject to a qualifying period of one year. The employer may agree to provide access to parental leave after a shorter qualifying period as a contractual right.

- The right is available to all employees – including part-time workers. The Directive refers to workers 'who have an employment contract or employment relationship' but leaves the decision to member states.

- The right to return to 'the same job or, if that is not possible, to an equivalent or similar job consistent with their employment contract or employment relationship' (*see* the discussion above on the rights of return after ordinary maternity leave). An employee may terminate their contract of employment after parental leave with due notice.

- The employment contract during parental leave is continued (*see* the earlier outline of provisions under the taking of maternity leave). The period of parental leave counts towards continuous service.

- Protection against dismissal and against detriments is provided for employees exercising this right. These are the same as those provided for those taking maternity leave.

- Collective and workforce agreements: Where a trade union is recognised, an employer may negotiate an agreement that provides for enhanced parental leave arrangements. The enhancements may include, for example, payment for the leave; more flexible arrangements for taking the leave; entitlement to a longer leave period; and a leave entitlement covering children beyond the age of five years. In a non-union organisation, the employer may agree a 'workforce agreement' with employee representatives. (The establishment of such an agreement is the same as that set out under the Working Time Regulations 1998 – *see* Chapter 11.)

- Individual agreements: these may be reached between the employer and individual employees.

- Enforcement of the rights will be through an employment tribunal. Also the services of ACAS conciliation will be used.

Time off for dependants

Every employee, irrespective of length of service, is entitled 'to take a reasonable amount of time off during the employee's working hours' (ERA 1996, s 57A) without pay. 'Reasonable' is not defined. There is no limit to the amount of time that might be taken off. The employee should tell the employer of the reason for the absence 'as soon as reasonably practicable'. The purposes of the time off are:

- To provide assistance on an occasion when a dependant falls ill (either physical or mental), gives birth or is injured or assaulted.

- To make arrangements for the provision of care for a dependant who is ill or injured.

- As a result of the death of a dependant.

- Because of the unexpected disruption or termination of arrangements for the care of a dependant.

- To deal with an incident which involves a child of the employee and which occurs unexpectedly in a period during which an educational establishment which the child attends is responsible for the child.

Dependant means, in relation to an employee, 'a spouse, a child, a parent, a person who lives in the same household as the employee otherwise than by reason of being his employee, tenant, lodger or boarder' (ERA 1996, s 57A(3)). It also includes 'any person who reasonably relies on the employee for assistance' (when that person is ill, injured or assaulted) or 'to make arrangements for the provision of care in the event of illness or injury'.

A person exercising this right is protected against dismissal and detrimental treatment.

Paternity leave

From April 2003 (under the Paternity and Adoption Leave Regulations 2002), employees with 26 weeks' continuous service at the qualifying week (i.e. the fifteenth week before the expected week of childbirth) are entitled to two weeks' paid paternity leave in respect of birth or adopted children. The leave must be completed within 56 days of the child's birth date. Entitlement is determined on the basis of the employee's relationship with the child and its mother. It can be available to a person who is not the biological father. It is intended that an employee will be entitled to all contractual benefits, except wages or salary, and will have the right to return to the same job.

As with maternity leave, where an employee's contract of employment makes its own provision for paternity leave, an employee may not benefit from both the contractual and the statutory provision. The employee may take advantage of whichever right is more favourable in any particular respect.

Adoption leave

From April 2003 (under the Paternity and Adoption Leave Regulations 2002), male and female employees with 26 weeks' continuous service at the qualifying week who are adopting a child (under the age of 18 years) are entitled to Ordinary Adoption Leave (OAL) of 26 weeks, paid at a flat rate. Additional Adoption Leave (AAL) (which is unpaid) of a further 26 weeks, is possible, giving a total leave period of one year. This broadly mirrors the provision of maternity leave. The start date is either the date on which the child is placed for adoption or no more than 14 days before that date. Adoption leave is not available where the child is already known to the adopters (e.g. in step-family adoptions) or where existing foster carers adopt. In joint adoptions, either partner can choose to take the adoption leave. The other partner may, if eligible, take statutory paternity leave.

During OAL, an employee is entitled to the benefit of the terms and conditions of employment (excluding remuneration) which would have applied if they had not been absent. The employee is bound by any obligations arising under those terms and conditions. The employee on OAL is entitled to return from leave to the job in which they were employed before the absence with their seniority, pension and similar rights intact.

Reflecting the position under AML, the employee is entitled to benefit from the employer's implied duty of mutual trust and confidence; and any terms relating to notice of dismissal, redundancy compensation and disciplinary and grievance procedures. The employee continues to be under the duty of fidelity and any terms relating to notice on resignation, disclosure of confidential information, the acceptance of gifts or other benefits and participation in any other business.

If it is not reasonably practicable to return to the job in which they were previously employed, then, the employee might be employed in another job which is suitable and appropriate in the circumstances. This must be on terms and conditions as to remuneration not less favourable than those that would have applied had the employee not been absent.

A person exercising their rights to parental leave and adoption leave is protected against dismissal and detrimental treatment.

Draft Regulations are currently before Parliament on entitlements to paternity and adoption leave.

13.4.7 Detrimental treatment and unfair dismissal

Detrimental treatment

The right not to suffer detrimental treatment at work starts as soon as a woman has told her employer that she is pregnant and lasts up to the end of her OML or AML. It is also provided for those taking parental leave and time off for dependants. Detrimental treatment does not include dismissal or selection for redundancy. Complaints can be made to an employment tribunal.

Unfair dismissal

The Employment Rights Act 1996 protects a pregnant employee from dismissal in two specific instances: where the reason for the dismissal is her pregnancy, and where there is a denial of an employee's right to return to work.

First, the dismissal of an employee by reason of the fact that she is pregnant or for any other reason related to her pregnancy is automatically unfair (ERA 1996, s 99). This protection is available irrespective of length of employment. English courts have been increasingly liberal in their interpretation of this section and the words 'any other reason related to her pregnancy' have been held to include illnesses such as post-natal depression. Whether it will include practical reasons, such as lack of childcare facilities, remains to be tested. The case of *Caledonia Investment and Property* v *Caffrey* [1998] IRLR 110 concerned an employee failing to return to work through illness. The EAT extended the protection beyond the end of the maternity-leave period. The illness had arisen during the maternity period and was a direct consequence of the pregnancy. In this case, the dismissal was also held to amount to discrimination on grounds of sex.

The second protection afforded in statute concerns the denial by an employer of an individual's right to return to work (ERA 1996, s 96) (*see also* Fig. 13.3). Where there is such a refusal (and the employee has satisfied the notification requirements), there will be a deemed dismissal. The dismissal is deemed to have taken place on the notified date of return. This right is only available to those who qualify for the right to return to work (currently, two years' continuous service). Such a dismissal is not automatically unfair. An employer might be able to show that it was fair. The employer has two special defences (ERA 1996, s 96(2)–(5)). First, the employer may show that they have made an offer of suitable alternative

> The Northern Ireland Court of Appeal ruled that replacing a contract worker who went on maternity leave with a permanent employee was unlawful discrimination. It was found that:
>
> ■ There was a job available for a contract worker when Ms Patefield went off work in March 1998.
>
> ■ If she had not gone on maternity leave at that time, the Belfast City Council would have kept her in post indefinitely.
>
> ■ By replacing her with a permanent employee when it knew that she wanted to return to her post after the birth of her child, the Council subjected her to a detriment. It effectively removed the possibility of her returning to work.
>
> ■ By acting in this way, the Council treated her less favourably than it would have treated a man who would not have become unavailable for work because of pregnancy.

Figure 13.3 A contract worker

Source: Summarised from *Patefield* v *Belfast City Council* [2000] IRLR 664, NICA.

employment which has unreasonably been refused. Secondly, if there are five or fewer employees, the employer may show that it was not reasonably practicable to take the woman back at all – either in her old job or any other.

An employee who fails to exercise her right to return may still have a remedy against dismissal if her contract is held to have continued throughout the maternity period. Whether an employee's contract continues is a question of fact and depends on the intention of the parties in each case. This intention can be shown inadvertently. In one case (*Lewis Woolf Griptight Ltd* v *Corfield* [1997] IRLR 432, CA), a woman's exchange of correspondence with her employer, after her return to work was delayed through illness, constituted an affirmation of the continuation of the contract. However, in such circumstances, the employee will not benefit from the presumption (ERA 1996, s 96) that the reason for her dismissal was the failure to allow her to return to work.

An employee dismissed at any time during pregnancy or statutory maternity leave is entitled to receive from her employer a written statement of the reasons for her dismissal – regardless of whether or not she has requested one and regardless of her length of service. If her employer unreasonably fails to provide a statement or provides one that she considers inadequate or untrue, she may complain to an employment tribunal.

Redundancy

During maternity leave, it may not be practicable because of redundancy for an employer to continue to employ an employee. In this situation:

■ There must be a genuine redundancy situation. This means that the employee is not selected because of her pregnancy, her childbirth or the fact that she has taken maternity leave.

■ If there is a suitable vacancy, the returning employee is offered this alternative employment on terms and conditions which are not substantially less favourable to her than those to which she would have been entitled if she had continued to be employed under her previous contract. This employment can be with her employer, his successor or an associated employer.

13.4.8 Statutory pay

Statutory maternity pay

A pregnant woman is entitled to 26 weeks of statutory maternity pay (SMP). To qualify, she must have been in continuous employment for at least 26 weeks ending with the week immediately preceding the fourteenth week before the expected week of childbirth. Her average earnings must not exceed the low earnings limit for payment of National Insurance. The woman must give the employer advance notification of her intentions. She may continue working up to the date the baby is born and still retain her entitlement to full SMP.

There are two rates of SMP. The first six weeks are paid at the higher rate, which is based on nine-tenths of the woman's normal salary. Normal salary is calculated by averaging the woman's salary over the eight-week period which precedes the start of her maternity leave. On the seventh week she will move to the lower rate, which is calculated at £100 per week (April 2003), which is payable for a further 20 weeks. Employers are reimbursed from public funds for a proportion of the SMP they have paid.

A woman on extended maternity leave will receive no further payment after the expiry of the 26 weeks unless she is entitled to do so under her employment contract.

Statutory paternity pay

Statutory paternity pay (SPP) is introduced from April 2003 at the rate of £100 per week or 90 per cent of the employee's normal weekly earning – whichever is the lower. This is payable for a period of two consecutive weeks within a period of 56 days beginning with the date of the child's birth.

Statutory adoption pay

Statutory adoption pay (SAP) is introduced from April 2003 at the rate of £100 per week or 90 per cent of the employee's normal weekly earning – whichever is the lower. This is payable for a period not exceeding 26 weeks commencing on the day that OAL starts. It is only possible to receive SAP if the person has chosen not to receive SPP.

13.5 Employment policies and practices

There are several broad issues considered here: the creation of an appropriate workplace culture; employers' approach to 'work-life balance'; employees' needs in general; employers' knowledge of statutory entitlements; leave entitlements;

flexibility of working time; decisions on the place of work; the provision of specific facilities; and communication and consultation about 'work-life balance' policies.

13.5.1 Workplace culture

In a facilitating workplace culture there would be a climate in which there was ready acceptance of the need to reconcile family and work responsibilities for individual members of staff. 'Like any other corporate system, a reconciliation policy depends for its success on strong support from senior management . . . A company and personnel philosophy which underlines the importance and legitimacy of family needs is necessary if working practices are to be supportive' (European Commission, 1996). Such a culture would take into account 'the rhythms of family and social life'. So, it would avoid 'as far as possible evening and weekend work'. The creation of such a culture requires, particularly, an imaginative and creative exploration of working-time arrangements and the location of work.

An organisation would need to adopt a strategic approach to work-life balance. This would involve considering the feasibility of various employment practices (*see* below); and ways of tackling the 'take-up gap' (Kodz *et al.*, 2002). This would inevitably lead into an audit of the current patterns of work and working time which were inhibiting effective work-life balance.

This tension between 'work-life balance' and the dominant culture of organisations clearly shows that the government's aspiration of 'a transformation in the culture of the workplace' is necessary – but it is not easy to effect. For an organisation, the issue is: how far does 'work-life balance' facilitate or inhibit the achievement of business goals? There is no simple answer. However, it might be that the combination of business need and minimum statutory entitlements will prompt employers to reappraise the cultural, managerial and structural obstacles to 'work-life balance' and also see achieving this balance as in their business interests.

13.5.2 Facilitating work-life balance

Various forms of flexible working practices and working-time arrangements can be considered. These effectively form a menu from which employers might accommodate the needs of employees. The *Baseline Study* (Hogarth *et al.*, 2001) reported that management at individual workplaces retained considerable discretion about the form of and eligibility for work-life balance practices.

As a preliminary, it is important to remember several key issues:

- that there are gender differences in respect of work-life balance needs;
- that a creative and imaginative approach to the issue could be helpful;
- that stereotypes and assumptions are avoided;
- that geniune consultation should be established.

Finally, monitoring of work-life balance practices is essential. The *Baseline Study* (Hogarth *et al.*, 2001) found that 64 per cent of workplaces had no mechanism in place to monitor these.

The following sections elaborate on some of the key working arrangements that might be considered.

13.5.3   Leave entitlements

Leave entitlements are particularly important at specific times in a person's life. These reflect initiatives by the EU to reconcile work and family life. Those defined in the European Commission guide (1996) are:

■ *Maternity leave*: This is for 'the protection of the mother and the unborn child in the last weeks of pregnancy and during childbirth'. It is designed to help 'the full recovery of the mother after childbirth and to accommodate breast-feeding in early infancy'. It would also be augmented by ante-natal leave.

■ *Paternity leave*: 'This is to enable fathers to be present at the birth of their child, to spend time with their new baby in order to promote the relationship and to develop caring skills and to make an additional contribution to family responsibilities immediately after childbirth.'

■ *Parental leave*: 'This is for mothers and fathers. It is normally available after maternity leave. Its main purpose is to enable an employed parent to spend more time at home, caring for his or her young child. Amongst other objectives, parental leave is particularly important because it increases parental choice in combining employment and family responsibilities. For this and other reasons, parental leave should be equally available to both parents.'

■ *Emergency family leave*: This should be available to both men and women. It is for circumstances 'which require personal attendance'. Examples include the illness of a child, the illness of either a partner or someone else who looks after the child during working hours, or to accompany the child to a medical appointment. 'This type of leave could be applied to workers with other types of caring responsibility, for example for a disabled or sick elderly relative.'

The European Commission guide (1996) states that the reconciliation of family and work responsibilities 'is only likely to be achieved if all four types of leave are available to all workers'. The *Baseline Study* (Hogarth *et al.*, 2001) found that the provision by employers of leave other than maternity leave, bereavement leave, paternity leave and leave to care for others was relatively limited. Employees felt that should they need to take leave, their employer would accommodate their request.

For employers, there are several issues in respect of leave entitlements that could be considered:

■ *Minimum entitlements and enhancements*: These statutory entitlements are, of course, minimum entitlements. They can be enhanced by employers. However, the *Baseline Study* (Hogarth *et al.*, 2001) found that only a small proportion of employers provided benefits in addition to the statutory minimum maternity and parental leave entitlements.

■ *Payments*: One area where enhancement might be called for is in relation to payment.

■ *Procedures for determining enhancements*: Entitlements can be enhanced by employers (either under collective agreements or workforce agreements or at the employer's own discretion).

13.5.4 Flexible working time

The right to request flexible working (implemented from 2003) should encourage employers to think about the feasibility of accommodating proposals from individual workers. Additionally, a more wide-ranging policy establishing flexibilities might be advisable. Certainly, the interest is there among workforces. Despite a current low take-up by employers of flexible working-time, there was a substantial demand for flexible working-time arrangements from employees. Forty-seven per cent of employees not currently using flexitime would like to do so; 35 per cent would like to adopt a compressed working week. More men wanted flexitime, compressed hours and annualised hours than women. Women were more likely to want term-time working or reduced hours. The preference to switch to part-time working was greater amongst women than men. Given a choice, 55 per cent of women who had taken maternity leave said that they preferred greater flexibility over working hours to a longer period of maternity leave (Hogarth *et al.*, 2001).

Some further evidence from the *Baseline Study* (Hogarth *et al.*, 2001) suggests that some tentative steps are being taken. For example, 40 per cent of women returning from maternity leave had greater flexibility over their hours of work. Of those women formerly working full-time, around 70 per cent switched to part-time working.

13.5.5 Place of work

As indicated earlier, technology can now more easily shift the location of some work to the home (*see* Chapter 2). In some circumstances, this can help reinforce family-friendly policies. However, it is important to remember that such a dispersal and relocation of work activity is not pursued primarily for reasons of family-friendly policies.

It has been argued that, certainly, in the 'demographic timebomb' of the late 1980s, teleworking 'was seen as a way of recruiting or retaining women with children in the labour market, or holding on to existing staff by minimising commuting and improving the "quality of life" for employees' (Stanworth, 1996: 17). But the situation is now changed: 'The predominant emphasis is to use telework in order to reduce costs'. She points out that:

> the overhead costs of employment of teleworkers can also be cut by eroding terms and conditions. The most extreme form of this is the casualisation of teleworkers, where they become self-employed rather than remaining employees. Employers need not provide sick pay, holiday pay or pensions, neither do they pay NI contributions or have to administer income tax. Self-employment also shifts the risk of ensuring an adequate income flow onto the individual (1996: 18).

It could be that teleworking at home helps overcome some childcare and other dependency problems for particular employees. However, such a decision must be considered in the context of wider employment policies: the need to provide and maintain good standards of remuneration, conditions of employment and health and safety. Furthermore, consideration needs to be given to the negative aspects of working at home, as reported by teleworkers: isolation, the intrusion of work into domestic life, etc.

There is a long way to go in this area. The *Baseline Study* found that 22 per cent of employees worked from home at least occasionally. Where staff worked at home they were usually professional and managerial staff. Of those employees not currently working from home, around a third said they would like to occasionally – although around 87 per cent felt that their employer would not allow them to work from home (Hogarth *et al.*, 2001). Kodz *et al.* (2002) found that formal homeworking was less commonly offered, usually due to technological issues and management concerns

13.5.6 Facilities

The European Commission guidance (1996) comments that 'working parents report that their concentration and productivity at work is better if they are confident that their children are in safe and high-quality care'. Some employers offer a variety of supportive measures including:

- workplace nurseries;
- referrals to community childcare schemes;
- childcare vouchers;
- after-school programmes.

Of all the elements of family-friendly policies, these are the most costly. According to the Daycare Trust (www.daycaretrust.org.uk), the typical cost of a nursery place for a child under two is £6200. Childminders are less expensive, but a full-time place would cost almost £6000 per year. The *Baseline Study* found that overall just under 18 per cent of workplaces provided some kind of help with childcare needs but this usually related to providing information. Only 2 per cent of workplaces provided workplace facilities such as a creche; 1 per cent provided subsidised nursery places; and 3 per cent financial help with employees' other caring needs (Hogarth *et al.*, 2001).

13.5.7 Communiction and consultation about 'work-life balance'

As work-life balance develops as an employment issue – particularly in respect of leave entitlements and the right to request flexible working – the adequacy of information and the effective use of communication and consultation channels with employees are particularly important in respect of operational and human resource management.

Kodz *et al.* (2002), in a case study survey of large organisations that were promoting work-life balance, reported a number of inhibitors. First, there were information gaps – with some employees and managers not knowing what was available. Furthermore, there was considerable latent demand for provision which enables employees to balance their working and non-working lives, but many employees did not realise that change was possible.

The *Baseline Study* (Hogarth *et al.*, 2001) reported that the extent of consultation over work-life balance between employers and employees varied across workplaces and workforces. It was greatest in large and unionised workplaces. Perhaps surprisingly, 69 per cent of employees reported that their employer consulted them about work-life balance issues. This mostly related to hours of work rather than leave entitlements or working from home.

Case study 13.1 Dependency scheme in the Royal Borough of Kingston upon Thames

The context

The Royal Borough of Kingston upon Thames was among pioneering employers which, in 1989, voluntarily developed a more coherent policy on dependency rights. The stated aims were to ensure consistency of treatment and 'formalise circumstances which formerly would have otherwise been dealt with at the discretion of a department under the special leave provision'.

The scheme was conceived in the context of wider managerial and human resource objectives. In particular, it was an essential complement to the Borough's equal opportunities policy. This was initiated in 1986 and was associated with a range of measures to support, in particular, female staff. These measures comprised a career-break scheme, the encouragement of women returners to employment and the promotion of job sharing.

By itself, commitment to the moral case for equal opportunities was insufficient. The personnel function was operating in an environment of divergent political opinions and constraints on public expenditure. Consequently, the 'business case' for these policies was particularly important. So the rationale for the package of measures was also founded in a human resource planning strategy. This had several dimensions – two of which are significant here. Both are, in effect, factors concerned with cultural change. The Borough aimed to use these measures as change levers.

First, it would send messages to the workforce and job applicants about workplace culture. The local authority was to be perceived as an employer which, while wanting a flexible and well-motivated workforce, was also able to acknowledge that, for its staff, there could be tensions between work and non-work life. So, attempts should be made to accommodate these as far as practicable. Secondly, it was anticipated that a greater climate of openness and honesty in dealing with employees' problems could be encouraged.

Trade unions were consulted at the formulation stage in the Equal Opportunities Forum.

The contribution of the dependency scheme

The dependency-leave scheme signalled to employees a number of messages about day-to-day employment practice. First, that reconciling non-work demands with working life could be achieved within the context of an open and clearly understood system. Secondly, that the previous expedients of using 'fictionalised' sickness to take time off was unacceptable. Thirdly, that the need to take time off from work could be for a variety of reasons – childcare for both female and male staff, the adoption of children, care of elderly or disabled relatives and partners and bereavement. Fourthly, that given such a facilitating scheme, abuse would not be condoned.

The key provisions of the dependency scheme

Who is a dependant?

The provisions of the scheme will recognise a dependant under the following relationships:

- a wife, husband, cohabitee or partner;
- a person to whom the employee is next of kin or nominated next of kin;
- a parent/guardian/foster parent;
- a brother or sister;
- a son or daughter;
- a grandparent or grandchild;
- a person with a disability for whom the employee is normally responsible;
- in-laws may be recognised where there is a demonstrable close dependency.

The scheme states that 'it is essential to the operation of the scheme that a dependent relationship exists and it is recognised that sickness may create a dependency where it has not previously existed'.

Who may apply?

Those eligible are:

- all permanent employees (full-time or part-time) whether officers or manual workers, provided that they have a minimum of one year's service with the Borough;
- those employees not meeting the service qualification are offered an equivalent amount of unpaid leave.

How much leave?

Directors and heads of department have delegated authority to grant leave in accordance with guidelines. It would not total more than ten paid days per year during the dependency-leave year (April–March). Bonus earners would receive the basic rate of pay for dependency leave. Senior managers can extend leave by an equivalent unpaid period where appropriate.

How are applications verified?

In ensuring that the scheme is not abused, wherever possible it will be necessary to request proof of an employee's circumstances. This would not always be available in emergency situations and would usually be provided with a request for dependency leave after the event had taken place. Employees are expected to complete an application/certification form on their return or prior to taking the leave if it is known in advance. This should be accompanied by the appropriate form of verification.

Three months' notice of paternity leave and adoption leave would be expected.

Monitoring arrangements

An application/certificate system will ensure:

- that adequate records are maintained of individuals' applications in order to calculate the entitlement for the year;
- that records are kept of the total number of applications across the local authority;
- that details of applications are available to enable a breakdown both by circumstances and by department for future analysis;
- that details of unusual requests outside the proposed scheme are recorded and incorporated into the scheme where appropriate.

Operation of the scheme

In practice, the circumstances in which leave was requested encompassed taking children to hospital, illness of a child, illness of a parent, death of a parent and, occasionally, funerals of distant relations. Definitional problems of 'dependency' have not arisen.

The personnel department reports that managers across the authority have taken a consistent approach. A manager has power to refuse if abuse of the scheme is suspected, and furthermore can take disciplinary action for misconduct. This, however, has not been an issue. Employees can raise grievances about the operation of the scheme with the personnel department. None are recalled.

Unions now see the scheme as a 'fact of life' and a dimension of the Borough's equal opportunities perspective.

The scheme is viewed as 'neutral' in cost terms.

Exercise 13.1   **Developing a dependency policy**

Devise a dependency leave policy for your organisation, answering the questions below.

1 What are you trying to achieve?
2 What would be the provisions of the policy?
3 Which of these would comply with the statutory minimum requirements?
4 Which would be enhancements over and above the statutory minima?
5 Do you think there are constraints within the organisation that might prevent the achievement of your objectives?

References

Advisory Conciliation and Arbitration Service (2000) *Code of Practice or Disciplinary and Grievance Procedures.* London: ACAS.

Department of Trade and Industry (1998) 'Fairness at Work', White Paper. Cm. 3968. London: Stationery Office.

European Commission (1996) *Work and Childcare: Implementing the Council Recommendation on Childcare – a Guide to Good Practice.* Luxembourg: the Commission.

Felstead, A., Jewson, N. *et al.* (2002) '*Opportunities to work at home in the context of work-life balance*', *Human Resource Management Journal*, 12(1).

HM Treasury and the Department of Trade and Industry (2003) *Balancing Work and Family Life; enhancing choice and support for parents.* London: Stationery Office.

Hogarth, T. *et al.* (2001) *Work-Life Balance 2000: results from the Baseline Study.* London: Department for Education and Skills.

The Home Office (1998) *Supporting Families: a Consultation Document.* London: Stationery Office.

Kodz, J. *et al.* (2002) *Work-life Balance: beyond the rhetoric*, IES Report No. 384. Brighton: Institute for Employment Studies.

Office for National Statistics (2001) *Living in Britain: results from the 2000 General Household Survey*. London: Stationery Office.

Phillips, J. *et al.* (2002) *Juggling Work and Care: the experiences of working carers of older adults*. London: Policy Press.

Reeves, R. (2002) *Dad's Army: the case for father-friendly workplaces*. London: The Work Foundation.

Stanworth, C. (1996) *Working at Home – a Study of Homeworking and Teleworking*. London: Institute of Employment Rights.

Taylor, R. (2002a) *Britain's World of Work – myths and realities*. Swindon: Economic and Social Research Council.

Taylor, R. (2002b) *The Future of Work-Life Balance*. Swindon: Economic and Social Research Council.

Young, M. and Willmott, P. (1973) 'The Symmetrical Family', in Butterworth, E. and Weir, D. (eds) (1984) *The New Sociology of Modern Britain*. London: Fontana.

PART FIVE

Collective rights at work

Introduction to Part Five

PRELIMINARIES

There are three dimensions to the law relating to collective rights: processes of employee relations, industrial action and individual trade union membership.

The processes of employee relations

This relates to:

- trade unions and their activities (particularly collective bargaining and consultation);
- non-union representation (where employers are under a statutory duty to consult about specific issues).

Industrial action

This concerns:

- the role and liability of trade unions for industrial action;
- the position of individual workers who take part in industrial action (particularly relating to dismissal and pay deduction).

Individual trade union membership

This relates to:

- the admission to, or exclusion from, trade unions of individual workers;
- the rights of individual members of a trade union to participate in the internal democracy of their trade union.

In Part Five we will focus, principally, on the first two of these broad areas and only make occasional reference to individual rights of trade union membership, as appropriate.

THE ROLE OF TRADE UNIONS

The role of trade unions is central to the two chapters in Part Five. In this brief section we will consider a number of facets:

- their purposes;
- their organisational structure and relationship with their members;
- the historic legal status of unions;
- trade union immunities;
- trade union independence.

Trade union purposes: The purposes of unions must be seen in the context of the individual employment relationship. In Chapter 2 of this textbook we described the vulnerability of individual workers in what is an asymmetrical relationship with the employer. Lord Wedderburn (1986) commented that 'the individual employer is from the outset an aggregate of resources, already a collective power in social terms'. Trade unions provide the organisational basis for countervailing *collective* action by individual workers. Essentially, using the mechanism of collective bargaining, unions aim to:

- limit the unilateral power and authority of employers;
- lessen the dependence of employees on market fluctuations; and
- lessen the dependence of employees on the arbitrary will of management.

A long-standing historic definition of a trade union was provided in the late nineteenth century by Sidney and Beatrice Webb, two Fabian socialist writers. They described a union as 'a continuous association of wage earners for the purpose of improving the conditions of their working lives' (1896). As a starting point, this is still a useful definition. We will look at several aspects.

First, the recognition of the permanence of trade union organisation is important. They are not temporary groupings. This helps them develop expertise, enables them to acquire and use resources to provide services to their members and confers 'political' strength upon them in the power relationship with employers. Some commentators have noted the danger of unions being diverted from primarily looking after their members' interests to a greater concern for the protection of the organisation and in particular the full-time officers of that organisation (*see* the following subsection). Clearly, there will always be a tension within individual trade unions about the balance to be struck between the interests of members and the interests and survival of the organisation as a whole.

Secondly, the Webbs' characterisation of unions as organisations of 'wage earners' is nowadays too limited. Many salaried and professional workers are organised into unions (e.g. teachers, nurses, university lecturers, bank staff, scientists, etc.). This is a contemporary echo of a trend noted in the past: those with something to protect are likely to group together defensively. In the nineteenth century, significant trade union growth was found among skilled workers wishing to regulate entry into their trade and so protect wage rates. These were described as 'the aristocracy of labour'. In contrast, unskilled workers – often employed in casual and other forms of insecure employment – only

gradually organised into unions. In the present day, it is unsurprising that trade unionism has developed among those with careers, incremental pay scales and pensions to
protect. This contrasts with the lack of union protection for many 'atypical' workers.

Thirdly, the Webbs' statement of trade union purpose – 'improving the conditions
of their working lives' – deserves further elaboration. Although the specific issues may
have changed over the decades, there are five generic union objectives that have
remained broadly the same:

- the protection and improvement of remuneration;
- the regulation of working time;
- the promotion of job security;
- the provision of a healthy and safe working environment; and
- the ability to represent the interests of members and jointly to regulate terms and
  conditions of employment with an employer.

These objectives relate to the 'sectional interests' of union members – i.e. their concerns
at the level of the workplace or industry in which they work. Four major implications
follow from the pursuit by unions of these 'sectional interests'.

First, unions need to develop and preserve cohesion for effective collective action.
This is reflected in union slogans like 'unity is strength'. Unions are concerned about
perceived threats to 'solidarity'. These can involve the division of workers on grounds of
sex or race; and, in particular, the weakening of bargaining power through the presence
of non-unionists. As a consequence, there has been a long-standing commitment of
many unions to the principle of 'the closed shop' – the situation where, in a particular
workplace, union membership is a condition of employment. (Under present employment law, such arrangements have effectively been unenforceable since 1990.)

Secondly, employers have to consider the extent to which they are prepared to 'share
power' with a union. Effectively, this involves conceding the unilateral 'right to manage'
in respect of decisions on certain terms and conditions of employment. It can result
in 'joint regulation' through collective bargaining or the establishment of 'genuine'
consultation. (The processes of collective bargaining and consultation are discussed
in Chapter 14.)

Thirdly, although unions pursue their 'sectional interests', they may have to respond
to the wider implications of their actions in the economy as a whole. Unions have
increasingly in recent years been faced with a dilemma. Essentially, they are faced with
two broad questions:

- How far is a union prepared to see the achievement of its members' objectives
  within a wider framework of decision-making in respect of economic, political and
  social policy?
- How far, in acknowledging the relevance of these wider policies, is a union in danger of becoming less accountable to its members and, effectively, more responsive
  or accountable to government?

There is a clear tension here which can, at times, be difficult for union leaders to
manage. Allan Flanders (1975) has commented that 'it is wrong to expect trade unions

to abandon their primary responsibility to look after the interests of their own members and transform themselves into instuments for the execution of government policy. But it is equally wrong for trade unions to act as if they had no other responsibilities in present day society and were under no obligation to consider the wider social impact of their conduct.' Elsewhere in this work, he pointed to the continuing tension for trade unions in the pursuit of their objectives and from the concessions and compromises that, necessarily, they must make: 'once trade unions appear to be acting as servants of employers or servants of the government, they are bound to be written off by their own members who will turn, as they sometimes do already, to unofficial leaders to take up their demands'.

The fourth and final implication is the need for trade unions to determine their own wider 'political interests', to articulate these and pursue them through the political system. Such an approach is essential for two reasons. Workplace 'sectional interests' are invariably moulded and influenced by wider economic, social and political policies. For example, government commitment to 'public-private partnership', while designed to achieve certain objectives in terms of public service delivery and public expenditure, will also have profound implications for job security and terms and conditions of employment for the workers affected by the changes of employer. Furthermore, unions will see the promotion of certain policy as only being delivered effectively through legislation (e.g. the promotion of equal pay) and other government action; and will resist legislation that they see as restrictive (e.g. in respect of industrial action).

The mechanisms for articulating union political interests are varied. They participate in lobbying and ad hoc meetings with government ministers. (They are prepared to do this irrespective of the political complexion of the government in power.) They have representatives on various quangos (e.g. ACAS, the Equal Opportunities Commission, the Low Pay Commission). Finally, about 30 unions are affiliated to the Labour Party and so participate in its policy-making and seek to influence decisions of the party and, if it is in power, the government. The Certification Officer (2002) reported that 38 unions had political funds for political campaigning – but not necessarily any party affiliation (*Annual Report 2001–02*).

Union organisational structure: Unions vary considerably in size. There are 221 unions listed by the Certification Officer. Many are very small. Some 82 per cent of union members are in the largest 16 trade unions (Certification Officer, 2002). Smaller unions tend to have more specialist membership. They recruit from particular grades of staff (e.g. the Association of Magisterial Officers) or from staff in a particular organisation (e.g. the Abbey National Group Union). The larger unions tend to be 'open' and 'general' in that they will recruit members widely across industry and services. The Trades Union Congress has a policy and an appeal system to regulate what is called 'competitive trade unionism'. This is designed to limit or prevent recruitment conflicts between unions. Under this policy, unions are regarded as having legitimate 'spheres of influence'.

It is common for large unions to be structured at three levels:

- *The branch*: This may or may not be specific to a particular workplace. It is the primary unit in the union organisation and the first point of contact for a member. It will have voluntary officers (a chairman, a secretary and a treasurer) who will adminster business. Normally, members are able to attend periodic branch meetings.

Workplace union representatives – staff representatives and shop stewards – are likely to be active participants in the branch.

■ *The district or region*: In some unions, both of these intermediate geographical areas exist. There may be some form of representational committee at this level – representing members from the area. Full-time officials are usually employed at this level, working from a district or regional office. These are paid employees of the union who are skilled negotiators with expert knowledge of particular industries.

■ *National level*: Here, there is likely to be an executive committee which, normally, comprises elected members. (The Trade Union and Labour Relations Consolidation Act 1992 regulates elections to these 'principal executive committees'.) Full-time officials also are employed at this level. The most senior is likely to be the General Secretary. He or she, apart from having responsibility for the administration of the organisation as a whole, is also 'the public face' of the union. General Secretaries will represent the interests of their members in the political arena. Again, the election of these postholders is regulated in law (TULRCA, 1992). There are also likely to be national negotiating officers, responsible for members in specific sectors or industries.

From this description, it is evident that trade union structure comprises two inter-connected dimensions running from bottom to top of the organisation. First, there is *the representational or democratic dimension*. This provides structures through which members can participate in union decision-making and policy forums. Secondly, there is *the administrative or 'bureaucratic' dimension* – those full-time officers and specialist staff of the union (training officers, research staff, health and safety officers, legal officers) who implement union policies and deliver the service to members.

Tensions can exist between the 'democratic' and 'bureaucratic' dimensions. Robert Michels, a German sociologist, writing in the early twentieth century, identified this tension in respect of democratic organisations generally. He formulated 'the iron law of oligarchy' (1962) – i.e. government of the few. Essentially, this is a pessimistic theory about democratic organisations, suggesting that they are prone to deviations from their proclaimed democratic principles. The elected leaders were said to become a self-perpetuating group concerned about protecting their own interests (rather than the interests of those who elected them).

While it is arguable that the tendency to oligarchy exists in unions, it is important to remember that there is a constellation of pressures on full-time officials. These pressures and influences include: periodic elections; workplace representatives' involvement in union decision-making and policy formulation; the possibility of workplace revolt against the union leadership; block resignations of members from the union.

The legal status of trade unions: Current law is deeply embedded in the historic circumstances surrounding the growth of trade unionism in the nineteenth century. These circumstances were characterised, first of all, by new collective forms of work organisation (particularly in factories). Secondly, considerable economic power was held by employers. This could be, and was, used in an arbitrary and exploitative manner with little acknowledgement of the interests of working people. So, for example, pay could be cut, and workers could be fined, victimised, discriminated against and required to work long hours, often in unsafe and unhealthy conditions. Thirdly, regulations imposed on employers by Parliament were minimal. Generally, courts were not concerned with the interests of working people (apart from limited protections under the Factories Acts). Their central concern was to protect the business interests of employers. Finally, for most of that century, working people, generally, had no stake in the political process. Most working men and all women were excluded from voting and had limited opportunities to make representations to government. Against this background, then, the legal emasculation of trade unions was particularly damaging.

This emasculation of unions arose for two reasons: their situation under common law, and their liability for criminal conspiracy. Under **common law**, they were seen as unlawful organisations that operated *in restraint of trade*. This doctrine, developed by judges, determined that it was unlawful to place unreasonable obstructions in the way of trade. This included trade in labour as well as commodities. As a result, the purposes of trade unions – to regulate relationships between employees and their employers – were regarded as unlawful. Essentially, the primary objective of unions was to attempt to limit the unilateral power of management to make decisions. Under **criminal law**, also, much trade union organisation and activity was at risk. For example, employees who went on strike, or threatened to do so, could be liable for criminal prosecution for the offences of obstruction, molestation, intimidation and conspiracy.

Towards the end of the nineteenth century, as a result, in part, of the reports of Royal Commissions, there came a wider recognition by politicians (both Conservative and Liberal) of the economic, social and political importance of the expanding urban working class and their organisations. It was determined that, for pragmatic reasons, the legal status of unions and their activities should be clarified. The Trade Union Act 1871 and the Conspiracy and Protection of Property Act 1875 reduced the dangers of criminal prosecution for taking part in the activities of a trade union and participating in industrial action.

A further development in the law took place in 1906 when it became necessary to clarify the legality of trade unions' role in organising industrial action. This arose from a series of cases, in the preceding ten or so years, whereby unions found themselves **liable in tort**. Essentially, under civil law, unions were found to have committed a tort (i.e. a wrong other than a breach of contract). The wrong was to encourage their members to breach their contracts of employment (and commercial contracts to which the employer was party) when they engaged in industrial action. Under the Trade Disputes Act 1906 unions gained protection from actions in tort. This legislation formed the basis of the present-day law. The device used to confer legality on unions is the enactment of 'immunity' under this statute law. In this way, Parliament overrides the strictures of common law.

Trade union immunities: Essentially, immunity involves legal protection against action in the courts for acting 'in restraint of trade'. So, unions are permitted to exist; permitted to seek the regulation, with employers, of the terms and conditions of employment under which their members work; and permitted to organise industrial action. In some other European countries, trade unions exist and operate under explicit constitutional rights. The failure in Britain to enact positive rights has resulted in their status continuing to be subject to some ambiguity. Some commentators, even today, hint at the fundamental illegality of unions. Others, including some recently retired judges and right-wing politicians, regard the immunities as 'privileges' which are said to put unions 'above the law'. However, it is important to note that the notion of immunity exists in a wide range of other situations – immunity from prosecution, diplomatic immunity, Crown immunity and limited liability for companies.

Since the 1870s (with a short break in the early 1970s during the operation of the now repealed Industrial Relations Act 1971), this basic framework of trade union immunities has remained as the foundation stone of collective employment law. There are two aspects of the immunities in current law. The first concerns trade unions pursuing their purposes. The Trade Union and Labour Relations Act 1992 (s 1(a)) in defining a trade union describes it as 'an organisation (whether temporary or permanent) which consists wholly or mainly of workers of one or more descriptions'. It then adds that the '*principal purposes*' of such an organisation include 'the regulation of relations between workers of that description or those descriptions and employers or employers' associations'. Clearly, on the face of it such purposes are contrary to common law under the doctrine of restraint of trade. However, the present immunity is set out as follows: 'the purposes of a trade union are not, by reason only that they are in restraint of trade, unlawful' (s 11(1)). The consequence is that this legal protection does not 'make any member of the trade union liable to criminal proceedings for conspiracy or otherwise' (s 11(1)(a)). Neither does it 'make any agreement or trust void or voidable' (s 11(1)(b)).

Immunity in respect of **industrial action** is outlined in the context of breaches of contract. By encouraging industrial action, trade unions are provoking the breach of the contracts of employment of their members and also of any commercial contracts in operation between the employer and customers and suppliers. Under common law, this is unlawful. It is a tort to encourage breaches of contracts. Parliament has enacted a legal protection which is currently in TULRCA 1992, s 219. This states that 'an act done by a person in contemplation or furtherance of a trade dispute' (i.e. to promote industrial action) 'is not actionable in tort' (i.e. subject to legal proceedings to claim damages and have an injunction imposed). The section adds that it is not actionable on the ground only 'that it induces another person to break a contract or interferes or induces another person to interfere with its performance' (s 219(1)(a)). Furthermore, it is not actionable on the ground only 'that it consists in his threatening that a contract (whether one to which he is a party or not) will be broken or its performance interfered with, or that he will induce another person to break a contract or interfere with its performance' (s 219(1)(b)). (This issue is explored in more detail in Chapter 15.)

Trade union 'independence': This is a formal legal concept. The Trade Union and Labour Relations Consolidation Act 1992 (s 5) defines an independent trade union as: 'a trade union which – (a) is not under the domination of control of an employer . . . ; and (b) is not liable to interference by an employer . . . (arising out of the provision of financial or material support or by any other means whatsoever) tending towards such control'. 'Liable' is to be interpreted as implying 'vulnerability to interference' rather than 'likelihood of interference' (*Squibb UK Staff Association* v *Certification Officer* [1979] IRLR 75).

It is a duty of the Certification Officer to determine whether or not a trade union should be granted a certificate of independence. The principal criteria used by the Certification Officer fall under the following headings: history of the organisation; membership base; organisation and structure; finance; employer-provided facilities; and negotiating record. The Certification Officer will consider all these criteria in reaching a decision.

Occasionally, a certificate of independence is refused, as in the case, in 2001, of the News International Staff Association.

An organisation may complain to the Employment Appeals Tribunal against the withdrawal or refusal of a certificate of independence.

THE TRADITIONAL MODEL OF BRITISH INDUSTRIAL RELATIONS

For the period from 1871 to the 1980s, it was possible to characterise British industrial relations as founded on trade unionism and collective bargaining. Consultation played a limited role. Trade unions were the 'single channel of representation'. Public policy generally supported the extension of collective bargaining as a means of managing the employment relationship (*see* the discussion in Chapter 1 on political approaches to employment law at page 5). Non-union forms of employee relations were generally regarded as deviant and of marginal importance, although some examples of good employment practice were seen in certain large organisations like IBM and Marks & Spencer.

By 1979, when the first Thatcher government was elected, the density of trade unionism in the workforce was just over 50 per cent, with some 13 million trade unionists. It was estimated that some 75 per cent of working people had their terms and conditions determined by collective bargaining. The 1998 Workplace Employee Relations Survey (Cully *et al.*, 1998) reveals the diminished significance of the traditional model that has occurred over the past 20 years. In 47 per cent of workplaces there were no union members at all. In the previous 1990 survey, the figure was 36 per cent. Union density overall was 36 per cent (*see also* Table B below). 'During the past decade, there has been a substantial fall in union recognition arrangements. Earlier surveys in the series showed a fall from 66 per cent of workplaces in 1984 to 53 per cent in 1990 and now we have recorded a further eight percentage point decline to 45 per cent' (Cully *et al.*, 1998: 16). A further significant indicator of a changing employee relations culture is the finding that 'younger workplaces are less likely than older workplaces to recognise trade unions – 28 per cent of those at their current address for less than 10 years recognise unions, compared with 53 per cent which have been at their current address for 10 years or more' (Cully *et al.*, 1998: 16).

THE 'BRITISH DISEASE'

The 1970s saw trade unionism and the so-called 'British disease' of industrial action and poor economic performance become a key focus of political attention. In 1979, a right-wing Conservative government was elected. A central economic policy platform was the tackling of trade union power, principally, though not exclusively, through legislation. Initially, the government was split between, on the one hand, those who acknowledged the legitimacy of trade unionism and who favoured limited restraint and, on the other hand, those who sympathised with more radical anti-union policies. Indeed, in the first Green Paper on industrial relations law issued by the Conservative government, a traditional affirmation of the legitimacy of unions was made: 'The freedom of employees to combine and to withdraw their labour is their ultimate

Table B   Union density by individual characteristics

	Percentages		
	All	Men	Women
Age group			
Under 20 years	5	6	4
20–29 years	19	18	20
30–39 years	30	30	30
40–49 years	38	39	36
50 years and over	35	37	32
Ethnic group			
White	29	30	28
Non-white	26	24	28
of which:			
Mixed	25	22	27
Asian/Asian British	25	25	26
Black/Black British	30	27	33
Chinese/other groups	22	20	24
Highest qualification			
Degree or equivalent	37	31	44
Other higher education	44	33	52
A level or equivalent	28	31	21
GCSE or equivalent	23	26	21
Other	25	29	21
No qualifications	24	29	20
All employees	**29**	**30**	**28**

Source: Brook, K. (2002) *Trade Union Membership: an analysis of data from the Autumn 2001 Labour Force Survey*, London: Labour Market Trends.

safeguard against the inherent imbalance of power between the employer and the individual employee. This freedom has come to be accepted as a hallmark of a free society' (Department of Employment, 1981: para 3).

However, in due course, 'decollectivisation' became the hallmark of government policy. In particular, statutory recognition rights for collective bargaining were repealed, an ever-more stringent legal framework was enacted to tackle industrial action and collective bargaining was increasingly discouraged as a means of managing employee relations. Its encouragement ceased to be public policy. This policy culminated in the removal, in 1993, of 'the promotion of collective bargaining' as a statutory duty placed upon ACAS.

Although the government made a clear link between legislative action and its economic objectives, it has been argued that 'there were also broader economic changes which were particularly unfavourable to organised labour' (Brown, Deakin and Ryan, 1997: 69). 'Labour markets slackened and product markets tightened, both very substantially.' For example, official measures of unemployment, which had averaged below 4 per cent of the workforce over the 15 years before 1980, rose to over 9 per cent during the subsequent 15 years. In the private sector, particularly in manufacturing, 'there was a massive increase in the exposure of the workforce to product market competition' internationally. In addition, 'the highly unionised public sector was greatly reduced in employment and subjected to a variety of market mechanisms'. In addition, 'the bargaining system continued to fragment' because of the growth of enterprise-based bargaining in the private sector and decentralisation in the public sector. 'This fragmentation greatly reduced the industrial basis of trade union power, tying the interests of union organisations increasingly to those of individual employers.'

Summing up these economic and institutional circumstances, the authors comment that they 'had consequences for trade unions which were in many ways similar to those intended by the legislation'. Certainly, in reviewing the trade union legislation of the Thatcher governments, Wedderburn (1991: 211) drew attention to various policy 'threads': 'disestablishing collectivism', deregulation, and 'enterprise confinement' (whereby the legitimate area of trade union activity was defined as the specific workplace). (This last issue is explored further in the context of industrial action in Chapter 15.)

A 'NEW MODEL' OF EMPLOYEE RELATIONS?

It is against this background that the Labour government, elected in 1997, implemented its employee relations policies. These do not focus solely on the issue of trade union representation – although this is seen as an ingredient. They also encompass individual rights, the promotion of consultation and the specific inclusion of non-union forms of employee representation. In his address to the Trades Union Congress in September 1997 the Prime Minister, Tony Blair, referred to two approaches. First, he said that 'the culture of modern trade unionism' would continue to be subject to scrutiny. In particular, he emphasised the need for unions to be genuinely democratic, representative of their members' interests (and not those of activists alone) and accountable to members. He envisaged a pragmatic (not dogmatic) trade union movement that is engaged in economic reality. Secondly, on the regulation of industrial action, he made clear that 'we will not go back to the days of industrial warfare, strikes without ballots, mass and flying pickets, secondary action and the rest of it'. The broad legislative framework, enacted by the Conservative governments, would remain with some minor modifications.

Essentially, the new government is shifting the focus from radical 'decollectivisation' towards a system that acknowledges varying forms of collectivism – under a myriad of terms: consultation, trade union bargaining rights and social partnership. It is a system where trade unions are no longer the only channel of representation. Non-union systems now exist and have legal backing. Furthermore, individual representation rights are given explicit legal support.

INTERNATIONAL INFLUENCES

The implication of the previous discussion is that the current law on trade unions in Britain is very much homegrown. Generally this is true as far as the details are concerned. However, there are a number of external agencies which set principles to be adhered to by democratic societies. These bodies are the International Labour Organisation (a United Nations agency), the Council of Europe and the European Union.

Because Britain's constitutional relationship with the European Union is significantly different from the relationship with the other agencies, we will consider that separately. The rights elaborated by the ILO and the Council of Europe are voluntarily subscribed to by governments. Britain is a signatory to the following:

International Labour Organisation

ILO Convention No. 87 (1948) on freedom of association and protection of the right to organise

This provides, among other things, for the right of workers to establish and join organisations of their own choosing without previous authorisation, and for these organisations 'to draw up their constitution and rules, to elect their representatives in full freedom, to organise their administration and activities and to formulate their programmes' (Art 3). The objective is to prevent political interference in the internal affairs of unions. The Convention also requires signatory governments 'to take all necessary and appropriate measures to ensure that workers and employers may exercise freely the right to organise' (Art 11). The ILO has always considered that the right to take industrial action is covered by Art 3.

ILO Convention No. 98 (1949) on the right to organise and collective bargaining

Under this, 'workers shall enjoy adequate protection against acts of anti-discrimination in respect of their employment' (Art 1). Examples of such discrimination are requirements by an employer that an employee does not join a union or relinquishes membership. Also, it protects against dismissal or the imposition of some other detrimental treatment on the grounds of union membership. Among other things, this Convention also protects trade unions against interference from employers (Art 2).

ILO Convention No. 135 (1972) concerning protection and facilities afforded to workers' representatives in the undertaking

This covers protection against victimisation and the ability to function as a union representative at workplace level.

ILO Convention No. 151 (1978) on protection of the right to organise in the public service

This outlines parallel rights to Conventions 87 and 98.

Council of Europe

European Convention on Human Rights and Fundamental Freedoms (1950)

This wide-ranging statement of human rights has been incorporated into British law through the Human Rights Act 1998 (*see* Chapter 1). It covers the freedoms of assembly and association (subject to certain restrictions) and the right to form unions and protect workers' interests through unions. As far as issues of collective employ-ment are concerned, the Convention states that 'everyone has the right to freedom of peaceful assembly and to freedom of association with others, including the right to form and to join trade unions for the protection of his interests' (Art 11.1). Certain possible restrictions on these rights can be provided for (Art 11.2). Among the possible restrictions that national law might impose are those that 'are necessary in a democratic society . . . for the protection of the rights of others'. So, compulsory trade union membership – the 'closed shop', where union membership was a condition of employment – would be unacceptable. As Wedderburn (1991: 150) points out, experience has shown that this positive right to associate also encompasses a ' "negative" right to dissociate'. This issue was ruled upon in a British 'closed shop' case (*Young, James and Webster* v *UK* [1982] 4 EHRR 38). The present Labour government has ruled out any return to legisla-tion enabling 'closed shops' to be agreed between employers and unions.

European Social Charter (1961)

Among other things, this Charter provides for the right for workers to organise in 'local, national or international organisations for the protection of their economic and social interests and to join those organisations' (Art 5). In addition, 'with a view to ensuring the effective exercise of the right to bargain collectively', the signatory governments undertake:

- 'to promote joint consultation between workers and employers';
- 'to promote, where necessary and appropriate, machinery for voluntary negoti-ations between employers or employers' organisations and workers' organisations, with a view to the regulation of terms and conditions of employment by means of collective agreements';
- 'to promote the establishment and use of appropriate machinery for conciliation and voluntary arbitration for the settlement of labour disputes' (Art 6).

In addition, governments agree to recognise 'the right of workers . . . to collective action in cases of conflicts of interest, including the right to strike, subject to obligations that might arise out of collective agreements' (Art 6.4).

In aggregate, then, these documents incorporate the basic human rights that should be central to a liberal democratic society: freedom of association; freedom of assembly; freedom of expression; plus protection against victimisation for trade union member-ship and participation in union activities; and also the right to participate in industrial action.

European Community influences

The social policies of the European Union affect collective employment rights both directly and, indicatively, by asserting certain principles. Such measures are framed within the context of 'social partnership'. Direct examples of social partnership are seen at specific levels of activity. First, at Europe-wide level, when Commission proposals on new Directives are discussed, the social partners (employers' and workers' representative organisations) are formally involved in the consultation procedures.

Secondly, the social partners have the facility for negotiating a Europe-wide framework agreement on specific social policy measures. Successful examples of this 'social dialogue' have resulted in the Framework Agreement on Parental Leave 1996 and that on Part-time Workers 1997. Such agreements have, then, been incorporated into Directives for transposition into national law.

Thirdly, the social partnership principle has been a specific part of particular Directives. Under these consultation and negotiation with workers' representatives have been required. Such provisions are found in the:

- Acquired Rights Directive 1977 (on transfers of undertakings);
- Collective Redundancies Directive 1975 (as amended by the 1992 Directive);
- Safety and Health Directive 1989;
- Working Time Directive 1993;
- European Works Council Directive 1994;
- Information and Consultation Directive 2002.

There are now relevant provisions on these consultation matters in British employment law (*see* Chapter 14).

The European Community, in 1989, sought a commitment from member states to a Charter of the Fundamental Social Rights of Workers. This was adopted by all member states apart from the United Kingdom. It does not have any direct legal status – although it can be taken into account by the European Court of Justice when it is ruling upon a particular issue. However, it is indicative of certain important principles adhered to by the EU. The provisions of the Community charter relating to collective relations (Arts 11–14) are:

- **'the right of association'** of workers and employers in 'professional organisations or trade unions of their choice for the defence of their economic and social interests';
- **'the freedom to join or not to join'** such organisations;
- **'the right to negotiate and conclude collective agreements'** under the conditions laid down by national legislation and practice;
- **'the right to strike'** is included as part of 'the right to resort to collective action in the event of a conflict of interest'. It is subject to 'the obligations arising under national regulations and collective agreements';
- **'conciliation, mediation and arbitration procedures'** should be encouraged to facilitate the settlement of industrial disputes.

The Conservative government of the day saw these measures as breaching the principle of subsidiarity. It argued that the most appropriate decision-making level for policy and law on collective relations and industrial action was that of the member state. To date, there have been no EU general measures relating to these matters. Where the EU has dealt with collective relationships it has, as mentioned above, generally concerned the piecemeal inclusion of statutory consultation rights in respect of particular issues. However, two notable exceptions are the general right to information and consultation in specified multinational companies (under the 1994 European Works

Council Directive); and the Information and Consultation Directive 2002 on general workplace consultation in certain undertakings (dependent on size).

CONCLUSION

The issues that are covered in Part Five involve, then, a number of factors. First, the interaction between the rights of individual workers and unions as their representative bodies. Secondly, the consequences of trade union activity upon an employer's business and upon the economy as a whole. Thirdly, the responses of government to such trade union activity and whether it is to be challenged or accommodated. Finally, the extent to which the framework of legal regulation instituted by government conforms to international standards relating to freedom of association.

References

Brook, K. (2002) *Trade Union Membership: an analysis of data from the Autumn 2001 Labour Force Survey*. London: Labour Market Trends, July.

Brown, W., Deakin, S. and Ryan, P. (1997) 'The Effects of British Industrial Relations Legislation 1979–97', *National Institute Economic Review*, 161, July, 69–83.

Certification Officer (2002) *Annual Report 2001–02*. London: Certification Office for Trade Unions and Employers' Associations.

Cully, M. *et al.* (1998) *The 1998 Workplace Employee Relations Survey; First Findings*. London: DTI.

Department of Employment (1981) *Trade Union Immunities*, Cmnd. 8128. London: Her Majesty's Stationery Office.

Flanders, A. (1975) *Management and Unions: the theory and reform of industrial relations*. London: Faber.

Michels, R. (1962) *Political Parties*. London: Collins. Reprint of translation of work first published in German in 1911, first translated into English 1915.

Webb, S. and Webb, B. (1896) *The History of Trade Unionism*. London: Longman.

Wedderburn, Lord (1986) *The Worker and the Law*. Harmondsworth: Penguin.

Wedderburn, Lord (1991) *Employment Rights in Britain and Europe*. London: Lawrence and Wishart; Institute of Employment Rights.

CHAPTER 14

Employee participation

Brian Willey and Huw Morris

Learning objectives

This chapter examines differing views on employee participation, reviews current policy and practice within the UK, and outlines the existing and evolving legal framework regulating employee participation. Having read this chapter you should be able to:

- Understand the key concepts relating to employee participation.

- Understand the political objectives underpinning legislation.

- Be aware of the content of legal regulations governing the organisation of employee participation and representation arrangements.

- Understand the various objectives of employers in implementing participation arrangements.

- Advise your employer on steps that should be taken to introduce or modify employee participation arrangements within the organisation.

14.1 Structure of the chapter

This chapter comprises the following sections:

- *Introduction*: The concepts of consultation, collective bargaining and industrial democracy.

- *Context*: The development of employee participation in the UK, and employee participation policy and practice in the UK.

- *Legal framework*: Low-level participation, financial participation and higher-level participation; statutory rights for representatives and statutory recognition for collective bargaining.

- *Employment policies and practices*: Traditional managerialist, progressive managerialist, industrial democrat and social partnership and social inclusionist.

14.2   Introduction

The extent to which working people can or should influence decisions affecting their working lives has been a subject for debate among social commentators, employers and politicians throughout the twentieth century. The aim of this chapter is to define and explore some of the ways in which this issue has been tackled by policy makers, practitioners and researchers. The main focus of attention is on experience in the United Kingdom in the post-war period.

Two terms that are often used in employee relations – sometimes interchangeably – are: *employee participation* and *employee involvement*. The term *participation* is most commonly used to refer to the extent to which employees are informed of *and* have an influence over, decisions affecting the administration and organisation of their working lives. This may include decisions affecting the organisation of work, the allocation of resources – including the terms and conditions under which staff are employed – and can on occasion extend to include matters relating to the objectives and organisation of an enterprise or group of enterprises. Employee participation may be direct (with a particular work group) or indirect (through workforce representatives). *Employee involvement* encompasses communication arrangements, team-working and quality circles – but is less likely to bring employees into decision-making processes. An important underlying issue here is the nature and management of the power relationship between the employer and the organisation's employees. The extent to which an employer is prepared to share decision-making power – i.e. to concede aspects of the 'right to manage' – is at the heart of the concepts of participation and involvement (*see also* Chapters 1 and 2).

There are various mechanisms for employee participation. It is possible to consider these in terms of the degree to which power is shared between the employer and the workforce. Perhaps, more accurately, the issue is the extent to which unilateral power over decision-making is conceded by management in favour of power-sharing. The scale in Fig. 14.1 suggests the tendency to which power is either retained by an employer or shared with the workforce and/or their representatives. This is, of course, a theoretical construct. In the real world of employee relations, the effectiveness with which these mechanisms operate is contingent on a range of factors. These include the commitment of both management and the workforce (and their representatives) to make the mechanisms work; the extent to which the organisation has a coherent – even strategic – approach to employee particpation; and the quality of the relationship between the parties – whether

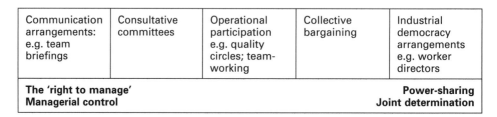

Communication arrangements: e.g. team briefings	Consultative committees	Operational participation e.g. quality circles; team-working	Collective bargaining	Industrial democracy arrangements e.g. worker directors
The 'right to manage' **Managerial control**				**Power-sharing** **Joint determination**

Figure 14.1   Mechanisms of employee involvement and participation

it is one of 'high trust' or 'low trust'. A further important factor is the particular nature of consultation and collective bargaining that exists (*see* sections below).

In the following sections we will look at three of the concepts mentioned in Fig. 14.1: consultation; collective bargaining; and industrial democracy.

14.2.1 The concept of consultation

Consultation is a process whereby the views of working people and/or their representatives are sought by management. Normally, it involves the discloure of information beforehand about some management proposal. The intention of management in particular is that decision-making power will remain with it. However, in its more developed form, consultation can result in an agreement to a particular change or course of action. Consultation can be a very difficult process to 'pin down'. There are two broad kinds:

'*Pseudo consultation*' (Pateman, 1970) is the situation which is essentially information giving by management. There is little, if any, expectation that a management decision or proposal will be changed as a result of discussion. This form of consultation maintains the 'right to manage'. In non-union organisations, this approach to consultation can be used to inhibit the emergence of genuine employee-based power (through trade union recognition and collective bargaining). This type of consultation has caused considerable scepticism about the concept and the failure of consultation to develop as a significant feature in the UK.

'*Genuine consultation*' can be assessed against various benchmarks. (Examples of these can be seen in European law on, for example, collective redundancies and transfers of undertakings). In particular, the indicators of such consultation include: the extent to which appropriate information is fully disclosed by management; the extent to which management representatives listen actively to the views of the workforce and its represenatives; the depth to which managers genuinely engage in discussion; the extent to which managers respond to the comments, views and ideas of the workforce; the willingness of management to amend a policy proposal or change a decision. It is possible for this form of consultation to develop into what is sometimes characterised as '*integrative consultation*'. This can focus on problem-solving or the implementation of substantial changes to the organisation of work and the deployment of staff. Necessarily, it involves detailed discussions about interrelated issues. These discussions, usually, need to be supported by substantial information disclosure. One example of this is the Company Advisory Board (or similar structure) introduced into some British plants by Japanese parent companies (*see* Fig. 14.2).

Marchington (1989) suggested that there were four models of consultation which derive from the relationship with the process of collective bargaining:

■ *Alternative to collective bargaining*: '[T]he stance adopted by employers in this model is essentially unitarist both in philosophy and practice, but it is more sophisticated than that of the traditional anti-union owner-manager' (1989: 386). The approach aims at persuading employees of the benefits of managerial policies. It tends to focus on the provision of information. It is 'fundamentally educative'.

The Nissan car factory came on stream in Sunderland in 1986. A corporate decision was made to recognise one trade union – the Amalgamated Union of Engineering Workers (now part of AMICUS). This union was selected through a 'beauty contest' in which management (rather than the workforce) considered the merits of three unions. A policy of the AUEW was to support single-union deals – pioneering and controversial in the 1980s. The recognition agreement reached between the company and the union set out certain general principles.

General principles
Economic considerations were a significant part of these:

■ Both parties agreed to the need 'to establish an enterprise committed to the highest levels of quality, productivity and competitiveness using modern technology and working practices and to make such changes to this technology and working practices as will maintain this position'.

■ They also agreed 'to avoid any action which interrupts the continuity of production'.

The union stated that it recognised 'the right of the company to plan, organise, manage and decide finally upon the operations of the company'.

Provisions
Among the key provisions were agreements on labour flexibility and single status conditions; and a commitment by the company to encourage union membership but not to have a 'closed shop'.

The Company Council
This was envisaged as part-negotiating and part-consultative. It comprised workforce representatives (who may or may not be union members) and company appointees. The purpose of the Council was to promote 'effective communication and harmonious relations between the company, its employees and the union' based on the recognition that 'all concerned have a mutual interest in ensuring the prosperity of the company and thus promoting the security of all employees'. Specifically, the Council had three roles:

■ *Consultation*: discussions on business issues, e.g. quality, production levels, market share, profitability, investment.

■ *Negotiations*: on salaries and terms and conditions of employment.

■ *Disputes*: matters referred to it under the grievance and dispute procedure.
If a dispute was not resolved at this stage then the issue would be referred to compulsory conciliation through ACAS. Further failure to resolve the matter could go to arbitration. (It is not a 'no-strike' deal but tries to minimise the likelihood of industrial action.)

The Council was also intended to be a major channel of information to employees.
The underlying purpose of the Council was to avoid adversarial industrial relations and to try and achieve consensus by having employees fully informed of and participating in company decisions.

Figure 14.2 Nissan

■ *Marginal to collective bargaining*: Here joint consultation 'achieves little or nothing for the parties, is marginal to any activity in the workplace and is in the process of stagnation' which could lead to 'the eventual collapse of the system' (1989: 387).

■ *Competing with collective bargaining*: This approach can be found in unionised workplaces. The aim of management is to 'upgrade' consultation. This will have an effect on the character and quality of collective bargaining. The aim is not to destroy collective bargaining but to provide a deeper understanding, through consultation, of, primarily, the business context in which negotiations take place. As an approach it is designed to be persuasive in favour of the management view. This approach may be complemented by other forms of employee involvement: e.g. quality circles, team briefings, company presentations.

- *An adjunct to collective bargaining*: Within this model, the two processes 'are kept strictly separate, although the representatives on each committee will be the same people. Collective bargaining is used for matters concerning wages, working conditions and aspects of a distributive nature, whereas joint consultation fills in the gaps, focuses on issues of an integrative character' (1989: 391). Management and unions are both committed to each process working alongside the other.

The nature of consultation will be particularly significant when the Information and Consultation Directive 2002 is implemented over the next few years. If the workplace context is facilitating – with genuine commitment by both management and the workforce to make the process of consultation work – much might be achieved in delivering more participative employee relations.

14.2.2 The concept of collective bargaining

Collective bargaining is a process involving an employer and union representatives. (Until the late 1980s, multi-employer bargaining was quite widespread – particularly in manufacturing industry and parts of the public sector. However, its significance has diminished considerably.) It is expected that through this process, the differences of interest, inherent in employment relations, might be resolved. Collective bargaining has been described as 'the great social invention that has institutionalised industrial conflict' that is endemic in the employment relationship (Dubin, 1954).

Conflicts of interest

These can be categorised under three broad headings: economic issues, power relations and values (Flanders, 1968: 29). The *economic issues* concern the distribution of an employing organisation's revenue or wealth between various competing interests: primarily, suppliers, shareholders, government and the workforce. So, a claim by the workforce for increased pay has to be considered in the context of, for example, the company's need to invest in new equipment, pay the shareholders increased dividends and pay corporation taxes to government. The issues concerning *power relations* (or the 'politics' of the organisation) largely concern the exercise of managerial power and the 'right to manage'. They concern the balance of decision-making power within the organisation – the extent to which it is shared; the extent to which it is retained by the employer. The issues concerning *values* concern the different standards used by the participants to judge behaviour and policies. So, for example, conflicts are likely to occur when an employer proposes employee relations changes in the interest of efficiency and cost effectiveness that jeopardise the job and income security of employees.

In any negotiations between an employer and union representatives all three conflicts of interest are likely to co-exist. The relative significance of the categories will depend on the circumstances of the negotiations. For example, if a company is facing a significant decline in demand for its goods and a reorganisation and redundancies are proposed, then, obviously, the emphasis will be different from that taken in bargaining in a profitable company which is negotiating improvements in terms and conditions of employment.

Forms of collective bargaining

Generally, the bargaining that is common within employee relations is described as *'distributive bargaining'*. It concerns the distribution of economic resources or power. Often it has a short- or medium-term focus. Collective agreements generally last for about one year and then are subject to renegotiation. This is because of constant change in the employment relationship: in product markets; in technology; in company profitability; in comparative pay with other groups of workers; and in the cost of living.

Another acknowledged form of collective bargaining is *'integrative bargaining'*. This theoretical concept may, in practice, blur into 'integrative consultation'. It is founded on a co-operative, high-trust and in-depth relationship between an employer and union representatives. Its purpose is to deal with such problems as work organisation, technological change or the fundamental restructuring of employment relations.

The bargaining process

Clearly, collective bargaining is based on the willingness of an employer to make concessions in the exercise of unilateral management power and the preparedness of union representatives to compromise on their original bargaining objectives. The negotiating process involves 'movement' – both parties shifting from their initial positions – and the identification of a 'settlement area' where an agreement might be reached.

Employer attitudes

Why might an employer be willing to engage in collective bargaining? There is no general legal requirement – unless the hurdles of statutory union recognition are met (*see* section 14.4.5). The arguments put forward by managers generally relate to two perceived benefits: the creation of order and stability in the organisation of employment relations; and the acquisition of workforce consent to terms and conditions and employment changes. The order and stability conferred through the use of collective bargaining is identified by Flanders (1968: 19) who saw the process achieving two important fundamental purposes: rule-making (i.e. setting the terms and conditions of employment to be observed by the employer and the workforce); and dealing with the politics of the workplace (i.e. regulating the power relationship between the employer and the workforce).

Of course, there is no common view among employers about the desirability of collective bargaining. Some are prepared to acknowledge the diversity of interests in the workplace and see union recognition and collective bargaining as a way of managing conflicts of interest. Managers with this perspective have been described as 'pluralist' (Fox, 1966: 4). Other managers, 'unitarists' (Fox, 1966: 3), see the employment relationship as essentially harmonious, founded on common interests between employers and employees. Any discontent is said to arise from poor management communication or agitation by trouble-makers. (Management attitudes to the organisation of employment relations is discussed in more detail in section 14.5 below.)

The breakdown of bargaining

The process of collective bargaining must also be seen in relation to the potential use of industrial action when the exercise of power becomes dominant. The resolution of an industrial dispute, nevertheless, requires re-entry into the bargaining process with the identification of a settlement area and the achievement of an agreement. Assistance in achieving this can be provided by the use of a conciliator or an arbitrator (usually from ACAS). (The issue of industrial action is discussed more fully in Chapter 15.)

'Free collective bargaining'

The pursuit and preservation of this is a key element in a 'voluntarist' system of employee relations – i.e. a system in which an employer and a trade union are relatively free to determine the nature of their relationship, the bargaining institutions they wish to create and the issues they wish to negotiate about. It has been a constant trade union objective.

Free collective bargaining, however, has, particularly in the post-war years, been subject to a number of criticisms and challenges. First, an issue of general importance has been government concern about the **economic consequences** of collective bargaining. Bargaining usually relates to the circumstances of a particular company (or maybe a group of companies). Trade unions, understandably, pursue the interests of their members to achieve optimum terms and conditions in organisation(s) concerned. This pursuit of *sectional interests* can create economic problems for government and its responsibility for the wider *public interest*. For example, a pay settlement might be regarded as inflationary. If it is seen as a benchmark for other groups of trade unionists who make wage claims, on the basis of comparability, for their members, then government might act against the actual or perceived general inflationary effects. In the post-war years, such action has been in the form of voluntary or statutory incomes policies designed to restrain the general increase in wages. Additionally, where government had a direct influence in the public sector, then, measures of cash restraint could be used. Furthermore, bargaining levels (particularly industry-wide multi-employer bargaining) came to be perceived by employers as irrelevant to highly competitive international product markets, particularly in manufacturing industry.

The second criticism of collective bargaining has been its inability to deliver effective and comprehensive **minimum standards**. Such minimum standards as did exist were provided on a sectoral basis and usually were restricted to the key ingredients of bargaining (i.e. minimum pay or earnings, premia shift working and overtime and holiday entitlements). As a consequence, it has increasingly been the responsibility of legislators to create an ever-widening framework of minimum standards for all workers (whether they are unionised or not) (*see* Chapter 1). Three key developments have been the creation of the national minimum wage, the Regulations on working time and the promotion of the principle of equal pay. Indeed, collective bargaining has been castigated for failing to address in any effective way the issue of **discriminatory treatment** (particularly against women) (*see* Chapter 4). Indeed, until 1970, discrimination was built into collective agreements – with specific pay rates for women. Only slowly have more serious attempts been made to deal with wider discrimination – usually as a consequence of legal requirements.

14.2.3 The concept of industrial democracy

The concept of 'industrial democracy' has fairly been described as 'incapable of definition' (Kahn-Freund, 1977). The term embraces a number of mechanisms. It is based on the notion of 'power sharing' and so, in the view of some, includes the process of collective bargaining. In the extensive debates on industrial democracy in the 1970s, the Trades Union Congress saw the extension of collective bargaining as its preferred way of promoting industrial democracy. Aside from the development of collective bargaining, industrial democracy has a limited track record in the United Kingdom. The other principal mechanisms tend to be found in continental European countries:

- *Co-determination* (whereby an employer and union representatives have, in law, to agree a particular decision). Examples of this process are seen, in particular, in certain European countries.
- *Worker directors*: These are elected representatives of the workforce who sit with shareholder representatives on the equivalent of the Board of Directors. In Germany a two-tier system exists comprising a supervisory Board (which includes worker directors) and a Management Board. Attempts by the European Commission, in the 1970s, to promote similar systems in other member states came to nothing. In the United Kingdom, a Committee of Inquiry on Industrial Democracy (under Lord Bullock) produced a report on the topic (1977). Its terms of reference required consideration of a trade union-based system of representation on company boards. It was, however, never acted upon because of a change of government in 1979.
- *Worker co-operatives*: Whereas the previous mechnisms can exist within existing patterns of private ownership, the worker co-operative changes the ownership base of the organisation. Workers, then, have stakes in both the financial interests of the organisation and its strategic and operational decision-making.

One attempt (Walker, 1970) to provide a structured consideration of the topic distinguished various levels of industrial democracy within an organisation. The schema enables the mechanisms to be located in a coherent way:

- *Democratisation of ownership*: This embraces co-operatives and employee share ownership schemes.
- *Democratisation of government*: In the private sector, this concerns, principally, the role of the Board of Directors and their legal responsibilities to look after particular interests. Under current British company law, their responsibilities are primarily to shareholders and not employees. A worker director scheme (if it was to be more than advisory) would require a change in company law.

- *Democratisation of terms and conditions of employment*: It is argued that such democratisation is taking place through collective bargaining and, to a lesser extent, through genuine consultation.

- *Democratisation of management*: This may be a consequence of collective bargaining, the process of genuine consultation and the adoption of more participative and less autocratic styles. Generally, it is unlikely that it will involve formal accountability of managers to employee representatives.

In contemporary British employee relations, the focus of government, unions and employers is primarily on the processes of consultation and collective bargaining relating to terms and conditions of employment. There is little drive towards the novel forms of industrial democracy.

14.3   The context

The issue of employee participation is influenced by economic, social, political/legal and technological factors. The significance of these will vary according to the circumstances in which the organisation is situated and the prevailing political climate. In this section we will review the contribution of these influences under the following two headings:

- the development of employee participation in the UK;
- employee participation policy and practice in the UK.

In the discussion that follows distinctions are made between participation arrangements in terms of the following two dimensions:

- **Issues**: the range of topics under discussion and subject to shared decision-making, i.e. does participation concentrate on information dissemination, task organisation, terms and conditions of employment, resource allocation and/or the goals of the enterprise?
- **Level**: the point within the organisational structure at which participation takes place, i.e. is participation organised at a low level covering office and shop-floor issues, or does it extend to higher levels involving elected or appointed employee or trade union representatives and senior managers?

14.3.1   The development of employee participation in the UK

For most of the first 70 years of the twentieth century, with the exception of the two world wars, UK governments avoided direct regulation of employee participation in general and trade union representation in particular. This approach changed fundamentally in the early 1970s and since that time legislation in this area has grown steadily in volume and complexity. One consequence of this incremental addition of minor reforms has been that the current regulation of employee participation is something of a legal patchwork quilt. In order to gain a fuller appreciation of the contents and effects of this legislation, this sub-section briefly reviews measures introduced by governments over the last 90 or more years under the following headings:

- collective laissez-faire (1906–70);
- from containment to support of trade unions (1971–9);
- regulation of trade unions and support for financial participation and employee involvement (1980–97);
- moves towards 'social partnership' (1997 to date)?

Collective laissez-faire (1906–70)

From 1906 to 1971, successive governments in the UK adopted policies designed to encourage trade unions but, apart from the recession of the mid-1920s and the two world wars, they steered clear of any direct legal regulation of employer and trade union activity in this area. This approach is often referred to as *legal abstention, voluntarism* or *collective laissez-faire* (Kahn-Freund, 1979). Underpinning this approach was a belief on the part of government ministers and policy-makers that managers could be persuaded to see the benefits of trade union membership and voluntarily concede to negotiate or consult with the representatives of these bodies over changes within the employers' organisations.

Government encouragement of this voluntary approach took four forms: setting an example, using its purchasing power, by promotion and by compliance with international standards.

Example

Governments of all political persuasions sought to promote trade union membership, organisation and the joint regulation of the employment relationship. This encouragement took the form of examples set by the personnel policies of the civil service and other public-sector bodies. It was seen as an advantageous way of managing workplace discontent by institutionalising conflict.

Purchasing power

Governments used the considerable purchasing power of public-sector bodies in order to encourage private-sector employers to promote trade union membership, recognition, consultation and negotiation. For example, the Fair Wages Resolution of the House of Commons in 1946 (rescinded in 1983) required government departments to include in their contracts with suppliers a clause which provided that the 'contractor shall recognise the freedom of his work people to be members of trade unions'. Although in practice this clause had limited effect, it was a significant gesture on the part of government in support of trade unions.

Promotion

Two major reviews of industrial relations practices, the Whitley Committee of 1919 and the Donovan Commission of 1965–8, were set up by Liberal and Labour governments respectively. The recommendations of these two bodies included suggestions for the improvement of industrial relations which were designed to promote collective bargaining between employers and trade unions at an industry, regional and/or organisational level. Although these reviews had no direct legal force, they helped to create a climate in which employers could arguably be more readily convinced of the virtues of collective forms of employee participation based on trade union membership and organisation. Elaborating on what was essentially public policy of the time, the Donovan Commission stated that 'properly conducted, collective bargaining is the most effective means of giving workers the right to representation in decisions affecting their working lives, a right which is or should be the prerogative of every worker in a democratic society' (Royal Commission on Trade Unions and Employers' Associations 1968, para 212).

International standards

At this level UK governments demonstrated their support for trade union organisation by ratifying a series of international Conventions which sought to guarantee the rights of employees to the freedom of association and collective organisation (*see* Introduction to Part Five).

The non-legislative encouragement of trade union representation for much of the twentieth century undoubtedly played a part in the steady growth of trade union membership in the post-war period. However, this largely favourable climate of public policy also needs to be seen in the context of wider economic and social changes. Thus, the pattern of growth of trade union membership (and by implication representation) between 1945 and 1979 has also been explained by reference to:

- low levels of unemployment;
- a steady increase in employer support for these arrangements;
- the expansion of the manufacturing sector and manual employment;
- a slow but growing recognition by white-collar, managerial and semi-professional employees that they might benefit from trade union membership.

From containment to open support of trade unions (1971–9)

In the 1970s the legal abstentionism which had traditionally characterised government involvement in issues associated with employee participation was replaced by more overtly interventionist initiatives. However, the nature of the intervention over this period varied considerably in tone and content. The policies of the Conservative government in the early 1970s were based, largely, on the containment of trade unions. The approach then switched under the Labour government in the mid-1970s to one of more open support.

The Conservative government's Industrial Relations Act 1971 (now repealed) introduced a number of significant measures on union membership, trade union recognition and the legal status of collective agreements. In the face of considerable opposition from the vast majority of unions, and antipathy from many employers, the 1971 Act had little impact on the day-to-day conduct of industrial relations in most UK-based companies. It was repealed by a newly elected Labour government in 1974 and replaced by the Trade Union and Labour Relations Act (TULRA) 1974.

This new Act moved government policy away from containment towards more open support for higher-level participation through trade union representatives.

New statutory trade union recognition procedures were enacted, the regulation of trade unions' internal rules was reduced, restrictions on closed-shop arrangements (whereby union membership is a condition of employment) were removed and the presumption that collectively bargained agreements were legally binding was rescinded. The Employment Protection Act (EPA) 1975 continued the then Labour government's policy of support for trade union involvement in higher-level participation with the following measures:

- union officials, including shop stewards, were provided with a right to paid time off for the performance of duties in connection with the conduct of industrial relations between employer and trade union (the current provision is in the Trade Union and Labour Relations Consolidation Act 1992, ss 168–70);

- employers were required to disclose to recognised trade unions information which might be relevant in negotiations (currently in TULRCA 1992, ss 181–5 and ACAS (1997) *Code of Practice on Disclosure of Information to Trade Unions for Collective Bargaining*);

- employers were required to consult with relevant recognised trade unions over proposals to make employees redundant (currently in TULRCA, ss 188–92 and associated amendment regulations). This measure supplemented other rights to trade union representation and consultation over pensions and health and safety matters, introduced by the Health and Safety at Work Act 1974 and the Social Security Pensions Act 1975;

- the application of negotiated agreements could be extended from one sector to another by ministerial order. In other words, terms and conditions collectively agreed by employers and unions could be applied to the workers of other employers who had not originally been involved in the negotiations.

Throughout the 1970s trade union membership and representation steadily increased and by 1979 more than half of the UK's labour force were trade union members, and 75 per cent had their terms and conditions of employment determined through collective bargaining. Government support for representation in the workplace and the political sphere played a part in this steady development of trade union power and influence, but the continuation of historically high levels of employment, an economy reliant on manufacturing industry and the growing presence of supportive employers also had an influence. However, economic recessions between 1972 and 1974, coupled with widespread industrial unrest in the so-called winter of discontent in 1978–9, arguably signalled the beginnings of the end of what had become a dominant pattern of trade union representation of workers' interests within British industry.

Regulation of unions and promotion of financial participation and employee involvement (1980–97)

Between 1980 and 1997 successive Conservative governments pursued a policy of regulating and restricting union organisation, while simultaneously promoting financial participation and employee involvement. The following measures were introduced:

Union organisation

- rescission of the Fair Wages Resolution 1946;
- prevention of the operation of 'closed shop' arrangements through the introduction of a right for employees not to be trade union members;
- repeal of existing statutory trade union recognition procedures;
- the ban on trade unions at Government Communication Headquarters (GCHQ);
- limitation stopping short of the abolition of paid time off for trade union activities.

Financial participation

- introduction of tax incentives for companies which operated employee share-ownership and profit-related pay schemes.

Employee involvement

- introduction of a requirement for companies to report on employee participation initiatives in their annual reports.

Despite the restrictive intent of Conservative trade union reforms, principally those affecting the organisation of industrial action (*see* Chapter 15), governments in the 1980s and early 1990s did not seek to rescind the commitments of previous administrations to international Conventions underpinning the rights of trade unionists. Government ministers preferred instead to emphasise the virtues associated with forms of employee involvement including quality circles, team-working and team-briefing. This, they argued, coupled with forms of financial participation including share-ownership schemes and profit-related pay, would promote more enterprising attitudes and behaviour on the part of managers and employees alike. It was even hoped that the spread of these measures would contribute to a movement away from collectivist values, and improvements in worker productivity as well as increases in company profitability and ultimately the renaissance of British industry.

EU social dialogue measures

The Conservative governments' domestic policies were coupled, at an international level, with a policy of opposition to the further extension of employee participation regulations. Thus, in response to proposals from the European Union for the extension of workers' rights to participation at a higher level within companies, Conservative government ministers opposed new initiatives and, wherever possible, sought to limit the impact of established provisions. This opposition to new initiatives was most evident, in particular, in the stance adopted by government ministers in discussions over the social dialogue procedures. In discussions on the Maastricht Treaty 1992, a specific 'opt-out' from social policy measures was agreed for the United Kingdom.

A key feature of this Treaty was the introduction of a form of supranational collective bargaining. Generally referred to as the 'social dialogue' procedure, this new negotiating mechanism brought together the 'social partners' (representatives of trade unions and private and public-sector employers' associations) to negotiate framework agreements dealing with employment-related matters. This new procedure would remove the need for Directives to be decided upon through the lengthier established procedures of the EU. The effect of Conservative governments' opposition to the development of EU regulation dealing with employment-related matters was relatively minimal. Over the six years of the opt-out (1993–9) only one Directive dealt with employee participation issues – the European Works Council Directive 1994 (*see* below).

Between 1979 and 1997 the incidence of financial and task-centred employee participation increased across most sectors of the UK economy. Meanwhile, union membership declined by half, the coverage of collective bargaining fell to 40 per cent of workplaces and less than 60 per cent of employees, and the range of issues subject to negotiation in British workplaces was narrowed considerably.

Moves towards 'social partnership' (1997 to date)?

The election of a Labour government in May 1997 led to some significant changes in the declared policy stance of government ministers. It is difficult to identify a coherent employee relations philosophy although a number of themes are discernible. Essentially these include a commitment to the principle of social partnership; the promotion of individual employment rights; support, within boundaries, for the principle of trade union recognition for collective bargaining; and the development of specified non-union forms of collective representation.

In the White Paper, *Fairness at Work* (DIT, 1998), the government proposed 'a framework in which the development of strong partnerships at work can flourish as the best way of improving fairness at work' (para 1.8). This framework was to 'help develop a culture in all businesses and organisations in which fairness is second nature and underpins competitiveness'. The White Paper added that 'such cultural change will lead in due course to more positive relationships between employers and employees than the letter of the law can ever achieve'.

It envisaged three main elements in the framework:

- Basic fair treatment for employees: 'unless minimum rights are established, effective relationships in companies cannot prosper' (para 1.9).
- New procedures for collective representation at work.
- Policies to enhance family life.

There are four essential ingredients in this approach. First a commitment to the view that employee relations – its processes and the standards to be achieved – must be seen in the context of business economic objectives and, more generally, Britain's international competitiveness. Secondly, that conflict in the employment relationship can be minimised through the promotion of fair treatment and the enactment of a range of minimum standards – relating to both terms and conditions of employment and workplace procedures. Thirdly, an implicit acknowledgement that the effective enforcement of individual employment rights is best achieved collectively. Finally, the view that collective representation is not only achievable through trade unions as the 'single channel of representation'. Other forms of collective representation can be developed dependent upon the views, at workplace level, of both employees and the employer.

Particular representation measures adopted by the government (and considered in this chapter and elsewhere in this textbook) are as follows.

Employee relations

- a statutory right of recognition for collective bargaining in organisations employing 20 or more people;
- a statutory right of derecognition;
- provisions to negotiate collective agreements (with trade unions) or workforce agreements (with non-union employee representatives) to implement aspects of the Working Time Regulations 1998, the Maternity and Parental Leave etc. Regulations 1999 and the Fixed-Term Employees Regulations 2002;
- clearer obligations on employers to consult on collective redundancies and transfers of undertakings in both unionised and non-unionised organisations;
- the implementation in 1999 of the European Directive on European Works Councils 1994 through the Transnational Information and Consultation Regulations 1999;
- the planned implementation of the Information and Consultation Directive 2002;
- making funds available to contribute to the training of managers and employee representatives in order to assist and develop partnerships at work.

(The government initally made available £5 million over four years for the Partnership Fund. In December 2001, the Secretary of State for Trade and Industry announced a further £20 million funding for best practice initiatives encompassing the Partnership Fund and other DTI schemes.)

Individual rights

- a statutory right to be accompanied by a fellow employee or a trade union representative in disciplinary procedures;
- a statutory right to be accompanied by a fellow employee or a trade union representative in grievance procedures;
- a prohibition on the blacklisting of trade unionists.

Essentially, the Labour government is shifting the focus from radical 'decollectivisation' towards a system that acknowledges varying forms of collectivism – under a myriad of terms: consultation, trade union bargaining rights and social partnership. It is a system where trade unions are no longer the only channel of representation. Non-union systems now exist and have legal backing. Furthermore, individual representation rights are given explicit legal support.

14.3.2 Employee participation policy and practice in the UK

The most recent comprehensive review of employee participation and representation arrangements is provided by the 1998 Workplace Employee Relations Survey (Cully *et al.*, 1998). Based on a detailed analysis of employee relations arrangements

Table 14.1 Spread of selected employee participation arrangements

Employee participation arrangements	% of workplaces
Most employees work in formally designated teams	65
Workplace operates a system of team briefing for groups of employees	61
Most non-managerial employees have performance formally appraised	56
Staff attitude survey conducted in the last five years	45
Problem-solving groups (e.g. quality circles)	42
Regular meetings of the entire workforce	37
Profit-sharing scheme operated for non-managerial employees	30
Workplace-level joint consultative committee	28
Most supervisors trained in employee relations skills	27
Employee share-ownership scheme for non-managerial employees	15

Source: Cully *et al.* (1998: 10).

in 2191 UK workplaces employing ten or more people, this survey has produced initial results that reveal the widespread and growing use of low-level information and task-based participation (e.g. team-working and team-briefing as well as problem-solving groups or quality circles); and slightly less evidence of higher-level representative-based systems of consultation and negotiation dealing with the organisation of tasks, the determination of terms and conditions and the allocation of resources (e.g. joint negotiating and joint consultative committees). (*See* Table 14.1.)

The survey revealed a continued decline in the extent of unionised forms of employee representation. In nearly half of all workplaces there were no trade union members at all – a substantial change from a little over a third revealed by a comparable survey in 1990. Meanwhile, respondents in 2 per cent of workplaces claimed that all employees were union members – down from 7 per cent in 1990.

Between these two extremes of growing non-unionism and declines in the incidence of *de facto* 'closed shops', there was a spread of union membership levels in the remaining half of the workplaces surveyed. Taking the survey as a whole, unions were officially recognised by managers for collective bargaining purposes in 40 per cent of workplaces. Despite the declines in trade union membership and recognition, the presence and position of trade union representatives appeared to be more robust.

On average there were four trade union representatives per workplace and 28 employees per union representative. However, despite these high levels of representation, the scope of union activity appears to have narrowed over recent years. Indeed, according to the information obtained from these workplaces, the activity of local union representatives was mostly confined to handling grievances (43 per cent), dealing with pay (30 per cent) and overseeing health and safety arrangements (22 per cent).

Declining union involvement and influence was further revealed by evidence that in a significant proportion of workplaces with union recognition, management was not supportive of a union role in joint negotiation or even consultation. In many of these workplaces it appears that management prefers to deal with employees directly rather than through a union channel. Indeed, when asked how they had sought to consult over the most significant workplace change in the last five years, managers were almost twice as likely to have consulted employees as individuals or members of small groups (57 per cent), rather than discuss the issues with trade union representatives (32 per cent). Moreover, in over 41 per cent of cases there was no union involvement at all, as opposed to 8 per cent of cases where there was no individual employee consultation.

Interestingly the survey did not ask any questions about the presence of employee directors or non-union works councils, which in itself suggests that these practices are rare. However, the authors did find evidence of an increased use of profit-related pay and employee share-ownership schemes (*see* Table 14.1).

These overall estimates of the adoption of employee participation arrangements conceal significant variations between enterprises reflecting differences in size, sector and the presence of trade union members.

All forms of employee participation and union representation are more common in large than in small organisations. Thus, because there are many more small than large organisations within the UK, measures which concentrate on the number of workplaces do not give a good indication of the number of employees affected. In other words, many more employees are covered by employee participation arrangements than would at first appear to be the case from a cursory reading of Table 14.1 or the results of the survey.

Direct and representative systems of employee participation are also more prevalent in private-sector manufacturing companies and the public sector than in private-sector services. The exception to this general trend is provided by systems of financial participation which, unsurprisingly, are more common in large private-sector companies in general and within the financial services sector in particular. The wider prevalence of direct and indirect forms of participation in public-sector bodies and manufacturing workplaces appears to reflect the larger size of these organisations. Meanwhile the greater incidence of financial participation arrangements in private-sector services is widely seen to have arisen as a consequence of the greater reliance on direct selling by the staff in these organisations.

Participation arrangements, with the exception of financial participation, are more frequently found in unionised than in non-unionised settings. When surveys in the 1980s initially revealed this finding it was treated with some surprise by employee relations commentators. However, further case study investigations suggested that the greater presence of task-based participation arrangements in unionised settings had arisen as a consequence of both campaigning by union representatives and managers' attempts to win the 'hearts and minds' of their employees (Millward, 1994).

In addition to the effects of size, sector and union presence, there are signs that many employee participation practices are used in combination. Thus, three-quarters of the workplaces covered by the 1998 Workplace Employee Relations Survey used three or more forms of employee participation, just over 20 per cent of workplaces used one or two forms of participation and only 2 per cent of workplaces reported no formal arrangements. The authors of this 1998 survey report that the grouping together of techniques is most prevalent in manufacturing organisations. In these settings they found a high degree of correlation between the presence of team-working, problem-solving groups and line management training in employee relations matters (Cully *et al.*, 1998: 11).

The legal framework

In this section the legal regulation of employee participation and arrangements for union representation will be examined in more detail under the following headings:

- low-level participation;
- financial participation;
- higher-level participation;
- statutory rights for representatives;
- statutory recognition for collective bargaining.

14.4.1 Low-level participation

As indicated earlier, the legal regulation of low-level participation has not traditionally been a feature of UK employment law. Thus, although schemes for low-level participation have grown rapidly in number and importance over the last 20 years, employers are faced with little legal compulsion or encouragement to develop or extend these initiatives. As this section aims to demonstrate, despite increased interest in these forms of participation, UK and EU policy-makers have concentrated on support and guidance rather than legislation to promote further initiatives by employers.

At present legal support for low-level employee participation in the UK is limited to two statutory provisions introduced in the early 1980s. The first of these measures, the Companies Act 1980, required directors to have regard for the interests of their employees as well as those of their shareholders when performing their duties. However, employees are effectively prevented from enforcing this duty because it is owed to the company rather than the employees directly. Furthermore, it is unlikely that shareholders at their annual general meeting or unions with a minority shareholding in the company would resolve to take action against a company or successfully prove that the directors had not acted in the *bona fide* interests of the company.

The second statutory measure designed to promote wider employee participation was enacted in 1982. It is now subsumed in the Companies Act 1985 (s 235). It requires the directors of companies with more than 250 employees to comment in their annual reports on what they have done over the year to promote arrangements for employee involvement. This statement must, amongst other things, include details of what has been or is being done to:

- systematically provide employees with information on matters concerning them as employees;
- achieve a common awareness on the part of all employees of the financial and economic factors affecting the performance of the company.

Assessments of the effects of the statutory reporting requirements for employee involvement suggest that they have had limited effect. For example, an analysis of annual reports in the late 1980s found that only three-quarters of affected companies had complied with the regulations (Department of Employment, 1988). There was also little sign of significant improvements in the quantity or quality of arrangements for employee participation as a consequence of these regulations. However, the absence of statutory encouragement for forms of low-level employee participation should not be taken to mean that the UK government and other bodies have not sought to encourage these practices.

14.4.2 Financial participation

This section reviews the statutory regulation of financial participation. In particular, it concentrates on legislation designed to encourage employee share-owning plans (ESOPs), profit-related pay (PRP) and 'gain sharing'. The growth of employer practice in this area has been directly prompted by both legal reform and the encouragement of policy-makers in the UK and the EU.

Schemes linking employee reward to company profitability and/or share performance have a long history in the UK, with the earliest recorded use dating back to the nineteenth century. However, despite this, there was no direct statutory support for such schemes until 1978. A Labour government (with Liberal encouragement) introduced Approved Discretionary Share Trust Schemes (ADSTs) under the Finance Act 1978. Although subsequently removed from the statute book, this scheme paved the way for a flurry of legislative activity over the next 19 years under a succession of Conservative governments. Examples included Save As You Earn Schemes in 1980; Discretionary Share Option (DSO) Schemes in 1984; Profit Related Pay in 1987; Approved Profit Related Pay in 1988; and Approved Company Share Option Plans in 1996. All were covered by the Finance Acts of the respective years. In different ways, each of these legislative schemes provided tax exemptions and advantages designed to encourage managers to tie the earnings of staff more directly to profitability or the share performance of their employing organisation.

The election of a Labour government in 1997 led to a change in policy on PRP. A timetable for the phased withdrawal of Approved PRP was announced. The reason for the withdrawal was the high cost to the Exchequer, estimated to be £1.5 billion in 1998. Despite the phasing out of income tax relief, profit-related pay schemes remain popular with employers. So, while the removal of tax relief has prompted many employers to end the schemes previously operated, others have decided to maintain these forms of employee reward.

Aside from changes in the operation of statutory PRP schemes, there are few signs that the political interest in financial participation schemes has abated. For example, in the 1999 Budget, the Chancellor of the Exchequer announced the launch of Share Incentive Plans (SIPs) and Enterprise Management Initiatives (EMIs) as well as the reform of DSOs under the new name of Company Share Option Plans. These changes were given statutory footing under the Finance Act 2000.

As a consequence of these changes, there are at the time of writing four sets of financial participation arrangements which receive statutory support and qualify for various forms of tax relief:

- Share Incentive Plans
- Savings Related Share Option Schemes
- Enterprise Management Initiatives
- Company Share Option Plans.

The key features of these are outlined in Table 14.2.

Table 14.2 Key features of statutory financial participation schemes

Type of scheme	Eligibility	Operation	Tax concessions
Share Incentive Plans (SIPs)	All employees	Employers provide employees with either up to £3000 of shares per financial year (Free Shares) or an option to buy £125 of shares per month (Partnership Shares) and up to two free shares for every partnership share purchased (Matching Shares). Employees may also use up to £1500 of dividend income to purchase additional shares (Dividend Shares). Shares obtained in any of these ways are held in trust for between three and five years.	Employees gain exemptions from income tax, national insurance contributions and capital gains tax if shares are kept in the scheme for five years.
Savings Related Share Option Schemes (SAYE)	All employees	The employer grants to all employees with a specified length of service of up to five years the right to purchase in 3, 5 or 7 years' time shares at today's price or at a discount of up to 20% off that price. The employee must save between £5 and £250 per month in the SAYE scheme.	Employees are exempt from income tax when they buy shares through a SAYE scheme and normally also exempt from income tax when they exercise the option to buy shares at the end of the scheme.
Enterprise Management Incentives (EMI)	All employees of trading companies with corporate assets of less than £30 million	Options over shares worth up to £100 000 at the time of grant can be granted to any number of employees.	Employees are exempt from income tax and national insurance when the options are exercised. Employees are not exempted from Capital Gains Tax when the options are exercised.
Company Share Option Plans (CSOPs)	All employees and directors	The company can choose which employees it wishes to provide with share options up to a total value of £30 000 at the time the option is granted. Options must be granted at the market price and can only be exercised after a minimum of 3 years and a maximum of 10 years.	Employees receive exemptions from income tax and national insurance.

Note: Further details of these schemes are available from Inland Revenue Guidance IR2002, IR97, Notes, available from Somerset House, London or www.inlandrevenue.gov.uk.

14.4.3 Higher-level participation

The law affects two processes of employee relations covered under this heading: **consultation** and **collective bargaining**. In addition, it provides rights which support and protect union and employee representatives.

Consultation

A statutory duty to consult, imposed upon employers, is a piecemeal obligation which derives, principally, from European Directives. However, the Information and Consultation Directive 2002 now imposes a more general duty to consult. We will look, in turn, at the following areas: workplace consultation under the

Information and Consultation Directive 2002; the information and consultation duties of multinational companies under the European Works Council Directive 1994; collective redundancies and business transfers (both of which areas should be read in conjunction with Chapter 3); and health and safety (*see* Chapter 12).

Information and Consultation Directive 2002

The gestation period of this Directive was long. There was considerable opposition to it – particularly in the UK and Ireland. In both these countries the effect of the Directive will be considerable because neither has an established system of works councils. The 2002 Directive is intended to complement the information and consultation requirements of other European Directives; and is a companion to the European Works Council Directive 1994 relating to multinational companies.

The key provisions of the 2002 Directive may be summarised as follows:

- *Minimum requirements* are established for undertakings and establishments within each member state.
- *Who is covered?* It will apply, according to the choice of each member state, either to undertakings employing at least 50 employees in that member state; or to establishments employing at least 20 employees in that member state. (The British government intends that in the UK the legislation will cover undertakings of 50 or more employees.) Undertakings are defined as public or private undertakings carrying out an economic activity. In its consultation document, (DTI, 2002: 5) the government points out that undertakings with 50 or more employees constitute one per cent of UK enterprises but they employ 75 per cent of employees.
- *When is it implemented?* The implemenation date for the Directive is early 2005. However, in the UK, the Directive is restricted initially to organisations with 150 or more employees. After a further two years (by 2007) it will apply to organisations with 100 or more employees; and after a further year (by 2008) to those with 50 or more employees.
- *Information and consultation rights*: The detailed provisions cover:
  - information on the recent and probable development of the undertaking's activities and economic situation;
  - information and consultation on the situation, structure and probable development of employment within the undertaking and on any anticipated measures (particularly where there is a threat to employment);
  - information and consultation on decisions likely to lead to substantial changes in work organisation and contractual relations;
  - the grounds on which an employer might withhold information (e.g. commercial confidentiality).
- *The timing and nature of information disclosure*: Information should be given at such time, in such a way and in sufficient detail to enable employee representatives to conduct an adequate analysis of the material and, where necessary, prepare for consultation.
- *Consultation*: This should be at an 'appropriate' time, using 'appropriate' methods and should cover 'appropriate' issues. It should involve the relevant

level of management and relevant representatives. It should be arranged that the employees' representatives can meet with the employer; obtain a response from the employer to whatever views they express; and be given reasons for the employer's response. Consultation should be with a view to reaching an agreement on decisions.

■ *Non-compliance*: Member states are to provide enforcement arrangements. Penalties for non-compliance should be 'effective, proportionate and dissuasive'.

The Department of Trade and Industry consultation paper on the Directive, *High Performance Workplaces* (2002), asserts a number of principles, indicating the government's attitude to the Directive. These can be summed up as follows:

■ *A balance of fair treatment and economic benefit*: This view echoes that already promoted in previous employment measures and set out in the *Fairness at Work* White Paper (1998). 'Fair treatment' can minimise conflict. Consultation can 'aid understanding on the part of staff of the reasons for a particular proposal and hence smooth its implementation' (para 1.8).

■ *No 'one size fits all' approach*: The Directive 'respects the wide diversity of employee involvement practices throughout Europe'. There is no commitment by the UK government to a 'works council model' as adopted in, for example, France and Germany. Indeed, the government notes that 'there is no single European model and the Information and Consultation Directive does not seek to impose one' (para 5.2).

■ *Acknowledgement of existing good practice*: The government notes that the Directive 'will allow us to introduce arrangements in the UK that respect and build on the best of our tradition and experience and at the same time help to spread existing best practice'.

■ *Freedom to choose*: The government is not advocating a compulsory specific model. 'The government wants to see business and employees agreeing arrangements that best suit their needs. Where agreement is not reached, there will be a statutory minimum requirement for formal information and consultation procedures consistent with the arrangements laid out in the Directive' (para 1.9). There is no commitment to a 'works council model' as adopted in, for example, France and Germany.

■ *Small and medium-sized enterprises*: The phasing in of the Directive, permitted in the UK, means that special consideration can be given to the interests and concerns of small organisations. 'The government will be considering with small business stakeholders how best to promote information and consultation among SMEs, by non-legislative means' (para 5.5).

There are a number of implications arising from the Information and Consultation Directive. Many of these revisit issues already discussed in the chapter. The key issues are:

■ How is agreement to be achieved in a particular workplace on the structures to be adopted for information and consultation?

■ What is consultation? Is it to be genuine 'social dialogue'? How can this be achieved?

- Who are the employee representatives? If the organisation is a non-union undertaking, how can their credibility and independence be assured?
- To what extent will the new rights give greater coherence to the existing piece-meal information and consultation rights?
- In unionised organisations, how well will the new consultation machinery 'fit' with established collective bargaining machinery?
- What are the obstacles to maintaining employer commitment? How might they realistically be overcome?

Exercise 14.1	**Implications of the Information and Consultation Directive**
	Think about these questions and, in groups, discuss them, suggesting possible answers.

Consultation in multinational companies

In 1994, a European Directive provided for the establishment of a European Works Council (EWC) or a procedure for the purposes of informing and consulting employees on strategic issues. This Directive has been implemented since 1996. However, initially Britain opted out under the Maastricht Treaty 1992. The Directive has now been extended to Britain and, since 1999, has been implemented by relevant British multinationals (Transnational Information and Consultation of Employees Regulations 1999). It was calculated that over 50 British multinationals (although not bound, in the period 1996–9, to comply with the Directive) voluntarily set up works council arrangements.

1996–2000: The purpose of the 1994 Directive is to improve the right to information and to promote consultation in specified 'Community-scale' undertakings or groups of undertakings. Essentially, this refers to multinational companies that operate within the EU (and the EEA). A relevant undertaking is defined as having a total of at least 1000 employees within these member states, including at least 150 employees in each of two or more member states (Art 2). (The number of employees refers to the average of full-timers and part-timers employed in the preceding two years.) It is estimated that some 800 multinational companies are covered by the Directive. Some 300 of these companies have headquarters in the UK.

The Directive provided an opportunity prior to implementation (in September 1996) for companies to establish information and consultation arrangements that met the objectives of the Directive (Art 13). The advantage of this provision was that some flexibility was available in tailoring the information and consultation arrangements to the structure and operational circumstances of the multinational company concerned.

The issues discussed included: the economic position of the company; investment plans; product market and sales information; technological change; restructuring; research and development. The agenda is generally drafted by management. The extent to which any particular issue is explored in detail is, usually, a matter for the company concerned. Few schemes provide for formal consultation and agreement. They tend to involve the sharing of information, discussion and exchanging views. Indeed, in this respect they reflect the Directive's own description of 'consultation' as 'the exchange of views and establishment of dialogue' (Art 2). There is a provision in the Directive prohibiting the disclosure of confidential information (Art 8).

Generally, EWCs meet in plenary session for one day once a year. However, there are occasional examples of biannual meetings. Representatives are elected according to the law of the member state concerned (Art 2).

2000 onwards: The Transnational Information and Consultation of Employees Regulations 1999 (the TICE Regulations) came into force on 15 January 2000. They set out various provisions to implement the 1994 Directive in the UK. The key provisions are as follows:

- *An EWC agreement*: This is achieved through negotiations between management and employees in the relevant undertaking. The negotiating process is triggered after a written request from at least one hundred employees (or their representatives) in two or more EU member states. Alternatively, negotiations may start on management's own initiative.

- *'Special Negotiating Body' (SNB)*: Employees are represented in the negotiations by this body. It comprises representatives from all EU and EEA member states in which the undertaking has business operations. The number of representatives and the way in which the SNB members are selected is determined by each member state. The TICE Regulations 1999 prescribe one representative from each of the EU/EEA countries. Additional members, up to a maximum of four, may be included, depending on the proportionate size of the undertakings' European workforce in particular member states. In the UK, members of the SNB are selected by a ballot of the UK workforce. If there is a pre-existing consultative committee (whose members were elected by the UK workforce and which carries out an information and consultation function on their behalf), then, this committee may elect the SNB representatives.

- *The 'statutory model'*: If management refuses to negotiate within six months of the request; or there is a failure to agree on transnational information and consultation procedures within three years, then, the EWC must be set up in accordance with the 'statutory model' (TICE Regulations 1999).

- *Disclosure of information*: The Regulations provide that management may withhold information or require the EWC to hold it in confidence where 'according to objective criteria it would seriously harm the functioning of the undertaking or be prejudicial to it' if it were disclosed. The EWC members can appeal to the Central Arbitration Committee (CAC) if they believe that management is not complying with the law in this respect. The CAC would rule on a case-by-case basis.

- *Enforcement*: There are two aspects to the enforcement process. The CAC hears disputes about whether an undertaking is subject to the Directive and about the procedures leading to the establishment of an EWC. In the first two years, the Committee reported that it has received only one application, which was subsequently withdrawn (Annual Report 2001–02). The Employment Appeals Tribunal hears disputes about the operation of an EWC or its non-establishment. It also hears appeals on points of law from the CAC. Both the CAC and the EAT may refer cases to ACAS if conciliation is considered useful.

A study (Weber *et al.*, 2000), among ten UK multinationals which complied with the 1994 Directive, reported the following on the working of the EWC system:

■ Eight of the ten concluded voluntary agreements under Article 13 mainly because of the greater flexibility provided.

■ All companies were 'concerned not to exclude their employees in the UK from their European-wide bodies for information provision and consultation'.

■ 'All the companies had prior experience of information and consultation arrangements in one of several member states where they had subsidiaries. However, all reported that they would not have set up European information and consultation bodies had it not been for the Directive'.

■ Employee representatives were selected according to the national rules and practices of each member state. In the UK, most companies opted for 'split representation' – with one group nominated by the recognised union(s) and the other directly elected by ballot of the relevant workforce.

■ In terms of costs, the mean cost of annual meetings was £53 000. The cost per employee representative was between £900 and £4500. 'The most variable element' in the costs of employee representatives was translation and interpretation. Understandably, this 'was relatively low for those organisations with a very high proportion of their workforce in the UK'.

The views of the respondent companies was summarised as follows:

> Some companies said that EWCs lead to unnecessary duplication of information and consultation provision between EWCs and national information and consultation bodies, raised unrealistic expectations amongst some employee representatives about what they could achieve and, in the longer term, might lead to calls for transnational collective bargaining. On a more positive note, most perceived some symbolic value in demonstrating companies' concern about their employees. However, others saw value in contributing to increased trust, employee involvement in the business, better understanding of the factors affecting managerial decisions and developing a corporate culture (Weber *et al.*, 2000).

Collective redundancies

This legislation derives from the 1975 Directive on collective redundancies (as amended by the 1992 Directive). The duty to consult applies where 'an employer is proposing to dismiss as redundant twenty or more employees at one establishment within a period of ninety days or less' (TULRCA 1992, s 188(1)). The consultation 'shall begin in good time . . . before the first of the dismissals takes effect' (s 188(1A)). Elaborating this, the statute states that where the employer is proposing to dismiss 100 or more employees, the consultation take place 'at least ninety days' before the dismissals, and in other cases, 'at least thirty days'. The consultation 'shall be undertaken by the employer with a view to reaching agreement' with the employee representatives (s 188(2)). It shall include discussion about ways of:

■ avoiding the dismissals;

■ reducing the numbers of employees to be dismissed;

■ reducing the consequences of the dismissals.

The employer must 'disclose in writing' (s 188(4)) to the employee representatives the following information:

- the reasons for the proposed redundancies;
- the numbers and descriptions of the employees whom it is proposed to dismiss as redundant;
- the total number of employees of any such description employed by the employer at the establishment in question;
- the proposed method of selecting the employees who may be dismissed. The importance of non-discriminatory criteria must be remembered;
- the proposed method of carrying out the dismissals, with due regard to any agreed procedure, including the period over which the dismissals are to take effect;
- the proposed method of calculating the amount of any redundancy payments to be made to dismissed employees (in excess of the statutory minimum).

The employer may claim exemption from this duty to consult if there are 'special circumstances which render it not reasonably practicable for the employer to comply' (s 188(7)). (An example of this might be the immediate closure of an organisation.) However, he must take 'all such steps towards compliance' as are reasonably practicable. For example, it may not be practical to consult for at least 90 days, but genuine consultation for a shorter period might be reasonbly practicable.

The representatives with whom an employer should consult might be either:

- employee representatives elected by the appropriate workforce; or
- representatives of an independent trade union that is recognised for the appropriate workforce (s 188(1B)).

A failure by an employer to comply with any aspects of the duty to consult (set out in s 188) can result in a complaint to an employment tribunal. If the complaint is well founded, the tribunal must 'make a declaration to that effect and may also make a protective award' (ss 189–90). Such a complaint must be made before the date upon which the last of the dismissals takes effect, or within three months of that date (unless the tribunal agrees an extended period) (s 189(5)).

Transfers of undertakings

This legislation derives from the 1977 Acquired Rights Directive and is found in British law in the Transfer of Undertakings (Protection of Employment) Regulations 1981 (as amended) (the TUPE Regulations). The duty upon the relevant employers to consult is potentially wide ranging. 'Where an employer of any affected employees envisages that he will, in connection with the transfer, be taking measures in relation to any such employees he shall consult.' This consultation shall be with appropriate representatives of the employees for whom he will be 'taking measures'. The consultation shall be 'with a view to seeking their agreement to the measures to be taken' (reg 10.5).

Several points of elaboration need to be made in respect of this duty. First, it applies to the transferee (the organisation to which the undertaking or part of the undertaking is being transferred and is likely to become the new employer of the working people concerned) as well as the transferor (the organisation which is shedding the staff). This arises because **both** employers may have employees who are 'affected' by 'a relevant transfer' (reg 10.1).

The nature of the consultation is developed in the TUPE Regulations in the following way: 'The employer shall (a) consider any representations made by the appropriate representatives; and (b) reply to those representations and, if he rejects any of those representations, state his reasons' (reg 10.6).

The employer of any 'affected employees' (the transferor and/or the transferee) must inform representatives 'long enough' before a relevant transfer of the following (reg 10.2):

- the fact that the relevant transfer is to take place;
- when, approximately, it is to take place;
- the reasons for the transfer;
- the legal, economic and social implications of the transfer for the affected employees;
- the measures which the employer envisages taking, in connection with the transfer, in relation to the 'affected employees';
- if no measures are envisaged, then, that fact;
- information from the transferee about measures (if any) affecting those employees who will become employees of the transferee.

The 'measures' that might be considered are permitted dismissals for an 'economic, technical or organisational reason entailing changes in the workforce of either the transferor or the transferee before or after a relevant transfer' (reg 8.2).

The representatives with whom an employer should consult might be either:

- employee representatives elected by the appropriate workforce; or
- representatives of an independent trade union that is recognised for the appropriate workforce (reg 10.2A).

If an employer fails to inform and consult the appropriate representatives, a complaint can be made to an employment tribunal. The tribunal shall, if the complaint is well founded, make a declaration and may award 'appropriate compensation' to the 'affected employees' (reg 11).

Health and safety

There is a general duty upon 'every employer' to consult with union or employee representatives 'with a view to the making and maintenance of arrangements which will enable him and his employees to co-operate effectively in promoting and developing measures to ensure the health and safety at work of the employees, and in checking the effectiveness of such measures' (Health and Safety at Work etc. Act 1974, s 2(6)).

There are four alternative consultation arrangements provided under health and safety legislation. These are:

1 through the representatives of recognised independent trade unions (Safety Representatives and Safety Committees Regulations 1977);

2 through non-union employee representatives (Health and Safety (Consultation with Employees) Regulations 1996);

3 direct with the relevant workforce (Health and Safety (Consultation with Employees) Regulations 1996);

4 through representatives off-shore (Offshore (Safety Representatives and Safety Committees) Regulations 1989).

These arrangments are outlined in Chapter 12.

Occupational pensions

Employers are required to consult with independent recognised trade unions on certain matters relating to contracting out of the state scheme (Pensions Scheme Act 1993). Also, there are requirements on pension trustees to disclose information about their stewardship (Occupational Pensions Schemes (Disclosure of Information) Regulations 1996).

European Company Statute

In 2001, a European Regulation and an accompanying Directive were adopted by the Council of Ministers. The Regulation comes into force in October 2004. The Directive concerns worker involvement in European companies. A European company will be a new legal entity, available on a voluntary basis to companies operating in more than one EU member state. Arrangements for employee involvement in the European company must be in place before such a company can be registered. This may include worker representation on the board of a company. Voluntary negotiations are possible within the company about the form of involvement. If these do not lead to an agreement, then, a set of standard arrangements prescribed in the Directive will apply. These provide for a representative body similar to that under the European Works Council Directive 1994. This body is to be informed and consulted about the company's current and future business plans, production and sales levels, implications of these for the workforce, management changes, mergers, divestments, potential closures and layoffs.

Collective bargaining

A duty upon employers to bargain with trade unions is enacted under the Employment Relations Act 1999. It is hedged about with various conditions. This section considers the legal framework within which this duty is located. It also provides a broad review of the issues that are likely to arise under a scheme for statutory recognition:

- the meaning of recognition;
- the meaning of collective bargaining;
- the legal status of collective agreements;

- the transfer of collective agreements;
- prohibitions on pressure to enforce recognition upon an employer;
- information for collective bargaining;
- workforce agreements, protection for representatives;
- facilities for union representatives;
- the statutory recognition process.

The meaning of recognition

In the Trade Union and Labour Relations (Consolidation) Act 1992, 'recognition' in relation to a trade union means 'the recognition of the union by an employer, or two or more associated employers, to any extent, for the purpose of collective bargaining' (TULRCA, s 178(3)). The 'extent' may be slight – over a few key issues (e.g. pay, hours and holidays). Alternatively, it may be extensive – covering, for example, terms and conditions, deployment of staff and technical change. The employer's view on the acceptable 'extent' of bargaining normally prevails.

The meaning of collective bargaining

In TULRCA (s 178(1)–(2)), collective bargaining means negotiations relating to or connected with one or more matters. These matters are specified as:

- terms and conditions of employment, or the physical conditions in which any workers are required to work;
- engagement or non-engagement, or termination or suspension of employment or the duties of employment, of one or more workers;
- allocation of work or the duties of employment between workers or groups of workers;
- matters of discipline;
- a worker's membership or non-membership of a trade union;
- facilities for officials of trade unions;
- machinery for negotiation or consultation and other procedures relating to any of the above matters including the recognition by employers or employers' associations of the right of a trade union to represent workers in such negotiation or consultation or in the carrying out of such procedures.

Clearly, they encompass both the substantive and procedural issues of employee relations.

The legal status of collective agreements

A collective agreement 'shall be conclusively presumed not to have been intended by the parties to be a legally enforceable contract' (TULRCA, s 179(1)). If it is to be regarded as legally enforceable, the agreement must be in writing and must contain a provision 'which (however expressed) states that the parties intend that the agreement shall be a legally enforceable contract' (s 179(1)(a), (b)). If only part of the agreement is to be legally enforceable, then this must be clearly identified (s 179(3)).

The transfer of collective agreements

In the event of a transfer of an undertaking, certain legal provisions apply (TUPE Regulations 1981). Effectively, collective agreements (including recognition agreements) are transferred from the transferor to the transferee. So, where there are collective agreements between a transferor and a trade union that affect the conditions of employment of transferred employees, 'that agreement, in its application in relation to the employee, shall, after the transfer, have effect as if made by or on behalf of the transferee with that trade union' (reg 6). Where an independent trade union is recognised by a transferor employer 'to any extent' in respect of the employees transferred, 'the union shall be deemed to have been recognised by the transferee to the same extent' (reg 9.2).

Prohibitions on pressure to enforce recognition

As part of its policy on trade union recognition, the Conservative governments in the 1980s introduced certain restrictions to limit the pressure to be exerted by trade unions on non-union employers (TULRCA, ss 186, 187 and 225). These remain in force:

- **A contract to supply goods or services**: A term or condition of such a contract is void if it requires a party to the contract to *recognise* one or more trade unions; or *negotiate or consult* with a union or union official (TULRCA, s 186).
- **A refusal to deal with a supplier or prospective supplier of goods or services**: This is unlawful if 'the grounds or one of the grounds' is the supplier's non-recognition of trade unions or failure to negotiate or consult with unions. Evidence of such unlawful action would be a list of approved suppliers of goods, exclusion of a supplier from a tender list, failure to permit a supplier to submit a tender or the termination of a contract to supply (s 187).
- **Industrial action**: Industrial action to pressurise an employer to break the provisions of ss 186 and 187 is unlawful (s 225(1)), as is any attempt to force an employer to recognise or negotiate or consult with a union (s 225(2)).

Information for collective bargaining

In the 1970s, when, as outlined earlier, public policy strongly supported the extension of collective bargaining, a general duty was placed upon employers who recognised independent unions to disclose information for the purposes of collective bargaining to union representatives (TULRCA, s 181). It is stated that:

> the information to be disclosed is all information relating to the employer's undertaking which is in his possession, or that of an associated employer, and is information (a) without which the trade union representative would be to a material extent impeded in carrying on collective bargaining with him and (b) which it would be in accordance with good industrial relations practice that he should disclose to them for the purposes of collective bargaining (s 181(2)).

There are restrictions on the information that an employer is required to disclose (including, for example, that which would breach national security or an existing statute or which is confidential information) (s 182). Furthermore, the employer is not obliged to engage in work or expenditure to produce information that is 'out of reasonable proportion to the value of the information in the conduct of collective bargaining' (s 182(2)(b)). A complaint for non-disclosure can be made to the Central Arbitration Committee (ss 183–5).

This right is further elaborated in the ACAS *Code of Practice* (1997).

Workforce agreements

So far we have considered the issue of collective agreements. A new term has emerged under the Working Time Regulations 1998 (WTR 1998): 'workforce agreements', which will be applicable in non-union workforces (*see also* Chapter 11). Under these Regulations there are three types of 'relevant agreement', which enables some flexibility to be introduced into its implementation: a collective agreement, a workforce agreement or any other written agreement between a worker and their employer that is legally enforceable (reg 2). The flexibilities possible through the negotiation of a collective agreement or a workforce agreement are:

Working time
■ defining working time (reg 2.1).

Maximum working week
■ determining the reference period (potentially up to 12 months) for the 48-hour average working week (reg 23).

Night work
■ determining the period during which work is classified as night work (reg 2.1);
■ defining a night worker (reg 2.1);
■ defining the reference period applicable in respect of the limit on the length of night work (reg 6.3);
■ determining the types of work that involve 'special hazards or heavy physical or mental strain' for night workers (reg 6.8).

Rests and breaks
■ determining the starting point of a seven-day period for the weekly rest entitlement (reg 11.4);
■ deciding the length of rest breaks where the working day is longer than six hours (reg 12.2).

Annual leave
■ deciding the start date of the holiday year (reg 13.3).

A workforce agreement is described in the following terms (WTR 1998, Sch 1):

■ it has to be in writing;
■ it is to be effective for a specified period not exceeding five years;
■ it can apply to all or a part of a workforce;
■ it has to be signed by representatives of the workforce or a majority of the workforce (if the employer employed 20 or fewer workers on the date of the agreement);
■ advanced copies of the text and guidance are to be provided by the employer before signature.

Requirements are set out for the election of 'representatives of the workforce'. These include the requirement that 'the election is conducted so as to secure that (i) so far as reasonably practicable, those voting do so in secret and (ii) the votes given at the election are fairly and accurately counted' (Sch 1, para 3).

Workforce agreements have also been provided for under the Maternity and Parental Leave etc. Regulations 1999 and under provisions relating to fixed-term employees (Fixed-Term Employees Regulations 2002).

14.4.4 Statutory rights for representatives

Facilities for representatives

These fall into two categories: those relating to trade union representatives, and those specified for employee representatives who are elected to consult about particular issues.

- **Union representatives**: Officials of independent, recognised trade unions (e.g. shop stewards and staff representatives) have a statutory right to 'time off during his working hours for the purpose of carrying out any duties' and 'training in aspects of industrial relations' (TULRCA, s 168). The amount of time to be taken and the exercise of the right must be 'reasonable in all the circumstances' (s 168(3)). An ACAS Code of Practice (No. 3, *Time off for Trade Union Duties and Activities*, 1991) provides guidance on the operation of this provision. The duties are principally negotiations with the employer on collective bargaining issues (s 178(2)). Arrangements for payment for the time off are indicated (s 169).

  There is also a companion right available to all employees who are members of an independent union which is recognised by their employer (s 170). Under this, an employee has the right to take time off during working hours to take part in 'any activities of the union' and 'any activities in relation to which the employee is acting as a representative of a trade union'. The exercise of this right must be 'reasonable in all the circumstances'. There is no requirement upon an employer to pay for time off for trade union activities. Complaints about the exercise of all these rights can be made to an employment tribunal.

- **Employee representatives**: In relation to consultation on collective redundancies, 'the employer shall allow the appropriate representatives access to the employees whom it is proposed to dismiss as redundant and shall afford to those representatives such accommodation and other facilities as may be appropriate' (s 188(5A)). A similar provision occurs in the TUPE Regulations (reg 10.6A). The nature of these facilities is unspecified. However, paid time off is provided for (Employment Rights Act 1996, ss 61–2).

Protections against victimisation

Representatives are also protected from victimisation and discrimination by employers.

Those elected or standing for election as representatives in redundancy consultation or consultation on transfers of undertakings have 'a right not to be subjected to any detriment by any act, or any deliberate failure to act, by his employer done on the ground that' the person was an employee representative or a candidate for election (ERA 1996, s 47).

In addition, a trade union member has a right 'not to have action short of dismissal taken against him as an individual by his employer' if this is for the purpose of preventing the person from taking part in the activities of an independent trade union at 'an appropriate time' (TULRCA, s 146). A parallel protection is provided against dismissal (s 152).

14.4.5 Statutory recognition for collective bargaining

The scheme implemented in 2000, under amendments to the Trade Union and Labour Relations (Consolidation) Act 1992 (Sch A), is the third attempt to enact such a system in the post-war period. Previous attempts were between 1972 and 1974 and 1975 and 1980. These were subsequently reviewed in the literature of employee relations (Weekes *et al.*, 1975; Dickens and Bain, 1986; Ewing, 1990). The starting point of the new scheme is 'voluntary agreement'. The statutory procedure is for circumstances where such agreement 'proves impossible' (para 4.15).

The statutory recognition procedure

Any independent trade union (or a group of such unions acting jointly) should be able to invoke this. The government expects competing claims from unions to be resolved beforehand with the possible assistance of the Trades Union Congress, although this will not be part of the statutory procedure (para 4.19). Small organisations are to be excluded from these statutory requirements. The procedure will not apply to employers with 20 or fewer employees.

The steps involved in this statutory procedure can be summarised as follows:

1 A **formal request** in writing to the employer specifying the group of employees on behalf of whom recognition is sought (i.e. the bargaining unit).

2 The employer's **response** within 14 days. This response might take one of three forms:

   (a) agreement to the union's/unions' request. The statutory recognition procedure is then closed;

   (b) willingness to discuss the details of the request with the union/s. ACAS might be asked to assist in the achievement of an agreement;

   (c) no response or refusal. The union/s may make an immediate application to the Central Arbitration Committee (CAC).

3 The **responsibilities of the CAC:**

   (a) to determine *whether the union-proposed bargaining unit is appropriate*, and if not, to specify what would be an appropriate bargaining unit;

   (b) to determine *whether the union has the support of a majority* of the employees in the appropriate bargaining unit (drawn, perhaps, in the first instance, from membership records).

4 The **CAC process**:

(a) 'It will first try to **broker an agreement** between the employer and the union, allowing up to 28 days for this stage';

(b) if agreement is not achieved, it will (normally within seven days) **determine the appropriate bargaining unit**. In making this decision, the CAC:

should take particular account of the bargaining unit's compatibility with the need for effective management as well as:

- the views of the employer and of the union;

- any existing national or local bargaining arrangements;

- the desirability as a general rule of avoiding small, fragmented bargaining units within an undertaking;

- the characteristics of the employees in the bargaining group proposed by the union and of any other of the employer's employees whom the CAC consider relevant; and

- the location of the employees.

5 Once the **bargaining unit is agreed or determined**, two alternative courses of action may then follow:

(a) the **employer may accept** that the union enjoys majority support and the CAC will issue a declaration that the union is recognised for the bargaining unit concerned;

(b) a **secret ballot of the bargaining unit** is to be conducted by an independent body (within 21 days of the bargaining unit being determined). An employer will be under a legal duty to co-operate with the body conducting the ballot and with the union. The cost of the ballot will be shared equally between the employer and the union. The union will be declared as recognised provided that a majority of those voting and at least 40 per cent of those eligible to vote have supported recognition.

6 Then 'the employer and the union must try to reach **a procedure agreement** to give effect to recognition and set out how they will conduct collective bargaining'. The parties may seek the assistance of ACAS. Under existing law, this agreement may be legally enforceable (TULRCA, s 179). Even if it is not legally binding, an employer or an independent union can apply to the CAC to impose a legally binding default procedure agreement (*see* below) because it considers that the other party is not honouring the terms of the voluntarily agreed procedure.

7 If three months after the agreement to give effect to or the determination of recognition, no procedure agreement has been reached, then the union may apply to the CAC to have '**a default procedure agreement**' applied. After a further attempt at brokering an agreement, the CAC can impose this. It would be legally binding on both parties. It would provide for collective bargaining 'on pay, hours and holidays as a minimum'.

Enforcement

A legally binding procedure agreement will be 'a deemed contract between employer and union'. If a complaint is made that a party is in breach of the procedure agreement then a court may make an order for specific performance, and any failure to comply with the order would be contempt of court.

The usual consequences of contempt of court are that the offending party is liable to pay a fine (this is unlimited and depends on the view of the court). Imprisonment is also an option. The way of 'purging contempt' is to apologise to the court and comply with the order. (*See* Chapter 15 for examples of where these proceedings were used, particularly in the 1980s against unions under industrial action law.)

Derecognition

Employers will have available a parallel procedure to end recognition arrangements if employee support for them reduces significantly.

Experience of the new statutory recognition procedure

The Central Arbitration Committee, in its Annual Report (2002) recorded 175 applications under the statutory recognition procedure over the period from 2000 to 2002. The number of cases grew in the second year of operation (2001–02). The Chairman noted that the number of live cases at any one time was about 50. The majority of cases came from three sectors: manufacturing (43 per cent); printing and publishing (21 per cent); and transport/distribution (19 per cent). Geographically, 37 per cent came from London and the south-east; 25 per cent from the north and north-west of England; and 19 per cent from the Midlands. Few came from other parts of the United Kingdom. It was reported that 'continuing the trend noted in last year's report, 57 per cent of all applications received to 31 March 2002 involved organisations employing less than 200 staff' (CAC, 2002: 18).

The Chairman reported that four decisions of the CAC had been subject to judicial review – three in the second year. He added that 'as employers, unions and their advisers increase their familiarity with the system, they are also liable to become more inclined to challenge CAC decisions' (CAC, 2002: 3). However, in one of these cases, the Court of Appeal signalled the inappropriateness of judicial review for challenging CAC decisions. It was stated that the CAC was intended by Parliament to be a decision-making body in a specialist area that was not suitable for intervention by the courts. This may deflect further applications – unless there is serious irregularity in the CAC proceedings.

One notable decision, which was the subject of judicial review, concerned the determination of an appropriate bargaining unit. The Chairman of the CAC commented that 'probably the most complex part of the recognition process for a panel is when it is required to decide the issue of the appropriateness of the bargaining unit. This can involve the panel in detailed discussions on the rationale behind the union's proposed bargaining unit and any counter-proposal by the company. Each party will seek to demonstrate why the other's proposal is unsuitable' (CAC, 2002: 3) (*see* Fig. 14.3).

The company structure: It has 646 centres in Britain, 110 of which are located in London, in two divisions. London comprises 20 per cent of the company's employees.

Union objectives: The Transport and General Workers' Union had for two years been recruiting and organising employees in the London area. In October 2001, it applied for statutory recognition.

The first step: The CAC held a hearing to decide, as required, the appropriate bargaining unit.

TGWU's view: The union contended that the two London divisions were different in employment terms from the rest of Kwik-Fit. They had a London weighting and, until recently, operated a particular pattern of working-time. Also, they had a separate management structure, where final discipline and dismissal decisions were taken without reference to head office.

Kwik-Fit's view: The company stated that it was an integrated and centralised organisation. All fitters and centre managers (subject to seniority of service) were on the same terms and conditions of employment. National procedures on discipline were followed. The company was concerned that a London 'bargaining unit' would lead to fragmentation and the possibility of multi-unionism.

CAC's view: It saw nothing particular about the London divisions – except that London had a distinctive labour market. However, there were some aspects that were persuasive: the relative autonomy of the London divisions in disciplinary matters; and the local delivery of training by a local manager. So, other aspects of employment relations, such as collective bargaining, could be applied to the London divisions. It did not see collective bargaining affecting management approaches in the company. The divisional management team were seen as capable of conducting collective bargaining within a national framework; and developing working relationships. So, the statutory requirement – to ensure that the bargaining unit was compatible with effective management – was satisfied.

Ballot of employees: The CAC proposed a ballot of the workers in the bargaining unit to decide whether a majority supported recognition by the TGWU for collective bargaining on wages, hours and holidays.

Judicial review: Before the ballot could be held, Kwik-Fit applied to the High Court for judicial review of the CAC's decision. The company argued that the CAC had not considered the company's counter-proposal. The CAC was said by the court to have 'misdirected' itself and its decision was set aside. The CAC should not have considered the union's proposal first. The CAC appealed to the Court of Appeal.

Court of Appeal decision: The Court had to decide whether or not the CAC had erred in law in understanding the statutory provisions. It found that the CAC was entitled to consider the union's proposal for a bargaining unit against the statutory tests and then the employer's arguments. It was not responsible for determining the most appropriate bargaining unit. The CAC is not under a statutory duty to treat the union's proposal and the employer's proposal on an equal footing.

Figure 14.3 The Kwik-Fit case

Source: *R* v *Central Arbitration Committee and another ex parte Kwik-Fit* [2002] IRLR 395.

14.5 Employment policies and practices

In the UK there is considerable variability in employers' approaches to participation and representation. As indicated earlier, some organisations have adopted comprehensive systems of employee participation which combine low-level employee involvement, high-level representation and profit-sharing and/or employee share-ownership schemes. In other companies, employee involvement is extremely limited. Between these two extremes, the vast majority of UK-based organisations operate systems of employee participation which demonstrate a marked preference for particular forms of employee involvement. This variability indicates differences in the importance attached to participation and representation by managers in different organisations. It also shows wider variations in beliefs of policy-makers and academics about the advantages and disadvantages of different forms of these schemes. More specifically, it reflects differences of view about answers to the following four questions.

1   Why should employees participate?
2   What areas of decision-making and action should be covered?
3   Who should be involved in employee participation?
4   How, when and where should participation mechanisms be organised?

This section explores different answers to these questions, looking at four different theoretical approaches: traditional managerialist, progressive managerialist, industrial democrat or partnership, and social inclusionist. These terms are used as heuristic devices and therefore it should not be assumed that the writers reviewed in this section would willingly apply these labels to their own work, nor that practitioners and politicians would use these labels when attempting to define the approaches that they have adopted. However, it is hoped that the use of these categories may reveal some enduring differences of opinion between writers about appropriate forms of employee participation.

14.5.1   Traditional managerialist

The term *traditional managerialist* is used to group writers and practitioners who argue for a strict division between the work of managers and employees. These include those associated with particular schools of management thought: Scientific Management, Classical Management Theory and Business Process Re-Engineering. For these commentators participation should be limited to the minimum required for employees to undertake their allotted jobs. The reasoning behind this judgement is commonly based on the following two arguments.

First, it is suggested that employees do not own the organisations they work in and, therefore, they should not expect to be involved in decisions about how their work is organised and administered. In the UK, property owners have certain legal rights to determine how their belongings will be used. Thus, those who receive a wage or salary for their work and who do not own the materials or equipment with which they work are bound to respect and abide by the decisions of the organisation's owners. Indeed, for some this lack of ownership rights means that employees can be treated by their employers as a factor of production like any other raw material (*see* discussion of the 'right to manage' in Chapter 1).

Secondly, it is suggested that organisations exist to pursue the objectives of their owners or sponsors. In commercial organisations these objectives will tend to include measures designed to enhance profitability, increase sales, improve productivity and ultimately ensure the long-term survival of the enterprise. By contrast, within public-sector bodies and voluntary organisations the main objectives will tend to be the achievement of objectives defined by nominated representatives.

For example, the trustees of a charity or local politicians may define the objectives and means of operation of their respective organisations.

However, whatever the form of ownership, it is suggested that the objectives of the employer will frequently conflict with those of the employee. Employees, it is suggested, will tend to concentrate on their employment prospects and rewards, while managers will concentrate on the financial viability of the wider organisation. Because of these differences in objectives, it is argued that someone has to have the power to make the final decision on any issue.

For writers adopting a traditional managerialist perspective those best placed to make these decisions are the organisation's managers. As these commentators point out, managers have been recruited and trained to make these decisions according to financial and technical criteria which other employees may not fully understand or be capable of understanding. In other words, individual employees do not know enough about the organisation and the broad sweep of its activities in order to make informed judgements about what should be done. Furthermore, the division of decision-making responsibilities between managers and employees is likely to be in the employees' own best interests because this approach will lead to quicker and more effective decision-making.

Writers associated with the traditional managerialist perspective are apt to suggest that employees should be fully informed about management decisions after they have been taken. The information in these written communications and briefings should include areas subject to legal regulation including details of the employee's terms and conditions of employment, operating and technical instructions relating to the performance of the job, health and safety information and details of the organisation's disciplinary and grievance procedures. However, these same writers tend to warn against the provision of information or any measures which may increase employee influence over decisions about the overall objectives of the organisation or how resources are allocated. Allowing involvement in these areas, they suggest, is likely to undermine the overall effectiveness of the organisation and should, therefore, be resisted.

14.5.2 Progressive managerialist

This approach draws together a series of common assumptions underpinning the analyses of mainstream writers associated with schools of management thought which have been labelled: human relations, the quality of work life movement (QWL), 'soft' human resource management (HRM) and total quality management (TQM). In different ways, the main protagonists of these approaches have argued that the most effective organisations provide opportunities for employees to influence how their own work is structured and performed. This is normally taken to mean that employees should not play a direct role in decisions concerning the strategic direction of the organisation or the allocation of resources, but should be informed of these decisions and be entrusted with a greater say in how particular tasks are organised and informed about the organisation's current position and future prospects (*see* Fig. 14.4). It also means that employees should be provided with greater opportunities to share in the financial rewards of organisational success.

Policy-makers and practitioners associated with the progressive managerialist label arrive at their conclusions about the importance of low-level employee involvement and financial participation as a result of assessing four factors: the

Employees have a strong interest in what is happening in the company. Information going beyond matters of direct and personal relevance which should be given to employees will vary according to whether the organisation is in the private or public sector, in manufacturing, construction or services, and on its size and structure. Management should normally report to all employees on the organisation's:

- objectives and policies
- past and present performance and progress
- future plans and prospects.

Under these broad headings information can be given about:

- financial performance
- management and manpower changes
- state of the market and order book
- changes in products or services
- technological developments
- investment.

The emphasis should be on successes and problems and the reasons for them. This information should be provided as part of a regular programme. When successes are achieved employees need to be told promptly; similarly they should be given early warning of problems. Employees tend to distrust managers who communicate only when there is bad news.

In most organisations information on the performance of the company will normally contain financial data about:

- sales
- income and expenditure
- turnover
- profit and loss
- assets and liabilities
- cash flow
- return on investment
- added value.

Much of this information has to be made public by law – for example in the Annual Report to Shareholders – and is indirectly available to employees. Often it is not readily understood in this form and may be misinterpreted by employees or give a misleading picture, unless it is carefully explained in a separate employee report.

Special efforts are needed by management to provide information about performance, progress and prospects in subsidiary companies, private companies or partnerships, and in non-commercial organisations.

Job security is a major concern of all employees. Changes in technology or market conditions can cause fears among employees which become exaggerated if based on rumour or false information. Advance information and discussion of the organisation's prospects can help alleviate such fears and assist employees to adapt to necessary change.

Where information may affect the share price of a company, Stock Exchange regulations also prevent the organisation informing employees before the market is notified, although they may be informed simultaneously.

Figure 14.4   Extracts from ACAS advice on what information should be communicated to employees

Source: ACAS (1998: 7–12).

significance of technological change, the need for effective resource utilisation, the value of employee morale and the economic benefits of participation. Arguments supporting the promotion of such participation relate to these developments.

Technological change

This view is based on the assumption that the nature of private and public-sector organisations has changed radically over the last 50 years. The spread of new technologies and more intensive forms of knowledge work have meant that it is now difficult, if not impossible, for managers to gain and retain a detailed understanding of the work of their employees. Without this understanding of the tasks performed by each employee, it is not possible to separate the tasks of planning and executing work as suggested by traditional managerialists. Recognising these difficulties, it is argued that it is essential that employees are involved in decisions about how work will be performed, if only because they have useful information necessary to ensure that the right decisions are taken.

Effective resource utilisation

This is the second argument for increased participation. It is based on the assumption that there has been increased competition between organisations in both the private and public sectors. This, it is suggested, means that it is now essential for managers to ensure they use resources effectively. The most expensive of these resources is likely to be staff. While traditional managerialists suggest that the contribution of employees should be limited to physical activities, their more progressive counterparts argue that managers should also attempt to tap the mental capabilities of their employees. The advocates of this approach suggest that team-working, quality circles, problem-solving groups, working parties and team-briefings provide appropriate means for encouraging employees to help managers when dealing with decisions about how particular tasks should be performed. In the most advanced forms of these arrangements self-managed teams might even replace managers completely (*see* Fig. 14.5).

A number of studies of the implementation and operation of quality circles and problem-solving groups suggest that the presence of the following factors is likely to have a key bearing on the success of these schemes:

■ visible commitment and encouragement from top management;
■ time and money allocated for training and meetings;
■ senior managers should be available to attend meetings;
■ management support for the implementation of solutions to problems, with resources where necessary;
■ open operation with full recognition given to their achievements;
■ the circle or group should be able to select their own problems to solve, not just those selected by managers;
■ trade unions should be consulted and encouraged to become involved;
■ initial objectives should be modest and any scheme should begin with a pilot project.

Figure 14.5 The implementation of quality circles and problem-solving groups

Employee morale

The third set of arguments used to support task-centred employee participation is based on the motivations of staff. It is argued that employee participation provides a means of increasing employees' feelings of control over the work they perform, their job satisfaction, commitment to the organisation and trust in managers' actions. They argue that employee morale increases where individual members of staff are given more control over the work that they do. This improvement is said to have direct positive effects on the quantity and quality of work performed by staff and as a consequence the overall financial health and viability of the organisation. To help the organisation's managers directly gauge the state of employee morale, the supporters of the progressive management techniques frequently call for the use of staff attitude surveys, the high visibility of senior managers, periodic meetings of the whole workforce and measures to improve the direct people management skills of line managers.

Economic benefits

The final set of arguments used by progressive managerialists emphasises that employees should be encouraged to see the links between their individual contributions and the success of the organisation. This, it is suggested, can be achieved through the introduction of profit-related pay, gain-sharing plans and employee share-ownership schemes. These schemes are frequently referred to as forms of financial participation, although the inability of employees to influence the form and operation of most of these schemes suggests that this is probably an inappropriate label.

Proponents of financial participation frequently argue that by tying a proportion of employees' pay to the financial performance of departments, divisions or the organisation as a whole, it is possible to promote a greater shared understanding of the common interests of employees and managers. They also suggest that the adoption of these techniques will promote more enterprising behaviour by all sections of the workforce. Some advocates of these schemes have even argued that by allowing employees' wages and salaries to increase and decrease in line with the performance of the organisation it should be possible to avoid the need for redundancies and lay-offs when there is a business downturn.

14.5.3 'Industrial democrat' or partnership

The third group includes a range of writers associated with movements or labels like stakeholding and social or industrial partnership. Advocates tend to adopt pluralist assumptions about appropriate forms of social and business organisation. They maintain that the objectives of any organisation and decisions about how it should operate are always contested and the subject of disagreements. This conflict over the objectives of the organisation, it is argued, most commonly occurs between employers and their employees (or union and employee representatives). Supporters of this approach base their claims for the extension and consolidation of employee participation on three political and social arguments, rather than the more economic and business rationales.

Employees as corporate citizens not salaried subjects

The first and perhaps most important argument advanced by the 'industrial democrats' is that individual employees should be treated as citizens rather than subjects – civil rights do not end at the workplace gate. They suggest that employees, as citizens, should have the right to influence decisions affecting their working lives, rather than just a duty to perform tasks defined by their employers. While these writers frequently concede that ownership of the organisation confers certain rights on the employer, they go on to argue that the payment of a salary does not entitle an employer to treat their employees as waged slaves. Furthermore, they argue that the owner's property rights over land, materials and equipment have been granted by the members of the society within which they operate. Thus, if they don't take account of the wishes of employees these privileges could be restricted or rescinded in the future. In short, if the employer wishes to retain a 'licence to operate' they need to provide opportunities for employees to participate in decisions affecting their working lives. More pointedly, effective management requires the consent of those who are managed.

Difficulties of drawing boundaries

Writers associated with the 'industrial democrat' tradition recognise that managers can never know everything about the operations in their organisations. However, unlike their progressive managerialist counterparts, they frequently go on to argue that it is inappropriate or impossible to draw distinctions between employee participation which on one hand deals with work-related tasks, and on the other with the allocation of resources and the goals to which tasks are addressed. In other words, they suggest that it is difficult to draw hard and fast distinctions between decisions about individual employees' tasks and the overall goals of the organisation. This difficulty, they suggest, arises because decisions about what the organisation does and how resources are allocated will inevitably impact on deliberations about how specific tasks should be undertaken. Similarly, how a particular job is performed might have an impact on views about what the organisation could do in future and how these activities will be supported by the internal allocation of resources.

Agreement and compromise

'Industrial democrats' also tend to believe that the objectives of employers and managers on one hand, and employees on the other, are frequently competing and often contradictory. However, rather than suggest that managers should always have the unilateral right to determine how contentious issues are dealt with they suggest that it is possible to accommodate differences of opinion or reach compromises.

Because of the assumed links between tasks and goals and a recognition of the competing or contradictory objectives of managers and employees, 'industrial democrats' are apt to call for forms of employee participation which rely on employers and managers consulting, negotiating or jointly deciding with union or employee representatives issues associated with the organisation's objectives, the allocation of resources, the form of jobs within the workplace and the rewards that employees should receive for their efforts. The most commonly advocated mechanism for this participation is collective bargaining through joint negotiating and consultation committees. These bodies usually provide a forum for managers and elected or appointed trade union representatives to discuss and agree proposals for changes within the organisation. The range of issues dealt with by these committees might cover one or more of the following:

- task-related issues like job definitions, job evaluations and health and safety matters;
- allocation decisions affecting the pay and conditions of the workforce;
- strategic issues such as investment in new equipment, relocations and redundancy programmes.

Where unionised forms of representation are to be adopted, it is often suggested that there should be early agreement and possibly periodic revision of understandings about the most appropriate scope and breadth of consultation, negotiation and joint decision making.

Unionised forms of consultation, negotiation and joint decision making are not the only forms of employee participation advocated by 'industrial democrats', although these have been the predominant form in the UK in the post-war period. Other suggested systems of employee participation include works or company councils these bring managers together with employees and on occasion other representatives regardless of their union membership status. As indicated earlier in the chapter, this form of employee participation has been particularly popular in many continental European countries during the post-war period and has also been seen as a model by many voluntary organisations and a few private and public-sector organisations, e.g. the John Lewis Partnership and the Scott Bader Commonwealth.

The influence of continental European traditions on approaches to employee participation has become more pronounced in recent years and finds expression in debates about social and industrial partnership. In some respects social partnership is a difficult concept to define because it overlaps with the progressive managerialist and industrial democrat traditions outlined above. For example, while writers associated with the social or industrial partnership approach tend to argue that employers should consult and negotiate with unions over a range of issues including the organisation of work, terms and conditions of employment and strategic decisions with employment implications, they also tend to suggest that ultimate decision-making power should rest with the managers of the enterprise. In addition, these same writers tend to suggest that trade unionists and employee representatives should be more prepared to recognise the commercial constraints within which modern organisations operate. In short, employee representatives are encouraged to adopt a more business-orientated approach.

14.5.4 **Social inclusionist**

The last group of writers, practitioners and policy makers to be considered in this section has been labelled social inclusionist. This label groups together writers, practitioners and policy-makers who have drawn attention to the deep-seated

Table 14.3 Some of the most commonly cited forms and sources of structured exploitation and disadvantage

Ideological perspective	Elite group	Exploited group	Means of exploitation	Description of process
'Marxist'	Bourgeoisie/ capitalists	Proletariat/ working class	Capitalism	Capitalists as the owners of the means of production are able to extract surplus value in the form of money from the work of the working classes who do not own what is needed to produce their own goods and services
'Feminist'	Men	Women	Patriarchy	Men structure relationships, behaviour and attitudes at work and in the home in order to advance their own interests at the expense of women
'Black'	White people	Ethnic minorities	Racism Colonialism Imperialism	The legacy of colonial relationships and socially ingrained racial prejudices influence behaviour and attitudes to limit the opportunities of ethnic minorities
Ability awareness	Able bodied	Less able Disabled	Exclusion	Prejudice and the influence of decisions based on the presumption that everyone shares the same physical capabilities combine to limit the opportunities of the less able bodied or disabled

influence of wider social and economic conditions on patterns of employee participation and representation in the workplace. In particular, the label is used in relation to writers associated with Marxist, feminist, black and other movements who draw attention to divisions inside and outside the workplace based on class, status, gender, ethnicity, religion, physical impairment, sexuality, age and political allegiance. (*See* Table 14.3.)

These writers tend to draw upon one or more of the following four arguments in order to advance the case for changes in the ways in which employees with particular characteristics are represented within organisations.

Participation and representation as an expression of wider social forces

With few exceptions, writers associated with the social inclusionist approach suggest that organisations provide a setting within which broader economic, social and physical forces operate to bolster the position of elites at the expense of exploited groups. Although definitions of elite and exploited groups vary, along with discussion of the precise sources of advantage and disadvantage, all of these approaches question the fairness of situations in which the interests of particular groups are subservient or secondary to those of other more powerful groups. More specifically, they suggest that their chosen group or groups are equal to other sections within society and, therefore, deserve equivalent forms of representation.

Overcoming institutional exclusion

The second common theme in radical analyses is the assumption or prescription that the position of disadvantaged groups would be improved if there was greater awareness of their difficulties among the members of important decision-making bodies. For many of these writers the precise form of employee participation and representation arrangements is less important than the extent to which a recognition of the exclusion of particular groups is taken into account within these groups and committees. In other words, whether it is quality circles, works councils or joint negotiating committees, the most important consideration is the extent to which the concerns and interests of economically and socially disadvantaged groups are considered.

Achieving equal representation

For many of the most vocal critics of contemporary patterns of social exclusion and marginalisation the only effective way of ensuring that improvements are made is to take steps to increase the proportion of employee representatives drawn from disadvantaged groups. Ideally, as many of these accounts imply, the proportion of representatives from these different groups should reflect their presence within wider society.

Gaining power and influence

For the most strident advocates of the social inclusionist approach, participation in low-level task-related decisions about the organisation of work is really only ever pseudo or partial participation, which is unlikely to advance the real interests of disadvantaged groups. It is only when representatives are involved and able to exert influence over higher-level bodies, including boards of directors, industry associations and government committees, that full participation will have been achieved. This increased representation, they suggest, is a necessary prerequisite to the longer-term economic and social advancement of these disadvantaged groups.

14.5.5 Summary of employer approaches

As this section has attempted to demonstrate, writers and practitioners have produced different answers to questions dealing with why employees should participate and the form that this participation should take. For *traditional managerialists* employee participation should be limited to providing information to employees about decisions that have been taken by managers. This is best achieved by means of newsletters, videos and other means of information dissemination.

By contrast, *progressive managerialists* suggest that organisations benefit from allowing employees to participate in low-level decisions about the organisation of work and tasks as well as from providing them with access to forms of financial participation. This is best achieved by means of problem-solving groups, quality circles, team-working and profit-sharing or employee share-ownership schemes.

Industrial democrats or partners tend to argue that participation should extend to higher-level decisions affecting not only the organisation of work, but also the allocation of resources. Examples of participation mechanisms available to advance these aspirations include joint negotiating and consultation committees, works councils and worker director schemes.

Finally, commentators concerned with the advancement of *social inclusion* suggest that employees in general and disadvantaged groups in particular need to be considered if not involved in all aspects of organisation decision-making.

14.6 Conclusion

As this chapter has demonstrated, the legal regulation of employee participation and representation in the UK developed slowly over the first 70 years of the twentieth century. However, over the last 30 years the coverage of legislation in this area has expanded and the speed of change has increased. The recent frequent revision of laws in this area reflects the politically contentious nature of union representation rights in particular. Thus, between 1971 and 1999, there have been attempts to use statutory law to increase the incidence of low-level employee involvement, a steady increase in the number of Acts of Parliament and Inland Revenue regulations designed to encourage financial participation and a see-sawing between laws designed to encourage or discourage union representation. Over the last 20 years, these changes, together with wider economic shifts, have contributed to a steady decline in union membership, recognition and representation, as well as increases in low-level task-based employee involvement and financial participation.

Despite the apparent presence of general trends in the pattern of employee participation in the UK, there is still considerable variation between employers' practices. Thus, large unionised organisations in the public or manufacturing sectors remain much more likely to have adopted a variety of different forms of employee participation than their smaller, private, non-unionised counterparts in the service sector.

While legal and economic changes may explain much of the change in the general pattern of employee participation, deeper-seated differences in the values, attitudes and prevailing operational styles of managers in particular organisations probably do more to explain the form of participation in specific organisations. For the purposes of this chapter, these variations in predominant approach have been labelled traditional and progressive managerialist, industrial democrat or partnership and social inclusionist.

Looking back over the last 20 years there appears to have been some increase in the number of managers and employees subscribing to a progressive managerialist or industrial partnership approach at least at the level of published policy statements. Looking to the future, the influence of these approaches, together with legal changes proposed by the European Commission and the Labour government, appear to be indicating a growth in non-union and possibly unionised forms of higher-level employee representation in the UK over the next five years. It also seems likely that this will be accompanied by a further expansion and consolidation of low-level employee involvement and financial participation schemes. However, whether these changes will be accompanied by an increase in the participatory and representative franchise of traditionally excluded groups remains in question. In short, there are few signs of concerted attempts to introduce legislation or management actions designed to increase the representation of women, ethnic minorities, the disabled or other traditionally disadvantaged groups within the workforce.

Further reading

Central Arbitration Committee (2002) *Annual Report 2001/02*. London: CAC.

Cully, M., O'Reilly, A., Millward, N. and Forth, J. (1998) *The 1998 Workplace Employee Relations Survey: First Findings*. London: HMSO.

Department of Trade and Industry (1998) 'Fairness at Work'. White Paper, Cm. 3968. London: Stationery Office.

Wood, S. (1997) *Statutory Union Recognition*. Issues in People Management, No. 17. London: Institute of Personnel and Development.

References

ACAS (1991) *Code of Practice No. 3. Time off for Trade Union Duties and Activities*. London: ACAS.

ACAS (1997) *Code of Practice on Disclosure of Information to Trade Unions for Collective Bargaining*. London: ACAS.

ACAS (1998) *Workplace Communication*. Advisory Booklet No. 8. London: ACAS.

Central Arbitration Committee (2002) *Annual Report 2001–02*. London: CAC.

Certification Officer (2001) *The Annual Report 2000–01*. London: The Certification Office for Trade Unions and Employers' Associations.

Cully, M., O'Reilly, A., Millward, N. and Forth, J. (1998) *The 1998 Workplace Employee Relations Survey: First Findings*, London: HMSO.

Department of Employment (1988) 'Reporting Employee Participation Initiatives', *Employment Gazette*, October, 574.

Department of Trade and Industry (1998) 'Fairness at Work'. White Paper, Cm. 3968. London: Stationery Office.

Department of Trade and Industry (2002) *High Performance Workplaces*, consultation paper. London: DTI.

Dickens, L. and Bain, G. (1986) 'A duty to bargain? union recognition and information disclosure', in Lewis, R. (ed.) *Labour Law in Britain*. Oxford: Blackwell.

Dubin, R. (1954) 'Constructive aspects of conflict', in Kornhauser, A., Dubin, R. and Ross, A. (eds) *Industrial Conflict*. New York: McGraw-Hill.

Ewing, K. (1990) 'Trade union recognition – a framework for discussion', *Industrial Law Journal*, Vol. 19, 209–27.

Flanders, A. (1968) 'The Nature of Collective Bargaining', in Flanders, A. (ed.) *Collective Bargaining*. Harmondsworth: Penguin.

Fox, A. (1966) *Industrial Sociology and Industrial Relations*, Research Paper 3 for Royal Commission on Trade Unions and Employers' Associations. London: HMSO.

Kahn-Freund, O. (1977) *Industrial Democracy*. Oxford: Industrial Law Journal.

Kahn-Freund, O. (1979) *Labour Relations: Heritage and Adjustment*. Oxford: Oxford University Press.

Marchington, M. (1989) 'Joint Consultation in Practice', in Sission, K. (ed.) *Personnel Management in Britain*. Oxford: Blackwell.

Millward, N. (1994) *The New Industrial Relations*. London: Policy Studies Institute.

Pateman, C. (1970) *Participation and Democratic Theory*. Cambridge: Cambridge University Press.

Royal Commission on Trade Unions and Employers' Associations 1965–68 (1968) The Report of the Donovan Commission. Cmnd. 3623. London: HMSO.

Walker, K. (1970) 'Industrial Democracy', The Times Management Lecture. London: Times Newspapers Ltd.

Weber, T. *et al.* (2000) *Costs and benefits of the European Works Council Directive*. Employment Relations Research Series No. 9. London: DTI.

Weekes, B. *et al.* (1975) *Industrial Relations and the Limits of Law: the Industrial Effects of the Industrial Relations Act 1971*. Oxford: Blackwell.

15 Industrial action

This chapter considers the roles of individual employees and trade unions in industrial action and how their participation is regulated by the law. Having read it you should understand:

- The nature and extent of industrial action.
- Political concerns about the use of industrial action.
- The political purposes involved in enacting legislation.

15.1 Structure of the chapter

This chapter comprises the following sections:

- *Introduction*: Definition of 'industrial action', and the phenomenon of industrial action.
- *The context*: Political approaches to industrial action, a 'dual track' policy and the position of individual employees.
- *The legal framework*: Individual employees and industrial action – dismissal, pay deduction, the right not to take part; unions – breach of contract, immunities, trade dispute, secondary action, union membership issues, balloting, essential services, picketing and liability.

15.2 Introduction

In this section, industrial action will be defined. In addition, the nature and manifestations of conflict of interest in the employment relationship will be explored.

15.2.1 What is industrial action? Sociological definitions

Generally, the term 'industrial action' is equated with strikes because they have a high 'social visibility' (Hyman, 1984). However, in practice, it covers a considerably wider range of sanctions imposed by working people against their employers. Definitions of strikes occur both in law and in sociological studies. A notable example of the latter describes a strike as 'a temporary stoppage of work by a group of employees in order to express a grievance or enforce a demand' (Griffin, 1939). Each aspect of this definition is particularly important. It recognises the expectation of a return to work. It distinguishes a strike qualitatively from other forms of industrial action – in that no work takes place. It identifies the collective character of the act. And it indicates that 'a strike is almost always a calculative act' (Hyman, 1984) and a 'demonstration in force' (Knowles, 1952). A strike is, clearly, a weapon in a power relationship.

It would be misleading, however, to see any strike as a homogeneous phenomenon. Surveys reveal much variety in the characteristics of strikes – in terms of purpose, duration, numbers involved, status as official or unofficial, and legality. So, 'stoppages of work are in fact part of a continuum of behaviour' (Hyman, 1984). They can range from a massive and protracted confrontation ('**a trial of strength**') to a half-hour protest by half a dozen workers ('**a demonstration stoppage**'). Increasingly strikes are discontinuous events (a series of one-day strikes) as part of a longer-term campaign.

Non-strike action (or 'action short of a strike') covers an extremely diverse range of sanctions by employees against their employer. Such action is probably best defined by way of example. Perhaps the most clear-cut examples are overtime bans, 'blacking' (or boycotting) specific work and working to rule. Under these sanctions, the consequences are clear – certain tasks are not carried out and the economic consequences for the employer are likely to be evident.

At the other end of the spectrum of non-strike action are some rather nebulous forms of industrial action that can, and probably do, shade into individual sanctions against an employer (e.g. working without enthusiasm, withdrawal of co-operation and sabotage).

15.2.2 What is industrial action? Definitions from legislators

The definitional problems set out above are not assisted by the law. Given the vast body of legal regulation in this area, more clarity might be thought to exist. The Trade Union and Labour Relations Consolidation Act 1992 (s 246), in respect of the balloting provisions, defines a strike as 'any concerted stoppage of work'. In this way, it reaffirms the view that it is collective. It is action by a group of people acting together.

Non-strike action frequently appears in employment law as 'action short of a strike' or 'other industrial action' and is not defined.

The inadequacy of these statutory definitions has, however, been compensated for by some case law. Judges have elaborated certain characteristics of both broad categories of industrial action (*see* section 15.4: The legal framework).

15.2.3   **The phenomenon of industrial action**

Any exploration of the phenomenon of industrial action involves consideration of three issues:

1   the nature and sources of conflicts of interest between employees and employers;
2   the collective and individual manifestations of conflict;
3   the legitimacy of industrial action and the 'public interest'.

The nature and sources of conflicts of interest

As indicated in Chapter 14, in the discussion on collective bargaining, conflicts between employers and employees are likely to arise from any of three broad sources. First, they can be about the **economics of employment**. This would encompass, for example, the allocation of resources to pay wages, to increase investment, to meet other labour costs, to pay dividends, to meet tax obligations, etc. Clearly, an employer faces competing demands which, as far as practicable, would have to be reconciled.

Secondly, conflict can arise about the **distribution of power** in decision-making processes. This will relate to views about the extent to which management can or should retain freedom of decision-making, and the extent to which decision-making power over certain issues (e.g. pay and working time) is jointly shared with employees and their trade unions.

Finally, conflict of interest can arise in respect of the **values and standards** used by managers to guide their decision-making. One illustration of this, frequently evident in recent years, has involved, on the one hand, managerial promotion of cost effectiveness (through the introduction of new technology and reductions in and the redeployment of workforces) and, on the other hand, employees' concerns about job and income security.

In any negotiation or dispute between employers and employees, aspects of all three sources of conflict might be evident – with the difference of emphasis depending on the circumstances of each organisation's employee relations at that specific time.

Further exploration of the source of conflict must consider *latent* and *manifest* conflict. If any trade unionist on strike were asked why they were on strike, the answer would probably be 'for a pay rise' or 'to stop the redundancies'. Records of the causes of industrial action show that, for example, 67 per cent of strikes and 62 per cent of non-strike action were about pay-related issues (Workplace Industrial Relations Survey, 1990 – *see* Millward *et al.*, 1992). These reflect the 'manifest' cause of the dispute.

However, any analysis of a strike will show that underlying it are likely to be other issues of complaint. These may relate to management style, the existence of a relationship of low trust between employees and their employer, or employees' general insecurities about their jobs and income. These 'latent' causes can be difficult to express and organise as a focus for industrial action. So, more tangible matters like pay and redundancy programmes are likely to emerge as the central publicly stated issue. So, conflict resolution has to address both dimensions – the 'latent' and the 'manifest'.

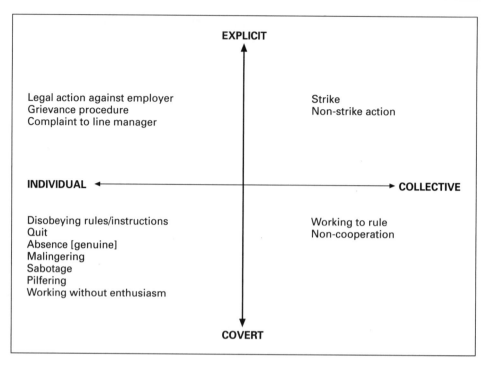

Figure 15.1 Manifestations of conflict

Collective and individual manifestation of conflict

In defining industrial action above, both the collective and the individual dimensions have been recognised. These need some further brief exploration (*see* Fig. 15.1).

As Fig. 15.1 shows, manifestations of conflict may be explicit or covert, as well as individual or collective. In addition, many of these examples may be adopted at the same time. So, for example, although a workgroup may be engaged in non-strike action (like an overtime ban), there may also be suffcent discontent with the quality of employee relations to provoke some, as individuals, to engage in low-level sabotage and various forms of non-cooperation. In non-union organisations, of course, the probability of formal industrial action is slight. However, recourse to individual sanctions is more likely.

The legitimacy of industrial action and 'the public interest'

As discussed earlier, the various forms of industrial action are means through which conflicts of interest in the employment relationship are expressed. Clearly, these expressions of 'sectional' interest (by particular workgroups or workforces) may have consequences for the wider community. For example, train drivers may be concerned about the length of the shifts and so work to rule to put pressure upon their employer, or nurses may be concerned about the grading and pay of their jobs and, consequently, refuse to undertake non-emergency duties. Particularly in these public-service jobs, there is a clear 'public interest' about possible economic disruption or about ensuring public safety. It is in these circumstances that governments may adopt policy measures to restrict industrial action in what are described as 'essential services'. (This issue will be covered further in section 15.4: The legal framework.)

Keeping in mind the notion of 'public interest', there is a fundamental issue affecting any liberal democracy. This is whether, despite the economic consequences and any possible social or political upset, it is legitimate for working people to withdraw their labour at all. Various international Conventions have asserted that this should be a basic right in a free society – though it may be qualified in some ways. For example, the right to take industrial action might be limited to those taking 'lawful' industrial action (as determined in the country concerned). Also, it may be proscribed where interruption of a service would endanger 'life, personal safety or health' (International Labour Organisation).

A climate of opinion developed in Britain during the 1980s and 1990s which appeared to reject the legitimacy of industrial action – except when certain publicly favoured groups take action (e.g. ambulance drivers and nurses). Public policy (evident in legislation and other government action) has largely focused on the phenomenon – striking – rather than the reasons why working people strike. Consequently, there is now in place an extensive and intricate body of industrial action law. Arguably, however, less attention has been paid to improving in any systematic way the quality of employee relations and working life.

15.3   The context

The incidence of industrial action has, throughout the post-war period, been a concern to both Conservative and Labour governments. This receded during the 1990s as the incidence of strikes and other forms of industrial action fell considerably from the high levels reported in the 1970s. So, for example, it is recorded in official statistics that in 1997 there were 216 strikes and 235 000 working days lost. This contrasts with the average of 2300 strikes and 11.4 million working days lost in the period 1975–9. *The Workplace Employee Relations Survey* (Cully *et al.*, 1998) reported that 'the incidence of industrial action is very low, with only 2 per cent of workplace managers reporting action of any kind in the year preceding the survey' (Cully *et al.*, 1999: 125). In these workplaces, 52 per cent experienced strikes, 57 per cent non-strike action and 9 per cent both forms. Industrial action is more likely to take place in larger establishments and in the public sector.

Several factors caused this decline. In part it was a result of changing economic circumstances (with two major recessions commencing in 1980 and 1990). It was also a consequence of the decline of trade union membership and recognition – particularly in the heartlands of manufacturing industry and the public sector. Parts of manufacturing had been characterised as strike prone (Smith *et al.*, 1978). The public sector had witnessed a significant number of major *trials of strength*. Furthermore, the decline in incidence of industrial action was also a response to the considerable range of legal constraints introduced in successive Acts of Parliament from 1980 onwards.

Nevertheless, sporadic outbursts of industrial action do occur and keep the issue briefly on the political agenda. Furthermore, the regulation of industrial action still provokes a division of opinion between the major governing parties. Although there may be some shift towards a consensus on issues like balloting, other matters are still in contention.

15.3.1 **1945–79**

During this period, advocates of policies to deal with this perceived or actual 'problem' of industrial action tended to be identified with one of two broad strands of opinion:

■ those proposing a reformed 'voluntary system', wherein free collective bargaining was encouraged and permitted to operate;

■ those wanting to initiate a detailed and prescriptive legal framework for trade union activities.

By the late 1960s, the distinction between the two broad groupings had become clear.

On the one hand, the Donovan Commission Report 1968 (the Royal Commission on Trade Unions and Employers' Associations) focused on attempts to reform the 'voluntary system' of industrial relations. Included among its recommendations were suggested changes to collective bargaining machinery and to grievance and dispute-handling procedures. These measures were supported by a broad range of employers, trade unions and the Labour government (of 1964–70).

On the other hand, the Conservative opposition was simultaneously devising a radical new legal framework for industrial relations drawn, to some considerable extent, from practice in the United States. On the election to office of the Conservatives in 1970, this was enacted in the Industrial Relations Act 1971 (now repealed). It was criticised and undermined, in some essential respects, not only by trade unions but also by employers. It was widely perceived to be disruptive of good industrial relations, liable to provoke industrial action and generally unworkable (Weekes *et al.*, 1975).

With the election, in 1974, of a Labour government, there was the restoration of a legal framework that encouraged the development of an industrial relations system based on trade union recognition and collective bargaining and also on a range of individual statutory rights (e.g. in respect of unfair dismissal, equal pay and discriminatory treatment). As far as industrial action was concerned, this framework re-enacted the 'immunities' (*see* below) for organisers of strikes originally developed in the nineteenth century.

15.3.2 **1979 to date**

By the late 1970s, concern about industrial action re-established itself as a major issue of public and political issue – particularly during the so-called 'winter of discontent' (1978–9). Although a considerable amount of political rhetoric infused the debates on industrial action, several issues emerged that deserved both close scrutiny and reflection. These concerned, on the one hand, the economic consequences of industrial action and, on the other hand, trade union behaviour in the course of such action:

- The voting systems used by unions to decide on industrial action were frequently defective. Mass meetings were often held resulting in some dubious decisions to approve industrial action. Individual secret ballots were the exception.

- There was some use of industrial action before negotiations had been completed and/or a company's disputes procedure had been exhausted.

- There was political concern and concern among employers about the extent to which it was appropriate for workers to take supportive, sympathetic secondary action to assist other groups of working people in their disputes.

- The economic consequences of both spontaneous stoppages (or 'wildcat' strikes) and prolonged 'trials of strength' were seen to be damaging to the national economic interest.

- The extent to which trade union leaders appeared to control their members who were taking action, particularly in essential services (like hospitals, the fire service, etc.), was also a matter of public concern and debate.

As a result of the 1979 general election, it became the responsibility of a Conservative government to address these issues. Unlike previous post-war Conservative governments, that led by Margaret Thatcher was characterised by a radical shift in political ideology and objectives. It moved decisively away from the broad bipartisan consensus on both economic management and social policy objectives that had, generally, prevailed since 1945. It pursued a radical policy of deregulation and free-market economics.

In relation to trade unions and industrial action, the new government pursued a policy which was more explicitly, over time, anti-trade union. It has been seen as part of a wider policy of 'disestablishing collectivism' (Wedderburn, 1991: 211) – aimed at curbing trade union economic power and promoting non-union workplaces and the curtailment of collective bargaining. Union activities were seen as constraining the development of a free market economy. So, the first Employment Act in 1980 began a rolling programme of both statutory requirements for industrial action and also restraints on the exercise of trade union power. This was still being supplemented well into the 1990s.

15.3.3   A 'dual track policy'

Auerbach (1990: 153) has suggested that the Thatcher government had a 'dual track policy' for tackling trade union power and industrial action. It comprised a *policy of restriction* and a *policy of regulation*.

The policy of restriction

The policy of restriction focuses on trade union 'immunities' (*see* Introduction to Part Five and also below). These legal protections from civil proceedings were narrowed, so creating a wide set of circumstances in which certain forms of industrial action could be declared unlawful. This policy of restriction had two underlying components: the promotion of 'enterprise confinement', and the 'depoliticisation' of trade union activity. The main thrust of the legislation, however, was towards the former.

The notion of 'enterprise confinement' (Wedderburn, 1991: 219) describes the view that industrial action could only be lawfully permitted in respect of employees and their *own* employer. So, 'sympathetic' secondary industrial action would be generally unlawful. This reflected a widely held view in the Conservative government that, if trade unions were to exist and function, their only legitimate sphere of interest was workplace industrial relations and not the wider economic sphere.

Trade unions argued, however, that this restriction of their interest could, in many cases, weaken their collective power in relation to an employer. One 'employer' might be a division or an 'associated employer' of a much larger corporate group of companies. Real decision-making power may lie with the 'ultimate employer' – and so would be distant from a specific workplace. Industrial action at this lower level might, consequently, be comparatively ineffective.

A corollary to 'enterprise confinement' is the view that unions should not pursue political objectives. So industrial action was deemed unlawful if it was undertaken for 'political' purposes. Trade unions, however, argued that industrial action against political policies was legitimate. Government action, policy initiatives and legislation could affect their members' job and income security and their conditions of employment. Examples of this could be seen in the resistance to both public-sector competitive tendering and the liberalisation of markets (as in telecommunications), as well as in responses to economic policies.

The policy of regulation

The policy of regulation is closely interconnected with these restrictions on trade union immunities. This policy involves the enactment of an extensive set of statutory provisions for regulating the operations and activities of unions in the course of industrial action. They can be categorised under two headings:

- those which relate to the conduct of industrial action balloting;
- those which concern a union's liability for the actions of its members and its officials.

This policy of regulation (in respect of ballots) involves the use of a different technique – i.e. detailed prescriptions on how ballots approving industrial action are to be conducted. This is set out in legislation (the Trade Union and Labour Relations (Consolidation) Act 1992) and in a supporting code of practice. Immunity is conditional upon compliance with these balloting requirements. The political purpose behind this regulation is identical to that in the policy of restriction – to shift the balance of industrial relations power.

Although, on the face of it, many of these provisions appear to improve trade union internal democracy, it has been argued that they have an ulterior purpose. In fact, they have created a myriad of legal trip-wires in the way of industrial action. It has become increasingly difficult for trade unions to call for and to undertake lawful primary industrial action without the danger of an inadvertent infringement of these complex regulations.

One positive aspect of balloting has been suggested. Quoting one research report (Elgar and Simpson 1993), the *Workplace Employee Relations Survey 1998* states that balloting 'has served to defuse the strike option as it provides a signal to workplace management of the depth of discontent among the workforce: a high proportion voting "yes", it is said, will bring management back to the bargaining table' (Cully *et al.*, 1999: 125).

The Labour government elected in 1997 accepted the essential framework of law enacted by the Conservative governments. However, in the 'Fairness at Work' White Paper (DTI, 1998), two principal amendments were proposed to the 'policy of restriction'. First, the Balloting Code of Practice was to be simplified. 'Present provisions are unnecessarily complex and rigid. This makes it difficult for trade unions and their members to understand their rights and responsibilities' (para 4.26). Secondly, the disclosure to employers of the names of those taking industrial action was to be amended to 'identify as accurately as reasonably practicable the group or category of employees concerned' without giving names (para 4.27). These changes were included in the Employment Relations Act 1999; and the amended Code of Practice on Balloting came into force in 2000.

15.3.4 The position of individual employees

The discussion above has focused, primarily, on measures directed at trade unions as the organisers of industrial action. In parallel legal developments, the situation of individual employees who participate in industrial action has also been addressed since 1979. This has arisen, generally, from judicial decisions relating to an employee's obligations under the contract of employment. Case law has elaborated a number of new principles in respect of both breach of contract and pay deduction as a result of industrial action.

So, in aggregate, the restriction of immunities for trade unions, unions' liability for industrial action, and the legal consequences for individual employees have created a considerable framework of legal restriction. This led to a re-emergence of the 'right to strike' as an issue in political debate and among some academic lawyers.

For the individual employee, there is no legal 'right to strike' in Britain. When this term is used, it is invariably to affirm a moral right or a freedom not to work because of a dispute with an employer. However, in Britain, there are legal consequences for exercising this freedom.

These arise from the employee's position under the common law of contract. When an employee takes strike action – or participates in most other forms of industrial action – that employee breaches the contract of employment. In the case of strike action this can be (and, usually, is) regarded as a repudiatory breach. Until 2000 (when the law on unfair dismissal was amended) the employer could sack the employee immediately. Although such actions are relatively rare, there have been well-publicised examples in recent years – at News International (1986), at Timex (1993) and on the Liverpool docks (1996).

As discussed in Chapter 2, there are significant problems of vulnerability for individual employees in the employment relationship. It is a power relationship which has been characterised as 'asymmetrical' (Brown, 1988) in the sense that more power resides with the employer than with the employee. Whilst the contract of employment regulates that employment relationship for most working people, it does little to redress this imbalance of power. Generally, industrial action is viewed as 'a challenge to the legitimate authority of the employer as embodied in the contract of employment' and, consequently, is seen as a 'violation' of the contract (Mesher and Sutcliffe, 1986: 243).

This vulnerability of individuals, under common law, has existed since the nineteenth century. It has only been modified in a limited way by the introduction in 1975, for the first time, of unfair dismissal provisions. However, as discussed below, these provide only limited protection.

One way of modifying the common law would be to introduce a rule that industrial action suspends rather than breaches the contract of employment. Indeed, most European countries have accepted the principle of suspension of contracts in industrial disputes as part of the provision of a positive right to strike. However, such suspension is often only accepted in the case of a lawful strike. It has generally been necessary, therefore, to draw a line between those strikes and the unlawful strikes for which a system of termination of contract was still to be applicable.

If a government in Britain were to introduce such a provision on suspension of contract, it might be similarly qualified – i.e. providing protection solely for those participants in lawful industrial action. (The criteria for what might be considered 'lawful' industrial action are considered below in section 15.4: The legal framework.)

Certainly, Britain has been criticised by international agencies for its failure to enact a legal right to strike. The International Labour Organisation Convention 87, to which Britain subscribes, includes (by implication) this right. In a formal 'observation' on legal practice in Britain, the ILO asked the government to introduce legislative protection against dismissal for industrial action (Ewing, 1989).

In the 'Fairness at Work' White Paper (DTI, 1998) the government discussed this issue. It is stated that it had 'no plans to change the position in relation to those dismissed for taking unofficial action. However, in relation to employees dismissed for taking part in lawfully organised official industrial action, the Government believe that the current regime is unsatisfactory and illogical'. It continued that, 'in general employees dismissed for taking part in lawfully organised official industrial action should have the right to complain of unfair dismissal to a tribunal. In any particular case the tribunal would not get involved in looking at the merits of the dispute; its role would be to decide whether the employer had acted fairly and reasonably taking into account all the circumstances of the case' (para 4.22). The law was amended under the Employment Relations Act 1999 and the limited further protection came into force in April 2000.

15.4 The legal framework

This section considers the existing legal framework covering both the individual employee and unions (as organisers of industrial action).

15.4.1 Individual employees

The legal position of individual strikers will be explored in more detail in order to answer the following questions:

- What can happen to an employee who takes strike action?
- What can happen to an employee who takes other forms of industrial action?

The answers to these questions will cover the issues of dismissal and pay deduction and any protected stoppages of work (in relation to health and safety).

Strike action

In the introduction to this chapter, the inadequacy of the definition of a 'strike' was mentioned. Judges have, in various cases, elaborated an important principle relating to strikes and the contract of employment. Phillips J has said that 'a "real" strike' would be a repudiatory breach of the contract (*Simmons* v *Hoover Ltd* [1976] 3 WLR 901, EAT). The consequence, for the employee, of participation in a strike, then, is that the employer might accept the repudiation of the contract and immediately terminate the employee's employment. However, this is subject to rights under the law on dismissal.

Non-strike action

This is a much more complex area. As indicated earlier, such action is not defined in statute law. Nevertheless, case law has produced a number of issues to take into account. The starting point is the contract of employment. Initially, the issue is whether the sanction used by the employee relates to a term of the contract or to a non-contractual practice. Let us look at each of these in turn.

A contractual term can be express or implied. So, for example, the refusal of Inland Revenue staff to use new computer equipment was determined to be a breach of the implied term requiring employees to obey the employer's lawful and reasonable instructions (*Cresswell and Others* v *Board of Inland Revenue* [1984] IRLR 190, HC).

The issue, then, is whether this breach of the contract is fundamental and so constitutes a repudiatory breach – with a possible consequence being the employee's termination of employment. Usually, such breaches are not viewed as fundamental. The employer might, however, reciprocate by withholding part or all of the employee's pay for the duration of the industrial action. (This sanction by the employer is considered in more detail below.)

One very notable case from the early 1970s concerned a work-to-rule by train drivers – using the rules specified by British Rail. The industrial action involved the meticulous preparation of trains for departure with the consequence that delays were caused to the scheduling of services. Lord Denning ruled that this rigorous compliance with the lawful and reasonable instructions in the contract was unacceptable. He said that '[a man] can withdraw his goodwill if he pleases. But what he must not do is wilfully to obstruct the employer as he goes about his business' (*Secretary of State for Employment* v *ASLEF (No. 2)* [1972] 2 All ER 949, CA).

Lord Buckley added, in the same case, that 'I have no hesitation in implying a term into the contract of service that each employee will not, in obeying his lawful instructions, seek to obey them in a wholly unreasonable way . . . I prefer to rest my decision that work to rule is a breach of contract on this ground.'

This represents one illustration of a marked tendency for the courts to be 'creative' in their use of implied terms (e.g. the duty to co-operate with the employer;

the duty to obey lawful and reasonable instructions; the duty of fidelity). This judicial creativity has caused concern to some academic lawyers. Commenting on the decisions of Denning and Buckley, in the *ASLEF* case, Mesher and Sutcliffe (1986) say: 'The combined effect of the judgments in this case is to establish a negative duty on the employee not wilfully to disrupt the employer's undertaking and a positive duty to promote the commercial interests for which he is employed.'

Whilst the negative duty might be permissible; the positive duty, arguably, inhibits any industrial action (apart from, possibly, refusing non-contractual overtime and 'working without enthusiasm').

Non-contractual terms have posed some particular uncertainties in recent years with the consequence that judges have tended to find them to be contractual under broad implied terms. So, for example, the refusals by schoolteachers to carry out lunchtime supervision duties were thought to be voluntary and non-contractual. However, Templeton LJ stated that 'any form of industrial action by a worker is a breach of contract' (*Metropolitan Borough of Solihull* v *National Union of Teachers* [1985] IRLR 211).

A second example concerned not only lunchtime supervision but also attendance at out-of-hours meetings. The contract of employment was silent on these issues. Scott J asserted that 'it is, in my view, a professional obligation of each teacher to cooperate in running the school during school hours in accordance with the timetable and other administrative regulations or directions from time to time made or given' (*Sim* v *Rotherham Metropolitan Borough Council* [1986] IRLR 391). Ewing (1991) commented: 'The lack of specificity in the contracts . . . was turned to the advantage of the employer.'

Clearly, the use of implied contractual terms which was considered earlier has effectively disposed of the notion of 'non-contractual issues' as a possible sanction against an employer. Indeed, Ewing (1991) says that 'it can safely be assumed that all forms of industrial action (with the possible exception in some cases of a refusal to work voluntary overtime) will be a breach of contract by the individuals concerned'. So, this gives a green light to employers to impose appropriate sanctions themselves.

Sanctions by employers

There are two sanctions that an employer might impose on an employee who takes part in industrial action: **dismissal** and **pay deduction**.

Dismissal

The vulnerable situation of individual employees, described above, has existed, under common law, since the nineteenth century. In recent years, Parliament has passed various Acts which have affected the circumstances in which an employer might dismiss an employee who is participating in industrial action.

There are four sets of circumstances to be considered:

- Dismissal and protected industrial action.
- Unlawful selective dismissal.
- Lawful and unlawful selective re-engagement.
- Lawful selective dismissal.

Dismissal and protected industrial action

Under legislation implemented on 24 April 2000, it is unlawful to dismiss an employee who is taking part in 'protected industrial action'. Such industrial action must be lawful and approved by the trade union concerned. If the union repudiates the industrial action, the protection ceases – on the working day after the repudiation. Otherwise, the protection lasts for eight weeks. However, in circumstances where the employer fails to take 'reasonable procedural steps' to deal with the dispute, the period of protection for the employee can be extended. These reasonable steps could include the employer's unreasonable refusal to seek conciliation, mediation or arbitration. Alternatively, it could include the failure to offer to start or re-start negotiations. An employee who is dismissed during the course of protected industrial action can complain to an employment tribunal irrespective of length of service or age.

Unlawful selective dismissal

Since 1975 an employer must sack all participants in industrial action if he is to avoid a complaint of unfair dismissal. If an employer attempts to dismiss selectively, then (apart from the special circumstances introduced in 1990), these dismissals will be automatically unfair. The employees concerned are then likely to receive compensation, but not necessarily re-employment, through a complaint to an employment tribunal. If all those taking part in industrial action were sacked, an employment tribunal would decline jurisdiction if any complaints alleging unfair dismissal were made.

Selective re-engagement

In 1982, this legal framework against selective dismissal was amended with the introduction of the possibility of re-engaging, selectively, former employees. This can only be undertaken when three months have elapsed since their dismissal for participation in the industrial action.

Lawful selective dismissal

In 1990, the principle of selectivity was extended to permit the lawful selective dismissal in the circumstances where an employee was taking part in 'unlawful' industrial action. Effectively, this covers a union member who is involved in industrial action that has been 'repudiated' by the trade union because it does not comply with all the legal requirements for the organisation of industrial action (*see* next section). It would be 'unofficial' also – in that it did not have the authorisation of the union. In such a case an employee has no right to complain to an employment tribunal about unfair dismissal. This framework of unfair dismissal protection is now enacted in TULRCA 1992 (ss 237–9).

Clearly, one of the critical issues for sacked employees is whether or not they did 'take part' in the industrial action. There is, however, no statutory definition. For the overwhelming majority of participants, this will be clear-cut. However, there can be cases where uncertainty exists and the employee contends that, for whatever reason, they were not involved. In a complaint alleging unfair dismissal, an employment tribunal will decide the issue of 'participation' on the facts. Generally, participation concerns the behaviour, not the motives, of the person concerned. The burden of proof is on the employer. A number of cases suggest the decisions that a tribunal might reach.

Sick absence might not preclude an employer from taking the view that the employee was taking part in the industrial action. In *Williams* v *Western Mail & Echo* [1980] IRLR 222 EAT, an employee, who was already engaged in a range of different forms of industrial action (including one-day strikes, 'blacking', work-to-rule, non-cooperation), was absent through genuine sickness on the day when the employer's ultimatum demanding normal working was to be effective. He, along with others who did not comply, was dismissed. The Employment Appeals Tribunal ruled that once industrial action has commenced, an employee will be regarded as participating until this employee informs the employer that they are not involved. So 'part association' is enough to constitute participation.

In *Bolton Roadways Ltd* v *Edwards and Others* [1987] IRLR 392, the EAT said that the key question was: 'what was the employee actually doing at the time of dismissal?' In this case, the driver was sick at the time that both the employer's ultimatum and, consequently, his dismissal were effective. He had, on the day before, crossed the picket line and had informed his employer that he would not join the strike. However, on leaving the depot, he spoke to the pickets and gave advice on the conduct of further industrial action. This was deemed to be participation.

A final aspect of employee participation concerns threats of industrial action. In *Winnet* v *Seamarks Brothers Ltd* [1978] IRLR 387 the EAT determined that an employee's participation in the strike had started from the moment he told his employer in unequivocal terms of his intention to start the strike from the beginning of his next shift. This view was further elaborated in *Midland Plastics* v *Till and Others* [1983] IRLR 9, EAT. In this case, a distinction was drawn between:

- a threat to take industrial action at some future date where such action had not yet commenced (as in the *Winnet* case); and
- a statement by employees that they will be taking industrial action when next due to work where the action has already been started by others.

So, it was decided what while the former does not constitute 'taking part' in industrial action, the latter normally would. As Wedderburn (1986) said of the declaration of intent or notice to take part in industrial action, 'the notice announces a forthcoming breach, and is therefore itself in law an "anticipatory" breach, which the employer can waive or accept'.

As a result of these cases, an employee could be seen as taking part in industrial action if they associated with a strike, attended a picket line or participated in other activities of the strikers in order to further their aims, or in certain circumstances, declared an intention to participate. Consequently, the employee will be vulnerable to instant dismissal.

In one set of circumstances an employee (or group of employees) is protected from dismissal when they stop work. This is in respect of workplace hazards, where an employee 'in circumstances of danger which he reasonably believed to be serious and imminent and which he could not reasonably have been expected to avert, left or proposed to leave or (while the danger persisted) refused to return to, his place of work or any dangerous part of his place of work' (Employment Rights Act 1996, s 100(1)(d)) (*see also* Chapter 12).

Pay deduction

For the individual employee, a second important consequence of participation in industrial action is the likelihood of pay deduction. Both statute law and case law have defined the current framework. In 1986, the former Wages Act (now Part II of the Employment Rights Act 1996) specified that the usual requirements relating to pay deduction did not apply to deductions of wages 'where the worker has taken part in a strike or other industrial action and the deduction is made by the employer on account of the worker's having taken part in the strike or other action' (ERA 1996, s 14(5)). The consequence is that an employer may deduct pay without the employee being able to complain to an industrial tribunal.

Case law has elaborated the ways in which this might happen. The key issues have been:

- whether there has been a breach – fundamental or not – of the individual's contract of employment;
- whether the employee 'took part' in the industrial action;
- the nature and extent of the 'partial performance' of the individual's contract of employment in non-strike action;
- whether the employer accepts or rejects this 'partial performance' of the contract;
- the appropriate amount of deduction for no work and for 'partial performance'.

In the context of a strike, the principle of 'no work, no pay' usually prevails, but the situation is more complex with other forms of industrial action and partial performance of the contract.

The issue of **rejected partial performance** was considered in a leading case, *Wiluszynski* v *London Borough of Tower Hamlets* [1989] ICR 493. In this Court of Appeal hearing, Fox LJ set out several important principles:

- employees are 'not entitled to pick and choose' what work they do under their contract of employment;
- an employee 'could not refuse to comply with his contract and demand pay under the contract';
- an employer 'having told [an employee] that he was not required to attend for work [as a result of the employee's partial performance] and that if he did so it would be on a purely voluntary basis . . . could not, when he in fact attended, give him directions to work and at the same time not pay him';
- an employer 'could not be expected to take action physically to prevent those members of staff who were refusing to comply with their contracts from entering [his] premises';
- the character and volume of work was also a consideration. (In this case, the industrial action involved a refusal by NALGO members to answer queries from elected councillors. So, although the work was comparatively small when assessed in terms of time, it was of 'considerable importance'.)

In a later case, the Court of Appeal enhanced employers' powers in respect of rejected part performance. In *British Telecommunications plc* v *Ticehurst* [1992] IRLR 219, CA it was judged that two managers could be sent home without pay because they refused to sign an undertaking to work in accordance with the terms of their contracts of employment. They had previously participated in a short strike and had also withdrawn their goodwill. The court asserted that managers' contracts contained an implied term requiring them to further their employer's interests. The concerted withdrawal of goodwill was a breach of this term.

There have been instances whereby employers have **accepted partial performance** of contracts of employment. Here some, or most, of the contracted work is carried out. The difficult issue has been the calculation of appropriate remuneration for part performance. The probability is that 'rough justice' will prevail.

For example, in *Royle* v *Trafford Borough Council* [1984] IRLR 184, HC a schoolteacher refused to accept into his class of 31 pupils another five. However, he carried out all his other contracted duties including extramural activities. Despite this, it was determined to be 'part performance' and he sustained a deduction of 5/36ths of his salary over the relevant period. The deduction represented 'the notional value of the services not rendered.'

The right not to take part

Since 1990, individual employees have had an escape route, in law, from the obligation to comply with a collective decision by trade union members to embark on industrial action. This takes the form of the right 'not to be unjustifiably disciplined' by their trade union for non-participation in the industrial action (TULRCA 1992, ss 64–7). It has been subject to considerable contention. As one commentator has observed, it is an 'unqualified right' which is 'enjoyed without any special justification'. The member does not need to show anything special about their motives – 'they may be as malicious, selfish or directed to the common good as he pleases' (Leader, 1991).

This first section on the legal framework relating to industrial action has focused on the participation of the individual employee. It should be clear that an employee's situation is particularly vulnerable given the combined effect of the imbalance of power in the employment relationship, the creative use by judges of the implied terms of the contract of employment, the ability of employers, in certain circumstances, to sack those taking part in industrial action, and the opportunities for employers to deduct pay for partial performance of contracts.

This weak situation of individuals has never been tackled systematically by legislators to provide a well-defined statutory right to withdraw labour and to participate in industrial action. If this were to happen, then, the critical issues to be addressed would be the automatic dismissal of those taking industrial action and the position in which contracts of employment are, in law, breached (not suspended) by industrial action. Such a right to take industrial action might of course be qualified by a requirement that such action be 'lawful'.

This is a matter that we turn to next. In the framework developed for trade unions as organisers of industrial action, particularly since the early 1980s, the determination of what is 'lawful' and what is 'unlawful' has been given great attention.

15.4.2 Trade unions

The most substantial body of law on industrial action is that which governs trade unions. They are organisers of industrial action and the bodies which induce employees to breach their contracts of employment by taking part in that action. This law is founded on a set of **immunities** or legal protection from proceedings in the civil courts for damages.

Breach of contract

To explain the nature and significance of *immunities* it is necessary, first of all, to recap on the contractual situation between employees and their employer. As stated earlier, when employees participate in most – if not all – forms of industrial action, they breach their contracts of employment. When a trade union 'calls' upon its members to take industrial action it is, in law, inducing or encouraging a breach of each member's contract of employment. In addition, a union is likely to be interfering with commercial contracts agreed between their members' employer and other companies. Under common law, it is unlawful to induce people to break contracts or to interfere with the performance of a contract – or to threaten to do either of these things.

Inevitably, this means that, without some special protection, trade unions or trade union officials would face the possibility of legal action (i.e. an injunction and/or a claim for damages) for inducing breaches of contract every time they called a strike. Unions would be liable for committing economic torts (i.e. civil wrongs other than a breach of contract).

Immunities

As outlined in the Introduction to Part Five, trade union 'immunities' were enacted in the nineteenth century in legislation to override the common law situation created by judges. These provide, in effect, that trade unions and individuals can, in certain circumstances specified by Parliament, organise industrial action without fear of legal proceedings. This permission to organise a strike or other industrial action was qualified by the phrase (still enacted in law today) 'in contemplation or furtherance of a trade dispute'. This means that any industrial action must relate to a 'trade dispute' between an employer and their employees (*see* below).

By the late 1970s, the circumstances in which these immunities applied had been widened considerably so that the organisation of virtually all forms of industrial action was protected. Since 1980, however, this situation has been gradually reversed and the extent of the immunities has been narrowed. Certain forms of industrial action, which hitherto had been lawful, ceased to be so (e.g. action concerned with political matters, inter-union disputes, secondary industrial action and most action related to industrial relations matters occurring overseas).

In 1982, Parliament also introduced provisions whereby unions, as organisations, could be sued for unlawful industrial action. This established a clear framework of 'liability' for industrial action which was unlawful – i.e. was not protected by the immunities. Then, in 1984, immunity became conditional upon a union obtaining support, first of all, from its members through a secret and properly conducted ballot before it called for the industrial action to start. The current enactment of the immunities is set out in TULRCA 1992, s 219.

What is lawful industrial action?

The determination of whether industrial action is lawful centres on four key sets of issues. The first three relate to the reasons for the industrial action, and the final one concerns appropriate balloting and organisational procedures. The questions that need to be asked are as follows:

1 Is there a 'trade dispute'; and has the industrial action been called 'in contemplation or furtherance of that trade dispute'?
2 Is the industrial action 'secondary action'?
3 Is the industrial action being taken or threatened to prevent work being done by non-union companies; or in support of certain prohibited trade union membership issues?
4 Has the industrial action been approved in an individual secret ballot in accordance with the code of practice?

A 'trade dispute'

A lawful trade dispute:

■ must be between workers and their own employer or a Minister of the Crown; and

■ must be *wholly or mainly* about employment-related matters, such as pay and conditions, jobs, allocation of work, discipline, negotiating machinery or trade union membership (TULRCA 1992, s 244).

There are two issues of potential difficulty here: who is the employer? and who determines 'wholly or mainly'? The question of who is the employer is considered under 'Secondary action'. The determination of 'wholly or mainly' is judged on the facts. Consequently, much will depend on what particular judges make of these facts. Subjectivity is clearly an important element.

For example, in 1983, telecommunications engineers working for British Telecom refused to connect Mercury Communications (then a new company) into the BT network because it was said to infringe a job security agreement with BT. Mercury sought an injunction to stop this 'blacking' or boycott. The High Court refused to grant it. However, on appeal, the Court of Appeal ruled that the dispute was not a 'trade dispute' (i.e. wholly or mainly about employment-related matters). It was said to be 'political' – concerned with the 'liberalisation' of the telecommunications markets. Consequently, it was ruled as unlawful and an injunction was granted.

In this case, both employment and political elements were involved. In certain disputes they inevitably inter-penetrate – particularly in the public sector or in those parts of the private sector where government policy is influential. In practice, it can become difficult to disentangle these two elements in any kind of realistic way. There is no objective standard to guide the judiciary. The decision is based on their assessment of the facts of the case.

'Secondary action'

Secondary action is defined as action taken by workers (in breach of their contracts of employment) whose employer is not a party to the trade dispute (TULRCA 1992, s 224). In everyday language, this is 'sympathetic' industrial action designed to support a group of fellow trade unionists in another company. Since 1990, all secondary action has been determined to be unlawful.

This blanket prohibition might appear simple. However, one critical difficulty is again the question of who is the employer. On one level, it is straightforward enough – a person's employer is the other party to that person's contract of employment. However, given the complexity of some organisational structures, particularly within corporate groups of companies, this is unlikely to be the 'ultimate employer'. But, this 'ultimate employer' may well be the person who makes the final decisions.

So, defining a lawful trade dispute in this restrictive way (as a dispute between an employee and their own employer) may result in the industrial action being aimed at a part, a subsidiary, of a larger conglomerate. It illustrates the concept of 'enterprise confinement' (Wedderburn, 1991: 219) which can have the effect of limiting the effectiveness of such trade union pressure. It can create an incentive to certain employers to fragment their organisational structures into separate companies in order to marginalise industrial action. So, for example, in the 1988 seafarers' dispute, P&O's operations at different ports were run by distinct companies within the P&O Group (Auerbach, 1988). As Lord Wedderburn asserted, 'the right to strike is put entirely into the hands of the employer' (*Hansard*, House of Lords, 10 July 1990, col. 172).

The ILO has expressed concern about Britain's limitations on secondary action. Such action is protected by Convention 87. The government was asked 'to introduce amendments which enable workers to take industrial action against their "real" employer' (Ewing, 1989). Such a step would have to deal with two issues: the common or allied social and economic interests of the workers involved; and the need to determine who the 'real' employer was. On this last issue, courts have been resistant to exploring organisational structures and determining who the 'ultimate employer' is. In 1984, Lord Diplock commented in a case involving interlocking printing and publishing companies that Parliament had not required the courts 'to pierce the corporate veil' (*Dimbleby and Sons Ltd* v *National Union of Journalists* [1984] IRLR 161).

Issues concerning trade union membership

In relation to issues of trade union membership, there are four circumstances where industrial action cannot be used lawfully (i.e. does not attract immunity):

1 to prevent an employer using non-union labour;

2 to pressurise a contractor, used by the employer of a unionised workforce, to recognise, negotiate with and consult with a trade union;

3 to pressurise an employer to establish or maintain a 'closed shop' practice;

4 to prevent an employer from dismissing an employee who has been sacked for participating in unofficial industrial action.

Balloting

Since 1984, immunity for trade unions intending to organise any industrial action (in breach of contracts of employment) has been conditional upon an individual secret ballot having been held (TULRCA 1992, s 226). So, unless a ballot is held and the requirements of the *Code of Practice* (DTI 2000) are satisfied, the industrial action will be regarded as unlawful and the employer may take action in the courts to secure an injunction and claim limited damages.

The *Code of Practice* is complex. Among its key requirements are the following:

- a majority of those voting must say that they wish to take part, in the industrial action (TULRCA 1992, s 226(2)(a)(iii));
- the entitlement to vote in the ballot must be given to all those members who it is reasonable for the union to believe will be called on to take part, and to no one else (TULRCA 1992, s 227);
- the ballot must be held before the trade union gives its authority for the action, but not more than four weeks before the action begins. (An extension to 12 weeks in this timescale is possible in some cases where there is a legal dispute with an employer);
- the ballot must be secret by means of marking a ballot paper. Prescriptions are given on the content of the ballot paper (TULRCA 1992, s 229) (*see also* Fig. 15.2);

'If you take part in a strike or other industrial action, you may be in breach of your contract of employment. However, if you are dismissed for taking part in a strike or other industrial action which is called officially and is otherwise lawful, the dismissal will be unfair if it takes place fewer than eight weeks after you have started taking part in the action, and depending on the circumstances may be unfair if it takes place later.'

This statement must not be altered, qualified or commented upon by anything else on the ballot paper.

Figure 15.2 Obligatory statement on industrial action ballot paper

Source: DTI (2000) *Code of Practice: Industrial Action Ballots and Notice to Employers*, Annex 2. London: DTI.

- in respect of discontinuous action, the union must notify the employer of the dates or give seven days' notice of each new piece of action (TULRCA 1992, s 234A(3)(b));
- the ballot must be by post;
- where 50 or more members are voting, the votes must be accurately and fairly counted and scrutinised by an independent scrutineer. Provisions are set on the appointment of a scrutineer (TULRCA 1992, ss 226B and 231B);
- where votes are given to members at different places of work, they may be aggregated if it is reasonable for the union to believe that the aggregated group consists of:

- all its members;
- all its members employed by one or more employers;
- members who share a 'common distinguishing factor' (such as a factor relating to their terms and conditions of employment) (TULRCA 1992, s 228);

■ no 'call' for industrial action must be made before the date of a ballot (TULRCA 1992, s 233(3)(a));

■ it is possible for a union to delegate authorisation to 'call' industrial action to a 'specified person'. This can include delegation by the General Secretary (on behalf of the executive committee) to district and regional officers.

Finally, the *Code of Practice* (DTI, 2000) requires, as appropriate, the provision of various notices and information from the trade union to employers:

■ unions have to give an employer at least seven days' written notice of intention to ballot on industrial action, plus a description of the workers to be balloted (para 14);

■ employers must get a sample voting paper (para 19);

■ employers must see details of the result (para 43);

■ employers are entitled to a copy of the scrutineer's report on request (para 48);

■ seven days' written notice will have to be given by unions of intended industrial action, the dates of the action and a description of which workers are likely to be involved (para 50).

There is now a political consensus on the importance of balloting prior to industrial action. The ILO criticised the law on industrial action in Britain for being too complex. Certainly, Convention 87 states that 'worker's . . . organisations shall have the right to draw up their constitutions and rules . . . the public authorities shall refrain from any interference which would restrict this right or impede the lawful exercise thereof' (Art 3).

What is the situation in essential services?

The wide framework of law regulating industrial action does not specifically restrict strikes in 'essential services'. Indeed, there is no accepted statutory definition of such services. Auerbach (1990: 115) has commented, in his investigation of Conservative government policy, that 'it was generally reckoned that there was no simple direct way of legislating to control strikes of this kind, while a number of the legal and non-legal measures, especially some of those adopted since 1979, might help alleviate the problem'. He adds that 'the Government itself on several occasions expressed the view that "strike ballot provisions could help with the essential services problem"'.

A general criminal proscription has been available since 1875, but although 'there have been many disputes where it could have been invoked . . . there is no record of any prosecutions under it' (Morris, 1986: 234). This states that:

A person commits an offence who wilfully and maliciously breaks a contract of service or hiring, knowing or having reasonable cause to believe that the probable consequence of his so doing, either alone or in combination with others, will be –
(a) to endanger human life or cause serious bodily injury, or
(b) to expose valuable property, whether real or personal, to destruction or serious injury (TULRCA 1992, s 240).

Aside from these general civil and criminal legal situations, the only proscriptions on industrial action in essential services relate to specific categories of working people: viz. armed forces, police officers, prison officers, merchant seamen, postal workers and telecommunications workers (both in certain circumstances).

At present, in political debates, two alternative policy routes are advocated for dealing with this area: amending the existing general framework on immunities to outlaw strikes in essential circumstances; or providing compulsory dispute mechanisms like arbitration, mediation or conciliation to decide on industrial relations outcomes. While the former seems superficially clear-cut and attractive, it is likely to experience definitional problems. The second route is more pragmatic. It keeps the disputing parties in an industrial relations context where they can influence and determine possible outcomes. It could be more constructive.

Lawful picketing

During the 1970s and 1980s, picketing as a feature of industrial disputes provoked considerable political and public concern. This arose from the characteristics of some picketing at that time. There was some mass picketing, where large numbers of people would congregate at the entrance to an employer's premises, causing an obstruction. Also there was the use of 'flying' pickets, whereby numbers of people would move from site to site of an employer's business when an industrial dispute was in progress. These examples of picketing, although rare, given the number of industrial disputes, were frequently characterised by violence and were well publicised in the media. There were no restrictions on those present on picket lines, and they could include any supporters of the employees on strike. A consequence of this was an early change in the law, in 1980, by the Conservative government together with the introduction of a statutory *Code of Practice* on Picketing (DTI 1992).

The law relating to picketing encompasses both civil and criminal law. Immunity from civil proceedings creates the foundation for lawful picketing. The criminal law is involved when the behaviour of a picket results in public order offences, a breach of the peace or offences against property. So, for example, under civil law, picketing is lawful if it is 'in contemplation or furtherance of a trade dispute' and is in the following circumstances:

- where a person attends at or near their own place of work; and
- their purpose is peacefully to obtain information or communicate information; or peacefully to persuade a person to work or not to work (TULRCA 1992, s 220).

If the picketing is not 'peaceful', then the police may charge and arrest individuals for specific offences. These can include: breach of the peace, assault, affray, obstruction of a police officer in the execution of his duty, intimidation, criminal damage.

Several questions arise in respect of the operation of picketing.

Where is a person's 'own place of work'?

This is not precisely defined in law. However, the *Code of Practice* states:

> Lawful picketing normally involves attendance at an entrance to or exit from the factory, site or office at which the picket works . . . The law does not enable a picket to attend lawfully at an entrance to or exit from any place of work which is not his own. This applies, for example, even if those who are working at the other place of work are employed by the same employer or are covered by the same collective bargaining arrangements as the picket (DTI, 1992: paras 17–18).

So, for example, in the *Stockport Messenger* dispute (1983) and in the miners' strike (1984), injunctions were successfully obtained by the employers in question to prevent strikers picketing at different locations (from where they worked) of their own employer.

The only exceptions for employees are the following people who may picket an administrative centre: a person who does not normally work at one particular place, and employees for whom it would be impractical to picket their place of work (e.g. lorry drivers).

Can non-employees attend a picket line?

This is possible only in the following circumstances: if the person is either a trade union official accompanying members or an ex-employee in dispute over a sacking.

What is 'secondary picketing'?

This phrase does not exist in legislation. It is used in everyday language to describe a situation where a person (not employed at a particular place of work) attends there to support strikers. It is unlawful. It is a matter for the employer, not the police, to identify and take civil proceedings against such a picket – i.e. to obtain an injunction and to claim damages. The *Code of Practice* is very clear on this: 'An employer cannot require the police to help in identifying the pickets against whom he wishes to seek an order from the civil court' (DTI, 1992: para 46).

How many employees can attend a picket?

This is a matter for police discretion. However, the *Code of Practice* states that 'pickets and their organisers should ensure that in general the number of pickets does not exceed six at any entrance to, or exit from, a workplace; frequently, a smaller number will be appropriate' (DTI, 1992: para 51).

In recent years, picketing has tended to be a low-key activity. There has been general compliance with the law. For example, the Workplace Industrial Relations Survey 1990 found that in 58 per cent of primary pickets up to six people attended; in 17 per cent of cases, between seven and 20; and in 7 per cent of cases, between 21 and 100. It has been relatively rare for an employer to seek injunctions. Also, in general, the criminal law has been observed. In the sub-sequent decade, the situation has remained broadly the same.

Liability for unlawful industrial action

In 1982, the law was amended to enable civil proceedings to be used against trade unions, as organisations, in relation to unlawful industrial action. Essentially, this enabled an 'injured' party to seek an injunction and claim limited damages. This area of the law will be considered under the following headings:

- Who can be sued?
- Who can sue?
- What remedies are available?

Who can be sued?

Normally, the trade union organising the unlawful industrial action is liable to be sued. In the case of unlawful picketing, however, it may also be possible to sue, as well as the organisers, the individual pickets who are inducing breaches of contract. The liability of a trade union is extensive. It encompasses the unlawful acts of its officials and members. Also, the union is liable for any unlawful act authorised or endorsed by any official or any committee of the union. The excep-tions to this overall liability are:

- where the official or committee who authorised or endorsed the act was forbidden to do so by the union's own rules; or
- where the executive committee, the General Secretary or the President 'repudiates' or disowns the unlawful industrial action. (The requirements in respect of this are set out in TULRCA 1992, s 21.)

Who can sue?

Those who are 'injured' by the unlawful industrial action are able to claim damages and seek an injunction. Normally, the injured party would be an employer. However, it is possible for other parties to contracts and for trade union members to take certain action (*see* Fig. 15.3). The 'injured' party would have to show:

- that an unlawful act has been done or is threatened;
- that the injured person is party to contracts which will be or have been inter-fered with by the unlawful act; and
- that the injured person is likely to suffer loss or has done so as a result.

What remedies are available?

There are two available remedies: an injunction and damages. An **injunction** is a court order to prevent the industrial action or to have it stopped. If the case is urgent, courts may grant such an order on an interim basis without waiting for a full hearing of the case (i.e. an interlocutory injunction). Generally, it is employers who have sought injunctions. However, since 1988, trade union members have

---

Background

A pupil, P, was excluded from school on the direction of the headteacher. This decision was overturned by the Governors and P returned to school. There were further behavioural problems with P. The teaching staff expressed concern about the effect of these on other pupils and about his behaviour towards them. Eventually, staff were instructed by the headteacher to continue teaching him in class. Contractually, teachers are required to carry out their duties under any direction which might 'reasonably' be given by the headteacher.

The union decided to ballot its members with a view to industrial action. It gave the Local Education Authority proper notices in relation to such a ballot. The result of the ballot was 25 members to 1 in favour of strike action; and 26 to nil in favour of non-strike action. The union stated that it intended to call for continuous industrial action short of a strike. This was in the form of a refusal to accept the headteacher's 'unreasonable direction' to teach P. This action began on 1 December 2000. From that date, P was mostly taught on his own by supply teachers.

P started action in the High Court to restrain the teachers from refusing to teach him. The matter, then, went on appeal to the Court of Appeal.

Is this a 'trade dispute'?

In the Court of Appeal, it was ruled that there was a trade dispute. There was a dispute about the teachers' terms and conditions of employment. This was about whether the headteacher could give a direction to teach an allegedly disruptive pupil. This amounted to a trade dispute (under the legislation). Consequently, P failed in his attempt to secure an injunction.

What if it had been unlawful industrial action?

If the industrial action had been unlawful – for example, if the ballot had not been conducted properly – P might have been successful. In that case, the union would have been required to instruct its members to call off the industrial action (i.e. take P back into the classroom). If the union had failed to instruct its members in this way, then, it would have been in contempt of court and liable to be fined by the court.

Figure 15.3   A disruptive pupil

Source: Based on *P* v *National Association of Schoolmasters/Union of Women Teachers* [2001] IRLR 532 CA.

been able to apply in the High Court or (in Scotland) in the Court of Session) for an injunction where they are to be called on to take part in industrial action that has not been endorsed in a ballot.

If an injunction is granted by the courts, but disobeyed, those who sought it (usually the employer in the dispute) can go back to court and have those concerned ruled to be in 'contempt of court' (i.e. disobeying the court order). Anyone found to be in contempt of court may be fined an unlimited amount or even imprisoned. An employer does have the choice whether or not to seek 'enforcement proceedings'. It is a matter of judgement by the employer whether it might be preferable to pursue industrial relations options to deal with the industrial action. Since the late 1980s, it has been very rare for a trade union to face the ultimate penalty of sequestration, which is likely to arise if fines are not paid to the court. The general policy of the trade union movement has been to acquiesce to the legal requirements.

An **action for damages** may be preceded by an application for an injunction, but this is not a requirement. Claims for damages go to a full hearing of the case. There are limits on the scale of damages against trade unions. These are related to the unions' size:

Number of members	
Up to 4999	£10 000
5000–24 999	£50 000
25 000–99 999	£100 000
100 000 or more	£250 000

15.5 Conclusion

In this chapter, consideration has been given to both the practical employee relations issues that arise in respect of industrial action and also the nature and impact of the legal framework. Clearly, industrial action is perceived as a 'problem', but it is also, arguably, a 'right'. So, the issue for any government is to consider two sets of policy matters: what law? and what other policy measures?

In respect of the first, the question inevitably arises as to whether the 'right to take industrial action' can be acknowledged formally in employment law. This is far from the case in Britain at the present time. The development of the law on strikes in Europe has been described as evolving through three phases:

1 The strike is treated as a crime.
2 The strike becomes a 'liberty' or freedom.
3 The 'right to strike' emerges.

Britain, according to Wedderburn (1991: 279) 'has been left retarded in the second phase'. So we have a 'moral' or 'social' right, but no legal right. A task for the future might be to determine how an effective 'right to withdraw labour in combination' might be enacted. This would bring Britain into conformity with the overwhelming majority of its EU partners and with the ILO. The limited protection against dismissal (TULRCA 1992, s 238A) is a limited step towards a right. But in no way does it confer one.

An ancillary legal issue must be the definition of 'lawful' in respect of industrial action. This is inextricably enmeshed, at the moment, with the extensive constraints on trade union activity. The complexity of this law has been criticised by the ILO. So, a clearer and less onerous definition of a 'lawful' trade dispute and industrial action could form the context in which an individual right to take industrial action might be enacted.

As far as other policy measures are concerned, these are the responsibility of government and employers as appropriate. For example, government could take the view that the 'problem' of industrial action could be more effectively tackled by the use of third-party intervention in employee relations. This would involve a wider use of the processes of arbitration, mediation and conciliation. Furthermore, it might encourage employers to focus on pre-emptive measures. This could involve tackling the root causes of workplace discontent. This would involve addressing the issues of managerial style, managerial policies, standards of good HR practice, acceptable and fair terms and conditions of employment, the quality of employee relations.

Case study 15.1

A bakery in Liverpool is a division of a large food conglomerate. Due to adverse changes in the market for certain packaged cakes, the parent company has decided to close the Liverpool bakery.

Industrial relations at the bakery have not been good for a number of years. The Food and Bakery Workers' Union (FABWU) is recognised for the production workers. The drivers, who transport the finished products to the retailers, are employed by a separate company owned by the conglomerate. The Road Transport Workers' Union (RTWU) is recognised for the drivers.

News about the closure of the Liverpool bakery has not yet been announced. However, rumours have been spreading through the plant all morning (Tuesday, 2 March). Billy Baker, the FABWU convenor, had heard unofficially from a secretary in the personnel department. 'It's not on! All the unemployed in this area – and we're going to be added to the heap', he told the shop stewards' committee. 'We've got to do something now!' At Billy's instigation, the committee decided to call the bakery production workers out on strike.

'What about the drivers?' asked Tracy Jones. 'Can't we get them to support us?' The committee thought this was a good idea and contact was to be made with the drivers' senior steward.

At lunchtime on Tuesday, 2 March, the production workers present in the canteen had a hurried mass meeting. Billy told them about the threatened redundancies and closure and that the personnel manager would not discuss the issue with him. He said that the only way to resist the anticipated management action was for the workforce to strike immediately. On a show of hands there was an overwhelming majority in favour of an immediate walkout. By 2 pm, all production workers were outside picketing the plant. The drivers delivering goods were 'persuaded' to go away and those about to transport packaged cakes did not leave the depot.

The production manager and the personnel manager discussed the situation and made immediate contact with the district officer of the FABWU, telling him to come down urgently and get his members back to work.

After long discussions with the shop stewards' committee, the district officer, Fred Bland, told the stewards that what they were doing was unlawful and that they must return to work. If they did not, the union would be forced to repudiate them.

Billy Baker, who had been elected convenor because he was the most vocal of the stewards, vehemently opposed this course of action. 'You are not employed by us to implement these laws!' he exploded. 'You are supposed to looked after your members' interests. So do it!' Further discussions were fruitless. Eventually, Bland left saying that he was going to report the issue to the union's general secretary.

The picketing lasted until 5 pm and all present resolved that the strike would continue the next day. At 6 am on Wednesday, 3 March, pickets were outside the gates of the plant and no production took place. A message was received from the senior steward of the drivers, employed by a delivery company, who said that all the drivers had stopped work in support of the production workers.

The production manager had been told by the managing director, at the head office in Berkshire, that it was essential that production was re-started. The previous day's disruption to production had caused one major supermarket chain to question whether to place further orders with the company. Although the plant was to close, the rationalisation of the organisation was, at this stage, incomplete – so it was essential that production in Liverpool continued for a while longer. The same message was transmitted from the personnel director to the plant personnel manager.

The production manager and the personnel manager had a further meeting with FABWU district officer, Fred Bland, who reported to them that the union's national executive committee had told him to instruct his members to return to work and to open consultations with management about the prospective redundancies.

Bland went to see the shop stewards' committee to pass on the message. The committee was furious. Its members told him of the support they had from the drivers as well as among the production workers themselves. 'It won't do you any good. If you don't do what the union tells you, you're on your own,' Bland told them.

By lunchtime, the strike was still continuing. The managing director gave the production manager instructions to have the firm's solicitors go to court to obtain injunctions. He told Bland of his intention. This threat was sufficient for the strike committee to call off the action. At 2.30 pm, the production workers were ready to return to work.

The production manager told Fred Bland and Billy Baker that he did not want full production to start until 6 am on Thursday, 4 March. The union officials protested that management could not stop them working and prevent them earning any pay. They said that management was breaking their contracts.

The following day full production did start. In their pay packets for that week, the production workers had two days' pay deducted.

Permission has been granted to reproduce this case study (with adaptations) from Huw Morris and Brian Willey (1996) *Corporate Environment*. London: Financial Times Management.

Exercise 15.1   **Granny's Pride Bakery**

1   What could have happened in law to the FABWU and RTWU if they had persisted with the industrial action, and why?

2   If the shop stewards' committee had continued with the industrial action after it had been repudiated by the FABWU, what might have happened in law, and why?

3   In law, what right does the management have to make the deduction from the employees' pay packets that they did?

4   Do the workers, as individuals, have any protection from dismissal for taking part in the industrial action?

Feedback on this exercise is provided in the Appendix to this book.

Further reading

Department of Trade and Industry (1998) 'Fairness at Work'. White Paper, Cm. 3968. London: Stationery Office.

Department of Trade and Industry (2000) *Code of Practice: Industrial Action Ballots and Notice to Employers*. London: DTI.

Ewing, K. (1989) *Britain and the ILO*. London: Institute of Employment Rights.

References

Auerbach, S. (1988) 'Injunction Procedure in the Seafarers' Dispute', *Industrial Law Journal*, (17)3, 227–37.

Auerbach, S. (1990) *Legislating for Conflict*. Oxford: Clarendon Press.

Brown, R.K. (1988) 'The Employment Relationship in Sociological Theory', in Gallie, D. (ed.) *Employment in Britain*. Oxford: Blackwell.

Cully, M. *et al.* (1998) *The 1998 Workplace Employee Relations Survey – First Findings*. London: DTI.

Cully, M. *et al.* (1999) *Britain at Work*. London: Routledge.

Department of Trade and Industry (1992) *Code of Practice: Picketing*. London: DTI.

Department of Trade and Industry (1998) 'Fairness at Work.' White Paper, Cm. 3968. London: Stationery Office.

Department of Trade and Industry (2000) *Code of Practice: Industrial Action Ballots and Notice to Employers*. London: DTI.

Elgar, J. and Simpson, B. (1993) 'The impact of the law on industrial disputes in the 1980s', in Metcalf, D. and Milner, S. (eds) *New Perspectives on Industrial Disputes*. London: Routledge.

Ewing, K. (1989) *Britain and the ILO*. London: Institute of Employment Rights.

Ewing, K. (1991) *The Right to Strike*. Oxford: Clarendon Press.

Griffin, J. (1939) *Strikes: a Study in Quantitive Economics*. New York: Columbia University Press.

Hyman, R. (1984) *Strikes* (3rd edn). London: Fontana.

Kahn-Freund, O. (1977) *Labour and the Law*. London: Stevens.

Knowles, K.G. (1952) *Strikes: a Study in Industrial Conflict*. Oxford: Blackwell.

Leader, S. (1991) 'The European Convention on Human Rights, the Employment Act 1988 and the Right to Refuse to Strike', *Industrial Law Journal*, 20(1), 39–59.

Mesher, J. and Sutcliffe, F. (1986) 'Industrial Action and the Individual', in Lewis, R. (ed.) *Labour Law in Britain*. Oxford: Blackwell.

Millward, N., Stevens, M. *et al.* (1992) *Workplace Industrial Relations in Transition*. London: Dartmouth.

Morris, G. (1986) 'Emergencies and Essential Supplies', in Lewis, R. (ed.) *Labour Law in Britain*. Oxford: Blackwell.

Royal Commission on Trade Unions and Employers' Associations 1965–68 (1968) The Report of the Donovan Commission. Cmnd. 3623. London: HMSO.

Smith, C.T.B. *et al.* (1978) *Strikes in Britain*. London: HMSO.

Wedderburn, Lord (1986) *The Worker and the Law*. Harmondsworth: Penguin.

Wedderburn, Lord (1991) *Employment Rights in Britain and Europe: Selected Papers in Labour Law*. London: Lawrence and Wishart; Institute of Employment Rights.

Weekes, B. *et al.* (1975) *Industrial Relations and the Limit of the Law*. Oxford: Blackwell.

16 Conclusion

Employment law is continually changing – in some periods with great rapidity. Yet it is possible to discern certain continuing themes in both legislation and case law. These themes frequently reflect social and political attitudes and objectives. In this concluding chapter, we review several which are likely to be key to the development of employment law in the next few years. The principal ones considered are: ethical standards, minimum standards, juridification, business interests, labour-market flexibility and employment status, the accommodation of non-work life, individualisation, representation rights, qualified access to statutory rights, enforcement processes and remedies.

16.1 Ethical standards

There are two very significant and related bodies of law that affect employment standards: the established and growing body of discrimination law, and the Human Rights Act 1998. Their effect is felt and will continue to be felt both in respect of substantive issues (terms and conditions of employment) and also in relation to the procedures used to conduct employment relations. Action against discrimination, in society at large as well as in employment, continues to expand. New wrongs are being formulated in law – in respect of sexual orientation, religion and age.

Human rights legislation infuses all aspects of society. It 'will have a momentous impact on our legal system. It is the most important piece of constitutional legislation in Britain for many years' (Wadham and Mountfield, 1999). It concerns, for example, rights of individuals (as citizens and as working people), decisions of public authorities and the treatment of individuals in judicial processes. The pervasiveness of this legislation will be considerable.

16.2 Minimum standards

It is in the context of these ethical standards that a wider range of specific statutory minimum standards is being developed in employment relations. Standards of treatment in employment can, in fact, be enacted as absolute standards or as minimum standards. Examples of the former exist particularly in health and safety law, but the tendency of most governments in the post-war period has been to create minimum standards. The present government is likewise committed to this approach. It is reflected in provisions on, for example, contractual information, redundancy pay, maternity leave, notice to terminate employment, the minimum wage and paid annual leave. It still allows an employer discretion to provide enhanced conditions of employment above the statutory minimum.

Reinforcing the approach, the Prime Minister signalled the need for a balance between flexibility, job creation and economic growth, on the one hand, and the development of a framework of minimum standards, on the other. Reporting to Parliament after the 1997 Amsterdam European Council meeting he said that 'Europe needs a new approach to employment and growth, based on British ideas for competitiveness, introducing more flexible labour markets and employability. That means creating a more skilled and adaptable workforce, better equipped to cope with economic change . . . Basic minimum standards are not, in our view, inconsistent with economic prosperity' (*Hansard*, 18 June 1997).

16.3 Juridification

Standards for determining the treatment of working people have, over the past 30 years, increasingly been determined in law. Employers, as we have seen, still have some discretion but this is narrowing. In most organisations, decisions relating to human resource management are now more likely to be reached by reference to these legal standards. Even where trade union recognition has been conceded by an employer, the standards set in collective agreements must reflect legal standards where they exist.

It can be argued, of course, that this juridification of HRM and of employment relations is more likely to be found in larger organisations which have the professional support and advice of personnel departments. Certainly, evidence suggests that some managers, particularly in smaller organisations, either are ignorant of legal standards or deliberately flout them (NACAB, 1997: para 7.4). Clearly, if a minimum standards employment culture is to be promoted by government, then, adherence by employers to such standards must likewise be promoted (*see* discussion below on enforcement of statutory rights).

16.4 Business interests

Legal standards are, of course, designed to mould the behaviour of employers. Inevitably, tensions can exist. Two business reactions have been voiced. These are certain to recur: employers' concerns about the cost of legal regulation, and the extent to which human rights and minimum standards can be effectively implemented into business organisations.

The government asserted in 'Fairness at Work' (DTI, 1998), that 'in particular, [it] is determined that all the changes proposed in this White Paper should avoid bureaucracy and unnecessary burdens on business'. However, representations from employers (particularly on the Working Time Regulations and the national minimum wage) strongly suggest that this objective has not been achieved. More generally, concern is also expressed about the cost to employers of responding to employment tribunal claims.

Tensions between the promotion of business interests and the achievement of ethical standards are frequently reported in the news media and in academic studies and commentaries. Several examples illustrate what is likely to be a continuing tension and a continuing failure, in some cases, to achieve standards of fair treatment – in Britain and internationally.

First, in respect of conditions of employment, the Citizens' Advice Bureau is experiencing a growing caseload of employment complaints. These focus on three broad categories – redundancy, dismissals and unilateral variations of terms and conditions of employment (Abbott, 1998: 262). This illustrates the continuing vulnerability of certain people – particularly those working for small organisations. A second example is the international concern voiced about supply-chain arrangements of multinational retail organisations – in particular, whether exploitation of working people and the use of child labour was evident in developing countries. Attempts have been made by the ILO and charities (such as Oxfam) to have a code of practice adopted by multinational companies.

Thirdly, globalisation and the operational size and scale of private business has created further anxieties. Charles Handy (1998: 8) has outlined what he calls 'the critical ethical challenge for the next century' in this way: 'when half of the world's 500 biggest economies are corporations answerable only to themselves and effectively stateless, then we have to rely on their own internal values to keep them honest and decent. We have to hope that those values are focused on what is best for all of us, not just themselves and that they think of themselves as communities fuelled by purposes rather than as the personal properties of their owners.' It is, of course, arguable whether such a laissez-faire approach can be acceptable.

How this 'ethical challenge' will be met can only be speculated upon. Pessimists expect that profit, shareholder value and corporate survival will remain the driving forces behind business activity. Those who are more optimistic see possible accommodation between business interests and ethical standards. Mary Robinson, the United Nations High Commissioner for Human Rights, commented that 'in many ways business decisions can profoundly affect the dignity and rights of individuals and communities. Business is coming to recognise this and I welcome the growing activities in the business community to establish benchmarks, promote best practice and adopt codes of conduct' (1998: 14). So, tension exists between business interests and ethical values. In a global economy, this is further aggravated as 'footloose' multinational companies pursue cost-effective investment opportunities.

In this context, the issue of 'corporate social responsibility' (CSR) has been promoted by both the British government and the European Union. The Department of Trade and Industry (2002) has defined the 'responsible organisation' in the following terms:

- It recognises that its activities have a wider impact on the society in which it operates.

- In response, it takes account of the economic, social, environmental and human rights impacts of its activities across the world.
- It seeks to achieve benefits by working in partnership with other groups and organisations.

The concept of CSR must start from an ethical premise. Although it covers a wide range of business activities, implicit in the ethical framework are many concepts recognisable to human resource practitioners: 'fair' and non-discriminatory treatment; the promotion of equal opportunities; 'fair' pay; non-exploitative conditions of employment; and a duty of care to workers.

One driver of ethical standards may be consumers. The DTI (2002) quoted opinion surveys which reported that 'the proportion of people who regard an organisation's social responsibility as "very important" when selecting a product has risen from 28 per cent in 1998 to 46 per cent in 2001'. The extent to which this can be translated into consumer action is indicated by the fact that 'research suggests that as many as one-fifth of consumers now boycott or select products on social grounds'.

In practice, there is likely to remain a marked differentiation between employers and their espousal of standards of good employment practice. The literature of employee relations provides various categorisations of management style (e.g. Purcell and Sisson, 1983). In summary, there are probably three broad theoretical 'types' of organisation:

- *'Sophisticated' organisations*, which have a strategic perspective and develop policies which generally reflect professional standards of human resource management and comply with employment law. Faced with successful tribunal complaints, they may well revise corporate policy to ensure no repetition of any breaches of good practice;
- *'Pragmatic' or 'opportunistic' organisations*, which react to situations as they arise and, generally, will only comply with good employment practice if there is a legislative 'stick' used against them;
- *'Exploitative' organisations*, which are ignorant of the law or deliberately do not comply.

The social policy challenge is to ensure compliance with employment across this diverse range of organisations. The difficulty is that the final two categories, in aggregate, cover by far and away the largest number of employers.

16.5 Labour-market flexibility

The values, ethics and minimum standards that have just been considered are to be applied in a flexible labour market. In such a labour market there will, inevitably, be a tension between economic interests (e.g. the minimisation of unit labour costs) and standards of good practice. This makes universal compliance difficult to achieve.

The 'flexible workforce' is likely to remain a significant feature of the British labour market. Indeed, its economic significance is central to government policy objectives. At the same time, a key social policy issue concerns the extent to which employment protection is afforded to workers who have a diverse range of employment statuses (part-time, casual, agency workers, etc.).

The progressive inclusion of these 'atypical' workers into a framework of employment rights is set to continue. As we have seen (Chapter 2) piecemeal attempts at employment protection deriving from case law have produced some patchy outcomes. Nevertheless, the courts have outlined legal approaches to discerning a person's employment status and access to statutory rights (e.g. whether or not a particular casual worker has certain rights). As far as statute law is concerned, part-time workers, homeworkers and agency workers, for example, will benefit from strengthened employment rights.

Furthermore, the problematic distinction drawn between an 'employee' and a 'worker' is being tackled. The government is following up its commitment in 'Fairness at Work' (DTI, 1998: para 3.18) to extend statutory employment rights to 'workers'. The ability to make such changes is provided for in the Employment Relations Act 1999, s 23.

16.6 The accommodation of non-work life

The growing feminisation of the labour market, the persistence of traditional caring responsibilities remaining with women, flexibility of working time and the long-hours working culture have all been factors in discussions on social policies designed to accommodate working life and non-work life. Action to date has been piecemeal (primarily through the enactment of rights to maternity leave and maternity pay). However, the concept of 'family-friendly policies' is now an explicit dimension of government policy. It is certain to infuse a range of policy measures which, in theory, should make the accommodation of work and certain dependency responsibilities easier. These measures include: enhanced paid maternity leave, unpaid parental leave, limited statutory paternity leave, greater opportunities for flexible patterns of work and limits on working time.

16.7 Individualsation and collectivism

Part of the rhetoric of the 1980s and early 1990s concerned the relative significance of 'individualism' and 'collectivism' in employment relations. The prevailing political policy, then, was designed to eradicate collective action and promote individualism. In a new political climate, there has been some change of emphasis.

The inheritance from the Conservative governments has been reviewed recently in a survey of companies (Brown, 1998). A distinction is drawn between '**substantive individualisation**' and '**procedural individualisation**'. On substantive matters, the research found that as far as non-pay terms and conditions were concerned, standardisation 'has **increased** rather than diminished at firms which claimed to have taken steps to individualise contracts' (1998: 6). This was a reflection of 'a long established national trend of "harmonising" non-pay terms'. Even the 'individualisation' of pay was problematic for employers. The opportunity to link pay to individual performance was 'valued'. But performance-related pay was 'notoriously difficult' to manage. Some reported that it 'damaged team work'.

Brown (1998: 8) concludes that 'all this suggests that the recent individualisation of employment contracts in Britain has not been primarily concerned with greater diversification of the substantive content of individual employees' contracts. By implication, then, the individualisation has been procedural and not substantive.'

A number of issues arose from the survey of procedural practice (in organisations that had individualised procedures by de-recognising unions). These could be relevant to some of the anticipated developments in respect to representation rights (discussed below).

First, as far as the handling of **individual grievances** was concerned (in firms which had de-recognised unions):

> there were considerable differences in the warmth or hostility with which firms tolerated their employees' unions for individual grievances . . . It was often more difficult for ex-shop stewards to pursue members' cases without the protection of formal recognition (1998: 9).

Secondly, in respect to **consultation**, some companies, having de-recognised unions, felt that:

> there was no need to develop further institutional arrangements to tap a collective employee voice. Their efforts were concentrated on the individual employee. Others attempted to construct consultative machinery without unions. Many of them found this difficult in practice. They typically found it difficult to get volunteers to join consultative bodies when they were not backed by a trade union, in some cases because employees feared it might harm their job prospects (1998: 9).

Finally, where **unions were still recognised**, then, managers reported some advantages:

> One frequent theme was that unions could help in the process of talking the workforce through both the need and the manner of adjustment to change . . . A strong senior shop steward was often reported as taking the lead in manoeuvring through a succession of changes . . . Another related and recurring theme in employers' reasons for retaining recognition was that the involvement of unions greatly reinforces the legitimation of management action (1998: 22).

16.8 Representation rights

As indicated in the previous section, there is a three-tiered structure of representation: on individual matters (grievances and disciplinary action), in consultation processes and in negotiations about terms and conditions of employment. The thrust of government social policy is to improve, through legislation, some of these areas of representation. The historic tradition, in Britain, of trade unions being the single channel of representation (particularly collective representation) has clearly been broken. It is unlikely to be restored. A dual channel will remain. In addition stronger emphasis and support is given to individual representation in grievances and disciplinary cases.

The Employment Act 2002 provides for minimum statutory procedures (on grievances and discipline and dismissal) to be implied into contracts of employment. This is supported by the statutory **right to be accompanied** whereby in a disciplinary or a grievance hearing a worker may be accompanied by a union official or a fellow worker (Employment Relations Act 1999, ss 10–15; ACAS, *Code of Practice on Discipline and Grievance Procedures*, 2000).

Such statutory **consultation** rights as exist (on redundancies, health and safety and transfers of undertakings) are augmented by information and consultation rights placed upon certain multinational companies (under the European Works Council Directive 1994). More general information and consultation rights are being implemented in a phased way by 2008.

Legal **rights to negotiate terms and conditions of employment** are enacted under the Trade Union and Labour Relations Consolidation Act 1992, s 70A and Sch A1. In addition, collective representation through non-union employee representatives is provided for under the Working Time Regulations 1998, whereby workforce agreements (to utilise derogations) can be negotiated and agreed.

16.9   Qualified access to statutory rights

Access to employment protection can be restricted in various ways, for example by:

- the need to be an 'employee' working under a contract of employment;
- the need to have a qualifying period of continuous employment;
- the exclusion of those who work for an employer of a particular size;
- the need to be working a given number of hours each week;
- the exclusion of those of a particular age;
- restricted application to specific occupations, sectors or industries.

In recent years, many of these restrictions have gradually been eroded, providing greater access to working people.

First, as outlined earlier, much employment protection is extending beyond those with a contract of employment to embrace all 'workers' who have an employment relationship (*see* section 16.5). Secondly, in 1999 the qualifying period of employment of two years in unfair dismissal cases was reduced to one year. In 2001, the 13-week qualifying period for paid annual leave was removed as a result of a ruling by the European Court of Justice. Thirdly, the restricted access to the Disability Discrimination Act 1995 of working people in small organisations has been reduced: access is now open to those working in firms employing 15 people (formerly 20) and this restriction will be abolished in 2004. Fourthly, hours restrictions on access to statutory employment rights have already been removed (in 1994) as indirectly discriminatory on grounds of sex. Fifthly, age restrictions for young people exist, for example, under minimum wage legislation and under redundancy law. At the same time, under unfair dismissal legislation, the restriction on applications by particular retired men is being challenged as indirect sex discrimination. Finally, restrictions in respect of specific occupations and sectors can be varied. So, in respect of working time regulation, they are currently being removed under further European law.

16.10   Enforcement processes

The evolving framework of statutory employment rights that has been outlined in this text inevitably brings into focus two important related questions: whether the enforcement processes for aggrieved individuals are effective and also whether the remedies available are just and equitable. There has been an ongoing debate about various aspects of the enforcement process. This surfaced in the consultation on 'Fairness at Work' (DTI, 1998). It will undoubtedly persist because many of the issues are still unresolved. The aspects of the enforcement process considered here are: knowledge about employment rights, the means and resources of applicants, representation arrangements, operational weaknesses in the tribunal system, and (in the next section) the value of the remedies.

It is obvious to say but **knowledge** of an entitlement is an essential preliminary to the assertion of statutory rights. It is, however, a hit and miss process. Some rights are common knowledge (e.g. the right not to be unfairly dismissed) even if the specifics are not fully understood, but many other rights may be unknown or sketchily known. Indeed, the NACAB (1997: para 7.24) has recommended that the Department of Trade and Industry 'should have a statutory duty to make available free information and advice on employment rights'.

The **means and resources** available to individuals vary widely. Trade unions have played, and continue to play, an important role in advising, funding and representing certain members before employment tribunals. However, the past 20 years have seen a substantial reduction in trade union membership and, simultaneously, a massive increase in the jurisdiction of employment (formerly industrial) tribunals. One consequence of these developments is that non-unionists who believe their employment rights have been infringed may either do nothing or alternatively turn for advice, guidance and, possibly, help with representation to other agencies (e.g. law centres, women's groups and local racial equality councils).

One important body whose role in employment relations is increasingly being recognised and documented is the CAB. In one survey in Greater London (Abbott, 1998), the CAB reported that 'between 1994–1995 the number of employment inquiries received . . . ranged from just under 1000 to over 3000, accounting for between nine and fifteen per cent of their workload'. It may be that these figures are an underestimate, given that the initial problem presented to advisers 'often appeared to have little to do with employment issues and it was only after closer investigation and probing that it became clear that the problem was of an employment nature'. Employment inquiries 'are now the third largest category after debt and social security matters'.

Abbott reports different approaches used by the CAB. First, 'some use paid community lawyers with responsibility for employment law and these act as specialist caseworkers and as a resource for other advisers'. Secondly, 'others have a system of paid specialists supporting volunteers'. Thirdly, 'other bureaux have advisers with a keen interest in employment issues'.

Whether the role of the CAB as 'a new industrial relations actor' will continue and develop is dependent, in part, on the use made of a new legislative initiative. This is the extent to which trade unions can capitalise on the right of workers to be accompanied in grievance and disciplinary hearings. Should such issues, ultimately, lead to an employment tribunal, then, the union would be well placed to be adviser and representative.

Operational weaknesses in the tribunal system have been documented over several years (Dickens, 1985; Leonard, 1987; Lewis and Clarke, 1993). Further corroborative evidence has been reported by the National Association of Citizens' Advice Bureaux (1994 and 1997). Among the evidence produced was, first of all, an extreme reluctance by employees to take discrimination cases to tribunals. The reasons for this were 'perceptions about the low probability of winning a case', 'fear of not being believed' and 'fear of being seen as having overreacted to "normal behaviour"'. Secondly, there was concern about the extensive delays in the tribunal system.

Moves are under way to deal with some of the procedural flaws and delays. These include having a wider range of people authorised to agree compromise agreements, and an increased number of circumstances when tribunal chairmen might sit alone.

One other procedural route to expediting the handling of complaints was the introduction of an optional arbitration scheme (initially for unfair dismissal complaints) under the auspices of ACAS. This came into operation in 2001. It is a less legalistic and less intimidating forum for dispute resolution than that previously available. It might be that, in due course, this option might be available to deal with other infringements of statutory rights.

16.11 The value of the remedies

Fair and effective procedures for dealing with infringements of employment rights must be complemented by effective remedies. It is debatable whether or not such remedies are available. The principal remedy available in most employment complaints is financial. This is unrestricted in respect of discrimination complaints but a ceiling exists in relation to successful unfair dismissal claims. In 1999, the latter was raised substantially, to £50 000, and is increased annually in line with inflation. The change is an acknowledgement of the erosion in real terms of compensation levels. Critics doubt, however, that it is an effective deterrent against unfair dismissal by an employer.

16.12   The future

It is dangerous to predict future developments and directions in employment law. Indeed, the field is littered with many unanticipated consequences. Those issues that are certain are the continued 'Europeanisation' of employment law, the likelihood of intricate arguments about employment protection for 'workers' in the flexible labour market, continued juridification of HRM and employment relations generally, and ever-present concerns about the extent to which working people have effective access to complaints procedures and remedies.

References

ACAS (2000) *Code of Practice on Discipline and Grievance Procedures*. London: ACAS.

Abbott, B. (1998) 'The Emergence of a New Industrial Relations Actor – the Role of the Citizens' Advice Bureaux?' *Industrial Relations Journal*, 29(4), 262.

Brown, W. (1998) *Individualisation and Union Recognition in Britain in the 1990s*. Cambridge: ESRC Centre for Business Research, University of Cambridge.

Department of Trade and Industry (1998) 'Fairness at Work', White Paper, Cm. 3968. London: Stationery Office.

Department of Trade and Industry (2002) *Business and Society: corporate social responsibility report 2002*. London: DTI.

Dickens, L. (1985) *Dismissed: a Study of Unfair Dismissal and the Industrial Tribunal System*. Oxford: Blackwell.

Handy, C. (1998) 'The Real Challenge to Business', in *Visions of Ethical Business*. London: Financial Times Management.

Leonard, A. (1987) *Judging Inequality: the Effectiveness of the Industrial Tribunal System in Sex Discrimination and Equal Pay Cases*. London: The Cobden Trust.

Lewis, R. and Clark, J. (1993) *Employment Rights, Industrial Tribunals and Arbitration: the Case for Alternative Dispute Resolution*. London: Institute of Employment Rights.

National Association of Citizens' Advice Bureaux (1994) *Unequal Opportunities*. London: NACAB.

National Association of Citizens' Advice Bureaux (1997) *Flexibility Abused*. London: NACAB.

Purcell, J. and Sisson, K. (1983) 'Strategies and Practice in the Management of Industrial Relations', in Bain, G. (ed.) *Industrial Relations in Britain*. Oxford: Blackwell.

Robinson, M. (1998) 'The Business Case for Human Rights', in *Visions of Ethical Business*. London: Financial Times Management.

Wadham, J. and Mountfield, H. (1999) *Blackstone's Guide to the Human Rights Act 1998*. London: Blackstone Press Ltd.

Feedback on case studies and exercises

Purpose of feedback

- to help consider some of the practical issues involved in applying the law to employment practice; and
- to redirect readers to the legal issues outlined in the main text.

Chapter 1: An introduction to employment law

Exercise 1.2: How much freedom of expression?

- **Circumstances**: Examples include the prevention of sexual, racial and homophobic abuse; the need for child protection; the prevention of defamation of character.
- **Why selected?** Arguably to protect the rights of others to live in safety and security.
- **Restrictions**: These would be enacted through legislation and would probably confer powers on particular agencies to deal with specific problems (e.g. Social Service Departments; the police); and/or permit individuals to take complaints to the courts or employment tribunals.
- **Possible problems**: In particular, whether the legislative action was 'proportionate' (i.e. not excessive); whether due consideration was given to the rights of the alleged perpetrator.

Part One: The changing employment relationship

Chapter 2: Regulating the employment relationship

Exercise 2.2: Who has employment rights?

In these cases, the individuals are entitled to make claims at an employment tribunal. However, before lodging such a claim, they should raise their grievance with the employer to provide an opportunity for the complaint to be resolved.

1   Mick (whether he is an employee or a worker) is entitled to claim unlawful pay deduction irrespective of his length of service (ERA 1996 Part II) at an employment tribunal. (*See also* Chapter 10.)

2   Marion probably can claim continuity of service for 18 months, under the approach taken by the House of Lords and other courts in dealing with breaks in service. In which case, having over 12 months' continuous service, she qualifies to claim unfair dismissal at an employment tribunal if she believes she has a case (ERA 1996 Part X).

3   Indira is paid below the National Minimum Wage for adult workers and employees. She may make a claim at employment tribunal for the appropriate pay. The length of her working week and her length of service are not relevant. (*See also* Chapter 10.)

4   Sharon has short service. This does not prevent her claiming sex discrimination at an employment tribunal. Neither does the fact that she has resigned prevent a claim. She would presumably say that she was unfairly constructively dismissed. Presumably, she told her employer of her objection to the sergeant's behaviour and gave her employer an opportunity to take action. (*See also* Chapter 7.)

5   Jehan may have a right to claim unfair dismissal at an employment tribunal. Much will depend on the facts of the particular circumstances. He needs to establish that he is an employee (according to case law) and that there is mutuality of obligation. (*See also* the earlier section in this chapter on casual workers.)

Chapter 3: Managing change in the employment relationship

Exercise 3.1: Some problems of managing variation

1   The principal legal issue is what is in Samantha's contract of employment about her place of work. It may be that it is a condition of employment that she is mobile and so the manager is entitled to ask her to transfer between branches. If, however, she has been told to work at one branch and then is expected to transfer to another, the employer should obtain her agreement. To encourage her to agree, the employer might offer some 'consideration' (e.g. later starting and finishing times or financial assistance with transport). In practice, it would be sensible for the employer to discuss the transfer with the employee and attempt to deal constructively with any problems that she might have.

2   The starting point for considering this is the terms of the contract of employment. If employees have no contractual right to an annual pay increase, then the employer is entitled not to make a payment. Even if the employer commits to review pay annually, this is not a requirement to offer a pay increase. However, if there are contractual obligations to pay increases (e.g. on incremental pay schemes) then it would be a breach of contract for the employer not to pay this. Financial difficulties would not be a good enough reason for non-payment. The way out of the problem would be to discuss the matter with the staff in question and seek their agreement to a change in the contract

(i.e. not to pay the increase). If this course of action is not successful, the employer might terminate existing contracts of employment (with due notice) on the grounds of business need and offer new contracts.

3   It is unlikely that Beryl's contract of employment will contain a term committing her to working with manual files. The most likely and relevant contractual term will be the implied term requiring an employee to obey lawful and reasonable instructions. The employer would probably argue that it was reasonable, after proper training and support, to instruct Beryl to use the computerised system. If this course of action is not successful, then the employer might terminate her existing contract of employment (with due notice) on the grounds of business need and offer a new contract requiring her to undertake training. She may claim unfair dismissal, but her chance of success will depend on whether the employer behaved reasonably in all the circumstances.

4   Assuming that the break conforms with the requirements of the Working Time Regulations 1998, the employer is entitled to reaffirm the established arrangement and require staff to observe it. The threat of disciplinary action might be permissible technically. However, initially, for good employee relations, it might be advisable to use such action sparingly.

5   The issues here are whether the employer is requiring Jamila to undertake a task which is outside her contract of employment and whether or not there is a repudiatory breach of the contract. The relevant contractual term is the implied term requiring an employee to obey lawful and reasonable instructions. It is the duty of an employee to promote their employer's business. The task she was being required to undertake was (in the widest sense) a further selling task and clearly within her competence. She would not be able to establish a repudiatory breach of contract and, consequently, not be able, successfully, to claim unfair constructive dismissal.

Exercise 3.2: Some problems of managing transfers of undertakings

1   The central issue is the prospective redundancy of some security guards. Dismissal in the context of a relevant transfer is only defensible if it is for an economic, technical or organisational reason. If The Protection Company is involved in a reorganisation of staff then it might be possible to defend the dismissals. If so, the staff would have entitlements under the law on redundancy.

2   The managing director might be able to de-recognise the union, by giving notice to terminate the collective agreement. However, his ability to do this will be constrained by the law on union recognition and de-recognition. The terms of the contract which derive from collective agreements remain within the individual contracts until changes have been agreed with the staff concerned. The issues concerning variation of contract apply here. Unilateral variation would not be permissible in law. If, outside the transfer period, existing contracts are to be terminated with due notice and new contracts are offered to staff, then the Managing Director might be able to make the necessary changes. Such termination might result in unfair dismissal and redundancy claims before an employment tribunal.

3 Outside the transfer period (not specified anywhere in law), it is possible for an organisation to embark on such changes. Harmonisation can be achieved, provided the principles of contractual variation are adhered to. These involve providing information about the changes to be implemented, entering genuine consultation about the changes and reaching agreement. Failure to reach agreement can result in the employer terminating existing contracts with due notice and offering new contracts incorporating the new terms and conditions.

4 The facilities management company might be liable for the allegation if it has not taken steps in law, when it was negotiating the transfer, to indemnify itself from existing and prospective employment tribunal claims arising when the transferor was the employer of the staff in question. If it had not taken such steps, then it could be involved in the cost of defending the claim and in paying (unlimited) compensation if the applicant was successful.

5 The issue of self-employment can be difficult. An employer may call a person self-employed but that person may not be recognised as such by the courts. As discussed in the Chapter 2, the key issues in law are whether there is mutuality of obligation between the organisation and the individual concerned, whether there is (in transfer of undertakings situations) evidence of a contract of employment, and so whether or not the individual is an employee or an independent contractor. These questions can only be resolved by applying the law to the facts and circumstances of particular cases.

Exercise 3.3: Some problems in managing redundancies

1 The employer may have good reason for dismissal on grounds of redundancy and is intending to give due notice. However, the flaw in the process is his failure to consult. Even when fewer than 20 people are involved in redundancies, courts and tribunals require consultation with the individual concerned to consider any representations that they might make.

2 The suggestion is unlawful. Although the employer does not formally know that Michaela is pregnant, it is clearly common knowledge. The general manager is intending to use the information in the making of a decision. If Michaela were sacked then she could claim, irrespective of length of service, unfair selection for redundancy and unfair dismissal at an employment tribunal.

3 This is a possible course of action. In choosing to adopt it, the company needs to ensure that it is not likely to be exposed to allegations of indirect discrimination on grounds of sex or race in the selection of people for redundancy.

4 For Trisha, the alternative to accepting the new arrangements is redundancy. Her starting point in considering the situation is whether or not what she has been offered suitable alternative employment which she could reasonably refuse. She would need to consider a range of issues: whether or not her status is reduced; the preservation of her pay; the implications of a change in working hours; whether or not the change in working hours could be indirect sex discrimination.

Exercise 3.4:

The issues that arise are:

- The significance of the business circumstances.
- The business rationale for the reorganisation.
- The significance of the merger.
- Whether or not redundancies existed.
- The criteria for selection.
- The general notification of the redundancies.
- The notice of redundancy given to individual members of staff.
- The nature of discussion and consultation with the staff.
- Whether or not alternative employment was considered.

Part Two: Discrimination and equal opportunities

Chapter 4: Sex discrimination in the workplace

Exercise 4.1: Some discrimination problems

1   An employer can specify that work should be done in evenings and over occasional weekends. Women must not be automatically excluded from consideration on the assumption that they would create operational difficulties by taking time off to care for children. So, in sifting applicants for interview, men and women should be considered against objective criteria (e.g. relevant job experience, skills and qualifications). Any questioning in the interview must not relate to childcare responsibilities. Women applicants must not be asked questions not asked of men.

The essential issue for the employer to resolve in the selection process is: given the requirements of the job to work unsocial hours, is an applicant (irrespective of sex) able to meet those requirements? It is for each applicant to assure the employer of their availability. To treat women less favourably than men would be direct sex discrimination.

The employer might need to consider whether the requirement to work unsocial hours is necessary for operational reasons. If it cannot be justified then the organisation might be subject to an allegation of indirect sex discrimination.

2   As a pregnant employee, she is protected from dismissal on the grounds of her pregnancy or any reason connected with that pregnancy. She does not need any qualifying service. Consequently, if she were dismissed, the employer would probably face an unfair dismissal allegation at employment tribunal. The dismissal would be ruled as unfair because the reason for it was unlawful direct sex discrimination. The employer would, then, be liable to pay unlimited compensation.

3   In determining the person specification for a job, the employer should decide which qualities are essential and which are desirable. None of these should be directly discriminatory. Nor should they be discriminatory in effect. In this case the age barrier is probably indirectly discriminatory. It is likely that, in the labour market concerned, fewer women than men could comply in practice. More generally, good employment practice suggests that age is not used as the basis to distinguish between job applicants.

4   The potential danger in the section manager's approach is that the criteria he is proposing might be indirectly discriminatory on grounds of sex. A condition that applicants should have worked full-time for a number of years is likely to be detrimental to women. Women's working lives are more likely to be characterised by breaks in service. Furthermore, on return to employment, they are more likely to be work on part-time or temporary contracts. None of these factors is, in itself, evidence of poor 'commitment'. The requirement to work hours 'as and when required' can be an acceptable condition of employment. However, it may need to be justified as necessary to meet the organisation's operational requirements. Otherwise, it could be challenged as indirect sex discrimination.

5   Such requests are not uncommon. The employer can refuse it. However, he could face an allegation of indirect sex discrimination at employment tribunal. This could be defended if he could show that it was necessary for the job in question to be undertaken by someone working full-time. If the employer could not justify full-time working, then, he would be liable to pay (unlimited) compensation to the aggrieved employee. Each case would be considered on its own facts and circumstances.

Chapter 5: Race discrimination in the workplace

Exercise 5.1:

The legal issues
- The coverage of the legislation: including the provision of goods and service and, also, employment.
- Whether or not Rosemary's dismissal was on the grounds of race discrimination.
- The liability of the employer.
- The likely decision of an employment tribunal: a declaration and an award of compensation.
- The possibility of a formal investigation by the Commission for Racial Equality.

Other issues
- How such circumstances are handled by the staff concerned.

Chapter 6: Disability discrimination in the workplace

Exercise 6.1: Some discrimination problems

1 The company is covered by the legislation. It employs 15 or more staff. Applicants for employment are protected. Mental illness is a protected disability. The employer should consult with her about the issue and consider whether any reasonable adjustments might be made. This might involve adjusting workload and pace if the prospective employee finds difficulty in coping with stressful situations.

2 The employee has a disability within the meaning of the legislation. The employer should consult with her about two broad related issues: the medium-term prognosis in respect to her health; and whether reasonable adjustments can be made to enable her to continue work. It may be that the circumstances are such that the employer can justify not making reasonable adjustments and that consideration should be given to termination of employment on grounds of long-term ill-health.

3 The employee is disabled within the meaning of the legislation. The employer should consult with the employee to consider whether or not reasonable adjustments can be made. These might include the scheduling of work, opportunities for breaks in the working day and physical adjustments to a car. A trial period could be adopted and the situation reviewed.

Part Three: Regulating performance and conduct

Chapter 7: Harassment and bullying at work

Exercise 7.1:

The legal issues
- Defining harassment.
- Ensuring no breach of the contract of employment.
- Ensuring compliance with sex discrimination law.
- Action at employment tribunal.

Employee relations and organisational issues
- The importance of organisational culture.
- The difficulty of changing this culture.
- The image of the organisation to staff and clients if complaints publicised.
- The quality of employee relations.
- The commitment of senior and middle management.
- A grievance procedure covering harassment.
- A counselling service.
- Disciplinary action against perpetrators of harassment.

Chapter 9: Discipline and dismissal

Exercise 9.1: Misconduct cases: Scenarios

9.1.1 The supermarket manager: persistent misconduct?

In the view of the district manager, John Smith was dismissed for persistent misconduct. Under the Employment Rights Act 1996, this would be a fair reason for dismissal.

The question of whether it was reasonable in the circumstances for the employer to dismiss for that reason would depend a number of factors and on an employment tribunal's view about whether the employer behaved as a reasonable employer. The factors are:

- Whether John Smith has any mitigating circumstances or reasonable explanations for his conduct.
- Whether the employer listened to these.
- Whether the employer had given him warnings about his behaviour and set out clearly expectations about future conduct.
- Whether, if appropriate, the employer had offered counselling and support.
- Whether John Smith had attempted to improve his behaviour.
- John Smith's length of service.
- Whether John Smith had a good disciplinary record prior to the current instances of misconduct.
- His position of responsibility within the organisation.

Procedurally, the employer must, having made clear to the employee the nature of the allegation against him, investigate the misconduct and give him an opportunity to state his case and be accompanied. The employee should also be told of a right of appeal within the company.

9.1.2 The bakery shift manager: gross misconduct?

The reason for the dismissal: This was misconduct, which is a fair reason under the legislation. The employer is entitled to regard this theft as gross misconduct.

Is it reasonable in the circumstances to dismiss for that reason? In the circumstances of its business the company is entitled to take a tough line in respect of theft of stock to avoid having abuses by staff develop. Factors that the employer would probably take into account are:

- Alistair McDougal's position as a shift manager (he would be expected to set an example);
- his length of service;
- his disciplinary record;
- his knowledge of the company's disciplinary rules.

In cases like this, it is not the role of the employment tribunal to 'second guess' the employer's decision to dismiss and substitute, for example, a final written warning. The employer has to show that they regarded the misconduct as a sufficient reason for dismissal. In a similar case before an employment tribunal, a manager said that he 'could not conceive of any circumstances in which theft could result in any other penalty than dismissal'.

Procedural fairness: provided the company handled the disciplinary matter in accordance with the ACAS Code of Practice, then, it would be ruled to be a fair dismissal.

Exercise 9.2: Discipline at work: Scenarios

1   Suspension without pay is an acceptable form of disciplinary penalty. However, it can only be used if it is provided for in the employee's contract of employment and the employee has, consequently, consented to it. Otherwise, the withholding of pay can be a repudiatory breach of the contract of employment. Furthermore, before imposing the penalty, the employer must, as usually expected, carry out a proper disciplinary hearing in accordance with the ACAS *Code of Practice on Disciplinary Procedures* (2000).

2   It would be inappropriate to take disciplinary action in these circumstances. It could be discriminatory action and breach the protection provided to pregnant workers. The employee has justifiable medical reasons for being late. She has come into work and not taken the whole day off. Consequently, an agreement to permit occasional lateness for the duration of morning sickness would be a sensible compromise.

3   This could be viewed by the employer as theft. However, some organisations tolerate such behaviour. The employer needs to be clear on the organisation's disciplinary rules and on the way in which they have been applied in the past (i.e. what action has been taken in respect of similar incidents). An interview should be held with Gary and his explanation listened to carefully. His disciplinary record and length of service are relevant in deciding the action to be taken. His taking of an unused disk is unlikely to be seen as gross misconduct. An appropriate penalty might be some kind of warning.

4   The employer could, and probably would, consider some form of disciplinary action. Much would depend on what was in his contract of employment. It might state that if he lost his licence, he would be liable to dismissal. After a proper disciplinary hearing he could be sacked. However, Jason will get his licence back within a short period of time. So, he could subsequently continue working as a van driver. In the interim, he could be offered some alternative employment; or be required to take leave of absence.

5   Certainly, consideration would be given to disciplinary action and the holding of a proper hearing on his release from custody. Several factors would need to be considered in addition to those relating to length of service and previous disciplinary record. It is possible to hold open Simon's job. The nature of the offence is serious (non-compliance with a court order) but may not breach the trust relationship between the employer and employee. Staff in his section/ department will have a view on whether he should return to work or not and

this will affect the nature of working relationships. It would be possible to sack him for 'some other substantial reason' (his conduct outside work). However, this might be out of proportion to what he has done.

6   Karen's instant dismissal would be unfair for a number of reasons. First, procedurally, she was not given a proper opportunity to respond to the issues that had been raised. Secondly, the reason for her dismissal did not come within the ambit of any of the fair reasons. Presumably, it could be argued that it was for 'some other reason' (because other staff would not work with her). There is no evidence that Karen has any medical condition. There is considerable misinformation and prejudice about her situation. The employer is failing to provide her with appropriate support (arguably, breaching the implied term of mutual trust and confidence). The responsibility of the employer is to educate and inform staff and support Karen.

Part Four: Terms and conditions of employment

Chapter 10: Pay regulation

Exercise 10.1: Pay regulation: Scenarios

10.1.1 National minimum wage

1   Darren does not come within the protection of the legislation.

2   Sara is protected. However, she receives pay that is not consistent with the development rate (set at £3.60 in October 2002).

3   Sharon is not receiving pay in compliance with the National Minimum Wage. The pay reference period is four weeks. Her relevant pay comprises basic pay and tips paid through the till. In the four weeks in question her relevant earnings are: £42; £21; £30; and £56. In total this is £149. She worked a total of 40 hours. Her average hourly earnings in the pay reference period are £3.72 – below the statutory rate set at £4.20 in October 2002.

4   Hassan's situation is problematic. The pay reference period is four weeks. His relevant pay from the hotel comprises basic pay and tips paid through the till. A deduction is made in the sum of £22.75 per week for accommodation. In the four weeks in question his relevant earnings are: £37; £21; £26; and £32. In total this is £116. He worked a total of 40 hours. His average hourly earnings in the pay reference period are £2.90 – below the statutory rate. However, he is benefiting from accommodation to the value of £22.75 per week. This could in aggregate mean that his employer is complying with the statutory level – though it is unlikely.

5   Siobhan becomes eligible for a higher rate of Minimum Wage on her twenty-first birthday. Her dismissal is a detriment and she is entitled to claim unfair dismissal at an employment tribunal, alleging that her dismissal was to avoid such a payment.

6   Fiona's employer must keep appropriate records and permit her to inspect them.

10.1.2 Pay deduction

7 It is an unlawful deduction to withhold money in respect of a loan. The employee must agree to it.

8 It would depend on the terms of the collective agreement as incorporated into Bill's contract of employment. If the agreement says that the shift allowance should be paid, then the employer is deducting it unlawfully.

9 Employees are required to repay overpayment. However, the question of reasonableness arises. If it is a small amount and the employee may not realise that overpayment has taken place, the employer might choose not to recover the money. An overpayment as indicated in this scenario is a considerable sum. If the employee has spent the money, it is unreasonable to expect it to be returned at once. Some agreement should be made with the employer about repayment by instalments. This should take account of the normal outgoings that an employee might have.

10 The deduction of £155 seems to breach an agreement that Winston has made to repair the van himself. The other deductions were provisional and, so, based on little firm evidence. The employer may have good reason for wanting to withhold or deduct some money. But this should be done by agreement with the employee concerned.

11 Andreas is right! The maximum permissible deduction in retail employment (which a café is) is 10 per cent of a week's gross wages (i.e. £15) – unless it is the final week of employment.

Chapter 11: Regulation of working time

Exercise 11.1: Some scenarios

1 Presumably, only a proportion of the total workforce is likely to be required to work in excess of the maximum. These would be the relevant workforce. Two possible routes are available to the employer. The first is to seek individual voluntary agreements to disapply the maximum working week. The likely problem with this course of action is continuing operational uncertainty for the employer – an individual has the right to terminate such an agreement (giving notice of not more than three months, if stipulated in the agreement).

A second way of managing the issue is for the employer to negotiate a longer averaging period (of 52 weeks as opposed to the statutory 17 weeks) through a 'workforce agreement'. This would apply only to relevant members of the workforce. It would be signed by a majority, if not all, and would become a new condition of employment.

2 The issue of determining 'working time' and non-working time is a matter for the employer and their workers. The Working Time Regulations provide for agreements to be reached, at workplace level, whereby 'working time' and 'rest periods' can be clarified. The essential test of 'working time' is that it is 'any period (in relation to a worker) during which he is working, at his employer's disposal and carrying out his activity or duties'.

In this example, it is arguable that, for the eight hours of a shift, the worker is at the employer's disposal – dealing with incoming calls; waiting for calls;

and depending on the operational circumstances, available to cover colleagues at short notice; and to take over any other duties the employer might allocate. The worker is unlikely to have any freedom of action in that eight-hour period. The worker will not be permitted to leave the workplace without permission.

3   There are a number of factors which enter into this case. The starting point is whether Jez is working solely for the supermarket chain. If so, he is certainly a protected 'worker'. However, it could be that although he has an ongoing commitment to the supermarket chain, he is also able to undertake other work (e.g. repairing and installing domestic fridges and freezers) – provided he gives priority to the supermarkets, as and when required. Some of his work is then self-employment (which he can pick and choose to do) in the commonly understood sense. He can, however, still be said to be a protected 'worker' in so far as his contract with the supermarket chain is concerned.

 A final possibility is that the engineer has a contract with the supermarket chain to work as and when required – as part of a bank of such engineers in the region. He has the right to refuse particular work if he is not available to undertake it. In this event, the supermarket will approach another engineer in the bank. His status as a protected worker is more problematic. He could be regarded as an independent contractor (self-employed) and not be eligible to protection by the Working Time Regulations.

4   The entitlement to minimum paid annual leave is available to all workers (young and adult), provided they have completed 13 weeks' continuous employment with the employer. No derogations are permissible. It may not be replaced by a payment in lieu.

 Part-time workers are entitled (from November 1999) to be away from work for four weeks (which may be consecutive or at different times). So, a person working 16 hours per week is entitled not to attend work for four weeks and to be paid for each period of 16 hours. Where hours of work vary for each week, there is averaging and the same broad principle applies.

 Temporary workers are also entitled to paid annual leave. They may have some problems in establishing the 13-week qualifying period. However, two or more temporary contracts might in aggregate result in the necessary qualifying period. An employment tribunal will consider this on the facts of each individual case.

 Flexibility is available in determining the leave year; in deciding the taking of leave by instalments; and in requiring notice of intention to take leave.

5   Several issues arise here:
 –   the definition of night time;
 –   whether particular staff are night workers;
 –   the length of night work.

In this scenario, staff are normally working nine hours in a 24-hour period. Operationally, there are good reasons for this. However, in terms of their strict entitlements, it is not acceptable. If the hotel did not wish to change its shift-work arrangements, it could use the derogation provision and, as a non-union company, negotiate a workforce agreement.

6 The worker is entitled to terminate the agreement. In the absence of an agreed notice period she can do this with at least seven days' notice. It was short-sighted of the employer not to provide for a notice period in the written agreement. This period can be for up to (but not longer than) three months. The worker does not have to provide reasons for wanting to end the agreement. The implied threat of dismissal by the employer is unlawful.

7 It would be possible for the local authority to discuss an annualised hours contract with the recognised trade union under the terms of the Working Time Regulations. If the employer were a non-union private grounds maintenance contractor, a longer reference period might be negotiated under a workforce agreement. This agreement would be for a five-year fixed term and then would be subject to re-negotiation.

8 Maggie is entitled to paid annual leave on a pro-rata basis. This is calculated by referring to the proportion of hours that she has worked in comparison with a full-time worker. As far as pay is concerned, her pay is averaged by adding up all her pay for the preceding 12 weeks and dividing it by 12.

Chapter 12: Health and safety at work

Exercise 12.2: The VDU operators: a safety grievance

1 The issues that might arise are:

Operational issues
- the need to get work done;
- the availability of substitute staff for job rotation.

Job design
- the amount of time spent on the VDU;
- the feasibility of job rotation.

Health and safety requirements
- the work environment in the office (lighting, heating, ventilation, etc.);
- the layout of the workstation;
- the compliance of the equipment with approved technical standards;
- person issues (e.g. the incidence of headaches and other physical pains).

Employee relations
- the duty to consult;
- the implications of establishing a consultation scheme in a non-union organisation;
- provision of training for representatives;
- time off for representatives;
- the relationship of the supervisor with the staff.

2   The differences and areas of possible consensus that might arise are:

Objectives

Employer
- get work done;
- improve quality of working relations;
- minimise cost of any action.

Employees
- resolve grievance;
- improve working environment;
- ensure compliance with the Regulations;
- establish some form of regular consultation on health and safety issues.

Preferred outcomes

Employer
- discussion with Helen individually to try and resolve her grievance;
- some form of non-union consultation (as and when necessary) – possibly through team briefings.

Employees
- resolution of Helen's grievance;
- more breaks from VDU work and some job rotation;
- consultative committee to meet monthly, supported by a Head Office representative;
- possibly a claim for union recognition.

Constraints
- cost of any action;
- commitment of management to follow such action through;
- extent to which staff are committed to achieve their objectives.

Part Five: Collective rights at work

Chapter 15: Industrial action

Exercise 15.1:

The issues that arise in relation to the three questions are as follows:

The legal issues

- The implications in law of the two different companies in the corporate group.
- The employee relations issue(s) about which the trade dispute was called.
- The absence of a secret ballot to approve the strike by the production workers.
- The nature of the picketing and whether it was peaceful.
- The likely repudiation by the union of its members and the consequences for them, individually, of this.
- The action that might be taken in legal proceedings by the company.
- Breach of the employees' contracts of employment.
- Whether or not individual employees had a legal right to strike.
- Whether the industrial action is 'protected'.
- Whether or not the employer was able to sack the strikers.
- Whether or not the employer was entitled to deduct pay for non-performance of work.

The employee relations issues

- Deep-seated poor industrial relations between the union members and the company.
- Poor communications and rumour.
- Apparent absence of proper consultation about anticipated redundancies.
- Poor relations between the shop stewards and the full-time official.
- The employee relations consequences of the company taking legal proceedings against the union and/or its members.

Glossary

This glossary defines briefly those terms which generally occur in more than one chapter. To find a definition, look for the **key** word. For example, if you want to refer to the term '*wrongful dismissal*', then look for it under '*dismissal*'. More detailed discussion of the terms will, generally, be found in the relevant chapters.

Agency worker: Someone whose services are provided by an employment agency to an employing organisation. The employment relationship between the worker and the employing organisation might be on a casual basis or for a longer period of time. A contract of employment governing this relationship may be between the agency worker and the agency or between the agency worker and the employing organisation.

Arbitration: A process whereby a third party (usually appointed through the auspices of ACAS) makes a decision to resolve a dispute between an employer and an individual or groups of workers. The arbitrator has been invited to intervene at the request of the parties.

Atypical workers: A term used in HR literature to cover a wide range of people with non-standard (i.e. full-time permanent) employment relationships. Principally it covers part-time workers, those on temporary contracts, agency staff (q.v.), casual workers and those on zero hours contracts. Sometimes the terms 'marginal' and 'peripheral workers' are used.

Breach of contract: The circumstances in which one party to a contract does not comply with the terms of the contract (q.v.). Many breaches are minor and may be resolved by an employee lodging a grievance with the employer; or, alternatively, by an employer taking disciplinary action against an employee. Some breaches are serious (e.g. the non-payment of wages; persistent bullying). These are fundamental or repudiatory breaches – equivalent to tearing up the contract of employment.

Burden of proof (onus of proof): The duty of a party in tribunal or court proceedings to prove an allegation by reference to certain relevant facts.

Case law: A body of law set out in judicial decisions. In employment relations, cases that are brought before the courts and tribunals can be about rights and duties under the contract of employment (q.v.) or under statute law (q.v.). Judicial decisions can help clarify and interpret the law and create precedent (q.v.).

CEEP (the European Centre for Enterprises with Public Participation): This is a representative body for public sector organisations in the European Union. Along with ETUC (q.v.) and UNICE (q.v.) it is one of the *social partners* (q.v.) in the EU. It contributes to discussions on the Economic and Social Committee concerning legislative proposals. It can with the other social partners negotiate framework agreements for the implementation of European social policy (for example, the 1996 Framework Agreement on Parental Rights which was ultimately implemented through the appropriate directive).

Closed shop: An arrangement between an employer and specific unions whereby trade union membership is a condition of employment for particular jobs. Given the freedom in law (since 1990) for employees to choose whether or not to be union members, such arrangements are now rare and difficult to enforce legally. Closed shops have been categorised as *pre-entry* (where only trade union members were considered for employment) or *post-entry* (where after an offer of employment, an employee was required to join a recognised union).

Codes of practice: There are both statutory and voluntary codes. Voluntary codes have no legal significance but can be important in setting standards of good employment practice. Statutory codes (for example, the ACAS Code of Practice on Discipline and Grievance Procedures 2000) do have legal importance. They are used by courts and tribunals in considering the extent to which an employer is liable for a breach of particular statutory employment rights.

Collective bargaining: A process of negotiation, normally between managers and trade union officials. Generally it concerns levels of pay and conditions of employment (like hours and holidays). It is designed to reconcile differences of interest between employers and working people and to produce a collective agreement. The terms of such agreements will probably be incorporated (q.v.) into individual contracts of employment.

Common law: Part of English law based on rules developed by judges over many centuries.

Compensation: This is a monetary payment to compensate an aggrieved person for some loss or damage (e.g. loss of a job in unfair dismissal cases). It is the principal remedy in employment law.

Conciliation: A process whereby a third party, usually an officer employed by ACAS, intervenes in a dispute between an individual employee or a group of employees and an employer in order to try to promote a settlement. Individual conciliation is required under statute in those cases where an aggrieved employee or worker complains to an employment tribunal about the infringement of a statutory employment right. Collective conciliation usually arises when an employer and a trade union (where collective bargaining has failed) voluntarily seek the assistance of ACAS.

Consideration: The price whereby one party to a contract buys the promise of another. In a contract of employment, it is usually pay that is given to the employee in exchange for his/her promise to be ready, willing and able to work.

Constructive dismissal: This is an enforced resignation that is equivalent to dismissal from employment. It arises as a result of the employer's unacceptable behaviour showing that he does not intend to be bound by the contract's terms. The employer effectively tears up the contract of employment (a repudiatory breach) by, for example, refusing to pay wages that are due, failing to deal with allegations of bullying and harassment, or persistently providing a hazardous working environment without proper protection. On resignation an employee may claim unfair constructive dismissal at an employment tribunal.

Consultation: A process involving the representatives of an employer and his workforce. Discussions take place on changes and developments in employment relations. There are certain statutory duties to consult. These arise, in particular, in relation to redundancies, transfers of undertakings, and health and safety. It is possible for consultation to take place between an individual employee and a manager. In individual redundancies, case law requires this.

Contract: A legally binding agreement, normally between two parties (e.g. a contract of employment). It arises as a result of an offer (e.g. of terms of employment) and acceptance (e.g. by the employee of these terms). There must also be consideration (q.v.) and an intention by the parties to create legal relations. The contract cannot be illegal (i.e. agreement to do something which is contrary to law). In this case, it would be void. Because a contract is an agreement, it is a basic principle that it can only be varied by consent.

Culture: Organisational culture refers to the range of values, traditional practices and standards that apply. The culture of an organisation is important (in facilitating or inhibiting) the effective implementation of certain bodies of employment law – discrimination law and health and safety law in particular.

Custom and practice: This may be part of a contract of employment if it is well-known, reasonable and it is certain that the individual knows the effect of the custom on themselves.

Damages: A sum of money awarded by a court or tribunal as compensation (q.v.) for a tort (q.v.) or a breach of contract (q.v.).

Detriment: Action by an employer which causes harm or damage to an employee (e.g. by victimisation or harassment, overlooking in promotion, depriving of benefits, etc.). It is a factor in discrimination law and in the statutory protection provided for employee representatives and trade union officials.

Direct effect: This is a doctrine developed by the European Court of Justice for the implementation of European law. It is important where a member state has not implemented certain provisions of European law. An Article of a Treaty (e.g. the Treaty of Rome) will have direct effect if it is clear and unambiguous, unconditional and needs no further action to come into force (apart from legislative action by the member state). Such a Treaty Article (e.g. art 141 of the Treaty of Rome on equal pay) applies both horizontally (i.e. conferring rights on individuals against each other) and vertically (i.e. conferring rights that can be enforced against the state). Directives only have vertical direct effect, again where they are clear, unambiguous and require no further action to be implemented.

Directives: The principal means by which European employment law is made. A directive is binding upon member states of the EU and must, within a given timescale, be transposed into the law of the member state. In Britain, directives are enacted either through statute law (q.v.) (e.g. the Equal Treatment Directive 1976 is implemented through the Sex Discrimination Acts 1975 and 1986) or through Regulations (e.g. the Working Time Directive 1993 is implemented through the Working Time Regulations 1998).

Discrimination: In employment, it is generally unfavourable treatment based on stereotying and prejudice. Anti-discrimination law distinguishes between the concepts of direct and indirect discrimination.

Dismissal: The termination of an employee's employment – it may be with or without notice. The law requires that a fair reason be given for the dismissal, that the disciplinary process leading to dismissal conforms with standards of fairness and natural justice and that the decision to dismiss is reasonable in all the circumstances. An employee may allege at an employment tribunal that the dismissal is unfair (against the statutory criteria and relevant case law) or that the dismissal is wrongful (i.e. it has not been in accordance with the contract of employment). Wrongful dismissal usually arises where an employer fails to provide due notice of termination.

Duty: A legal obligation to carry out some action or to stop some particular act. Some are expressly set out in statute law (q.v.) – for example, the duty to consult in respect of collective redundancies. Some are implied under common law (q.v.) into the contract of employment – for example, the duty of mutual trust and confidence.

Emanation of the state: This term arises from European law. It describes those organisations which provide a public service, which are controlled by the state and have special powers. It covers local authorities, hospital trusts and some private sector organisations like water companies. In the law, this status is significant in the context of the direct effect (q.v.) of directives (q.v.).

Employee: Defined in law as someone who works under a contract of employment. Case law has developed a number of tests to establish employee status. Courts will look for the existence of mutuality of obligation.

ETUC (the European Trade Union Confederation): This is a representative body for trade unions across the European Union. Along with CEEP (q.v.) and UNICE (q.v.) it is one of the *social partners* (q.v.) in the EU. It contributes to discussions on the Economic and Social Committee concerning legislative proposals. It can with the other social partners negotiate framework agreements for the implementation of European social policy (for example, the 1996 Framework Agreement on Parental Rights which was ultimately implemented through the appropriate directive).

Fixed-term contract: A contract to carry out work for a specified period of time (e.g. three months). Such contracts can be extended. The Fixed Term Employees (Less Favourable Treatment) Regulations 2002 provides some statutory protection.

Flexibility: A term used in a large number of management employment practices. The concept of the flexible firm was used to provide a theoretical model which encompassed all forms of flexibility. Numerical flexibility describes the extent and ways in which an employer can vary the size of the workforce (through, for example, the use of casual and part-time workers). Functional flexibility concerns flexibility of task and arises when job demarcations are removed. Temporal flexibility is working-time flexibility. Geographic flexibility concerns the requirement of workers to be mobile and have various places of employment.

Freedom of association: This is a human right (q.v.) enshrined in the European Convention of Human Rights 1950. It asserts the right of citizens in a liberal democracy freely to join voluntary associations (such as trade unions). Such organisations generally are free to make their own rules and elect their own officials.

Genuine occupational qualification: A provision under discrimination law whereby it is permissible to specify that a person employed in a particular job should be male or female, married or of a particular ethnic origin. The circumstances permitting such specificiations are set out in sex and race discrimination law. Discrimination law on sexual orientation and religion or belief (implemented in 2003) refers to 'genuine occupational requirement'.

Harassment: Behaviour that is unacceptable to the recipient. It can range from gestures and verbal insults to physical assault and stalking. At the latter end of the spectrum it can result in criminal court proceedings.

Homeworker: A person who undertakes work for an employer and performs all or most of this at home. Such people may be traditional homeworkers (undertaking repetitive tasks for manufacturing companies) or teleworkers (with networked computer links). Increasingly, they are acquiring statutory employment protection.

Human rights: Standards of treatment for individual citizens as outlined in, for example, the European Convention on Human Rights and Fundamental Freedoms 1950. This is incorporated into UK law from 2000. It sets standards relevant to employment: on discrimination; the use of fair procedures; and freedom of association.

Immunities: The principal use of these legal protections in employment law arises in respect of industrial action (q.v.). Trade unions are protected from legal proceedings (claims for damages) (q.v.) by employers if the industrial action they are organising is 'in contemplation or furtherance of a trade dispute'. Certain conditions are stipulated in statute law about the nature of the trade dispute and the holding of an approval ballot is a condition of attracting immunity.

Industrial action: These are sanctions imposed by working people (usually organised by trade unions) against their employer. It arises because of a trade dispute (q.v.). Broadly, there are two categories of industrial action. The first is a strike, whereby work stops completely. The second is 'industrial action short of a strike'. This encompasses working to rule, boycotting various job tasks, overtime bans, etc.

Injunction: A court order requiring a person (including a company or a trade union) to stop a certain course of action. Usually a temporary or interlocutory injunction is granted initially, pending a full hearing of the claim. A person who breaches an injunction is guilty of contempt of court and may be subject to a fine or imprisonment.

Job share: Circumstances where a full-time job is split between, usually, two employees, who then receive pro-rata conditions of employment.

Liability: This arises in circumstances when wrongs have been committed (e.g. discrimination or breach of health and safety regulations) and concerns who is answerable in law for the wrong. Usually in employment law this is the employer. He may also be vicariously liable for the behaviour (acts or omissions) in the course of employment of his workforce or a contractor. A defence for the employer, depending on the legislation, may be that he took reasonably practicable steps to prevent the wrong being committed.

Natural justice: These rules are applicable in the courts and tribunals. Under dismissal legislation, they also influence the way in which disciplinary proceedings should be conducted. There are two principal rules: a person should have an opportunity to state his/her case and to answer the other side's case; and no one should be a judge in his own case.

Negligence: Carelessness or neglect. The most common examples in employment arise in the area of health and safety. An employer who is sued by an employee for damages in a negligence claim might himself claim that the employee was also negligent (e.g. failing to wear appropriate protective equipment). This would be an allegation of contributory negligence.

Part-time worker: Someone who works less than the normal working week in a particular organisation. The Part-time Workers (Less Favourable Treatment) Regulations 2000 provides some statutory protection for these workers.

Precedent: A judgment or decision of a court, normally recorded in a law report, which is used as an authority for reaching decisions in subsequent cases.

Procedural issues: In employee relations, these concern the operation of the procedures that are adopted to structure relationships between an employer and his workforce (and, if relevant, any trade unions). The procedures concern grievances, discipline, consultation and negotiation of terms and conditions of employment.

Qualified majority voting: A system of majority voting used in the European Council to approve the adoption of new legislation. It weights the votes of participating member states. To date, it has been used principally for health and safety measures and not those extending employment protection.

Qualifying periods: The period of continuous employment that an employee or worker must have in order to claim certain statutory rights. For example, one year's qualifying service is required for taking most unfair dismissal allegations to an employment tribunal.

Regulations: Statutory instruments. They are delegated legislation. They are presented to Parliament and subject to its approval. Regulations are made under the authority of particular pieces of statute law (q.v.). For example, the Working Time Regulations 1998 were made under the authority of the European Communities Act 1972, s 2. Other Regulations are made under the authority of the Health and Safety at Work Act 1974.

Remedy: This is any method available at law for enforcing rights or for obtaining redress for their infringement. It can include an injunction (q.v.), damages (q.v.) or a declaration.

Self-employment: Someone who does not have a contract of employment and who is not a worker (under particular statute law). Usually, they are referred to as independent contractors.

Social partners: These are the representative bodies of European trade unions and public and private sector employers: ETUC, CEEP and UNICE (q.v.). Within the processes for making European law, these may negotiate framework agreements (e.g. on part-time working in 1996) and they are consulted regularly on new Commission proposals for social policy and employment legislation. A related term, 'social partnership', is used more generally in British employee relations to describe a more harmonious approach to the conduct of employee relations.

Standards of proof: There are two: beyond reasonable doubt; and balance of probabilities. The first is used in criminal cases to establish conviction. The second arises in civil proceedings and generally is construed as follows: that it is more probable than not that something alleged to have happened did happen.

Statute law: Law made by Parliament, usually reflecting the political policies of the government of the day. However, it also encompasses legislation proposed by backbench Members of Parliament (e.g. the Public Interest Disclosure Act 1998). Statute law is interpreted by judges. New statute law can overturn judge-made law.

Substantive issues: In employee relations this refers to the terms and conditions of employment upon which an employee is employed.

Summary dismissal: Instant dismissal (i.e. without notice).

Teleworker: see homeworker (q.v.).

Temporary worker: A worker who is on a contract of specific duration to carry out work for an employer. Such workers may also be covered by the terms casual worker, agency worker (q.v.) and fixed-term contract worker (q.v.).

Terms: These are the provisions of a contract of employment (q.v.). They may be express (e.g. outlining pay and hours, etc.) or implied from common law (e.g. the duty of care on the employer and the duty of trust and mutual confidence).

Tort: A civil wrong other than a breach of contract (q.v.). Obligations here are provided by law (e.g. under health and safety law).

Trade union recognition: This refers to the decision by an employer to negotiate with one or more unions about specific terms and conditions of employment. Decisions to recognise unions have generally been voluntary. However, since 2000, a statutory recognition scheme has been in force. This provides for the imposition of recognition in certain circumstances.

UNICE (the Union of Industrial and Employer's Confederation of Europe): This is a representative body for private sector employers in the European Union. Along with CEEP (q.v.) and ETUC (q.v.) it is one of the *social partners* (q.v.) in the EU. It contributes to discussions on the Economic and Social Committee concerning legislative proposals. It can with the other social partners negotiate framework agreements for the implementation of European social policy (for example, the 1996 Framework Agreement on Parental Rights which was ultimately implemented through the appropriate directive).

Vicarious liability: see liability (q.v.).

Victimisation: A form of detriment (q.v.). It involves singling out a person for unfair and usually unlawful treatment.

White Paper: A document published by government in which it sets out proposals for legislative action. Usually, White Papers are open to limited consultation (e.g. with employers' organisations and trade unions).

Worker: Generally a person who has an employment relationship with an organisation. It covers employees (q.v.) but does not cover the self-employed (q.v.). Definitions are set out in statute law (e.g. Employment Rights Act 1996, s 230 (3)).

Index

Page references to terms in the Glossary are shown in bold. Major entries include a separate 'legal framework' entry e.g.: 'disability discrimination'; 'disability discrimination, legal framework'.

adoption leave 470–1
adoption pay 473
Advisory Conciliation and Arbitration Service (ACAS)
    advice on information to be communicated to
        employees, extract from, Fig. 14.4 537
    code of conduct 10
    constitution and functions of 24, 33–4
    unfair dismissal arbitration scheme, Fig. 9.3 337
    unfair dismissal procedures 335–6
    voluntary regulation and 33–4
agency workers **601**
    employment protection 87–8, 208
    employment relationship 59
    race discrimination and employment protection 208
agricultural workers 378
alternative dispute resolution 29–30

betting-shop workers, unfair dismissal 329
business interests 577–8
    corporate social responsibility 578–9
    ethical standards, tensions with 578
    types of organisations 579

casual workers
    Carmichael and Leese case 86
    employment protection 84–5
Central Arbitration Committee, constitution and
    functions 26–7
change, managing *see* employment relationship
    change, managing
codes of practice 9–10, **602**
    Advisory Conciliation and Arbitration Service (ACAS)
        10
    Code of Practice for the elimination of
        discrimination in the field of employment
        against disabled persons 10, 243, 246, 253,
        254–7

    Commission for Racial Equality 10
    data protection 306–7
    Equal Opportunities Commission 10
collective agreements
    employment policies and practices 378–9
    legal status of 527
    national minimum wage 373
    terms and conditions 72, 356, 373, 378–9
    transfer of undertakings 118, 528
    working time, regulating 397
collective bargaining 516, 526–7, **602**
    bargaining process 504
    breakdown of 505
    collective agreements, legal status of 527
    collective agreements, transfer of 118, 528
    concept of 503–6
    conflicts of interest 503–4
    derecognition 533
    employer attitudes 504–5
    employment contract and 72, 356
    enforcement, statutory recognition 533
    forms of 504
    free 5, 6, 505–6
    information for 528–9
    Kwik-Fit case, Fig. 14.3 534
    meaning of 527
    prohibitions on pressure to enforce recognition 528
    recognition, meaning of 527
    statutory recognition procedure 531–3
    statutory recognition procedure, experience of new
        533–4
    voluntary regulation 33
    workforce agreements 529–30
collective rights 483–5, 498 (*see also* employee
        participation; industrial action; trade unions)
    'British disease, the' 492–4
    British industrial relations, traditional model of 492

collective rights (*continued*)
    Council of Europe 495–6
    employee relations, a 'new' model? 494
    European Community influences 496–8
    International influences 494–8
    International Labour Organisation 495
    trade unions
        immunities of 490–1
        independence of 491–2
        individual membership 485
        legal status of 489–90
        organisational structure 488–9
        purposes of 486–8
        role of 486–92
collectivism, conclusion 580–1
collectivism and employment relations 54–5
Commission for Racial Equality, constitution and
        Functions 25
common law **602**
    contract of employment, implied terms 73
    contract and pay 367–8
    discrimination and 137
    employment status tests 63, 64–5
    health and safety and 418–22
    Human Rights Act, effect 15–16
    legal regulation and 8–9
company, internal procedures 30
complaint, processes for 19–20
    Advisory Conciliation and Arbitration Service (ACAS)
        24, 33–4
    Central Arbitration Committee 26–7
    Commission for Racial Equality 25
    Court of Appeal 20, 23
    Disability Rights Commission 25–6
    effectiveness of 28–30
    Employment Appeals Tribunal 20, 23
    employment tribunals 20–3
    Equal Opportunities Commission 25
    European Court of Human Rights 20, 24
    European Court of Justice 20, 23–4
    health and safety 435
    Health and Safety Commission 26
    House of Lords 20, 23
    Low Pay Commission 26
conclusion, employment law in context, general
        576–85
consent, employment relations processes and 38–9
consultation **602–3**
    anti-harassment policies and trade unions 280
    conclusion 580–1
    employee participation and 501–3, 518–26
    health and safety 436–8, 525–6
    multi-national companies and 521–3

    pensions 526
    redundancy 122–3, 523–4
    transfers of undertakings 112, 127, 524–5
    voluntary regulation and 33
contract of employment 46, 49, 68, **603**
    atypical workers, employment protection 78–88, **601**
    characteristics of 68–71
    change
        agreement, by 103–5
        agreement to and continued working 104–5
        resignation of employee 104
        termination, by 105
        unilateral 104–5
        work under protest 104
    collective agreements 72, 356, 373, 378–9
    deductions from pay, no authorised 73–4
    dismissal, circumstances at end of 324–5
    employer and employees
        co-operation 74–5, 75, 106
        reasonable care obligation 74–5, 76–7, 269
    employment policies and practices 378–9
    enforcement of 69
    flexibility in existing terms 98–9, 105–6, **604**
    freely aimed at? 69
    maternity rights, status of 463–6
    minimum employment contract 355
    mobility 106, 120
    parties to 68–9
    place of work and mobility 106, 120
    role of 49–50
    signing 71
    statement of initial employment particulars 379
    statement of initial employment particulars, Fig. 2.4
        70
    termination 77–8, 105
    terms of 71, **607**
        breach of contract, industrial action 564, **601**
        collective agreements 72
        common law implied terms 73, 557–8
        custom and practice 73
        disabled person and 256
        employee's general duties 75–7, 105–6
        employer's general duties 73–5, 105–6, 269
        express and implied 71, 269
        flexibility of 98–9, 105–6, **604**
        'gagging' clauses 296
        harassment and bullying 269
        industrial action, strike and non-strike action
        557–8
        instructions to obey lawful and reasonable 75,
        105–6
        management's decision making freedom 71
        mobility 106, 120

contract of employment
  terms of (*continued*)
    statute law and 73
    terminating 77–8, 105
    trustworthy, employee's duty 76, 106, 269
    wages and salaries 73
    workplace rules 72–3
  transfers of undertaking, contract variations and
      harmonisation 127
  variation of 98, 102–3, 115, 126, 127
  verbal contract 69
  written information about 77
contract law
  discipline and dismissal 316
  legal regulation and 8, 137
contracting-out 99–100
Council of Europe 495–6
Court of Appeal 20, 23
criminal convictions 331

Data Protection Act 1988 288
  data covered 289–90
  data protection principle 288
  'data subjects', rights of 290–1
  enforcement action 292
  Information Commissioner, role of 291
  personal data 289–90
  privacy and surveillance 292
  processing, meaning 290
  who are the parties involved? 288–9
dependency leave 469–70
dependency rights *see* parental and dependency rights
direct discrimination
  harassment and detriments 271–3, 603
  race discrimination, in 210–11
  sex discrimination and 165–6
disability discrimination 229–30
  Access to Work Scheme 242
  accommodating disabled people 235, 236–7, 238,
      247–50
  advice 235, 236
  Code of Practice 1996, practical steps 253, 254–7
  context 230–42
  contracts and agreements 254
  Cornell University survey 238
  disabled people, experience of employing 234
  disability, defining 230–1
  discrimination problems, some, exercise 6.1 257
  Disability Service Teams 241–2
  employment barriers 254
  employment context 234–8
  employment policies and practices 234–8
  Equal Opportunities Review Survey 1997 237

European Employment Directive 2000 241
  individual applications of complaint 240
  Institute of Manpower Studies Survey 1993 234–5
  Kingston Business School Survey 1995 235–7
  labour market and 282–3
  legislation on 230, 238–9, 240, 243
  management approach 253
  management systems 254–5
  pension schemes 256–7
  political and historical background 238–40
  political and legislative context, developing 240–1
  promotion and transfer 256
  recruitment and selection 234, 255–6
  small firms exemption, removal of 240–1
  social context 231–2
  social welfare support 241–2
  Supported Employment Programme 242
  technological context 238
  termination of employment 257
  terms and conditions of service 256
  training and guidance 237, 256
  'Two Ticks' Scheme 242
  working time 249
disability discrimination, legal framework 241–3
  adjustments, duty to make reasonable
    adjustments, the 248–9
    duty, the 247–8
    justification 249–50
    knowledge of the impairment 248
  burden of proof 251, 601
  disability, meaning of 243–6
  Disability Rights Commission 25–6, 252–3
  discrimination, meaning of 246–7
  enforcement procedures 251
  legislation, coverage of 242
  less favourable treatment 246–7
  liability 250–1
  long-term effect 245
  normal day-to-day activities 245–6
  physical or mental impairment 243–4
  remedies 252
  sick absence, managing long-term 253
  statutory codes and regulations 243, 246, 253,
      254–7
  substantial adverse effect 244–5
  victimisation 247
  working time regulation 390
Disability Rights Commission, constitution and
    functions 25–6, 252–3
discipline 313–15
  anti-harassment policies, role of in 280
  context 315–21
  contract, common law of 316

discipline (*continued*)
  data protection code 306–7
  employment, handling 343–4
  employment policies and practices 342–50
  fines for disciplinary action 369
  harassment and bullying 275
  law's effectiveness, assessing 318–19
    employees 319–20
    employers 320–1
  reason for dismissal, breach of rules and standards
    344–5
  reasonableness in the circumstances 345–6
  sanctions 347–9
  standard discipline procedure, Fig. 9.4 348
  valuating regulation procedures 32–3
  work, at, scenarios, exercise 9.2 350, 594–5
discipline, legal framework
  appeal 332–3
  background 321
  disciplinary penalties 323–4
  disciplinary policy and rules 322
  disciplinary procedures 322–3, 346–7
  disciplinary procedures, good, Fig. 9.1 323
  law's effectiveness 318–21
  misconduct scenarios, exercise 9.1–9.1.2 334–5,
    593–4
  nature and purpose 322–4
  natural justice 332, **605**
  omissions of a procedural stage 332
  procedural fairness 332–5, 346–7
  representation 333
  statutory right to be accompanied, Fig. 9.2 333
discrimination and equal opportunities generally 135,
    147, **603** (*see also* disability discrimination; equal
    opportunities policies; race discrimination; sex
    discrimination)
  concepts, the 135–7
  criteria, objective and unlawful 135–6
  equal opportunities and/or equal treatment 136–7
  European Union law and 138
  law, the 137–8
  pay and 363
  positive action and discrimination 138–40
  voluntary action by employers
    equal opportunities policies 140–5
    managing diversity 145–7
dismissal 313–15, **603–4, 606**
  constructive 116, 276, **602**
  context 315–21
  contract, common law of 316
  data protection code 306–7, **602**
  disability discrimination 257
  disciplinary sanctions 349

economic, technical or organisational reasons
    116–17
  employment policies and practices 342–50
    sanction, as 349
  employment relationship, nature of 48, 315–16
  expectations and norms, context 343
  handling 343–4
  harassment and bullying 273–4, 275
  industrial action sanction 558–60
  law's effectiveness, assessing 318–19
    employees 319–20
    employers 320–1
  political action 318
  race discrimination and 208–9, 226
  reason for dismissal, breach of rules and standards
    344–5
  reasonableness in the circumstances 345–6
  redundancy decision 124
  sanction, as 349
  sex discrimination and 186
  social standards 316–18
  standard dismissal procedure, Fig. 9.4 348
  transfer, before a, Fig. 3.1 117
  transfer of undertakings and 116
  unfair, automatic 116
dismissal, legal framework
  ACAS scheme for unfair dismissal arbitration, Fig. 9.3
    337
  background 321
  compensation 340
    additional award 342
    basic award 340–1
    compensatory award 341–2
  contracts of employment, termination 77–8, 324–5
  disciplinary penalties 324
  fair dismissal 325–6
    reasons for 326–7
    capability and qualifications 326
    conduct 326–7
    redundancy 327
    statutory duty or restriction, contravening 327
    substantial reason, other 327
  law's effectiveness 318–21
  reasonableness in the circumstances 329–30
    alternative employment 331–2
    capability and ill-health 331
    consultation with employee 331
    criminal convictions unconnected with work 331
    different treatment for different employees 330
    evidence informants 330–1
    medical evidence 331
    misconduct cases 330, 593–4
    previous warnings 330

dismissal, legal framework (*continued*)
  redress procedures 225
    Advisory Conciliation and Arbitration Service
      (ACAS) 335–6
    compromise agreements 336
    employer's response 335
    employment tribunal, application to 335
    entitlement to complain, deciding 335
    full tribunal hearing 338
    interim relief 338–9
    pre-hearing review 337–8
    preliminary hearing 336
  re-engagement, unfair dismissal remedy 340
  reinstatement, unfair dismissal remedy 339–40
  remedies 339–42
  unfair dismissal 325–6
    assertion of a statutory right 328–9
    disability discrimination 328
    employment tribunal, processing application,
      Fig. 1.5 22–3
    national minimum wage and 329, 378
    pregnancy 471–2
    race discrimination 328
    sex discrimination 327–8
    shop workers and betting shop workers 329
    working time cases 329
dress and appearance
  race discrimination and 225–6
  sex discrimination and 186

economically driven change 45, 96, 359
employee participation 499 (*see also* employment
    relations, processes of; industrial action; trade
    unions)
  bargaining process 504
  breakdown of bargaining 505
  collective bargaining 503–6
  collective bargaining, form of 504
  collective *laissez-faire*, 1906–70 508–9
  conclusion 544
  conflicts of interest 503–4
  consultation 501–3, 518–26
  containment to open support of trade unions 509–10
  context 507–15
  development of, in UK 507–13
  employee relations 513
  employer approaches 543–4
  employer attitudes, collective bargaining 504–5
  employment policies and practices 534–4
  EU social dialogue measures 511–12
  financial participation 511, 517–18
  financial participation and employee involvement
    511

'free collective bargaining' 505–6
individual rights 513
industrial democracy, concept of 506–7
'industrial democrat' or partnership 539
  agreement and compromise 540–1
  difficulties of drawing boundaries 540
  employees as corporate citizens not salaried
    subjects 540
international standards 509
introduction 500–1
mechanisms of employee involvement and
    participation, Fig. 14.1 500
Nissan and, Fig. 14.2 502
participation policy and practice in UK 513–15
progressive managerialist 536–8
  ACAS advice on information to be communicated
    to employees, extract from, Fig. 14.4 537
  economic benefits 539
  employee morale 539
  quality circles and problem-solving groups,
    implementation, Fig. 14.5 538
  resource utilisation, effective 538
  technological change 538
promotion 508–9
purchasing power 508
regulation of unions and promotion of financial
    participation and employee involvement 510–12
social inclusionist 541
  equal representation, achieving 543
  overcoming institutional exclusion 542–3
  participation and representation as expression of
    wider social forces 542
  power and influence, gaining 543
  structural exploitation/disadvantage, forms and
    sources, Table 14.3 542
social partnership moves 512–13
spread of selected employee participation, Table 14.1
    514
trade union organisation 511
traditional managerialist 535–6
employee participation, legal framework 516
  collective bargaining, Kwik-Fit case, Fig. 14.3 534
  collective bargaining, statutory recognition 516,
    531
    experience of new procedure 533–4
    statutory recognition, procedure, the 531–3
  collective redundancies 523–4
  consultation 501–3, 518–26
  consultation in multi-national companies 521
    Directive, 1994 521–2
    Regulations, 1999 522–3
  European Company Statute 526
  financial participation 516, 517–18

employee participation, legal framework (*continued*)
  financial participation schemes, key feature of,
    Table 14.2 518
  health and safety, consultation 525–6
  higher-level participation 516, 518–30
  Information and Consultation Directive 2002
    519
    Department of Trade and Industry principles on
      520
    implications of, exercise 14.1 521
    key issues on 520–1
    key provisions 519–20
  low level participation 516–17
  pensions, consultation 526
  representatives, statutory rights for 516
    facilities for 530
    victimisation, protection against 530–1
  transfers of undertakings, consultation 524–5
employee participation model 5, 7–8
employees
  assistance programmes and counselling 444–8
  caring demands confronting 456–7
  co-operation with employer 73–5, 105–6
  corporate citizens, as, not salaries subjects 540
  definition **604**
  dismissal law's effectiveness 318–20
  general duties of 75–7, 105–6, 269
  health and safety, general duties of 424–5, 430
  health and safety rights of 432–5, 444–8
  individual and industrial action 555–6, 556–62
  lawful picketing 568–70
  non-strike action 557–8
  pay, importance to 359
  reasonable care of, employer's duty 74–5, 269
  resignation of 104
  right not to take part 562
  sanctions by employers 558–62
  strike action 557
  work, expectations about 456
  work under protest 104
employers
  disability, duty to make reasonable adjustments
    247–50
  discipline, law's effectiveness 320–1
  discrimination and voluntary action 140–7
  dismissal by 324–5
  general duties, contract of employment 73–5, 106,
    269
  health and safety, defences 422
  health and safety liability 417–18, 419–22, 423–4,
    427–30
  national minimum wage 372
  pay, importance of 359–60

  records, need to keep 374
  sanctions in industrial action 558–62
  vicarious liability 175, 215–16, 250–1, 274–5, 421–2,
    607
  voluntary regulation, discretion 31–2
  working time regulation 392
  work-life balance, expectations of 457
employment
  concepts of and employment relationship 50–1
  forms of 58–60
Employment Appeals Tribunal, constitution of 20, 23
employment law, generally
  contract law and 8, 137, 316
  political perspectives 5–8
  principles underlying 1, 34–40
  procedural aspects 4–5
  regulation, nature of legal and voluntary 1, 2–3, 31,
    40
  substantive aspects 3–4, 34–8
employment policies *see under* individual entries
employment policy, directives on, Table 1.1 11
Employment Practices
  Data Protection Code 298
  data protection, managing 298
  electronic communications, policy for, Fig. 8.5
    308
  employment records 302
    collecting and keeping 302
    discipline, grievances and dismissal 306–7
    disclosure requests 305
    equal opportunity monitoring 303–4
    mergers and acquisitions 305–6
    references 304–5
    retention of 301–2, 307
    security 302–3
    sickness and accident 303
    workers access to information about themselves
      304
  medical information 298, 311
  monitoring at work 298, 307–8
    covert monitoring 309–10
    in-vehicle monitoring 310
    monitoring communications 308–9
    video and auditing monitoring 309
    workers' private lives 310–11
  recruitment and selection 298–9
    advertising 299
    applications 299
    interviews 300
    pre-employment vetting 300–1
    recruitment records, retention of 301–2, 307
    shortlisting 300
    verification od applicant's details 299

employment protection 78, 356–7 (*see also under*
    transfers of undertakings)
  agency workers 87–8, **601**
  casual workers 84–5, **601**
  extended coverage of 355–6
  fixed-term contracts, workers with 82–4
  homeworking and tele-working 85–6, **605**
  part-time workers 78–81, **605**
  race discrimination and 207–9
  sex discrimination, and access to 163–5
  zero-hour contract workers 86–7
employment relations, processes of 38, 485
  consent 38–9
  employee relations, a 'new' model? 494
  freedom 39–40
  natural justice 38, **605**
employment relationship change, managing 91–2
        (*see also* employment relationships regulating;
        transfers of undertakings
  College, case study 3.1 129–30
  College, exercise 3.4 130, 590
  context 92–102
  contracting-out 99–100
  contracts of employment, variation of individual 98
  economic considerations 96
  employment policies and practices 126–7
  employment relations matters 96–7
  flexibility of contractual terms 98–9, **604**
  incidence and experience of change 98–102
  legal requirements, tensions with 97
  operational factors 95–6
  organisation's culture 94–5
  participation 512–13
  participation policy and practice in UK 513–15
  private and public sector change, overall view 92–4
  private sector enterprises, change in, Table 3.1 93
  problems of, some, exercise 3.1 107, 587–8
  redundancy 101–2, 119–25, 127–9
  strategic considerations 95
  transfers and 99, 100–1, 126–7
  transfers between posts 106–7
  variation 126
employment relationship change, managing, legal
        framework
  alternative employment 121
  change and tensions within 97
  contracts of employment
    change by agreement 102, 103–5
    place of work and mobility 106
    variation of 102–3
  pay 124–5
  redeployment 119, 121
  redundancy and redeployment 119

  consultation 122–3
  definition 119–20
  managing redundancy, some problems, exercise 3.3
    125
  selection criteria 120–1
  termination of employment 123–4
  time of work 122
transfers between posts 106–7
transfers of undertakings 108
  coverage of 108
  employee protection, nature of 112–18
  'going concern', a 111–12
  identity 109–11, 126
  information disclosure and consultation 112, 127
  'relevant transfer' 108–9
employment relationships, regulating 47, 88 (*see also*
        contract of employment)
  collectivism 54–5
  concepts of work and employment 50–1
  conclusions, general 60, 88
  context 50–62
  contract of employment 49
    characteristics 68–71
    employment protection for atypical workers
        78–88
    role of 49–50
    terms of 71–7
  defining the relationship 48, 315–16
  employment status, diversity 55–62
  European Directive and 11–13
  'flexible firm', the 45, 55–6
  flexible workforce? Exercise 2.1 62
  forms of employment 58–60
  'frontier of control' 48
  individualism 54–5
  labour market, snapshot of 57–8
  labour market trends, models and evidence 57
  parties' expectations, the 48–9
  psychological contract 51–4
  psychological contracts, three, Fig. 2.1 52
  rules, three sets of 49
  status, employee, worker or contractor? 62–8
employment relationship regulating, legal framework
        62 *see also* European Convention on Human
        Rights; Human Rights Act
  common law and 19–27
  complaint, processes for 19
  continuity of work 63, 66–8
  contract law and 8
  contracts to perform work 63, 68
  directives, EU
    employment policy, on, Table 1.1 11
    generally 11–13

employment relationship regulating, legal framework
(*continued*)
  employment status
    common law tests 63, 64–5
    establishing, Fig. 2.3 63
    worker or contractor? 62–8
  European Court of Justice, rulings of 13–14
  EU law 10
    impact of, some key cases, Table 1.2 14
    non-binding instruments 14–15
    procedures 11–15
    standards of treatment 11
    Treaty articles 10–11
  human rights and 15–19
  mutuality of obligation 63, 65–6
  nature of 1, 2–3, 8, 40
  procedural aspects, Fig. 1.1 3
  regulations, statutory instruments and 9, 356
  remedies, effective 27–30
  standards in law 8–19
  statute law 9
  statutory code of practice 9–10
  tort, law of and 8–9, **607**
employment rights
  access to and sex discrimination 163–5, 171–2
  statutory, access to key, Fig. 2.6 89
  who has? Exercise 2.2 88, 586–7
employment status
  changes in 46
  common law tests 63, 64–5
  continuity of work 63, 66–8
  contracts to perform work 63, 68
  distinctions 62–8
  diversity of 55–61
  employees and transfers of undertakings 113
  establishing, Fig. 2.3 63
  'flexible firm', structure and groups of workers 56
  'flexible firm', the 45, 55–6
  general conclusion 60
  immigrant workers 201–2
  labour market, snapshot of 57–8
  labour market structure, 2001, Table 2.1 58
  labour market trends, models and evidence 57
  managerial occupations, proportion of females,
    Table 4.3 155
  mutuality of obligation 63, 65–6
  workforce sex and employment status, Table 4.1 154
employment tribunals
  application, processing unfair dismissal, Fig. 1.5 22–3
  application to, unfair dismissal 335
  applications, strategy for reducing 29–30
  complaint to, health and safety 435
  complaint process 20–3

  process, characteristics of 28–9
  protected disclosure, detriment application 296
  redress, procedures for 335–9
enforcement of employment law, institutions and,
  Fig. 1.4 20
enforcement processes 583–4
Equal Opportunities Commission, constitution and
  functions 25
equal opportunity policies 140
  nature and scope 140–1
    diagnosis 141
    elements of, essential 141–5
    monitoring and review 145
    objective setting, action planning and
      implementation 141–5
equal treatment (*see also* discrimination and equal
    opportunities, generally; sex discrimination;
    sex discrimination, legal framework)
  EU Directive 162–3
  harassment and bullying 270
  pay claims and sex discrimination 169–70
  practices, Table A 144
  substantive issues as 36–8
ethical standards 576, 578
European Convention on Human Rights
  discrimination, prohibition against 17
  fair trial 17
  freedom of expression 17, 586
  legal regulation and 15
  legislation, effect on 16, 293
  privacy, right of 293
  public authorities, effect on activities of 16
  remedial action, case of Christine Goodwin, Fig. 1.3
    18–19
  rights of, key, Fig. 1.2 15
European Court of Human Rights, complaint process
  20, 24
European Court of Justice
  constitution of 20, 23–4
  rulings of and legal regulation 13–14
European Union, influences of 496–8, 511–12
European Union law (*see also*
  directives and legal regulation 11–13, 357
  discrimination and 138
  equal treatment legislation, harassment and 270
  European Company Statute 526
  health and safety, impact on 415–16
  Information and Consultation Directive 2002 519–21
  legal regulation and 10–19, 357
  non-binding instruments 14–15
  procedures 11–15
  standards of treatment 11
  Treaty articles 10–11

fair trial, European Convention of Human Rights and 17

fairness, as substantive issue 34–5

family friendly policies *see* parental dependency rights

fixed-term contracts, workers with **604**
   employment protection 82–4
   statutory regulations 2002 82–4

flexible workforce? Exercise 2.1 62

flexible working
   employment policy and practice 476
   flexibility, definition **604**
   requests for 467–8
   typology of, Fig. 2.2 61

free labour market model 5, 6–7

freedom
   employment relations and 39–40
   expression, of 17, 586
   expression of, exercise 1.2 17

full time workers, employment relationships 58

future, the 585

genuine occupational qualifications
   race discrimination and 214–15
   sex discrimination and 173–4

grievance
   data protection code 306–7
   harassment, procedure 279
   voluntary regulation, procedure 32

harassment and bullying 263–4, **604**
   approaches to allegations of 278
   characteristics of the workplace 267
   communications 280
   conclusions on 281
   context, the 265–9
   cultural factors 266–7
   defining harassment and bullying 277
   definitions 264–5
   disciplinary action, role of 280
   employment policies and practices 277–82
   Exercise 7.1 282, 592
   grievance procedure, role of 279
     procedures and counselling 279
     trade union consultation 280
     training 279
     victims, who might be possible? 278
   growing concern over 264
   managerial rules and responsibilities 278–9
   moneybrokers, case study 7.1 281–2
   moneybrokers, exercise 7.1 282, 592
   monitoring, grievance procedure 281
   parties involved, the 268
   possible consequences 268–9

power relations 266
procedures and counselling 279
trade union consultation 280
training 279
victims, who might be possible? 278

harassment and bullying, legal framework 269
   action against the perpetrator 274–6
   civil proceedings 276
   compensation against individual harassers, Fig. 7.4 277
   constructive dismissal claim 276
   contract of employment and 269
   criminal proceedings 275–6
   direct discrimination and detriments 271–3
   disciplinary action and dismissal 275
   discrimination claim 276–7
   dismissal 273–4, 275
   European equal treatment legislation 270
   Jones, case of Raymondo, Fig. 7.2 274
   liability 274
   Manning, Bernard, harassment by, Fig. 7.3 275
   Miles, case of Ms, Fig. 7.1 269
   remedies for victim, possible 276–7
   resignation, breach of contract claim 276
   third party harassment 274

harmonisation, as substantive issue 36–7, 38

health and safety 407
   accidents, incidence of major 415
   AIDS and HIV status, employee assistance 446
   background to increase in attention to 410–11
   concepts, the 408–10
   conclusion 449
   context, the 410–17
   drug, alcohol and other substantive abuse, employees 444–5
   economics of 411–12
   employee assistance programmes and counselling 444–8
   employment policies and practices 439–49
   European dimension 415–17
   health, meaning 408–9
   history of regulation 409
   introduction to 408–10
   major disasters, Fig. 12.3 416
   occupational health service 443–4
   psycho-social stressors, Fig. 12.2 414
   safety consultation and communication 442–3
   safety culture, creating a 440–1
   safety, meaning 409
   safety policy, a 441–2
   scope, extension of 356
   stress, work related 413–15, 421, 446–7
   technology and ergonomic factors 412–13

health and safety (*continued*)
VDU operators, safety grievance case, case study 12.1
448
VDU operators, safety grievance, exercise 12.2 449,
598–9
violence at work 447–8
welfare, meaning 409
workplace death and injury, some statistics, Fig. 12.1
410
Health and Safety Commisson, constitution and
functions 26
Health and Safety Executive, powers of 426–7
health and safety, legal framework 410, 417–18
assessing the risks? Exercise 12.1 430
breach of contract, repudiatory 420–1
civil law and 410, 417
common law, the 418–22
competent persons, appointment of 429
consultation and representation 436–8, 525–6,
602–3
criminal law and 410, 417–18
defences, employer's 422
designers, manufacturers, importers, suppliers,
general duties of 425
employees, general duties of 424–5, 430
employees, rights of
complaint to employment tribunal 435
detriments, protection from 432–4, 438–9, **603**
van driver, case of, Fig. 12.7 434
employer's liability 417–18, 419–22, 423–4,
427–30
health and safety arrangements 429
Health and Safety at Work Act 1974 422
enforcement machinery 425–6
general duties, what are they? 423–5
Health and Safety Executive powers 426–7
infringements of standards, liability for 427
nature of the Act 423
who is covered? 423
health surveillance 429
information, disclosure of 437–8
Jones, case of Simon, Fig. 12.4 418
legal action, diversity of 410, 417–18
liability and vicarious liability 421–2
negligence, test of 419–20
policy, written statement of 424
pregnancy 462–3
regulations, some key
Health and Safety (Display Screen Equipment)
Regulations 1992 430–2
Management of Health and Safety at Work
Regulations 1999 428–30
role of 428

representation, union and non-union, functions
436–7
risk assessment 428–9
safety representatives and safety committees 424,
433
elections/appointments 438
non-union representatives, functions of 437
union safety representatives, functions of
436–7
serious or imminent danger 430
statute law 422–7
unguarded machine, the, Fig. 12.5 419
Health and Safety at Work Act 1974 422–7
homeworkers and teleworkers **605**
employment protection 85–6
employment relationships 60
House of Lords, constitution of 20, 23
human rights **605** *see* European Convention on
Human Rights; Human Rights Act 1998
Human Rights Act 1998
common law, effect on 15
effects, fundamental 15–16
information privacy 293
legislation and European Convention on Human
Rights 16
public authorities, effect on activities 16
remedial action, direct and indirect effect 17–18

immigration control 220
illegal immigrants, employment of 220
work permits 219–20
immunities *see* industrial action, legal framework; trade
unions
indirect discrimination
detriment establishing a 168–9
justification 169
provision, criterion or practice 167
race discrimination, in 211–13
sex discrimination 166–9
smaller proportion, defining a 168
individualisation, conclusion 580–1
individualism and employment relationships 54–5
industrial action 547, **605**
bakery, case study 15.1 573–4
bakery, exercise 15.1 574, 600
collective and individual manifestation of conflict
550
conclusion 572
conflict manifestation, Fig. 15.1 550
context 551–6
definitions from legislators 548
definitions, sociological 548
'dual track policy' 553–5

industrial action (*continued*)
 historical background 551–2
  1945–79 552
  1979 to date 552–3
 individual employees, position of 555–6
 introduction 547–51
 legitimacy of and 'the public interest' 550–1
 nature and sources of conflicts of interest 549
 pay deduction 369, 561–2
 phenomenon of 549–51
 regulation of trade unions, policy of 554–5
 restriction, policy of 553–4
 trade union immunities 491
industrial action, legal framework 556
 disruptive pupil, a, Fig. 15.3 571
 employee's 'own place of work', lawful picketing 569
 essential services situation 567–8
 individual employees 556–62
 lawful industrial action, what is? 564–7
 lawful picketing 568–70
 liability for industrial action 570–1
 membership issues 565
 non-employees and picketing 569
 non-strike action, individual employee 557–8
 obligatory statements on industrial ballot paper,
  Fig. 15.2 566
 picketing, how many employees may attend? 569–70
 rejected partial performance 561–2
 right not to take part in action 562
 sanctions by employers 558
  dismissal 558–60
  pay, deduction of 561–2
 secondary action 565
 secondary picketing 569
 strike action, individual employees 557
 'trade dispute' 564
 trade unions 563
  balloting 566–7
  breach of contract 563
  employee's 'own place of work', lawful picketing
   569
  immunities 563–4, **605**
  lawful industrial action, what is? 564–7
  lawful picketing 568–70
information, privacy and surveillance 284–5
 background to growth in 285
 Bladon v ALM Medical Services, Fig. 8.4 297
 conclusions on 312
 context, the 285–7
 economic and security considerations 287
 employment policies and practices 296–8, 311
 privacy and surveillance 311
 social values and human rights 286–7

 technological developments 285–6
 whistleblowing 295, 311
information, privacy and surveillance, legal framework
 Data Protection Act 1998 288–92
 data protection principles, Fig. 8.1 288
 Employment Practices Data Protection Code 298
  employment records 298, 302–7
  medical information 298, 311
  monitoring at work 298, 307–11
  recruitment and selection 298–302
 Halford, Allison, case of, Fig. 8.3 294
 Human Rights Act 1998 293
 personal data in the workplace, Fig. 8.2 290
 privacy and surveillance 292–5
 public interest disclosure legislation 295–6
 Regulation of Investigatory Powers Act 2000 293–5
International Labour Organisation 495

juridification 577

labour market
 changes in since 1970 156–7
 disability and 232–3
 ethnic group participation 200–4
 flexibility 579–80, **604**
 participation by women in and sex discrimination
  153–5, 356–7
 snapshot of 57–8
 social trends, parental and dependency rights 452–4
 structure, 2001, Table 2.1 58
 trends, models and evidence 57
Low Pay Commission, constitution and functions 26

managing change, legal framework *see* employment
  relationship change, managing; transfers of
  undertakings
maternity leave entitlements 463–4, 465–6, 466,
  472–3
maternity pay, statutory 473
minimum employment contract 355
minimum standards 576–7
monitoring at work 298, 307–11
multinational companies, consultation in 521–3

national minimum wage 370
 agricultural workers 378
 atypical work patterns, and, Fig. 10.1 373
 cases, some successful, Fig. 10.3 376
 collective agreements and contractual terms 373
 coverage 370–2
 employer, the 372
 enforcement, civil proceedings 373–6
 enforcement, criminal action 377

national minimum wage (*continued*)
  hourly rates, calculating 372–3
  inspectors, role of 375–6
  National Minimum Wage Annual Report 2001/02,
    trends in, Fig. 10.2 375
  national minimum wage rates since 1999, Table 10.3
    371
  national rate, a 370
  progress to 364–5
  records, need to keep 374
  underpayment 374
  unfair dismissal 329, 378
  victimisation 377–8
natural justice 38, 332, **605**
negligence, tort of 419–20, **605**
'new model' employment regulation *see* contract of
    employment
non-work life *see* work-life balance

parental and dependency rights 451
  business benefits and disadvantages 458, 459–61
  caring demands of employees 456–7
  communication and consultation 477–8
  context, the 452–61
  dependency policy, developing a, exercise 13.1 480
  dependency scheme in Kingston Upon Thames,
    case study 13.1 478–80
  employees' expectations on work 456
  employers and work colleagues, expectations of 457
  employment policies and practices 473–80
  facilities 477
  family diversity 452–4
  flexible working time 476
  household and family, types of 452
  households in Great Britain, Table 13.1 453
  introduction 451–2
  labour market and socials trends 452–4
  leave entitlements 475–6
  managing patterns of work 458
  maternity pay 473
  paternity pay 473
  place of work 476–7
  political initiatives 456–61
  work context characteristics 456
  work-life balance
    concepts 454–9
    defining, Fig. 13.1 459
    defining and achieving 458–9
    facilitating 474–5
  workplace culture 455–6
parental and dependency rights, legal framework 461
  adoption leave 470–1
  adoption pay 473

ante-natal care 463
contract of employment, status of 463
  additional maternity leave 465–6
  benefits 464–5
  ordinary maternity leave 463–4, 466
contract worker, a (maternity leave) Fig. 13.3 472
flexible working requests 467–8
maternity leave
  entitlements 463–4, 465–6, 466, 472
  notice requirements, Fig. 13.2 464
  part-time work 466–7
  redundancy and 472–3
  returning to work 466–7
parental leave 468–9
paternity leave 470
pregnancy
  comparator, no 462
  detrimental treatment 471
  discriminatory treatment 462
  health and safety issues 462–3
  sickness and 462
  unfair dismissal 471–2
  statutory pay 473
parental leave 468–9
part-time workers **605**
  Directive, EU 79–81
  employment protection 78–81
  employment relationship 58
  maternity and 466–7
  working time, regulation of 384
paternity leave 470
paternity pay, statutory 473
pay *see also* pay regulation
  benefits and, race discrimination 224
  equal claims and discrimination 169–70, 363
  Equal Pay Act 1970 and Regulations 161–2, 363
  gender pay gap, major occupational groups, Table 4.4
    156
  redundancy and 124–5
  women's and sex discrimination 155–7, 161–3, 363
pay regulation 358–9
  context, the 359–66
  discrimination and pay 155–7, 161–3, 363
  economic issues 359–60
  employment policies and practices 378–81
  fair pay 362
  mean weekly earnings: full time workers by ethnic
    group, Table 10.2 363
  minimum pay, progress to 364–5
  new earning survey data, Table 10.1 361
  new social objectives 365–6
  pay, importance of 359–60
  payment systems 360

pay regulation (*continued*)
  political policy, market 'free play'? 360–1
  social policy 362–6
  social welfare factors 361
  status-based pay 362–3
pay regulation, legal framework 366 *see also* national
    minimum wage
  cash shortages and stock deficiencies in retail
    employment 370
  common law of contract and pay 367–8
  contracts of employment and collective agreements
    378–9
  deduction, industrial action sanction 369, 561–2
  definitions 366–7
  dependants, time off for 469–70
  employment policies and practices 378–81
    special agreements 379
  fines and disciplinary action 369–70
  industrial action, participation 369
  information about pay 368
  information and records 374, 379–80
  maternity pay, statutory 473
  national minimum wage, statutory 370–8
  overpayment 369
  paternity pay, statutory 473
  pay deduction 368–9
  pay regulation scenarios, exercise 10.1 380, 595
  payment methods 368
  regulating the pay transaction 367–70
  special agreements 379
pensions
  consultation on occupational 526
  disability discrimination and 256–7
  sex discrimination and 186
  transfers of undertakings and 114
performance and conduct 259–62 *see also* discipline;
    dismissal; harassment and bullying; information,
    privacy and surveillance
political perspectives 5
  disability discrimination 238–41
  dismissal and 318
  employee protection model 5, 7–8
  free collective bargaining 5, 6
  free labour market model 5, 6–7
  'free play' market? 360–1
  parental and dependency rights 459–61
  race discrimination and 199–200
  sex discrimination and 158–60
positive action
  legal concept 138–40
  positive discrimination, distinctions 139
  race discrimination and 215
  sex discrimination and 170–3

positive discrimination
  legal concept 138–40
  positive action, distinctions 139
  race discrimination and 215
  sex discrimination and 170–3
pregnancy
  comparator, no 462
  detrimental treatment 471
  discriminatory treatment 462
  health and safety 462–3
  rights 462–3, 471
  sex discrimination 174–5, 462
  sickness 462
  unfair dismissal 471–2
pregnant workers, sex discrimination and 174–5, 462
private and public sector change, overall view 92–4
private sector enterprises, changes in, Table 3.1 93
procedure
  aspects of, individual and collective 4–5
  aspects of, voluntary and legal regulation, Fig. 1.1 3
promotion
  disability discrimination and 256
  sex discrimination and 185–6
  transfer and race discrimination 224–5
psychological contract, the 51–4
public and private sector change, overall view 92–4
public interest disclosure legislation 295
  employment tribunal application 296
  'gagging' clauses 296
  'protected' disclosure, meaning 296
  'qualifying' disclosure, meaning 295
public sector, enforcement directives 12–13

race discrimination 191–2 *see also* discrimination and
    equal opportunities generally
  Britain's population by ethnic group, Table 5.1 193
  colour, concept of 195
  concepts, the 194–8
  context, the 198–205
  dismissal 226
  dress codes 225–6
  employment/economic status, labour market 200–1
  employment policy and practice 220–7
  ethnicity concept 194–5
  'genuine occupational qualification' 214–15, **604**
  Gilroy, case of Mark, Fig. 5.1 199
  historical background 192
  human resource strategy 221–2
  industries and sectors, ethnic group participation
    201–2
  labour-market participation 200–4
  migrant workers, contribution characteristics
    203–4

race discrimination (*continued*)
 migrants, the cumulative barriers to employment,
  Fig. 5.2 204
 pay and benefits 223
 political approaches 199–200
 population profile of Britain 192–3
 promotion and transfers 224–5
 race, concept of 194
 racism,
  concept of 195–6
  expressions of 196–8
  key factors in 197
 recruitment and selection 222–3
 restaurants, case study 5.1 226
 restaurants, exercise 5.1 227, 591
 social background 198–9
 social issues 204–5
 training and development 224–5
 unemployment 202–3
 unemployment by age, Table 5.2 202
 working time 223–4
race discrimination, legal framework
 compensation 218
 declaration 218
 direct discrimination 210–11
 dismissal, unfair, reason for 328
 employing workers from overseas 218–19
  free movement 219
  immigration control 219–20
 employment policies and practices 220–7
 employment protection, areas of 207
  agency workers and contract workers 208
  applicants 207
  employed people 207
  Race Relations (Amendment) Act 2000 209
  summarily dismissed employees 208–9
 enforcement 217
  burden of proof 217
  questionnaire 216–17
  recovery (Scotland, discovery) 217
 grounds for unfair discrimination 205–7
 indirect discrimination
  compliance in practice with condition or
   requirement 212–13
  condition or requirement 212
  definition and questions of analysis 211–12
  detriment 213
  justification 213–14
 liability 215
 pay and 363
 positive action and discrimination 215
 racial grounds and groups, definitions 205–7
 recommendation 218

remedies 217–18
 special provisions, 'genuine occupational
  qualification' 214–15
 three cable-layers, Fig. 5.3 205
 victimisation 214
racism 195–8
reasonableness, substantive issue, as 35–6
records, employment 298, 302–7, 374, 379–80,
 398
recruitment and selection
 disability discrimination 234, 255–6
 Employment Practices Data Protection Code
  298–302
 race discrimination 222–3
 sex discrimination, employment policies and
  180–2
redeployment 121
redundancy
 change, managing 101–2
 collective, multi-national companies consultation
  523–4
 consultation 122–3, 523–4, **602–3**
 definition 119–20
 dismissal decision and 124
 fair reason for dismissal 327
 managing 127–9
 managing, some problems in, exercise 3.3 125,
  589
 maternity leave and 472–3
 pay and 124–5
 procedural fairness 124
 selection criteria 120–1
 termination of employment 123–4
 unfair reason for dismissal, as 328
regulation *see also* employment relationship, regulating;
  voluntary regulation
 generally 2, 40
 principles, some underpinning 34
  employment relations, processes 38–40
  substantive issues 34–8
 purposes 2
 substantive 3–4, 34–8
remedies
 access to legal redress 27, 30, **606**
 alternative dispute resolution 29–30
 company, effective procedures in 30
 compensation **602**
  award, sex discrimination 176, 177–9
  disability discrimination 252
  harassment and bullying 276–7
  race discrimination 218
  unfair dismissal 340–2
 complaints procedure, effectiveness of 28–30

remedies (*continued*)
 declaration
  disability discrimination 252
  harassment or bullying 276
  race discrimination 218
  sex discrimination 177
 effective 27–30, 187–8
 harassment and bullying, possible 276–7
 Human Rights Act 1998, under 17–19
 injury to feelings payment, harassment or bullying 276
 interim relief, unfair dismissal 338–9
 recommendation
  disability discrimination 252
  race discrimination 218
  sex discrimination 179–80
 re-engagement and reinstatement, unfair dismissal 339–40
 reinstatement, harassment or bullying 276
 sex discrimination, adequacy of 187–8
 unlawful industrial action, for 570–1
 value of, conclusion 584
representation rights 581–2
reverse discrimination *see* positive discrimination

self-employed workers **606**
 employment relationships 59–60
 sex discrimination 164–5
sex discrimination 149–50 *see also* discrimination and equal opportunities generally
 changing perspectives 151–2
 conclusion overview 187–8
 context, the 152–60
 discrimination problems, some, exercise 4.1 188, 590–1
 dismissal 186
 dress and appearance 185–6
 employment policies and practices 180–6
 female economic activity by age, Table 4.2 154
 gender pay gap, major occupational groups, Table 4.4 156
 historic situation of women 139, 150–1
  conclusion on 187–8
  dismissal 186
  dress and appearance 185–6
 human resource strategy 180
 labour market, changes in and 156–7
 labour market participation 153–5
 managerial occupations, proportion of females, Table 4.3 155
 pay 155–7, 363
 political approaches 158–60
 promotion and career progression 184–5

recruitment and selection 180–2
 retirement and pensions 186
 social trends and influences 157–8
 terms and conditions of employment 182–3
 training and development 184
 workforce, sex and employment status, Table 4.1 154
 working time 183–4
sex discrimination, legal framework 160
 access to statutory rights 163
  applicants for employment 163–4
  employed people protection 164
  exceptions 165
  self-employed, the 164
 compensation award 177, 178–9
 declaration, remedy 177
 direct discrimination 165–6
 dismissal, unfair, reason for 327–8
 enforcement proceedings
  burden of proof 176–7, **601**
  discovery 177
  questionnaire 177
  recovery (Scotland) 177
  time limit 175–6
 Equal Pay Act 1970 and Regulations 161–2
 equal pay claims 169–70
 Equal Treatment Directive 1976 162–3
 financial loss, compensation 178–9
 genuine occupational qualifications 173–4, **604**
 indirect discrimination 166
  detriment, establishing a 168–9
  justification 169
  provision, criterion or practice 167
  smaller proportion, defining a 168
 injury to feelings 179
 interest and compensation 179
 liability 175
 positive action and discrimination 171
  employment, access to 171–2
  family-friendly measures 172
  organisational and cultural change 173
  training, access to 172–3
 pregnancy 174–5, 462
 recommendations, remedy 177, 179–80
 remedies 177–80, 187–8
 Sex Discrimination Act 1975 162
 special provisions 173–5
 structure of 160
 unlawful discrimination, grounds of 160–3
 victimisation 170–1
 working time regulation 390
shop workers, unfair dismissal 329
social justice model *see* employee protection model

statute law **606**
  contract of employment terms and 73
  discrimination and 137–8
  health and safety 422–7
  legal regulation and 9
statutory instruments, legal; regulation and 9, **606**
statutory rights, qualified access to 582–3
stress, work related 413–15, 421, 446–7
strikes *see* industrial action
substantive issues 34, **606**
  equal treatment 36–8
  fairness 34–5
  harmonisation 36–7, 38
  reasonableness 35–6

teleworking *see* homeworking
temporary workers **606**
  employment relationships 58–9
termination of employment *see also* contract of
      employment; dismissal; redundancy
  contract of employment, under 77–8
  disability discrimination and 257
  redundancy and 123–4
terms and conditions of employment **607** *see also*
      contract of employment
  collective agreements 118, 356
  EU law, employment protection, extension of 357
  health and safety, extension of 356
  minimum employment contract 355
  regulatory procedures in workplace, new 356
  work and non-work life, reconciling 356–7
tort, law of **601**
  legal regulation and 8–9
  negligence and 419–20, **605**
trade unions **607** *see also* industrial action
  anti-harassment policies, consultation 280
  balloting 566–7
  'British disease', the 492–4
  containment to open support 509–10
  historical background 508–9, 551–3
  immunities of 489–90, 553–4, 563–4, **605**
  independence 491–2
  industrial action 491
  legal status of 489–90, **607**
  membership, individual 485
  membership issues 565–6
  organisation, 1980–97 511
  organisational structure 488–9
  purposes of 486–8
  regulation of, policy of 554–5
  regulation of and promotion of financial
      participation and employee involvement
      510–12

role of 486–92
transfers of undertakings and recognition 118
training
  access to and sex discrimination 172–3, 184
  development and, race discrimination 224–5
  disability discrimination and 237, 256
  harassment, procedures for 279
transfers of undertakings
  change, managing 99, 100–1, 108, 115
  collective agreements 118
  consultation 112, 127, 524–5, **602–3**
  contract harmonisation 127
  coverage of 108
  disclosure and consultation 112, 127
  dismissal before, Fig. 3.1 117
  economic unity transferred to transferee? 110–11
  employee protection 112–13
    changes relating to the transfer 115
    constructive dismissal 116
    continuity of individual's contract 114
    dismissal 116–17
    employee status 113
    employee's right to refuse transfer 115
    occupational pensions 114
    protection against unilateral worsening of
        conditions 115–16
    relevant date, the 113
    variation of contracts 115, 127
  employee relations decisions 127
  'going concern', a 111–12
  identifiable economic unity pre-transfer? 109–10
  identity 109, 126
  information, disclosure and consultation 112, 127
  problems of, some, exercise 3.2 119, 588–9
  'relevant transfer' 108–9
  trade union recognition 118

unfair dismissal *see* dismissal; dismissal, legal
      framework
unlawful discrimination *see under* sex discrimination,
      legal framework

victimisation **607**
  disability discrimination and 247
  national minimum wage and 377–8
  protections against, representatives and 530–1
  race discrimination and 214
  sex discrimination and 170–1
voluntary regulation
  consultation and collective bargaining 33
  disciplinary procedures 32–3
  employer discretion 31–2
  grievance procedures 32

voluntary regulation (*continued*)
  nature of 1, 2–3, 31, 40
  procedural aspects, Fig. 1.1 3
  third parties and 33–4
  working time, regulation of 385–6

wages councils 364
wages and salaries, contract of employment and 73
whistleblowing *see also* public interest disclosure
    legislation
  information, privacy and surveillance 295, 311
work, concepts of and employment relationship 50–1
work life balance 451, 454–5 *see also* parental and
    dependency rights
  conclusion on 580
  context, the 452–61
  defining and achieving 458–9, 477–8
  employment policies and practices 473–80
  facilitating, working practices 474–5
  introduction 451–2
work life balance, legal framework 461
  adoption leave 470–1
  contract of employment, status of 463–6
  dependency leave 469–70
  detrimental treatment, and unfair dismissal 471–2
  flexibility working, requesting 467–8
  maternity leave 463, 465–6
  parental and paternity leave 468–9, 470
  pregnancy 462–3
  redundancy 472–3
  returning to work 466–7
  statutory pay 473
work, place and mobility 106, 120
workforce reductions
  methods of 101
  reasons and selection criteria 101–2
working time, regulation of 382
  annualised hours scheme 383–4
  basic working week 383
  checklist for action 403–4
  compliance, costs of 388–9
  context, the 385–9
  economic considerations 387–9
  employment policies and practices 401–3
  estimated costs to employees, Table 11.1 388
  flexible hours 384

  introduction to 383–5
  job share 384
  long-hours culture, a growing 386–7
  overtime 383
  part-time working 384
  scenarios, some, exercise 11.1 404–5, 596–8
  shift work 383
  social issues 387
  unfair dismissal 329
  voluntary measures, historic use of 385–6
  weekend working 384
  work performance, long hours effect on 388
  zero hours contract 384–5
working time, regulation, legal framework 389
  annual leave, paid 394–5
  breach of contract 390
  children and young people 389–90
  collective agreements 397
  daily rest periods 393
  Disability Discrimination Act 1995 390
  employer, the 392
  employment policies and practices 401–3
  enforcement 398–9
  implementation, a strategic approach to 401–3
  individual opt-out 393
  key provisions, some 392–4
  night work 394
  piecemeal legal regulation 389–90
  records 398
  regulations, implementing the 395–7
  rest breaks 393
  sex discrimination law 390
  specific occupations 389
  weekly rest periods 393
  weekly working hours limits 392–3
  workforce agreements 397–8
  working people with entitlements 390–2
  working time, defining 392
  Working Time Regulations 1998 390
  Working Time Regulations, are they working?
      399–401
workplace rules 72–3

zero hour contracts
  employment protection 86–7
  employment relationships 59